World Art

THE ESSENTIAL ILLUSTRATED HISTORY

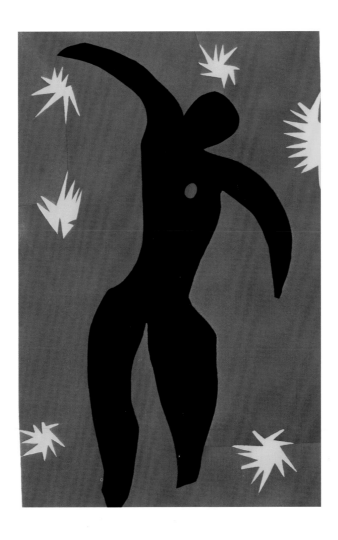

Foreword by Dr Mike O'Mahony
Contributors: Dr Robert Belton, Andrea Belloli, Ihor Holubizky,
Dr Julia Kelly, Dr James Mackay, William Matar, Tom Middlemost, Ian Zaczek,
Dr Mike O'Mahony, Tamsin Pickeral, Michael Kerrigan

FLAME TREE
PUBLISHING

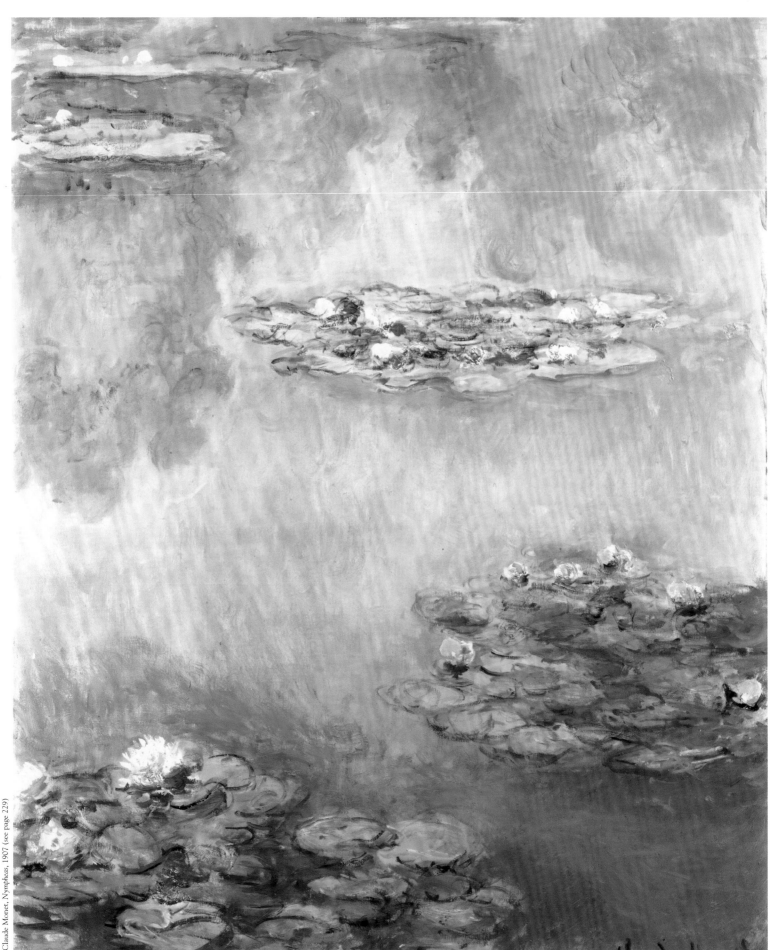

Claude Monet, *Nymphéas*, 1907 (see page 229)

Contents

Foreword

In our image-saturated epoch the eye, it seems, is rarely afforded the opportunity to linger. Life is constantly on the move and, increasingly, the images we encounter in our daily lives seem equally unhappy to remain at rest. Technological developments have enabled a panoply of fast paced, ever changing images to enter into the public arena and invade our consciousness. The flickering television screen, for example, is no longer confined to the domestic interior but has slowly crept into shopping malls, railway stations, bars and restaurants, indeed any space in which someone might be tempted to stop for more than a few minutes. Public advertising hoardings are gradually being replaced by huge scale, flat-screen television monitors and even our personal telephones now have the capacity to deliver a barrage of images from action movies and sports events to advertising and pop videos. In a world of visual over-stimulation it is all too easy to become little more than a passive spectator, casually watching one throwaway image rapidly replaced by another. We risk forgetting the importance and, indeed, the sheer pleasure of looking closely, in detail and at a more leisurely pace at the images presented before our eyes, of engaging with and examining such images thoughtfully and critically.

In such a world, the rich heritage of art produced in both the distant and more recent past can give us pause for thought. Paintings tend, by their very nature, to be static images and command our attention. Whether we encounter them hanging on the walls of a museum or gallery, or indeed beautifully reproduced as in this volume, they invite us to linger, to cast our eye more slowly over their surfaces, to engage with their subject matter and symbolism and to admire their formal qualities, their colour, texture and composition. We recognize them as highly valued objects, carefully conceived and produced by artists who, at different historical moments, have adopted a variety of techniques. We might marvel at their intricacy, be invigorated by their sheer energy, or even frustrated by their seeming lack of craft. Art also has the capacity to stimulate our emotions, generating a wide range of responses. It can instil a sense of excitement or tranquillity, destabilize our sense of the world around us or offer a reassuring mood of continuity and comfort. It can encourage us either to look with fresh eyes at what surrounds us, or even to contemplate what may no longer be there. Art can also provide us with something of a window into the past. What it shows us, however, is not so much a simple record of what the world was like in an earlier epoch. More importantly, it reveals what individuals, within certain societies and at certain times, thought about the world they inhabited, how they engaged with it, what was most important to them and what concerned them most.

This book provides a wonderful opportunity to contemplate this rich artistic heritage at leisure. Incorporating 350 full-colour illustrations, *World of Art* takes the reader on an incredible journey both through time and space: it includes some of the world's best-loved artists from Cimabue and Giotto in the Early Italian Renaissance period to Henri Matisse, Jackson Pollock and Lucien Freud in the Modern era, and represents works of art from all five continents. Each illustration is accompanied by a short text inviting readers to enhance their visual experience by learning more about the individual artists represented, the artistic movements they originated and worked within and the wider historical and cultural factors that influenced their work. More detailed information can also be found in the Introduction and section on Art Movements, which allow the reader to delve deeper into the history of art and to gain a greater understanding of the diversity of works presented throughout the book. Similarly, the section on Painting Techniques guides the reader through the various materials and methods used by artists throughout history.

World of Art is very much a book to linger over, to return to time and time again. It is a volume to treasure and escape into, both for the sheer visual pleasure of the works illustrated and to discover more about the artists who produced these works and the place such works occupy in the history of world art.

Dr Mike O'Mahony

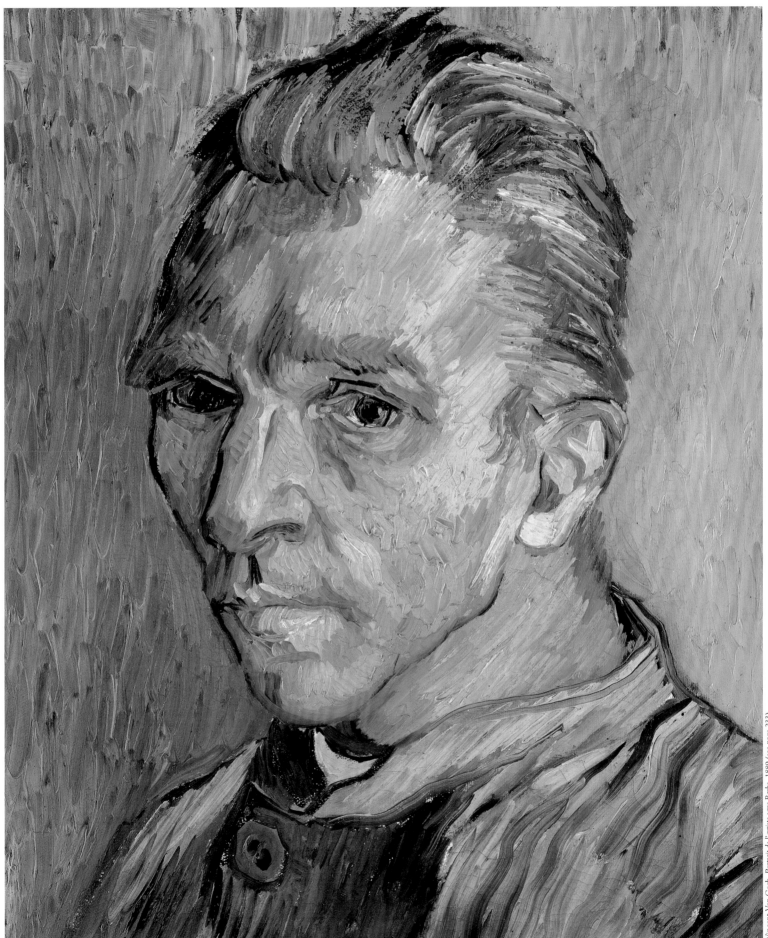

Vincent Van Gogh, *Portrait de l'artiste sans Barbe*, 1889 (see page 233)

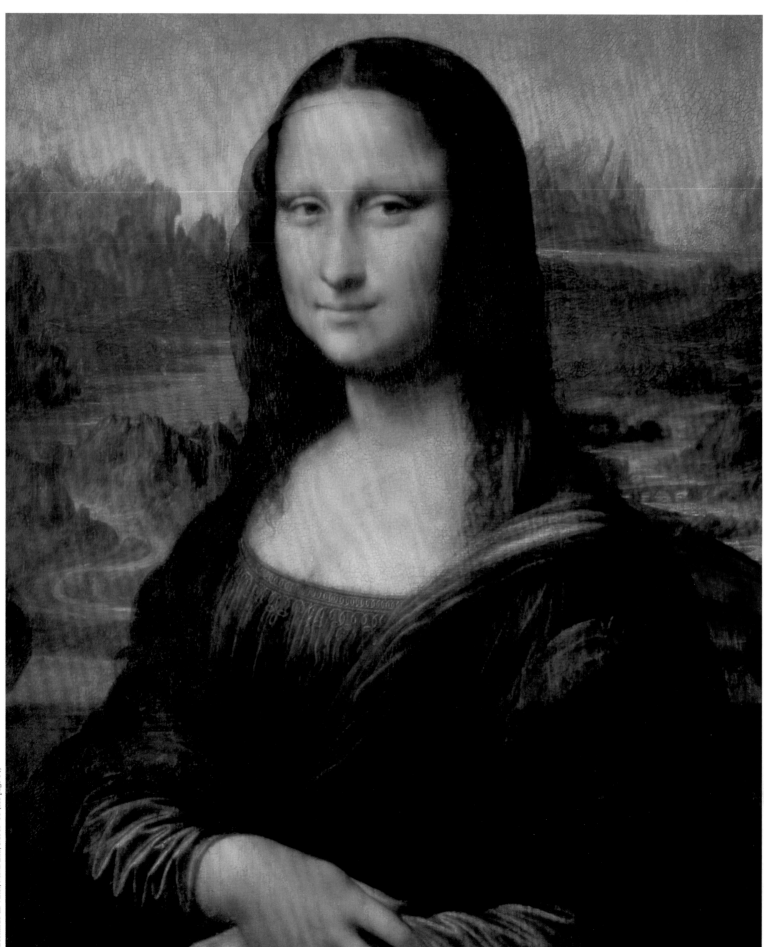

Leonardo da Vinci, *Mona Lisa*, c.1503–06 (see page 84)

Introduction

For most people the process of viewing something aesthetically pleasing can be a momentarily life-enriching experience. The same people might also feel that there is a big difference between looking at a painting for its own sake, and accepting the concept of art as a medium conveying a set of intellectual theories and arguments, and many would ask why should we bother with art? The enjoyment provided by the visual is an acceptable motivation in itself. However, it does not tell us very much about anything – after all, sweets can provide enjoyment too. Unlike sweets, though, art has the potential to enrich life in a manner that goes well beyond mere enjoyment, agreeable décor or a more superficial gratification through popular imagery. Moreover, because the art of our own time often simply reaffirms our own values and expectations, being familiar with the art of other times and places is a useful portal into others' aesthetics, ideologies, morals, philosophies, politics and social customs. This familiarity, in turn, may well invite us to question our own ideologies and social customs; in fact, much art was never meant to be *enjoyed* at all, in the common sense of the word. Art's most fundamental importance is therefore not as décor but as an avenue of intellectual communication. This makes insight into art an invaluable part of an advanced comprehensive education.

For a long time there was little doubt that one of the higher expressions of a culture was its advanced visual art. For the layperson, the word 'Renaissance' remains to this day more likely to conjure up the works of Leonardo da Vinci and Michelangelo than those of, for example, the composers Heinrich Isaac and Josquin des Préz. However, it is difficult to say the same of the visual art of our own time, unless we are speaking specifically of the mass media. With a few notable exceptions, such as Picasso, modern and contemporary art is much less likely than that of the Renaissance to spring to average people's minds as an example of their own culture's higher accomplishments. For the purposes of this book, when we talk about art we are really referring to paintings, since for most 'lay' people paintings act as their first serious introduction into art interpretation, and for many it is the medium that they find most accessible.

Why is Art Difficult?

Why is it that much recent art – even that deemed very important by the critical community of visual arts professionals – simply does not engage the imagination of the average person in the same way as traditional art? One conventional explanation is that over the past 150 years art has increasingly moved away from the familiarity and comfort of resemblance, in part because artists felt photography and film freed them from having to stick to straightforward representation. Another is that instead of clarity in the discourse around new and unfamiliar work, explanations are increasingly, and deliberately, obscure. This implies that what went into the making of the art object is more important than what it says to, or the effect it has on, an observer.

The development of the mass media means that a larger proportion of the population is exposed to visual art on a daily basis, and consequently exposed to the accompanying argument. In other words, art that was once intellectually challenging is now part of mainstream culture, and in order for those artists pursuing art as a pure 'academic' exercise, to push the boundaries of learning, the questions they ask have to become more cryptic. Yet another reason that more recent art fails to engage the populace is a general mistrust for the people who create the art, and a perception of them and their work as elitist, only inviting in a narrow section of the population to engage in the discourse.

The average person's apparent alienation from the advanced art of the late twentieth and early twenty-first centuries puzzles the professionals, for it seems to be based on several faulty assumptions. The most basic of these is that what makes art 'art' is how accurately it resembles something. This misapprehension ignores the fact that part of what makes even traditional art 'art' is its symbolism, codes and composition, regardless of the accuracy of its representation. A well-crafted object with nothing to say is impoverished as art, whereas something that shows intelligence, imagination and creativity can sometimes be good art even if its technique is ostensibly poor.

Attributing too high a value to the *making* of art is clearly what lies behind frequently heard objections like 'my five-year-old daughter could do that', but these are not complaints that have been levelled solely at difficult contemporary art. The nineteenth-century sculptor Harriet Hosmer was criticized for her figures of heroines from history and literature because she did not make the final stone versions of her sculptures with her own hands. She defended herself by explaining that art is not the technique but the 'design' – the intellectual component of the work. The average person's resistance to art is based on the presumption that art is not the design but the technique – that what makes art 'art' is its 'craft', glorifying the means over the end.

A related faulty assumption is that because the art of the last century is almost invariably accompanied and explained by words, the meaning of the piece resides in the words rather than the object itself. This position fails to recognize that traditional art was often accompanied by words and that the words themselves are merely a part of the context in which the piece exists. More will be said about this context presently. As for class-based mistrust, yes, there are those who traffic in very expensive art less as expressions of an artist's motives than as trophies of their own status, but this is also true of other signs of material wealth and it has no bearing on the meaning or intrinsic value of the art itself. In other words, this too is merely an expression of a contextual matrix surrounding the art.

What is Art For?

We must begin by asking several questions about context, the most basic of which are 'What is art?' and 'What is art for?' The average person might say, 'Art is decoration' or, more awkwardly, 'Art is the technically skilful representation of something absent in such a way as to create an illusion of its presence.' However, these answers ignore a host of important pieces that are not particularly attractive, realistic or well made. The history of art is filled with brilliant examples of disturbing and violent imagery, stylized or inaccurate likenesses, and objects that require constant care in order to prevent deterioration.

In addition to the aesthetic purposes of adornment and beautification, art's roles have included:

  aggrandizing oneself or others
  arranging disordered or dissimilar things
  associating one thing with another thing
  communicating
  complementing education and training
  contrasting familiarity and surprise for aesthetic excitement
  creating codes
  creating illusions
  documenting things and events
  educating the illiterate
  employing the thoroughly known characteristics of one thing as
     metaphors of the less well known characteristics of another to
     shed light on the latter by comparison
  enlivening a dull existence with change and variety
  entertaining
  executing a premeditated purpose
  exhibiting technical skill
  flattering patrons
  giving form to therapy
  heightening experience
  illustrating ideas and narratives
  indulging in fantasy
  indulging in sensuousness
  reconciling differing ideologies
  passing on folklore or family histories
  passing the time
  providing a means of personal expression
  providing an opportunity for self-examination
  persuading
  propagandizing
  providing testimony
  redefining reality
  redefining art itself

This is a list of ends or purposes, and while it is possible that they might all be achieved using only one means – for example, realistic painting – in practice artists have used many techniques, styles and approaches. The result is that a definition of art based primarily on

means is particularly unsatisfactory. All the definitions of art offered over the centuries include some notion of human agency, whether through manual skills (the art of sailing, painting or photography), intellectual manipulation (the art of politics) or public or personal expression (the art of conversation). As such, the word is related to 'artificial' – that is, produced by human beings rather than by nature. But it doesn't stop there: this definition of art is correct in a limited way but it is also essentially flawed because it does not allow one to distinguish the defined term from something else that correctly exemplifies the definition. 'A vacuum cleaner is a household appliance' is insufficient as a definition of a vacuum cleaner because 'vacuum cleaner' can be correctly replaced with 'refrigerator', and a vacuum cleaner is not a refrigerator. Saying 'Art equals artificial equals human-made things' fails to distinguish art from other things produced by human beings. It gives us a start, however, for it makes it clear that infinitely realistic painting would simply replicate the world. In so doing, realistic painting says nothing much about human agency and thereby ceases to be art in all but the most bankrupt way. It would be similarly unsatisfactory to try to understand art while limiting oneself to only one or two of the ends above. 'Art is decoration' fails to distinguish advanced art from simple ornament, and 'Art is the exhibition of technical skill' fails to distinguish art from sports and woodworking.

To fail to remain open to the wide range of art's purposes is to be indifferent to its contextual variations, even before we get to the seemingly infinite variety of means and ends. This cripples one's understanding of and openness to art. For example, those who say that art's goal is accurate representation ignore many cultures (such as African, indigenous Australian and Islamic, not just the modern West) in which realism is subordinate to emotional exuberance, imaginative visions anchored in faith or the expression of an idea. Some would declare that art, by definition, has to be beautiful, arbitrarily excluding innumerable depictions of social injustice, violence and tragedy. Still others might maintain that art's only real identity lies in redefining what constitutes art, but that is surely not what was on the mind of an artist whose work is effectively an anguished outburst.

Interpreting Art

So, the answers to the questions 'What is art?' and 'What is art for?' are that art is a particular way of saying something or producing an effect in an observer, and art is 'for' whatever it says or produces as an effect in an observer. The judges of what art is for must be the observers themselves, who are in some ways interpreters of this art. It does not follow, however, that one interpretation is just as good as the next one. Historians and older academics tend to encourage interpreters to 'perform the art' (the word 'interpret' means 'to perform' in some languages) subject to the constraints provided by the work itself. They do so because they believe that this produces more of a statement about the work itself than about the observer. However, observers have the right to interpret as they feel – like a musician improvising around a theme, i.e., they can pretty much refuse to 'perform the art' subject to its constraints, allowing themselves to be inspired in a way that produces more of a statement about themselves than about the work. Both attitudes, and every position between them, can be seen in current writing about art. This might all seem very complicated, but bear in mind that there are in fact only three categories of statements one can make about a work of art: Context, Form and Content. However, there are numerous possibilities for interaction between the elements within each category (for example, Form to Form), exponentially more possibilities for interaction between the categories themselves (for example, between Form and Content) and virtually infinite possibilities brought to one layer in one of the categories (Context), so we shall consider each of these in turn.

Context

'Context' refers to the circumstances surrounding the production and reception of a work of art rather than anything physically present in the work itself. Whether an artist was a man or a woman, religious or secular, academically trained or self-taught, is not something *in* the work, but it provides additional information that can certainly affect our understanding *of* the work. Whether the work was produced for public consumption in

a religious establishment or for the cabinet of a private collector also affects our interpretation and understanding of the piece. We would have to interpret a work made during the time of the Spanish Inquisition differently from a hypothetically identical one made, say, during the expansion of the railways in the New World because we would need to keep in mind the very different cultural expectations behind them.

Recognizing a contextual code can help an observer understand a lot more about a piece of art. In the absence of this knowledge, a conventionally representational painting might still give us something to look at, even though we do not really understand it at all. In a work that departs from the conventional – for example, art that uses scratchy, unpolished-looking graffiti marks and codes – we do not even have the comfortable familiarity of the contemporary *Zeitgeist* on art. If we do not know that a certain mark means 'the people who live here are friendly to the homeless', for example, then we do not understand the piece and we may have no meaningful experience of it. Without contextual information our interpretation is likely to be insufficient at best and faulty at worst.

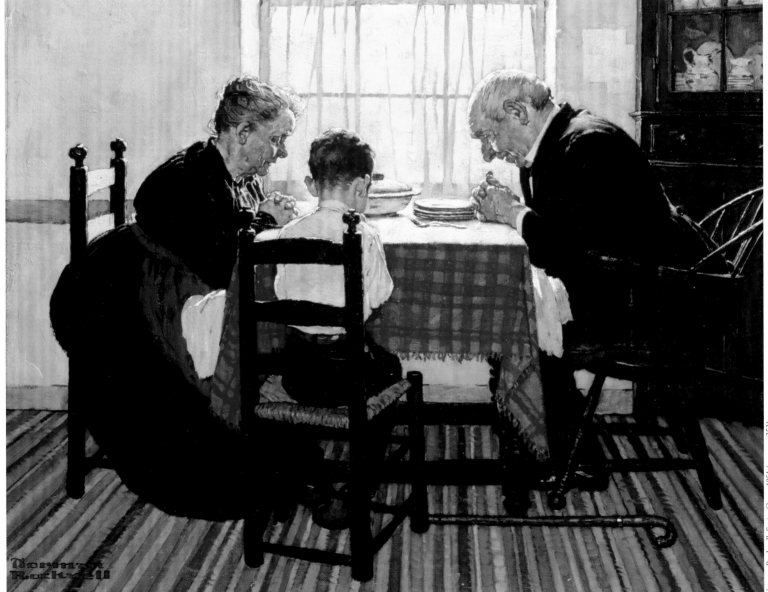

Norman Rockwell, *Saying Grace*, 1951 (see page 353)

Information about the artist is one of the major factors in the Context category. Although some might argue that details about the artist's social world are more significant, society in general did not produce the actual work, however much it may have influenced or affected its creation. Since there would be no work without its maker, primary Context is that which describes the circumstances of the work's production at the level of the individual artist. Contextual information is not a description of the production of the piece of art itself; it is the artist's attitudes and beliefs, education and training, gender and sexual preference, likes and dislikes, lifestyle and philosophy, politics and religion, social standing and personal wealth. As with all Context, none of these things has to appear in the work, but they all affect our understanding of it. For example, Artemisia Gentileschi (1593–1653) did not paint her experience of rape by her tutor Agostino Tassi in 1612, but knowing this detail of her life gives us license to interpret her depictions of male decapitations in a certain way.

We can consider secondary Context to be the broader cultural expectations, such as the philosophy, politics and religion of the observers or patrons of the work, which of course the artist might have shared. Again, none of these things appear in the work, but they can change our interpretation of it. For example, it can help us to understand that a swastika – a Greek cross with its arms bent in the same rotary direction – can be interpreted in one way in twentieth-century Europe where it is associated with Nazism, and in a completely different way in ancient China, India and Tibet where it is inextricably linked to Buddhism, Jainism and Hinduism.

The information we gain about a piece of art's context must be accurate and relevant (the sexual assault mentioned above is relevant, for example, whereas knowing that that artist was fond of a particular type of cheese would not be). One of the fascinating things about art history, however, is the way that later generations of observers sometimes retrieve and reuse an aspect of Context that an earlier generation found irrelevant. Every observer brings to a work his or her own secondary Context, and in this way the art is a reflection of ourselves. Secondary Context is theoretically infinite, unless we arbitrarily restrict our interpretations to a given range – for example, the lifetime of the artist or the patron. Because we have difficulty deciding where the boundary falls between acceptable and unacceptable circumstantial evidence, the proliferation of secondary Context makes the meanings of art seem inexhaustible.

Form

The second of the three basic categories, Form, differs fundamentally from Context. While the latter, by definition, does not appear in the work, Form *is* the work and its constituent elements, independent of any meaning they might have. For example, a work's colour, light, medium, shape, size, technique, and texture are all aspects of Form. The basic formal elements are primary when they are treated in isolation. For example, to speak of the character of a single shape in a painting as organic, geometric, static or dynamic is to refer to an aspect of primary Form. When we say something about how that shape relates to another shape, we shift to a secondary level of Form, in which elements relate to each other, as in balance, composition, contrast, distance, perspective, space, and so on. When we recognize shapes as particular things with particular identities – for example, identifying an arrangement of coloured stripes as a flag – we assign them a meaning and move from Form to Content. The mechanism that makes the change in the flag example is Context, because we know that certain stripes (Form) indicate a flag (Content) within the horizon of expectations of a particular culture. Moving from Form to Content is so natural to us that we find it difficult to distinguish between the categories. It is, however, a useful exercise, for Form, however interesting on its own, plays an important role in actually *creating* Content.

Content

'Content' refers to what a work says and the effects it produces in an observer. Some of these may actually be 'meanings' (in the sense that the artist meant or intended to convey them), and some may be better described as 'significances' (pseudo-meanings not intended or controlled by the artist but peculiar to an individual observer). Like the other categories, Content has primary and secondary levels. Primary Content corresponds approximately to the literal level of language – attributes, events, facts, objects, people, places and things, all representing what they appear to represent, as opposed to symbolizing something else. As soon as we point out that one thing symbolizes or stands for something else, we shift to a secondary level of Content. Every competent performer of

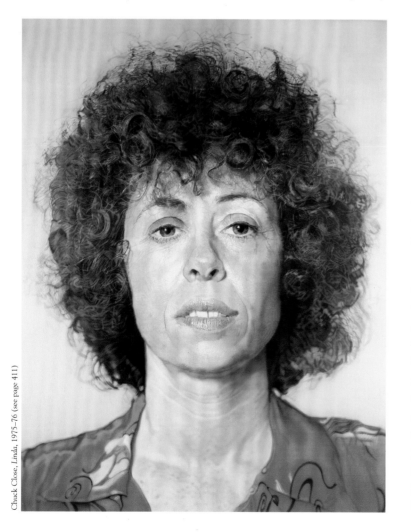

Chuck Close, *Linda*, 1975–76 (see page 411)

a language instinctively understands that figurative expressions are not to be taken as literal. 'She was on cloud nine' does not refer to someone floating in the sky; it pushes beyond the primary to a secondary layer of Content, 'happiness'. This is the core flaw in the theory that the value of art lies in its ability to render something accurately: to praise a work solely for its realism is to ignore the codes that may be utterly obvious to an observer who shares its artist's horizon of expectations. In other words, what you see may not be what you (are supposed to) get.

There are several mechanisms by which primary Content becomes secondary Content. Probably the most common of these is symbolism – the comparison of a literal element in the picture to another element, whether present or implied, until a different level of meaning emerges. Devices such as the metaphor work in exactly this way. A child blowing a bubble is just that if we take the scene literally, but if we are prepared to see it as a comparison of the child and the bubble, a metaphor is produced. The understood characteristics of the bubble – its beauty and fragility – imply something less immediately apparent but no less true about the child.

A good many of these tropes, as they are known, are conventional and widely understood by the culture or society in which the work has been produced. 'She was on cloud nine' would not be figuratively meaningful in a culture that had not standardized the expression. Other tropes are invented by the artist rather than simply borrowed from culture in general. Observers may recognize these spontaneously, or they may have to work at understanding them by filling in the gaps in their knowledge of the artist. That an observer's knowledge of the artist is never complete is another of the many ways in which the meanings of art seem to be inexhaustible.

Relationships between Context, Form and Content

That Form consists of elements independent of meaning does not mean that it does not affect the meaning of a piece of art. Just as Context influences Content, pushing it from primary to secondary, Form also affects Content, although it uses a less familiar method of category-shifting that we might call 'paralinguistic'. Though the term strictly applies to the spoken language, the same principles can be applied to the visual image. The term refers to the way changes in individual delivery (or performance) of a statement lead to changes in our understanding of what is meant. If one changes the Form of a literal image (that is, the way in which it is delivered or performed), one can produce a corresponding change of the literal meaning of the image to a metaphorical one. Like tropes, some of these shifts can be conventional, evoking an immediate response that is mediated by secondary Context. For example, in Western culture everyone spontaneously recognizes the difference between the look, sound, and meaning of 'fire' spoken normally and 'FIRE!' screamed loudly, even though the core meaning is the same. Moreover, everyone can tell the difference between 'fire!' yelled in a crowded theatre and 'fire!' shouted next to a line of aiming soldiers. Someone who fails to understand the difference has overlooked something important about the culture in which the expressions have achieved currency.

However, artists do not limit themselves to illustrating those

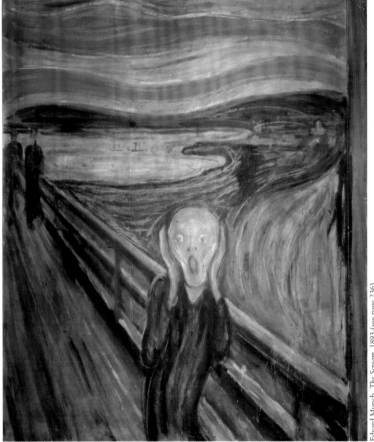

Edvard Munch, *The Scream*, 1893 (see page 236)

paralinguistic shifts that are already part of the popular culture. They routinely invent them for expressive and aesthetic purposes. This is most immediately apparent in works of an expressionist sort – for example, Van Gogh's *Starry Night*. Because of the painting's departure from conventional depictions of the night sky (and from Van Gogh's own usual style), it seems to evoke a deeply emotional response, and the scene almost cries out in mystical ecstasy. Trying to unravel the meaning-effects of contextual codes and formal nuances without falling prey to the assumption that good art is realistic, is key to understanding art as art, rather than art as craft.

No matter how complicated, then, all works of art involve the interplay of these three categories. This realization provides a way to create a workable definition of visual art that brings us at least a little closer to sufficiency. That is, visual art is the manipulation and interrelation of visible Form, invisible Context and primary Content to create secondary Content – that is, to say something or to produce an effect in the observer that goes beyond the literal – for the purpose of accomplishing one or more of the various ends listed above.

What is Good Art?

Notice that the new definition of art carefully avoids the question 'What is good art?'. This is because definitions of 'good' are always mediated by the values of secondary Context, the circumstances in which the piece is seen rather than in which it is created. One set of secondary cultural expectations sees goodness as 'quality', for example. But in one culture

'World Art'

Mark Rothko, *Untitled*, 1968 (see page 378)

In order to appreciate art it is helpful to keep our minds open to others' aesthetics and social customs by learning about the art of other times and places. It is interesting to think about what the expression 'World Art' implies in the light of differences in the viewpoints of the dominant European-American Context and what that Context deems somehow Other – that is, 'World' cultures. For example one can draw a distinction between world artists who work essentially within their indigenous traditions and those who consciously accept and manipulate international influences.

Curiously, the lay person seems to have less difficulty dealing with objects made by the indigenous branch of world artists than with works by those who accommodate and/or reinvent European-American approaches. One explanation is that average viewers might be thinking of the objects less as art per se than as ethnographic objects or charming curiosities. They might be tempted to justify this by alluding to the absence of a word equivalent to 'art' in some cultures, but some cultures probably also do not have a word for 'cystic fibrosis', the worldwide prevalence of which would not necessarily mean that the ailment cannot occur within their societies. So it is with art, which appears to be everywhere whether we know it by that name or not.

Perhaps the average person is more comfortable with indigenous objects than avant-garde objects because they do not expect the former to be art, so they do not run afoul of the perceptual fallacy that has been previously highlighted and therefore do not expect indigenous art to be a realistic portrayal of a subject or object. The same reasoning may lead some viewers to reject unconventional artworks from the European-American tradition, on the grounds that they don't accept such pieces as examples of a craft, preferring to think of them as some sort of fraudulent commodity at best, or tomfoolery at worst. In order for them to accept a craft there has to be a quality in the technique applied to the creation of the piece. They would hold that art is craft, and would reject some pieces of advanced art on these grounds.

If these hypothetical average viewers think of unconventional artworks in the Western tradition neither as craft nor as ethnographic objects, then it is possible to speculate that thinking of non-Western artworks as anthropological trophies is nothing more than a strategy to avoid engagement with them as works of art. This strategy of containment is exactly the opposite of our goal to keep our minds open to others' aesthetics and social customs. In fact, we should be so open to this that we pass beyond grounding our identity in self and other altogether, because there are those who think this process, however well-meaning, is parochial and in dire need of redefinition.

It is all the more important, then, to explore works in which world artists accommodate and transform Western models, because in them we see postcolonial approaches to contemporary art that might provide instructive models for future interpretations. In Africa, Australasia, Central America and South America indigenous artists were influenced by the trends of the European settlers, who worked in the prevailing European styles. It was only

quality is defined as formal orderliness whether or not it is really appropriate for the Content, and in another culture quality is interpreted as whether or not artists have achieved what they set out to achieve. Where some cultures have not seemed to care whether an artist's use of symbolism is purely conventional or original, another culture highly prizes 'innovation' – the deliberate striving of the artist to invent a new and unconventional way of expressing something. Today, innovation is in the ascendant and it is manifest in only about three ways. First, artists can innovate by portraying primary Content with Form that is unexpected and, ideally, previously unused in this connection in such a way that new secondary Content is produced. As raw subject matter, Picasso's famous weeping women are nothing new, but his inventive Form shifts them until they say something new and produce a new effect in the observer. Second, artists innovate by making unusual combinations of secondary Content. Judy Chicago's famous *Dinner Party* of 1979 (in which place-settings are decorated with flower motifs that pun on female genitalia) retrieves old associations – for example, women's art as flower painting – and reinvents them within the set of cultural assumptions that constitutes feminism. Third, artists innovate by developing and depicting idiosyncratic aspects of primary Content. Because this involves personal motivations that are often difficult to pinpoint, this third way to innovate is another contribution to the impression that art's meanings are inexhaustible.

the course of the twentieth century that indigenous art, some of it with traditions going back many centuries, received a wider audience. This resulted in distinctive national or regional movements that either paint traditional themes using Western techniques or blend ethnic motifs with Western styles; but it is only within relatively recent times that the arts of Africa, Asia, Australasia or Polynesia have inspired artists working in Europe and America, as part of the ongoing quest for distinctive styles arising out of a riotous mixture of eclecticism.

The Purpose and Structure of this Book

You may be wondering what the relevance is to this book, of this reflection on art's definition, purpose, characteristics, and potential for interpretation. The answer lies in the fact that an artwork's Form and its primary Content actually appear in the work, while its Context has to be brought to the work to give the observer a full and sufficient experience. This does not mean that experience of a work without knowing its Context is invalid any more than the statement 'A Hoover is a household appliance' is invalid. It is simply insufficient. So the purpose of this book is to introduce the general reader to a wide sample of artists and artworks from around the world, while providing some brief information necessary to enrich understanding.

Before sending you straight into the midst of the hundreds of artists and artworks that so richly populate this book, we begin with a small section devoted to setting the historical and contextual scene. 'Art Movements' discusses the main eras and their art since the Byzantine Empire, and the myriad styles, schools and movements that have occurred over the centuries, illustrating the text with relevant artworks. Many movements are readily identified by sets of stylistic traits, as in the ubiquitous paint-dots of Pointillism, which is to say that some movements are best characterized by aspects of Form. Other movements can be characterized as well by aspects of Content, as in Symbolism's preoccupation with 'clothing the Idea in sensual, perceptible form', to paraphrase Jean Moréas (French Poet 1856–1910). In other words, an idea or emotion became the starting point for the piece, and was expressed through the selective use of color (for artists) and words (for poets) so that the idea attained a physical form. Still other movements can be characterized by Context, as in Surrealism's preoccupation with Freudian thought and Postmodernism's reliance on abstruse literary, political and other theories. Ultimately, all movements are in fact contextual entities because they are historically specific. If we describe the work of an artist of the 1990s in terms of Cubism, which flourished 80 years earlier, we are probably addressing only its Form. Such a work is likely outdated and of little significance, although it is possible that the artist is trying to accomplish some other end that would have to be unearthed through contextual analysis.

In the latter part of this section Dr Julia Kelly deals with 'Modern Art' and its breakdown into the many and varied styles that exploded in art in the twentieth century. This is perhaps the type of art that is currently given most coverage by the media, and often the most baffling for the art novice, despite its supposed links with contemporary life. The twentieth century ushered in a period of rapid transition, with more scientific, technological and political change than at any other time. Dr Kelly outlines the dramatic effect these changes had on the development of art, describing the sociological environment and historical factors that gave rise to the modern art movements, and discussing whether modern art is a reaction against, or a reflection of modern society.

The art of the modern world tends to dwell on the internal world of the artist, more than that of any other era, so that instead of the art movements that reflected the consensus of a group of artists, modern art conveys many intensely personal messages, which can be baffling to the observer. Dr Kelly elucidates the logic behind the modern art movements, such as conceptual art, using individual works as examples and explaining the reasoning behind them, especially in cases where a movement or style might be considered by many to be particularly incomprehensible or enigmatic.

Finally, after the reader has sampled and studied a selection of artists and paintings from the many on offer in the heart of the book, the section on 'Painting Techniques' explores the physical constituents of art and their interrelations (or Form), through an investigation of methods and techniques. Here we present sketches of many of the more important techniques that have inspired artists and facilitated their expressions over the centuries. We provide brief technical explanations and descriptions of artists' processes, so that general readers can at least know how a print is created, and become wise to retailers promoting 'limited-edition prints' that are not true prints at all. Readers will also want to know how various techniques, in and of themselves, have 'voices' that inflect a work's Content.

How to Read this Book

We invite readers to make use of this book in any way they see fit. We do, however, ask them to keep in mind that its final purpose is to see art as a way to exercise our hearts, imaginations and minds, not only to expand our knowledge of others' ideologies and social customs but also to question our own. These poles of respect and critique provide the parameters within which this book will achieve its purpose.

You may find that you end up reading this book, or at least sections of it, more than once. Dipping into the entries selectively will allow you to be drawn into the subject of art through the artists, or pieces, that most appeal to you. Reading through the art movements and painting techniques sections at a slightly later stage will then allow you to learn more about the lie of the land in general. The concepts introduced in these sections will equip you to teach yourself more about the pieces on display as you work your way around a gallery as well as enable you to gain a deeper understanding of the works included in the sections, by seeing how their components work in sympathy with one another. Lastly, we discourage you from thinking of the book's selection of works as the final word on the subject – art history's canonical 'greatest hits', as it were. Think of them instead as exercises to prepare you for the great adventure of art – to explore a world that could never be encapsulated within the covers of one book.

Art Movements

Art in one form or another has been in existence for thousands of years. There is ample evidence not only that cave painting and engraving were widespread in Palaeolithic times, but also that it spanned many centuries and reflected many different styles and purposes. It is fascinating to observe the development of technique over the centuries and the improvement in the materials used to create a wider range of colours and styles. It is clear that cave-dwellers executed these works of art partly for decoration, partly for self-expression and partly for some other motive, perhaps in connection with their religious beliefs. The Aboriginal art of Australia, which has developed along distinctive tribal and community lines for almost 40,000 years, offers the best example of art which, in form and content, has retained its essential character and is still very much a living force.

There is a huge gap between the cave paintings of the Old Stone Age and the art of the Middle Eastern civilizations. It should not be supposed that art did not exist in the interim, merely that the media in which it was executed have not survived. Certainly the applied and decorative arts from 10,000 BC onwards in Anatolia and Mesopotamia, in metalwork and pottery, for example, reveal a high degree of artistic attainment. The fine arts of painting and sculpture evolved gradually all over the world and eventually attained high levels of sophistication and aesthetic sensibility in those parts of the world where 'civilization' in the broadest sense reached its peak. Thus we may find a high degree of technical skill manifest in the temple and tomb murals of Pharaonic Egypt, the friezes of Babylon, the wall-hangings of China and the mosaics and frescoes of Crete and Mycenae. Out of the art of the

Aegean, which flourished between 5,000 and 1,000 BC would develop the art of Greece and ultimately that of Rome. To the Greeks painting was a minor art, mostly confined to the decoration of vases but nevertheless revealing a very lively sense of composition and realism. The Etruscans derived their art from the Greeks but took it a stage further, reviving the art of painting on ceilings and walls – techniques later refined by the Romans. The murals of Pompeii and Herculaneum, engulfed by lava and volcanic ash in AD 79 and miraculously preserved as a result, are mute testament to the skills of Roman artists, notably in their clever use of line to create a three-dimensional effect.

Byzantine Art

As the Roman Empire pushed farther east it came in contact with the arts of the Orient and, after the collapse of the empire in the West in the fifth century, the Byzantine Empire increasingly looked to the East for both the form and content of its art. Silk-weaving, ivory-carving and glass mosaics all benefited from this Oriental influence. The sumptuously coloured illuminated manuscripts from the sixth century onwards, replete with gold leaf, reflect the influence of Persia, but it was not until the end of the ninth century that representational art, in the style of the Classical Greeks, was revived and then rose to new heights. Most of the surviving examples from the later Byzantine period are associated with imperial portraiture or the representation of saints, out of which developed the tradition for icon painting which continues in Orthodox countries to this day.

Although the western Roman Empire disintegrated under the incursions of the Goths, Vandals and other barbarian peoples and its civilization was destroyed, it did not vanish completely. Western Christianity, with its headquarters in Rome itself, was eventually embraced by the pagan tribes, and from this developed the petty kingdoms of the Dark Ages and the revival of empire under Charlemagne. Italy was reconquered (or liberated) by the Byzantines in the sixth century and in the ensuing period Ravenna and Venice became major centres of Byzantine art and architecture, noted for their religious mosaics. Although the Byzantine Empire briefly extended along the southern shores of the Mediterranean as far as Morocco, the rise of Islam in the seventh century gradually forced it back and Constantinople itself came under attack in the eighth century. Nevertheless, the Byzantine Empire endured until 1453, when its capital Constantinople fell to the Osmanli Turks. Its art had become somewhat stereotyped and what fresh impetus it had seems to have come from southern Russia (notably in the shape of icons), Turkey or Syria; but from the early 1300s there was a late flowering of Byzantine art, reflected in religious wall-painting, illuminated manuscripts and icons which, in turn, had a dramatic impact on Italian art in the fourteenth century.

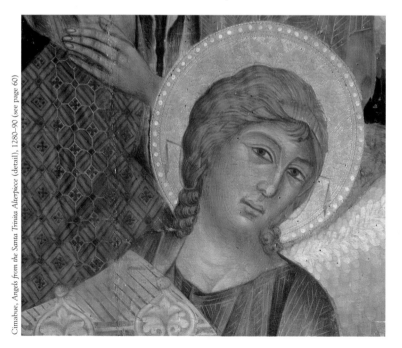

Cimabue, *Angels from the Santa Trinita Alterpiece* (detail), 1280–90 (see page 60)

Gothic Art

As the political and cultural heir of the western Roman Empire, the Holy Roman Empire founded by Charlemagne consciously imitated the art and architecture of the period before the fall of Rome. In architecture particularly this imitation was often crude and barbaric, and was contemptuously dismissed by Renaissance writers as 'Gothic'. Although the term is grossly inaccurate and misleading, it has been retained as a convenient name for the art and architecture from the end of the first millennium to the start of the Renaissance.

The Gothic style arose primarily out of a desire by newly Christianized peoples to build churches, monasteries and cathedrals on a grand scale; consequently, Gothic is largely associated with extravagant vaulting, spires, flying buttresses and elaborate tracery. These edifices were distinguished by their huge, tall windows which encouraged the development of stained glass, but whose walls left relatively little scope for mural painting. Fine art in this period made advances through the medium of illuminated manuscripts, but this was a skill practised in every monastery. Working on parchment, the limners outlined their pictures in various coloured inks and used tempera (a mixture of various pigments with egg-yolk, oil and water) and gold leaf to create everything from an ornamental initial letter to a complete illustration in the manuscript copies of the Gospels, psalters and breviaries. Before the invention of printing from movable type, the only books were those laboriously copied by hand, a labour of love for the greater glory of God. Inevitably there was also a secular parallel development when kings, princes and great merchants commissioned prayer-books, known as 'books of hours', which differed from the monastic works in their greater use of scenes drawn from everyday life. These books were produced by artists who might have learned their craft in a monastery, but who operated in purely commercial workshops. It is significant that while we know little of the identity of the monastic limners and scribes, the earliest identifiable artists in western Europe were those like Jean Pucelle of Paris and the Limbourg Brothers of Flanders, the respective creators of the magnificent *Belleville Breviary* and the *Très Riches Heures du Duc de Berry*.

Fresco Painting

Long before the fall of Constantinople brought a flood of refugees to western Europe with the accumulated learning, skills and technology of the East, the Byzantine influence was making itself strongly felt. In the thirteenth century a change in Italian ecclesiastical architecture left more wall space, which demanded suitable decoration. We shall probably never know who was the genius who first stumbled upon the technique of painting on wet lime plaster, using colours ground and mixed with lime water. As the plaster dried the colours were fixed, just as if they had been applied to pottery then fired in a kiln. The problem with this technique was that the plaster set quickly, so fresco painting (as it was termed) had to be executed swiftly to a careful plan, because it was impossible to repaint once the plaster had dried. Although this style of painting was

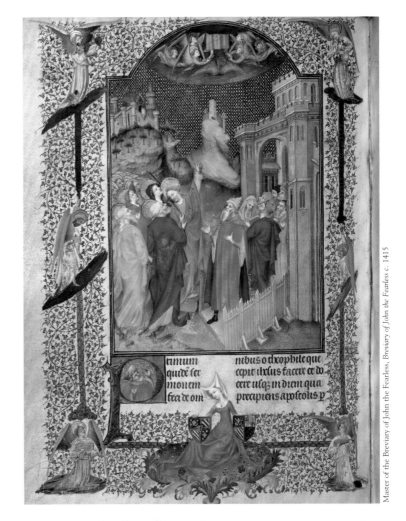

Master of the Breviary of John the Fearless, *Breviary of John the Fearless c. 1415*

immensely popular all over Europe, by its very nature it was unsuited to the prevailing damp climate of northern Germany, the Low Countries or Britain, with the result that few medieval frescoes have survived intact. Even in Italy, many of the frescoes painted for churches have not stood the ravages of time and weather.

The greatest impetus to fresco painting came in the late thirteenth century, when the Franciscan order created the magnificent foundation at Assisi in honour of St Francis. The Franciscans recruited the best artists from all over Italy and thus Assisi briefly became an important centre where painters came together, argued and exchanged ideas. A large part of the decoration at Assisi was carried out by Benevieni di Pepo, nicknamed Cimabue ('ox-head'), in around 1280. Trained in the Byzantine tradition, Cimabue (c. 1240–c. 1302) transformed it and laid the foundations for a distinctive Italian style. Few frescoes by this Florentine painter have survived, but those that are still extant reveal his role in effecting the transition. The influence of Byzantine icon-painting is still very strong in his *Maestà* (1280), but the Madonna on her majestic throne has a much softer, more human expression than one would find in icons of the period. The artist's radical departure from the Byzantine tradition was continued by his pupil and successor Giotto di Bondone (1266–1337), who combined a more flexible approach to composition with portraiture, a style that conveyed both the feelings and character of the subject in a manner never previously attempted, far less achieved.

The Sienese School

Although there were at this time a number of artists at Rome who, like Cimabue and Giotto, had been schooled in the Byzantine tradition and who had turned from mosaics to painting, the work of Giunta Pisano (c. 1229–c. 1254), Coppo di Marcovaldo (c. 1225–c. 1274) and their colleagues did not immediately follow the new style. In Siena, however, there was Duccio di Buoninsegna (c. 1255–c. 1318), whose *Ruccellai Madonna* of 1285 was the equal of the masterpieces by Cimabue and Giotto. Like his contemporaries, Duccio was raised in the Byzantine tradition, and he too breathed new life into it, independently of Cimabue and Giotto, with works that displayed an increased sense of spatial awareness and narrative. His studio in Siena became the well-spring for a school of art which developed along parallel lines with that of Florence. The Sienese artists of the next generation included Simone Martini (c. 1284–1344) and the Lorenzetti brothers Pietro (c. 1280–1348) and Ambrogio (d. 1348). The latter completed his art training in Florence which, by the middle of the fourteenth century, had emerged as the predominant force in Italian painting.

The Early Flemish School

Elsewhere in western Europe, the outstanding painter of his generation in Flanders was Jan Van Eyck (1390–1441). Not only did Van Eyck inject an unprecedented realism into his paintings, particularly in his delineation of the texture of robes and the surface of stone or brick, but he was also responsible for the introduction of painting in oils – a method that would revolutionize the medium. The appearance of his great altarpiece of the Mystic Lamb, with its 12 interior panels and matching exterior compartments was a *tour de force* that placed the Flemish School in the forefront of painting in northern Europe – a position it retained for more than a century – and even influenced developments in Italy itself. A prime example of this was the painting of himself and his wife, which was commissioned by Arnolfini at Bruges; this piece is still widely regarded as the exemplar of realism and precision that was the hallmark of Flemish painting. Rogier Van der Weyden (1400–64) and later Hugo Van der Goes (c. 1440–82) continued the tradition, adding their own special brand of pathos and expression.

Early Renaissance Art

Although France was at the nadir of its fortunes as a result of the Hundred Years' War with England (which occupied Paris itself), a few artists managed to maintain standards at Avignon, then a papal fief. Among them was Jean Fouquet (c. 1420–c. 1480), who raised portraiture to a new level (painting on canvas instead of the more usual wood support), in full-scale works as well as in miniatures, and demonstrated how, even in vicissitude, a country can still produce great art.

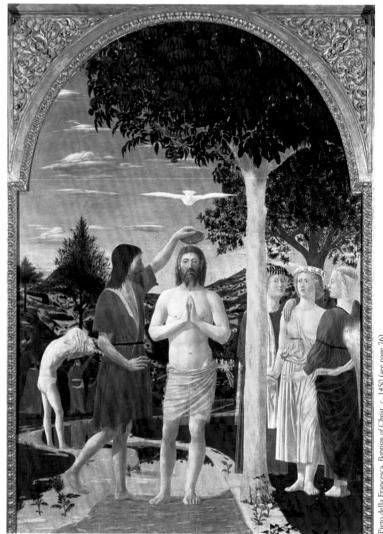

Piero della Francesca, *Baptism of Christ*, c. 1450 (see page 76)

The wealth of the merchant princes who controlled the affairs of the great Italian cities created a patronage of the arts that has not been exceeded since. This period coincided with the rise of the papacy, and an unparalleled era of church building in the Italian style which yielded huge expanses of interior walls for decoration. This was the golden age of frescoes and elaborate altarpieces as artists vied with each other in painting the Holy Family and biblical scenes, into which was breathed the fresh air of the new Renaissance humanism. Religious works were given a contemporary slant and made free use of ordinary everyday scenes. A new realism pervaded these paintings, enhanced by much greater attention to detail. Pisanello (1380–1456) and Masaccio (1401–28) pioneered the study of the human form and made the nude figure a respectable subject for ecclesiastical decoration – a notion taken to its logical conclusion by Masolino da Panicale (1385–1447) in his great *Baptism of Christ*.

In the background architecture of Masaccio's paintings we can see the striving towards a mastery of perspective; had he not died so young, who knows what he might have achieved. As it was, it was his colleague Paolo Uccello (1397–1475) who solved the problem. Indeed, Uccello became obsessed with creating a three-dimensional illusion that might emulate the great bronze bas-reliefs of Lorenzo Ghiberti (1378–1455), in whose workshop he had originally been employed as a mosaicist. Andrea del Castagno (1423–57) also experimented with perspective and the use of space and lighting. Piero della Francesca (c. 1420–62), though not a Florentine, subsequently came under the influence of Uccello and Masaccio and likewise sought the solution to the problems of perspective, eventually writing a couple of treatises on the subject.

Painters were held in the highest esteem in the early Renaissance era, and the Dominican monk Fra Angelico (1387–1455) was even beatified by the Church in recognition of the profound effect his powerful but simple religious paintings had on those who saw them. By contrast, the Carmelite monk Fra Filippo Lippi (c. 1406–69) brought an earthy realism into his works and is best remembered for liberating the altarpiece, removing the artificial divisions of the centrepiece and side panels to create one large continuous surface.

High Renaissance Art

Painters who had begun their careers as stone carvers or sculptors included Sandro Botticelli (1444–1510), Antonio Pollaiuolo (c. 1429–98)and Andrea Verrocchio (1435–1488), and they too strove to achieve those attributes which would give their paintings a proper sense of distance. These artists came to the fore just at the time the Renaissance ideals of secularism and humanism were at their most pervasive, but were overshadowed by the next generation. Foremost, of course, was Leonardo da Vinci (1452–1519), whose life was synchronous with the High Renaissance and who was the most perfect example of the Renaissance man, excelling in an extraordinary diversity of disciplines, as an architect, sculptor, designer, military engineer and inventor as well as a painter. Not only did he produce one of the greatest masterpieces of all time, the *Mona Lisa*, but he was also one of the first Italian artists to employ landscape as an extension of the subject rather than merely to fill the background.

Michelangelo (1475–1564) had many of Leonardo's attributes, as well as being a poet of considerable ability. Though best known as a sculptor, in later life he produced paintings of such sublime power as to place him in the first rank; his decoration of the Sistine Chapel is rightly regarded as one of the greatest masterpieces of all time. His near contemporary was Raphael (1483–1520), trained in the effete Umbrian School but later acquiring the positive qualities of the Florentine School, and having the good sense to graft on the best precepts from Leonardo and Michelangelo. The end result was a noble style that transcended the sum of its parts and was universally regarded as the quintessence of a pure and perfect harmony. The religious

Leonardo da Vinci, Vitruvian Man, c. 1492

paintings of Raphael are so well known that it is difficult to realize how startlingly novel they struck his contemporaries. He breathed new life into the hackneyed subject of the Madonna and Child and other aspects of the Holy Family, which were an obligatory part of the repertory of every artist of the period. To Raphael more than any other artist of the High Renaissance is due the credit for establishing Rome as the artistic centre of the Western world – a position that remained unchallenged for more than 200 years.

Mannerism

It became the goal of every aspiring painter and sculptor to travel to Rome and study under the great masters. Returning to France, Germany or the Low Countries, they would spread the teachings of Rome, a process that endured long after Rome's status as Europe's cultural capital had diminished. The rising powers of northern Europe compounded this by hiring Italian artists to decorate palaces which themselves were designed by Italians or slavishly followed the example of Italian architects. This Italian predominance led indirectly to the rise of Mannerism, a style that evolved in the sixteenth century as the successors of Michelangelo and Raphael tried to surpass them. The buzzword was *maniera* ('stylishness'), but in striving to achieve this its practitioners indulged in a rather self-conscious refinement which reached its peak in the 1570s. Exaggeration of form, colour and expression characterized the works of Andrea del Sarto (1486–1531) and his pupil Jacopo Pontormo (1494–1577) but culminated in the frescoes of Giorgio Vasari (1511–74), better known today as an art historian than an artist in his own right. Mannerism was relatively short-lived, and the reaction to it produced a return to more naturalistic styles.

The Later Flemish School

While the Italianate influence was accepted unquestioningly in France, it was not embraced quite so wholeheartedly in the Low Countries, where Quentin Metsys (1466–1530), founder of the Antwerp School, modified Italianism to produce a more humanist style imbued with natural expression and a distinctive grace. Hieronymus Bosch (c. 1450–1516) harnessed Italian techniques to his own highly idiosyncratic style, creating a brand of fantasy and visionary painting which in many respects anticipated the Surrealists by several centuries. Pieter Brueghel (c. 1520–69) accepted the basic tenets of the Italian style, but his approach to painting was wholly original. We may detect the influence of Bosch in his Gothic scenes, but his development of genre scenes, full of down-to-earth humour, was without precedent. His son, Pieter Brueghel the Younger, tried to go one better, with grotesque paintings of devils and hags which inspired terror in their beholders, but the wheel came full circle in the case of younger brother Jan, known as 'Velvet' Brueghel because of his anodyne paintings of flowers, still-lifes and religious themes that conformed to mainstream ideas.

The German School

Something of the anarchic attitudes of Bosch and Brueghel was also evident in the paintings of the German engineer, architect, engraver and artist Matthias Grünewald (c. 1470–1528), who rebelled against Roman Classicism. The parallel with da Vinci is very close: a man of many talents and prodigious intellect, whose visionary passion comes across vividly in his great masterpiece, the Isenheim altarpiece. His exact contemporary was Albrecht Dürer (1471–1528), whose Classical training never impeded his Germanic genius. If he lacked the versatility of Grünewald, he had da Vinci's enquiring mind and fascination for the

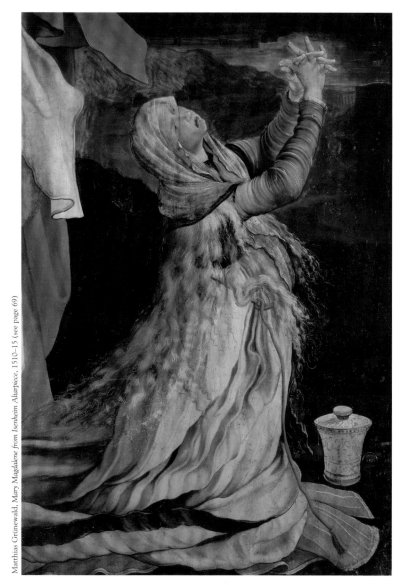

Matthias Grünewald, *Mary Magdalene from Isenheim Altarpiece*, 1510–15 (see page 69)

minutiae of nature, evident in his numerous anatomical studies of animals and humans. Lucas Cranach (1472–1553) lived far longer, and so his art was strongly influenced by the Reformation. Working as court painter at Wittenberg, he was an eye-witness to the dramatic events surrounding Martin Luther from 1517 onwards. Thus his earlier work, comprising mainly religious paintings and Classical allegories, gave way to portraits (including the reformers Luther and Melancthon) and more secular subjects, all imbued with a sense of realism and immediacy.

Portraiture had been comparatively neglected in the Italian convention, although there had been some outstanding exceptions – Leonardo's portraits of Ginevra di Benci (c. 1476) and the *Mona Lisa* (the wife of Zanoki del Gioconda) 30 years later were quite extraordinary examples of purely secular portraiture in an age when idealized pictures of the Holy Family and the saints were the norm. The example of Cranach was followed by Hans Holbein (1497–1543) who, though German by birth, trained in Italy then worked in Switzerland and finally in England. One of the first truly cosmopolitan artists, he combined Teutonic precision with Italian elegance to create some of the greatest documentary portraits of the early sixteenth century, notably his series devoted to Henry VIII and his wives. Holbein produced full-scale easel-paintings, but also helped to establish the tradition of the portrait miniature, which attained its zenith with Nicholas Hilliard (1547–1619) in the reign of Elizabeth I and continued unabated in Britain until the advent of photography in the middle of the nineteenth century.

The Venetian School

The Venetian School also developed in the fifteenth century. Its progenitor was Andrea Mantegna (c. 1431–1506), a native of Vicenza who learned his craft in Padua and worked mainly in Mantua and other towns and cities of northern Italy. Mantegna's influence spread to Venice via his connection with Giovanni Bellini, his brother-in-law. Bellini's early years as an artist were inspired by Mantegna's style; particularly his sculpturesque figure style and sense of composition. Although Mantegna was employed as a fresco painter – his finest works were the series of tempera pictures *The Triumph of Caesar* and the ceiling of the Camera degli Sposi in Mantua – he exerted enormous influence on the next generation of northern Italian painters. Their vitality and exuberance brought renewed splendour to Italian painting at a time when the older-established schools were running out of momentum.

Actually the Venetian tradition can be traced back much further, to Gentile da Fabriano (c. 1370–c. 1427), who spent most of his life painting in Venice before studying in Rome, Florence and Siena in the 1420s. Gentile was the teacher of Jacopo Bellini (c. 1400–70), a Venetian artist whose few extant works reveal an intense fascination with landscape and architecture long before either subject was fashionable. Jacopo was the father of Gentile (c. 1429–1507) and Giovanni (c. 1430–1516), the Bellini brothers who helped to revolutionize and reinvigorate Italian painting in the late fifteenth century. Gentile Bellini was one of the first artists to appreciate the unique beauty of Venice and its canals, but he also excelled as a portraitist, and was invited to Constantinople in around 1480 to paint a portrait of Sultan Muhammed II. Giovanni Bellini was the first Italian artist successfully to wed figures to landscapes in a wholly naturalistic setting, and pioneered the naturalistic treatment of light.

Mantegna married Jacopo's daughter and was thus brother-in-law to Gentile and Giovanni, with whom he worked very closely. Also associated with them was Antonello da Messina (c. 1430–70), who migrated from southern Italy in the last decade of his life and was one of the first Italians to abandon tempera for oil paints and explore the potential of this Flemish innovation. Another early exponent of the Venetian School was Antonio Pisanello (c. 1395–c. 1455); working in a city in which the influence of the eastern Mediterranean was pervasive, Pisanello countered the prevailing Byzantine style with his own individual brand of International Gothic.

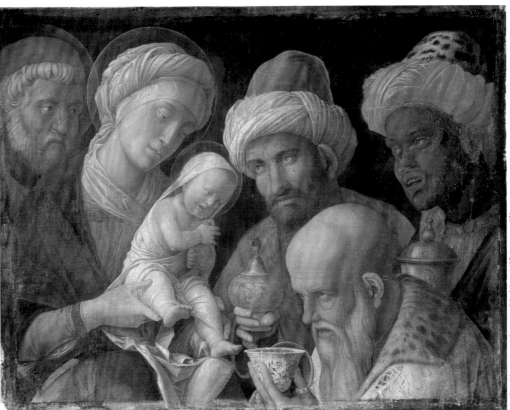

Andrea Mantegna, *Adoration of the Magi*, 1495 (see page 83)

The leading figures in the next generation of Venetian painters included Vittore Carpaccio (c. 1460–c. 1525), who combined religious themes with contemporary Venetian urban landscape, and Giorgione (c. 1476–1510), a somewhat shadowy figure whose chief interest is that he bridges the gap between Giovanni Bellini and Titian, who assisted him on the frescoes of the Fondaco dei Tedeschi.

The Venetian School attained its finest flowering in the sixteenth century, in the hands of Tiziano Vecellio, known as Titian (c. 1490–1576). He succeeded Giovanni Bellini as Painter to the Most Serene Republic in 1516 and, like his predecessor, executed a number of large paintings and altarpieces for various churches in and around Venice. He also undertook commissions for wealthy patrons, in which he concentrated on Classical subjects which enabled him to develop the painting of the female nude. In Florence nudes were invariably shown as standing figures in static poses, but Titian liberated the nude; his Venuses were recumbent or reclining in languid poses, invested with a new sensuality. This was a definite turning point: and in works such as *Sacred and Profane Love* Titian freed painting from its religious didacticism and enabled his successors to explore the infinitely wider world of sentiment. In his later works the quality of his brushwork led to an exceptional combination of form and content; the manner in which he used paint poetically to attain sublimity of expression has rarely been equalled, far less surpassed.

Of all the Venetian painters, Jacopo Tintoretto (1518–94) came closest to scaling Titian's great heights, and he went even further in taming perspective. Tintoretto produced some of the largest painted works of all time, but despite their great size, the quality was undiminished and he excelled both as a portraitist and

as an accomplished master of the human figure in every conceivable pose. The third of the great painters in this phase of the Venetian School was Paolo Veronese (c. 1528–88), noted for his great historical and biblical scenes conceived and executed on a heroic scale. Veronese pushed to the limits the secular treatment of religious subjects, an activity that led to charges by the Inquisition that he had treated sacred themes in a profane manner. His chief contribution to the development of painting was his exploration of colour and texture and the effects of light on different surfaces. The reflection of hard or polished surfaces such as metal and marble, the soft tones of human flesh, the sumptuous qualities of silks and brocades or the deep tones suggestive of velvet and fur or the glossy tints of human hair – these were attributes that the great Venetian masters raised to new levels, investing their paintings with qualities of pathos, nostalgia, melancholy, majesty or an inner radiance.

Italian Academicism

Throughout the course of the sixteenth century there was a great deal of cross-fertilization in the European art world. Venetians such as Titian worked in Rome on papal commissions. Others also found their way there: Sebastiano del Piombo (1485–1547), a pupil of Giovanni Bellini and Giorgione, assisted Michelangelo at Rome from 1510 onwards and was so strongly influenced by him that he was regarded as more Florentine than the Florentines. Conversely, there were also artists of great independence of spirit and originality of style flourishing in other parts of Italy. Antonio Correggio (c. 1499–1534) worked in Parma, a skilled decorator on a vast scale but also an

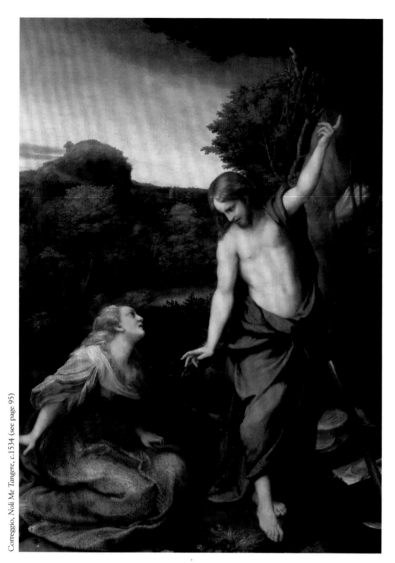

Correggio, *Noli Me Tangere*, c.1534 (see page 95)

Art in Spain

The chief reason for the preponderance of Italian art in the fifteenth and sixteenth centuries was that it was the part of western Europe that felt the greatest impact of the Renaissance. North of the Alps, a different set of forces were at work. The printing press revolutionized communications, enabling the rapid dissemination of new ideas in philosophy and religion, and the development of a humanism that challenged the teachings of the Church. In turn, this created the independent, free-thinking climate in which art developed along radically different lines. While Italian art continued to be dominated by religious paintings, in Germany and the Low Countries a more secular approach was reflected in the intimacy of small portraits, in the popularity of genre subjects and in the development of both landscapes and domestic interiors.

France went through a period of social and political upheaval before an uneasy peace between the Catholics and the Protestant Huguenots was agreed in the Edict of Nantes in 1598. Consequently, in the seventeenth century France gradually took over from Italy as the leading artistic centre. Spain, on the other hand, had only achieved political unity at the end of the fifteenth century. The expulsion of the Moors and Jews took place in the very year that Columbus landed in the New World. Religious conformity – enforced in Spain more rigorously through the Inquisition than anywhere else in the Catholic world – was a major factor in the development of art in the sixteenth and seventeenth centuries, while the vast influx of precious metals from the mines of Mexico and South America produced a period of unparalleled wealth and prosperity, in which architecture, sculpture and painting flourished as never before.

If the disparate elements of Spain were brought together through the marriage of Ferdinand of Aragon and Isabella of Castile, the political unions of their offspring would lead rapidly to the ascendancy of the Habsburg dynasty and the emergence of Charles V as the ruler of a vast European empire. The resulting cross-fertilization in Spanish art far exceeded the eclecticism in Italy during the same period. It is significant that the leading Spanish painter of the early sixteenth century was Antonio Moro (c. 1517–77), who was actually born Anthony Mor van Dashorst at Utrecht in Holland and trained under Jan Scorel (1495–1562) at Antwerp. One of the first great, although somewhat underrated, cosmopolitans, Moro enjoyed a high reputation as a portraitist at the courts of Brussels and London before being summoned to Madrid. His style was eclectic, combining Flemish realism with Spanish romanticism and Italian classicism. The result betrays more than a hint of Mannerism, the style that developed initially in Italy in the second half of the sixteenth century. Originally this was clearly defined as a tendency to exaggerate or distort features or form for the sake of effect; in Moro's case this was reflected in the elegant aloofness and haughty expressions of his royal sitters, but in later generations mannerism (with a small 'm') became a general term denoting an affected adherence to a particular style.

It was another foreigner who brought the Spanish version of Mannerism to its fullest flowering. Domenikos Theotokopoulos

accomplished master of the smaller easel painting. Agostino (1557–1602) and Annibale Carracci (1562–1609) were artists who developed in Bologna, outside the mainstream of the large schools. Ironically, they founded an academy which attempted to train young artists to paint according to clearly defined principals and formulae, thereby giving rise to the rather stereotyped 'academicism' of the seventeenth and eighteenth centuries. The greatest of the independent artists, however, was Michelangelo da Caravaggio (1573–1610), a restless and untamed spirit in every sense, whose wild lifestyle forced him to move frequently and hurriedly. Perhaps this constant need to be one step ahead of his creditors or enemies dictated his passionate, rapid, almost frenzied style of painting. Caravaggio was the great master of genre scenes from everyday life, often so lowly that few would have considered them fit for depiction; but he also produced some sublime religious masterpieces in which the subjects were handled with great realism. Stripping Christ and the saints from the idealization of earlier generations, Caravaggio made them more acceptable at a time when reform and the questioning of traditional religious values were becoming more commonplace. His revolutionary style struck a responsive chord throughout Italy and beyond; Rembrandt was one of the northern painters to come under his spell.

(1541–1614) was a native of Crete, part of the Venetian dominions at that time, but ethnically and culturally Greek. Trained in the Byzantine tradition, El Greco ('the Greek') went to Venice where he became a pupil of Titian in the latter's declining years, came under the influence of Tintoretto and the Mannerist style of Andrea del Sarto, and studied the works of Michelangelo and Raphael in Rome before settling at Madrid in 1577. El Greco developed a highly individual style. Faces and bodies were elongated and features distorted and his style influenced Spanish portrait painters of the ensuing generations, notably Diego Velázquez (1599–1660) and Bartolome Murillo (1617–82).

The French School

Religious and political stability came to France in 1610 with the accession of Henri IV, but it was his grandson, Louis XIV (1638–1715), who left his mark on the seventeenth century and created the era that is still known as Louis Quatorze. This was the era that witnessed the great glories of Versailles and an extraordinary flowering of the applied and decorative arts, from Gobelins tapestries to Sèvres porcelain. The era of Louis XIV would become almost synonymous with the age of the Baroque.

In the fine arts, France had lagged behind both Italy and Spain. Since the time of Jean Fouquet in the fifteenth century there had been little of note in French painting, other than the Clouets, father and son. Jehan Clouet (c. 1483–1541) hailed from Flanders and was successively painter to the Duke of Burgundy and François I of France. His skills as a portraitist were exceeded by those of his son François (c. 1516–72). Best remembered for his extraordinary portraits of Charles IX, Elizabeth of Austria and Mary, Queen of Scots, François also painted the remarkable *Lady in her Bath* (possibly the royal mistress, Diane de Poitiers), which betrays the influence of the Mannerists. There was no continuity such as existed in Italy at the same period, and the artists who emerged in the seventeenth century received their training elsewhere, or were influenced by the art of other countries. Simon Vouet (1580–1649) appears to have been self-taught, an infant prodigy whose skills by the age of 14 led to many international commissions which took him to England, Constantinople and Italy, where he worked in Venice, Florence and Genoa before being summoned by Louis XIII back to Paris in 1628. For the last 20 years of his life he ruled the French art establishment and although his own pictures are not highly appreciated nowadays, he had a tremendous influence on the development of French painting, not least on the work of Nicolas Poussin (1594–1665), who was only four years his junior. Poussin covered a wide range, from allegorical, classical and bacchanalian scenes in the first half of his career to great religious, heroic, historic and architectural subjects in his later years. Towards the end of his career (1648) he took up landscape

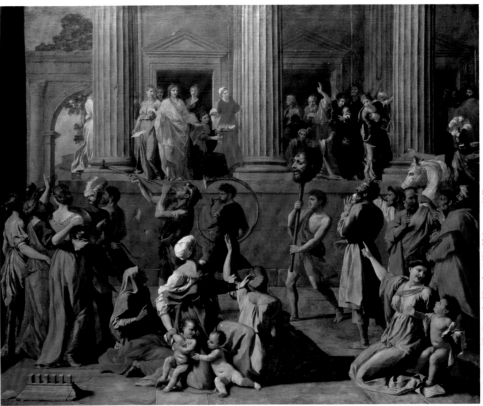

Nicolas Poussin, *The Triumph of David*, c. 1631–33 (see page 116)

painting. Poussin was precise and meticulous, every brushstroke clearly thought out, never indulging in whim and leaving nothing to chance. Not surprisingly, Poussin laid down the strict principles that would be slavishly followed by the Royal Academy of Painting and Sculpture (founded in 1648) until the closing years of the nineteenth century. By contrast, Claude Lorraine (1600–82) is classed as a French painter solely on grounds of birth, but early in his career he settled in Rome and spent most of his life there. Yet his landscapes were painted in a distinctive style that stands apart from the Roman manner. Regrettably, the demands of Louis XIV for colossal paintings designed to record the glories of France and depict the Sun King in the most heroic light did not inspire great or original painting.

The Flemish School

The marriage in 1495 of Joanna of Castile and Philip of Burgundy at Antwerp, and the birth of their son, the future Holy Roman Emperor Charles V, gave Spain control of the Netherlands. In 1579 the seven predominantly Protestant provinces proclaimed their independence and became a republic, although they remained under the control of a hereditary Stadholder, the Prince of Orange. While the remaining provinces (later known as the Austrian Netherlands and now Belgium) declined in importance, the United Provinces became one of the leading maritime powers of the seventeenth century. Amsterdam and Rotterdam took over from Antwerp and Brussels as great trading centres, and the arts flourished accordingly.

Peter Paul Rubens (1577–1640) was born in Westphalia but was educated in Antwerp and throughout his life remained loyal to the

Habsburg connection. A man of many talents, he was a scholar, antiquarian and career diplomat as well as one of the greatest European painters of all time. He was a devout Catholic and supporter of the Habsburgs and his greatest diplomatic achievement was the peace treaty he negotiated between Spain and England. It was as a result of his diplomatic activity that he was able to paint so many portraits in both Madrid and London, not to mention the extraordinary series of 21 large canvasses showing the life and times of Marie di Medici, Queen of France. An artist of the widest range, he was equally at home in intimate portraits and colossal heroic scenes and in his Antwerp studio he made use of a large number of pupils and assistants, including Anthony Van Dyck (1599–1641), Jacob Jordaens (1593–1678) and Frans Snyders (1579–1657); his influence on the later Flemish School was profound and long-lasting. Nor should it be overlooked that his style had a tremendous impact on such French painters as Eugène Delacroix (1798–1863) and Jean-Antoine Watteau (1684–1721).

Van Dyck was born at Antwerp and closely emulated the style of his master. Like Rubens, Van Dyck excelled as a portraitist and is best known for his magnificent paintings of Charles I and other members of the British royal family, as well as English nobles and celebrities of the early seventeenth century. In turn, Van Dyck exerted an enormous influence on the English portraitists, notably Thomas Gainsborough (1727–88).

The Dutch School

Long before the Dutch School emerged in all its glory, there were precursors whose originality and independence of mind set them apart from the main Flemish School. In this group may be named such painters as Lucas Van Leyden (1494–1533), whose portraits were boldly innovative, and Gerard de St Jean (c. 1465–93), a self-taught artist whose naïve religious paintings anticipate the Primitives of a much later period. But what led to a pronounced dichotomy between the older Flemish School and the emerging Dutch School were the social, political and religious differences that came in the wake of the Reformation.

The Reformers were iconoclasts who abhorred religious imagery of any kind. For this reason art was diverted from the religious subjects that dominated even secular painting in Catholic countries, and resulted in pictures that extolled the Christian virtues in a more subtle, natural manner. Dutch painters were free to indulge their passion for realism, constrained solely by what appealed to the increasingly wealthy middle classes. The rising bankers, merchants, manufacturers and ship-owners of Holland did not live in large palaces surrounded by opulence, but in relatively modest houses, which explains why Dutch paintings of the seventeenth century were generally small in scale. Despite this, there was still a vogue for large canvasses, commissioned by the wealthy guilds and corporations as well as the numerous paramilitary volunteer groups which stemmed from the protracted wars of independence. The personal element in Dutch painting ensured that portraiture assumed paramount importance. It is a singular fact that all the great Dutch masters were portraitists, first and foremost. Frans Hals (c. 1580–1666), a native of Antwerp who spent most of his life in Haarlem, is unusual in that he rarely painted anything else,

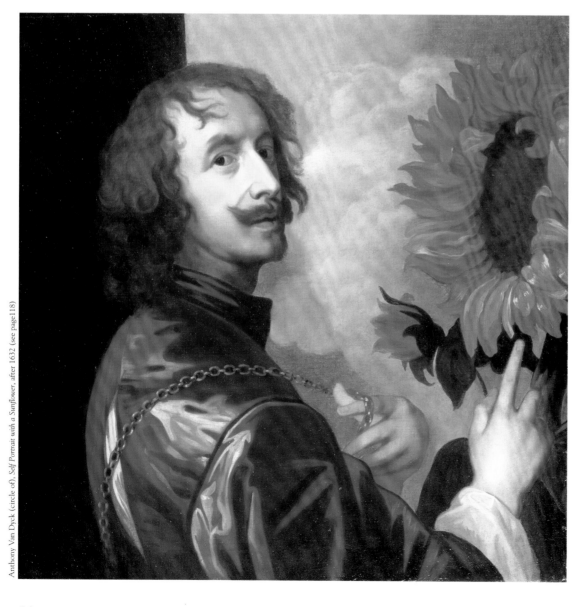

Anthony Van Dyck (circle of), *Self Portrait with a Sunflower*, after 1632 (see page 118)

although his work ranged from small individual portraits to those large militia groups that were a purely Dutch phenomenon.

The early Dutch masters reacted against the Mannerists and the religious painters by concentrating on genre scenes and landscapes. The artists in Haarlem who learned their trade from Frans Hals included Adriaen Brouwer (c. 1606–38), who specialized in genre subjects of a decidedly earthy, off-colour and sometimes downright vulgar character, which may be regarded as a healthy reaction against the extreme Calvinism of the period. Adriaen Van Ostade (1610–85) worked primarily as an etcher and watercolour artist, although he also executed a number of fine oil paintings. Like Brouwer, he had a penchant for Rabelaisian comedy, tinged in his case with satire, though his more serious work extolled the virtues of the peasantry. His pupil Jan Steen (1626–79) produced his own special brand of genre paintings, comic scenes of dysfunctional families in their disorderly homes – immensely popular with the Dutch who, in their own lives, were models of cleanliness and order.

Towering over all the others, however, is Rembrandt Van Rijn (1606–69), a native of Leyden who settled in Amsterdam at a time when that port was emerging as the most prosperous city in the Netherlands and the nation's commercial capital. Rembrandt was schooled by his master, Peter Lastman (1583–1633), in the traditions of the High Renaissance, but soon established his own distinctive style. Rembrandt was unusual in the Holland of his day in that he continued to paint large religious scenes long after they had fallen out of favour. Although he never went to Rome, he studied prints of the best classical works and in this manner imbibed the techniques of light and shade pioneered by Caravaggio. To his religious, mythological and historical subjects he brought a new realism, and these works are now regarded as his greatest masterpieces. In his own lifetime, however, what earned his daily bread were the portraits of individuals and groups. Even as the commissions dried up, Rembrandt continued to paint self-portraits and portraits of his family, including imaginary portraits derived from history or mythology. Like Dürer, he was also a prolific draughtsman who left a rich legacy of etchings and prints.

The generation of Dutch masters that followed Rembrandt was also noted for portraiture, but by the middle of the seventeenth century the prevailing fashion was for landscapes and domestic interiors – the sort of pictures that the Dutch bourgeoisie preferred to hang on their walls. The transition from the bonhomie of the militia groups and genre paintings of tavern scenes was almost imperceptible at first, Gerard Terborch (1617–81) having switched effortlessly from one to the other. Carel Fabritius (1622–54) was a pupil of Rembrandt who produced some unusual pictures which, in effect, combined still-life with landscape. The sort of pictorial geometry that delighted Fabritius also exercised painters like Samuel Van Hoogstraten (1627–78) and Pieter de Hooch (1629–84), the latter using this to good advantage in his domestic interiors, handling perspective with considerable skill. Jan Vermeer (1632–75) likewise specialized in domestic interiors of such precision that it has been speculated that he employed some form of camera obscura. The resulting paintings are highly objective, but lack feeling or passion, and their realism is counterbalanced by the lack of variety in texture and tone.

The Dutch painters, however, invented a style of art that had no motive beyond the precise reproduction of inanimate objects which had never excited any interest previously. These studies of still-life were generally small; they became very popular from the 1630s onwards and gave rise to a sub-school of Dutch painters who produced little else. In time the still-life was subdivided into distinct categories, so that there were artists who specialized in vases of flowers, dead fish or game, breakfast or banqueting compositions. Still others consisted of the careful juxtaposition of objects thath had some symbolic connotation. A popular theme, for example, was mortality, hence those pictures of human skulls and hour-glasses as a constant reminder that time was running out. Arrangements of crowns and jewels might symbolize the vanity inherent in the lust for wealth or power. Books and musical instruments were also popular subjects for pictures with a moral undertone. There were many exponents of still-life painting, but the most interesting works were produced by Davidsz de Heem (1606–83), whose use of a limited range of sombre colours emphasized the austerity of his subjects and emulated the work of Pieter Claesz (c. 1596–1661). Jan van Huysum (1682–1749) was a later exponent of the virtually monochrome still-life which at times veered towards the abstract. De Heem, however, later moved to Antwerp, where he was swept up in the Baroque fashion and switched to lavish still-life paintings, rich in colour and profuse in subject matter.

The Dutch painters were noted for their landscapes, and so diverse were the styles and their exponents that there was a tendency to specialize. Thus Aelbert Cuyp (1620–91) at Dordrecht and Jacob Van Ruysdael (c. 1628–82) from Haarlem produced vast landscapes that relied heavily on clouds and unusual lighting effects. Van Ruysdael's works often depicted rugged mountains in the background which, considering where he spent all his life, must have been largely a figment of his imagination. Cuyp's trademark was to depict cattle, sometimes individual cows but often herds, in the foreground. Other artists, such as Pieter Molijn (1595–1661) and Jan van Goyen (1596–1656), concentrated on seascapes and riverbanks, or placid views along the numerous canals of Holland. Jan Porcellis (c. 1584–1632) went a step further by creating dramatic stormy scenes in which ships featured prominently. Marine pictures became immensely popular later in the seventeenth century, reflecting national pride in the Dutch East India Company, which brought the wealth of the Indies and the Far East to Holland. Specialists in this medium included Willem Van de Velde the Younger (1633–1707), who painted particular ships and had a high reputation for pictures showing naval engagements.

Baroque Painting

The Baroque movement which swept across the rest of Europe in the seventeenth century was a marked contrast to the homely styles evolved by the Dutch School. It arose initially as a reaction against Mannerism in painting and sculpture and was triggered by the Caravaggisti, the followers of Caravaggio who were inspired by his dramatic naturalism. At its best, the Baroque style of painting resulted

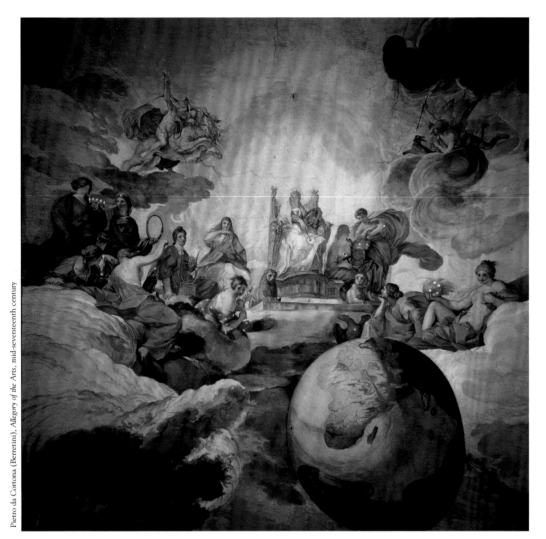

Pietro da Cortona (Berretini), *Allegory of the Arts*, mid-seventeenth century

short shrift. It made little impact on painting, though a noteworthy exception is the *Transparente* in Toledo Cathedral by Narciso Tomé (c. 1690–1742), which echoes Bernini in its combination of stucco and painting. Baroque, in fact, was a style most closely associated with architectural painting and lent itself particularly to the huge ceilings of palaces. Good examples are to be found as far afield as the Banqueting Hall in Whitehall, London (painted by Rubens), and Drottningholm Palace, Stockholm (painted by David Klöcker Ehrenstrahl) appropriately entitled *Great Deeds of the Swedish King*s.

Rococo Style

The term Rococo was derived from the French word *rocaille*, signifying the rockery and shell work which became immensely popular in sunken gardens, dells and grottoes in the late seventeenth and early eighteenth centuries. Indeed, a spin-off from the same movement was the Grotesque (literally pertaining to caves and grottoes). Just as the craze for all things Baroque swept across Europe like a plague, so also the fashion for Rococo assumed

in a riot of colour which appealed to the emotions rather than the intellect. The Baroque style was extensively used in architecture and every aspect of the applied and decorative arts, and as such had an enormous impact which survives to this day. Significantly, many of the finest paintings in this manner were architectural in concept. Elaborate architectural forms can be seen in the great frescoes of Pietro da Cortona (1596–1669) and, most of all, in the illusionistic ceilings and murals of Andrea Pozzo (1642–1709). The finest exponent of the Baroque at its most extravagant was Gianlorenzo Bernini (1598–1680), the most accomplished master of all the artifice and illusionistic tricks. He was first and foremost an architect and sculptor, but he succeeded admirably in translating the three-dimensional to the two dimensions of painting and, by the clever use of lighting and perspective, creating masterpieces that seem to leap off the surface. Painting was also combined with stucco work to heighten the three-dimensional effect.

Elsewhere, there were many practitioners of the Baroque, but because of the sheer flamboyance of the style and the criticism heaped upon it in later periods, they have often been overlooked. In France, Baroque ideas fitted very neatly with the grandiose views held by Louis XIV, interpreted competently by such prolific painters as Hyacinthe Rigaud (1659–1743) and Nicolas de Largillière (1656–1746). Spanish painting of the comparable period, however, was so totally dominated by Velázquez, de Zurbarán and Murillo, that the Baroque style received

epidemic proportions. It manifested itself primarily in architecture and furniture, but soon extended to silver, glass, ceramics and all the minor decorative arts. Asymmetry was the key, with profuse application of scrollwork and curvilinear ornament. It fitted the mood of frivolity and gaiety that affected many countries during this period. On mainland Europe it mirrored the economic recovery after the long-term debilitating effects of the Thirty Years' War (1618–48), and in Britain it was a fitting climax to a liberalization in the arts that had begun with the Restoration of the monarchy in 1660 and attained its greatest heights in the reign of Queen Anne (1702–14).

More specifically Rococo developed in France in the closing years of the seventeenth century, when many of the noble families began to drift back to Paris from Versailles as the Sun King lost his brightness. The process was accelerated after the death of Louis XIV when the royal court no longer seemed to be the centre of the world. The aristocracy who built their villas and town houses in Paris laid out gardens to match, and it was in the artificial creation of 'natural' features such as dells and grottoes that the fashion for the Rococo developed.

The first painter to catch the spirit of the Rococo in a big way was Watteau, who neatly encapsulated all the wit, grace and elegance of the early eighteenth century – a time when France was the unchallenged arbiter of taste throughout the Continent. His paintings were neatly attuned to the boudoirs and salons of the aristocracy, in marked contrast to the great Baroque extravaganzas required for the grand palaces of Louis XIV. Watteau's paintings are frothy confections of light and colour, although towards the end of his very short life there is often an underlying air of melancholy, perhaps a premonition of the death from tuberculosis that lay ahead. He was an innovator whose *Fêtes galantes* ('pastoral scenes') reflected the obsession with rusticity when even the French royal family played at shepherds and shepherdesses. The delicacy of his brushwork was well-suited to subjects which were play-acting and pure fantasy, but underlying this was a keen observation of the ordinary and an uncanny feeling for human nature. He had a number of pupils and imitators, such as Nicolas Lancret (1690–1743) and Bonaventure de Bar, who did not take his style further but who enjoyed a certain vogue due to their lyrical quality, even if they seldom found their way beneath the surface as Watteau had done.

François Boucher (1703–70) was the leading French Rococo artist of the next generation. Compared with Boucher, Watteau seems a master of restraint, for the younger man created paintings which were a riot of colour, whose exuberance matched the extravagance of the subject. If there was an innocence about Watteau's *Fêtes galantes*, there was a much more sensual character to Boucher's bacchanals, derived from Classical mythology and therefore invariably executed in the best possible taste. Pink nudes suffused with golden light, cavorting all over the canvas, were perfectly acceptable so long as it was clear that they were classical gods and goddesses and not meant to represent real human beings. Under the patronage of Madame de Pompadour (the mistress of Louis XV) Boucher produced his greatest masterpieces dealing allegorically with the rising and setting of the sun, but there is no denying the eroticism of such paintings as *Odalisque*.

Significantly, interest in the Rococo style evaporated in France following the death of Madame de Pompadour in 1764, although it enjoyed a brief resurgence in the paintings of Jean-Honoré Fragonard (1732–1806). Early in his career he had copied the paintings of Boucher and the best of his later work was very much in the same style, even if the eroticism was generally more subtle as befitted the less licentious atmosphere in the reign of the worthy but dull Louis XVI who, along with his wife Marie Antoinette, were chief among Fragonard's patrons. In the 1770s and 1780s, the Rococo element in Fragonard's paintings was gradually replaced by something more sentimental.

Elsewhere, the great centre of Rococo art was Italy, where the style was nicely attuned to the lighter aspects of the Grand Tour. Italy in the eighteenth century had ceased to be a major player on the world commercial scene. Many of the great palaces and public buildings that had been erected in the heyday of the merchant princes and powerful prelates were now in decay, if not total ruin. Giovanni Battista Piranesi (1720–78) made a good living from his picturesque scenes of Roman ruins, although there was also a dark side to his art – the very antithesis of the Rococo – in his nightmarish visions, which were probably drug-induced. For Italianate Rococo at its frothiest we must turn instead to the ceilings and frescoes of Giovanni Battista Tiepolo (1696–1770). Elegance, lightness and grace are personified in the glorious decorations which he executed for the churches and palaces of his native Venice, as well as further afield all over northern Italy,

southern Germany and latterly in Spain. However, Tiepolo was a deeply religious man who never strayed over the boundaries of decorum. His cherubim and putti may frolic all over the place but they are innocent and sexless. He also painted a number of large historical works derived from events of the Middle Ages but invariably (and rather incongruously) executed in the Rococo style. His brother-in-law, Francesco Guardi (1712–93), shows some affinity with the Rococo in his paintings, but this is more evident in the form than the content, for his forte was the urban landscape of Venice, a medium in which he was second only to Antonio Canaletto (1697–1768). While Canaletto travelled to England and produced some of the finest eighteenth-century paintings in London, his nephew Bernardo Bellotto (1720–80) went to Poland where he introduced a late flowering of the Rococo to Warsaw in the dying years of the Polish kingdom. Many of his architectural paintings served as the basis for the meticulous post-war restoration of the Polish capital after its wholesale destruction in 1944.

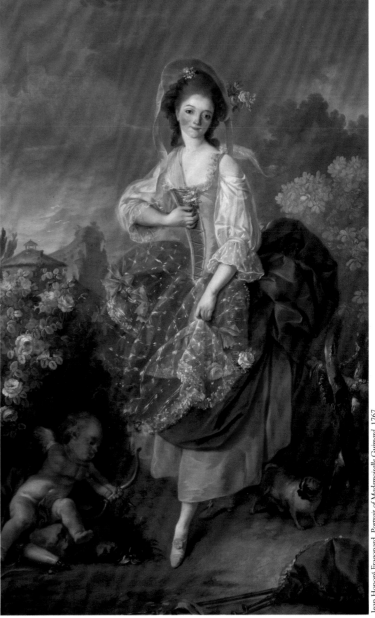

Jean Honoré Fragonard, *Portrait of Mademoiselle Guimard*, 1767

French Academicism

There was a more serious side to the art of the eighteenth century, exemplified by Jean-Baptiste Chardin (1699–1779). Although in some respects one of the pedestrians of the French academic tradition, who spent much of his career as a sign-writer but who also worked on the restoration of the royal paintings at Fontainebleau, Chardin had his moments of glory. In 1728 he made his debut at the Academy with two large still-lifes which combined richness of colour and subtlety of draughtsmanship with a feeling of intimacy but, above all else, a lyric quality, a sense of rejoicing in the humble things of everyday life. These canvasses were a hint of things to come; Chardin would go on to paint pictures of peasant and domestic scenes imbued with charm and integrity. His pictures were wholesome but unpretentious and foreshadowedg the paintings of Jean-Baptiste Camille Corot (1796–1875) more than a century later. In the next generation this example would be taken up by Jean-Baptiste Greuze (1725–1805). In the first half of his career Greuze concentrated on historical subjects, but after visiting Rome in 1755 he switched to genre subjects, mainly featuring young women and often with an underlying edge of satire which redeemed his more sentimental works teetering on the edge of mawkishness.

The English School

Greuze is sometimes compared unfavourably with William Hogarth (1697–1764), an English engraver who turned to portrait painting but achieved renown with his great moral and satirical works, crammed with detail and subtexts. Hogarth visited Paris in 1743 and thereafter concentrated on genre subjects drawn from low life. Hogarth, in fact, was the first great English indigenous painter. Britain, on the edge of

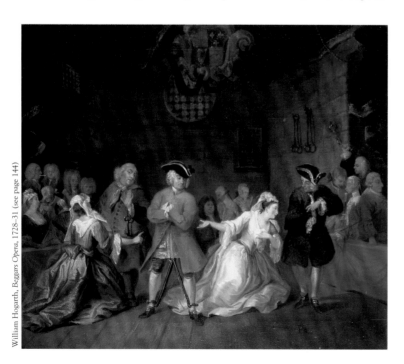

William Hogarth, *Beggars Opera*, 1728–31 (see page 144)

Europe, produced very few painters of any eminence in earlier periods. Instead, the court and nobility relied on European artists to fill the gap. To Holbein, Mora, Rubens and Van Dyck may be added Pieter van der Faes (1618–80) and Gottfried Kniller (1646–1723), who anglicized their names as Peter Lely and Godfrey Kneller respectively.

Sir Anthony Van Dyck, ennobled by Charles I, may be regarded as the father of the English School. As Van Dyck was first and foremost a portraitist, it was in the realm of portraiture that the British artists excelled. The Reformation deprived them of the rich field of religious subjects, but Classical mythology was little known or understood in Britain and thus did not fill the gap. Like the Dutch, the British painters concentrated on portraits, followed by landscapes and genre subjects. Whereas the Dutch also perfected the intimate street scene and the small domestic interior, the British did not diversify from portraiture until relatively late in the eighteenth century. Nevertheless, artists of the calibre of Allan Ramsay (1713–84), Sir Joshua Reynolds (1723–92), George Romney (1734–1802), Sir Henry Raeburn (1756–1823) and Sir Thomas Lawrence (1769–1830), as well as Gainsborough, raised the art of portraiture to new levels. Gainsborough alone in this group was equally versatile as a landscape painter, and established the pattern later followed by John Constable (1776–1837) and J. M. W. Turner (1775–1851). Although lacking the formal guidance provided on the Continent by the guilds of St Luke and the various academies, the foundation of the Royal Academy in 1768 placed the English School on a proper footing at last. It should be noted that attempts to establish an Academy of St Luke in Edinburgh were short-lived and Scottish artists such as Ramsay and Raeburn gained their training, and to a large extent earned their living, in England.

Neoclassicism

In 1755 archeologists unearthed the ruins of Herculaneum and Pompeii, which had been engulfed by lava from Mount Etna in AD 79, and electrified the world by the beauty and naturalism of the mosaics and frescoes thus brought to light. Archeology was then in its infancy, but the notion of lost civilizations that lay just below the surface of the modern world fired the popular and artistic imagination. Johann Winckelmann (1717–68) studied theology then medicine before turning to art history, and it was while working as a librarian in Rome that he was inspired by the discoveries at Pompeii to embark on his great *History of the Art of Antiquity* (1764), which had a tremendous impact on the art world throughout the later years of the eighteenth century and right through the nineteenth century.

The first artist to exploit this resurgent interest in Classical subjects was J. M. Vien (1716–1809), whose paintings *Marchandes d'Amour* and *Belisaires* excited favourable comment. He and his pupils, Vincent and Regnault, took to heart Winckelmann's famous dictum that beauty depended on calmness, simplicity and correct proportion, exemplified in Greek sculpture. These qualities were the direct opposite of Rococo and the reaction against its excesses resulted in the great movement known as Neoclassicism.

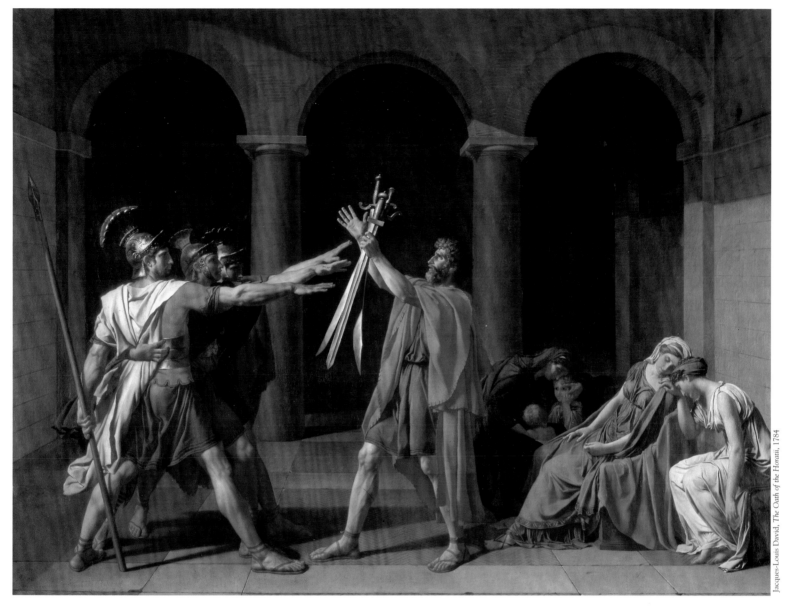

Jacques-Louis David, *The Oath of the Horatii*, 1784

Its finest exponent was another pupil of Vien, Jacques-Louis David (1748–1825). Ironically, he gained little from studying under Vien but was inspired by the writings of Quatremère de Quincy, who seized on Winckelmann's doctrine and expanded it for the benefit of his French audience. Greek painting of the Classical period had long since vanished but de Quincy urged French painters to study Greek statuary, and for this reason the earliest works by David and his contemporaries have a rather static appearance. Thus David's great painting *The Oath of the Horatii* (1785) bears an uncanny resemblance to a Classical bas-relief in which form triumphs over colour. It was an immediate sensation, whose vigour and austerity were hailed as shining examples of all that was best in 'republican virtues'. What was meant, of course, was the ideals of the Roman Republic, but the term would soon have an unfortunate resonance for France as the country was plunged into revolution. When the French Revolution erupted David shot to the top of the new artistic establishment, abolished the Academy and even designed a revolutionary uniform based on Classical lines. When Charlotte Corday stabbed Jean Paul Marat in his bath-tub, creating the first great martyr of the Revolution, David

hastened to the gory scene to capture it in oils. His *Death of Marat* evoked patriotism in the highest Roman republican ideal, painted with noble simplicity in the best Classical tradition.

Ironically, the man who dictated the doctrinaire precepts of the new republican art ultimately found himself in prison, as the Revolution took an uglier twist, but he survived the ordeal and was restored to favour under Napoleon Bonaparte. In this period he concentrated on portraiture, his great masterpiece being *The Coronation of Napoleon I* (1804). Driven into exile after the decisive Battle of Waterloo, he spent the last years of his life in Belgium, where he helped found the Belgian School, which reached maturity just as Belgium won its independence from Holland in 1831. In France, David strongly influenced Pierre Narcisse Guérin (1774–1833), a Neoclassicist who outdid even David in his sense of the melodramatic. Both Guérin and Antoine Jean Gros (1771–1835) became pillars of the French art establishment and received peerages in recognition of their achievement. Guérin passed on his Neoclassicist principles to Théodore Géricault (1791–1824) and Delacroix, but they, like their master, later turned to Romanticism, unlike poor Baron Gros, whose attempts to keep Classicism alive led to his work being ignored – an unhappy situation that drove him to suicide. Infinitely more successful in fighting the rearguard action on behalf of Classicism was Jean-Auguste-Dominique Ingres (1780–1867), who studied under David and regarded himself as the custodian of the Davidian tradition. He succeeded because he strove towards a greater purity and in so doing created a style of expression that was all his own. But he was sometimes accused of being 'Gothic' or even 'Chinese', and he waged an artistic duel with Delacroix that lasted for many years. Ironically, Ingres did what Gros failed to do, and eventually moved with the times, producing portraits – thoroughly modern in their realism – of the self-satisfied upper middle classes of the Second Empire when he was in his eighties.

The chief exponent of Neoclassicism in Germany itself was Anton Raffael Mengs (1728–79), who painted religious and historical subjects conveying the restrained emotions and heroic style of the neo-classical period (working as a painter to the royal courts of Saxony, Poland, Naples and Spain). Mengs lacked the passion and patriotic fervour of David, but in the last years of his life he worked in Madrid, where he created the great *Apotheosis of the Emperor Trajan* for the dome of the grand salon in the Escorial. Perhaps his greatest contribution to the development of European art was the fact that he taught Francisco Goya (1764–1828). It should be noted that Goya, the spiritual heir of Velázquez, was very much his own man, who derived inspiration and technique from many sources and refashioned them in his own inimitable style, and it is significant that whatever Neoclassicism he had imbibed from Mengs was quickly subsumed in the extremely versatile range of Goya's output. The last of the great eighteenth-century painters, he was also the father of nineteenth-century art and the precursor of modern art.

The Age of Reason

A second Renaissance occurred in the middle of the eighteenth century, dominated by the pursuit of truth and knowledge. An entirely new, scientific approach was applied to every discipline. Archeology replaced the vague antiquarian pursuits of previous generations and led to a reappraisal of history. Mathematics, physics, chemistry, astronomy, biology, philosophy, logic, politics and economics were put under the spotlight of rational thought. This intellectual revolution went hand in hand with a technological revolution, as steam mechanized industry and soon transformed communications. The Age of Reason was therefore also the Age of Steam, of the industrial and agrarian revolutions and ultimately the overturning of long-accepted systems of government.

It was inevitable that these intellectual and technological upheavals should have a profound effect on the fine arts. Perhaps because Britain was at the cutting edge of the Industrial Revolution, it tended to be British artists who led the way. The prime example of an artist who revelled in the wonders of the Industrial Revolution was Joseph Wright of Derby (1734–97). Although an accomplished portraitist and painter of genre scenes, his reputation was secured by

his exploration of – indeed revelling in – the great mechanical wonders of the age that were rapidly transforming the way that people lived and worked. Wright was also brilliant in his handling of artificial light, which considerably enhanced his treatment of the industrial subjects he drew from his environment. Other painters applied scientific procedures in furthering their art. George Stubbs (1724–1806) was not the first artist by any means to study anatomy as a prelude to painting human or animal subjects, but few artists went to the extremes of endlessly dissecting carcasses as he did, in order to impart greater realism to his work.

Even if he had acquired the most perfect knowledge of equine anatomy, Stubbs could not have produced such wonderful paintings had he not also possessed a powerful imagination. It was this attribute that marked out a number of other artists active in the second half of the eighteenth century and, letting their imagination, reveries and dreams run riot, they created some of the most extraordinary paintings of that or any other period. Many of the great symphonies of light and colour painted by Turner were in the latter part of his career, when he was becoming increasingly reclusive. In these paintings Turner used paint to recreate the effects of light, which was in turn used to convey the moods associated with his increasingly pessimistic vision of the world, as in *The Slave Ship* (1840).

Paradoxically, therefore, the Age of Reason also produced great paintings that seemed devoid of reason. Long before the time of Freudian psychoanalytical technique, painters were attempting to interpret their dreams and nightmares and record them on canvas. Henry Fuseli (1741–1825) was born in Switzerland, worked in England as a translator (1763–70) then studied painting in Italy (1770–78) before returning to London. Although best remembered for the two series of paintings illustrating the works of Milton and Shakespeare, he painted *The Nightmare* (1781), a truly disturbing work with its overtones of sexuality, sadism and death. It was the precursor of many other works that explored the deepest and darkest recesses of the mind. It was rumoured that Fuseli ate or drank

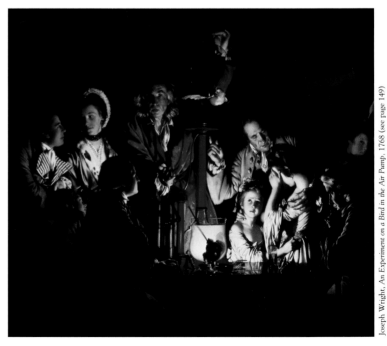

Joseph Wright, An Experiment on a Bird in the Air Pump, 1768 (see page 149)

certain substances to make his consciousness more receptive to these horrific images. He may therefore have been the first – but certainly not the last – artist to resort to drugs to conjure up the lurid or the psychedelic as the basis of their paintings.

There were also mystics and visionaries who rejected the theories of rational thought altogether and strongly objected to the scientists and mathematicians who would reduce everything to geometric principles. Foremost among the rebels against Reason was William Blake (1757–1827). Blake was essentially a poet, but he was also a competent engraver and illustrator. As a poet, he fought long and hard against the tyranny of rationalism and materialism and championed the freedom of the imagination, which eventually found expression in the 537 coloured illustrations that he produced for Edward Young's *Night Thoughts* (1797), as well as a number of individual works, such as *The Marriage of Heaven and Hell* (1791).

Blake inspired a veritable army of followers and imitators whose work carried on well into the nineteenth century and, in turn, influenced some of the artistic developments that come, broadly speaking, under the heading of the Romantic movement. John Martin (1789–1854) produced some highly disturbing images, charged with passion, in his illustrations for Milton's *Paradise Lost*. At one end of the spectrum was Samuel Palmer (1805–81), whose visionary paintings were ultimately more accessible (and therefore more successful) than Blake's because he managed to effect a compromise between an inner mystical vision and the external reality of nature. Furthermore, in an age when conformity was the watchword, eccentricity and idiosyncrasy in art might so easily be regarded as evidence of a deranged mind. In the nineteenth century there would be all too many examples of artists – from Richard Dadd to Louis Wain, from Vincent Van Gogh to Edvard Munch – who were mentally disturbed to a greater or lesser degree. In spite of, or perhaps because of, their affliction some of them at least would produce great art.

Romanticism

The year 1815 was one of the great watersheds of history. The defeat of Napoleon at Waterloo brought to an end his dreams of a European order, but the Congress of Vienna did not entirely turn back the clock. The archaic Holy Roman Empire disappeared, and in its place emerged new nation states. However, Belgium and Holland were forced into an uneasy union which would eventually be dissolved, while the struggle between Austria and Prussia for supremacy in the German-speaking world would be a source of instability in Central Europe. The unification of petty states to form Germany and Italy was a violent process spread over many years. Europe was engulfed by revolutions in 1848–49, but the only major continental conflict to involve Britain between 1815 and 1914 was the Crimean War (1853–56), a relatively localized campaign, while the wars with Denmark (1864), Austria (1866) and France (1870–71) which charted the rise of Prussia and the formation of the German Empire, were short-lived.

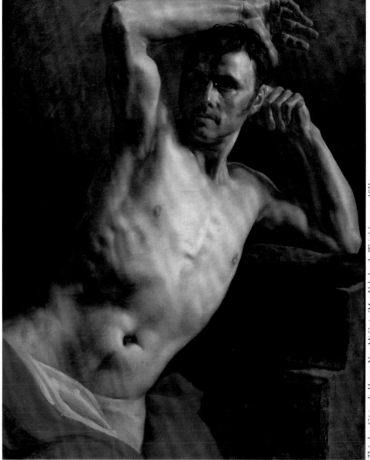

Théodore Géricault, *Homme Nu a Mi-Corps (Man Naked to the Waist)* (see page 183)

The period was one of relative peace and enormous material progress. Britain had a head start, being at the forefront of the Industrial Revolution. Britain took the raw materials from a third of the world and converted them into manufactured goods which were then exported to every country. The population and material wealth of the United Kingdom expanded out of all recognition throughout the nineteenth century. The fine arts flourished in Britain as never before, and for a time a country that had hitherto been on the fringes of artistic development now took on a more prominent role. Yet France, despite the demoralizing effects of defeat in 1815 and 1871, and punctuated by revolution and political instability in the intervening period, continued to be the centre of Western art in the widest sense, and Paris the Mecca that drew aspiring artists from every part of Europe and, increasingly, from the New World.

Thus it was in France that most of the great nineteenth-century art movements had their origins and their greatest exponents although, significantly, most of the others began in England. Neoclassicism was already on the wane when Napoleon commissioned large paintings – heroic in scale and content – to chronicle his imperial exploits. Confronted by the harsh reality of modern warfare, even a convinced Neoclassicist like Gros could not help depicting *The Plague House at Jaffa* (1804) as it really was; full of emaciated, dying men. But the artist who led the revolt against the Neoclassicism of David was Pierre Paul Prud'hon (1758–1823). Having trained at Dijon, he worked in Rome and thus was absent from France during the revolutionary period. He only returned to the latter part of the Empire when his skill as a portraitist brought him the patronage of Napoleon's empresses. He shared David's fascination for Classical sculpture without demonstrating David's dogmatism, and in his great allegorical works – noted for their rich colours, fluid composition and exquisite charm – he led the return to a style akin to that which was popular under the Ancien Régime, yet invested with a freshness that foreshadowed the Romantics.

François Gérard (1770–1837) was a pupil of David who started out as a staunch upholder of art in the service of the Revolution but who ended his career as a baron under Louis XVIII. His *Cupid and Psyche* (1798) is in the Neoclassicist mould, but relieved by an elegance that was quite distinctive. In contrast, his epic canvas of the *Battle of Austerlitz* (1808) was only one of several large works that marked a return to a more realistic approach. Paul Delaroche (1797–1856) was a pupil of Gros, from whom he learned the technique of executing vast historical canvasses. Apart from his murals for the École des Beaux-Arts, where he was a professor, he is chiefly noted for dramatic scenes from English history, such as *The Death of Queen Elizabeth* (1828) and *The Execution of Lady Jane Grey* (1834).

Géricault is another interesting artist who marks the transition from the rigidity of Neoclassicism to the flights of fancy characteristic of the Romantics. Though trained in the style of David, he was also influenced by the Flemish School and showed considerable originality, not to say unorthodoxy, in a number of paintings, notably the *Raft of the 'Medusa'* (1819). In this painting Géricault portrays the true and horrific story of the shipwreck of La Méduse. Nowadays this is regarded as one of those great seminal works that mark a turning point; here are realism and Romanticism wonderfully fused, a splendid example of inspiration at its loftiest. But it was greeted with outrage and vehement criticism which drove the artist into exile in England. Gérard and Géricault were the role models for Delacroix, one of the most intellectual artists of his generation, whose *Journal* provides a rare insight into his attitudes towards art in general as well as a careful analysis of his own and other painters' efforts.

Delacroix made his debut at the Salon of 1824 (the Salon was the name given to the official exhibition of members of the French Royal Academy of Painting and Sculpture) with *The Massacre at Chios*, an action-packed canvas alluding to an incident in the Greek struggle for independence, then at its height. Between this work and his great masterpiece, *The Taking of Constantinople by the Crusaders in 1204*, exhibited in 1840, Delacroix established himself as the undisputed champion of Romanticism. Unlike most other French painters of his generation, he drew on the great writers of English literature for inspiration, from Shakespeare to Byron and Scott. It may be said that while Delacroix never repudiated his Classicist origins, there was much of the Romantic in Ingres. In fact, their differences lay rather in their approach and individual character: the one instinctive where the other was intellectual, the former more concerned with form and the latter more interested in dramatic expression.

The Barbizon School

One aspect of the Romantics that hardly ever arose in earlier art movements in France was an interest in landscape for its own sake. This arose in the closing period of the Revolution, although it did not attain maturity for several decades after this, in the hands of a group of painters who were only born in the last years of the First Empire. The eldest of this group was Alexandre Gabriel Decamps (1803–60), a leading Romantic and a great colourist who specialized in Oriental scenery and biblical subjects and who broke new ground with his evocative landscape entitled *The Watering Place*. Jules Dupré (1811–89) studied in England under John Constable and went on to become one of the leaders of the Barbizon School. Théodore Rousseau (1812–67) had a conventional academic training but by 1833 was sketching from nature in the forest of Fontainebleau. Although he had a measure of success with his *Forest of Compiegne* (1834) he endured more than a decade of disappointment. In the 1840s he settled in the village of Barbizon, where he helped to found a colony of like-minded artists.

Unlike most of his colleagues, Jean-François Millet (1814–75) actually came from a peasant background and grew up with an appreciation of nature, while living and working with his father in a

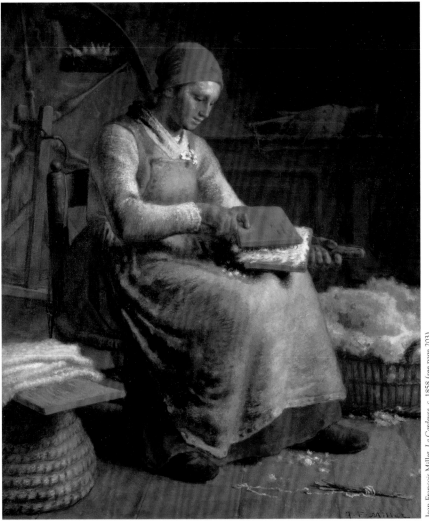

Jean-François Millet, *La Cardeuse*, c. 1858 (see page 203)

small farm at Gruchy, and he received his art education not in Paris or one of the other major centres but at Cherbourg. He continued his studies in Paris before settling in Barbizon and producing such works as *Peasants Grafting* (1855) and *The Gleaners* (1857). Masterpieces of social realism, they were regarded at the time as politically subversive for daring to treat peasants as noble subjects.

Charles François Daubigny (1817–78) specialized in moonlight scenes and river landscapes, of which his *Banks of the Oise* (1872) is a typical example. Constant Troyon (1810–65) injected interest into his landscapes by including animals. What the Barbizon painters had in common, apart from their fascination with landscape, was a desire to represent nature in every aspect, from the awesome to the mundane and ordinary.

Although he also worked at Barbizon for many years, Camille Corot (1796–1875) differed quite radically from the other artists associated with this district. Corot by virtue of his training was more of a Classicist, interested in landscape only in so far as it served his purpose in achieving a harmony between sky and trees, the play of lightand the composition of figures in the foreground. Corot, in fact, stood apart from the Romantics and anticipated the Impressionists.

Naturalism and Realism

Millet's paintings of peasant subjects broke new ground and triggered a movement in France that combined naturalism with realism in order to make a statement with political undertones. France in the period of the Second Empire was still coming to grips with industrialization and the drift of the peasantry from the land to the burgeoning industrial towns. It was a period of great deprivation and social injustice. What Emile Zola and Victor Hugo achieved through their polemical novels, artists such as Gustave Courbet (1819–77) and Honoré Daumier (1810–79) sought to create through their paintings. Courbet believed that the common people were the only true custodians of real values and simple truths, a viewpoint perhaps that comes across very vividly in the vigour and passion of his pictures. Not surprisingly, Courbet was severely criticized and reviled for coarseness and vulgarity when his paintings were exhibited at the Salon. Undaunted, Courbet persevered, and his later canvasses became even more dedicated to putting across his notions of primitive socialism. True to his principles, he took an active part in the ill-starred Paris Commune of 1870–71. Daumier went much further, neatly avoiding the cloying sentimentality that occasionally reduced the paintings of Corot and Millet to mawkishness. His chief forte was the lithograph, a medium that he used extremely effectively to put across his satirical and often savage comment on the ills of society. After the Revolution of 1848 he took up painting, and became increasingly strident in his attacks on the corruption and hypocrisy of the bourgeoisie after Louis Napoleon seized power. He was too satirical to be regarded as a Naturalist, but his use of Realism as social comment has never been surpassed.

Offshoots of Romanticism

Although France dominated the Romantic movement, as it had done Neoclassicism, it had its counterparts in other parts of Europe. The German artist Caspar David Friedrich (1774–1840) is usually regarded as belonging to this movement, although there was a fundamental difference between the French Romantics, who tended to regard nature as a substitute for God, and Friedrich, who saw painting as a medium for worshipping God. His preference was for grandeur of lofty and rugged mountains and wild places, invariably painted by moonlight or at dawn or sunset in order to make the most of the special effects of the sun's rays. He was something of a loner, supremely confident in his own talents without the need to seek out like-minded artists from whom he might learn, or to whom he could impart his ideas. To be sure, there was a group of German painters who sought a spiritual aspect to their work, but they were expatriates, working in Rome, where they formed a quasi-monastic order known as the Brotherhood of St Luke. This group was founded by Friedrich Overbeck (1789–1869) and Franz Pforr (1788–1812) as a reaction against the doctrinaire academicism of Vienna. After Pforr's death the group was reformed as the

Gustave Courbet, *Nuages sur la Lac Leman, c.1856*

Nazarenes, whose later members included Peter Cornelius (1783–1867) and Julius Schnorr von Carolsfeld (1794–1872). Their paintings of biblical subjects and historic scenes were distinguished by their bright colours and deliberately medieval appearance.

The counterpart of the Nazarenes in Britain was the Pre-Raphaelite Brotherhood, founded in 1848 by Dante Gabriel Rossetti (1828–82), William Holman Hunt (1827–1910) and John Everett Millais (1829–96) as a reaction against the prevailing Neoclassicism of the Royal Academy. They consciously strove to return to the early Italian Renaissance, before the advent of Raphael (hence their name). Like the Nazarenes, they had a penchant for sharply incised outlines and brilliant colours. Although the Pre-Raphaelites soon went their individual ways, they exercised a profound influence on the next generation of English painters, notably Edward Burne-Jones (1833–98) and Lawrence Alma-Tadema (1836–1912), while their principles were also endorsed by William Morris (1834–96).

Impressionism

Although this term did not come into use until 1874 when Claude Monet exhibited a painting entitled *Impression, Sunrise, Le Havre* – provoking the comment by Louis Leroy that pictures of this kind were an 'impression' of nature, nothing more – the movement had been evolving for more than a decade. Camille Pissarro (1839–1903) had been a pupil of Corot, whose open-air landscapes pointed the way towards Impressionism. Edouard Manet (1832–83) had been influenced by Goya, whereas Edgar Degas (1834–1917) had studied under Ingres. Alfred Sisley (1839–99), Claude Monet (1840–1926) and Pierre-Auguste Renoir (1841–1919) were among the other

leading figures. While they were primarily preoccupied with landscape, Renoir became one of the leading exponents of the female nude, while Manet excelled in animated groups and Degas was renowned for his paintings of ballet dancers. On the fringe of Impressionism was Paul Cézanne (1839–1906), who felt uneasy at the lack of discipline in this style and wished to return to a greater reliance on form and content without sacrificing the feeling for light and brilliant colours. Out of this evolved Post-Impressionism, a term that originally meant merely 'after Impressionism', but which became the springboard to all the varied 'isms' that come under the heading of modern painting.

Apart from Cézanne, the leading Post-Impressionists included Georges Seurat (1859–91), an early practioner of Pointillism, the technique of applying small strokes or dots of pure colour so that from a distance they appear to blend together. Neither of these artists were particularly concerned with the emotional content of their paintings, but this was the principal feature of the works of Henri de Toulouse-Lautrec (1864–1901), Van Gogh and Gauguin.

Art Nouveau

French for 'new art', this term was used in the English-speaking world to describe a style that came to prominence in about 1895 and continued until World War I, being derived from the Paris shop of that name opened by the Hamburg entrepreneur Samuel Bing. Paradoxically, in France it was generally known as *le style anglais* and in Italy more specifically as *lo stile Liberty*, after the London department store which did so much to promote it. In the German-speaking countries it was *Jugendstil* ('Youth Style'). All of these names embraced a style distinguished by its sinuous curves, swirling lines and ethereal quality. Figures were elongated and in some cases distorted and its practitioners relied heavily on plant forms; tulips, lily pads and thistle heads being particularly favoured. It manifested itself in every medium of the applied and decorative arts, from the architecture of Gaudi and Horta to the furniture of Mackintosh and the Wisteria glass of Tiffany. In the fine arts it was manifest in the drawings of Louis Anquetin and Aubrey Beardsley, and the paintings of Edward Burne-Jones, Alphonse Mucha and Jan Toorop.

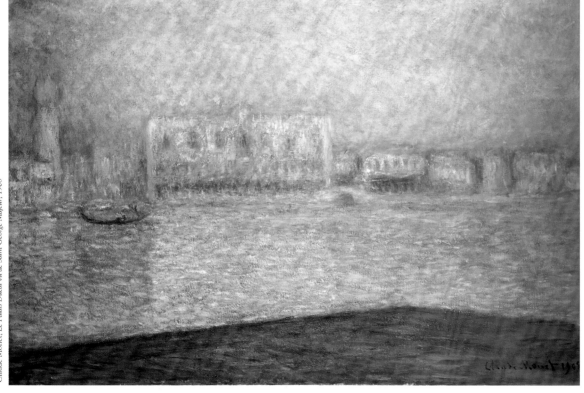

Claude Monet, Le Palais Ducal ou de Saint George Majeur, 1908

Modern Art

The twentieth century saw many radical changes in people's lives: an increased pace of technological and industrial change; the rapid spread of large urban centers; the development of new means of transportation and communication; innovative scientific discoveries such as the X-ray and the theory of relativity; the growth of consumerism on a large scale; and the chilling reality of mass warfare. Against this background of social, political and technological developments, Western art also underwent a series of radical shifts. For the preceding four centuries, painting in Europe had been based on illusionism – a desire to represent external reality through a series of pictorial conventions, such as single-point perspective and the modelling of depth through light and dark tones. In the twentieth century, however, these conventions were abandoned and a whole new range of possibilities opened up with regard to the effects and meanings that could be created in paint on a two-dimensional surface. Painting no longer had to take on the task of recording historical events – one of its central nineteenth-century roles – as this function was now fulfilled by the newer media of photography and especially film. Changes in the structure of the art market, too, away from the grand public 'Salons' which promoted large-scale works, to a system of private galleries and collectors, meant that paintings could be smaller, more personal and more experimental. Artists could respond to the changing reality around them in a variety of ways: embracing modern experience, reacting against it, or seeking to make an impact upon it through their art. They could also aim to be 'modern': to produce paintings that were innovative and exciting, different from anything that had been seen before, full of radical new effects and new meanings. Art in the twentieth century, like the social environment in which it was produced, would undergo a process of constant and rapid change.

From Symbolism to the Fauves and the Expressionists

In 1890, the French painter Maurice Denis (1870–1943) famously claimed: 'a picture before being a battle horse, a nude woman or some anecdote, is essentially a flat surface covered in colours arranged in a certain order.' Denis' definition has been seen as ultimately pointing towards abstract painting, but at the time he made this comment he was more concerned with downplaying the need for realism in art in favour of effects of line and colour. His paintings were of recognizable subjects – religious scenes, women in forest settings, bathers – but depicted in heightened, unreal colours bounded by flowing, decorative contours. His compatriot Paul Gauguin (1848–1903) used strong, contrasting colours

and dark outlines around the different elements of his compositions, drawing attention away from the subject depicted and towards the artist's use of paint. Symbolism was a broad artistic movement that encompassed painting, literature, music and theatre in the late nineteenth and early twentieth centuries, and manifested itself in a diverse range of styles. Painting associated with the movement, such as that by Denis and Gauguin, was often based on literary themes, myths and legends, but also on personal fantasy and dream. A striking tendency within Symbolist works was a move away from narrative, away from the depiction of scenes that could 'tell a story' in an accessible way, in favour of the evocation of a mood or feeling. A common motif in Symbolist painting is a group of figures who do not interact in any straightforward way, whose eyes do not meet and whose gestures and gazes suggest that each one is lost in their own private reverie. The arrangement of a Symbolist composition can thus seem more artificial than truthful, more about art than about reality. In the works of Gauguin and Denis, this sense of artificiality is heightened by an emphasis on colour and line and on the ways in which different parts of the painting relate to one another within an overall 'pattern'.

The Symbolist interest in colour in painting as an evocative element in its own right was crucial to the development of the young painter Henri Matisse (1869–1954). Matisse trained in the studio of Gustave Moreau (1826–1898), a Symbolist artist who created extraordinary jewel-like effects in his paintings, building up layers of coloured paint, sometimes squeezing it directly on to the canvas, to evoke luxuriant details of dress and architectural décor within biblical and mythological scenes. In 1905, Matisse exhibited a painting that caused a great stir in the Salon des Indépendants, an artist-run and unjuried exhibition forum in Paris; this painting, *Luxe, calme et volupté* (painted in 1904) is now seen as one of the key Fauvist works. (Fauvism

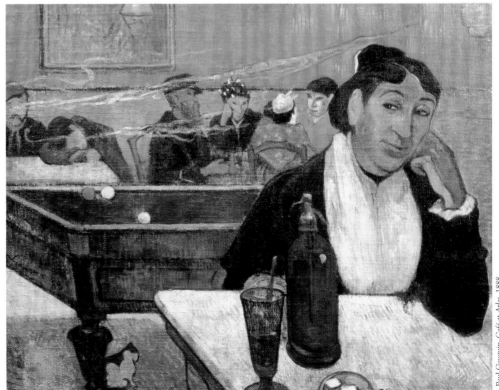

Paul Gauguin, *Café at Arles*, 1888

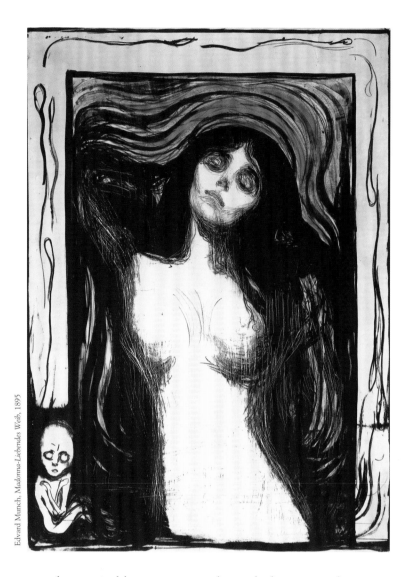

Edvard Munch, *Madonna-Liebendes Weib*, 1895

was characterized by a primitive style in which intense colours were used, often to create deliberate clashes. This technique completely freed colour from its depictive role, so that it could be truly expressive.) The piece took its title from a refrain in a poem by Charles Baudelaire (1821–67), who was himself a Symbolist. Matisse did not attempt to 'illustrate' this poem – a suggestive homage to the sensual pleasures of travel; rather he created his own vision of a beach scene with a moored boat and a group of languid female nudes. The whole composition was made up of small patches of colour, a technique known as 'Pointillism' which had been developed in the nineteenth century by Georges Seurat (1859–91). At a distance, these colour patches would fuse to suggest effects of light and volume, but seen close to, the painting would begin to break up into a series of juxtaposed markings. Matisse exaggerated this effect, making some marks bigger than others, as well as distorting the forms of his nudes using thick curving contours. The subject matter of *Luxe, calme et volupté* was ostensibly serene and restful – a lunch party on the beach – but Matisse's handling of the paint and treatment of the human figure were expressive and almost violent.

In the autumn of 1905, an exhibition of works by artists including Matisse, André Derain (1880–1954) and Maurice de Vlaminck (1876–1958) earned them the name 'Fauves' or 'wild beasts'. This term, coined by the art critic Louis Vauxcelles (b. 1870), was intended as

derogatory, a response to what he saw as a spontaneous and reckless handling of paint and use of colour. Derain produced landscapes full of striking contrasting colours, reds and greens, which appeared to have been painted very freely and quickly, while Vlaminck aimed to express himself instinctively, after the model of the painter he most admired, Vincent van Gogh (1853–90), later describing himself as a 'tender-hearted savage, filled with violence'. The Fauves generally chose traditional subject matter in their paintings – landscapes, nudes and portraits – which they made modern through their radical treatment. A powerful example of this is Matisse's 1906 portrait of his wife, whose composition is brought to life by a bold green stripe extending down from her forehead and along her nose.

In Germany in 1905, a group of painters based in Dresden who called themselves 'Die Brücke' ('the bridge') felt a similar desire to inject youthful vigour and energy into the practice of painting as the Fauves did. Die Brücke also admired Van Gogh, as well as the Norwegian Edvard Munch (1863–1944) and the art of non-Western cultures, particularly Africa, all of whom to them achieved a kind of untrammelled expressiveness. Artists such as Ernst Ludwig Kirchner (1880–1938) and Karl Schmidt-Rottluff (1884–1976) painted portraits and landscapes in bright colours with large, simplified forms, and were drawn to depictions of nudes in outdoor settings, suggesting a return to nature and to basic origins. Emil Nolde (1867–1956), who was associated with the group for a few months, used distorted forms and angry combinations of colour to explore his own religious beliefs. The term 'Expressionism' was first used in 1911, primarily in relation to art in France, and then to refer to the painters of Die Brücke, who by 1913 had drifted apart. It would continue to be applied to the work of artists like the Austrian Oskar Kokoschka (1886–1980) and the German painter Max Beckmann (1884–1950). Beckmann translated his traumatic experience during the first World War into distorted self-portraits and figure scenes, such as his disturbing vision of torture and murder *The Night* (1918–19). His later paintings depicted circus performers, with himself as clown or king, reflecting the anxiety caused by the social events that surrounded him.

The use of painting as a means of communicating personal experience and emotion – a central aim of the Expressionists – was manifested in a more subtle and controlled way in the work of the painters of the Munich-based group Der Blaue Reiter ('the blue rider'). In an almanac published in 1912, the Blauer Reiter artists, including Franz Marc (1880–1916), Wassily Kandinsky (1866–1944) and Paul Klee (1879–1940), put forward their vision of new ways of self-expression, including art, design, poetry and music. Kandinsky's painting, inspired by Fauvism, began to focus less on subject matter than on the lyrical force of colour and the strokes of his brush, seeking to communicate with the viewer in a direct and spontaneous way in the manner of a piece of music. Kandinsky's works of 1910 to 1914, such as *Improvisation No. 23*, are considered to be the first abstract paintings of the twentieth century. Klee's awareness of the evocative use of colour was encouraged by a trip to Tunisia in 1914, and he went on to create small-scale paintings of exotic landscapes, still-lifes and figure scenes, all depicted in a schematic and magical child-like way, a style that he described as 'taking a line for a walk'.

Cubism

Cubism was one of the most influential twentieth-century art movements, and one whose works can seem the most 'difficult' and inaccessible to the observer. Cubist works would provide a radical challenge to the painterly conventions for producing an illusion of depth, and they would attack the tradition of 'high' art by including within two-dimensional paintings and collages a range of extraneous, materials not traditionally associated with high art, such as newspaper clippings, scraps of sheet music and stencilled lettering. Cubism flourished in Paris between 1907 and the outbreak of the First World War in 1914, and its impact was felt in artistic developments throughout Europe during this period.

The French painter Georges Braque (1882–1963) had worked initially in a Fauvist style, but after seeing a major retrospective exhibition of the work of Paul Cézanne (1839–1906) in Paris in 1907, he pursued a new artistic vision. Cézanne's work was an inspiration, particularly in its use of 'passages', the unification of parts of the picture surface through colour and tone, which meant that the difference between foreground and background was no longer sharply maintained. Braque made trips to the village of L'Estaque in southern France to paint the same sites depicted by Cézanne, and his resulting series of landscapes were exhibited in Paris in 1908, showing houses, trees and roads as simplified geometric forms squeezed into a shallow picture space. The box-like appearance of houses in these landscapes led the critic Vauxcelles – who had been quick to label the Fauves – to describe them mockingly as 'cubes', inspiring the term 'Cubism'.

In 1907 Braque had also made the acquaintance of the Spaniard Pablo Picasso (1881–1973), who that same year had produced his extraordinary large-scale painting *Les Demoiselles d'Avignon*. This work managed to bring together several radical and shocking elements. It showed five prostitutes with sharply distorted naked bodies within a room whose space seemed shattered into fragmentary shards, while the women's faces derived from Egyptian, Iberian and African art, the latter still viewed as something crude and savage in this period. Picasso's friends and collectors were unable to accept this painting, which they felt was 'mad' and 'monstrous', and it remained rolled up in his studio for almost 10 years. To the dizzying handling of space inspired by Cézanne's landscapes, Picasso added a disregard for the European canonical treatment of the human body influenced by his interest in African art, preferring startling deformations and exaggerations to idealized proportions.

By the end of 1909, Picasso and Braque were close friends, and often painted together, producing works very similar in appearance. The period of 'Analytical Cubism', which lasted until 1912, saw the creation of paintings that took traditional motifs, such as still-life elements, landscapes and nudes, and broke these up into a series of facets, often incorporating fragmentary glimpses of an object or figure from different points of view. These motifs could sometimes become barely recognizable within an overall fluctuating mass of planes, painted in a limited colour palette of greys and browns, suggesting an emphasis on the conceptual process of coming to terms with the subject depicted. The practice and problems of painting became the content and meaning of these Cubist works, where the central question was no longer what to represent, but how to represent it. The need to create an illusion of depth ceased to concern Picasso and Braque as painters; in fact they deliberately drew attention to the point that their explorations of objects in space were in themselves as paintings completely flat. In *Pitcher and Violin* (1909–10), Braque included a trompe-l'oeil nail at the top of the canvas, as if to suggest that the painting itself was simply tacked to the wall, and in 1911 he began to include stencilled lettering in his oil paintings. Picasso created the first Cubist collage in May 1912 when he included a piece of imitation chair-caning in a still-life of a table top. This fragment of oil cloth, painted to give the illusion of a chair seat, seemed to imply that all oil painting was a game, a means of fooling the spectator into believing what he or she sees. Cubist works after 1912 began to include pasted papers, textures such as sand and a greater range of colours – a phase known as 'Synthetic Cubism'. If 'analysis' consisted in breaking objects down from their starting point in the real world, 'synthesis' meant that they were built up again from the basis of the simple geometrical forms of a piece of collaged paper or a block of colour. The Spanish-born Juan Gris (1887–1927), who came to Paris in 1906 and was strongly influenced by Picasso, produced synthetic Cubist works using a variety of colours and collage elements such as wallpaper and newspaper which were carefully cut and positioned, creating the impression of meticulous control over the objects depicted.

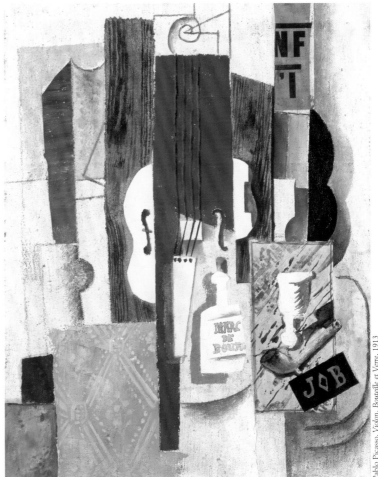

Pablo Picasso, *Violon, Bouteille et Verre*, 1913

Picasso and Braque produced no manifesto, and in their later careers gave little explanation of their Cubist works. Many of their paintings and collages were small-scale, experimental works, which were not necessarily intended for public view. They did not exhibit during the Cubist period, relying instead on the support of the dealer Daniel-Henry Kahnweiler (1884–1979), who agreed to buy the whole of their output at fixed prices, giving them financial security and encouraging experimentation. But this private orientation did not mean that the Cubism of Picasso and Braque declined to engage with the outside world. In fact, their Cubist works are full of references to popular culture, to music hall, café life and advertisements. From 1912 to 1913, Picasso produced a series of pasted papers using newspaper clippings that referred to the Balkan Wars then raging in central Europe.

Cubism did, however, have a public face in the form of the so-called 'Salon Cubists', a group of artists who exhibited together and whose leading figures, Jean Metzinger (1883–1956) and Albert Gleizes (1881–1953), produced a theoretical tract, On Cubism, in 1912. The group included the young Marcel Duchamp (1887–1968) along with his two older brothers, as well as Robert Delaunay (1885–1941) and Fernand Léger (1881–1955). Léger had learned from Cézanne's distortions of pictorial space, and broke the forms in his paintings up into cylindrical geometrical shapes, which were dubbed 'tubist'. In 1913 he began to produce a series of works entitled Contrasting Forms – lively compositions based on abstracted discs highlighted with primary colours: red, blue and yellow. These paintings were inspired by Léger's interest in the shiny metallic forms of machines, and in the simplified designs on advertising billboards, both of which for him epitomized the dynamic potential of new, modern experience. Delaunay and his wife Sonia Delaunay-Terk (1885–1979) also began to create paintings using circles and arcs of contrasting colour which aimed to capture effects of light and movement. Their work was based initially on scenes of modern city life, particularly the motif of the Eiffel Tower, but paintings such as Robert Delaunay's 1912 Circular Forms relied less on recognizable subject matter, reflecting Sonia's abstract designs for fabrics and book-bindings. Delaunay's use of colour, as well as the Cubist handling of space, were both important inspiration for the Russian painter Marc Chagall (1887–1985), who lived in Paris between 1910 and 1914. Chagall combined these effects and modern motifs like the Eiffel Tower with subject matter drawn from his own upbringing to produce dream-like poetic paintings.

The poet Guillaume Apollinaire (1880–1918), a crucial supporter of modern art before the First World War, called the Delaunays' work 'Orphic', a variant of Cubism which would rely on colour and form rather than subject matter for its meaning; the name was drawn from the ancient myth of Orpheus, who created a kind of 'pure' music. In his seminal collection of writings The Cubist Painters (1913), Apollinaire claimed: 'We are moving towards an entirely new art which will stand, with respect to painting as envisaged up to now, as music stands to literature. It will be pure painting, just as music is pure literature.' The painters of Orphism, who also included Francis Picabia (1879–1953), did not, however, produce purely abstract works: 'pure painting' should rather be understood as a desire to create works which had their own internal coherence independent of the motif represented, and which could convey some of the dynamism of modern experience that to these painters was much more important than the depiction of external reality.

Futurism and Vorticism

'Dynamism' was one of the names considered by the Italian writer Filippo Tommaso Marinetti (1876–1944) for a new movement which he planned to establish; he eventually opted for 'Futurism', which also suggested his fascination with the technology and speed of the modern world. Futurism was the first major twentieth-century art movement to be launched explicitly through a series of written manifestos, sets of ideas which preceded the development of new ways of painting. Marinetti lived and worked in Milan, but he published his 'Founding Manifesto of Futurism' in French on the front page of Le Figaro in February 1909, as he wished to make an impact upon Paris, still the most important centre for art in Europe. This manifesto was a passionate and provocative attack on culture and tradition, calling for the destruction of museums

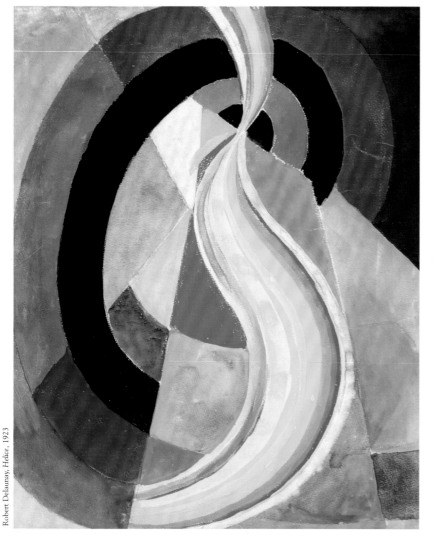

Robert Delaunay, Hélice, 1923

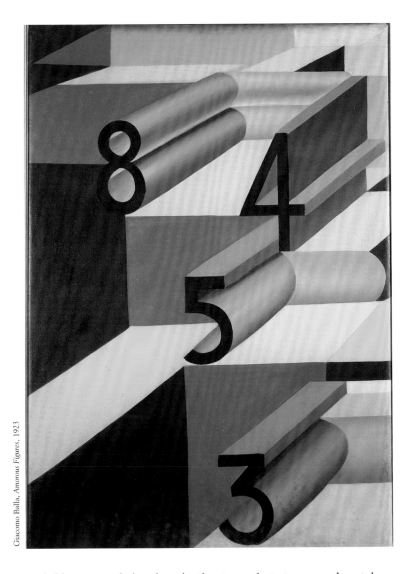

Giacomo Balla, *Amorous Figures*, 1923

Futurist painting was just one part of an overall assault on the art world, and was intended above all to illustrate ideas laid out in? Futurist manifestos. Boccioni's 'Technical Manifesto of Futurist Painting' of 1910 sought to overthrow the art of the past, and described the swift succession and perceptual overloading of images of the modern world that this new art should strive to capture: galloping horses which appeared to have 20 legs; hurtling trams that seemed to merge with the houses around them; the human body becoming part of the furniture on which it is sitting. Balla's *Dynamism of a Dog on a Leash* (1912) drew upon time-lapse photography to evoke the successive movements of a woman walking a small dog. Boccioni's *The Street Invades the House* (1911) showed a woman leaning from a balcony, her form merging with the tumultuous activity in the street below. Futurist painters used vibrant colours, thrusting diagonals and energetic, swirling compositions in order to convey speed and movement. They drew upon painterly techniques that had already been established in the late nineteenth century, such as the principle of colour divisionism, a variant of Pointillism, as well as taking inspiration from Cubism. The faceted appearance of Futurist works, where the subject represented began to disappear beneath an overall pattern of shifting planes, and the use of lettering in the work of Carrà and the Paris-based Gino Severini (1883–1965), both derived from Cubist painting. To some extent Futurist painting could not live up to the strident requirements of its manifestos, and it relied more on other artistic developments than may have been intended.

The impact of Cubism and Futurism was felt in many European countries, and in Britain just before the First World War the dynamic treatment of the forms of the modern world found expression in the works of the Vorticist movement. The Futurist Boccioni had stated that all art should find its source in what he called an 'emotional vortex', and this terminology was taken up by the poet Ezra Pound (1885–1972) to describe a kind of imagery which would not be flat 'surface art', but 'a VORTEX, from which, and through which, and into which ideas are constantly rushing'. The paintings of Wyndham Lewis (1882–1957), the central figure of Vorticism, are a good illustration of Pound's definition. Lewis used simplified angular forms suggestive of cityscapes in his compositions, arranged in such a way as to create the impression of plunging recessions and vertiginous depths. Edward Wadsworth (1889–1949) painted abstracted intersecting shapes of buildings, while David Bomberg (1890–1957), an associate of the group, fragmented his motifs, initially based on groups of moving figures, into a brightly coloured overall grid-like pattern. Bomberg's paintings were the most radical in appearance: *In the Hold* (1913–14) was made up of a myriad of jostling flat triangles of colour, its original subject matter indicated only by its title. Vorticism crystallized around the publication of the periodical *BLAST*, which appeared in two issues in 1914 and 1915, and which proclaimed the aim of these artists was to overthrow the legacy of Victorian Britain in an aggressive and violent way. The brutal energy that was one of Vorticism's central principles, along with its interest in machine technology, strikingly prefigured the mass warfare that brought the movement to an abrupt end.

and libraries and for the glorification of rioting crowds, violent revolutions and war. Beauty in this period, for Marinetti, was to be found in the products of modern technology and industry, and above all in speed, and he claimed that a car was superior in this respect to one of the Louvre's most prized and famous antique statues: 'a screaming automobile that seems to run on grape shot, is more beautiful than the *Winged Victory of Samothrace*'.

The exaggerated rhetoric of the Futurist manifestos was an important part of their aim to raise the maximum publicity for themselves, and to communicate their ideas to as wide an audience as possible. The Futurist group included the artists Umberto Boccioni (1882–1916), Giacomo Balla (1871–1958) and Carlo Carrà (1881–1966), who were involved in a series of widespread publicizing events. Futurist evenings were staged, which could include the showing of paintings, the reading of manifestos, theatrical sketches or the painter Luigi Russolo (1885–1947) playing his cacophonous 'Noise Machines'. These evenings would often begin with the Futurists hurling insults at their audience, and sometimes ended in brawls and street fights, reported – to their delight – in the press the following day. Between 1912 and 1914 an 'Exhibition of Futurist Painters' toured extensively, from Paris via Berlin and London to Chicago and Moscow, accompanied by a series of lectures and publications.

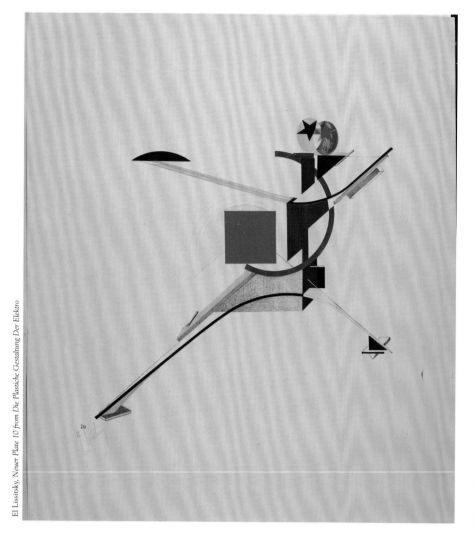

El Lissitsky, Neuer Plate 10 from Die Plastiche Gestaltung Der Elektro

Suprematism and Constructivism

Cubism had initiated the idea of reducing a motif from the external world to its most basic elements, and of presenting a motif in a painting in such a way as to make apparent the canvas's inevitable flatness. The Cubist style became familiar to Russian artists via the numerous exhibitions of Western contemporary art in Moscow, from 1912 onwards. Both Matisse and Picasso were patronised by wealthy Russian merchants, who exibited their works to the public. The Suprematism of the Russian artist Kasimir Malevich (1878–1935) took the essential aspects of Cubist painting to their extremes. Malevich believed that art could be free from the representation of recognizable figures and objects. By no longer having to worry about how to depict external reality, art could develop its own language of forms and create new realities 'no less significant than the realities of nature itself'. The key elements of Suprematist art for Malevich were the straight line and the square, which reflected his emphasis on the man-made rather than the forms found in nature. In Leningrad in 1915 the artist exhibited a series of works that he claimed he had worked on since 1913, including a notorious painting of a black square on a white background. The square was a form not to be found in nature; it was a deliberate negation of artistic illusionism as well as a

provocative comment on the art of the past. Painted canvasses themselves are on the whole flat, square and rectangular forms; Malevich's squares, however, were also intended to carry their own meanings for the artist himself, mainly of a spiritual nature. The elementary act of painting a line or square was, for Malevich, a gesture of humility, and he talked about the empty backgrounds of his compositions in terms of infinite spaces. After a series of coloured compositions with groups of diagonally placed rectangular shapes, Malevich produced a series of 'White on white' paintings in 1918. These works, which suggested a kind of ultimate freedom from the material world, took painted representation to its limits, and proved a crucial inspiration for later generations of artists.

While Malevich felt strongly that art should have no connection with society, and that the artist should be able to pursue spiritual ideas in complete independence, other painters in Russia in this period, known broadly as the 'Constructivists', had a more pragmatic and rigorous approach to non-representational painting. In around 1911, Mikhail Larionov (1881–1964) had developed a style he called 'Rayonnism', a means of breaking up objects through rays of light, colours and textures, which was also explored in the work of his partner Natalia Goncharova (1881–1962). Alexander Rodchencko (1891–1956) worked on paintings based on abstract principles, which he would later call 'non-objective', such as a series of works created in 1914 with the help of a ruler and compass. Lyubov Popova (1889–1924) produced linear architectonic compositions. All of these painters were involved in the applied arts, creating theatre designs, book-bindings, textiles and posters, so that their artistic experiments had a public, practical application.

After the Russian Revolution of 1917, the concerns of 'non-objective' art as something divorced from reality were justified as 'laboratory research' – a means of trying out ideas which ultimately would contribute to the progress of the new socialist state. Some of the most important works of Constructivism would be posters and photomontages destined for a mass audience, but more significant even than these were the sculptural and architectural projects, which could directly benefit the public. Designs for constructions and buildings had their roots, however, in radical developments in painting, as explorations in three dimensions of the spatial possibilities of the painted surface. El Lissitzky (1890–1941) had trained as an architect and in the 1920s produced a series of paintings based around his concept of 'Proun', taken from the Russian word meaning 'new art forms'. Proun was a means of working in which the fundamentals of form such as space, proportion, flatness and rhythm were allied to function in the creation of utilitarian objects. Lissitzky's paintings, such as Proun 99 (c. 1924), resembled architectural plans, depicted through rectilinear shapes and in muted tones. Lissitzky also travelled widely in the 1920s and was an important disseminator of Russian Constructivist theories to artists throughout Europe.

Purism

In France after the First World War, concern with the functionality of objects and links to architectural principles were central to the development of Purism. The movement was conceived in relation to Cubism, seen as a logical successor to it in the book *After Cubism* (1918), written by the painters Amédée Ozenfant (1886–1966) and Charles Edouard Jeanneret (1887–1965), now better known as the architect Le Corbusier. The Purists took up the still-life motifs from the Cubism of Picasso and Braque – bottles, glasses and guitars – which they saw as 'type objects' uniting the positive qualities of precision and simplicity. Ozenfant and Jeanneret were critical of the development of Cubism towards decoration, and they called for a return to the values of order and objectivity which they felt it had originally pursued. These values were also to be found in the material world of man-made and machine-made things, which for the Purists were a much more fascinating subject for art than the human figure; this, they believed, suggested too many associations and feelings and was thus distracting. Both Ozenfant and Jeanneret painted still-lifes in mainly interior settings, consisting of groups of bottles, cups, vases, pipes and musical instruments (all traditional still-life motifs, from the seventeenth century onwards), depicted in muted pastel colours. Their works appear quite similar, as both used a smooth painted finish in order to maintain an impersonal, objective effect. In works such as Jeanneret's *Still Life* of 1920, the round openings at the top of these objects were shown as a series of full circles placed around the canvas, ignoring traditional perspective as the Cubists had done, and creating a sense of rhythmic regularity and order. The Purist periodical *L'Esprit nouveau* ('The New Spirit') appeared between 1921 and 1925, and acted as a vehicle for the celebration of architecture, engineering and industrial design as key elements of a new functionalism and efficiency. Jeanneret began to pursue architectural projects in the early 1920s under the name Le Corbusier, famously declaring in 1923 that 'a house is a machine for living in'. Purism also had a noticeable influence on the design principles of the German Bauhaus school of architecture and design, which had been founded in 1919 by Gropius.

Bauhaus

Largely a reaction against the florid, fussy styles in the applied arts of the late nineteenth century, the Bauhaus style developed in the early twentieth century under the inspiration and guidance of Walter Gropius, a German architect and designer who was influenced by the writings of John Ruskin and William Morris. Unlike these mentors, he did not reject mechanization but sought ways of harmonizing industrial methods to design. He was appointed Director of the Grand Ducal schools of art in Weimar in 1919, collectively known by the name Bauhaus (literally 'architecture house'). Gropius and his colleagues strove to marry form and function in the applied arts, architecture and industrial design. When the Nazis came to power Gropius and his disciples went to France, Britain and the USA,

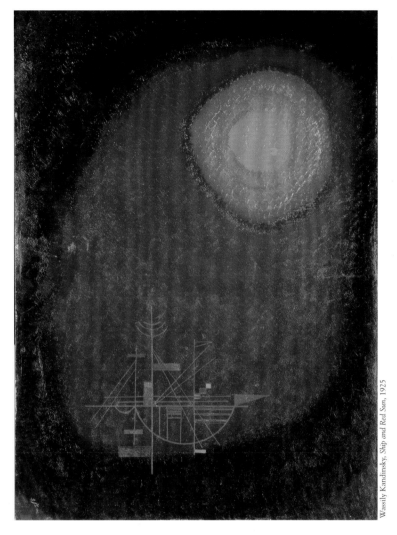

Wassily Kandinsky, *Ship and Red Sun*, 1925

spreading the gospel and laying the foundations for the clean lines of modern industrial design. In the decorative arts their ideas influenced the development of Art Deco and Art Moderne in the 1920s and 1930s. Paul Klee and Wassily Kandinsky were among the artists who taught at the Bauhaus and were, in turn, imbued with its concepts, leading to the development of Abstract art.

De Stijl and Neoplasticism

Several artists in the first decades of the twentieth century, such as the Delaunays, Kandinsky and Malevich, had experimented with non-representational paintings. In France, Matisse had progressed from his Fauvist works to paintings like *The Piano Lesson* (1916), which asserted the flatness of the picture plane, eliminating depth and volume in favour of the abstract play of lines and colours. These developments, however, were to find their most extensive and coherent exploration in the work of the Dutch artist Piet Mondrian (1872–1944), and of the group to which he belonged, De Stijl ('the style'), active between 1917 and 1932.

Mondrian's early work was inspired by Fauvist painting, showing brightly coloured and expressively painted landscape motifs, and between 1911 and 1914 he lived and worked in Paris, absorbing the new developments in Cubist art. A group of works based on single trees from this period show the artist's paring down of his motif, reducing the leaves and branches to a series of schematic markings or signs on a flat surface, and creating an overall pattern which appears to be held in place by fragments of rectangular and squared-off lines. The abstract paintings that Mondrian produced in these years had their origins in landscapes or still-life, which were now totally integrated into a rhythmic grid of squares and rectangles composed in muted shades of grey, pale blue and ochre. In the most extreme works of 1914–17, the shapes of the sea and pier at Scheveningen, near The Hague, were indicated only through a succession of monochrome 'plus' and 'minus' shapes. In his writings, Mondrian felt that this point of departure in nature was hindering his art, as nature aroused feelings and emotions that got in the way of what he called 'universal harmony'. He wanted to reduce the markings of his paintings even further, and create a new harmonious reality using elements of form and design.

Around 1917, Mondrian met the painter Theo van Doesburg (1883–1931), who was the leading figure behind the founding of the De Stijl group and the editor of a journal of that name through which ideas could be propagated. For van Doesburg and for the designer Gerrit Rietveld (1888–1964), another member of the group famous for his *Red-blue Armchair* (1917–18), colour was crucial. Under their influence, Mondrian began to use colour as a fundamental part of his compositions in its most basic form: the three primary colours of red, yellow and blue; and the three non-colours black, white and grey. According to his own theory of what he termed 'Neoplasticism', published in *De Stijl* in 1919, Mondrian's ultimate aim in painting was to reduce representation to its most elementary function: 'In painting you must first try to see *composition, colour and line* and not the representation *as representation*. Then you will finally come to feel the subject matter a hindrance.' Mondrian's best-known works pursue this aim, consisting of a series of rectangles in primary colours separated by a grid of black vertical and horizontal lines. These separating lines were necessary so

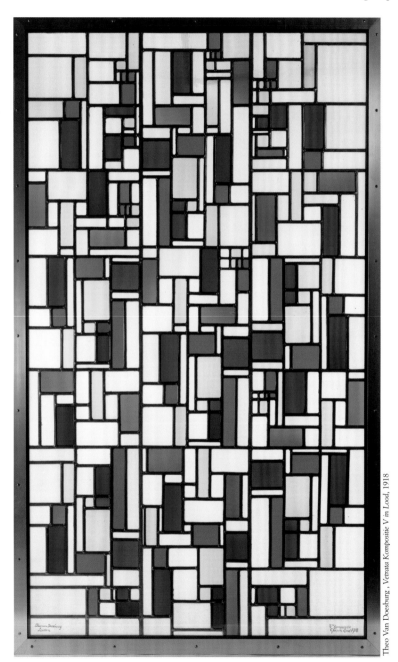

Theo Van Doesburg, Vetrata Kompostie V in Lood, 1918

that a painted rectangle would not suggest any illusion of depth. Paintings such as *Composition with Red, Yellow, Blue and Black* (1921) were intended to be completely impersonal, controlled and harmonious, creating a sense of balance that for Mondrian had a strong spiritual meaning. Mondrian would maintain his austere artistic vision rigorously throughout the rest of his career, developing variations on the essential principles of his compositions, such as lozenge-shaped canvasses as the basis for his groupings of lines and colours. Towards the end of his life, in 1940, he moved to New York, where the excitement of the metropolis was captured in the vibrant patterns of paintings such as *Broadway Boogie-Woogie* (1942–43), based on much smaller units to create a greater sense of movement and jazz-like rhythm.

Van Doesburg's work had made a crucial contribution to the development of De Stijl in his use of a strong asymmetricality, shown, for example, in his painting *The Cow* (1917), with its carefully placed flat blocks of colour – in this case pink, blue, yellow and black – on a plain white background. Van Doesburg also created a series of compositions based on diagonal forms, whose pattern of horizontal and vertical lines and rectangles were shifted through 90 degrees, to dynamic effect. Mondrian's belief in contrasting pictorial elements was extended by Van Doesburg to a vision of all of the arts: painting, sculpture, music and architecture. Architecture and applied design, particularly interior décor, furniture and typography, were an important part of De Stijl's overall programme. A style with clean, straight lines and no decoration was in part a reaction against the flowing qualities of Art Nouveau, and an assertion of the dominance of the man-made over the forms of nature. Van Doesburg's interest in design and in the creation of functional objects also led him, in a manifesto of 1923 entitled 'The End of Art', to praise everyday items like bicycles, cars, irons and bathrooms, and to pronounce any attempt to renew art as it had previously existed as bankrupt: 'Let us rather create a new life-form which is adequate to the functioning of modern life.'

Dada

The urgent need to liberate art from its past was nowhere more strongly felt in the early twentieth century than among the artists and writers internationally who were associated with the Dada movement. For the Dadaists, the 'end of art' was already taken for granted: art had been discredited by its connection with the world of consumerism, and was the preserve of the 'bourgeoisie' – a past generation whose values were seen to be stifling and defunct. The Dadaists reacted strongly against the generation of their parents and its associated morality, and responded to what they saw as the absurdity and mindless horror of the First World War. Dada came into being in Zurich in 1916, when a group of expatriate young artists in refuge from the war, including the Romanian writer Tristan Tzara (1896–1963) and the Alsatian Jean Arp (1887–1966), founded an arts center called the 'Cabaret Voltaire'. The name 'Dada' was taken either from a dictionary definition of a child's term for a rocking horse, or from the Romanian for 'yes'; either way it was intended to be deliberately child-like and nonsensical. The Cabaret Voltaire was a forum for artistic events: readings of nonsense poetry, recitals of folk songs and performances of raucous music, frenetic dancing and the display of new pictures. There was no stylistic principle to these manifestations: Dada was not a style but an attitude. Its tone caught on in other European centres, as well as in the United States during the war, where Duchamp and Picabia had got to know the artist Man Ray (1890–1977).

Arp was a poet as well as an artist and he later talked about the need to find an elementary means of creation which would save mankind from the madness of the times, by responding in an appropriate manner, summed up in his paradoxical claim 'Dada wanted to replace the logical nonsense of the men of today with the illogically senseless'. Arp used words and sentences chosen at random from newspapers in his poetry, and began to produce compositions based on torn-up pieces of paper dropped in chance formations. He also made woodcuts, reliefs, and later paintings and sculptures based

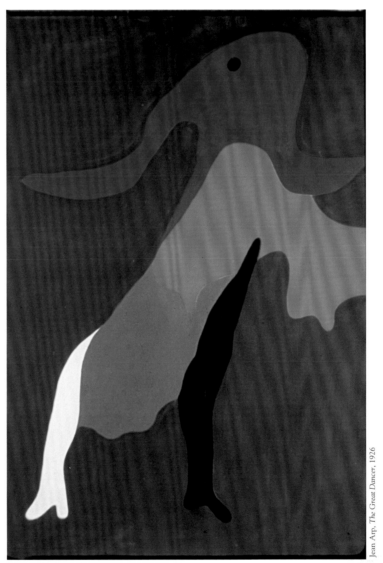

Jean Arp, *The Great Dancer*, 1926

on simple, organic forms, often with absurd titles, like the relief *Navel, Shirt and Head* (1926). The principle of random combinations was also central to the work of Kurt Schwitters (1887–1948), a Dada artist working in Hanover. Schwitters used the term 'merz', a fragment from the word 'Kommerzbank' ('corporate bank'), to describe his collage works, which consisted of scraps of coloured paper and discarded bits of rubbish arranged in two and three dimensions.

An emphasis on the absurd and on chance was one of the means by which Dada artists responded to events in the wider world; a very particular attitude towards modern technology was another. Back in 1912, Duchamp had submitted a strange canvas entitled *Nude Descending a Staircase* to a Cubist exhibition called the 'Golden Section'. The painting had been rejected, and in a series of subsequent paintings had shown combinations of human and machine parts with titles that evoked love and desire. In contrast to the celebration of the machine that underpinned Futurism, Duchamp, along with Picabia, Man Ray and the German artist Max Ernst (1891–1976), produced works which ironized the new mechanized society. Picabia's diagrammatic drawings of mechanical parts, complete with labels, depicted nonsense machines which would never work in reality. The title of his painting *Amorous Parade* (1917) suggests that the dysfunctional collection of isolated parts he represents – levers, a piston and a large screw – are ironically symbolic of modern sexual relationships. Paintings like these had the appearance of scientific diagrams, precise and neutral, deliberately lacking any sense of the artist's unique powers of expression, as a commentary upon the nature of art itself. Ernst, working in Cologne, used a wide range of source materials in his paintings, drawings and collages, including illustrations from encyclopedias and engravings from technical manuals and sales catalogues, which he would juxtapose with other elements to create new and bizarre combinations. In his painting *The Elephant Celebes* (1921), a large metal corn bin is transformed into a grotesque imaginary creature.

Central to the Dadaist attitude was the nonsense gesture, intended to turn the very idea of art on its head. Duchamp presented for exhibition in New York in 1917 under a pseudonym an upturned urinal that he entitled *Fountain*: this man-made object was rejected from the show, an outcome that was undoubtedly intended. Duchamp turned his back on painting in 1912, preferring to concentrate on 'ready-mades' like *Fountain*, and on interventions into famous paintings, like his addition of a moustache and an obscene caption to Leonardo da Vinci's *Mona Lisa*. The sanctity of great works of art was rudely undercut by Dada: Duchamp also once suggested that a Rembrandt could be used as an ironing board. Picabia's painting *L'Oeil cacodylate* (1921) was an intentional mockery of the financial value attached to the artist's signature: a piece of untreated canvas covered in the scrawled signatures, dedications and cut-out photographs of his friends and Dada associates.

In post-World War I Berlin, Dada took the form of a virulent political protest against society, and against the moral values of the Weimar Republic. The writer Richard Hülsenbeck (1892–1974) had been a founder member of Zurich Dada, and in 1917 he returned to his native Germany. In his 'First German Dada Manifesto' he claimed that: 'The highest art will be that which in its unconscious content presents the thousandfold problems of the day'. The 1920 Berlin Dada fair – an art exhibition which showed paintings and collages accompanied by slogans painted on the gallery walls – included a stuffed effigy of a Prussian officer with a pig's head suspended from the ceiling. George Grosz (1893–1959) produced drawings and paintings which brutally satirized figures of authority – the police, the army and the clergy – showing them as morally corrupt, greedy and sexually depraved, in line with his Communist convictions. In the hands of Hannah Höch (1889–1978) and John Heartfield (1891–1968), photomontage became a powerful tool for social commentary, for absurd and grotesque juxtapositions of words and images. Heartfield continued to use photomontage in the 1930s, to mock and undermine Hitler's regime.

Germany's moral decay was also evoked in the work of Otto Dix (1891–1969), whose paintings depicted subjects such as war cripples and prostitutes, figures on the margins of society who represented the fallout from a materialistic state. Dix often worked in tempera on wooden boards

– an Old Master technique – and used a realistic style heightened by minutely observed details. This close attention to immediate surroundings, treated in an uncompromising and even 'ugly' way, was a feature of a painting style which developed in Germany in the 1920s, known as 'Neue Sachlichkeit' (or 'New Objectivism'), and represented by artists like Grosz, Dix and Christian Schad (1894–1982), whose portrait paintings have smoothly worked surfaces and an almost photographic realism.

Surrealism

The term 'surrealism' was first used by the poet Apollinaire in 1917 to suggest a heightened sense of realism, but in Paris in the mid-1920s it came to designate a new art movement, whose influence was widespread and lasting. Dada activities in Paris, centering around Francis Picabia, had fizzled out by 1922, and a group of young artists and writers led by the poet André Breton (1896–1966) had begun to search for a more positive means of expression – one that would say 'yes' where Dada had said 'no'. The former Dadaist Max Ernst settled in Paris in 1922, and his work was praised by Breton for its strange juxtapositions, but above all for the new poetic vision of reality that these suggested. In order to try to stimulate new visions and ways of seeing, Breton, Ernst and a group of writers including the poets Paul Eluard (1895–1952) and Louis Aragon (1897–1982) experimented with mind-altering drugs and hypnotic trances. In 1924 Breton produced the 'First Surrealist Manifesto', in which he set out a definition of Surrealist activity as 'pure psychic automatism', a way of thinking that would be completely free of 'any control exercised by reason', as well as 'exempt from any aesthetic or moral concern'. As a kind of philosophical belief, Surrealism also set store by 'the superior reality of certain forms of previously neglected associations' and by 'the omnipotence of dream'.

Surrealism was primarily a literary movement, dominated by writers and poets, and the definitions of its manifestos were intended to apply to writing more than to painting. The Surrealists set out to produce 'automatic writing' – a free-flowing chain of thoughts and associations coming from the subconscious mind, inspired in part by treatments for psychiatric patients. Some members of the group questioned whether painting could ever be free of conscious control, as it was dependent on the artist's technical and compositional intentions. However, some artists did produce work which was seen to be – to some degree – 'automatic'. Surrealist journals such as *The Surrealist Revolution*, a crucial means by which the movement could express its ideas, were full of reproductions of drawings by the artist André Masson (1896–1987). Masson's paintings and drawings such as *Birth of the Birds* (1925), used flowing calligraphic lines to evoke figures, fruit, birds, fish and radiant suns caught up in a kind of swirling flux.

Surrealist artists found ways of creating works which suggested the absence of a controlling rationality. Masson

Otto Dix, *Der Salon I*, 1921

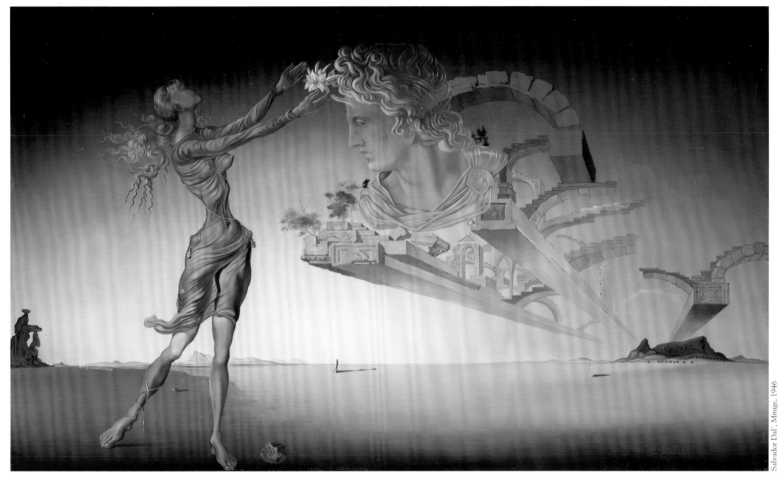

Salvador Dalí, Mirage, 1946

also experimented with sand and paint poured on to the canvas, taking inspiration from the random forms which resulted. Ernst used the technique of 'frottage' ('rubbing'), in which he took the patterns of wood graining, stones or leaves as a starting point to create pencil or wax crayon rubbings which could then become the basis of mysterious compositions such as *The Great Forest* (1927). The Catalan artist Joan Miró (1893–1983) created paintings using simplified marks and signs – schematic stick figures, body parts, animals and insects, suns and stars – combined with drawn lines and sometimes written inscriptions. These paintings, for example *The Hunter* (1923–24), had a child-like and spontaneous appearance, as if they were a more basic means of expression, freed from the limitations of a 'civilized', Western mentality.

Surrealism and the Subconscious Mind

The Surrealists looked to the creativity of children and the mentally disturbed as models of an untrammelled vision – the eye in a 'savage' state, as Breton once wrote. But they also looked within themselves, to the subconscious world opened up by the writings of the Viennese psychoanalyst Sigmund Freud (1856–1939), and to the manifestation of this world in dreams and desires. The Surrealists were fascinated by the work of the Italian artist Giorgio de Chirico (1888–1978): they interpreted his paintings of deserted sunlit Italian piazzas with isolated statues, looming dark arcades and tall chimneys, such as *The Enigma of a Day* (1914), as full of hidden sexual symbolism. The dream-like atmosphere of de Chirico's works also had a great influence on Surrealism, realistically painted and subtly disorienting

the spectator through shifting points of perspective. The Spaniard Salvador Dalí (1904–89) produced works which suggested dream scenarios, and which explored his own sexual fantasies and fears. He used his own personal symbols to evoke taboo themes such as masturbation and castration anxiety: a hand swarming with ants; the sticky insides of an egg; a floppy extended limb supported by a crutch; and a snarling lion's head to represent his feared father. Dalí's oil paintings were meticulous in their use of illusionistic detail, a technique that was crucial to his development of what he called 'paranoiac-critical' activity, the cultivation of painted double images. In *The Metamorphosis of Narcissus* (1937), a large hand holding an egg is echoed by the forms of a crouching figure and its reflection in a lake, suggesting the power of the mind to play tricks and reveal hidden subconscious thoughts.

The paintings of the Belgian artist René Magritte (1898–1967) also took up the idea of art as an illusion. Magritte used striking distortions of scale, paintings within paintings and strange juxtapositions (a bottle becoming a carrot), to force his viewers to question what they saw. He also explored contradictory combinations of images and words. *The Key of Dreams* (1930) depicted a series of objects including a hat, a shoe and a candle alongside handwritten labels which did not designate them at all.

The Surrealist 'revolution' in ways of seeing went beyond painting, moving into the fields of photography, film and object-making, and its combination of the cultivation of new artistic techniques along with new attitudes to social morality based on an acceptance of unconscious desires, was an inspiration to artists internationally. The exploration of personal, autobiographical events and feelings through disturbing images, was a key feature of the work of artists such as the American painter Dorothea Tanning (b. 1910) and the Mexican Frida Kahlo (1907–58). Kahlo's paintings evoked her own anxieties and physical distress using strange details, such as the scattered locks of her own hair in her *Self-Portrait with Cropped Hair* (1940). The Chilean artist Roberto Matta (b. 1911) expressed his own subconscious feelings in paintings of free-floating forms suggesting scenes of violence and bodily deformation, which he called 'psychological morphologies'. Matta worked first in Paris, then from 1939 in the United States, and his work was an important influence on a new generation of American artists after the Second World War.

Surrealism was also a significant context for the development of the work of Picasso in this period. The surrealist leader André Breton had praised Picasso's Cubist works as seminal precursors in their creation of a 'window' on to a new world. In his large painting *The Three Dancers* (1925), Picasso combined flattened areas of colour and an interior setting deriving from Cubism with an evocation of magic ritual, violence and sexuality. Human figures in his paintings, particularly women based on his wife, Olga, and his lover, Marie-Thérèse Walter, began to be grotesquely deformed, with swollen limbs, bulging faces and screaming mouths. These expressive distortions were used to powerful effect in Picasso's 1937 painting *Guernica*. In response to the bombing of a Basque town by General Franco's forces during the Spanish Civil War, Picasso produced a horrific vision of an assault upon humanity. Twisted bodies and terrified women and children are depicted in a fragmented way suggesting the shattering impact of an air attack, in a black-and-white palette recalling newspaper photographs. The new painting styles of the twentieth century made possible visually striking and disturbing reactions to social and political events.

Paris Post War and Tachisme

Picasso remained in Paris during the German Occupation, producing still-lifes and figure studies which reflected the physical constraints and deprivations of wartime. Painting in Paris in the post-war period was marked by a sombre mood: subject matter that suggested the isolation of the individual, often executed in a limited palette. The existentialist philosophy of Jean-Paul Sartre (1905–80) began to reach a wide audience in 1945, and emphasized the absurdity of human existence and the importance of personal responsibility. Sartre also wrote on art, providing prefaces for exhibitions of the work of Swiss artist Alberto Giacometti (1901–66). Giacometti had created Surrealist sculptures in the 1930s, and had spent the war in neutral Switzerland. On his return to Paris, he began to produce a series of tall, elongated figure sculptures with roughly modelled surfaces, and in the 1950s he worked on painted portraits of his mother, wife and writer friends. These paintings show single figures almost disappearing beneath a mass of crosshatched lines, situated against yawning backgrounds which seem about to swallow them up. Giacometti used

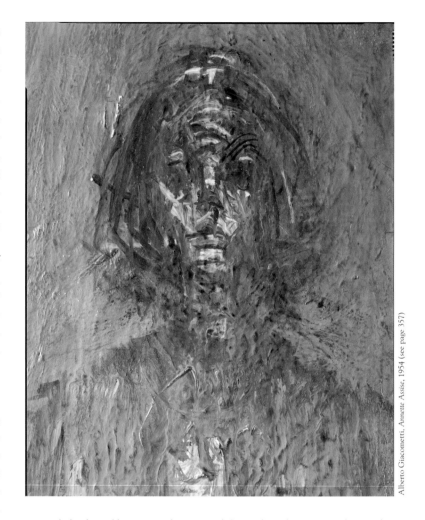

Alberto Giacometti, *Annette Assise*, 1954 (see page 357)

muted shades of brown and grey, and fine white lines to pick out the volumes of his figures. His mother in the painting *The Artist's Mother* (1951) takes on a skeletal, ghostly appearance.

Existentialism seemed to account, above all, for the experience of urban living: the alienating feeling of struggling alongside a mass of other individuals. The theme of urban existence was explored in the paintings of the French artist Jean Dubuffet (1901–85), who depicted single figures against graffiti-scrawled walls, or bustling group scenes full of men in suits and hats failing to interact with one another, such as *The Busy Life* (1953). Dubuffet developed a radical and characteristic painting technique, using thick, encrusted layers of paint which looked like smeared mud, sometimes enhanced with added glue, plaster or asphalt, and which were described by critics as 'living matter' and 'filth'. Dubuffet's technique sprang from his rejection of art-school training and of conventional notions of artistic beauty: he had abandoned art for almost 20 years to run the family wine business. He cultivated a deliberately naïve style, depicting the human body in a child-like way, as a simple outline with caricatural, often grimacing features. Dubuffet had a strong interest in the art of children as a source of authentic expression, and in the art of the insane, assembling an important collection of what he termed *art brut* ('raw art').

A thick surface impasto or textured pigment was also a feature of the paintings of Jean Fautrier (1898–1964), where it took on harrowing connotations. Fautrier had heard the cries of tortured prisoners from his studio just outside Paris during the war, and the series of works that he produced with the title *Hostages* reflected this experience. In these paintings, light-coloured oil paint was built up to create rugged fragmentary heads and torsos, whose flesh looked mottled and bruised, while areas of red paint suggested bleeding wounds. The artistic treatment of the human body as a formless mass of matter, and the expressive improvised lines in Fautrier's compositions were characteristics of a style known as 'art informel' ('art without form'). The tendency towards abstracted markings suggesting emotive states of mind in French painting of this period was also known more specifically as 'Tachisme', from the French word *tache* ('blot' or 'mark'). The watercolours of Henri Michaux (1899–1984), evoking primordial mental states and sometimes produced under the influence of hallucinatory drugs, and the explosive scratched and scribbled paintings of the German-born Wols (1913–51), were representative of this style.

Abstract Expressionism

The expressive qualities of paint's colours and textures were an essential feature of the movement that developed in the United States during the 1940s that became known as Abstract Expressionism. The Abstract Expressionists were a loose grouping of painters in New York, working in varying styles, but sharing a desire for a freedom from traditional artistic values. Art in the United States had begun to evolve in the 1930s and 40s, rising to prominence over that emerging from the old centre of Paris, as European imperial dominance began to wane, and with it cultural dominance over the old art of the West. In addition a new community of artists and intellectuals had begun to arrive from Europe, fleeing political upheaval and persecution, and including some of the major exponents of the Purist-Abstract and Surrealist art movements. American artists were receptive to both styles, so that the previously mutually distinct movements were assimilated into a third, new style.

One of the dominant tendencies in 1930s American painting had been a realistic and often documentary style, depicting rural and small-town life, epitomized by the work of the Iowa-based Grant Wood (1892–1942). The Abstract Expressionists reacted against what they saw as the conservatism and dryness of this kind of painting, preferring spontaneous and personal expression. Cubism and Surrealism were important sources for the development of this new movement. The Armenian painter Arshile Gorky (1905–48) was a close friend of Roberto Matta, and developed in his own work strong personal imagery using brightly coloured biomorphic forms. In paintings such as *One Year the Milkweed* (1944), Gorky created a bursting mass of daubed shapes overlaid with blurring, dripping colours full of emotional and irrational intensity. Gorky wrote about his paintings as transcriptions of childhood recollections, as well as explorations of joy, anxiety and pain. Gorky was a significant link between the European art movements and the new generation of American painters. The artist Hans Hofmann (1880–1966) also had a considerable influence. Hofmann, born in Germany, had worked in Paris and Munich before moving to New York in 1932, where he taught some of the artists that would rise to

prominence in the following decade. Hofmann's paintings of still-lifes and landscapes bore the marks of Cubism, but he also began to experiment with bold brushwork, strong colours and most importantly, with techniques of dripping and dribbling paint on to the canvas.

Jackson Pollock (1912–56) developed an abstract style based initially on mythic imagery inspired by the work of Picasso, Masson and Miró, and evoking sexual and violent themes expressed in a spontaneous way similar to Surrealist 'automatism'. Pollock had undergone psychoanalysis based on the teachings of the Swiss psychologist Carl Gustav Jung (1875–1961), which revolved around a series of collective, subconscious archetypes, such as the opposition of male and female qualities. Powerful, universal forces were suggested in the large-scale paintings that Pollock began to produce from 1946. He placed his canvasses horizontally on the floor and poured paint on to them in splashes and dribbles from all directions. Works like *Full Fathom Five* (1947) present a rhythmic mass of dripped paint, supplemented with small found objects such as cigarettes, nails and buttons, without any recognizable subject matter. Great arcs and curving forms reflect Pollock's vigorous gestures in creating the work, moving freely around the canvas using dried-out brushes, sticks and trowels to apply his paint from a distance. This process was known as 'action painting'. Pollock's work had great significance within the development of modern

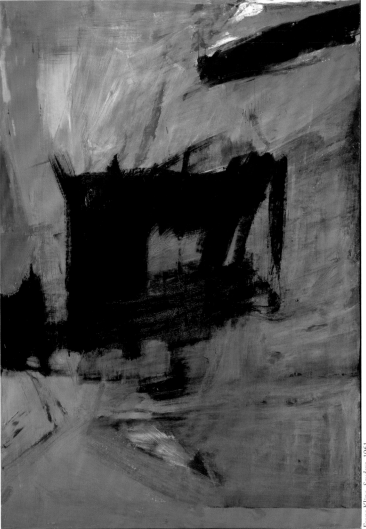

Franz Kline, *Scudera*, 1961

47

Ellsworth Kelly, *Orange Relief with Green*, 1991

The Colour–Field Technique

A very different tone and tendency was explored in New York in the work of Clyfford Still (1904–80), Barnett Newman (1905–70) and Mark Rothko (1903–70). All three passed through a stage of experimenting with mythic themes – chaotic, archetypal landscapes and primordial forms – to eventually develop personal abstract works known collectively as 'colour-field' paintings. In colour-field paintings the artists applied pure pigments to the canvas to create subtle variations in colour that were evocative of mood. From 1945, Still began to produce paintings using large planes of colour which dominated most of the canvas, at its edges making room for jagged fragments of other layers of paint. Still used a palette knife to apply paint evenly, creating a sense of emptiness, particularly in the centre of the canvas where we would expect the focus of a composition to be. In a similar vein to that of the less well-known 'Post-Painterly Abstraction' movement, which featured Ellsworth Kelly among others, Still was adamant in his rejection of a painterly tradition, which he characterized as 'dust and filing cabinets', and he was scathing of the spectator's attempts to be comforted or uplifted by art. Still's works are deliberately inaccessible and difficult to read, an assertion of his own perception of his 'solitary' and 'outside' status.

Barnett Newman was more receptive to the spiritual potential of his abstract paintings. In *Onement I* (1948) Newman laid a strip of masking tape painted orange-red vertically down the centre of his rectangular, deep-red canvas, originally intending to remove it later, but liking the result so much that it remained. A series of works ensued, known as the 'zip paintings' because of their single vertical stripes. These stripes echoed the edges of the canvas, making the process of framing the composition an integral part of the painting. The use of the whole canvas is a crucial characteristic of colour-field painting, and Newman once described how he reached a stage with his work 'where I got to the edge and didn't fall off'. Newman frequently gave his works suggestive titles, often on biblical themes, imparting to his paintings the sense of a search for simple, elemental forms.

Mark Rothko, who was of Russian origin, also talked in terms of 'ritual' and 'a transcendent realm' with regard to his paintings after 1947. His works were conceived to be seen up close in an atmosphere of silence, in order to encourage an intimate response. Their large scale was a corollary of this, allowing the spectator to enter into the experience of viewing them, as Rothko suggested: 'A large picture is an immediate transaction: it takes you into it.' The artist used veil-like layers of colour of varying warmths and coolnesses, creating an effect of soft depth which seems to engulf the onlooker. Patches of luminous colour are characteristically arranged as a stacked series of horizontally aligned rectangles in Rothko's works of the 1950s, such as *Number 10* (1950), creating an impression of calm meditation and otherworldly mystery. Warm reds and maroons gave way to more sombre colours in Rothko's later work as he succumbed to depression. The artist thought of his paintings not as totally abstract, but he was interested in how they could convey basic human emotions.

painting through its insistent treatment of the canvas as a flat – in this case horizontal – surface, and through its emphasis on the painter's own processes of creation.

Gestural energy and an emotive 'unfinished' appearance were important features of the painting of other artists associated with Abstract Expressionism, such as Lee Krasner (1911–84), Pollock's wife, and the Dutch-born Willem de Kooning (1904–97). De Kooning's work maintained a tension between abstraction and figuration, using the female nude in particular as the basis for compositions in violent reds and pinks. De Kooning was less interested in the processes of 'automatic' creation than in the relationship between the flat picture surface and the illusion of volume of the human figure, between the drawn line and the fleshy presence of colour. These concepts he had derived from Cubism, and from the work of Picasso in particular, whose grotesque deformations of women's bodies were a forceful inspiration upon De Kooning's *Woman* series of the early 1950s. The exuberance of this strain of Abstract Expressionism had a formative influence on the work of the 'Cobra' group of young painters in Europe, which included the Dutchman Karel Appel (b. 1921), with his stridently coloured, child-like animal and figure scenes, and the Dane Asger Jorn (1914–73), whose paintings are full of furious brushstrokes and disorderly forms in primary colours. The American Cy Twombly (b. 1928) was also inspired by the spontaneity of Abstract Expressionism as well as by the child-like vision of Paul Klee, creating complex scribbled works midway between painting and drawing.

Pop Art

Pop Art first emerged in the mid-1950s in both America and Britain. In part it was a reaction against the emotional seriousness and introspection of Abstract Expressionism, which had been affected by the experience of the Second World War. In the United States, John F. Kennedy's presidency, which began in 1960, marked a new era of optimism and a celebration of middle-class consumer values. The term 'Pop Art' was coined by the British-born critic and curator Lawrence Alloway (1926–90) in 1954 to describe the 'popular art' and imagery produced by a mass culture which 'high' art had begun to pick up and use: flags, jukeboxes, badges, advertising logos, comic strips and magazines. This interest in 'low' art forms as a means of rejuvenating artistic tradition had its precursors in American modern art in the work of earlier painters like Charles Demuth (1883–1935) and Stuart Davis (1894–1964). Demuth's painting *I Saw the Figure Five in Gold* (1928), for example, had recalled the industrial look of mechanically produced billboard lettering. After the intensity of Abstract Expressionism, Pop Art favoured irony and impersonal techniques in the creation of art works, as well as a return to figurative painting.

Bridging the Gap: Abstract Expressionism to Pop Art

The work of Robert Rauschenberg (b. 1925) and Jasper Johns (b. 1930) was influenced by the use of everyday, 'found' materials in Cubist collage and in the 'ready-mades' of Marcel Duchamp. From 1954, Rauschenberg began to produce works that incorporated collage elements and everyday objects, existing part way between two and three dimensions. For the artist, the activity of making these works was somewhere between art and life. In *Bed* (1955), Rauschenberg suspended a bed vertically on a wall and splashed it with coloured paint, a parody of the Abstract Expressionists' 'drip paintings', suggesting that their ideas had been brought into the realm of the banal and the everyday. The 'all-over' effect created by Rauschenberg's combines, where no single element appeared compositionally more important than the others – whether painted, reproduced or found – was also similar to the 'all-over' paintwork of Abstract Expressionism.

A painterly style deriving from Abstract Expressionism was employed by other artists of the so-called 'Beat generation' of the 1950s, such as the jazz musician-turned-painter Larry Rivers (b. 1923) and the performance artist Jim Dine (b. 1935). Jasper Johns, too, in his paintings referred ironically to the mode that he had pursued in his early work, by using expressive, gestural brushstrokes. His individualistic technique, however, was characteristically applied to subject matter common to everyone: familiar mass imagery such as flags and targets. In the painting *Three Flags* (1958), Johns depicted three American flags of decreasing size, one on top of the other, creating an image that was at once recognizable, but also formed a kind of abstract pattern. In works like this, attention was drawn away from the subject represented, with its well-known forms and colours, towards the handling of the paint itself. The representation and incorporation of real objects in Johns' paintings, and his sculptures of beer cans and flashlights in real-life scale and detail, raised the issue of

art as a process of thought, making Johns an important forerunner of Conceptual Art. His use of bold, iconic imagery, however, was a crucial inspiration for the Pop artists.

The world of advertising and graphic design was a major source for Pop Art. James Rosenquist (b. 1933) worked as a billboard painter before incorporating the large-scale, clear-cut forms and slick realism of advertising into his works. The painting *F-111* (1965) put together a jumble of images from the mass media, including a jet bomber and a child's smiling face, to suggest the jarring juxtapositions of modern urban life. Ed Ruscha (b. 1937) painted isolated words and signs as striking graphic elements in their own right. Most famously, Andy Warhol (1928–87) first worked as an illustrator producing advertisements and fashion designs, creating in the early 1960s a series of stencilled paintings using industrial paint which depicted cans of Campbell's tomato soup, dollar bills and Coca-Cola bottles. Warhol, like Johns, deliberately chose motifs that were part of a common

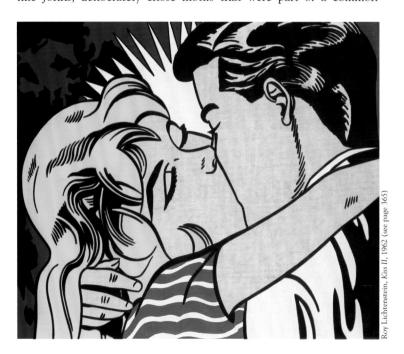

Roy Lichtenstein, *Kiss II*, 1962 (see page 365)

American culture, and he developed a technique of screen-printing his images so that they could be mass reproduced.

A stylistic neutrality and lack of emotion were important aspects of Warhol's paintings, so that they maintained a deliberate distance from the realm of 'fine' or 'high' art. His studio, known as 'The Factory' and comprising many acolytes and hangers-on, produced a large amount of work in an intentionally machine-like way. Warhol also used repetition to emphasize this idea of industrial-style production and, in his works depicting famous personalities like Marilyn Monroe and Elvis Presley, to suggest the superficiality of celebrity and media culture. His painting *Marilyn Diptych* (1962), created just after the film star's death, evoked a melancholy sense of the inadequacy of the iconic image through the blurring and fading of Marilyn's repeated face.

The importance of the visual image as a form of mass communication which had superseded the written word, in the form of film, television and comics, was a key feature of the work of Roy

Lichtenstein (1923–98). Lichtenstein's paintings were composed of a series of tiny, meticulously painted 'Ben Day' dots – the basic components of printed imagery – and they depicted isolated comic-strip frames, often complete with words and captions. The painting *Girl with Hair Ribbon* (1965) showed a glamorous blue-eyed blonde with an anxious expression, suggesting the small-scale mundane dramas of American suburban life.

Pop Art in Britain as it developed in the early to mid-1950s expressed a desire for an American lifestyle of consumer plenty, in contrast to the atmosphere of post-war rationing and privation. In a collage entitled *"Just what is it that makes today's homes so different, so appealing?"* (1956), the artist Richard Hamilton (b. 1922) put together magazine images including an advertisement for a vacuum cleaner, a tin of preserved ham, a Ford motor-car insignia and a muscle-bound bodybuilder as an ironic, but also celebratory, homage to aspirational consumerism. The Scottish-born Eduardo Paolozzi (b. 1924) also drew upon popular American magazines, using a spicy women's magazine called 'Intimate Confessions' in his early piece *I Was a Rich Man's Plaything* (1947). Peter Blake (b. 1932) took inspiration above all from popular music, using collaged photographs, but also the traditional technique of oil paint on canvas or board, to represent magazine covers featuring Elvis or Bo Diddley. His own role as a fan and collector of pop ephemera and souvenirs is evoked in the painting *Self-Portrait with Badges* (1961), which suggests a certain nostalgia rather than an enthusiastic embrace of modern technology. Blake's association with pop music was cemented by his creation of the album cover for the Beatles' *Sergeant Pepper's Lonely Hearts Club Band* in 1967.

The early work of David Hockney (b. 1937), born in the north of England, drew upon popular culture, most notably in the form of graffiti, but after he visited and eventually settled in California from the mid-1960s his painting style became flatter, reflecting a shift from oil paint to smooth acrylics. Hockney used simplified shapes – the horizontal forms of houses, lawns, hedges, pools and the blue Californian sky – in a series of works depicting the different movements of water. His painting *A Bigger Splash* (1967), showing a white spray of water from an immaculate swimming pool, evoked a wealthy and laid-back lifestyle, while in *Sunbather* (1966), a homoerotic male nude lies beside a calm pool, its shimmering surface suggested by graphic undulating lines. Hockney was an important mediator between British and American Pop Art.

Nouveau Réalisme

The use of found objects and remnants of everyday life, as well as an ironic attitude towards the new consumer society, were features that Pop Art shared with the work of a group of artists in France in the 1960s, known as the Nouveaux Réalistes ('new realists'). These artists, who included Yves Klein (1928–62), Arman (b. 1928) and Jean Tinguely (1925–91), wanted to involve contemporary society directly in their work through references to consumerism and the mass media, in an attempt to engage with 'the passionate adventure of the real'. To this end, they experimented with performances and events, and with three-

dimensional 'assemblages' based on the principle of collage. The artist Niki de Saint-Phalle (b. 1930) created a series of 'shooting paintings': large collections of assembled objects at which she and fellow artists would fire small cloth bags filled with paint, to produce a spattered, violent effect. Born into a society family, Saint-Phalle rebelled against the traditional female roles that were expected of her, depicting grotesque 'crucified' women in a combination of paint and other media.

Yves Klein, who had no formal art training, made paintings which had a direct link to performance. He produced a series of charred works on paper, made with the aid of a blowtorch. His *Anthropometries*, whose title suggested the scientific measuring of human proportions, were based on the bodily imprints of nude models on paper or canvas, and were often created during notorious public 'happenings'. These paintings were both literally figurative – a kind of portraiture of each individual body – and also abstract, an effect reinforced by Klein's predominant use of the colour blue. His favourite shade was patented as 'International Klein Blue': the cultivation of his provocative personality was an important part of his artistic activity. The Italian artist Piero Manzoni (1933–63) met Klein in 1957, and under his influence moved away from figurative painting to the creation of plain canvases enhanced with simple details such as a covering of white objects, which he called 'Achromes' ('without colour'). *Achrome* (1960) was a canvas covered in a fine clay material and bunched up into horizontal folds

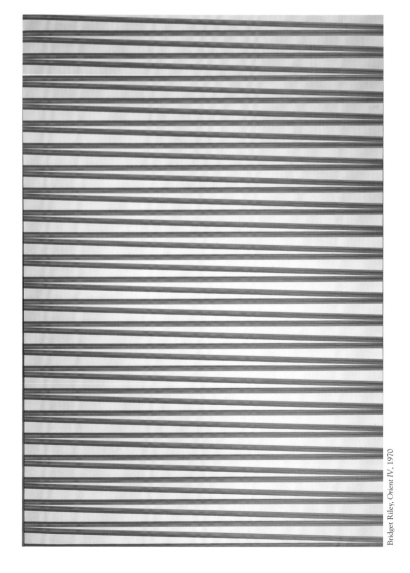

Bridget Riley, *Orient IV*, 1970

in the centre of the composition, and Manzoni also slashed and stitched his canvasses to draw attention to them as objects in themselves. The notion of art as performance, central to Nouveau Réalisme, was taken up by Manzoni in his famous gestures of signing balloons filled with his own breath, and tins containing his own faeces.

Op Art

While Pop Art relied on recognizable images to get across its celebration or parody of contemporary culture, the 1960s tendency known as 'Op Art' was uncompromisingly abstract. Op Art had its sources in Russian Constructivism and in the Suprematism of Malevich, in developing a painting style that was all about the spectator's perception of abstract forms and about the sensations and illusions that these could provoke. The term 'Op' is a shortening of 'optical', and Op Art aimed to explore the effects of different kinds of retinal stimulation, using closely spaced black-and-white or coloured patterns. In line with other modern developments, Op Art sought not to provide the illusion of representation – one of painting's traditional roles – but to make the viewer question his or her processes of seeing. But Op Art was not only confined to the realm of 'high' art: when the term was first coined in the American media in 1964, it also quickly came to refer to a characteristic design scheme used for fabrics, wallpaper and other household objects.

The Hungarian-born painter Victor Vasarély (1908–97), who worked for most of his life in France, trained as a graphic designer, creating works in black and white, before devoting his career from the late 1940s onwards to abstract painting using optical effects to suggest movement and depth. He believed that the standardized forms in his works could lead to a new, urban art replacing easel painting. Vasarély's coloured works with their pulsating squares and circles came to be seen as the epitome of Op Art. In Britain, Bridget Riley (b. 1931) also had a background in commercial design and advertising, going on to produce works like *Burn* (1964) – a composition in emulsion on hardboard, using repeated black-and-white triangles, which appear to fluctuate and move, disorienting the viewer. Riley's paintings combine a neutral and meticulous technique with a spectacular and psychologically affecting visual result.

Minimalism

Minimalism or Minimal Art of the late 1950s and early 1960s sought to eliminate all self-expression from the work of art. Like Op Art, it looked to earlier twentieth-century movements like Suprematism and the Neoplasticism of Mondrian as precedents in the creation of works that were meaningful in their own right without representing anything, and that were conceived in the artist's mind rather than found in nature. The painter Agnes Martin (b. 1912), born in Canada but working in New York in the 1960s, entitled a work of 1965 *Harvest*, which consisted of a fine grid of criss-crossing pencil lines on a plain cream canvas. Martin created these thousands of lines with a ruler, to

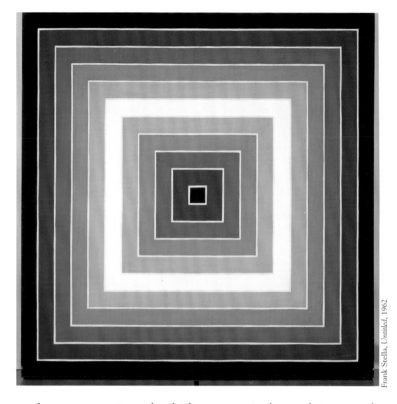

Frank Stella, *Untitled*, 1962

produce a geometric work which was emotionless and impersonal, bearing an oblique relation to the natural motif of its title.

Minimal Art had in part evolved out of Abstract Expressionism, from the increasingly pared-down paintings of Barnett Newman. Ad Reinhardt (1913–67) had been a close associate of the Abstract Expressionists, but partly through the inspiration of Oriental art had begun to produce paintings using a single colour and simple symmetrical rectilinear forms. In 1960, Reinhardt created a series of 'black paintings' which consisted of nine even squares of black paint on a canvas, only barely distinguishable from each other, to make the shape of a cross. In a statement of 1962 entitled 'Art as art', Reinhardt claimed that the only aim of abstraction could be to make art 'purer and emptier, more absolute and more exclusive'. The young artist Frank Stella (b. 1936) also produced 'black paintings'. In 1959 an exhibition at the Museum of Modern Art in New York included four large radical works by Stella, then aged 23. These paintings, such as *Die Fahne hoch!* ('The Flag High!') of 1959, were based on symmetrical patterns of regular pinstripes. Stella applied stripes of black enamel using a housepaint brush, leaving small gaps between them through to the canvas beneath. The evocative titles of these works, with their potential for private associations in the mind of the spectator, sat uneasily with their blank formal effects. The title *Die Fahne hoch!*, for example, derived from a German Nazi anthem, while the work's cruciform pattern recalled a 1923 painting by Malevich called *Black Cross*. These paintings also stood out from the walls against which they were displayed to an unusual extent, due to Stella's use of thick stretcher bars for his canvasses, making them more like three-dimensional objects. Many of the artists associated with Minimalism turned away from painting towards sculpture, including Donald Judd (1928–94) and Carl Andre (b. 1935), famous for his floor-based groups of commercial firebricks.

Conceptual Art

Both Pop artists and Mimimalists had been concerned to some degree with art as a means of thinking – 'art as idea' – which could go beyond the boundaries of the traditional media of painting, drawing and sculpture to include gestures, performances and happenings. The common starting point of these different manifestations was the rejection of the conventional art object: something tangible and unique that could be exhibited and sold. The work of Marcel Duchamp in the 1910s was a crucial inspiration for this, through his designation of objects – a bicycle wheel, a bottle rack and a row of coat pegs – as well as transactions – a cheque for his dentist, a bond for a roulette game – as 'art'. Conceptual Art, an international movement bridging the 1960s and 1970s, often resulted in events and activities which were short-lived, existing for posterity only in the form of photographs, film or written documentation. However, painting was also used by Conceptual artists to raise questions in the mind of the observer, whose role now became more important than ever by participating in and 'completing' the work of art.

A shift of emphasis away from the art object itself and towards a set of ideas about the role and function of art led to the frequent use of language as an integral part of an art work. The Italian-born artist Ben Vautier (b. 1935), working in France, painted bold slogans in acrylic on canvas which were intended as a kind of anti-establishment propaganda. The painting *Art is Useless, Go Home* (1971) consisted of the sentence 'L'art est inutile rentrez chez vous' in large white capital letters on a bright red background, a playful and provocative piece which transforms painting into a paradoxical 'anti-art' activity. The American artists Joseph Kosuth (b. 1945) and Lawrence Weiner (b. 1940) used words printed on the gallery wall or as images to be reproduced in different contexts such as billboards or even advertisements in newspapers. Kosuth characteristically employed dictionary definitions, blown up in large scale and printed white on black, of words related to his art-making processes, such as 'idea'. The British group Art and Language, which included the artists Michael Baldwin (b. 1945) and Mel Ramsden (b. 1944), saw the production of communal texts as an integral part of their art practice, as well as producing ironic paintings based on Socialist Realist icons like Lenin and Stalin in the style of Pollock's Abstract Expressionism.

If ideas were the main subject of Conceptual Art, the process of creating a work became just as important as the 'finished' result. The Japanese artist On Kawara (b. 1933), based in New York, has worked since 1966 on a series of 'date paintings', each of which is a neutral white-on-black transcription of the date on which the work is made, in the language of the country he is working in. The Pole Roman Opalka (b. 1931) began in 1965 an extensive series of paintings called *1 to Infinity*, in which canvasses are filled with infinite sequences of numbers, each one recorded into a tape player at the same time as it is painted. Each of Opalka's paintings in this series is regarded as a 'detail' from the larger overall work. The work of these two artists shares an emphasis on painting which is almost anonymous, a vehicle rather than an end in itself. The French artist Daniel Buren (b. 1938)

reduced his paintings to simple stripes as a protest against individual artistic style, and in 1966 decided that he would henceforth use only stripes of white and one colour and of a consistent width, in all his subsequent work. Buren uses his striped format on paintings, billboards or on panels of fabric to be shown in spaces both inside and outside the art gallery, in order to criticize the elitism of the art world.

Conceptual Art was often austere and unrelenting in its appearanceand its attitude towards artistic tradition, seen as ideologically loaded and unacceptable. The movement began to fade in the mid-1970s, when artists began to take a renewed interest in painting's materials and subject matter. It had, however, brought to the fore the use of irony, humour and autobiographical content which would all be taken up by new generations of artists.

New Painting and Neo–Expressionism

The late 1970s saw a concerted return to painting as a central artistic concern, in reaction to the explosion of different kinds of art activity in previous decades, such as photography, video and installation art. The painting that was produced differed in style, often harking back to earlier twentieth-century modes. One common feature was a rejection of the conception of painting seen as a specifically flat medium, whose subject matter and treatment should reflect this inevitable flatness. The so-called 'New Painting' of the late 1970s and 1980s turned away from this emphasis on flatness, which had been seen as key aspect of the development of pictorial abstraction, preferring to use painting to represent external reality in its traditional function as a 'window on to the world'. The resurgence of painting took place primarily in the then West Germany, Italy, the United States and Britain.

One of the features of the revival of painting was a reappraisal of the work of an older generation of artists whose work had always been figurative, despite changing artistic fashions. In London in 1976, the artist R. B. Kitaj (b. 1932), who had been born in America and who had played an important role in British Pop Art, organized an exhibition of figurative painting that included the work of Lucian Freud (b. 1922) and Francis Bacon (1909–92), painters known together as the 'School of

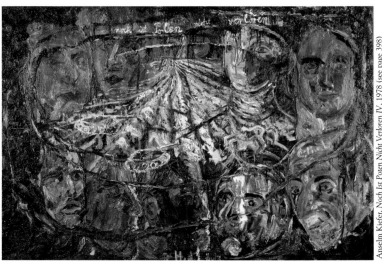

Anselm Kiefer, *Noch Ist Poem Nicht Verloren IV*, 1978 (see page 398)

London'. Kitaj's own work comprised landscapes and figure scenes, often quoting from 'high' art sources like Renaissance paintings, with a stress on painting's narrative content. Freud's paintings were nude studies and portraits, often seen close to or from unusual angles, with a powerful, painterly handling of flesh and an honest, sometimes frankly ugly, treatment of the naked human body. Freud's visceral and psychologically unnerving approach to the figure has continued in his painting up to the present day. Since the late 1940s, Francis Bacon had painted in an expressive mode, using distorted depictions of the human body to evoke sharpened emotions of pleasure and pain. Bacon had a strong interest in portraiture, particularly self-portraiture, and in narrative history painting. In his painting *Triptych – August 1972*, Bacon used a traditional religious format to depict three different views of his friend George Dyer in an austere empty room, both seated, and in the central panel, apparently writhing on the floor. The artist's use of paint to create flesh which is beautiful and repulsive simultaneously was part of his aim to 'bring the figurative thing up onto the nervous system more violently and more poignantly'. It was significant for these artists of the School of London that the human figure had never gone away as one of painting's central concerns.

In the United States, the painter Leon Golub (b. 1922) had also worked in a figurative style, in line with his deep left-wing political commitments. In 1976 he began a series of paintings called *Mercenaries*, whose raw realism was intended to reflect the violence of international conflicts – in Vietnam, Africa and Latin America. Golub used press and media photographs for details of weapons, uniforms and even bodily gestures, but believed that his large-scale paintings had a role as a kind of modern history painting, despite the extensive media coverage of wars and atrocities, which he saw as manipulated and tendentious. His works, with their bold coloured backgrounds and scraped-away painted flesh (an effect achieved by Golub's use of a small meat-cleaver as a painting tool) were intended to be shocking. Through their large size, the figures depicted – laid-back killers or interrogators – are, Golub insisted, 'inserted into our space and we're inserted into their space', forcing the spectator into confrontation.

History painting, which had been the dominant mode of nineteenth-century painting, was rejected in the first half of the twentieth century in favour of more intimate and experimental modes. In the work of the German Neo-Expressionists in the late 1970s and early 1980s, however, it was revived as a means of commenting upon Germany's past and of expressing distrust for political developments like the desire for the unification of East and West. These painters used exuberant brushstrokes and bright colours in their works, prompting identification with the early twentieth-century Expressionist movement, as well as with Fauvism through the designation 'Neue Wilden' ('the new wild ones').

Investigating Concepts of Art

The artist Jörg Immendorff (b. 1945) had been trained under the seminal Conceptual artist Joseph Beuys (1921–86), who drew heavily upon his German roots in the creation of a personal mythology. Beuys served in the Luftwaffe during the Second World War, and was shot down over the Crimea in 1943. His rescue by nomads was to shape his

philosophy as an artist; the felt and fat in which they covered him, enduring as two of his favourite materials (expressing warmth and comfort), and their Shamanic beliefs influencing his view that the role of an artist was akin to that of a Shaman: channelling energy through objects to give them symbolic power.

Immendorff's large, complex compositions, such as his *Café Deutschland* series, brought together military and political characters like Lenin, Stalin and Hitler, as well as using symbols of German identity such as flags, eagles and tanks. Anselm Kiefer (b. 1945) included the name of Joseph Beuys alongside those of the Romantic painter Caspar David Friedrich and the composer Richard Wagner in his 1973 painting *Spiritual Heroes of Germany*. His large-scale works of the 1980s also explored the theme of Germany's past, often evoking myths in a manner deliberately and pointedly reminiscent of the Nazis. Kiefer used highly textured, expressive surfaces, but combined with problematic and distancing subject matter, questioning painting's role as direct self-expression. The artist Georg Baselitz (b. 1938) distanced the viewer from his emotionally charged brushwork by turning his compositions upside down, counteracting conventional ways of looking at art. Unlike that of Immendorff and Kiefer, Baselitz's art is sensual and anti-intellectual, focused on the act of painting and breaking down the barriers between abstraction and figuration, in order to be, as the artist put it, 'delivered of all ballast, delivered from tradition'.

The Italian painter Francesco Clemente (b. 1952) produced highly eclectic works drawing on a range of different religious, cultural and mythological motifs, using the traditional fresco technique of painting into wet plaster that had been perfected in the Renaissance. Working in different international locations, principally Italy, India and New York, Clemente created paintings in the 1980s that took on references specific to the place in which he found himself. Clemente was seen as the foremost representative of a new *Transavanguardia* ('beyond the avant garde'). The principle of referring to different artistic subjects and styles within the same painting was characteristic of the so-called 'Bad Painting' that developed in the United States in the 1980s. The young artist Julian Schnabel (b. 1951) was one of the leaders of this trend, creating energetic large-scale paintings in which 'high' art themes such as motifs from the Classical tradition are mixed with 'low', popular art forms like broken crockery. His work *Blue Nude with Sword* (1979–80) used a dramatic fragmented surface of smashed plates upon which were painted Classical columns and a vigorous squatting male nude brandishing a sword. Schnabel also attached unconventional materials such as lino, velvet and fake fur to his canvasses which, along with his fragmentary quotations from Old Master paintings, created a confusing and even infantile effect.

The work of Keith Haring (1958–90) and Jean-Michel Basquiat (1960–88) also employed a child-like style, derived from the popular cultural forms of graffiti and street art. Haring was trained as an artist, but began his career decorating empty advertising hoardings in the New York subway before his brightly coloured scenes of dancing cartoon-like figures were accepted by art galleries and museums. A series of untitled works in acrylic on muslin from 1984 combined his trademark figures with motifs from the world of comic books and pop culture – aeroplanes, flying saucers and computers – rendered in simple thick black outlines. Basquiat, of Puerto-Rican and Haitian parentage and born in Brooklyn, brought to his paintings his favourite boyhood obsessions: cars, weapons, war, old movies, Richard Nixon and J. Edgar Hoover, as well as referring to Cajun, Hispanic and black American culture. Basquiat used a combination of acrylic, oil paint and wax crayons, enclosing his simplified figures and symbols with white lines, like chalk on a blackboard. His figures' grimacing, skeletal faces, in paintings like *Profit I* (1982), recall the caricatural style of the French artist Jean Dubuffet, while his graffiti-like scratches and scribbles suggest an ironic take on 'primitive' art.

In contrast to the profuse, energetic style of Schnabel, Haring and Basquiat, other American painters associated with the revival of figurative painting, preferred a more neutral, realistic mode. Eric Fischl (b. 1948) used a relaxed, casual style to depict subjects full of simmeringrepressed desires such as *Bad Boy* (1981). The directness of his scenes of young adolescent boys in sexual situations, combined with subtle lighting effects, makes the viewer a prurient voyeur of these explorations of suburban American anxieties. The artist Mark Tansey (b. 1949) created deadpan figure scenes which play tricks on the viewer in the manner of the paintings of René Magritte. *Action Painting II* (1984) was realistically painted in a monochrome range of blues, like a black-and-white photograph, and shows a group of easel painters depicting the launch of a space rocket in mid-air: the visual joke is that they could not possibly have captured their motif so quickly. The work refers both to American patriotism, through its inclusion of a flag and the space shuttle,and to the classic American art movement Abstract Expressionism in its title. Realistic painting was used with an ironic awareness of previous modern art movements.

Postmodernism and Contemporary

One of the issues at stake in the revival of painting was the sense that in the wake of the profusion of artistic experimentation of the twentieth century, no really new and original style could be created. Rather, hybrid forms of painting and pastiches of former styles were the only way forward, a belief which fully acknowledged the impossibility of the artistic expression of real, 'authentic' feelings and emotions – so central a principle in the creation of 'modern' art. The term 'postmodernism' signalled that this belief in originality and authenticity was now defunct, and that assumptions about what art could be were no longer valid in a new era of cynicism. In the mid-1980s, the cultural theorist Jean Baudrillard described the dominance of what he called 'hyperreality' in our experience of images. In the face of the ever-increasing growth and saturation of the mass media and the commercial world, the existence of something 'real' behind this surface proliferation of imagery was being called into doubt. The 'postmodern' artist would knowingly play with this 'hyperreal', exploring the impact of its simulated reality.

Postmodernism can be used to describe the work of a variety of artists from the mid-1970s up to the present. 'Neo-Expressionism' and American 'Bad Painting', in particular the work of Julian Schnabel, have features that can be seen as postmodern. The idea of making a painting by copying another visual source is a striking way of suggesting the end of art's uniqueness, a postmodern trait which had its roots in Dada and Pop Art. The German artist Gerhard Richter (b. 1932) used amateur snapshots from the 1960s onwards as the basis for blurry grey images made with paint dragged across the surface of the canvas, and talked about the liberating effect for his art of discovering 'that a stupid, ridiculous thing like copying a postcard could lead to a picture'. Richter's 'photographic' paintings, such as *Venice – Stairs with Isa (586-3)* (1985), are deliberately perverse: knowingly creating the appearance of photographs by the wrong means. Richter also creates abstract paintings with striking colours spread over the canvas using squeegees and spatulas, avoiding the unique touch of the artist's hand. A later example of photorealism can be seen in the works of Richard Estes. Richter often worked closely with the Polish-born Sigmar Polke (b. 1941), another artist originally associated with German Pop. Polke's works of the 1980s used incongruous superimpositions of illustration-like motifs and decorative surfaces like wallpaper, blankets and screen-printed 'Polke' dots, his trademark feature. The painting *Alice in Wonderland* (1983) combined references to sport, opium smoking and the children's story, carefully mixing different visual registers – the poetic and the trivial, the manually produced and the industrially manufactured – to create an overwhelming blend of changing images. The German artist Rosemarie Trockel (b. 1952) ironized painting techniques in her computer-knitted paintings of the 1980s, reproducing familiar imagery like the Playboy bunny or the Soviet hammer and sickle in a way that raised the question of women's artistic production. The contemporary British artist Chris Ofili (b. 1968) uses collage elements from pornographic and celebrity magazines, as well as beads and elephant dung, heavily varnished, to provocatively tackle the Western perception of the black body.

The work of the postmodern American 'Neo-Geo' artists blurred the boundaries between artistic and industrial manufacture. The abstract paintings of Peter Halley (b. 1953) use fluorescent paints and metallic paints alongside acrylic and Roll-a-Tex to create a mixture of smooth and rough surfaces reminiscent of institutional paintwork and décor effects. The term 'Neo-Geo' was used in the 1980s to suggest a revival of geometric abstraction stripped of its spiritual meanings. For Halley, Day-Glo paint represented 'low-budget mysticism', while the austere rectilinear forms in works like *CUSeeMe* (1995) were intended to evoke the confining architectural spaces of prisons, hospitals, schools and cheap motels. Halley's fellow New York artist and friend Ross Bleckner (b. 1949) drew upon Op Art to produce abstract works which were ironic, but also had a curious spiritual quality in their treatment of radiant lighting effects.

In Britain, the painter Gary Hume (b. 1962) originally produced life-size paintings of hospital doors in grim institutional colours. In the mid-1990s he began to create works in household paint on aluminium, based on celebrities, supermodels, angels or the shape of leaves and

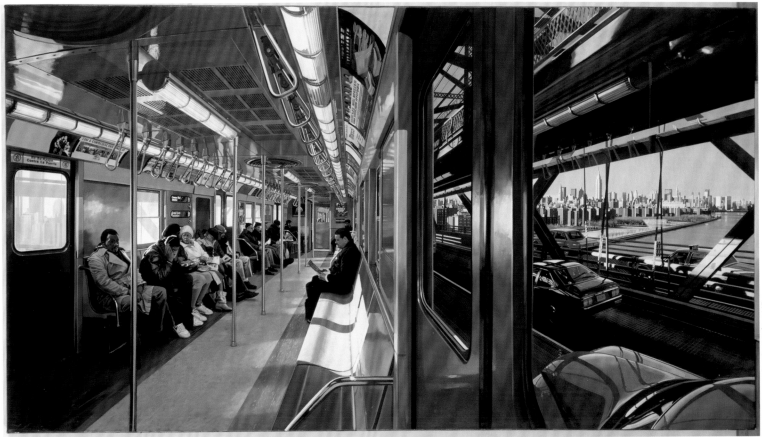

Richard Estes, *Williamsburg Bridge*, 1987

flowers, reduced to simplified areas of high-gloss colour. Hume feels his paintings – such as *Kate* (1996), based on the model Kate Moss – to be about beauty and without deep meaning, claiming 'all you ever get from me is surface'. Another Young British Artist, Fiona Rae (b. 1963), samples different abstract styles in her paintings: large, expressive brushstrokes, neat circular forms, splashes and dribbles, dragged and smeared paint. Her work combines an appearance of spontaneity with carefully calculated composition, giving a sense of vibrant energy without recognizable meaning.

While the label 'postmodern' might suggest a certain shallowness in art and the presentation of diversity without any commitment on the part of the artist, contemporary painters working in a whole range of styles do create work that communicates meanings and moods as well as taking account of the long painting tradition behind them. The British artist Howard Hodgkin (b. 1932), a member of an older generation of contemporary artists, creates abstract paintings on wood which are full of personal resonances, transforming motifs like landscapes and still-lifes into a luxuriantly-coloured array of forms. Hodgkin refers to artistic tradition by painting his frames as part of his compositions, in the manner of the late nineteenth-century painter Georges Seurat. His paintings are not ironic, however, but intimate and contemplative, painted slowly over a period of years. Marlene Dumas (b. 1953), born in South Africa but based in Amsterdam, works from photographic materials to capture the poses of her models, as well as taking subjects from art history. Of paramount concern in her works is their emotional effect, more than the familiarity of her figure subjects. Her four-panel painting *The First People (I-IV) (The Four*

Seasons) (1990) is based on photographs of her first child, shown in awkward poses on plain backgrounds, with putrid and deathly flesh tones which create a strong sense of anxiety. Dumas' works suggest a process of coming to terms with human vulnerability, without moral or social judgment. The Belgian Luc Tuymans (b. 1958) also bases his paintings on photographs as well as film. His disturbing images, often close-ups which impose themselves on the spectator such as *Der Diagnostische Blick IV* (1992), use badly applied cheap paint in washed-out empty colours, creating an air of desperation. The content of his work refers to Flemish, American and German history, and Tuymans regards his role as artist not as the documenter of events, but as a potential perpetrator. His paintings evoke a troubled detachment, drawing their effect from what Tuymans describes as a 'tremendous intensity of silence ... the silence before the storm'.

The variety and diversity of painting at the end of the twentieth and beginning of the twenty-first centuries reflect the artists' own individual approaches. The pursuit of personal ideas and feelings in painting seems more important today than the artistic allegiances and rivalries of painters previously, throughout the twentieth century. Painting is seen as less 'cutting-edge' than other artistic forms, such as video and installation art, and painters now are less caught up in the trends and fashions of the art world. Painting has also come a long way since the start of the twentieth century, from its traditional format of oil on canvas, to embrace all sorts of other materials, often taken from outside the realm of 'fine' art. The range of experimentation with content and technique that continues today demonstrates that painting's scope has most certainly not been exhausted.

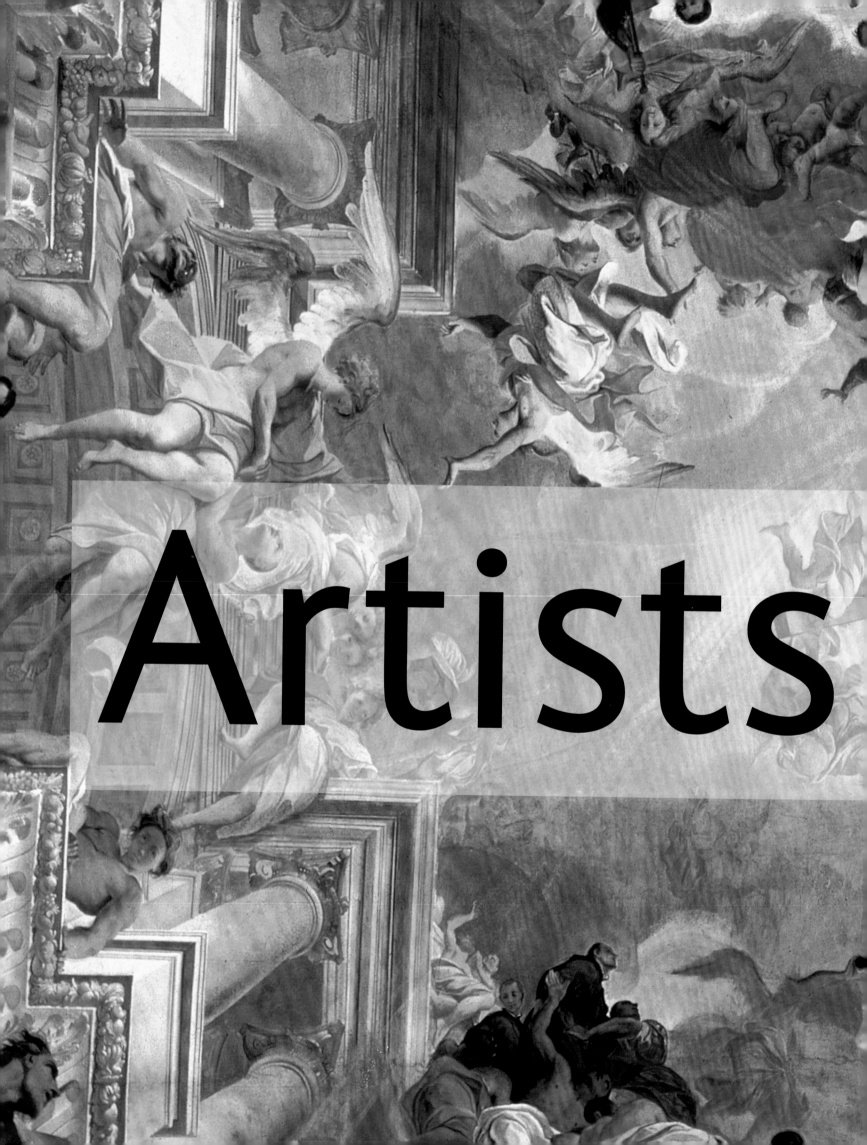

Artists

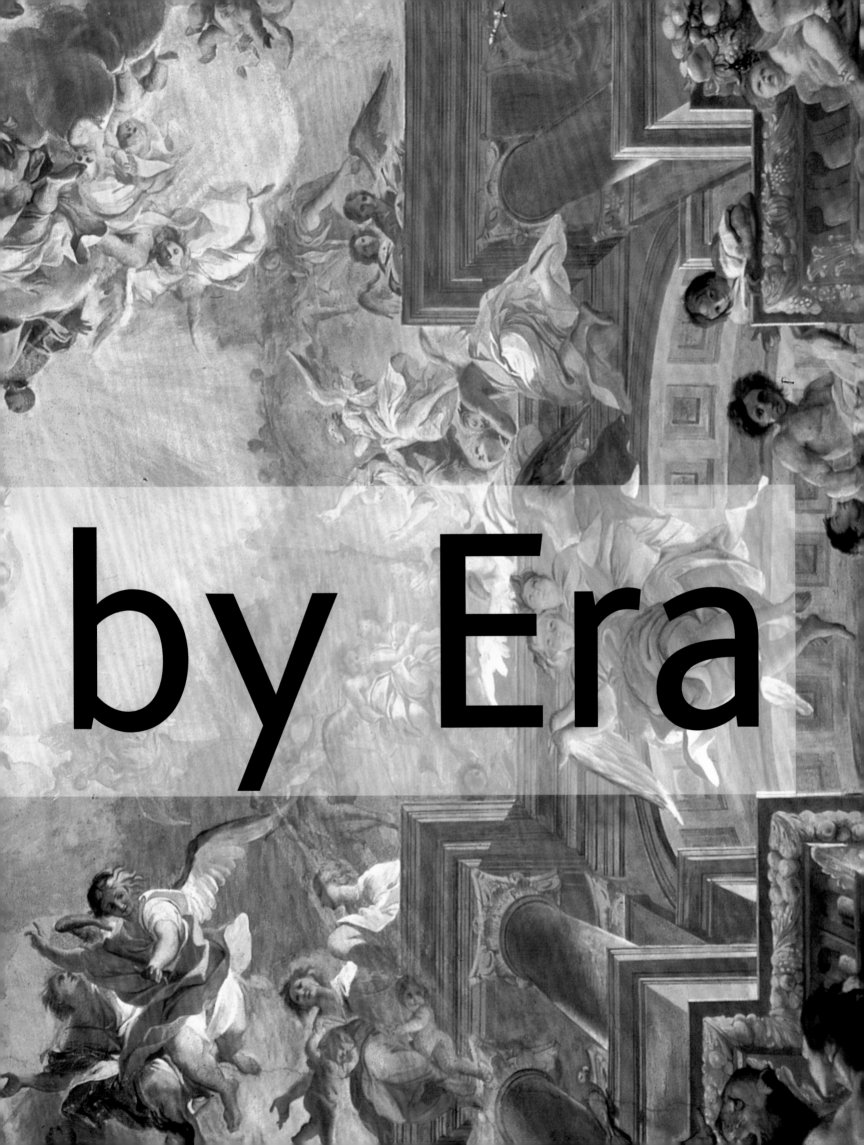

by Era

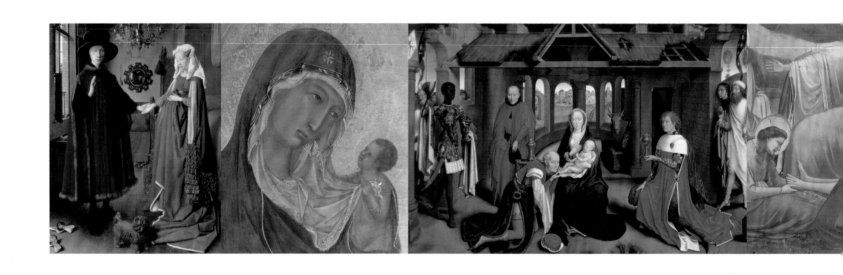

The Gothic & Medieval Era

The Gothic & Medieval Era
The Gothic & Medieval Era
The Gothic & Medieval Era
The Gothic & Medieval Era
The Gothic & Medieval Era
The Gothic & Medieval Era
The Gothic & Medieval Era
The Gothic & Medieval Era
The Gothic & Medieval Era
The Gothic & Medieval Era
The Gothic & Medieval Era
The Gothic & Medieval Era
The Gothic & Medieval Era
The Gothic & Medieval Era

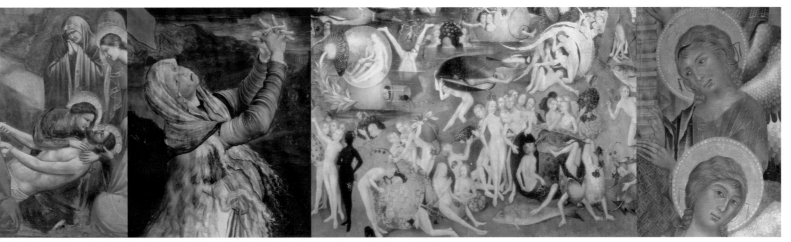

The Gothic & Medieval Era
The Gothic & Medieval Era
The Gothic & Medieval Era
The Gothic & Medieval Era
The Gothic & Medieval Era
The Gothic & Medieval Era
The Gothic & Medieval Era
The Gothic & Medieval Era

Giovanni Cimabue   Angels from the Santa Trinita Altarpiece, 1280–90

Born *c.* 1240 Florence, Italy   Painted in Florence   Died *c.* 1302 Florence
MOVEMENT: Florentine School   **OTHER WORKS:** *St John* (Pisa Cathedral)   **INFLUENCES:** Byzantine, Romanesque

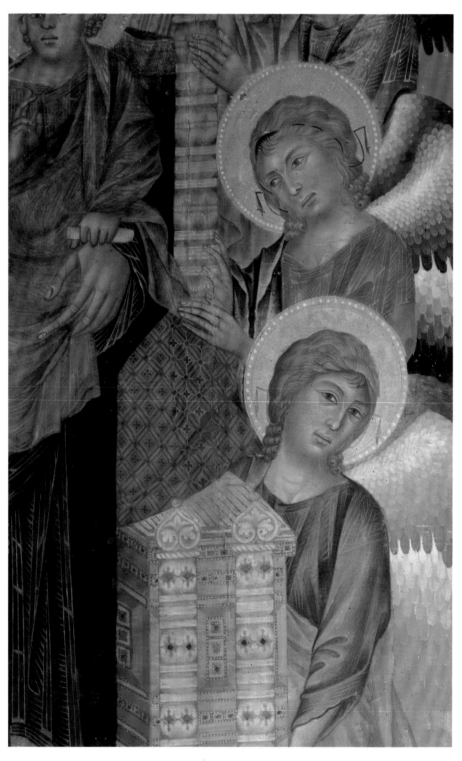

CIMABUE WAS the nickname of Genni di Pepo or Peppi, who was born in Florence around 1240. He began his career by imitating the Byzantine styles then prevalent, but soon developed a style of his own which earned for him the title of 'Father of Italian Painting'. There were certainly distinctive Italian painters before his time, but he was the outstanding artist of his generation and a role model for his successors. His fame rested mainly on the enormous altarpiece in the chapel of the Rucellai in Santa Maria Novella, Florence, although this was later proven to have been painted by Duccio. Works that are definitely attributed to him include the frescoes in the church of St Francis of Assisi and a number of paintings of the Madonna. He was the precursor of Giotto, whom he is supposed to have discovered as a 10-year-old shepherd boy and recognized his artistic potential.

Giotto (Giotto di Bondone)   Lamentation of Christ, c.1305

Born c. 1267   Painted in Italy   Died 1337

MOVEMENT: Renaissance **OTHER WORKS:** *Arena Chapel Frescos, Madonna and Child, Ognissanti Madonna* **INFLUENCES:** Cimabue, Pietro Cavallini

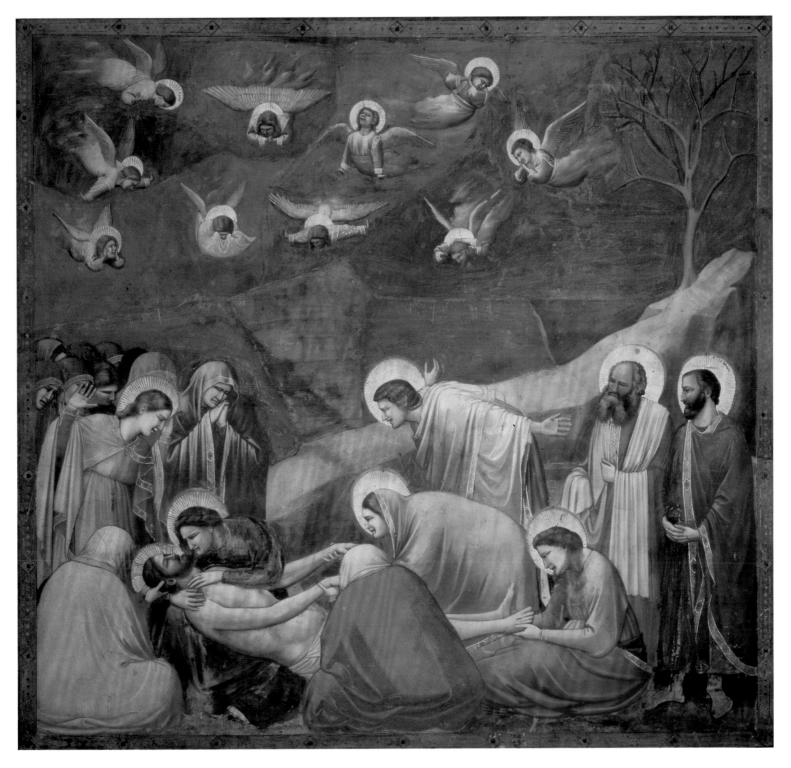

ONE OF the founding fathers of the Renaissance, Giotto was revered by early commentators as the greatest artist since antiquity, and it is clear that he was still influencing painters more than a century after his death. His greatest achievement was to rid Italian art of the repetitive stylizations deriving from Byzantine painting. In the process, he became one of the first Western artists to stamp his own personality on his work. In particular,

Giotto displayed an unparalleled degree of naturalism, both in his ability to depict solid, three dimensional forms and in his grasp of human psychology. He was also a gifted storyteller, conveying his religious narratives with absolute clarity and simplicity.

The details of Giotto's own life are, however a mystery. There is a tale that his master, Cimabue, first spotted his talent when he saw him as a

shepherd-boy, sketching a lamb on a slab of rock. This is probably apocryphal, however, and the identification of Giotto's pictures presents even greater problems. The marvellous frescoes in the Arena Chapel, Padua, are usually cited as his masterpiece, but most other attributions are hotly disputed. Even his three signed altarpieces may only be workshop pieces.

Duccio di Buonisegna   Madonna & Child, *c.*1315

Born *c.* 1255 Siena, Italy   Painted in Siena and Florence   Died 1319 Siena

MOVEMENT: Sienese School, Italy   **OTHER WORKS:** *The Crucifixion, Majestas, Madonna with Three Franciscans*   **INFLUENCES:** Byzantine illuminations

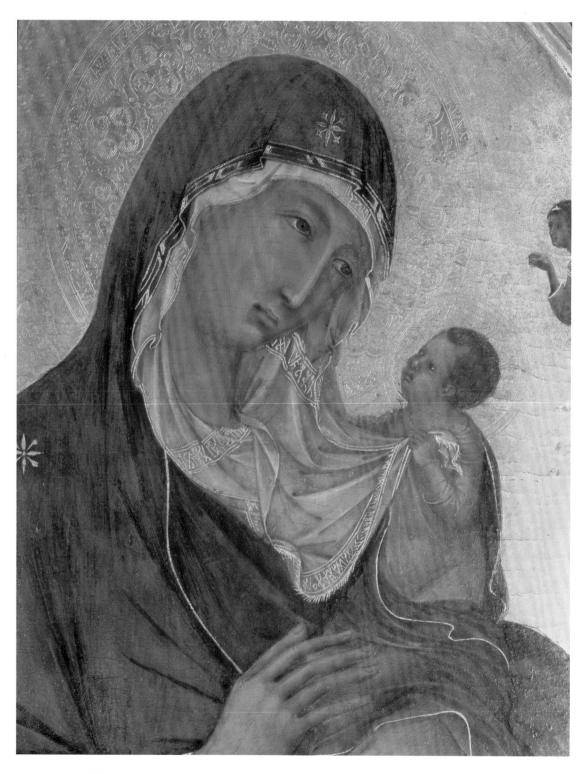

WESTERN ART begins with Duccio di Buonisegna, who learned his craft from studying the illuminated manuscripts created by unknown Byzantine limners. His earliest recorded work, dating about 1278, was to decorate the cases in which the municipal records of Sienna were stored. In 1285 he was commissioned to paint a large Madonna for the church of Santa Maria Novella. This is now known as the Rucellai

Madonna, for centuries attributed to Cimabue. Duccio painted the magnificent double altarpiece for the Cathedral of Siena, regarded as his masterpiece and one of the greatest paintings of all time. Many other works documented in the Sienese records have been lost, but sufficient remain to establish Duccio as the last and greatest of the artists working in the Byzantine tradition, as well as the founder of the

Sienese School, and thus the progenitor of modern art. In his hands the degenerate painting of the Gothic style was transformed and the principles of expressive portraiture established.

Jan Van Eyck   Portrait of Giovanni Arnolfini and Wife (Arnolfini Marr), 1434

Born *c.* 1389 Maastricht, Holland   Painted in Maastricht and Bruges   Died 1441 Bruges
MOVEMENT: Bruges School of Flemish Painting **OTHER WORKS:** *A Man in a Turban* **INFLUENCES:** Hubert van Eyck

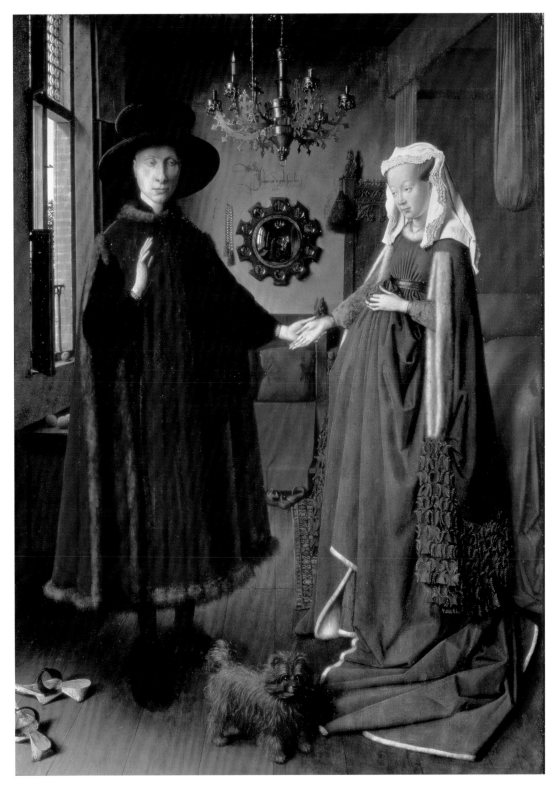

JAN VAN EYCK settled in Bruges in 1431, where he became the leading painter of his generation and founder of the Bruges School. He and his elder brother Hubert are credited with the invention of oil painting. Van Eyck's paintings have a startlingly fresh quality about them, not only in the dazzling use of light and colour but also in their expression and realism, which was something of a quantum leap in portraiture. Van Eyck was very much a pillar of the establishment, being successively court painter to John of Bavaria, Count of Holland, and Philip the Good of Burgundy. He was equally versatile in painting interiors and outdoor scenes, and exhibited a greater attention to detail than in the works of his predecessors. It is not surprising that he should not only sign and date his paintings but add his motto *Als ich kan* ('as I can').

Jean Fouquet   The Nativity, *c.*1445

Born *c.* 1420 Tours, France   Painted in France and Italy   Died *c.* 1481 Tours, France
MOVEMENT: French Primitives   **OTHER WORKS:** *Virgin and Child, Saint Margaret and Olibrius, Jouvenal des Ursins*   **INFLUENCES:** Van Eyck, Piero della Francesca

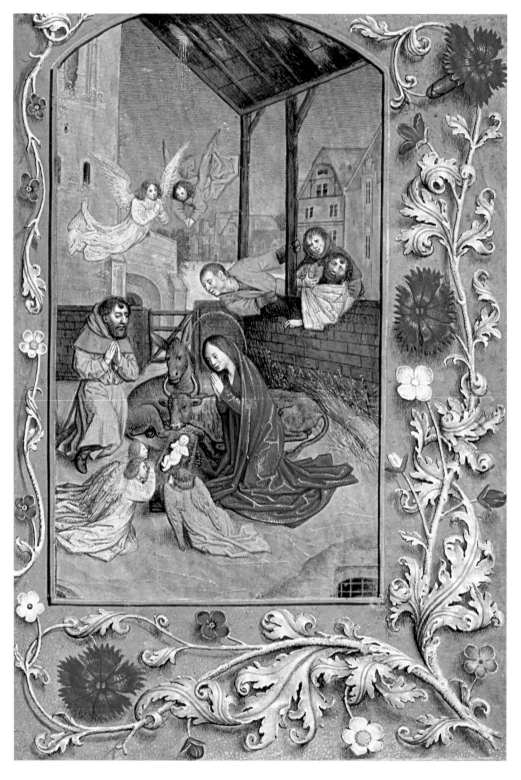

THE MOST representative French painter of the fifteenth century, Jean Fouquet originally came under the influence of Van Eyck, but a period in Italy – where he was commissioned to paint the portrait of Pope Eugenius IV – brought him in contact with the new styles emerging in Tuscany. On his return to France he combined the Flemish and Tuscan elements to create a wholly distinctive French style. Highly influential on the succeeding generation of French artists, Fouquet's supreme importance was not fully realized until 1904, when his surviving works were brought together for an exhibition in Paris. His painting combines the skills and precision acquired during his early career as a limner and miniaturist with a new-found expressiveness that places him in the forefront of the painters who could get behind the eyes of their subjects and reveal the underlying character.

Rogier Van der Weyden   Crucifixion, 1468

Born 1399 Belgium   Painted in Tournai and Brussels   Died 1464 Brussels
MOVEMENT: Flemish School   **OTHER WORKS:** *Deposition, The Last Judgment*   **INFLUENCES:** Robert Campin

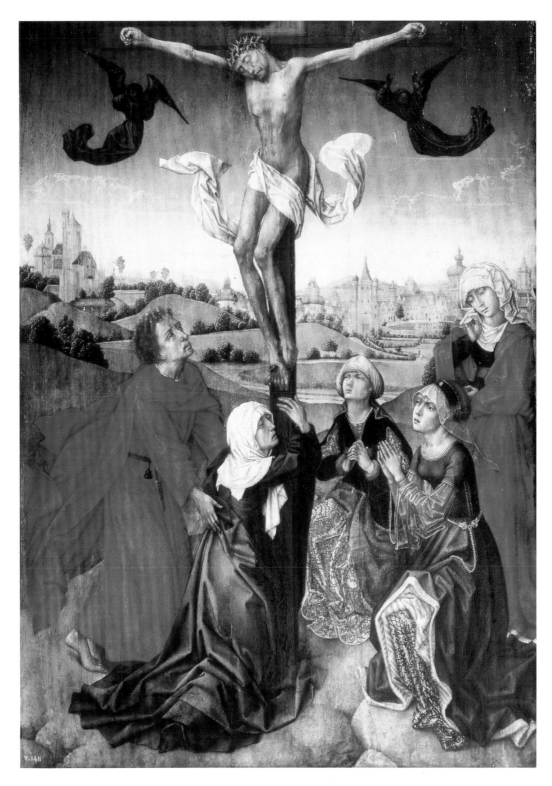

ROGIER VAN DER WEYDEN studied under Robert Campin in his native city of Tournai before going to Brussels, where he made his mark both as an artist and as a prominent citizen. From 1436 he was the official painter to the city as well as the Burgundian Court. Although he visited Rome in 1450 it had no impact on his style. A very accomplished technician, he excelled not only in form and composition but also in his use of colour. But his main contribution to the progress of art was in his highly expressive portraiture, one of the first painters to convey the character and psychological profile of the model or the subject. He combined deep religious feeling with a desire to make the maximum impact on the spectator and in this he succeeded admirably. He wielded enormous influence over his contemporaries and the ensuing generation of Flemish artists.

Hans Memling   Adoration of the Magi (Central Panel of Triptych), *c.*1470

Born *c.* 1433 Germany   Painted in Bruges, Belgium   Died 1494 Bruges
MOVEMENT: Flemish School   **OTHER WORKS:** *The Mystic Marriage of St Catherine, The Virgin Ethroned*   **INFLUENCES:** Rogier van der Weyden

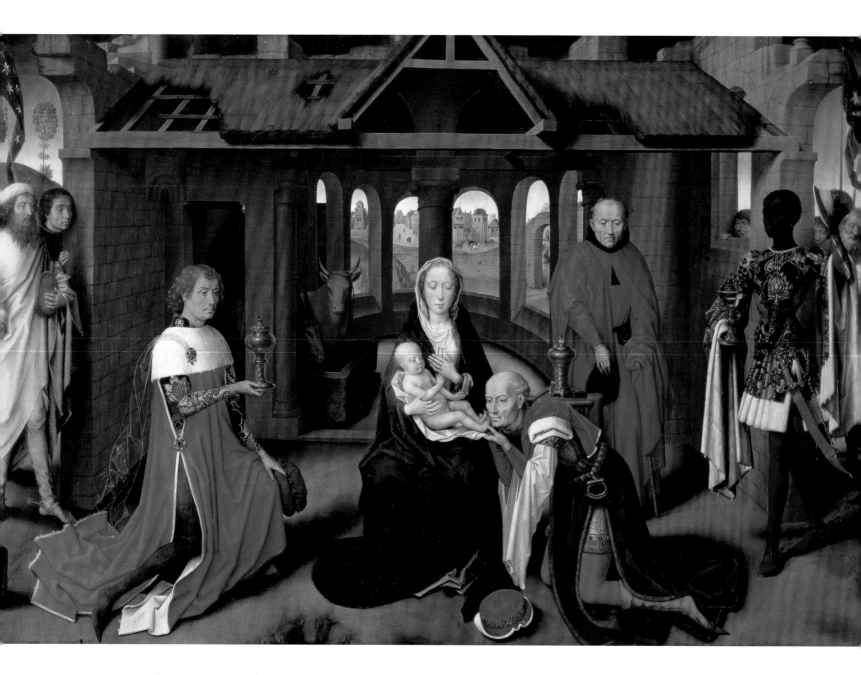

ALTHOUGH BORN in Germany Memling spent most of his life in Bruges (now in Belgium), where he was probably a pupil of Rogier van der Weyden. This is borne out by the great triptych, whose central panel was painted by Rogier but the wings by 'Master Hans'. Bruges, which had been the commercial centre of the duchy of Burgundy, was then in decline and it has been said that Memling's genius alone brought lustre to the city. He was certainly residing in Bruges by 1463 and four years later enrolled in the painter's guild. In 1468 he painted the triptych showing the Virgin enthroned, flanked by the family of the donor, Sir John Donne, who was in Burgundy for the wedding of Charles the Bold that year. Although best known for his altarpieces and other religious paintings, Memling also produced a number of secular pieces, mostly portraits of his contemporaries. His paintings are characterized by an air of serenity and gentle piety enhanced by the use of vivid colours and sumptuous texture.

Hugo Van der Goes   The Fall, after 1479

Born *c.* 1440 Ghent, Belgium   Painted in Ghent   Died 1482 Ghent

MOVEMENT: Flemish School   **OTHER WORKS:** *Fall and Deposition, Adoration of the Magi, Death of the Virgin*   **INFLUENCES:** Rogier van der Weyden

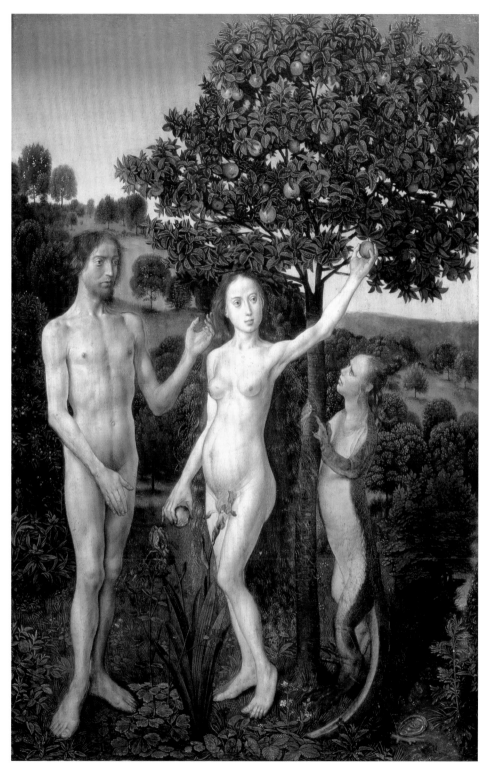

HUGO VAN DER GOES was the Dean of the painters' guild in that city from 1467 to 1475, before retiring to the monastery of Rouge Cloître near Brussels, where he continued to execute religious paintings. The outstanding Flemish artist of his generation, his reputation rests mainly on a single work: the magnificent altarpiece which was commissioned by Tommaso Portinari for the chapel in the hospital of Santa Maria at Florence. It is a vast triptych, crammed with figures, the great centrepiece representing the Adoration of the Shepherds, while the wings portray Portinari and his sons praying under the protection of Saints Anthony and Matthew and Protinari's wife and daughters on the other, protected by Saints Margaret and Mary Magdalen. A number of easel paintings have been attributed to this artist, while he also designed stained-glass windows and frescoes.

Hieronymus Bosch The Garden of Earthly Delights, (detail) *c.*1500

Born *c.* 1450 Hertogenbosch, Holland (now in Belgium)   Painted in Hertogenbosch, Holland   Died 1516 Hertogenbosch, Holland
MOVEMENT: Flemish School **OTHER WORKS:** *The Temptation of St Anthony, Last Judgment* **INFLUENCES:** Gothic art

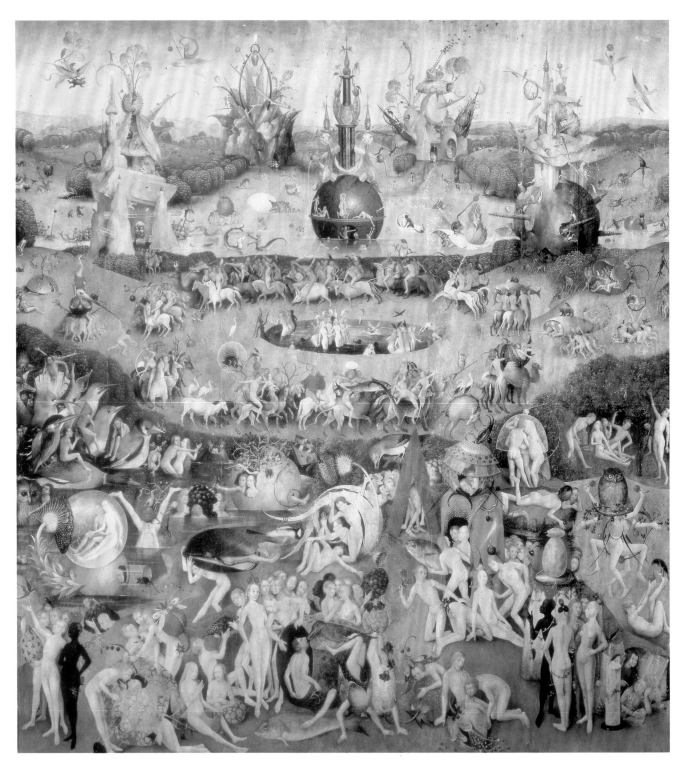

BORN JEROME VAN AKEN but known by the Latin version of his first name and a surname from the shortened form of his birthplace 's Hertogenbosch in North Brabant, where he spent his entire life, he painted great allegorical, mystical and fantastic works that combined the grotesque with the macabre. His oils are crammed with devils and demons, weird monsters, dwarves and hideous creatures, barely recognizable in human form. His quasi-religious and allegorical compositions must have struck terror in the hearts of those who first beheld them, but centuries later he would have a profound influence on the Surrealists. In more recent times there have been attempts to analyse his paintings in Jungian or Freudian terms, the theory being that he tried to put his more lurid nightmares on to his wood panels.

This is his best-known work, executed on four folding panels, in which he develops the story of the Creation and the expulsion of Adam and Eve. At the core of the work is a vast sex orgy, symbolizing the sins of the flesh that caused man's downfall.

Matthias Grünewald Mary Magdalene
from Isenheim Altarpiece, 1510–15

Born c. 1470 Bavaria, Germany   Painted in Frankfurt, Aschaffenburg, Mainz, and Colmar   Died 1528 Halle
MOVEMENT: German Gothic **OTHER WORKS:** *The Crucifixion, The Mocking of Christ* **INFLUENCES:** Albrecht Dürer

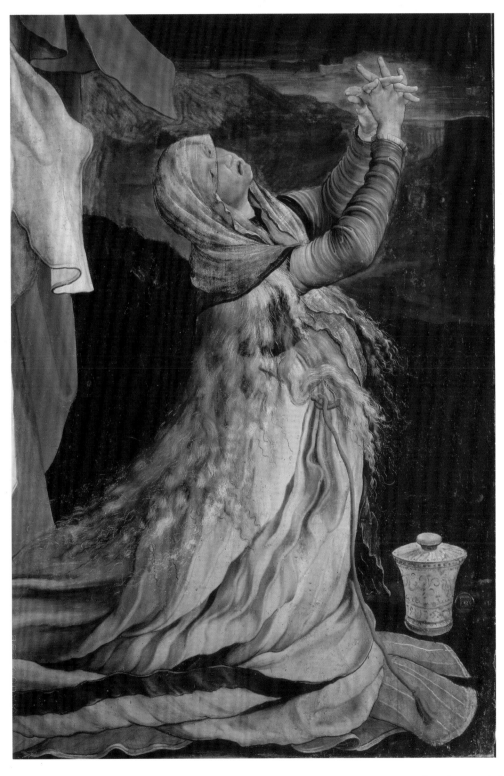

BORN MATHIS Gothardt-Neithardt, probably in Würzburg, he flourished at Frankfurt, Mainz, Aschaffenburg and Upper Alsace between 1500 and 1528, where he worked as an architect and engineer. Very little is known of his origins and early life, and he only came to artistic prominence in 1508 when he was appointed court painter at Mainz, taking up a similar post at the court of the Elector of Brandenburg in 1515. It was during the latter period that he undertook the great altarpiece at Isenheim, now preserved in the Colmar Museum. In his heyday he was ranked equal with Dürer and Cranach and is regarded as the last great exponent of German Gothic art, at a time when the ideas of the Italian Renaissance were making inroads into northern Europe.

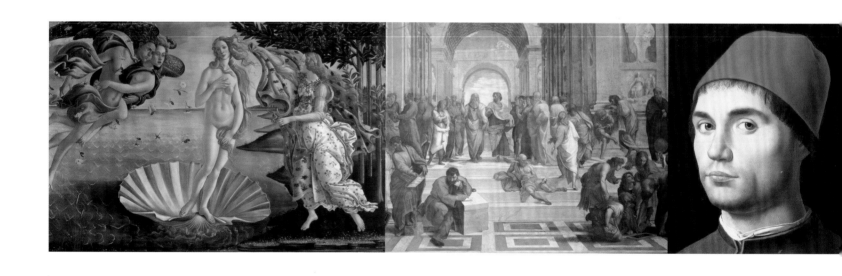

The Renaissance Era

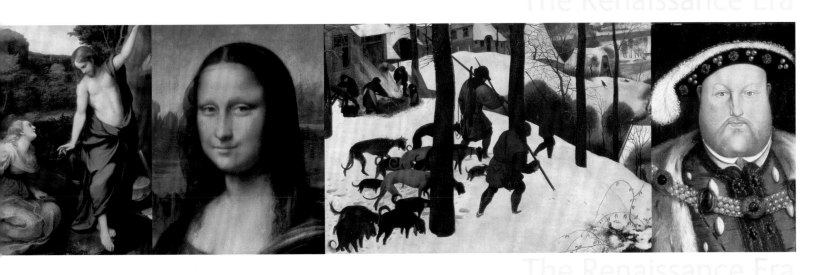

Fra Angelico (Guido di Pietro)   The Annunciation (detail), *c.*1420

Born *c.* 1400   Painted in Italy   Died 1455

MOVEMENT: Renaissance **OTHER WORKS:** *The Annunciation, Linaiuoli Triptych, Coronation of the Virgin* **INFLUENCES:** Masaccio, Monaco

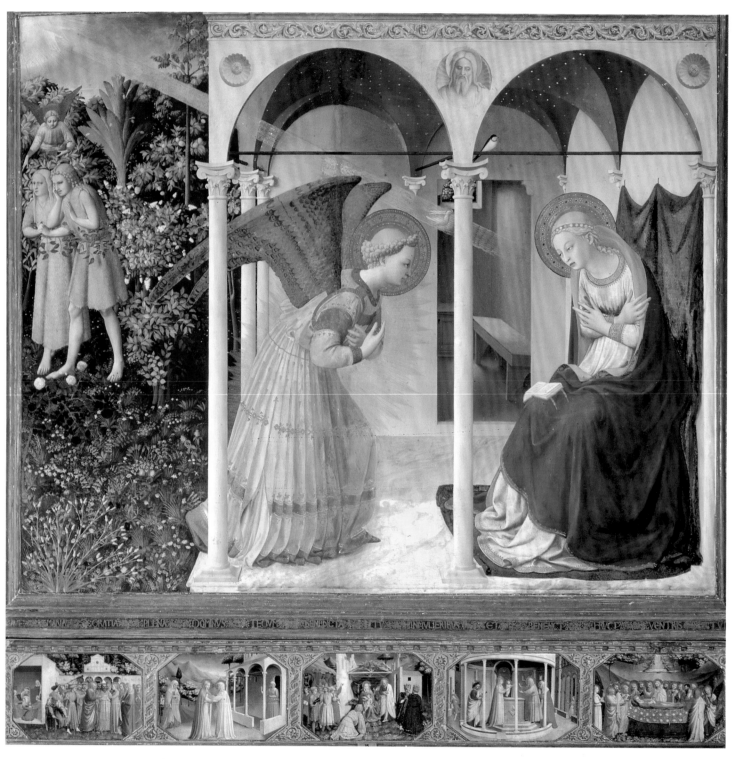

FRA ANGELICO was one of a select band of Renaissance artists who combined the monastic life with a career as a professional painter. Little is known about his early years, apart from the fact that he was born at Vicchio, near Florence, and that his real name was Guido di Pietro. He became a Dominican friar c. 1418–21, entering the monastery of San Domenico in Fiesole. For the remainder of his life,

he placed his art at the service of his faith, earning the nickname 'Angelic', by which he has become known to posterity.

Angelico's earliest surviving works are small-scale and betray an astonishing eye for detail, suggesting that he may have begun his career as a manuscript illuminator. They also display the influence of the International Gothic style, which was starting to

fall out of fashion. The painter-monk learned quickly, however, absorbing Tommaso Masaccio's revolutionary ideas about the organization of space and perspective. He also tackled the most prestigious form of religious art: frescoe painting. In this field, Angelico's greatest achievement was a magnificent cycle of frescoes at the newly restored monastery of San Marco in Florence (c. 1438–45).

Gentile Da Fabriano   The Adoration of the Magi, detail of Virgin and Child with Three Kings, 1423

Born *c.* 1370 Fabriano, Italy   Painted in Venice, Brescia, Rome, Florence and Siena   Died *c.* 1427 Venice

MOVEMENT: Florentine School **OTHER WORKS:** *Madonna and Child, Madonna with Angels* **INFLUENCES:** Filippo Brunneleschi

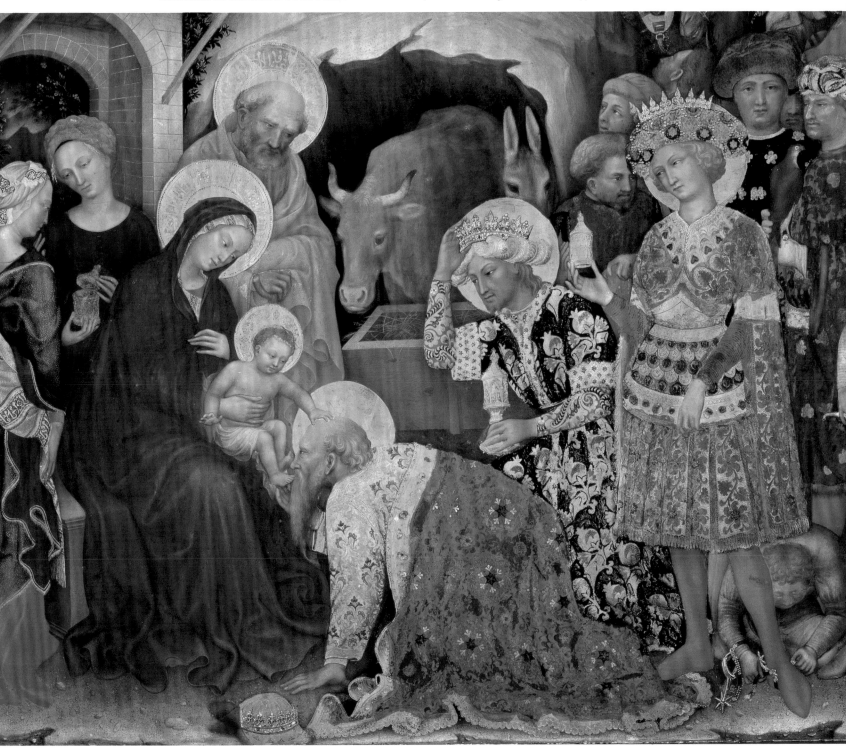

BORN IN the little north Italian town of Fabriano, Gentile worked as a painter mainly in Venice and later Brescia before settling in Rome in about 1419, although subsequently he also worked in Florence and Siena. There he executed a great number of religious paintings, although regrettably comparatively few of these works appear to have survived. His most important work was probably carried out at Florence where he enjoyed the patronage of Palla Strozzi, the richest magnate of the city in his day. About 1423 Strozzi commissioned him to paint the magnificent altarpiece depicting the Adoration of the Magi for the sacristy-chapel in the church of the Holy Trinity, intended by the patron as a memorial to his father Onofrio Strozzi. This is Gentile's undoubted masterpiece. The very epitome of the Italian Renaissance, it is now preserved in the Uffizi Gallery. It is an extraordinary work, crammed with figures – among whom we may discern the Strozzi family and their friends.

Tommaso Masaccio   Madonna Casini, after 1426

Born 1401 Italy   Painted in Milan and Florence   Died 1428 Rome

MOVEMENTS: Italian Renaissance, Florentine School   **OTHER WORKS:** *The Virgin and Child, The Trinity with the Virgin and St John*   **INFLUENCES:** Donatello

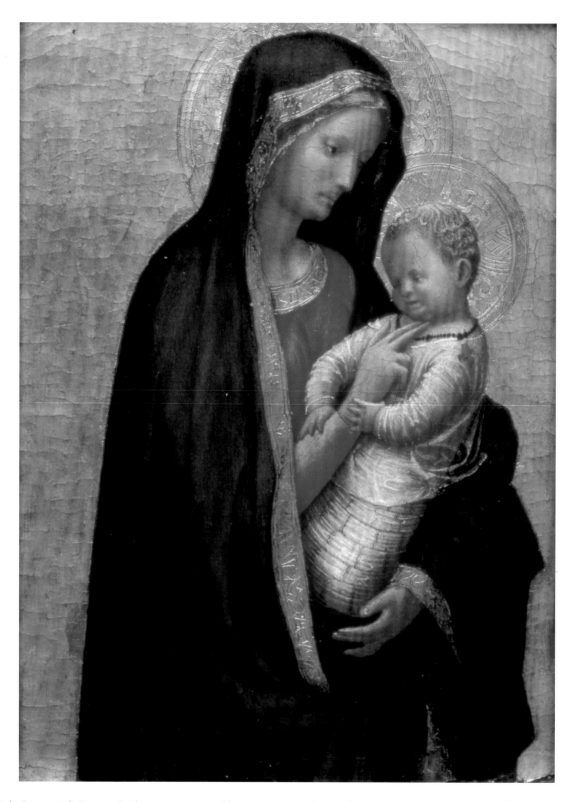

BORN TOMMASO de Giovanni di Simone Guidi at Castel San Giovanni di Altura in the duchy of Milan, he was nicknamed Masaccio ('massive') to distinguish him from another Tommaso who worked in the same studio. Who taught him is not recorded, but Masaccio was one of the most brilliant innovators of his generation, ranking with Brunelleschi and Donatello in revolutionizing painting in Italy. Biblical figures and scenes became infinitely more realistic in his hands. The human body is more fully rounded than before and Masaccio's handling of perspective is a marked improvement over his predecessors. He wielded enormous influence over his contemporaries and successors, notably Michelangelo. His greatest work consisted of the series of frescoes for the Brancacci Chapel in the Church of Santa Maria del Carmine in Florence (1424–27).

Paolo Uccello   The Flood and the Subsidence of the Waters, 1447–8

Born 1397 Pratovecchio, Italy   Painted in Florence and Venice   Died 1475 Florence
MOVEMENT: Florentine School **OTHER WORKS**: *The Battle of San Romano, St George and the Dragon* **INFLUENCES:** Donatello

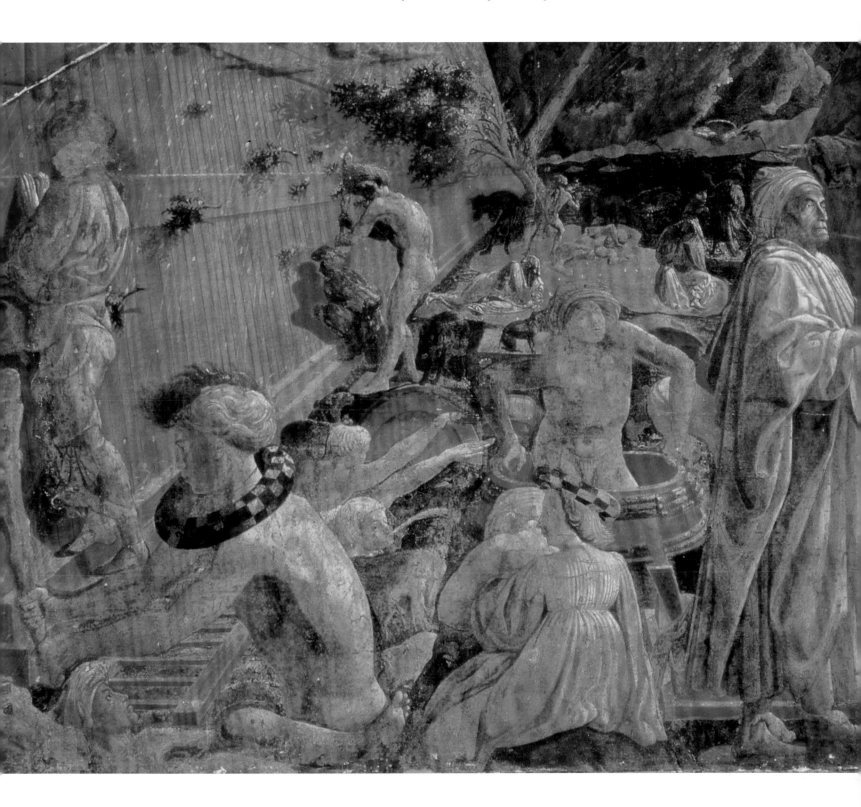

PAOLO DI DONO acquired his nickname from his love of painting birds. At the age of 10 he was apprenticed to Lorenzo Ghiberti, who was then working on the doors of the Florentine Baptistry, but it is not known from whom Paolo received his instruction in painting. He went to Venice in 1425 and worked on mosaics. In 1433 he painted the figure of Sir John Hawkswood, a fourteenth century knight errant, for Florence cathedral, the first equestrian painting of the Renaissance. Most of his work consisted of frescoes, few of which have survived intact, but he also painted tempera on pane, sufficient of which have come down to posterity to reveal Uccello as a master of perspective and foreshortening. He also made a major contribution to the art of showing natural objects in three-dimensional space.

Piero della Francesca   Baptism of Christ, 1450s

Born *c.* 1420 Italy   Painted in Florence and Borgo San Sepolcro   Died 1492 Borgo San Sepolcro
MOVEMENT: Florentine School **OTHER WORKS:** *Resurrection, The Legend of the True Cross, Constantine's Dream* **INFLUENCES:** Veneziano, Donatello, Masaccio, Uccello

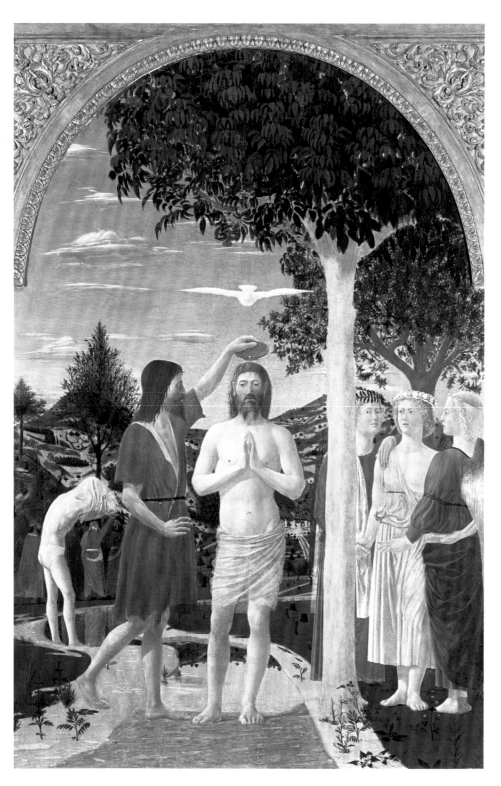

PIERO DELLA FRANCESCA began his career as a pupil of Veneziano in Florence, although he spent most of his working life in his home town of Borgo San Sepolcro, where he attained some eminence in civic affairs. Although strongly influenced by Donatello, Masaccio and Uccello, he was fascinated with mathematics and problems of perspective.

Indeed, from 1470 onwards, he abandoned painting and concentrated on these subjects, writing treatises dealing with geometry and perspective. He was a rather slow, perhaps dilatory, artist who took a long time to complete commissions – one of his greatest masterpieces being the unfinished *Nativity* now in the National Gallery, London. His

work was neglected and underrated for many years, but he was rediscovered in the nineteenth century and his stature as one of the major artists of the Renaissance has been re-established.

Benozzo Gozzoli   Angels, *c.*1459

Born 1420 Florence, Italy   Painted in Florence, Rome, Orvieto and Montefalco Gimignano and Pisa   Died 1497 Pistoia
MOVEMENT: Florentine School   **OTHER WORKS:** *St Thomas Receiving the Girdle of the Virgin*   **INFLUENCES:** Fra Angelico

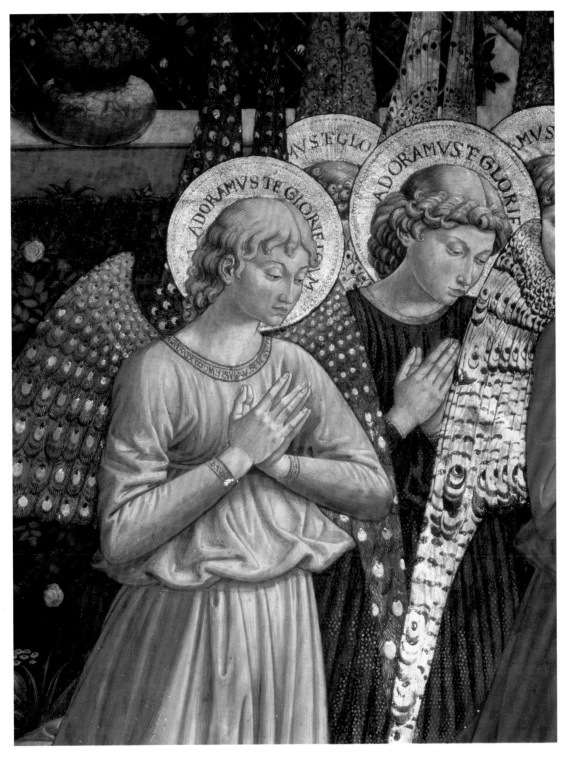

BORN BENOZZO di Lese di Sandro, he studied painting under Fra Angelico and assisted his master in the decoration of the Palazzo Medici-Riccardi in 1456–60. Gozzoli's major contribution was the *Journey of the Magi*, an ambitious work crammed with the portraits of the Florentine council and members of the Medici family. Later he moved with his master to Rome and later worked in Orvieto, also executing numerous frescoes and large murals for churches in Gimignano and Pisa. After leaving Angelico he went to Montefalco in Umbria, where he painted a number of smaller, individual works and altarpieces. As well as the obligatory religious subjects he painted a number of portraits, including Dante, Petrarch and Giotto. His paintings are characterized by their light, lively appearance, their vivacity enhanced by his use of bright, brilliant colours.

Antonello da Messina   Portrait of a Man, *c.*1475

Born *c.* 1430 Italy   Painted in Messina and Venice   Died 1479 Messina
MOVEMENT: Italian Renaissance   **OTHER WORKS**: *Ecce Homo, Madonna*   **INFLUENCES:** Jan Van Eyck, the Flemish School

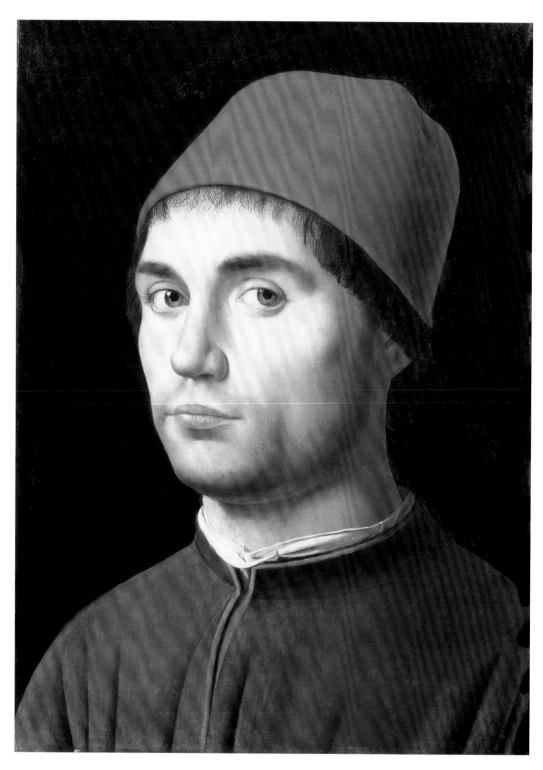

PROBABLY BORN at Messina, Sicily, whence he derived his surname, Antonello travelled in north-western Europe and spent some time in the Netherlands where he studied the techniques of the pupils of Jan Van Eyck, taking them back to Messina about 1465. Subsequently he worked in Milan and then in 1472 settled at Venice, where he executed commissions for the Council of Ten.

His paintings are remarkable for their blend of Italian simplicity and the Flemish delight in meticulous detail, although some of his earlier works do not always result in a perfect blend of techniques. The majority of his extant authentic works are religious subjects, mainly painted in oils on wood panels, but he also produced a number of half-length portraits of Venetian dignitaries in the

last years of his life. By introducing Flemish characteristics Antonello transformed Italian painting, notably in the use of oil paints, which revolutionized technique.

Sandro Botticelli   The Birth of Venus, c. 1485

Born 1445 Florence, Italy   Painted in Florence and Rome   Died 1510 Florence
MOVEMENT: Florentine School   **OTHER WORKS:** *Venus and Mars*   **INFLUENCES:** Fra Lippo Lippi, Verrocchio

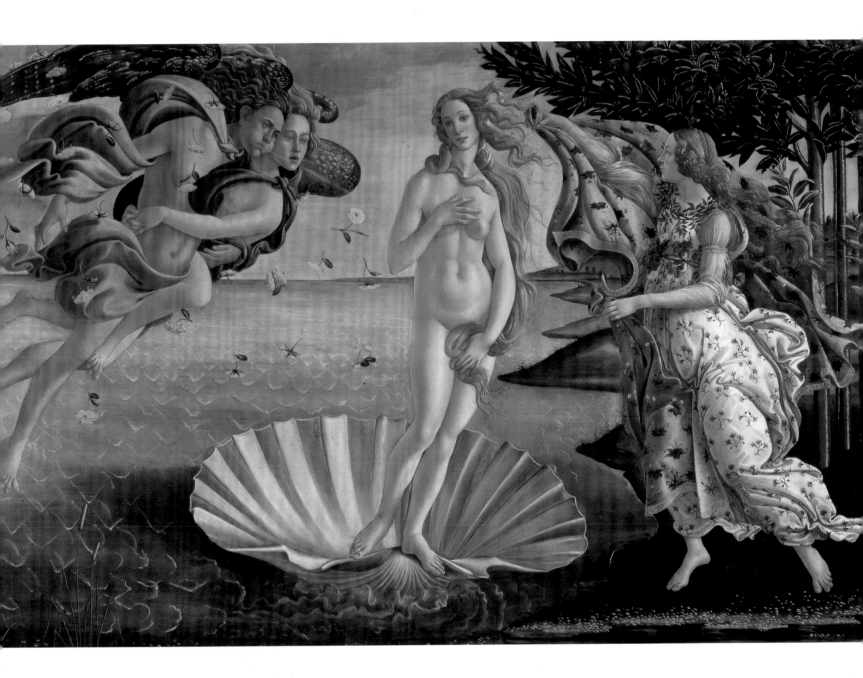

BORN ALESSANDRO Di Mariano dei Filipepi, he acquired his nickname ('little barrel') from his brother Giovanni, who raised him and who was himself thus named. From 1458 to 1467 he worked in the studio of Fra Lippo Lippi before branching out on his own. By 1480 he was working on the frescoes for the Sistine Chapel and his lesser works consist mainly of religious paintings, although it is for his treatment of allegorical and mythological subjects that he is best remembered. Outstanding in this group are his paintings *Primavera* (1477) and *The Birth of Venus* (1485), both now in the Uffizi. He also excelled as a portraitist, and provided the illustrations for Dante's *Divine Comedy*, which he executed in pen and ink and silverpoint (1402–5).

Domenico Ghirlandaio Portrait of a Young Man, c.1490

Born 1449 Italy   Painted in Florence and Rome   Died 1494 Florence
MOVEMENT: Florentine School   **OTHER WORKS:** *Adoration of the Magi, The Visitation, Virgin and Saints*   **INFLUENCES:** Alesso Bigordi

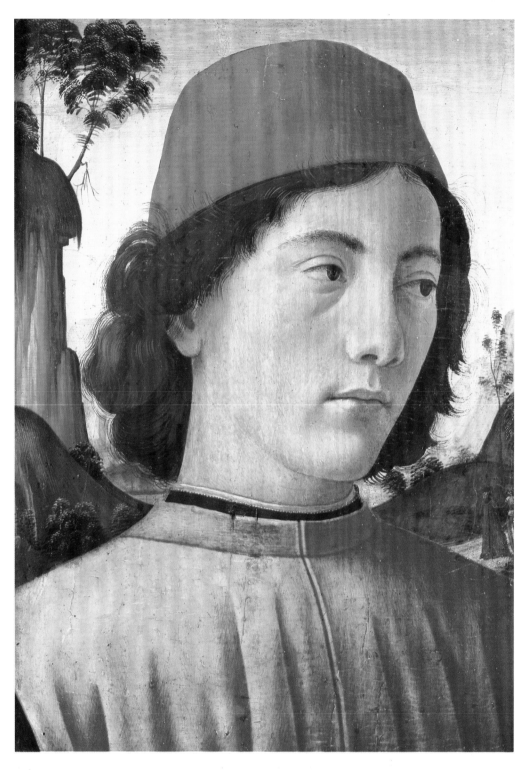

DOMENICO GHIRLANDAIO was the son of Tommaso Bigordi, under whom he trained as a goldsmith; he later studied painting and the art of mosaic under his uncle Alesso Bigordi. None of his early works has survived, but from 1475 onwards he was renowned as a painter of wood panels and frescoes mainly for church decoration. In 1481 Pope Sixtus VI summoned him to Rome, where he painted a number of frescoes as well as individual religious works in which the subject was placed in a secular setting, often with figures of contemporary personalities as spectators on the sidelines. Ghirlandaio ran a large workshop, employing many pupils (including the young Michelangelo). Although these frescoes incorporate numerous portraits, there are relatively few individual works by Ghirlandaio in this genre.

The best of these, however, is the touching portrait of an old man with his grandson; the identity of the sitters is unknown.

Pietro Perugino Madonna & Child with two Angels, late fifteenth century

Born *c*. 1450 Città delle Pieve, Umbria, Italy Painted in Parma, Florence and Rome Died 1523 Fontigano, Italy

MOVEMENT: Umbrian School **OTHER WORKS:** *The Virgin and Child with Saints, Francesco dell'Opera* **INFLUENCES:** Piero della Francesco, Andrea del Verrocchio

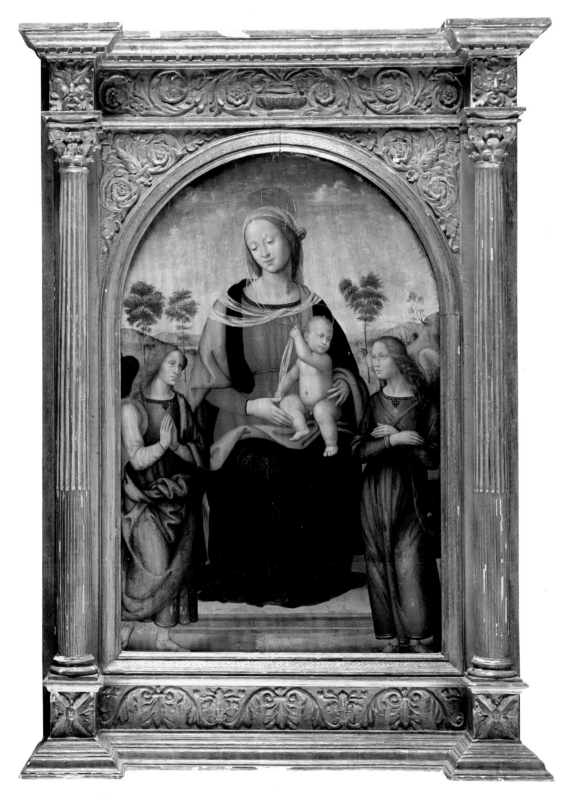

BORN PIETRO di Cristoforo Vannucci, he is better known by his nickname, from Perugia, the chief city of the district where he grew up and spent much of his working life. Apprenticed to a Perugian painter at the tender age of nine, he showed precocious aptitude. Later he worked under Piero della Francesca at Arrezzo and then was a fellow-pupil of Leonardo under Verrocchio at Florence. In 1480-82 he worked on the frescoes in the Sistine Chapel, Rome, before returning to Perugia, but thereafter worked on various church commissions, occasionally in Rome but mainly in Florence where he had Raphael as one of his pupils for several years. Apart from frescoes and altarpieces he was a prolific painter of individual works, mainly religious subjects but also including a few contemporary portraits.

Piero di Cosimo   A Young Man, *c.*1521

Born *c.* 1462 Florence, Italy   Painted in Florence and Rome   Died *c.* 1521 Florence

MOVEMENT: Florentine School   **OTHER WORKS:** *A Satyr Mourning Over a Nymph, Immaculate Conception*   **INFLUENCES:** Cosimo Rosselli, Luca Signorelli, Leonardo da Vinci

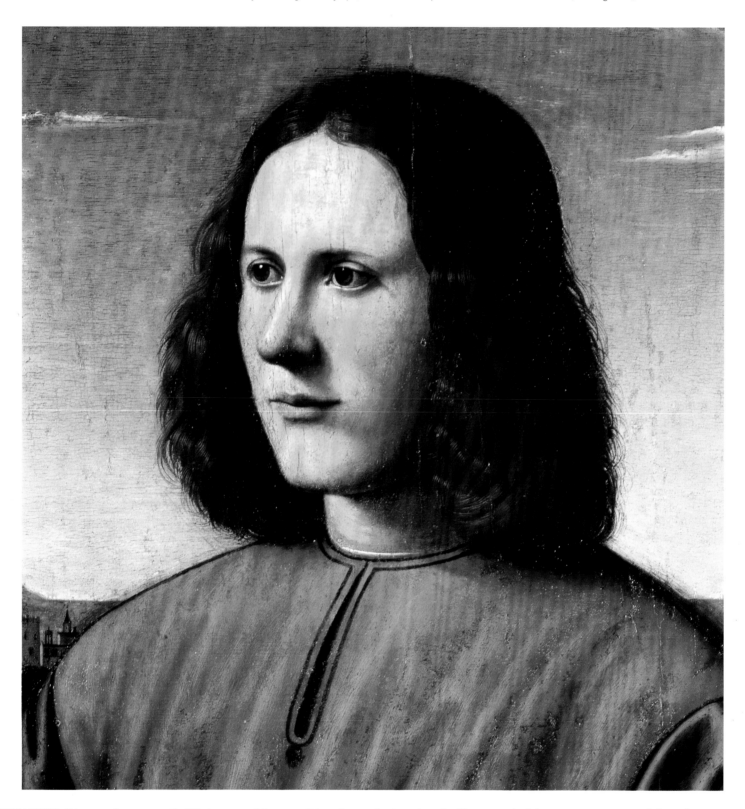

BORN PIERO di Lorenzo, he was a pupil of Cosimo Rosselli, whose name he adopted. In 1482 he accompanied his master to Rome, where they worked on the frescoes of the Sistine Chapel, and it was during this period that he became imbued with the images of classical mythology which, along with the obligatory religious themes, dominated much of his later work. He also painted a number of portraits and landscapes which are notable for their cheerful accessories. His later style was influenced to some extent by Signorelli and Leonardo da Vinci, although he developed his own highly distinctive approach which his contemporaries regarded as rather eccentric; his interpretation of certain subject matters being, at times rather strange. His reclusive character and diet of hard-boiled eggs tended to reinforce this opinion. Nevertheless, his paintings are distinguished by their mastery of light and composition.

Andrea Mantegna   Adoration of the Magi, 1495

Born c. 1431 Vicenza, Italy   Painted in Italy   Died 1506 Mantua, Italy

MOVEMENT: Italian Renaissance **OTHER WORKS:** *The Dead Christ, The Agony in the Garden* **INFLUENCES:** Francisco Squarcione, Andrea del Castagno, Donatello

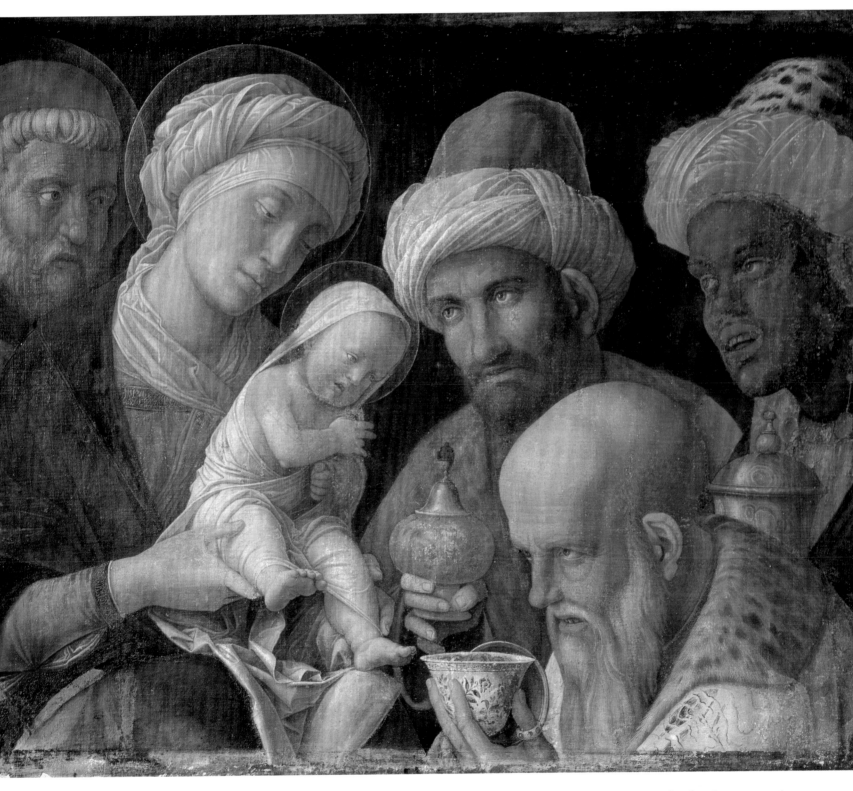

ANDREA MANTEGNA was originally apprenticed to Francisco Squarcione, a tailor in Padua who later adopted him. Squarcione was a self-taught painter and it was from him that the young Mantegna learned the rudiments of art. About 1450 he completed an altarpiece for the church of Santa Lucia, which immediately established his reputation. Later he studied the works of Donatello in Florence and Castagno in Venice and mastered the newly developed techniques of perspective. He worked in Verona and elsewhere, executing religious paintings. In 1459 he was recruited by Ludvico Gonzaga, Duke of Mantua, to decorate his palaces and to the subsequent period belong his great masterpieces, the series of tempera paintings of the Triumph of Caesar, executed between 1482 and 1492, later purchased by Charles I and now preserved at Hampton Court.

Leonardo da Vinci   Mona Lisa, c.1503–06

Born 1452 Italy   Painted in Italy and France   Died 1519
MOVEMENT: Renaissance **OTHER WORKS:** *Mona Lisa, Virgin of the Rocks, The Last Supper* **INFLUENCES:** Verrocchio

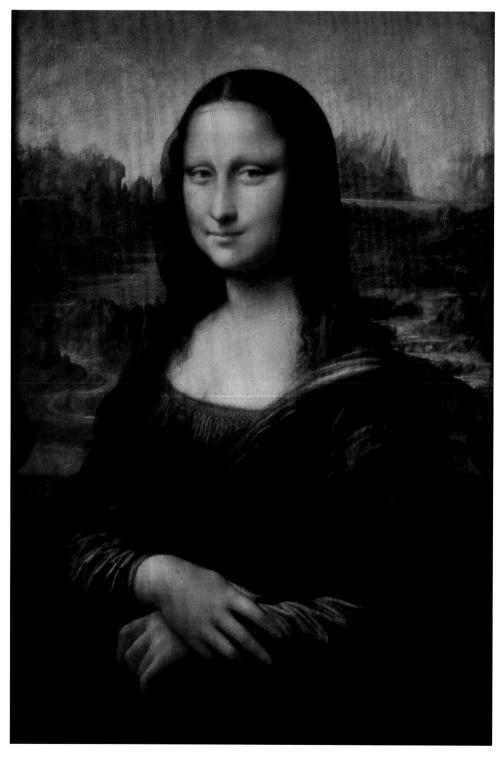

FLORENTINE PAINTER, scientist and inventor; the supreme genius of the Renaissance. Leonardo was the illegitimate son of a notary and probably trained under Verrocchio. In 1482 he moved to Milan, where he worked for the Sforzas. His chief work from this period was a majestic version of *The Last Supper*. The composition dazzled contemporaries, but Leonardo's experimental frescoe technique failed and the picture deteriorated rapidly. This was symptomatic of Leonardo's attitude to painting: the intellectual challenge of creation fascinated him, but the execution was a chore, and many of his artistic projects were left unfinished. Leonardo returned to Florence in 1500, where he produced some of his most famous pictures, most notably the *Mona Lisa*. These were particularly remarkable for their *sfumato* – a blending of tones so exquisite that the forms seem to have no lines or borders. Leonardo spent a second period in Milan, before ending his days in France. Leonardo's genius lay in the breadth of his interests and his infinite curiosity. In addition to his art, his notebooks display a fascination for aeronautics, engineering, mathematics and the natural world.

Tang Yin The Immortal Ge Changgeng Sitting on his Three-legged Toad, 1506–10

Born 1470 Suzhou, China   Painted in Suzhou   Died 1524 Suzhou

MOVEMENT: Wu School of China **OTHER WORKS:** *Moon Goddess Chang-e* **INFLUENCES:** Zhou Chen, Wen Zhengming

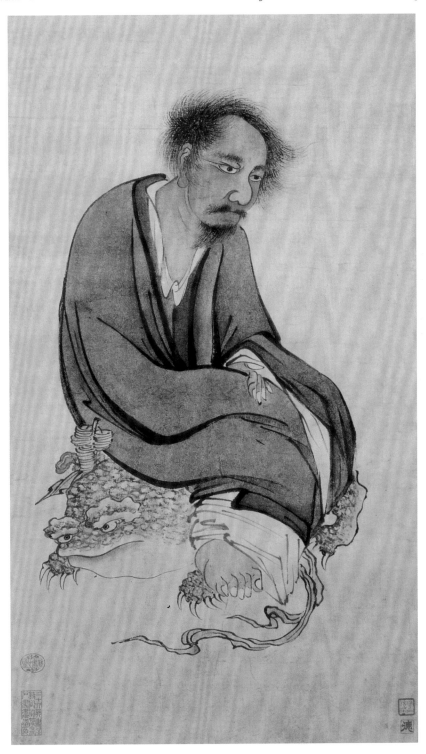

AN EXACT contemporary of Wen Zhengming, Tang Yin came from a prosperous middle-class family and had a brilliant academic education. Under the patronage of Wen Lin (Wen Zhengming's father) he seemed destined for the highest ranks in the civil service but he was caught trying to bribe the examiner, imprisoned and later returned to Suzhou in disgrace. His hopes of becoming a mandarin now dashed, Tang Yin took up painting and excelled to such an extent that he came to be regarded as one of the Four Great Masters of the Wu School. Studying under Zhou Chen, he achieved mastery of a very wide range of styles and subjects. Apart from handscrolls and wall hangings, Tang Yin was adept at the difficult art of painting on bamboo. He painted landscapes, scenes from Chinese mythology and portraits of beautiful women with equal skill. Most of his work was executed on paper using pen and ink with restrained use of colour, but combined with poetry and calligraphy in the finest tradition of the scholar-painters.

Giorgione The Three Philosophers, *c.*1508

Born *c.* 1478 Castelfranco, Italy   Painted in Venice   Died 1510 Venice
MOVEMENT: Venetian School **OTHER WORKS:** *The Sleeping Venus, The Tempest* **INFLUENCES:** Giovanni Bellini

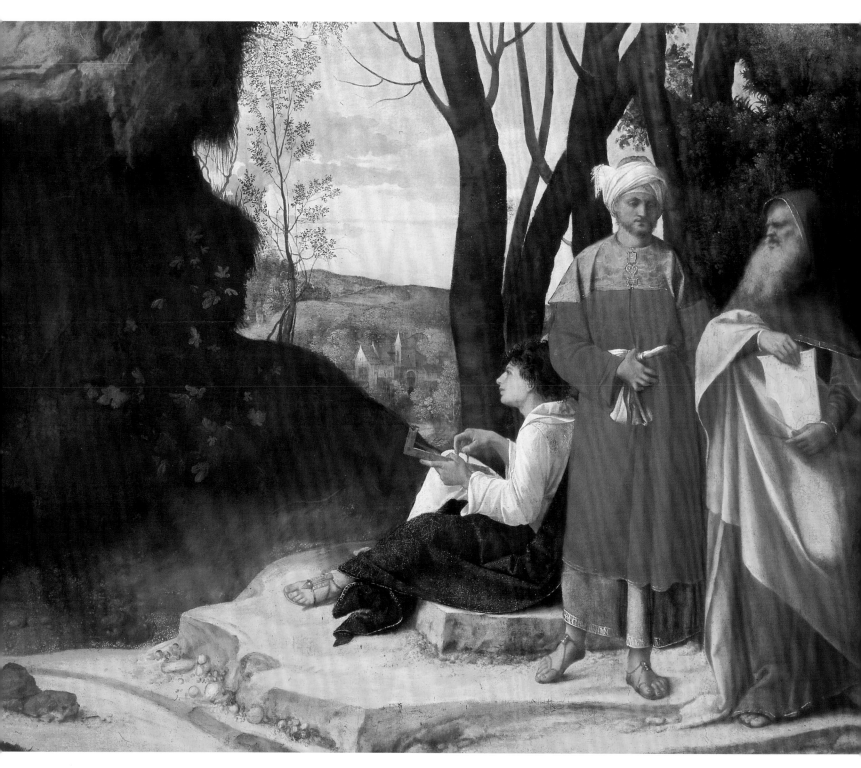

BORN IN Castelfranco, Italy he is sometimes known as Giorgio da Castelfranco or even Giorgio Barbarelli, from the unsubstantiated legend that he was the natural son of the scion of the powerful family of that name. Giorgione (often spelled Zorzon in the Venetian dialect) is a somewhat shadowy figure, a man of apparently considerable musical and poetic talents whose career was cut short by the plague. His output consisted largely of frescoes which have not survived, but his reputation rests mainly on the small, intimate paintings of Christ, the saints and some contemporary figures. He was also responsible for great improvements in the depiction of figures in landscapes and an ability to convey senses and moods in these pictures. He learned his craft from Bellini and, in turn, passed on his expertise to Titian. Many paintings once attributed to Giorgione have since been disproved, but the few that remain confirm his position among the foremost artists of the early sixteenth century.

Michelangelo   Creation of Adam, Sistine Chapel detail, 1510

Born 1475 Italy   Painted in Italy   Died 1564 Italy

MOVEMENT: Renaissance, Mannerism   **OTHER WORKS:** *David, Pietà*   **INFLUENCES:** Ghirlandaio, Giotto, Masaccio

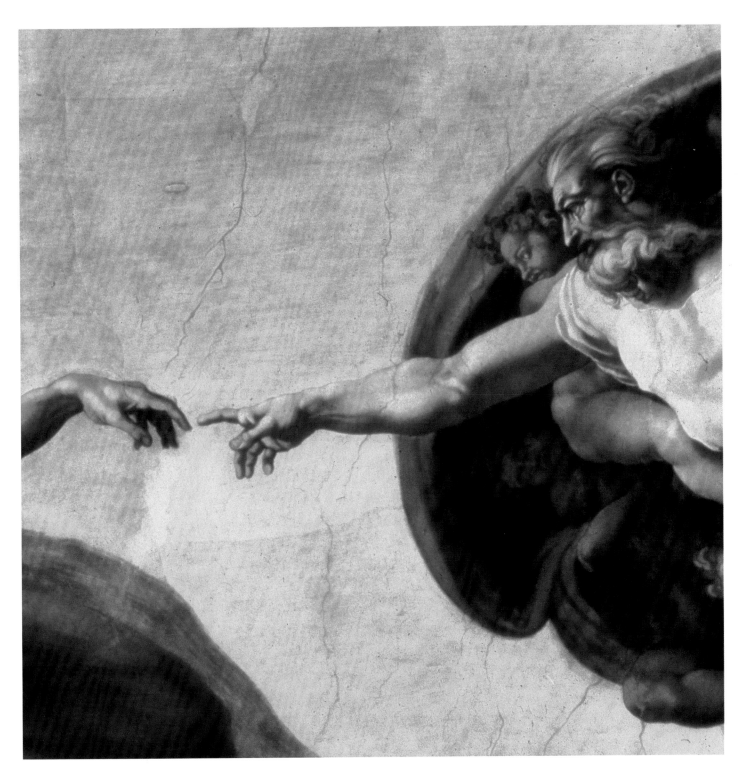

ITALIAN PAINTER, sculptor and poet, one of the greatest artists of the Renaissance and a forerunner of Mannerism. Michelangelo was raised in Florence, where he trained briefly under Ghirlandaio. Soon his obvious talent brought him to the notice of important patrons. By 1490, he was producing sculpture for Lorenzo di Medici and, a few years later, he began his long association with the papacy.

Michelangelo's fame proved a double-edged sword. He was often inveigled into accepting huge commissions, which either lasted years or went unfinished. The most notorious of these projects was the Tomb of Julius II, which occupied the artist for over 40 years.

Michelangelo always considered himself primarily a sculptor, and he was extremely reluctant to take

on the decoration of the Sistine Chapel. Fortunately, he was persuaded, and the resulting frescoes are among the greatest creations in Western art. The ceiling alone took four years (1508–12), while the *Last Judgment* (1536–41) was added later on the altar wall. In these, Michelangelo displayed the sculptural forms and the *terribilità* ('awesome power'), which made him the most revered artist of his time.

Raphael (Raffaello Sanzio)   School of Athens, 1510–11

Born 1483 Urbino, Italy   Painted in Italy   Died 1520

MOVEMENT: Renaissance   **OTHER WORKS:** *Galatea, The Sistine Madonna*   **INFLUENCES:** Pietro Perugino, Leonardo da Vinci, Michelangelo

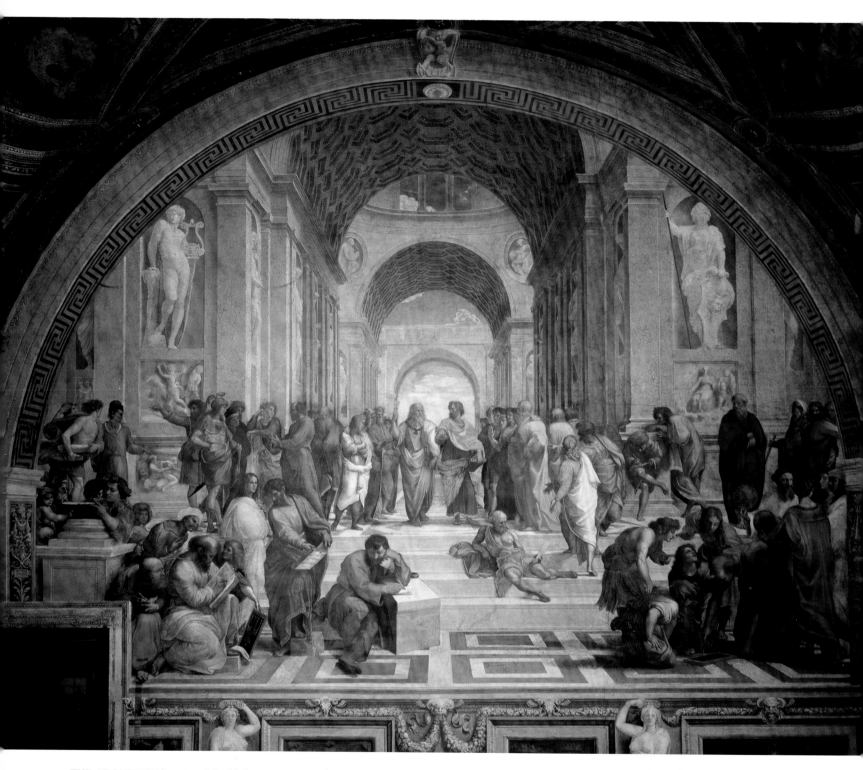

THE ARCHETYPAL artist of the High Renaissance, Raphael received his education in Perugino. In 1504, he moved to Florence, where he received many commissions for portraits and pictures of the Virgin and Child. Soon, his reputation reached the ears of Pope Julius II, who summoned him to Rome in 1508. Deeply influenced by Michelangelo he added a new sense of grandeur to his compositions and greater solidity to his figures. Michelangelo grew jealous of his young rival, accusing him of stealing his ideas, but Raphael's charming manner won him powerful friends and numerous commissions.

The most prestigious of these jobs was the decoration of the Stanze, the papal apartments in the Vatican. This was a huge task, which occupied the artist for the remainder of his life. *The School of Athens* is the most famous of these frescoes. Other commissions included a majestic series of cartoons for a set of tapestries, which were destined for the Sistine Chapel, and a cycle of frescoes for the banker, Agostino Chigi. In the midst of this frantic activity, however, Raphael caught a fever and died, at the tragically young age of 37.

Albrecht Dürer   Melancholia, 1514

Born 1471 Nuremberg, Germany   Painted in Nuremberg   Died 1528 Nuremberg
MOVEMENT: German School   **OTHER WORKS:** *Wing of a Hooded Crow*   **INFLUENCES:** Leonardo da Vinci, Bellini, Mantegna

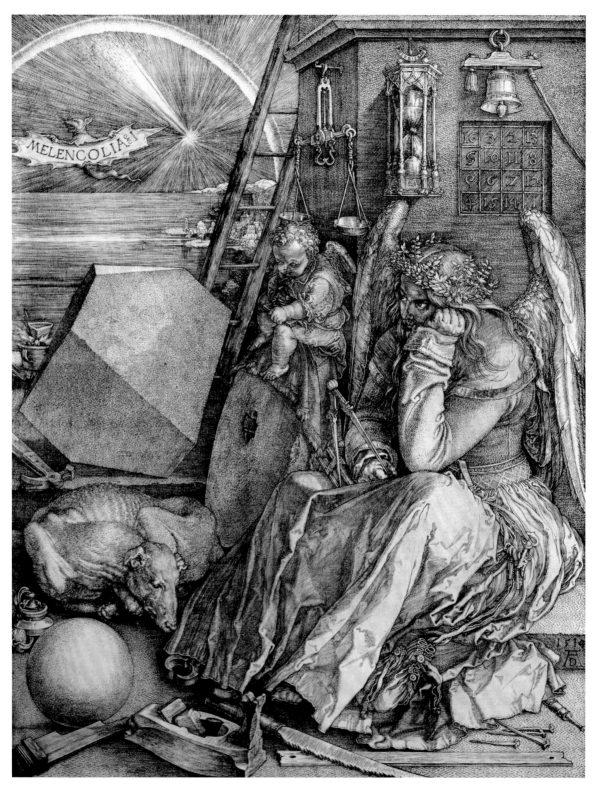

ALBRECHT DÜRER was the son of a goldsmith who taught him the art of drawing in silverpoint. In 1484 he was apprenticed to the leading Nuremberg painter and book illustrator of his time, Michael Wolgemut (1434–1519), from whom he learned the techniques of woodcut engraving. He then travelled extensively in Italy, where the works of Leonardo, Bellini and Mantegna had a profound influence on his later career, both as a practising artist and as an art theorist who wrote extensively on the subject. Dürer was thus responsible for introducing many of the ideas of the Italian Renaissance to northern Europe. Although now remembered chiefly for his engravings (including the *Triumphal Car*, at nine square metres the world's largest woodcut), he was an accomplished painter whose mastery of detail and acute observation have seldom been surpassed.

Albrecht Altdorfer Landscape with Footbridge, *c.*1518–20

Born *c.* 1480   Painted in Regensburg, Bavaria   Died 1538 Regensburg

MOVEMENT: Danube School of German painting   **OTHER WORKS:** *St George, Battle of Arbela, Landscape at Regensburg*   **INFLUENCES:** Lucas Cranach, Albrecht Dürer

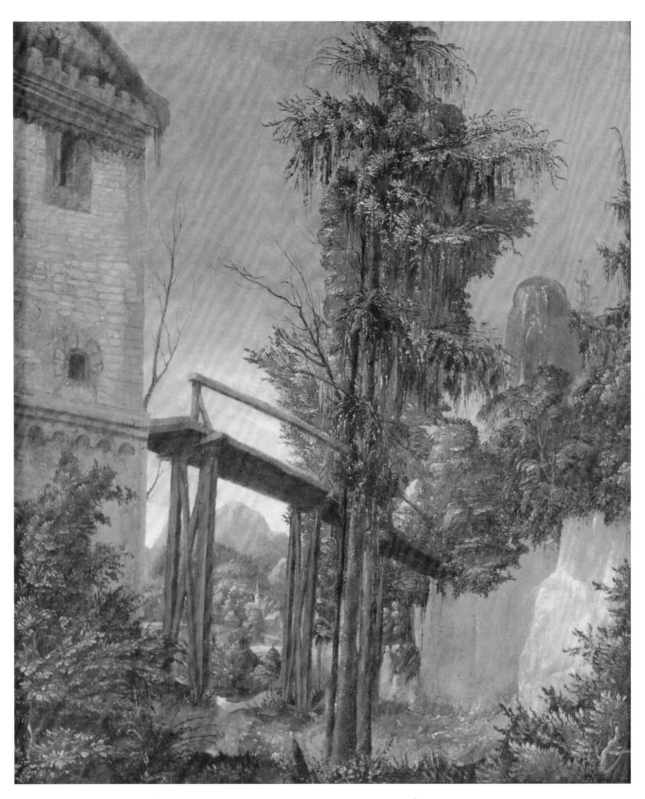

ALBRECHT ALTDORFER was born in Regensburg, Bavaria about 1480 and spent his whole life there. A Renaissance man in the true sense, he trained as an architect and was responsible for the design of many of the buildings in his native city, as well as rising to prominence in the city council. He also worked as an engraver, strongly influenced by Dürer, and was a pioneer of the technique of copperplate etching, but it is for his landscapes painted in oils on wood that he is best remembered. He specialized in biblical and historical subjects set in backgrounds, that gave free rein to his fertile imagination. After a prolonged tour of the Alps and Danube basin in 1511, however, he tended to concentrate on more realistic landscapes that were unusual for the time in that they were devoid of human figures and vividly conveyed a sense of atmosphere.

Andrea del Sarto   The Virgin and Child with a Saint and an Angel, 1522

Born 1486 Florence, Italy   Painted in Florence and Paris   Died 1530 Florence

MOVEMENT: Florentine School   **OTHER WORKS:** *Baptism of Christ, Dance of the Daughter of Herodias*   **INFLUENCES:** Leonardo, Michelangelo, Franciabigio

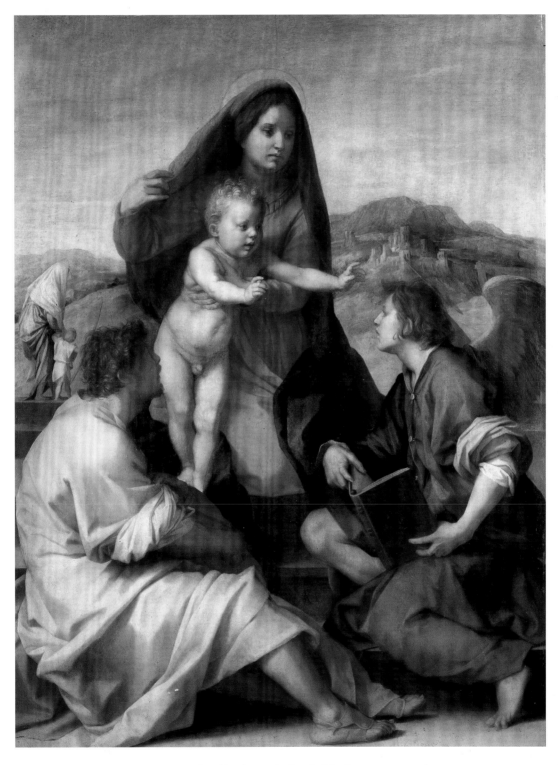

THE SON of a tailor (*sarto*), hence his nickname, Andrea was originally apprenticed to a goldsmith but his early aptitude for drawing led to him being sent to Piero di Cosimo for training in draughtsmanship and colouring. The measure of how well he learned his lessons is evident not only in his surviving works but also in the epithet applied to him in his lifetime as 'Andrea the Unerring'. Between 1509 and 1514 he was employed by the Brotherhood of the Servites to paint a series of frescos illustrating the life of the Servite saint Filippo Benizzi, and this established his reputation for his extraordinary mastery of colour and tone. Widely regarded as the finest fresco painter of his generation, Sarto was later commissioned by François I of France and spent some time in Paris before returning to Florence, where most of his later religious paintings were executed. As well as large wall paintings he excelled in smaller, more intimate portraits and he would undoubtedly have gone on to greater things had he not been struck down by the Plague at a relatively young age.

Qiu Ying   Zhao Mengfu Writing the Heart Sutra in Exchange for Tea

Born *c.* 1494, Taicang, Jiangsu, China   Painted in Suzhou, China   Died *c.* 1552, Suzhou
MOVEMENT: Chinese Landscape School   **OTHER WORKS:** *Golden Valley Garden, Landscape after Li Tang*   **INFLUENCES:** Shen Zhou, Zhou Chen

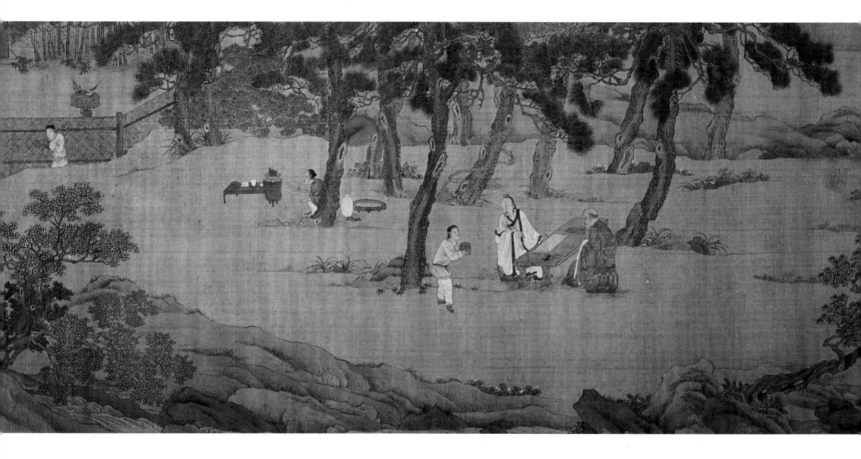

REGARDED AS one of the Four Great Masters of the Ming Dynasty (along with Shen Zhou, Wen Zhengming and Tang Yin), Qiu Ying was by far the most versatile of the four. In contrast to his great contemporaries, he was born of humble peasant parents, but his aptitude enabled him to study painting in the Wu School at Suzhou. Unlike the scholar-painters, he relied solely on commissions from wealthy patrons and for that reason he was always more alive to the slightest change in fashion or taste. He painted flowers, gardens, figures, religious subjects and landscapes that revelled in colour and form, very much in line with the sensuousness then prevailing in Ming society. A prolific artist, he frequently copied works of earlier masters or incorporated elements of their work into his own. His technique likewise varied considerably and his palette ranged from the deep, bright colours which give his sensuous and erotic paintings a jewel-like quality, to the paler, more muted shades found in many of his scroll paintings of landscapes, imparting a poetic or contemplative character.

Parmigiano   Self Portrait at the Mirror, *c.*1524

Born 1503 Parma, Italy   Painted in Parma, Rome and Bologona   Died 1540 Cremona, Italy
MOVEMENT: Lombard School   **OTHER WORKS:** *Madonna with St Zacharias, Madonna with the Long Neck*   **INFLUENCES:** Correggio, El Greco

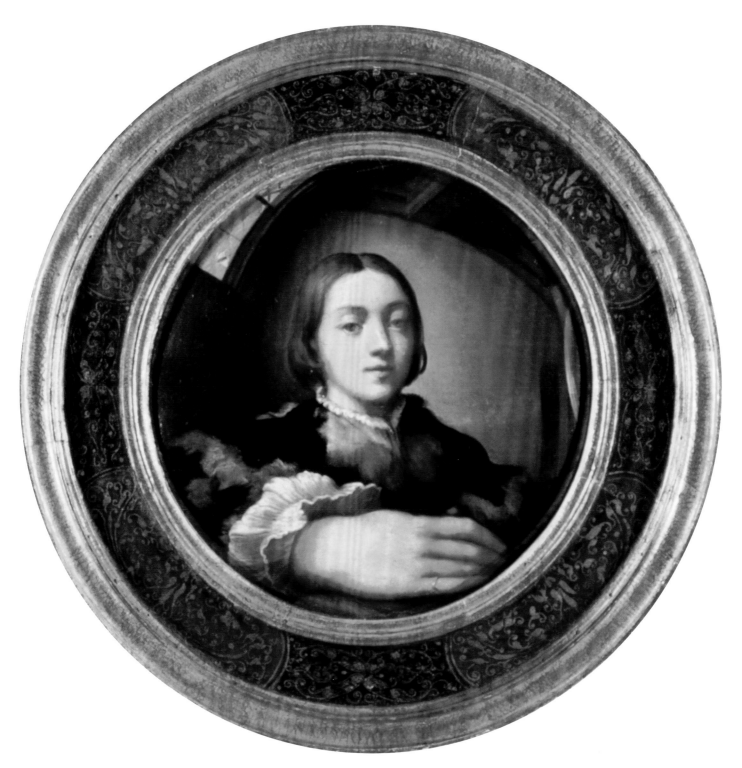

GIROLAMO FRANCESCO Maria Mazzola was generally known as Parmigianino ('the little Parmesan') or Parmigiano from his birthplace of Parma. His father and two uncles were painters and from them he learned his craft. Later he followed the style of Correggio, who settled in Parma, and they worked together on a number of frescoes for churches in Parma. Around 1523 he went to Rome, where he

worked on the ceiling of the Sala dei Pontifici and painted his earliest individual work, *Vision of St Jerome*. Following the sack of Rome in 1527 he fled to Bologna, where he painted the great Madonna altarpiece for the convent of St Margaret. He returned to Parma in 1531 and was commissioned to paint a series of church frescoes, but defaulting on the job resulted in his imprisonment. On his

release he decamped to Cremona, where he died in 1540. His few surviving paintings are distinguished by their grace and serenity.

Lucas Cranach   Venus with Cupid the Honey Thief, 1530

Born 1472 Kronach, Germany   Painted in Saxony   Died 1553 Weimar, Germany
MOVEMENT: German School   **OTHER WORKS:** *Jealousy, The Crucifixion*   **INFLUENCES:** Albrecht Dürer

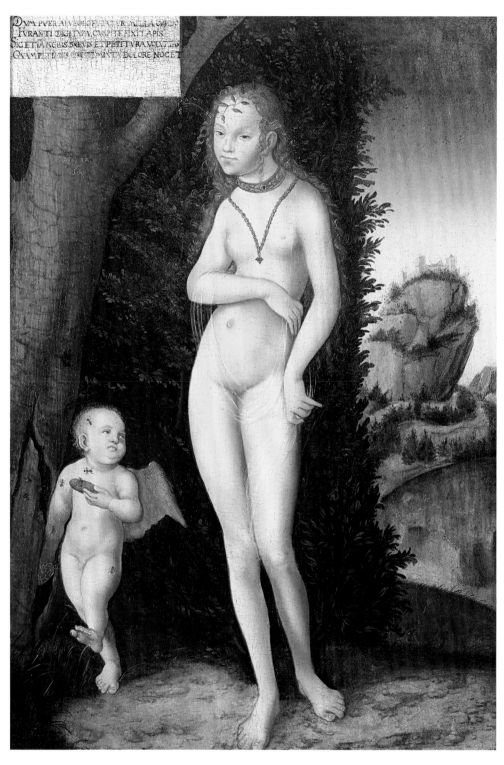

BORN AT Kronach in Germany, whence he derived his surname, Cranach learned draughtsmanship from his father. In 1504 his paintings came to the attention of the Elector of Saxony, who appointed him court painter at Wittenberg. Thereafter he designed altarpieces, etched copper, produced woodcuts and engraved the coinage and medal dies for the Saxon mint. In 1509 he visited the Netherlands and painted the portraits of the Emperor Maximilian and his son, the future Charles V. Although Cranach produced many religious paintings, it should be noted that he sided with the reformers and painted the earliest authentic likeness of Martin Luther, while also executing numerous paintings of an allegorical or mythological character. Nevertheless, it is as a painter of very life-like portraits that he is chiefly remembered, especially as a chronicler in oils of the leading personalities of the German Reformation. All three sons, including Lucas Cranach the Younger, were painters.

Correggio   Noli Me Tangere, *c.*1534

Born 1494 Correggio, Italy   Painted in Correggio and Parma   Died 1534 Correggio

MOVEMENT: Parma School **OTHER WORKS:** *Mystic Marriage of Saint Catherine, Ecce Homo* **INFLUENCES:** Leonardo da Vinci, Andrea Mantegna, Lorenzo Costa

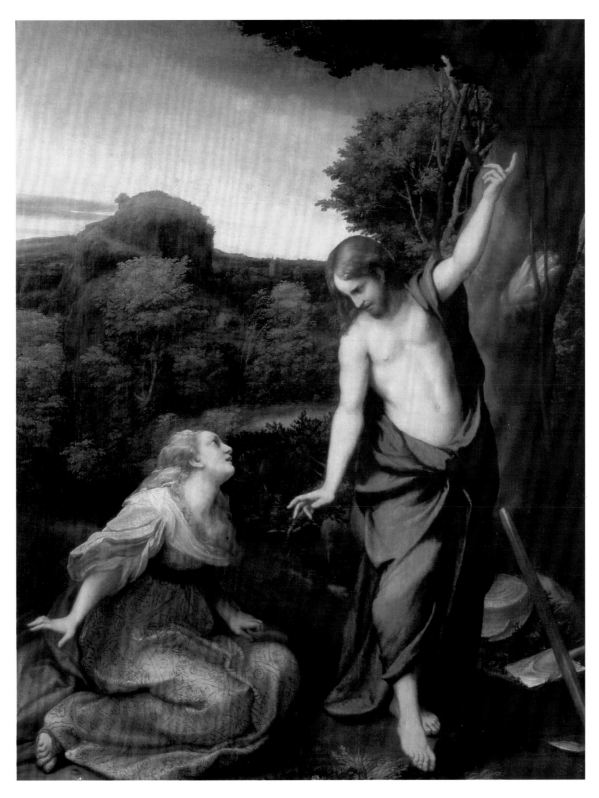

ANTONIO ALLEGRI, known to posterity by his nickname of Correggio, was born in the town of that name in the duchy of Modena. Originally he began training as a physician and surgeon, and studied anatomy under Giovanni Battista Lombardi – believed to be the doctor portrayed in the painting entitled *Correggio's Physician.* In 1518 he embarked on his epic series of frescoes for the Convent of San Paolo in Parma, and followed this with the decoration of Parma Cathedral. He was the first Italian artist to paint the interior of a cupola, producing *The Ascension* for the church of San Giovanni in Parma. He also executed numerous religious and biblical paintings, but also occasionally drew on classical mythology for inspiration. His wife Girolama (b 1504) is believed to have been his model for the *Madonna Reposing*, sometimes known as *Zingarella* ('Gipsy Girl').

Il Bronzino   Madonna & Child with Infant Saint John the Baptist

Born 1503 Monticelli, Florence, Italy   Painted in Florence   Died 1572 Florence

MOVEMENT: Mannerism **OTHER WORKS:** *Guidobaldo della Rovere, Eleanora Toledo and her Son* **INFLUENCES:** Raffaeline del Garbo, Jacope da Pontormo, Michelangelo

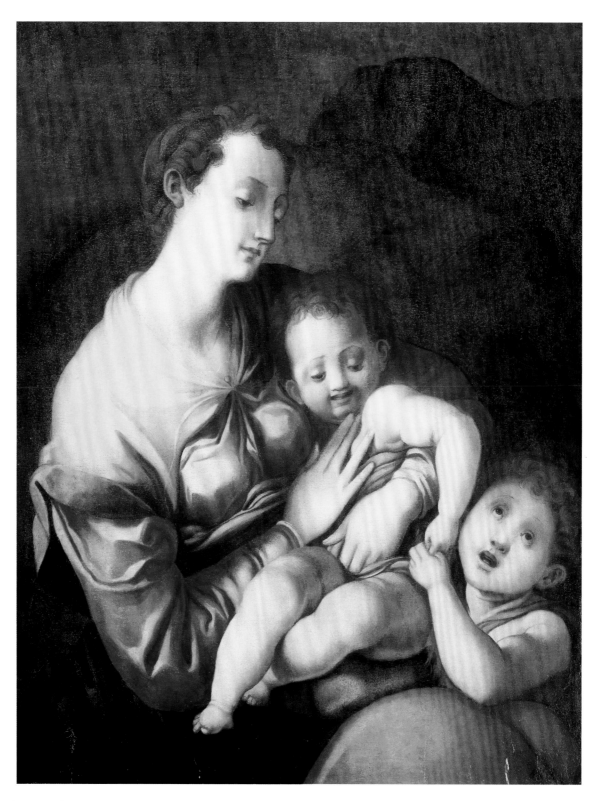

BORN AGNOLO di Cosimo di Mariano, he became the leading court painter of the Florentine School in the mid-sixteenth century. He studied under Raffaellino del Garbo and Jacopo da Pontormo (working with the latter on religious frescoes) as well as being strongly influenced by Michelangelo. He spent his entire working life in Florence where he was court painter to Cosmo I, Duke of Tuscany. Second only to Andrea del Sarto among the Florentine portraitists, he also excelled as a painter of religious works. His talents extended to the written word, for he was also a notable poet and a member of the Florentine Academy. From Pontormo he developed a passion for light, resulting in the rich, brilliant colours that dominate his paintings. These are also striking on account of their fascination for the female nude, without precedent or parallel up to that time.

Hans Holbein   Henry VIII *(after Holbein), c.1540s*

Born 1497 Augsuburg, Germany   Painted in Germany, Switzerland, France and England   Died 1543 London, England
MOVEMENT: German School   **OTHER WORKS:** *Dead Christ, The Triumphs of Wealth and Poverty*   **INFLUENCES:** Hans Holbein the Elder, Hans Herbst

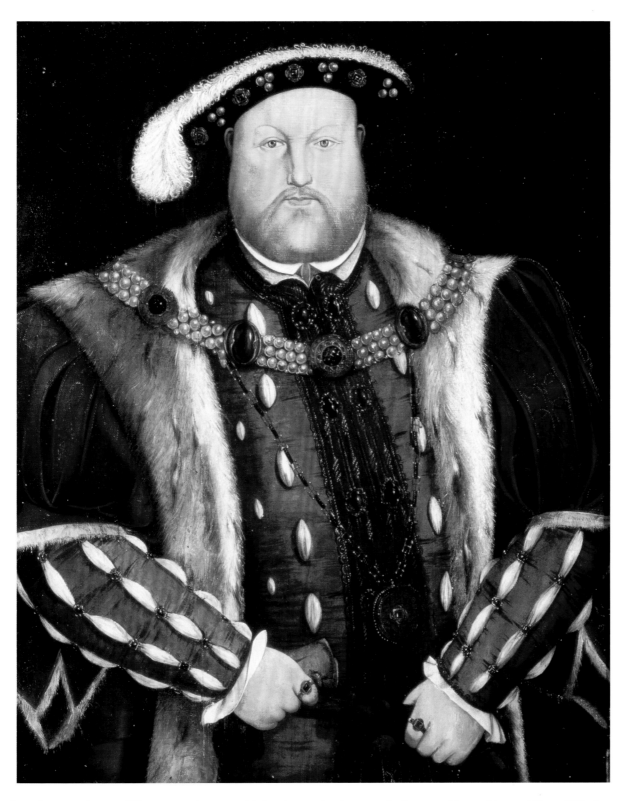

BORN AT Augsburg, Germany, the son of Hans Holbein the Elder, Holbein studied under his father and then went to Basle with his brother Ambrosius as apprentice to Hans Herbst. Subsequently he worked also in Zurich and Lucerne. He returned to Basle in 1519, married and settled there. To his Swiss period belong his mostly religious works. In 1524 he went to France and thence to England in 1526, where he finally took up residence six years later. There being no demand for religious paintings in England at that time, he concentrated on portraiture, producing outstanding portraits of Sir Thomas More and Henry VIII, whose service he entered officially in 1537. From then until his death he produced numerous sensitive and lively studies of the King and his wives, his courtiers and high officials of state. He also designed stained-glass windows and executed woodcuts.

Titian (Tiziano Vecellio) Venus & Adonis, 1555–60

Born *c.* 1485 Painted in Italy and Germany Died 1576

MOVEMENT: Renaissance **OTHER WORKS:** *Bacchus and Ariadne, Man with a Glove, Sacred and Profane Love* **INFLUENCES:** Bellini, Giorgione

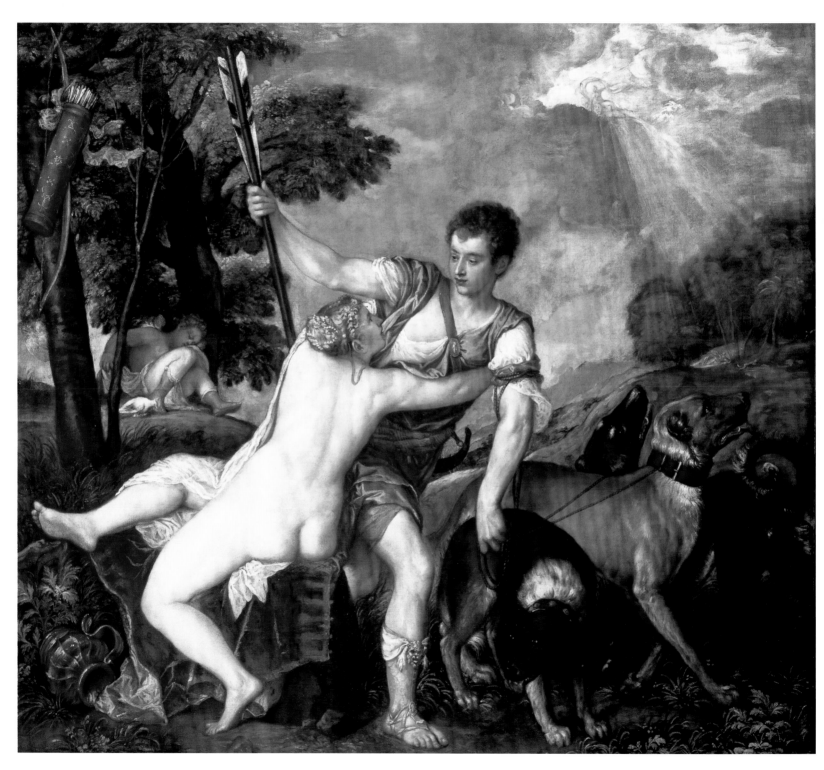

THE GREATEST and most versatile artist of the Venetian Renaissance, Titian excelled equally at portraiture, religious pictures and mythological scenes. Born in the Dolomite region, he arrived in Venice as a boy and was apprenticed to a mosaicist. Turning to painting, he entered the studio of Giovanni Bellini, before joining forces with Giorgione. After Giorgione's premature death

(1510), Titian's star rose quickly. He gained a major commission for frescoes in Padua (1511) and, in 1516, was appointed as the official painter of the Venetian Republic.

This honor enhanced Titian's international reputation and, soon, offers of work began to flow in from the princely rulers of Ferrara, Urbino and Mantua. The painter did not always accept these

commissions, as he was notoriously reluctant to travel, but some patrons could not be refused. The most distinguished of these was the Emperor Charles V. After their initial meeting in 1529, Titian was appointed Court Painter in 1533 and given the rank of Count Palatine. In 1548, he worked at the Imperial Court at Augsburg, and his services were also prized by Charles's successor, Philip II.

Sofonisba Anguissola   Self Portrait, 1556

Born *c.* 1527 Cremona, Italy   Painted in Cremona and Madrid   Died 1625 Palermo, Italy
MOVEMENT: Spanish School of Portraiture   **OTHER WORKS:** *Three Sisters Playing Chess, Portrait of a Young Nobleman*   **INFLUENCES:** Titian, El Greco

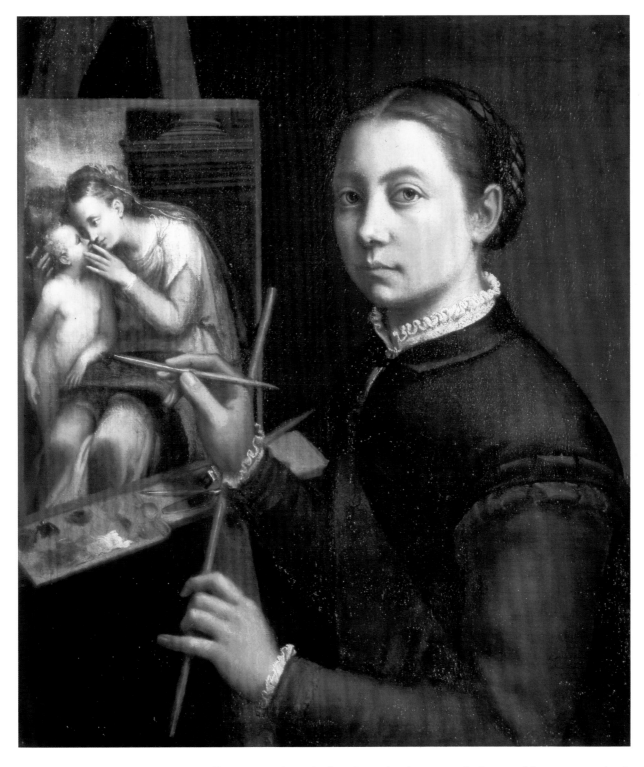

SOFONISBA ANGUISSOLA was born into an aristocratic family. Her mother died when she was quite young, but her enlightened father ensured that Sofonisba and her four clever sisters received a sound classical education, including lessons in painting. Her extraordinary talent enabled her to overcome contemporary prejudices against female artists (reflected in the subterfuge of pretending that this self-portrait was the work of a male artist) and eventually her lifelike portraits secured her an appointment at the Spanish court. Her paintings range from formal studies of Spanish grandees to charming genre subjects, notably her earlier pieces, in which her sisters provided the models. It is these which are now most highly regarded, not only on account of the lively rendering of their subjects but also because of the attention to detail in dress and background. Anguissola remained active almost to the end of her very long life.

Tintoretto The Concert of Muses

Born 1518 Venice, Italy Painted in Venice and Mantua Died 1594 Venice
MOVEMENT: Venetian School **OTHER WORKS:** *The Annunciation, The Last Supper, The Nine Muses* **INFLUENCES:** Michelangelo, Titian, Sansovino

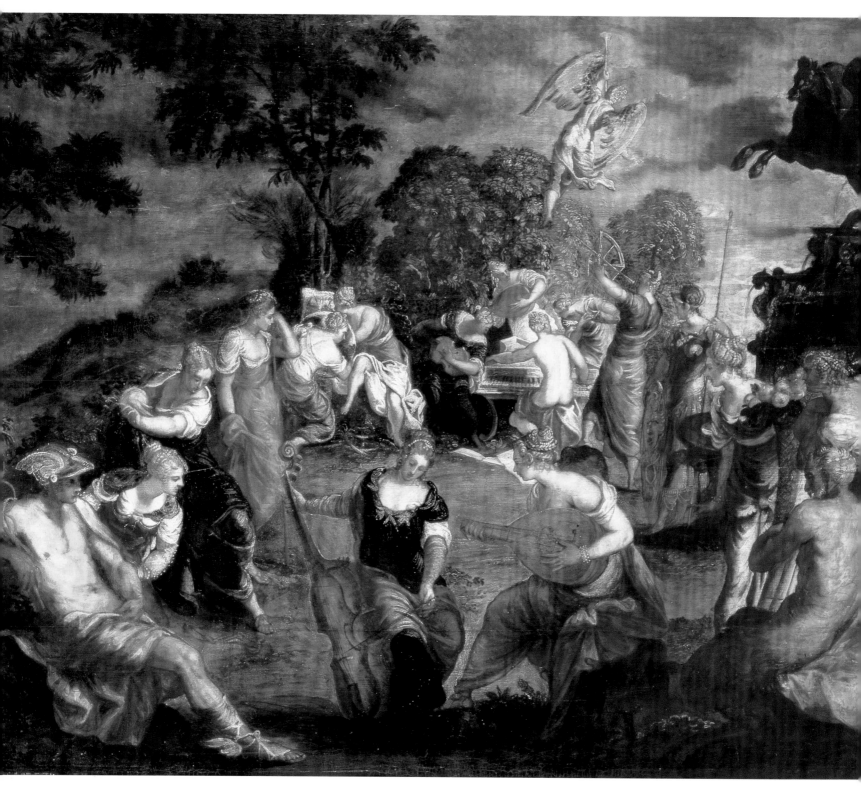

BORN JACOPO Robusti, he derived his nickname, meaning 'little dyer', from his father's trade. He was very briefly a pupil of Titian (who is said to have been jealous of the boy's talents) and though largely self-taught, was influenced by his master as well as Michelangelo and Sansovino. Apart from two trips to Mantua he spent his entire working life in Venice, painting religious subjects and contemporary portraits. His most ambitious project was the series of 50 paintings for the Church and School of San Rocco, but his fame rests on the spectacular *Paradise* (1588), a huge work crammed with figures. He was a master of dark tones illumined by adroit gleams of light. Three of his children became artists, including his daughter Marietta, known as La Tintoretta. His output was phenomenal and he painted with great rapidity and sureness of brushstrokes, earning him a second nickname of 'Il Furioso'.

Paolo Veronese   Christ and the Widow of Nain/Woman taken in Adultery

Born 1528 Verona, Italy   Painted in Verona, Mantua and Venice   Died 1588 Venice
MOVEMENT: Venetian School   **OTHER WORKS:** *The Adoration of the Magi, The Holy Family and St John*   **INFLUENCES:** Domenico Brussasorci, Paolo Farinato

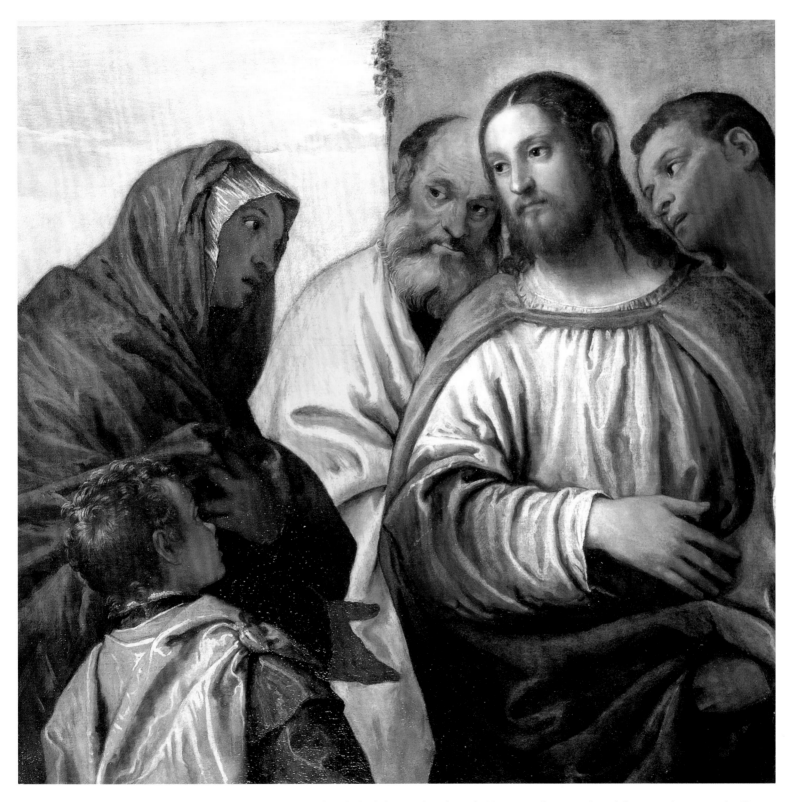

PAOLO CALIARI or Cagliari is invariably known by his birthplace. He was the son of a stone-cutter and originally trained as a stone-carver, but he showed more of an aptitude for painting and therefore switched to the profession of his uncle, Antonio Badile. According to Vasari he studied under Giovanni Caroto – though this left no mark on his style. He worked in Verona and Mantua before settling in Venice in 1555, where he ranked with Titian and Tintoretto in his range and technical virtuosity, reinforced by a visit to Rome (1560). He was a skilful master of genre subjects, which he used to imbue his religious works with humanity, but as a result of his painting *The Feast in the House of Levi* (1573), he fell foul of the Inquisition on a charge of trivializing religious subjects. His undoubted masterpiece is the colossal *Marriage at Cana*, which has over 120 portraits, including royalty and celebrities of the period.

Pieter Brueghel Hunters in the Snow, 1565

Born *c.* 1520 Brögel, Holland   Painted in Breda and Brussels, Belgium   Died 1569 Brussels
MOVEMENT: Flemish School **OTHER WORKS:** *Tower of Babel, Peasant Wedding* **INFLUENCES:** Pieter Coecke, Hieronymus Bosch

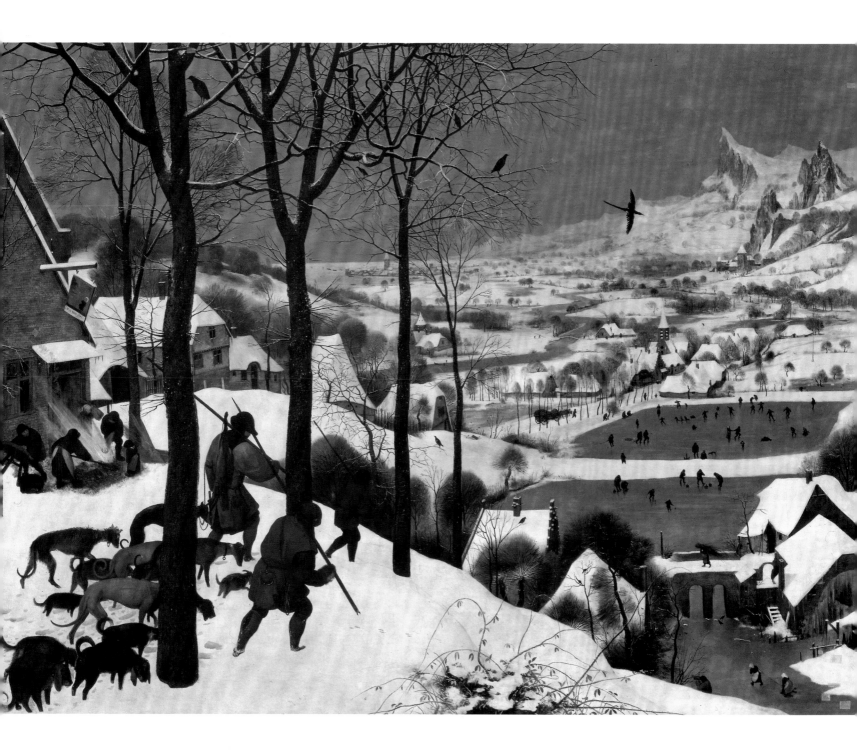

ALSO KNOWN as Brueghel the Elder (to distinguish him from his son Pieter and younger son Jan), he was probably born about 1520 in the village of the same name, near Breda. He studied under Pieter Coecke van Aelst (1502–50) and was greatly influenced by Hieronymous Bosch, from whom he developed his own peculiar style of late-medieval Gothic fantasy. About 1550 he travelled in France and Italy before returning to Brussels, where his most important paintings were executed. He was nicknamed 'Peasant Brueghel' from his custom of disguising himself in order to mingle with the peasants and beggars who formed the subjects of his rural paintings. Although he was a master of genre subjects his reputation rests mainly on his large and complex works, involving fantastic scenery and elaborate architecture, imbued with atmosphere and a sensitivity seldom achieved earlier.

Giuseppe Arcimboldo   Winter, 1573

Born 1527 Milan, Italy   Painted in Milan and Prague   Died 1593 Milan
MOVEMENT: Renaissaince ('surrealism')   **OTHER WORKS:** Summer   **INFLUENCES:** Medieval stained glass

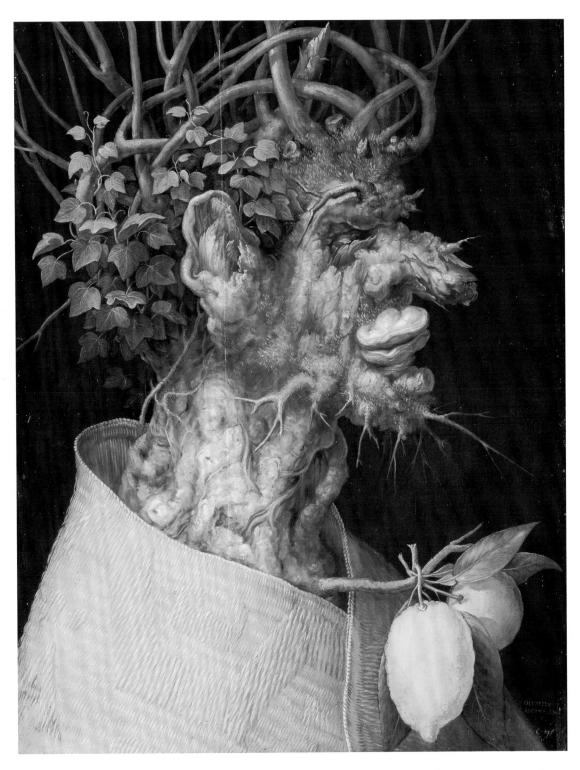

GIUSEPPE ARCIMBOLDO began his artistic career by working on the stained-glass windows in the Duomo (Cathedral) in Milan. Later he moved to Prague which, under Charles V, became for a time the centre of the Holy Roman Empire, and here he was employed by the Habsburg rulers as an architect (of the civic waterworks among other public projects), impresario of state occasions, curator of the imperial art collection and interior designer. It was in Prague that he painted the works on which his reputation now rests. In his exploration of human portraits composed of non-human and inanimate objects he was far ahead of his time, anticipating the Surrealists by several centuries. His fantastic heads symbolizing the four seasons were made up of pieces of landscape, flowers, vegetables and animals, even pots and pans and other mundane articles from everyday life, all executed in brilliant colours with an extraordinary attention to detail.

Caravaggio   The Young Bacchus, c.1591–93

Born c. 1572 Caravaggio, Italy   Painted in Venice, Rome and Malta   Died 1610 Porto Ercole, Sicily
MOVEMENT: Baroque **OTHER WORKS:** *Christ at Emmaus, The Card Players* **INFLUENCES:** Annibale Carracci

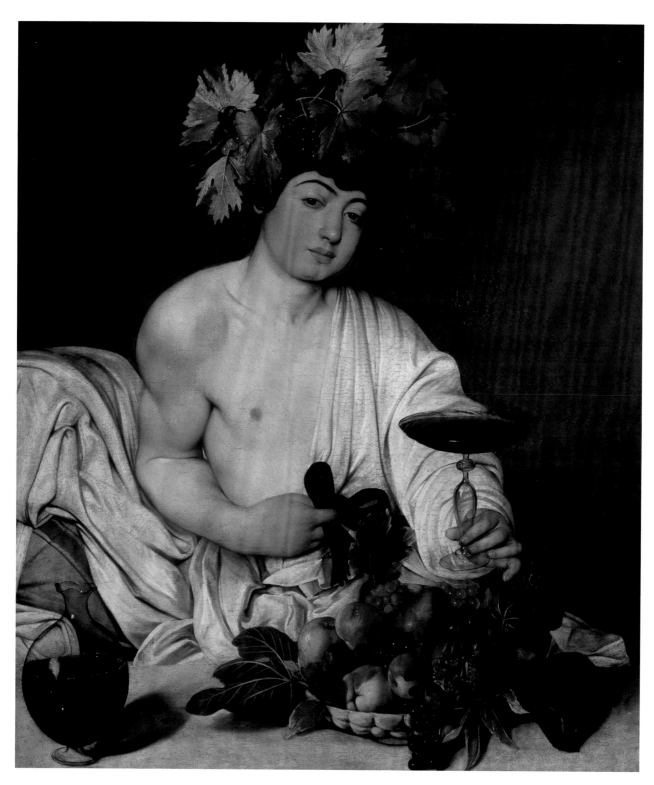

BORN MICHELANGELO Merisi in the village of Caravaggio, Italy, he studied in Milan and Venice before going to Rome to work under the patronage of Cardinal del Monte on altarpieces and religious paintings. His patron was startled not only by Caravaggio's scandalous behaviour but also by his rejection of the Roman ideals and techniques in painting. Instead, Caravaggio headed the *Naturalisti* (imitators of nature in the raw), developing a mastery of light and shade and concentrating on realism, regardless of theological correctness. As a result, some of his major commissions were rejected and in 1606, after he had killed a man in an argument, he fled from Rome to Naples and thence to Malta. On his return to Italy in 1609 he contracted a fever and died at Pontercole, Sicily. The years of exile produced one of his greatest portraits, the full-length of the *Grand Master of the Knights.*

El Greco   Christ on the Cross, 1600–10

Born 1541 Candia, Crete   Painted in Toledo, Spain   Died 1614 Toledo
MOVEMENT: Spanish School   **OTHER WORKS:** *Disrobing of Christ*, *Burial of Count Orgaz*   **INFLUENCES:** Titian, Tintoretto

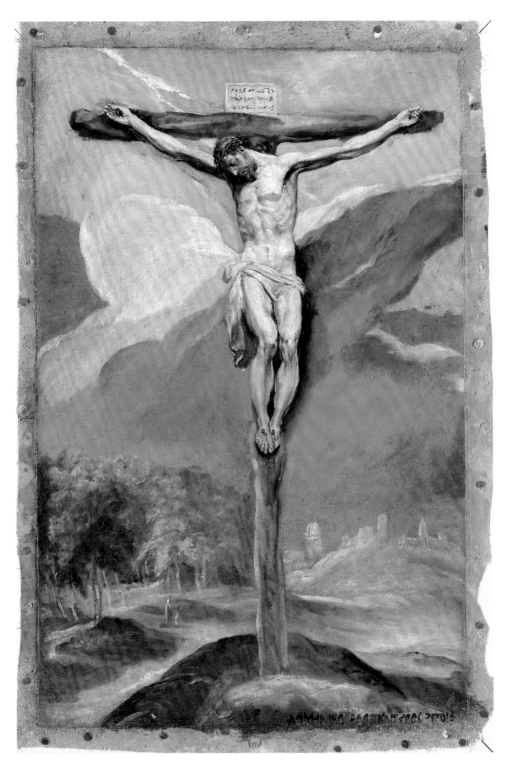

THIS NICKNAME, meaning 'the Greek' in Spanish, is the epithet by which Domenikos Theotokopoulos is better known. Born in Candia (Crete), which was then ruled by the Venetians, he worked as a painter of icons in the Byzantine tradition before moving to Italy, where he is believed to have become a pupil of Titian. He then settled at Toledo in Spain. His early portraits show the Venetian influence of his early training, but in Spain he evolved his own highly distinctive, mannered approach to portraiture, characterized by the elongation and distortion of the face and figure, combined with his penchant for sombre colours. These aspects are seen at their most dramatic and solemn in his large religious paintings, but they are also present to a lesser extent in his portraits of his contemporaries.

Inevitably, his treatment of his sitters' portraits was considered controversial at the time. Many of his extant works are preserved in the Museo El Greco in Toledo where he spent the last 44 years of his life.

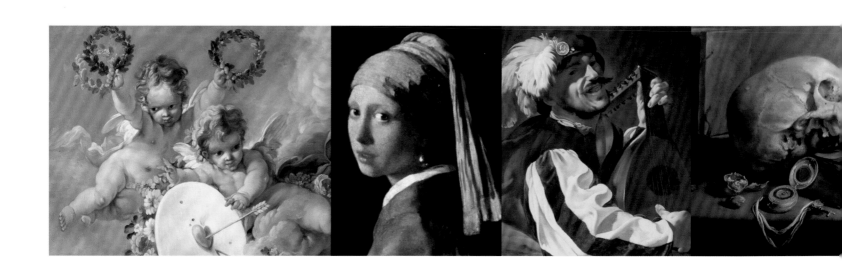

The Baroque & Rococo Era

The Baroque & Rococo Era
The Baroque & Rococo Era
The Baroque & Rococo Era
The Baroque & Rococo Era
The Baroque & Rococo Era
The Baroque & Rococo Era
The Baroque & Rococo Era
The Baroque & Rococo Era
The Baroque & Rococo Era
The Baroque & Rococo Era
The Baroque & Rococo Era
The Baroque & Rococo Era

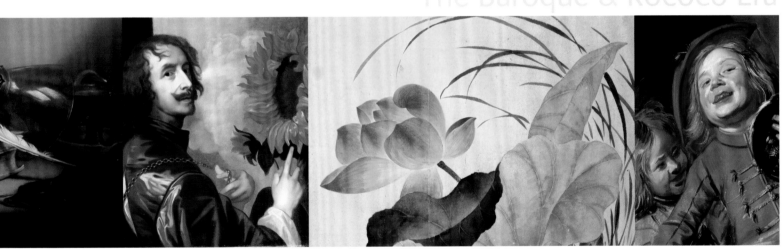

The Baroque & Rococo Era
The Baroque & Rococo Era
The Baroque & Rococo Era
The Baroque & Rococo Era
The Baroque & Rococo Era
The Baroque & Rococo Era
The Baroque & Rococo Era
The Baroque & Rococo Era

Annibale Carracci   The Veil of Saint Veronica

Born 1560 Bologna, Italy   Painted in Bologna and Rome   Died 1609 Rome

MOVEMENT: Neoclassical **OTHER WORKS**: *The Assumption of the Virgin, The Virgin Mourning Christ* **INFLUENCES:** Correggio, Raphael, Titian

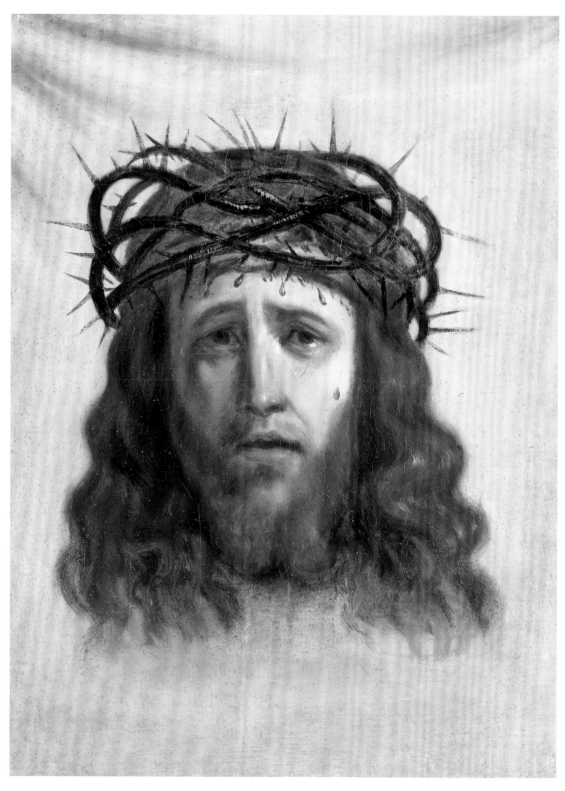

THE GREATEST of a talented family (which included his brother Agostino and his cousin Ludovico), Annibale Carracci was self-taught to some extent, although he was influenced by Correggio and Raphael. The three Carraccis founded an academy of painting in Bologna in 1585 and exerted a tremendous influence on Baroque artists of the next generation. In 1595 Annibale went to Rome, where he was employed by Cardinal Farnese in the decoration of his palace with a series of great frescoes whose motifs were mainly derived from classical mythology – an achievement which is surpassed only by Michelangelo's work in the Sistine Chapel. Carracci also produced numerous paintings of religious subjects, often placing the Madonna and saints in somewhat idealized classical landscapes. He thus combined the traditions of classicism with the advances in naturalism in the late sixteenth century.

Guido Reni St John the Baptist

Born 1575 Bologna, Italy Painted in Bologna Died 1642 Bologna

MOVEMENT: Bolognese School **OTHER WORKS**: *Massacre of the Innocents, Saint Jerome and the Angel, The Nativity* **INFLUENCES:** Raphael, Annibale Carracci

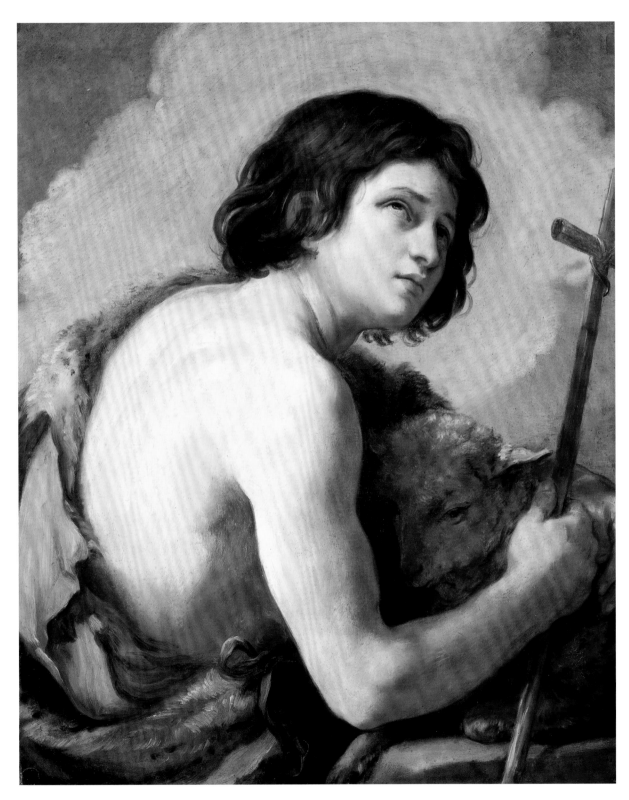

GUIDO RENI studied at the Carracci Academy in his native city of Bologna and acquired a mastery of drawing from life. In 1600 he went to Rome, where he studied the works of Raphael, but he was also strongly influenced by the paintings of other masters working on classical and mythological themes. Reni later painted frescoes, of which his *Aurora and the Hours* (1613–14) for the Borghese family is regarded as his masterpiece. After Carracci's death Reni became the most fashionable painter in Bologna and operated a large studio with numerous assistants. The pious sentimentality of his great religious canvasses had an enormous impact on later generations, although he went on to eclipse in the nineteenth century and has been restored to favour in more recent times, his technical mastery of lighting and composition being appreciated once more.

Peter Paul Rubens (attr.) Two Saints

Born 1577 Siegen, Germany   Painted in Antwerp, Rome, Madrid, Paris and London   Died 1640 Antwerp, Belgium
MOVEMENT: Flemish School **OTHER WORKS:** *Samson and Delilah, The Descent from the Cross, Peace and War* **INFLUENCES:** Tobias Verhaecht, Adam Van Noort

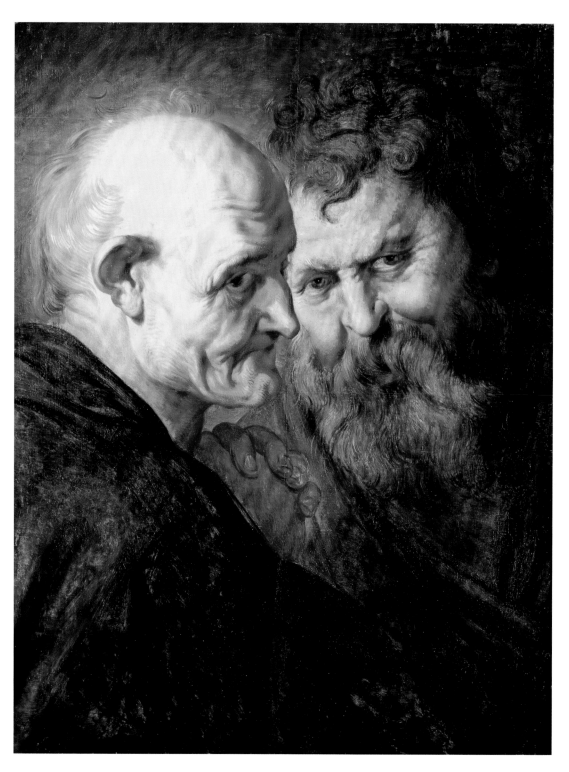

BORN AT SIEGEN, WESTPHALIA, now part of Germany, Peter Paul Rubens was brought up in Antwerp in the Spanish Netherlands. Originally intended for the law, he studied painting under Tobias Verhaecht, Adam Van Noort and Otto Vaenius and was admitted into the Antwerp painters' guild in 1598. From 1600 to 1608 he was court painter to Vincenzo Gonzaga, Duke of Mantua, and travelled all over Italy and Spain, furthering his studies and also executing paintings for various churches. Shortly after his return to Antwerp he was appointed court painter to Archduke Albrecht of the Netherlands. In the last years of his life he combined painting with diplomatic missions which took him to France, Spain and England and resulted in many fine portraits, as well as his larger religious pieces. He was knighted by both Charles I and Philip IV of Spain. In 1630 he retired from the court to Steen and devoted the last years of his life to landscape painting.

Abul Hasan   Squirrels on a Plane Tree, *c.*1610

Born *c.* 1570 India   Painted in India   Died *c.* 1640 Delhi, India
MOVEMENT: Indo-Persian School **OTHER WORKS:** *Elephant in a Palace Courtyard* **INFLUENCES:** Daswanth, Basawan

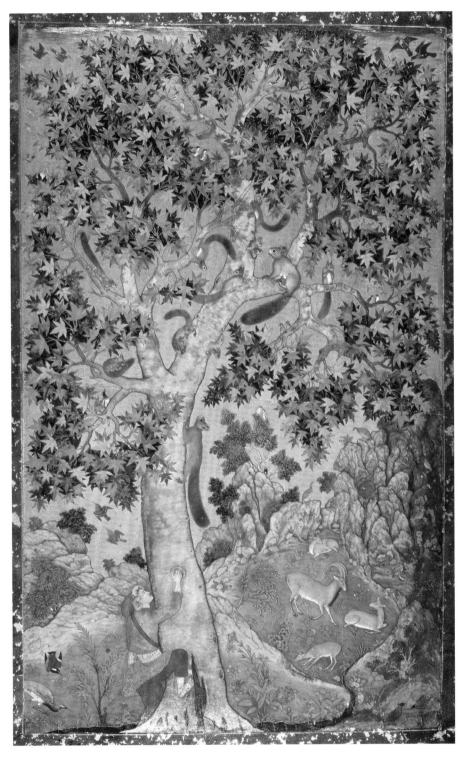

VERY LITTLE is known about the life of Abul Hasan, other than that he was one of the leading Muslim painters at the court of the Mughal emperors and was particularly esteemed by the Emperor Jahangir (1605–27), who conferred on him the special title of Nadir-uz-zaman. He appears to have been born about 1570 and came to prominence in the last years of the Emperor Akbar, but continued to paint in the reign of Shah Jahan (1627–58). He painted portraits of the emperors, courtiers and officials, as well as genre subjects and charming little studies of birds and animals. His technique matured from 1610 onwards and he was undoubtedly responsible for raising the standards of Indo-Persian painting to new levels. The old aggressive colouring was toned down and a general refinement of style and execution was cultivated. In the portraits of men and animals a little shading was introduced by a few delicate strokes, just enough to suggest solidity and roundness, in marked contrast to the flat, two-dimensional profile painting of the previous generation.

Sotatsu School   Herons & Grasses

Born 1576 Kyoto, Japan   Painted in Kyoto   Died 1643 Kyoto
MOVEMENT: Rinpa School, Japan   **OTHER WORKS**: *Deer Scroll, Zen Priest Choka, The Tale of Genji*   **INFLUENCES**: Ogata Korin, Honami Koetsu

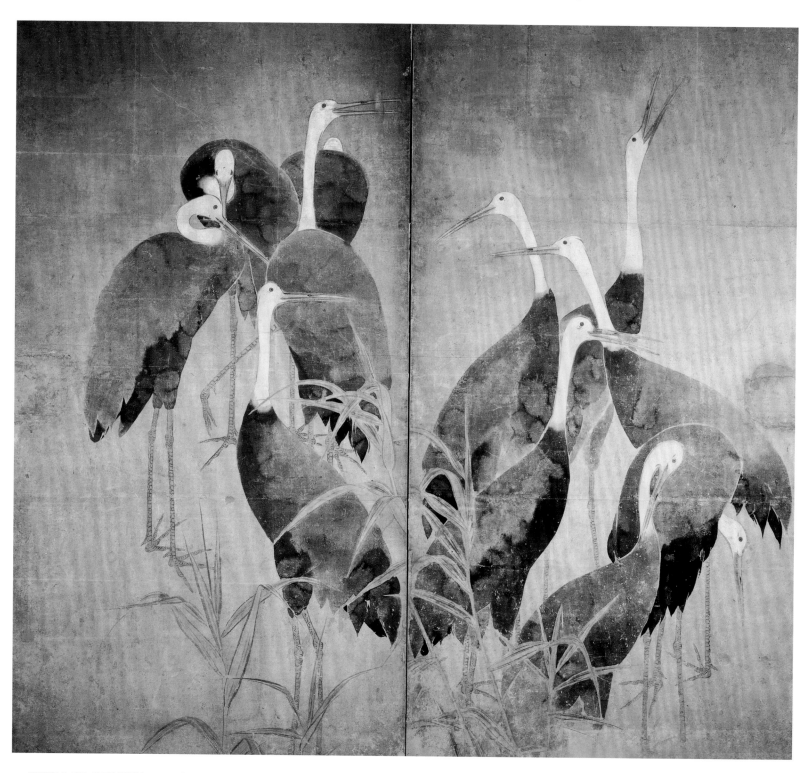

TAWARAYA SOTATSU operated a print shop in Kyoto that specialized in painted fans, but in 1621 he was commissioned to paint a set of sliding screens depicting pine trees and this appears to have been a major turning point in his career. Later he was closely associated with Ogata Korin in the Rinpa School, but as a result his own contribution to the development of Japanese art in the early seventeenth century was largely overlooked until relatively recently. A pair of two-fold screens depicting the gods of thunder and wind, however, reveals quite a radical departure from the style of the Momoyama painters, much bolder and ascetic, with greater emphasis on asymmetry and overall simplicity, coupled with greater use of colour. Rejecting the styles imported from China, he went back to earlier Japanese traditions both in subject matter and treatment. He also collaborated with Honami Koetsu in founding Takagamine, an artists' colony which reinvigorated Japanese art.

Artemisia Gentileschi   Judith Slaying Holofernes, 1612–21

Born 1593 Rome, Italy Painted in Italy and England   Died c. 1652

MOVEMENT: Baroque, Caravaggism **OTHER WORKS:** *Susanna and the Elders, Self-Portrait as the Allegory of Painting* **INFLUENCES:** Caravaggio, Orazio Gentileschi, the Carracci

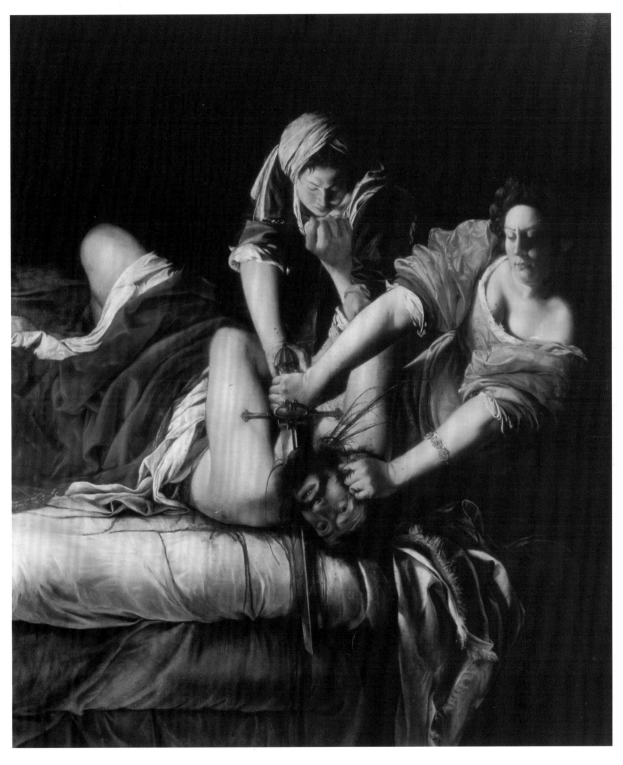

REGARDED BY many as the finest of all female artists, Artemisia was born in Rome, where she was trained by her father, Orazio. Both artists were heavily influenced by Caravaggio, sharing his fondness for unflinching realism and dramatic lighting effects. During her lifetime, Gentileschi was best known as a portraitist, but she has since become more famous for her powerful religious scenes. In these, she tended to focus on Biblical women, such as Susanna, Bathsheba and Esther but her favourite subject was Judith, the Jewish heroine who saved her people by killing an enemy general. Gentileschi produced at least six versions of this story and, although the theme was popular with other female artists of the time, hers are undoubtedly the goriest. This has often been ascribed to a trauma in her own life for, at the age of 19, she claimed that she was raped by an artist from her father's workshop. A five-month trial ensued, during which Gentileschi was tortured with thumbscrews, in order to 'verify' her evidence.

During her career, Artemisia worked in Florence, Naples, Venice. and also spent some time in London helping her father complete a commission for Charles I.

Jusepe Ribera   Saint Peter in Penitence

Born 1591 Jeatiba, Spain   Painted in Naples, Italy   Died 1652 Naples

MOVEMENT: Spanish and Neapolitan Schools   **OTHER WORKS:** *Saint Paul the Hermit, Portrait of a Bearded Woman*   **INFLUENCES:** Raphael, Correggio

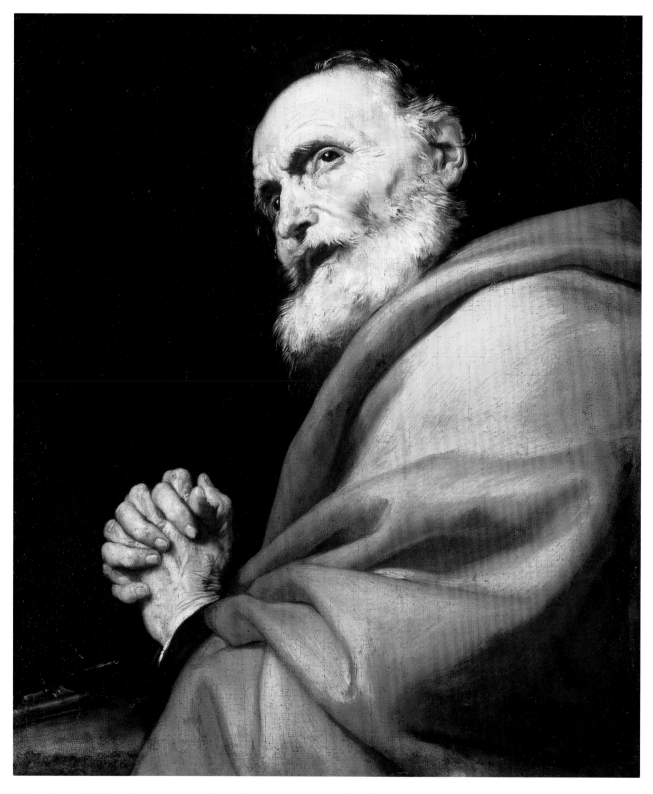

JUSEPE RIBERA, nicknamed Lo Spagnoletto ('the little Spaniard'), studied under Francisco Ribalta in Valencia and then went to Rome to study the frescoes of Raphael, and to Parma to learn from Correggio's works. He settled at Naples, where his paintings caught the eye of the Spanish viceroy.

As a result his career was assured and he became a prolific painter of intensely realistic religious and genre subjects. He delighted in the gory details of the martyrdom of the saints, thus provoking Lord Byron in *Don Juan* to quip that 'Spagnoletto tainted his brush with all the blood of all the sainted'.

He was also fascinated with the bizarre or grotesque in contemporary life; but by the 1630s his work assumed a more reflective, tranquil approach. Nevertheless it was the fervent spirituality of his earlier paintings that appealed to his predominantly Spanish clientele.

Hendrick Terbrugghen   A Lute Player, 1626

Born c. 1588 Holland   Painted in Utrecht, Holland   Died 1629 Utrecht

MOVEMENT: Utrecht School **OTHER WORKS**: *Jacob and Laban* **INFLUENCES:** Lorenzo Lotto, Caravaggio

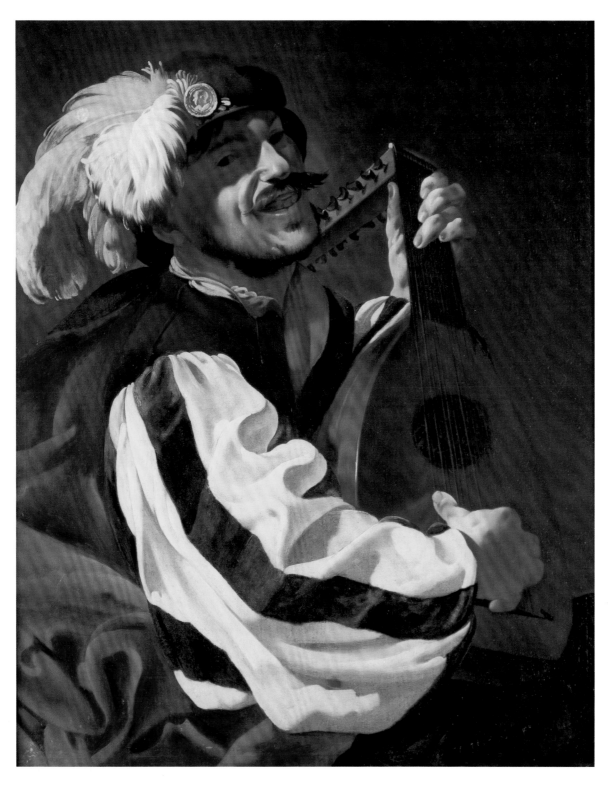

HENDRICK TERBRUGGHEN studied in Utrecht and in around 1612 went to Italy, where he was influenced by the paintings of Caravaggio and Lorenzo Lotto. Returning to the Netherlands in 1615 he settled in Utrecht, where he built up a reputation for his religious and genre paintings. He and Gerrit van Honthorst were mainly responsible for importing to the Netherlands the techniques of chiaroscuro and the dramatic use of light and shade which they had seen in Rome. Terbrugghen made a thorough study of anatomy, which he put to good advantage in his paintings and this, with his attention to detail in such matters as clothing and drapery, brought a new realism to Dutch painting. Dutch paintings in the early seventeenth century tended to have some underlying allegorical concept and it may be that *The Flute Player*, Terbrugghen's most famous work, executed towards the end of his career, was meant to symbolize Music.

Nicolas Poussin   The Triumph of David, c.1631–3

Born 1594 Les Andelys, France   Painted in Paris and Rome   Died 1665 Rome
MOVEMENT: Classicism   **OTHER WORKS:** *The Rape of the Sabines, The Worship of the Golden Calf*   **INFLUENCES:** Raphael, Bernini

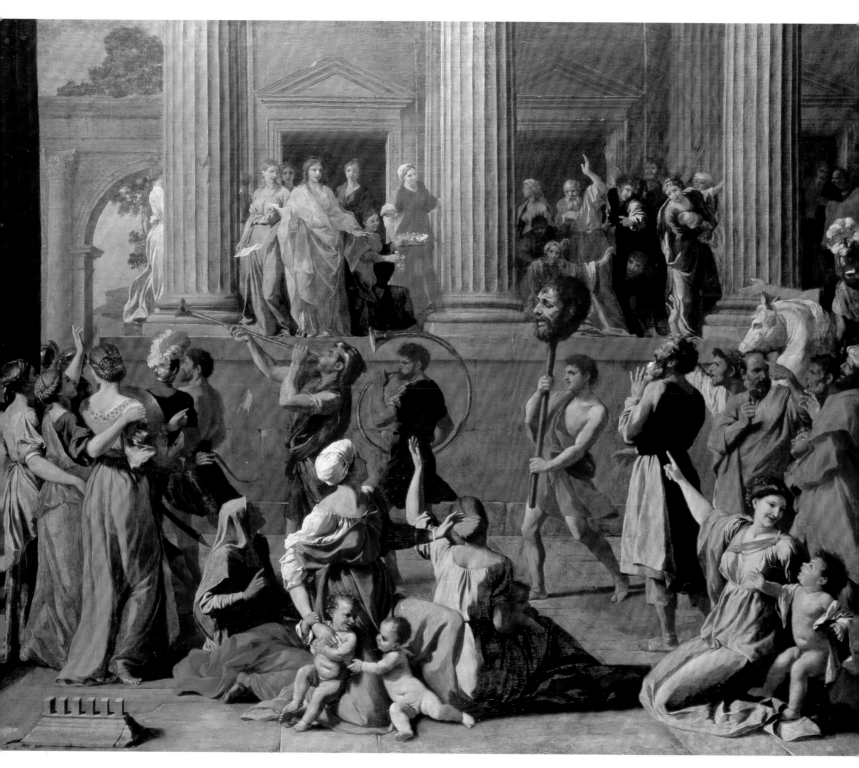

ONE OF the leading exponents of Baroque painting, Nicolas Poussin settled in Paris in 1612. Ignoring the Mannerist painting then fashionable, he took as his model Raphael and studied the great Classical works of the Italian Renaissance. He left Paris in 1623 and began travelling in Italy, studying the works of the Italian masters at first hand. He settled in Rome the following year. Apart from a brief sojourn in Paris (1640–42) he spent the rest of his life in Rome, executing commissions for Cardinal Barberini. Eschewing the increasingly popular Baroque style, he clung to the Classical style and became its greatest French exponent. He drew upon the rich store of Greek and Roman mythology for his subjects, while utilizing the techniques of colour developed by Titian. His greatest canvasses deal with vast subjects, crowd scenes crammed with action and detail. Later on he tended to concentrate more on landscapes, although still steeped in the Classical tradition.

Il Guercino Saint Luke

Born 1602 Cento, Italy   Painted in Rome and Bologna   Died 1666 Bologna
MOVEMENT: School of Bologna **OTHER WORKS:** *Jacob Receiving Joseph's Coat* **INFLUENCES:** Caravaggio

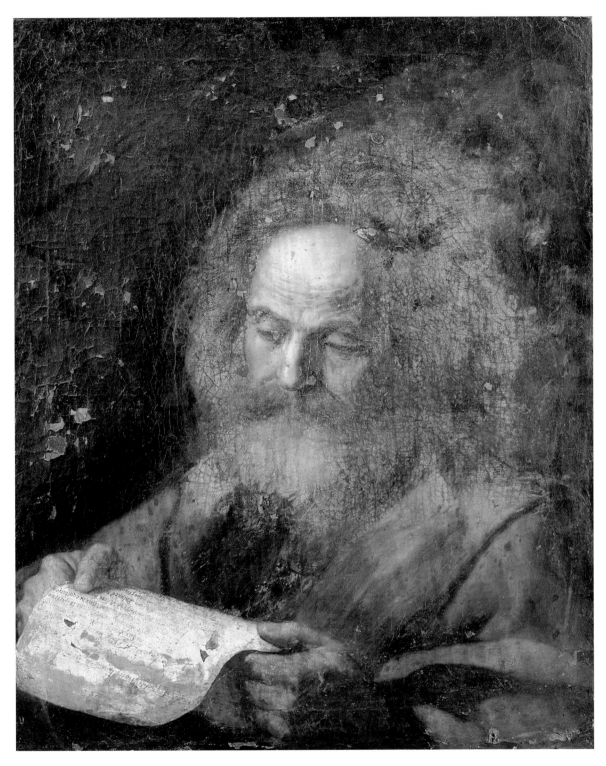

BORN GIOVANNI Francesco Barbieri, he is invariably known by his nickname, which means 'squint-eyed', but in spite of this handicap he showed early promise for sketching and drawing. He was trained in the rigorous classical mode at the Carracci Academy but was later influenced by the realism of Caravaggio, whose lighting techniques he modified by the richness of his colours. Like most artists of his generation he specialized in religious works – his major project being the fresco of Aurora which decorated the ceiling at the Villa Ludovisi, commissioned by Pope Gregory XV. From 1642 onwards he was the leading painter in Bologna, where he died. His oil paintings matched the rich density of their colours with the knack of conveying a wide range of emotions which heighten the dramatic impact of his work. There is invariably a dominant central figure, set against a background in the best Baroque tradition.

Sir Anthony Van Dyck   (circle of) Self Portrait with a Sunflower, after 1632

Born 1599 Belgium   Painted in Antwerp and London   Died 1641 London
MOVEMENT: Flemish School **OTHER WORKS**: *Charles I in Hunting Dress, The Three Royal Children* **INFLUENCES:** Peter Paul Rubens

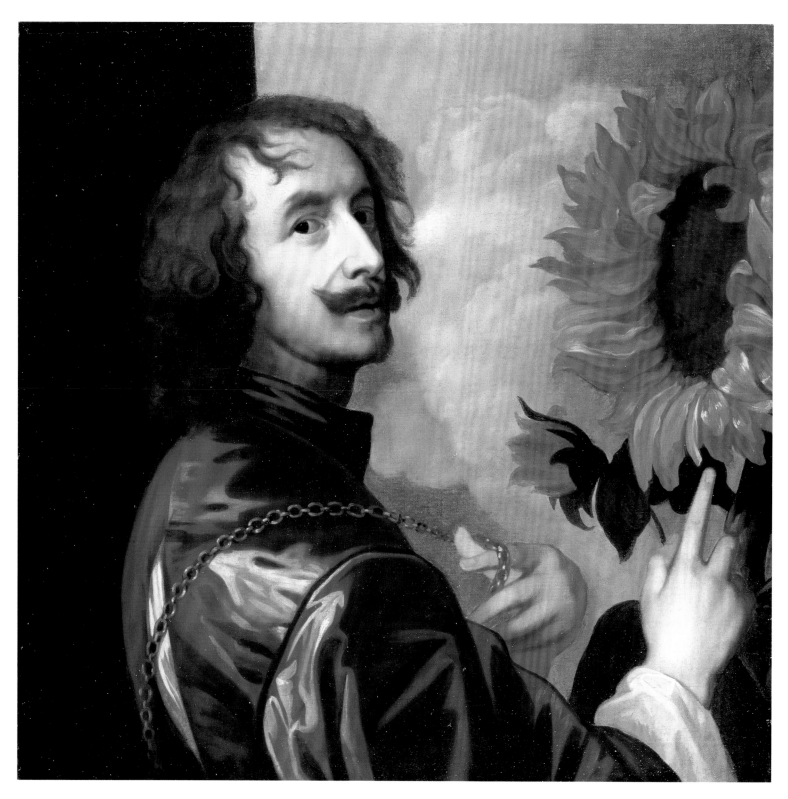

ANTHONY VAN DYCK worked under Rubens and later travelled all over Italy, where he painted portraits and religious subjects. He first visited England in 1620 and was invited back in 1632 by King Charles I, who knighted him and appointed him Painter-in-Ordinary. Apart from a two-year period (1634–35) when he was back in Antwerp, Van Dyck spent the rest of his life in England and on his return to London he embarked on the most prolific phase of his career. He not only painted numerous portraits of King Charles, Queen Henrietta Maria and their children, but also many pictures of courtiers and other notable figures, creating a veritable portrait gallery of the great and good of the period. His immense popularity was due not only to his technical mastery, but also his ability to give his sitters an expressiveness, grace and elegance, which few other artists have ever equalled.

Jan Van Goyen   River Landscape with Lime Kilns, 1640s

Born 1596 Leyden, Holland   Painted in Leyden and The Hague   Died 1656 The Hague
MOVEMENT: Dutch School **OTHER WORKS:** *A Castle by a River with Shipping at a Quay* **INFLUENCES:** Esaias van de Velde, Jan Porcellis

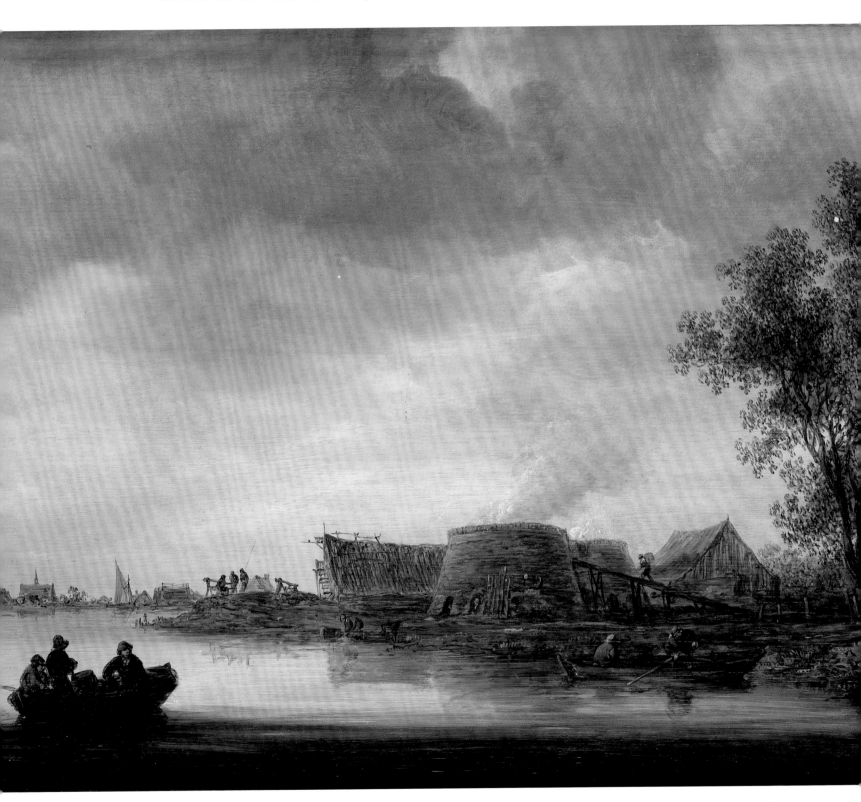

JAN VAN GOYEN visited France in his youth and may have been influenced by the painters in that country, but he also travelled all over Holland and imbibed the ideas of his older contemporaries. With Salomon van Ruysdael he helped to establish the Dutch School of landscape painters, and he had numerous pupils and imitators. In his travels he made countless sketches and drawings that formed the basis of his later oil paintings. He was a prolific artist but a poor businessman and died in debt. His landscapes divide into two periods, those dating from 1630 onwards being in more muted colours, predominantly shades of brown, but much more atmospheric. Towards the end of his life he began using a much greater range of colours again, coupled with that poetic sensibility which was the hallmark of the next generation of Dutch artists.

Pieter Claesz A Vanitas Still Life, 1645

Born c. 1597 Haarlem, Holland   Painted in Haarlem   Died 1660 Haarlem

MOVEMENT: Dutch School   **OTHER WORKS:** *Still Life with a Candle*   **INFLUENCES:** Ambrosius Bosschaert, Balthasar van der Alst, Caravaggio

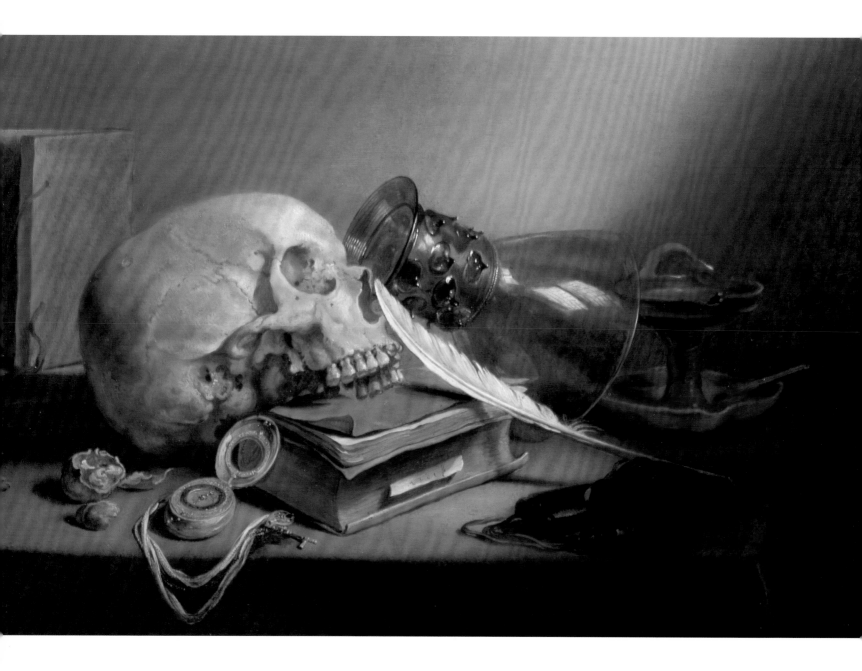

BORN AT Haarlem in the Netherlands in 1597 or 1598, Pieter Claesz grew up in a town which was the centre of the Dutch flower trade, so it was not surprising that he developed an early interest in floral painting. He grew up at a time when this style was being introduced to Holland by Flemish refugees, notably Ambrosius Bosschaert the Elder and Balthasar van der Alst. Claesz went on to develop the type of still life known as the breakfast or banquet picture – much less ebullient than the colourful flower paintings with more somber tones suited to the intimate atmosphere of domestic interiors. Claesz in fact took this further than his contemporaries, creating an almost monochrome effect and relying on the precise juxtaposition of each object which then took on a symbolic meaning. He pioneered a style that was emulated by many Dutch artists of the succeeding generation.

Ferdinand Bol   A Philosopher in his Study

Born 1616 Dordrecht, Holland   Painted in Dordrecht, Utrecht and Amsterdam   Died 1680 Amsterdam
MOVEMENT: Dutch School **OTHER WORKS:** *Vertumnus, Pyrrhus and Fabricius, Bacchus and Ariadne,* **INFLUENCES:** Jacob Cuyp, Rembrandt

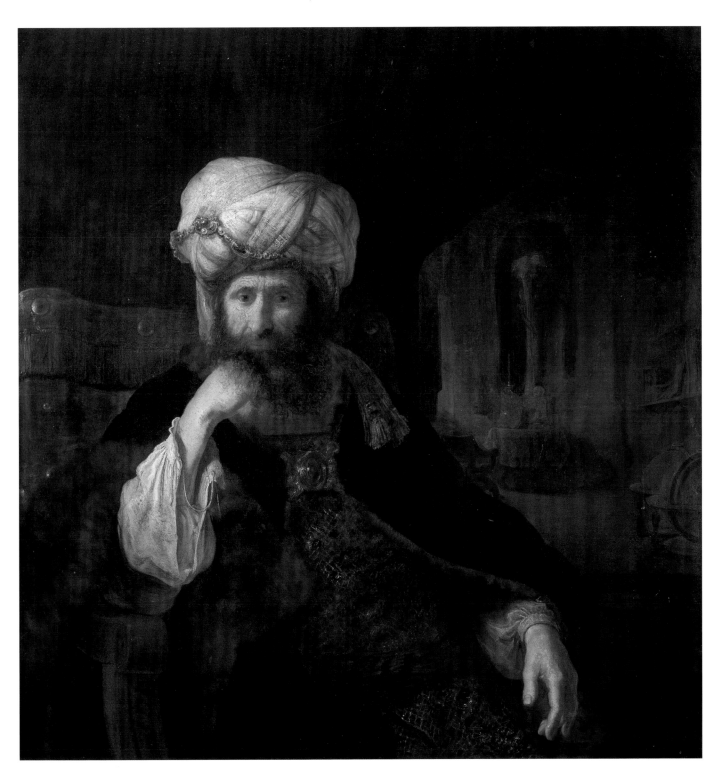

FERDINAND BOL was the son of a master surgeon and was originally intended to follow in his footsteps. He learned the rudiments of painting from Jacob Cuyp (father of Albert Cuyp) in Utrecht and also studied for a time under Rembrandt in Amsterdam in the late 1630s. Bol established his own studio in Amsterdam by 1642 and soon built up a reputation for his portraits and large groups as well as allegorical, religious and classical works. He was Rembrandt's most talented pupil and painted in a style so close to that of his master that some of his paintings have been wrongly attributed to Rembrandt. As well as executing paintings for wealthy patrons he received a number of major civic commissions, including the decorations for the town hall, leper asylum and admiralty building. Bol was a prominent member of the Guild of St Luke, and became its governor in 1665. He appears to have painted nothing after 1669 when he married a wealthy widow and thereafter devoted himself to business and civic affairs.

Georges De La Tour   The New Born Child, late 1640s

Born 1593 France   Painted in Luneville and Paris   Died 1652 Paris
MOVEMENT: French School   **OTHER WORKS:** *St Peter Denying Christ*   **INFLUENCES:** Caravaggio

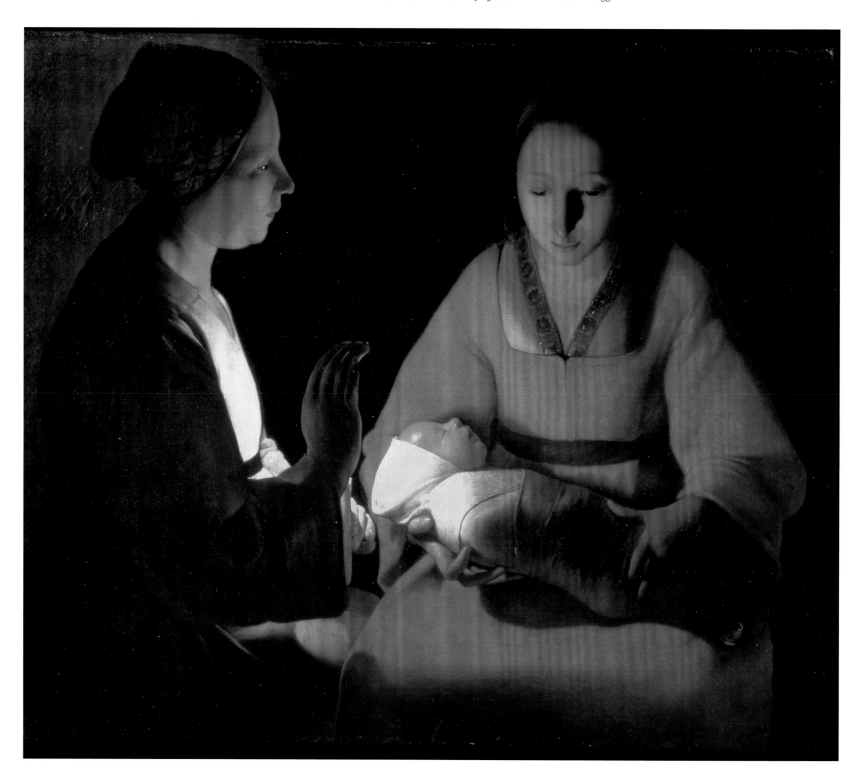

BORN AT Vic-sur-Seille, France, in 1593, Georges de la Tour established himself at Luneville about 1620, where he received many important commissions from the Duke of Lorraine. He also presented one of his paintings to King Louis XIII, who was so enchanted by it that he decided to remove paintings by all other artists from his private apartments. De la Tour concentrated on religious subjects, many of which were rather sombre with large areas of dark shadows and muted colours subtly illumined by a candle to create dark, dramatic and essentially realistic scenes. In this regard he was heavily influenced by Caravaggio and was, indeed, the leading French exponent of his particular brand of naturalism, although eschewing Caravaggio's penchant for the macabre. De la Tour's paintings exude serenity in keeping with their subject matter. Like his paintings, however, he languished in obscurity for many years and was not rediscovered until 1915.

Judith Leyster   Laughing Children with Cat, 1649

Born 1609 Haarlem, Holland   Painted in Haarlem, Utrecht and Amsterdam   Died 1660 Amsterdam, Holland
MOVEMENT: Dutch School **OTHER WORKS:** *Self Portrait, The Flute Player, The Gay Cavaliers* **INFLUENCES:** Hendrick Terbrugghen, Gerrit van Honthorst

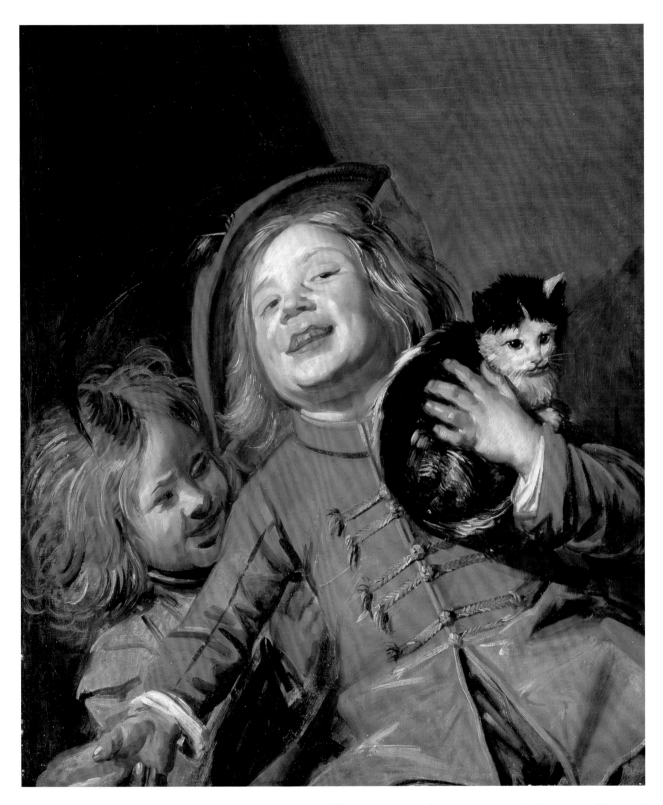

JUDITH LEYSTER was a child prodigy, but nothing is known about her formal art training, although after her family moved to Utrecht in 1628 she came under the influence of Terbrugghen and Honthorst. On her return to Haarlem the following year she studied under Frans Hals. She became a member of the Guild of St Luke in 1633 and by 1635 had several pupils of her own. In 1636 she married fellow artist Jan Miense Molenaer and they moved to Amsterdam. She specialized in genre subjects noted for the spontaneity of expression and her realism, heightened by her skilful control of light, tone and texture. These paintings ranged from little moments of domestic drama to exuberant scenes of revelry which have an underlying humour that sometimes bordered on the risqué. In addition she painted a few half-length portraits.

Frans Hals Portrait of a Gentleman, *c.*1650–52

Born *c.* 1580 Antwerp, Holland Painted in Antwerp and Haarlem Died 1666 Haarlem

MOVEMENT: Dutch School **OTHER WORKS:** *Man with a Cane, Regents of the Company of St Elisabeth* **INFLUENCES:** Van Noort, Van Mander

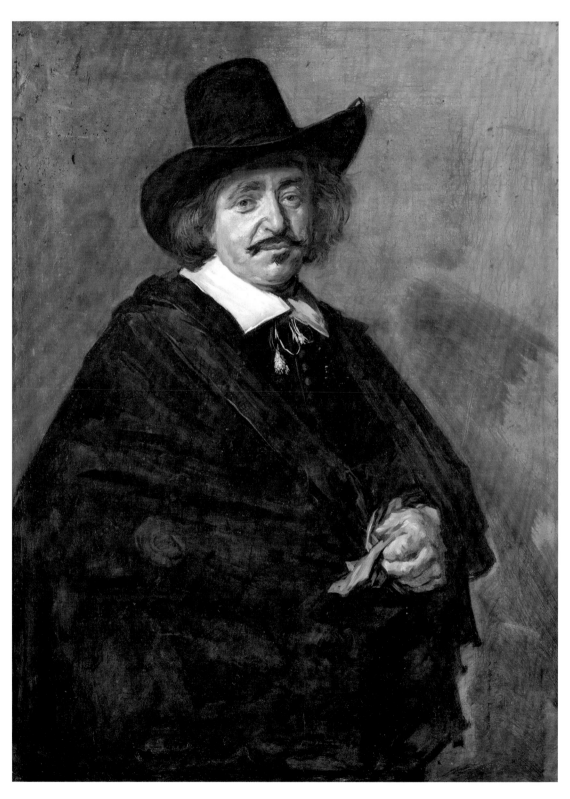

BORN AT Antwerp about 1580, Frans Hals moved with his family to Haarlem at an early age and spent the whole of his life there. It is believed that he received his earliest instruction from Adam Van Noort in Antwerp but continued his studies under Van Mander. None of his earliest works appears to have survived, but from 1618 onwards, when he painted *Two Boys Playing and Singing* and *Arquebusiers of St George*, his works show great technical mastery allied to that spirit and passion which made him the equal of Rembrandt in portraiture. His most famous work, *The Laughing Cavalier* is universally recognized, but it is only one of many expressive portraits, distinguished by a liveliness that was far ahead of its time and anticipating the work of the Impressionists. After 1640 his work mellowed and he adopted a darker and more contemplative style.

Sir Peter Lely   Portrait of Hon Mary Wharton

Born 1618 Soest, Holland   Painted in London, England   Died 1680 London
MOVEMENT: English School **OTHER WORKS:** *Two Ladies of the Lake Family, Flagmen, Susannah and the Elders* **INFLUENCES:** Pieter de Gebber, Van Dyck

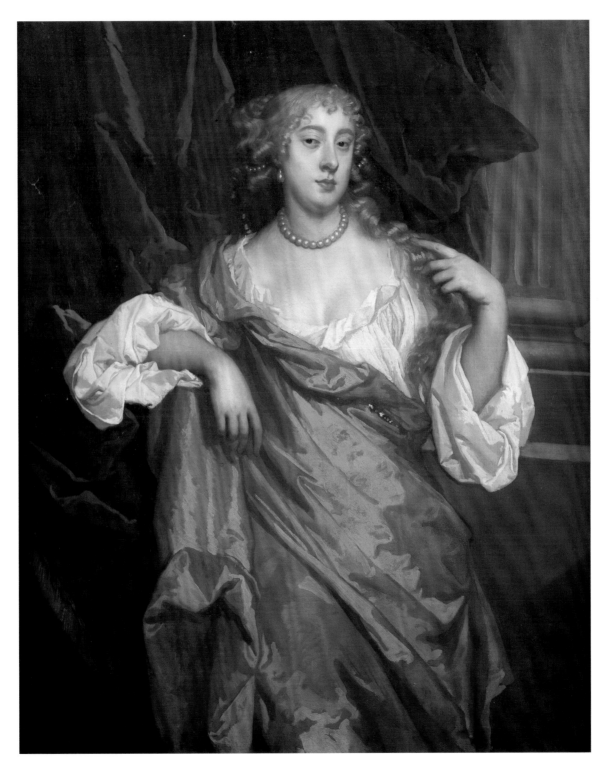

BORN PIETER van der Faes at Soest, Holland, he studied under Pieter de Gebber at Haarlem before settling in London in 1641, where he anglicized his name and adopted his father's nickname Lely as a surname. He rapidly became one of the most fashionable artists of the mid seventeenth century and managed to steer clear of politics, being patronized by both Charles I and subsequently Oliver Cromwell. In this early period he concentrated mainly on landscapes or historical and religious subjects, although a hint of things to come was given by his sensitive studies of the royal family during their imprisonment at Hampton Court. Following the Restoration of the monarchy in 1660 he was appointed court painter by Charles II in 1661 and changed his style of painting. Thereafter portraiture became the dominant theme, evinced in the magnificent series of *Windsor Beauties* now at Hampton Court, and the 13 portraits of British admirals at Greenwich. Lely was knighted in 1679.

Diego Velázquez Portrait of Juan de Pareja, 1650

Born 1599 Seville, Spain Painted in Seville and Madrid Died 1660 Madrid
MOVEMENT: Spanish School **OTHER WORKS:** *The Tapestry Weavers, Venus and Cupid* **INFLUENCES:** Francisco Pacheco

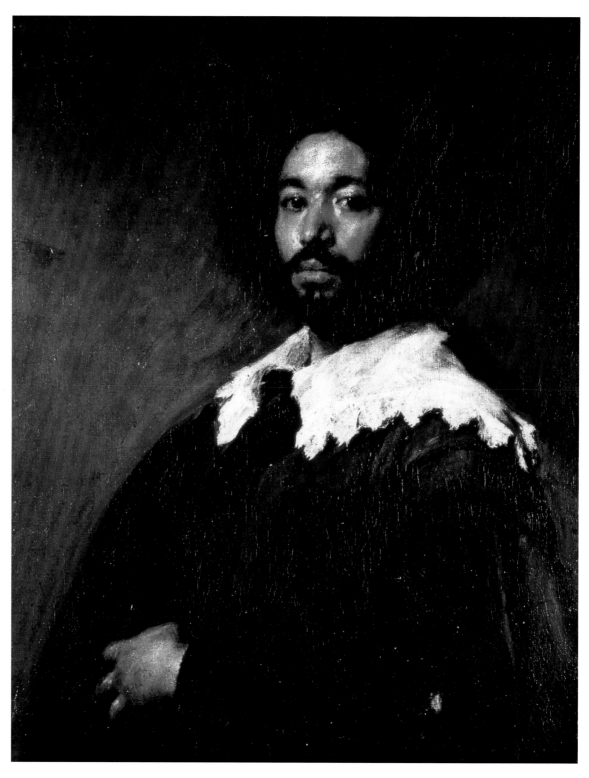

DIEGO RODRIGUEZ de Silva y Velázquez was the son of a prominent lawyer and studied languages and philosophy with the intention of following his father, but his aptitude for drawing induced him to become the pupil of Herera and then Pacheco, whose daughter he married in 1618. His earliest works were domestic genre subjects but after he moved to Madrid in 1623, and especially as a result of a visit to Italy (1629–31), he adopted a much more colourful approach. As the leading court painter of his day he produced numerous portraits of the Spanish royal family and nobility as well as scenes derived from classical mythology. Considering that he is now regarded as one of the greatest painters of all time, it is surprising that his work was little known outside Spain until the early nineteenth century, but his mastery of light and atmosphere had enormous impact on the Impressionists.

Yun Shouping   Lotus Flower

Born 1633 Wujin, Jiangsu, China   Painted in Changzhou, China   Died 1690 Changzhou
MOVEMENT: Early Ming Period, China   **OTHER WORKS:** *Bamboo and Old Tree, Peonies, Plum Blossoms*   **INFLUENCES:** Wang Yuanqi, Wang Hui, Wu Li

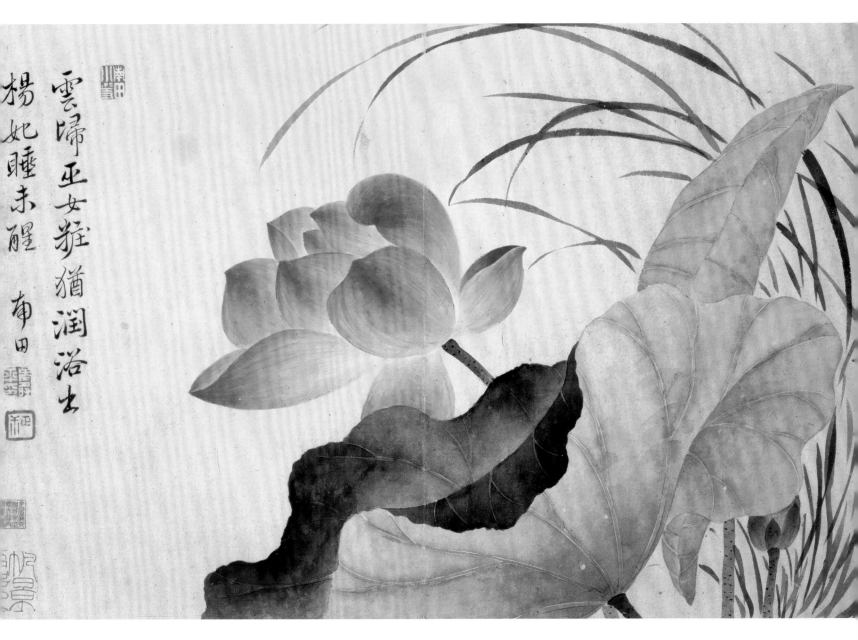

A NOTABLE poet and calligrapher, Yun Shouping was second only to Wu Li among the Chinese painters who were neither orthodox nor individualist, and therefore he does not fit into any exact category. He has often been dismissed merely as a flower painter, but this does not do justice to his art as a landscape painter. Of course, more than any other artist of his period, he loved to decorate his pictures with masses of flowers, but this does not detract from the fact that his landscapes themselves are among the most serenely beautiful and perfect productions among the later Chinese artists. In his studies of flowers and plants as such, however, he was unsurpassed for the delicacy and clarity of his draughtsmanship and the care he took with his compositions. He preferred a very wet brush so that the ink flowed freely, producing a very sharp, clean-cut line. His landscape paintings are very similar to those of the four Wangs and Wu Li, but it is in his use of floral ornament that he stands out from his contemporaries.

Frère Luc   Saint Bonaventure, *c.*1655

Born 1614 Amiens, France   Painted in France, Italy and Canada   Died 1685 Paris, France

MOVEMENT: French-Canadian School   **OTHER WORKS:** *Assumption, Guardian Angel*   **INFLUENCES:** Raphael, Guido Reni, Girolamo Muziano

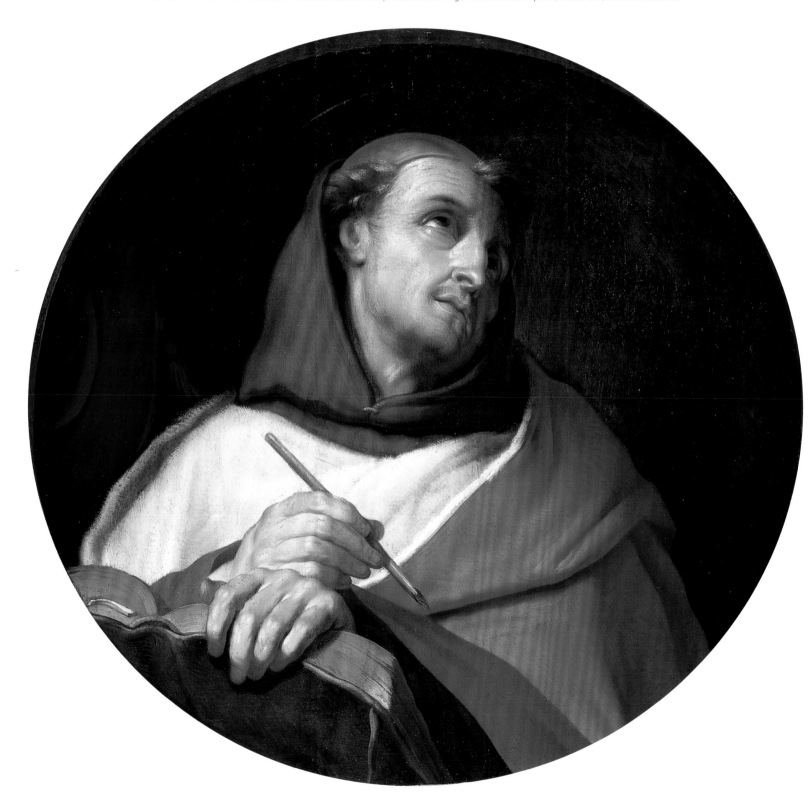

BORN CLAUDE FRANÇOIS, Luc trained under Simon Vouet between 1627 and 1634, when he went to Rome to study the great Masters. He returned to Paris in 1639, working on the decoration of the Louvre. In 1641 he joined the Franciscan Order, taking the name of Frère Luc and thereafter most of his paintings were devoted to the life and works of St Francis of Assisi, which he executed for various monasteries. In 1670 he went to Quebec, mainly as the architect in charge of the rebuilding of the monastery there. At the end of 1671 he returned to Paris and resumed his work as a painter of religious works. He is now chiefly of interest for the work he produced whilst in Quebec. These paintings influenced later generations of French-Canadian artists.

Gong Xian   Fantastic Mountains, 1655 (left, detail right)

Born c. 1619 China   Painted in China   Died 1689 China

MOVEMENTS: Individualist School, Qing Dynasty   **OTHER WORKS:** *A Thousand Peaks and Myriad Ravines*   **INFLUENCES:** Yuan Ji, Zhu Da, Kun-Can

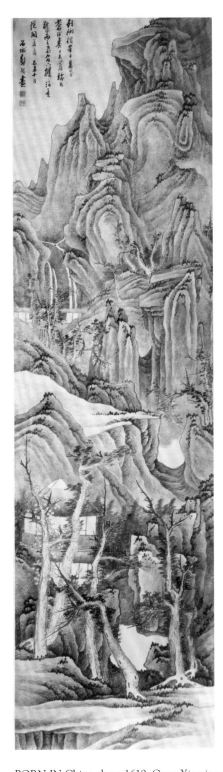
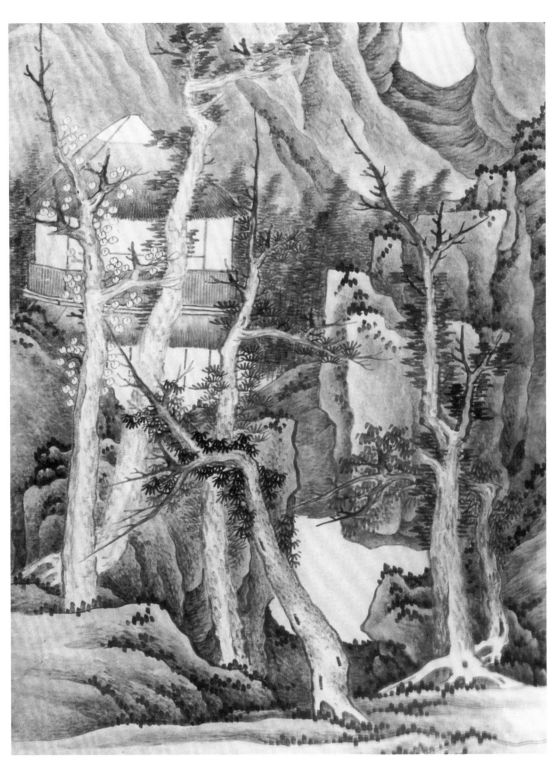

BORN IN China about 1619, Gong Xian is ranked among the greatest of the Individualists working in the Qing period. Although his was the most limited style, it was also the most forceful and dramatic in compact. His paintings have been described as gloomy, funereal and full of foreboding, peopled by ghosts and wraiths; or alternatively as the expression of a monumental genius of somber and passionate temperament. His preferred medium was the hanging scroll, painted in the richest, deepest, most sumptuous shades of black to be found in any Chinese painting, shading subtly in tones of grey, and contrasting with the sunless whites of clouds and mists. He painted empty landscapes; no figures either human or animal disturb the scene. In his experiments with light and shade he went far beyond any of his contemporaries, far less his predecessors and it has been suggested that this reveals the influence of Western artists whose work was beginning to enter China in his lifetime.

Albert Cuyp   The Maas at Dordrecht with Fishing Boats

Born 1620 Dordrecht, Holland   Painted in Dordrecht   Died 1691 Dordrecht

MOVEMENT: Dutch School   **OTHER WORKS:** *Dordrecht Evening, Cattle with Horseman and Peasants*   **INFLUENCES:** Van Goyen and Jan Both

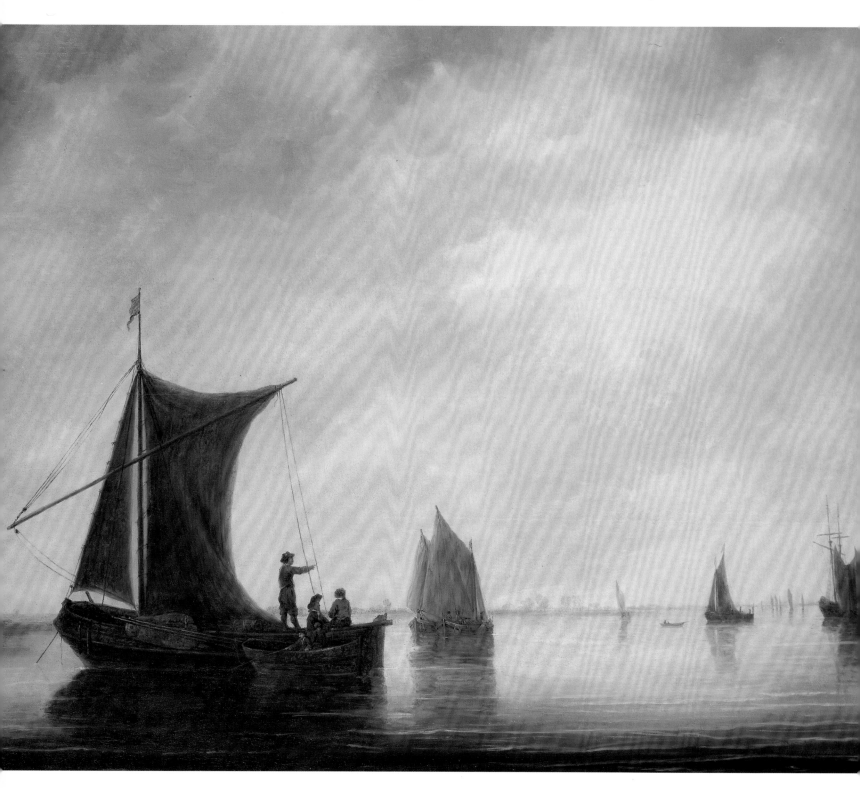

ALBERT CUYP, OR CUIJP, was the son of the painter Jacob Gerritsz Cuyp (1594–c. 1652), scion of a well-to-do family. Controversy continues to rage over the extent of his work, many paintings, particularly of still life, being merely signed with the initials AC. On the other hand, those paintings signed 'A Cuyp' are generally landscapes, whose startling lighting effects are very characteristic of his work. As the signed canvasses belong to his later period, it has been argued that the AC paintings are from his earliest years as a painter. He never strayed beyond the Netherlands, and his landscapes are bounded by the Maas and the Rhine, but what the flatness of the scenery lacks in variety is more than compensated for by Cuyp's mastery of conveying the different seasons and even different times of day, at their best suffusing the figures of humans and animals with brilliant sunshine.

Pieter De Hooch   The Courtyard of a House in Delft, 1658

Born 1629 Rotterdam, Holland   Painted in Rotterdam and Delft, Holland   Died 1684 Amsterdam
MOVEMENT: Dutch School   **OTHER WORKS:** *Woman and a Maid with a Pail in a Courtyard*   **INFLUENCES:** Carel Fabritius, Vermeer

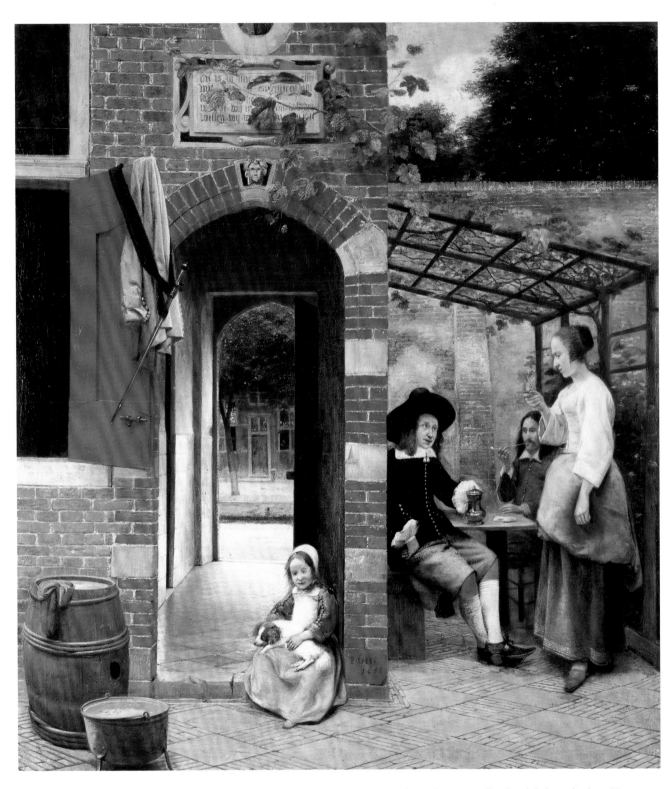

PIETER DE HOOCH spent his early life in Rotterdam but when he married in 1654 he settled in Delft. Here he came under the influence of Carel Fabritius shortly before the latter's untimely death in the explosion of the Delft Arsenal. De Hooch was subsequently influenced by the late artist's gifted pupil Jan Vermeer. De Hooch himself became one of the leading masters of paintings showing domestic interiors or courtyard scenes, with the emphasis on order, domestic virtue, cleanliness to the point of asceticism and benign tranquillity, shown through the careful arrangement of furniture and figures. His pictures are characterized by a dark foreground, often a doorway or gateway, leading to a bright interior suffused with light and colour. He was an accomplished technician, noted for his complete mastery of perspective which enabled him to create an almost three-dimensional effect.

Willem Kalf   A Kitchen with Vegetables

Born 1622 Rotterdam, Holland   Painted in Rotterdam and Amsterdam, Holland   Died 1693 Amsterdam, Holland
MOVEMENT: Dutch School **OTHER WORKS:** *Still Life with Lobster, Drinking Horn and Glasses* **INFLUENCES:** Vermeer, Pieter Claesz

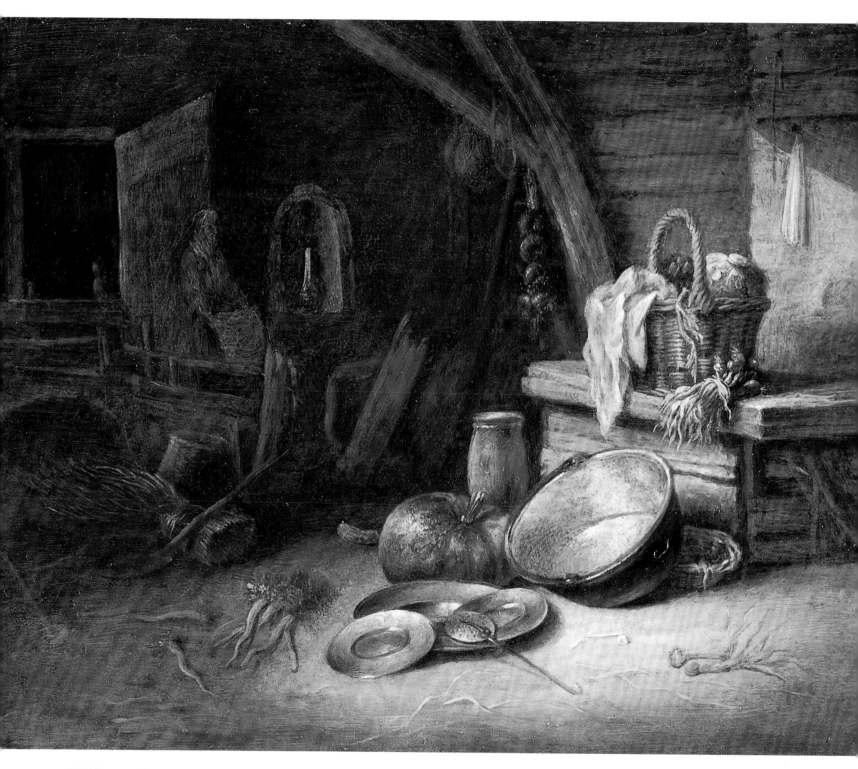

WILLEM KALF had a conventional art training in Rotterdam and then settled in Amsterdam, where he worked throughout his long but surprisingly undistinguished career. Very little is known of his life and work and although he had some recognition in his lifetime he appears to have not been particularly efficient at selling himself or his paintings. His work was all but forgotten until the twentieth century, when art historians restored his reputation. He is believed to have been influenced by his younger contemporary Jan Vermeer, whose own reputation had suffered similar vagaries in subsequent centuries. Kalf specialized in still-life compositions in which he delighted in placing unusual and exotic objects in unlikely juxtaposition. Rich, dark backgrounds contrast with the subtly lit objects painted in brilliant colours and exhibiting a wonderful mastery of intricate detail. The filigree work on silver ornament or the rich jewels set against a Turkish carpet really come to life and jump off the canvas in their intense realism – the kind of subjects which would have appealed to the rich bourgeoisie of seventeenth century Holland.

Harmensz van Rijn Rembrandt   Self Portrait, 1658

Born 1606 Leiden, Holland   Painted in Holland   Died 1669

MOVEMENT: Baroque **OTHER WORKS:** *The Night Watch, The Anatomy Lesson of Dr. Tulp, The Jewish Bride* **INFLUENCES:** Pieter Lastman, Jan Lievens, Rubens

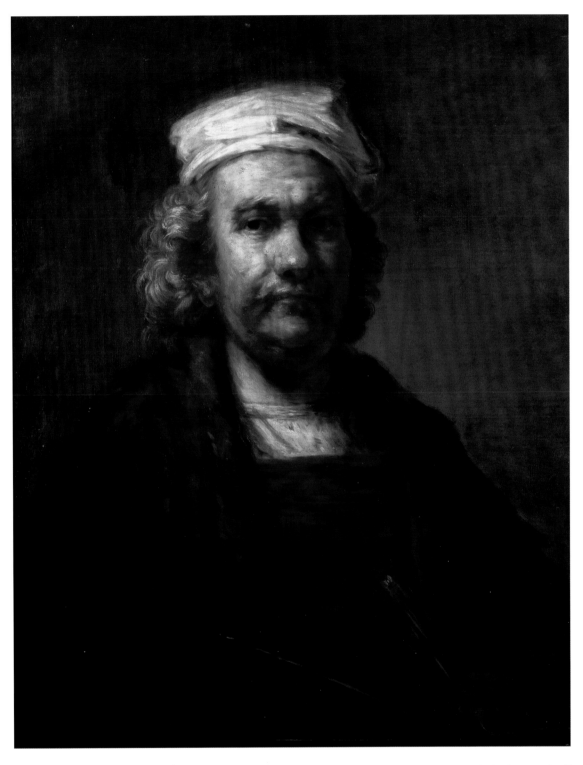

ONE OF Holland's greatest and most versatile artists. Rembrandt trained under several painters, the most influential of these being Pieter Lastman. For a time he shared a studio with Jan Lievens, but by the early 1630s he had moved to Amsterdam, where he established a formidable reputation as a portraitist. Rembrandt's approach to group portraiture, in particular, was extremely ambitious. He showed the anatomist, Dr Tulp actually performing a dissection, while his most famous canvas, *The Night Watch*, is a stunningly complex composition, portraying a local militia group.

As the 1640s progressed, Rembrandt's art entered a more reflective phase. He painted fewer fashionable portraits, preferring instead to depict the inner life. This can be seen in his magnificent religious paintings, in his intimate, unidealized portrayals of his two wives, Saskia and Hendrickje, and in a penetrating series of self-portraits – perhaps the finest ever produced by any artist. Rembrandt's later work was less commercially successful, and although this led to insolvency the popular image of him as a reclusive pauper is entirely fictitious.

Meindert Hobbema   A River Landscape with a Ruined Building and Figures, *c.*1660s

Born 1638 Amsterdam, Holland   Painted in Amsterdam   Died 1709 Amsterdam

MOVEMENT: Dutch School   **OTHER WORKS:** *Stormy Landscape, Road on a Dyke, Watermill with a Red Roof*   **INFLUENCES:** Jacob and Salomon van Ruysdael

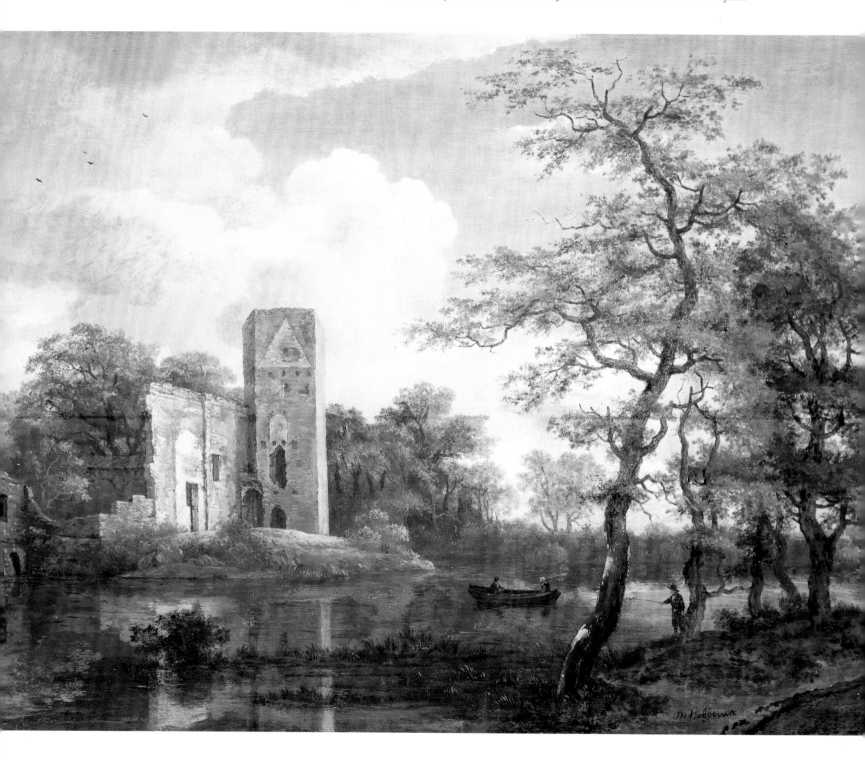

ORIGINALLY NAMED Meindert Lubbertszoon, Hobbema studied under Jacob van Ruysdael in his native city. They were close friends and often painted the same subjects; as Hobbema lacked his master's genius in raising the dramatic temperature in his landscapes, Hobbema languished in his shadow. This must also have been the attitude of the picture-buying public at the time, for eventually Hobbema was obliged to forsake painting and work as an excise man, an arduous occupation that left him little time or inclination for art. While it is true that many of his paintings are not particularly distinguished Hobbema at his best could be sublime, and in recent times his painting has been the subject of considerable re-appraisal. It is generally recognized that his greatest achievement was *The Avenue, Middelharnis* – deceptively simple, yet a painting of immense subtlety and complex detail.

Samuel Cooper   Miniature of James II as the Duke of York, 1661

Born 1609 London, England   Painted in London   Died 1672 London
MOVEMENT: English Miniaturists   **OTHER WORKS:** *John Aubrey, Mrs Pepys, Self Portrait*   **INFLUENCES:** John Hoskins

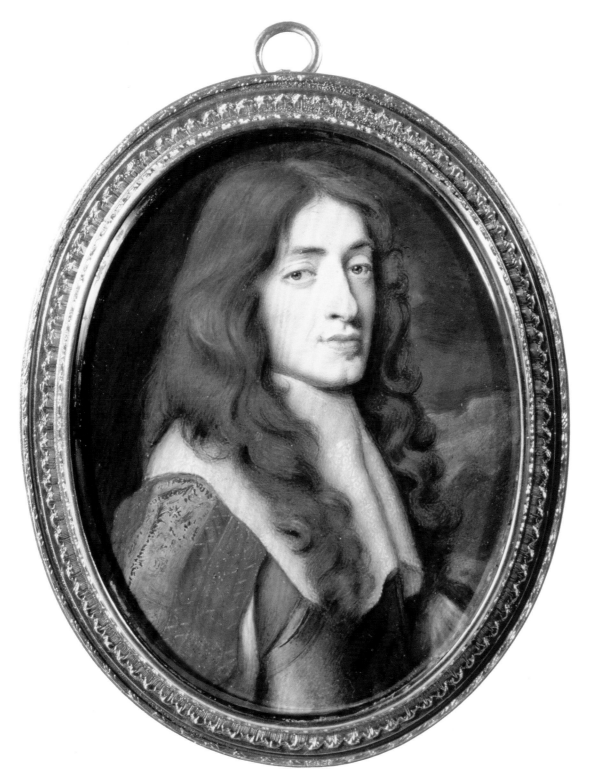

SAMUEL COOPER is often regarded as the greatest painter of miniatures who ever lived; certainly he was instrumental in raising the status of miniature painting to new heights. He learned his skills from his uncle, John Hoskins. Pepys mentions Cooper frequently in his diaries and noted that he was a fine musician and a good linguist in addition to his artistic talents. He lived through turbulent times and had the distinction of holding official appointments both under the Commonwealth and later the Crown following the Restoration of 1660. He painted several portraits of both Oliver Cromwell and King Charles II, including the effigy of the King used for the coinage. As well as miniatures, painted on ivory or fine parchment, he was also a prolific draughtsman, his collection of chalk drawings being preserved in the Oxford University gallery.

Bartolomé Estebán Murillo   Immaculate Conception, 1661

Born 1618 Seville, Spain   Painted in Seville   Died 1682 Seville

MOVEMENT: Spanish School   **OTHER WORKS:** *The Immaculate Conception of the Escorial*   **INFLUENCES:** Juan de Castillo, Velázquez

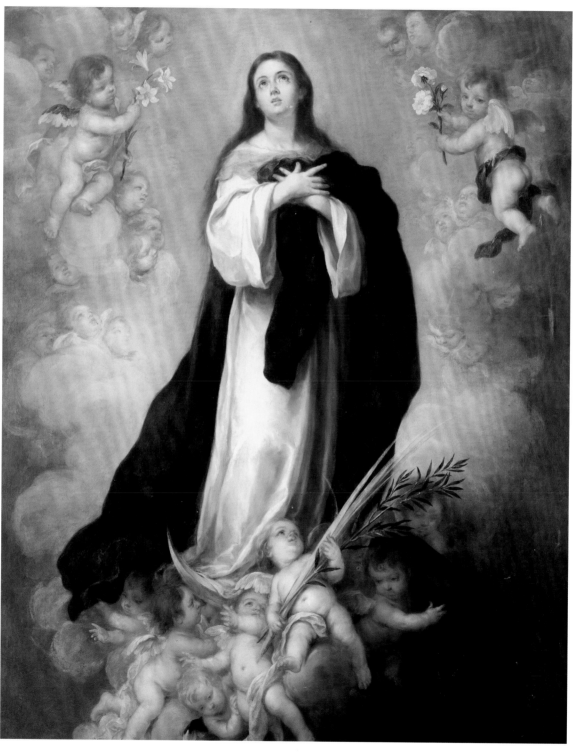

A GREAT master of sentimental religious paintings, Bartolomé Estebán Murillo received his brief artistic training from Juan de Castillo, but when his master moved to Cadiz Murillo scraped a living by painting cheap religious daubs, hawked at public fairs. It was an inauspicious start for the man who would co-found the Seville Academy in 1660 and become its first president. His career took off in 1648 when he went to Madrid and met his fellow townsman Velázquez, who not only helped him but also introduced his work to the royal court. Many of his earlier paintings were portraits of Franciscan saints, executed for the Franciscan monastery in Seville, but he went on to produce numerous works of a more general religious nature. In addition he produced many genre subjects, such as beggars, street urchins, fruit-sellers and other aspects of low life which reflect the hardships of his youth. He died from injuries sustained in a fall from scaffolding while painting an altarpiece at Cadiz in 1682.

Salomon van Ruysdael A Wooded Landscape with Cattle and Drovers on, 1663

Born *c.* 1600 Holland   Painted in Haarlem, Holland   Died 1670 Haarlem

MOVEMENT: Dutch School   **OTHER WORKS:** *Pellekussenpoort, Utrecht, Still Life*   **INFLUENCES:** Esaias van de Velde, Jan van Goyen

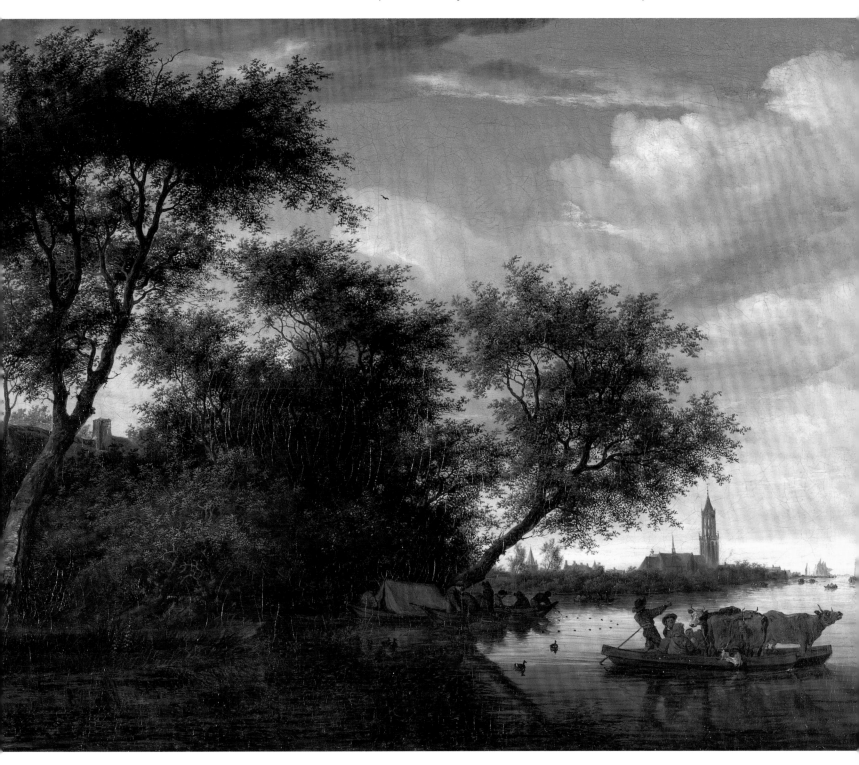

BORN AT Naarden in Gooiland, Salomon Jacobsz van Ruysdael was originally Salomon de Gooyer, but he and his brother Isaack (1599–77) adopted the name 'Ruysdael' from a castle near their father's home. Salomon joined the painters' guild at Haarlem in 1623, becoming Dean in 1648. From 1651 he also had a business supplying blue dyes to the Haarlem

bleachworks. His earliest dated works belong to 1626 and within two years of this his reputation as a landscape painter was assured. Although he remained in Haarlem all his life, he made occasional forays to other parts of the Netherlands in search of landscape subjects, noted for their fine tonal qualities, and laying the foundations for the great paintings of his

much more famous nephew Jacob van Ruysdael. As well as his tranquil landscapes and river scenes, he produced a number of still-life paintings towards the end of his career.

137

Jan Vermeer   Girl with a Pearl Earring, *c.*1665–6

Born 1632 Delft, Holland   Painted in Delft   Died 1675 Delft

MOVEMENT: Dutch School   **OTHER WORKS:** *Lady Seated at a Virginal, The Painter in his Studio, View of Delft* **INFLUENCES:** Carel Fabritius

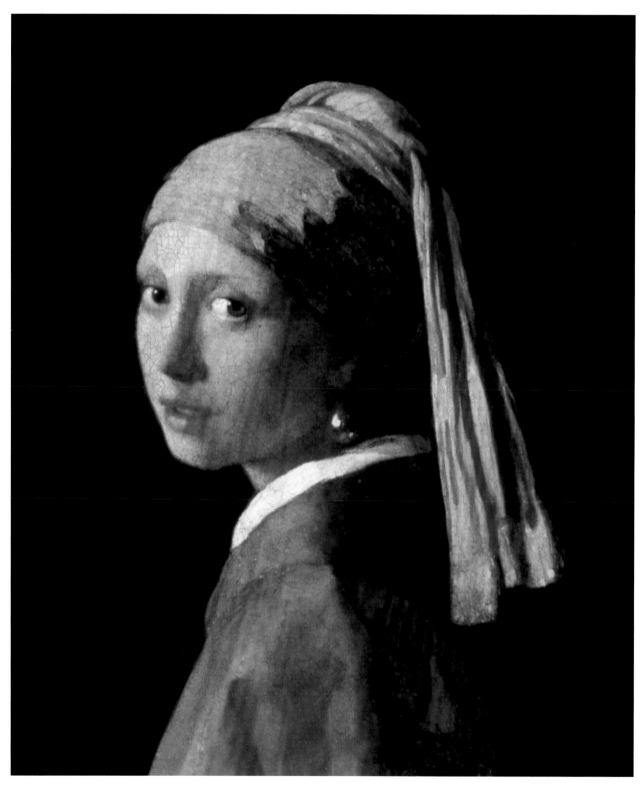

JAN VERMEER studied painting under Carel Fabritius. In 1653 he entered the Guild of St Luke taking the role of head there in 1662 and 1670. Diffident and a poor businessman, he died young, leaving a widow and eight children destitute. He was almost entirely forgotten until 1860, when he was rediscovered and works which had previously been attributed to other artists were properly identified as coming from his brush. He specialized in small paintings of domestic scenes, distinguished by their perspective and clever use of light to create subtle tones, as well as the fact that, unusual for the time, the figures in them are self-absorbed. Only about 40 paintings have definitely been credited to him, but they are sufficient to establish him as one of the more original and innovative painters of his time – second only to Rembrandt.

Ogata Korin Pampas Grass

Born 1658 Edo (now Tokyo) Painted in Edo Died 1716 Edo
MOVEMENT: Rinpa School of Japanese Decorative Painting **OTHER WORKS:** *Irises, Birds, White and Red Prunus in the Spring* **INFLUENCES:** Honami Koetsu, Tawaraya Sotatsu

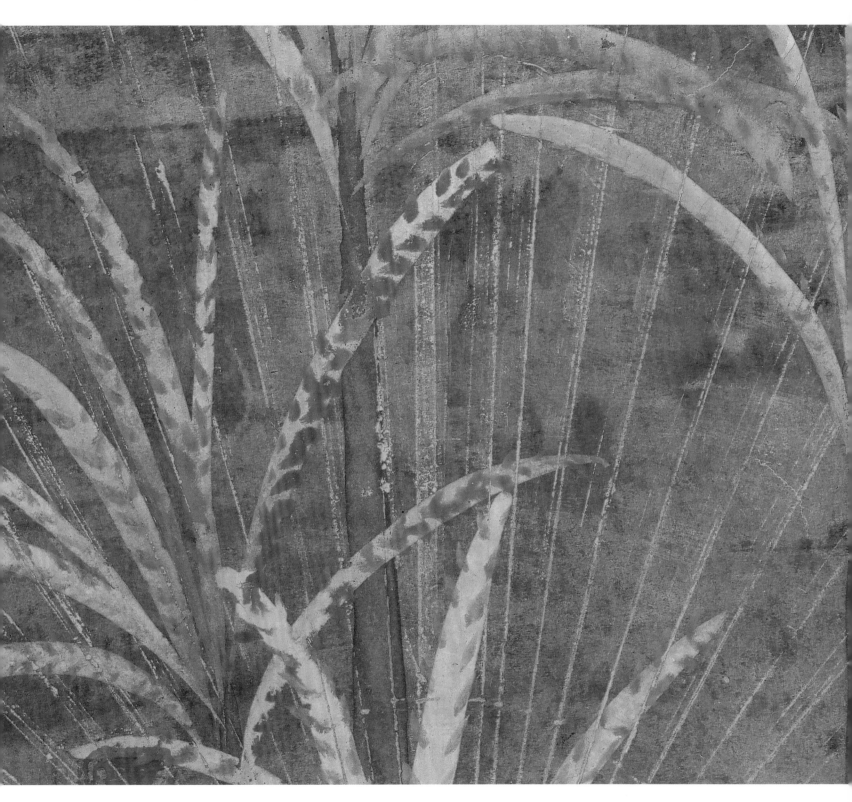

BORN AT Edo (now Tokyo), Ogata Korin came from an upper-middle-class Japanese merchant family, noted for their wealth and ostentation. He was once reprimanded by the court for flamboyant extravagance when at a party he wrote verses on gold leaf and floated them down a stream. He represented the rise of the merchant class in the Genroku era (1688–1703), which resulted in a distinctive culture and art forms. His paintings were carefully constructed and his brushwork shows great discipline, characterized by precise delineation and the even distribution of colour. His great masterpieces are the pair of six-fold screens featuring irises now preserved in the Nezu Art Museum, Tokyo. Like his kinsman and predecessor Koetsu, Korin worked in lacquer and ceramics as well as paint, producing boxes for writing implements or the tea ceremony, with delicate figure compositions worked in gold.

Rachel Ruysch A Carnation Morning Glory with Other Flowers, *c.* 1695

Born 1664 Amsterdam, Holland Painted in Amsterdam Died 1750 Amsterdam
MOVEMENT: Dutch School **OTHER WORKS:** *Still Life of Flowers* **INFLUENCES:** Willem Kalf, Vermeer

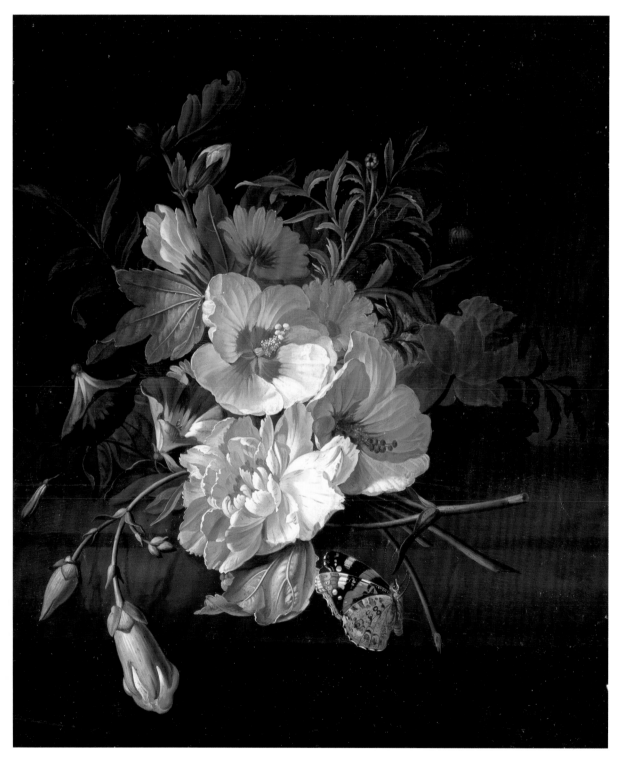

RACHEL RUYSCH had a conventional art education in the Classicist tradition, but was strongly influenced by Willem Kalf and Jan Vermeer – not only in the techniques of light and shade, but also in subject matter. Nevertheless she added her own distinctive contribution to the art of the still life, specializing in bouquets or vases of flowers made more interesting by the subtle inclusion of bees, butterflies or other insects. The vivid colours of the blossom contrasted with the muted tones of the backgrounds, which often featured classical buildings. She excelled in the painting of crystal vases, which positively sparkle and exquisitely set off the flowers, whose meticulous detail gives them an intensely realistic appearance and explains the popularity of Ruysch's work right up to the present time. Floral paintings were very fashionable in Holland in the late seventeenth and early eighteenth centuries, symbolizing the brevity of all life that is doomed to death and decay. Ruysch's bouquets have a sumptuous quality that has become timeless. She spent her entire life in Amsterdam.

Andrea Pozzo   The Entry of St Ignatius into Paradise, *c.*1707

Born 1642 Trento, Italy   Painted in Mondovi, Rome and Vienna   Died 1709 Vienna
MOVEMENT: Italian Baroque   **OTHER WORKS:** *St Francis Xavier Preaching, Investiture of St Francesco Borgia*   **INFLUENCES:** Andrea Sacchi, Pietro da Cortona, Bernini

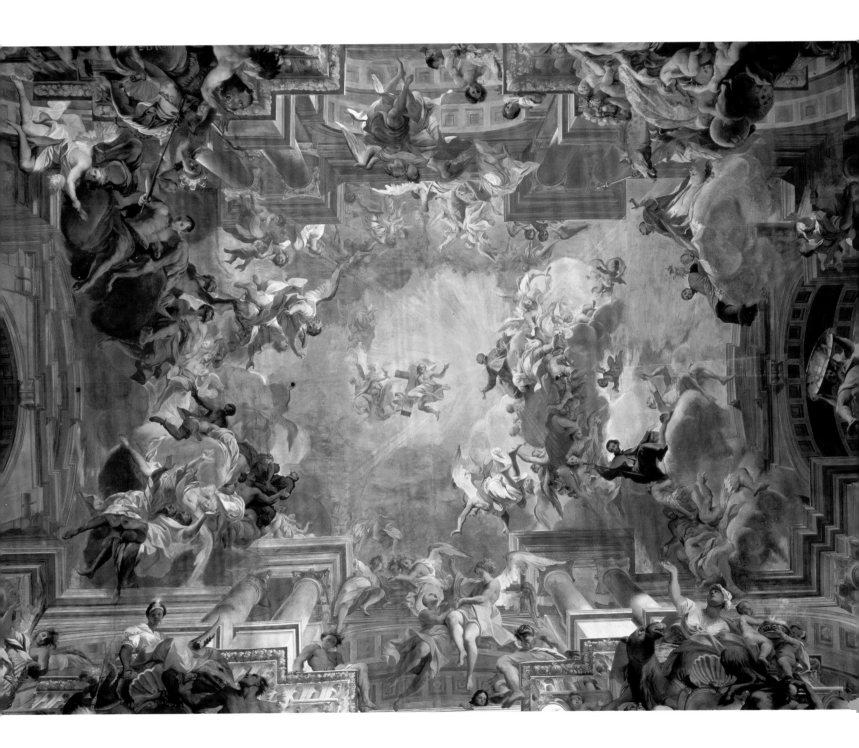

ONE OF the most brilliant painters and architects of his generation, Andrea Pozzo was the pupil of an unknown master whom he accompanied to Milan, where he became a Jesuit lay brother. In this connection he was responsible for the decorations of religious festivals and from this graduated to theatrical sets. In 1676 he painted the frescoes for the church of San Francisco Saverio in Modovi, a masterpiece of *trompe l'oeil*. This was a foretaste of his greatest illusionistic masterpiece, the ceiling of the church of Sant'Ignazio which, by an ingenious use of perspective, appears to expand the interior by hundreds of feet. In this immense achievement he united his talents as painter, architect and sculptor to great effect. In 1695 he designed the elaborate tomb of Ignatius Loyola, founder of the Society of Jesus. He worked on the decoration of many other churches in Italy and from 1703 onwards was similarly employed in Vienna.

Jean–Antoine Watteau   Les Plaisir du Bal, *c.*1714

Born 1684 France   Painted in Valenciennes and Paris   Died 1721 Nogent-sur-Marne, France
MOVEMENT: French School   **OTHER WORKS:** *The Music Party, Embarkation for the Isle of Cythera*   **INFLUENCES:** Claude Audran, David Teniers

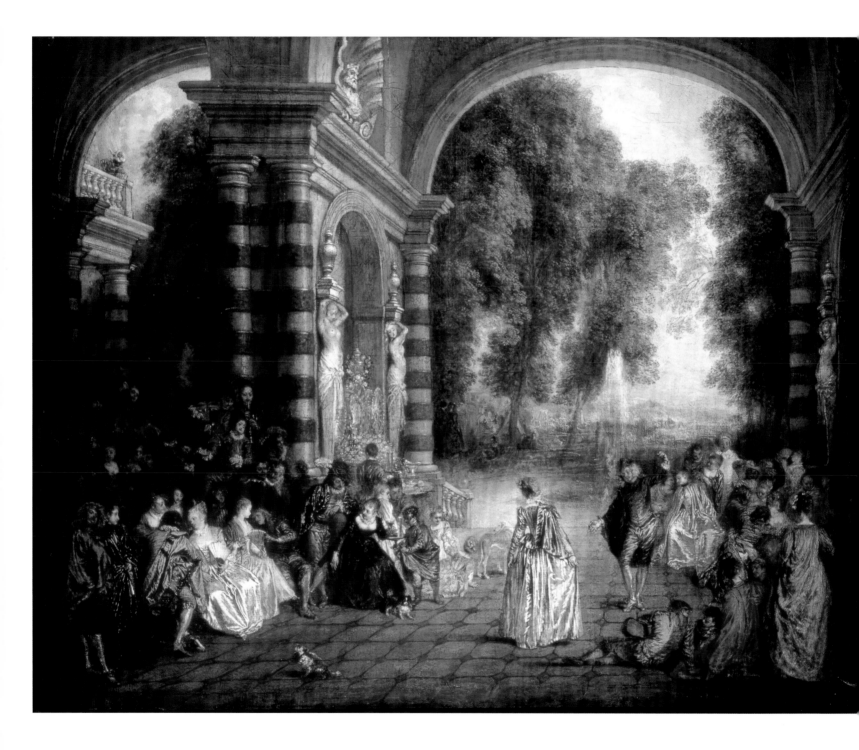

JEAN-ANTOINE WATTEAU studied under Gérin but learned more from the paintings of Ostade and Teniers. On his master's death, Watteau went to Paris, where he worked for the scene-painter Métayer and then in a factory where he turned out cheap religious pictures by the dozen. He was rescued from this drudgery by Claude Gillot and later worked under Claude Audran. The turning point came when he won second prize in a Prix de Rome competition (1709). He became an associate of the Academy in 1712 and a full member in 1717. He led the revolt against the pompous classicism of the Louis XIV period, and broke new ground with his realism and lively imagination. His early works were mainly military subjects, but later he concentrated on rustic idylls which were very fashionable in the early eighteenth century.

HuaYan   Falcon Hunting Prey, 1726

Born 1682 near Yangzhou, China   Painted in Yangzhou   Died 1756 Yangzhou
MOVEMENT: Chinese Eccentric School **OTHER WORKS:** *The Red Bird* **INFLUENCES:** Wang Fu, Badashanren, Shi Tao

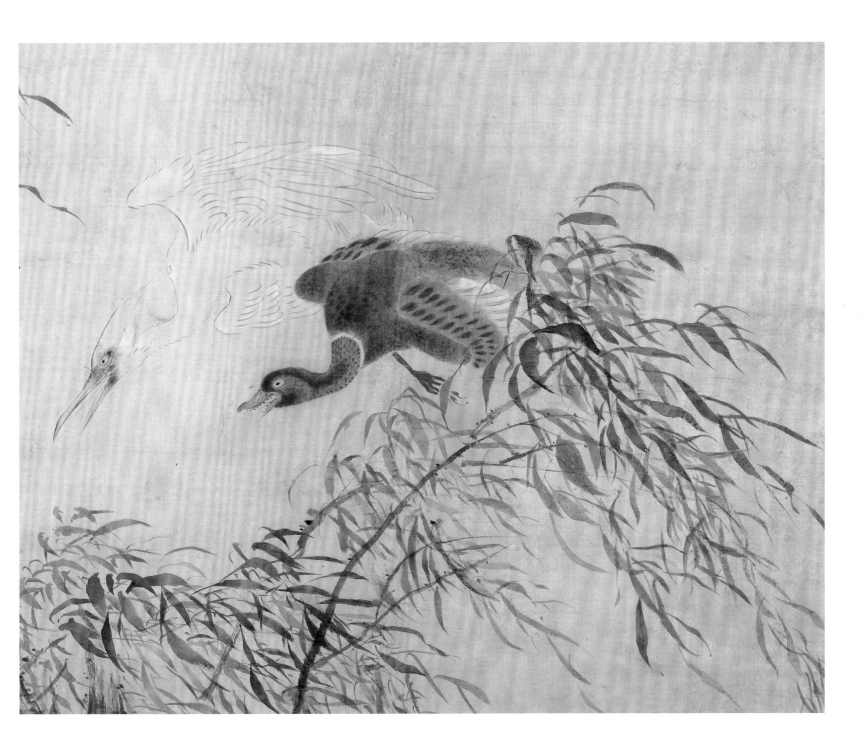

HUA YAN painted horses and figures, usually set in misty or windy weather. This created an atmospheric sense which was very rare in Chinese painting prior to that time, but had immense impact on the artists of the eighteenth and nineteenth centuries. His paintings evoked a realism and immediacy that was radically opposed to the timeless quality for which the painters of the classical tradition invariably strove. Hua Yan was one of the new generation of artists who were not employed in court circles and were thus free from the constraints of their predecessors, and therefore known as the Eccentrics. His works appealed to the rising middle classes of China and, unlike the dilettante artists in court circles, he had a keen sense of the value of his paintings. They found a ready market and he apparently made a fortune from the small pictures which he turned out in vast quantities.

William Hogarth   Beggars Opera, 1728–31

Born 1697 London, England   Painted in London   Died 1764 London

MOVEMENT: English School   **OTHER WORKS:** *Marriage à la Mode, Industry and Idleness, Garrick as Richard III*   **INFLUENCES:** Sir James Thornhill

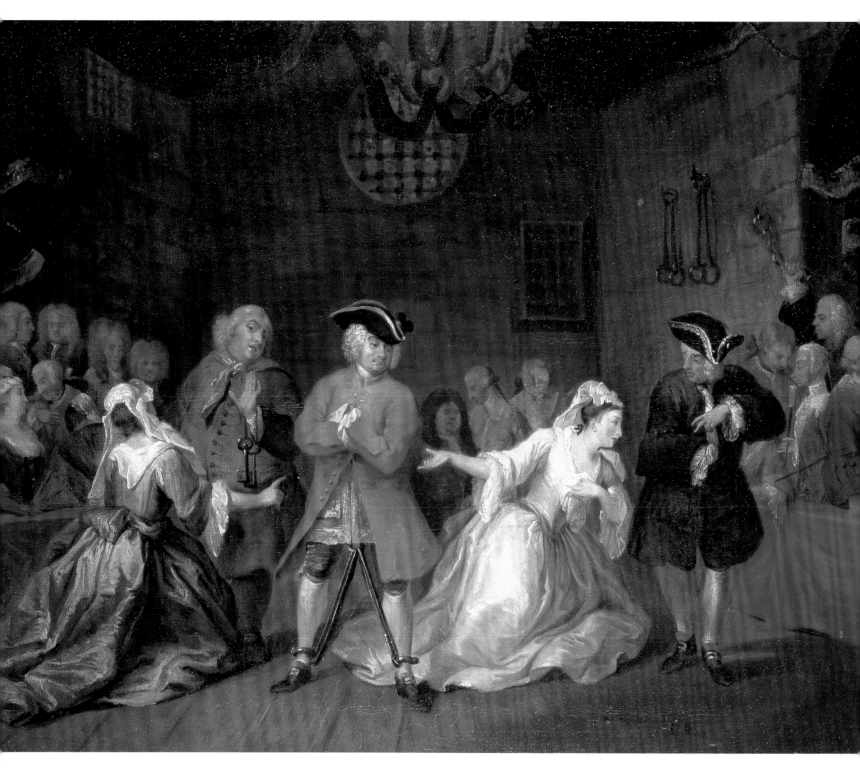

WILLIAM HOGARTH became the greatest English satirical artist of his generation. He was apprenticed to a silver-plate engraver, Ellis Gamble, and established his own business in 1720. Seeking to diversify into the more lucrative business of copper-plate engraving, however he took lessons in draughtsmanship under Sir James Thornhill. His early work consisted mainly of ornamental bill-heads and business cards, but by 1724 he was designing plates for booksellers and from this he progressed to individual prints, before turning to portrait painting by 1730. Within a few years he had begun to concentrate on the great satirical works on which his reputation now rests. His canvasses are absolutely crammed with figures and minute detail, sub-plots and side issues to the main theme. Following a visit to Paris in 1743 he produced several prints of low life and moral subjects. He also executed a number of portraits and oils of genre subjects.

Jean–Baptiste–Siméon Chardin   Still Life with Fowl, 1731

Born 1699 Painted in France Died 1779

MOVEMENT: Still life and genre **OTHER WORKS:** *Saying Grace, The Brioche* **INFLUENCES:** Nicolaes Maes, Jean-Baptiste Oudry

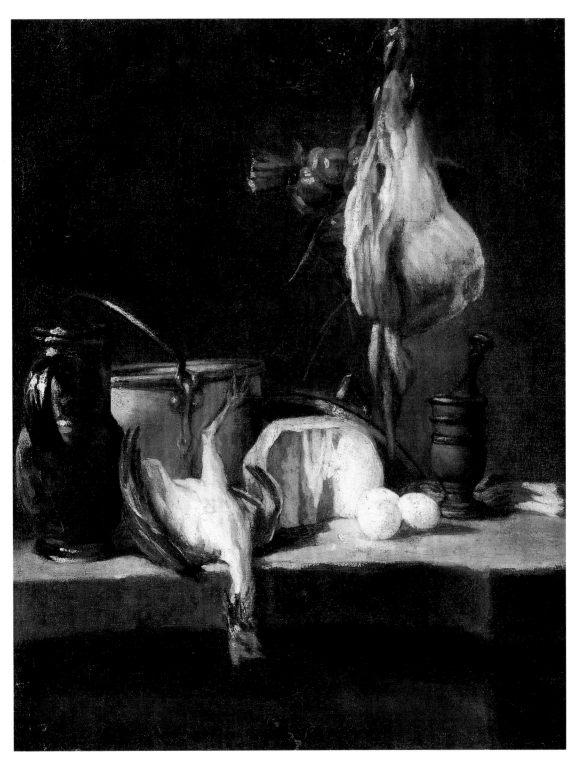

FRENCH PAINTER, specializing in still life and genre scenes. Chardin was born in Paris, where he spent most of his life. His father was a carpenter and, initially, he seemed destined to follow this trade, until his aptitude for painting became apparent. As a youth, Chardin trained under two very minor history painters, Pierre Cazes and Noel-Nicolas Coypel, but his real education came from copying Dutch and Flemish paintings in private art collections. These prompted him to concentrate on still-life pictures – a brave decision, since this type of painting had a low reputation and was very poorly paid.

Despite these drawbacks, Chardin's career flourished. In 1728, *The Skate* won such acclaim at a Paris exhibition that he was invited to become a full member of the Academy, an unprecedented honor for a still-life artist. Chardin was delighted and became a stalwart of the institution, holding the post of Treasurer for 20 years. Even so, he found it hard to make a living and, accordingly, extended his repertoire to include simple domestic scenes. These wonderful vignettes of everyday life displayed none of the affectation of the prevailing Rococo style, and proved enormously popular with the public.

Canaletto Grand Canal, *c.*1740

Born 1697 Venice, Italy   Painted in Venice and London   Died 1768 Venice
MOVEMENT: Venetian School   **OTHER WORKS:** *Piazza San Marco, Regatta on the Grand Canal*   **INFLUENCES:** Tiepolo

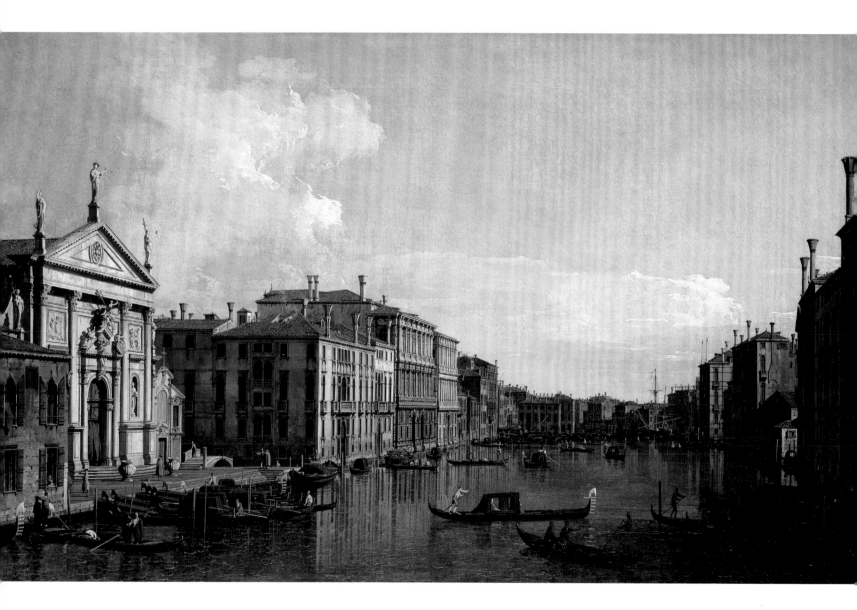

ORIGINALLY NAMED Giovanni Antonio Canale, Canaletto was the son of a scene-painter in whose footsteps he at first followed. In 1719 he went to Rome to study architecture and on his return to Venice he began painting those great architectural masterpieces with which he has been associated ever since. Although most of his paintings illustrate the buildings and canals of his native city – executed as souvenirs for wealthy patrons from England making the Grand Tour – he lived mainly in London from 1746 to 1753. This is reflected in his paintings of the Thames and the City, and other views in the Home Counties. He then returned to Venice where he became a member of the Academy in 1763. He established a style of architectural painting that was widely imitated by the next generation of Italian artists, notably Francesco Guardi and his own nephew Bernardo Bellotto, who slavishly imitated him and even signed his works 'Canaletto'.

Francesco Guardi   Still Life

Born 1712 Venice, Italy   Painted in Venice   Died 1793, Venice
MOVEMENT: Venetian School   **OTHER WORKS:** *Masquerade in the Ridotto*   **INFLUENCES:** Canaletto

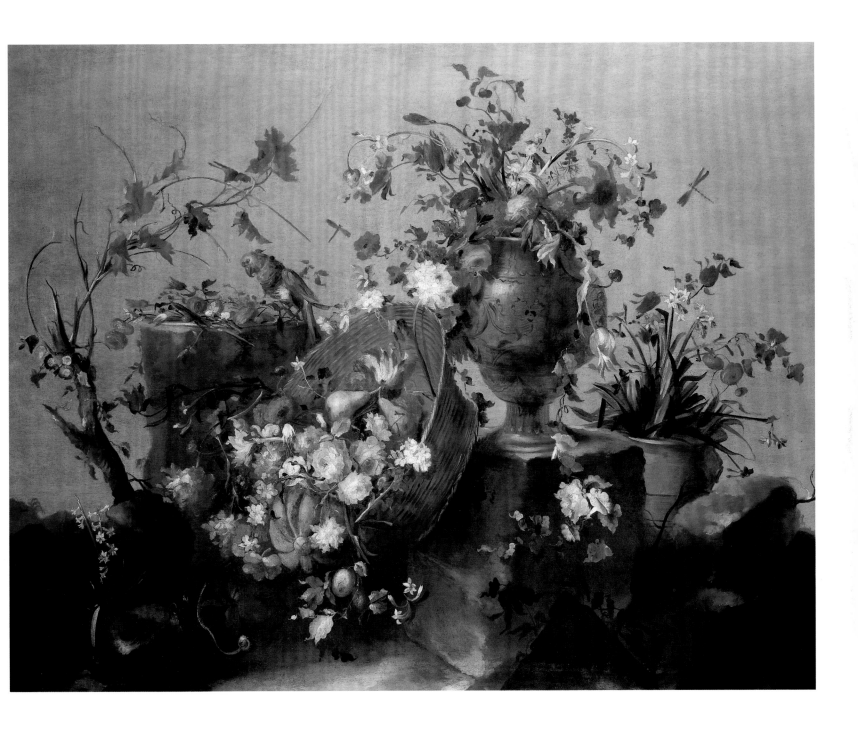

FRANCESCO GUARDI was a near-contemporary of Canaletto and probably also studied under him; certainly the latter's influence was strongly evident in Guardi's numerous paintings of Venetian scenes, but exceeding his master in his deft handling of lighting effects and above all his application of dazzling colours. Apart from his landscapes, Guardi excelled in interiors and architectural subjects, although he was also a master of the large and majestic subject, notably his paintings of great contemporary spectacles such as the Doge embarking in his state barge or the early balloon ascents of fellow-Venetian Vincenzo Lunardi. Guardi departed from the mathematical precision of Canaletto and developed a more impressionistic approach, anticipating the paintings of Turner.

Guardi also produced a number of religious works in collaboration with his brother Giovanni. His brother-in-law was Giovanni Battista Tiepolo.

François Boucher   (attr.) La Cible D'Amour (Love Target), 1758

Born 1703, Paris   Painted in France and Italy   Died 1770

MOVEMENT: Rococo **OTHER WORKS:** *The Triumph of Venus, Mademoiselle O'Murphy,* **INFLUENCES:** Watteau, Abraham Bloemaert, François Lemoyne

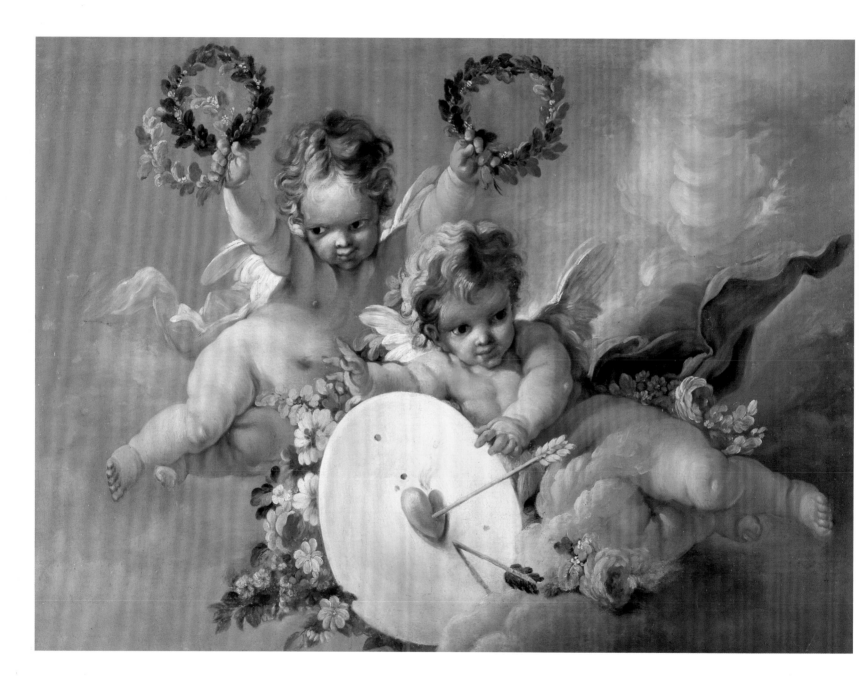

FRENCH PAINTER and designer, one of the greatest masters of the Rococo style. Born in Paris, Boucher was the son of a versatile, not particularly successful, artist and craftsman. As a result, he learned a wide variety of artistic techniques in his father's workshop before training more formally under François Lemoyne. Boucher's first significant job was to produce a set of engravings after Watteau's drawings, but he also found time to paint, winning the Prix de Rome in 1723. After making the traditional study-tour of Italy (1727–31), he began to gain official plaudits for his work. In 1735 he was granted his first royal commission and this secured his position as a court artist. This role governed the nature of Boucher's art. There were no grand, intellectual themes or moral dramas in his pictures. Instead, he painted light-hearted mythologies and pastoral idylls, which could serve equally well as paintings, tapestry designs or porcelain decoration. This is also evident in Boucher's work for his most distinguished patron, Madame de Pompadour. He immortalized her in a series of dazzling portraits, but also decorated her palace and designed sets for her private theatre.

Joseph Wright   An Experiment on a Bird in the Air Pump, 1768

Born 1734 Derby, England   Painted in Derby   Died 1797 Derby

MOVEMENT: British School **OTHER WORKS:** *The Air Pump, A Philosopher Giving a Lecture on the Orrery* **INFLUENCES:** Gerrit van Honthorst

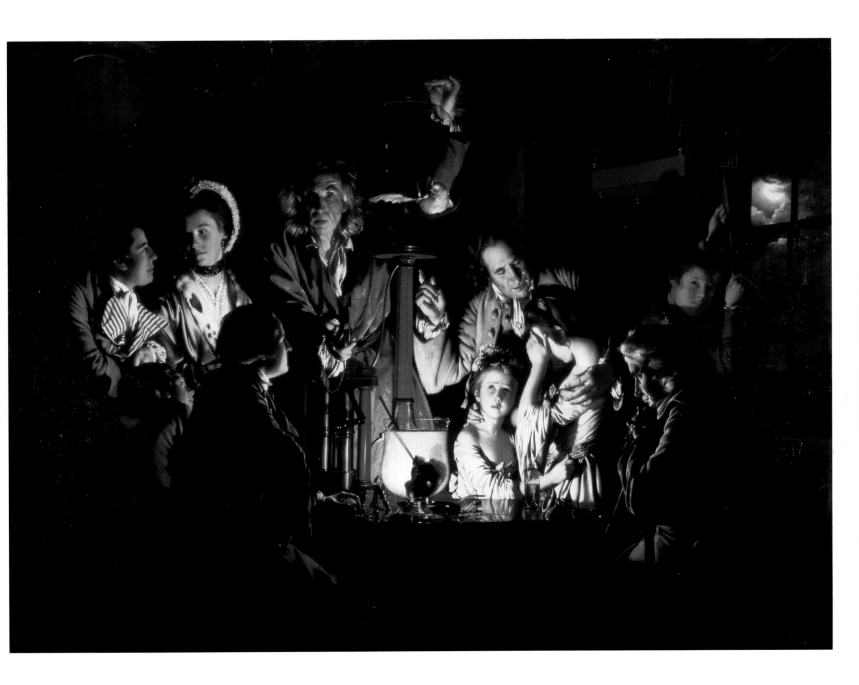

KNOWN AS Wright of Derby because he spent his entire life in that town, Joseph Wright was the first English painter of any significance to work in the provinces, although even he had to go to London for his formal art education. He established his own studio, where he flourished as a portraitist, and it was probably as a result of his contact with the rising industrialists of the 1760s and 1770s, such as Richard Arkwright and Josiah Wedgwood (whose portraits he painted), that his career eventually changed direction quite dramatically. Wright, in fact, was the artist of the Industrial Revolution, the right man in the right place at the right time, and it is for his spectacular canvasses depicting the wonders of modern science and technology in their infancy that he is chiefly remembered. His attention to the details of machinery was matched by his uncanny mastery of artificial lighting, which he used to good effect.

Thomas Gainsborough   Portrait of David Garrick, exhibited 1770

Born 1727 England   Painted in England   Died 1788

MOVEMENT: Rococo **OTHER WORKS:** *The Morning Walk, The Painter's Daughters Chasing a Butterfly* **INFLUENCES:** Hubert Gravelot, Van Dyck, Francis Hayman

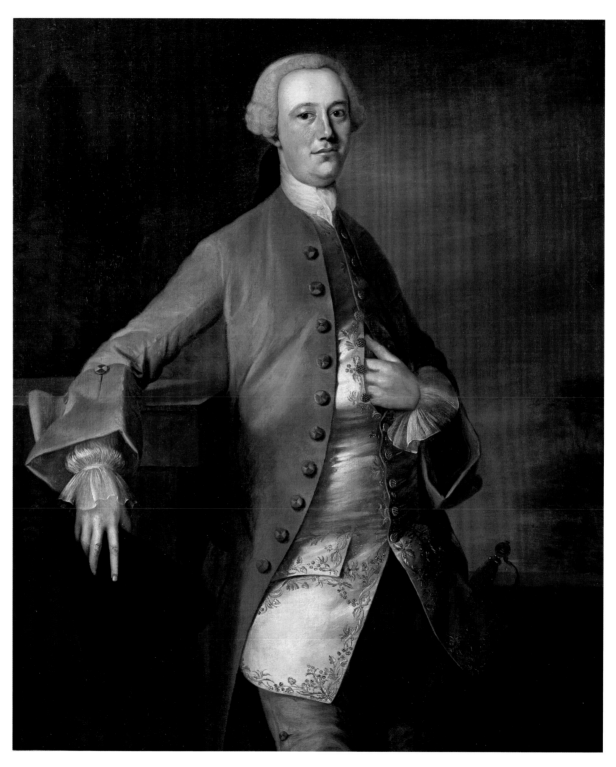

BORN IN Sudbury, Suffolk Gainsborough displayed precocious artistic skills. According to family legend, he helped catch a pear-thief in a neighbour's orchard by accurately sketching the culprit. Recognizing his obvious talent, his family sent him to London at the age of 13, where he was trained by the French Rococo artist Hubert Gravelot. In 1745, Gainsborough set up in business hoping to make a living selling landscapes, but the venture failed and he returned to Suffolk. Gainsborough preferred landscapes to 'face-painting', but found that portraiture was far more profitable. With this in mind, he eventually moved from Suffolk to the fashionable resort of Bath, where he was employed by a rich and illustrious clientele. Here, Gainsborough honed his skills to perfection, often painting by candlelight, in order to give his brushwork its distinctive, flickering appearance. By 1768, he was so famous that he was invited to become one of the founder members of the Royal Academy. Gainsborough accepted, and spent the final years of his career in London, vying with Reynolds for supremacy in the field of portraiture.

Jean–Honoré Fragonard   The Swing

Born 1732 France   Painted in France and Italy   Died 1806
MOVEMENT: Rococo **OTHER WORKS:** *The Progress of Love, The Bolt, The Love Letter* **INFLUENCES:** François Boucher, Hubert Robert, Tiepolo

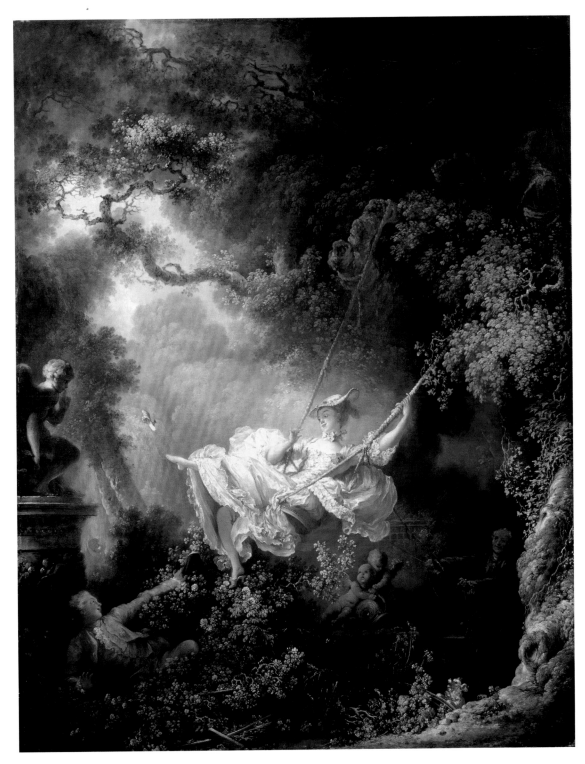

FRENCH PAINTER a leading exponent of the light-hearted Rococo style. Fragonard trained under Boucher (Madame de Pompadour's favourite artist) and won the Prix de Rome, both of which seemed to mark him out for a conventional career as a history painter. But he was too ill-disciplined to enjoy the business of copying Old Masters and his studies in Rome (1756–60) did not progress well. Instead, the

Italian countryside awakened Fragonard's interest in landscape painting while, on his return to France, the success of *The Swing* led his art in a different direction. *The Swing* demonstrated Fragonard's undoubted gift for playful eroticism, and it brought him a series of commissions for similar 'boudoir' pictures. Patrons were attracted by his dazzling, vivacious style and by his innate sense of taste, which strayed close to

the margins of decency, but never crossed them. In this sense, Fragonard became the archetypal painter of the Ancien Régime and ultimately shared its fate. By the 1780s, Neoclassicism had all but supplanted the Rococo style and, although he received help from David after the Revolution (1789), Fragonard's later years were marred by poverty and neglect.

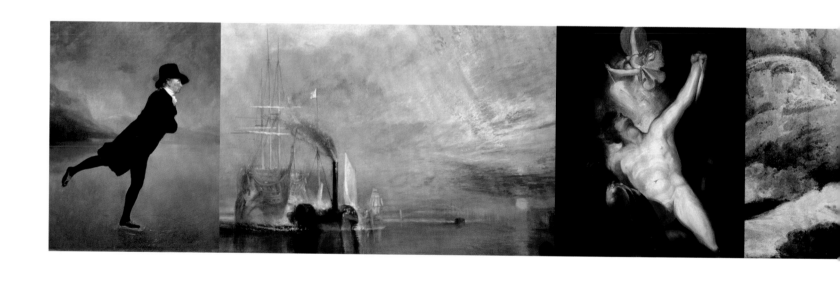

The Neoclassism & Romanticism Era
The Neoclassism & Romanticism Era
The Neoclassism & Romanticism Era
The Neoclassism & Romanticism Era
The Neoclassism & Romanticism Era
The Neoclassism & Romanticism Era
The Neoclassism & Romanticism Era
The Neoclassism & Romanticism Era
The Neoclassism & Romanticism Era
The Neoclassism & Romanticism Era
The Neoclassism & Romanticism Era
The Neoclassism & Romanticism Era
The Neoclassism & Romanticism Era
The Neoclassism & Romanticism Era
The Neoclassism & Romanticism Era

The Neoclassicism & Romanticism Era

The Neoclassism & Romanticism Era

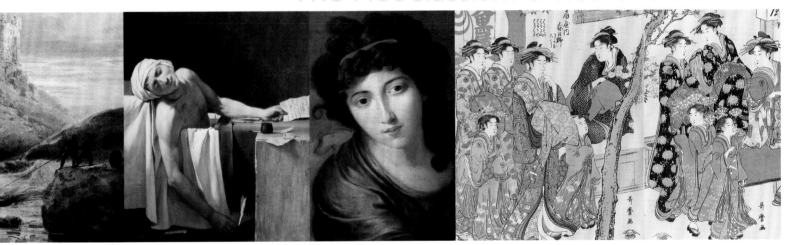

The Neoclassism & Romanticism Era
The Neoclassism & Romanticism Era
The Neoclassism & Romanticism Era
The Neoclassism & Romanticism Era
The Neoclassism & Romanticism Era
The Neoclassism & Romanticism Era
The Neoclassism & Romanticism Era
The Neoclassism & Romanticism Era
The Neoclassism & Romanticism Era

Allan Ramsay   Portrait of Sir Edward and Lady Turner, 1740

Born 1713 Edinburgh   Painted in Edinburgh, London, Rome and Paris   Died 1784 Dover, England
MOVEMENT: British School of Portraiture   **OTHER WORKS:** *Queen Charlotte and her Children, David Hume*   **INFLUENCES:** François Boucher, Pompeo Batoni

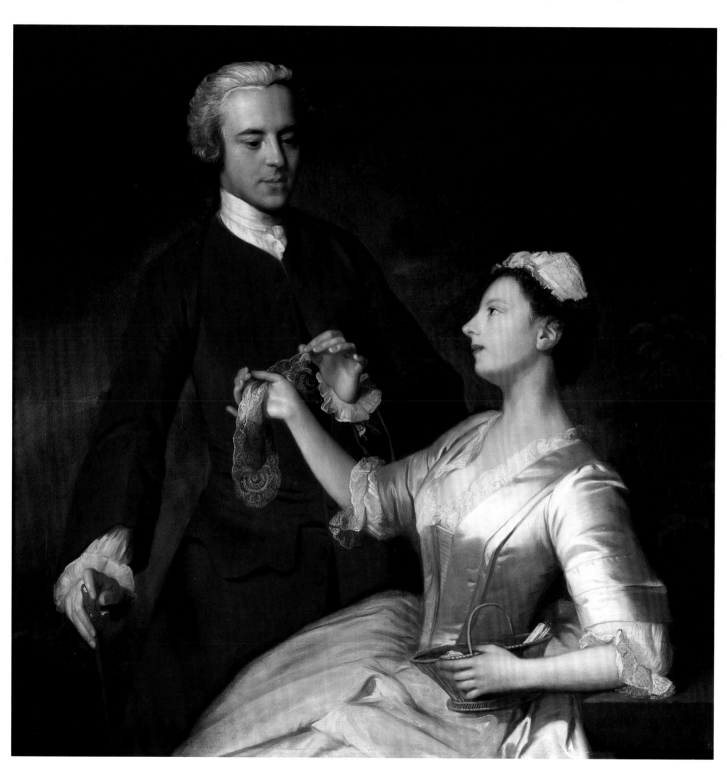

THE SON of the celebrated Scottish poet of the same name, Allan Ramsay was raised in Edinburgh and was one of the best-educated and most intellectual artists in Europe in his day. He trained in Edinburgh and Rome and was influenced by Pompeo Batoni, the most fashionable of the Italian portraitists. Ramsay settled in London in 1762 and was appointed Principal Painter to King George III

in 1767. The following year he became one of the co-founders of the Royal Academy. Ramsay was one of the outstanding portrait painters of his generation, the rival of Reynolds and Gainsborough.

In his lifetime he enjoyed an international reputation for the sensitive and expressive qualities of his portraits, especially of women. However, Ramsay was not content with mere likeness but

conveyed the feelings and emotions of his subjects in a manner which had seldom been achieved before. He was a prolific artist whose canvasses are a veritable portrait gallery of British society, but include a number of European celebrities. Living in the shadow of his father, Ramsay had literary ambitions and published a number of polemical and philosophical essays.

Sir Joshua Reynolds   George Townshend

Born 1723 England   Painted in London, England   Died 1792 London
MOVEMENT: English School   **OTHER WORKS:** *Nelly O'Brien, Samuel Johnson*   **INFLUENCES:** Thomas Hudson, Sir Peter Lely

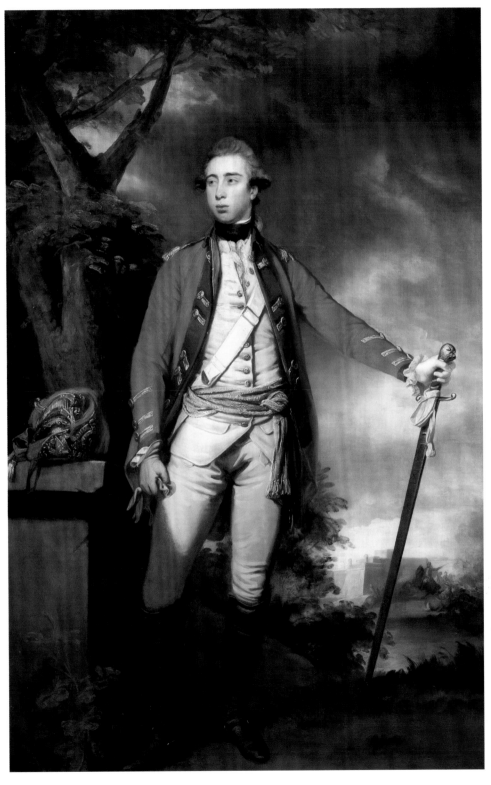

BORN IN Plympton, Devon, Joshua Reynolds was apprenticed in London to Thomas Hudson, a second-rate portrait painter, from whom he learned the rudiments of his craft. In 1743 Reynolds settled in Plymouth, but in 1744 he returned to London where his portrait of Captain John Hamilton, brought him recognition. Reynolds spent two years in Rome perfecting his technique, then visited other Italian art centres, before returning to England in 1752. By 1760 he was the most fashionable portrait painter in London, becoming the first President of the Royal Academy in 1768 and knighted a year later. A prolific artist, he produced over 2,000 portraits, many of which were subsequently published as engravings that further enhanced his reputation.

Jean–Baptiste Greuze Girl with Pet Dog

Born 1725 France   Painted in France and Italy   Died 1805
MOVEMENT: Rococo, Neoclassicism **OTHER WORKS:** *A Father's Curse, Girl with a Dead Bird* **INFLUENCES:** Chardin, François Boucher, Joseph-Marie Vien

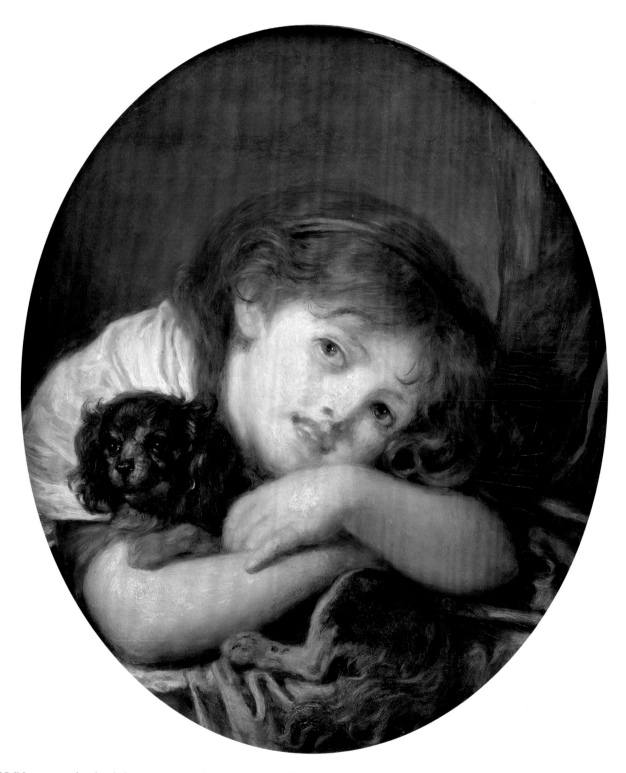

SPECIALIZING IN sentimental and melodramatic genre scenes. Greuze was taught by Grandon in Lyon, before completing his artistic training at the Académie in Paris. Apart from a brief spell in Italy (1755 –57), Greuze's career revolved around his exhibits at the Salon. There, he achieved his first notable success in 1755 and soon carved out a niche for himself. Profiting from the contemporary cult of sensibility, he created a unique combination of Dutch-style domesticity and lachrymose sentiment or sermonizing. This approach caught the mood of the times and it won the approval of the influential critic Diderot, who described Greuze's pictures as 'morality in paint'. These moralizing overtones were somewhat ironic, given that the artist's own marriage was a disaster due to the extravagance and infidelity of his wife.

The vogue for Greuze's work was short-lived. Conscious of the growing popularity of sober Neoclassical themes, he tried to emulate this in *Septimus Severus*, but the move backfired. The picture was universally mocked and Greuze was only admitted to the Academy in the demeaning category of 'genre painter'. By the time of the Revolution, he was a forgotten man.

Angelica Kauffmann   Portrait of a Lady as the Muse Enterpe

Born 1741 Switzerland   Painted in Switzerland, Rome and London   Died 1807 Rome, Italy
MOVEMENT: Rococo and Classicism   **OTHER WORKS:** *David Garrick, Joshua Reynolds Aged 48*   **INFLUENCES:** Sir Joshua Reynolds

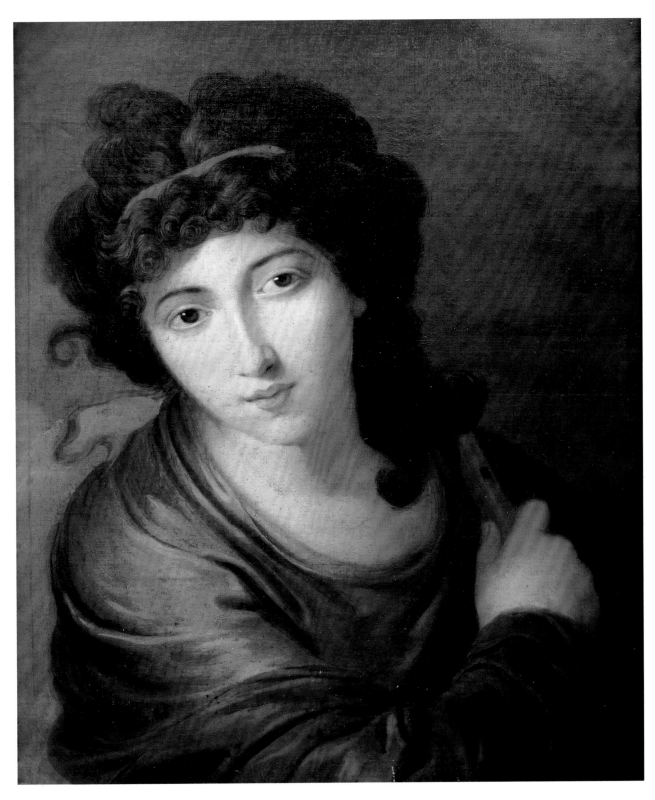

MARIA ANNA CATHARINA Angelica Kauffmann was a child prodigy, whose reputation as an artist and musician was well established by the age of eleven. Taught by her father, John Joseph Kauffmann, with whom she travelled to Italy, she developed her own highly distinctive version of Rococo portraiture. In 1766 she came to London where she was befriended by Sir Joshua Reynolds (they painted each other's portrait) and became a pillar of the artistic establishment and a founder member of the Royal Academy in 1769. In 1781 she married the Venetian artist Antonio Zucchi and returned with him to Italy soon afterwards, settling in Rome. As well as a large number of portraits, she executed a number of wall paintings for Robert Adam; she also decorated St Paul's and the Royal Academy's lecture room at Somerset House.

Benjamin West   A Group Portrait of a Lady and her two Children

Born 1738 Pennsylvania, USA   Painted in Philadelphia, New York and London   Died 1820 London
MOVEMENT: English School **OTHER WORKS:** *Self Portrait, Treaty of William Penn with the Indians* **INFLUENCES:** John Smibert, JohnWollaston

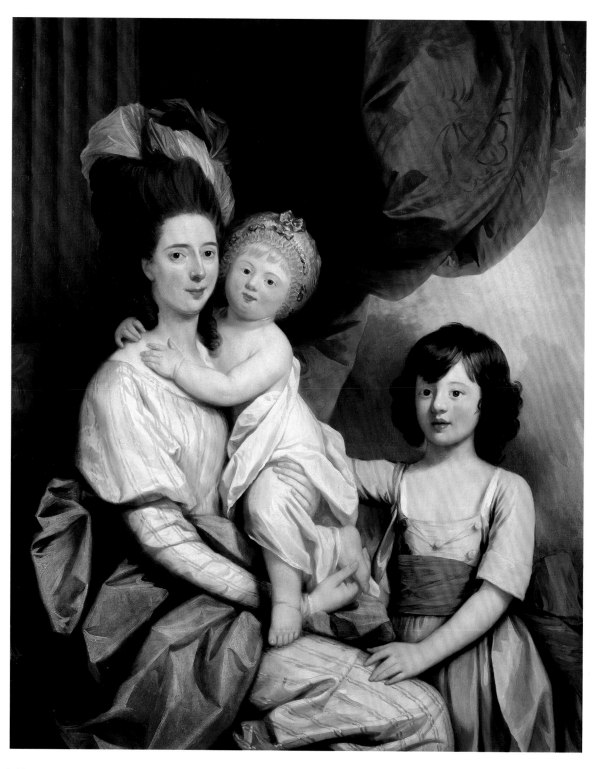

BORN AT Springfield, Pennsylvania in 1738, Benjamin West came from an old Quaker family originating in Buckinghamshire. He showed a talent for drawing when very young, and at the age of 18 settled in Philadelphia as a portrait painter. Later he worked in New York and in 1760 travelled to Italy, where he lived for almost three years. In 1763 he settled in London as a painter specializing in

historical subjects which brought him the patronage of King George III, who appointed him his historical painter in 1772. In 1768 he was one of the four artists who submitted a plan to the King for the establishment of the Royal Academy, which came to fruition the following year. In 1792 he succeeded Reynolds as President and was for many years a prominent figure in the English art establishment,

producing numerous religious, allegorical and historical works. His adoption of modern dress in his great masterpiece *The Death of General Wolfe* was an innovation in English historical painting.

John Singleton Copley   Portrait of Colonel Baker, 1781

Born 1737 Boston, USA   Painted in Boston, and London, England   Died 1815 London
MOVEMENT: English School   **OTHER WORKS:** *The Death of Major Pierson*   **INFLUENCES:** Sir Joshua Reynolds

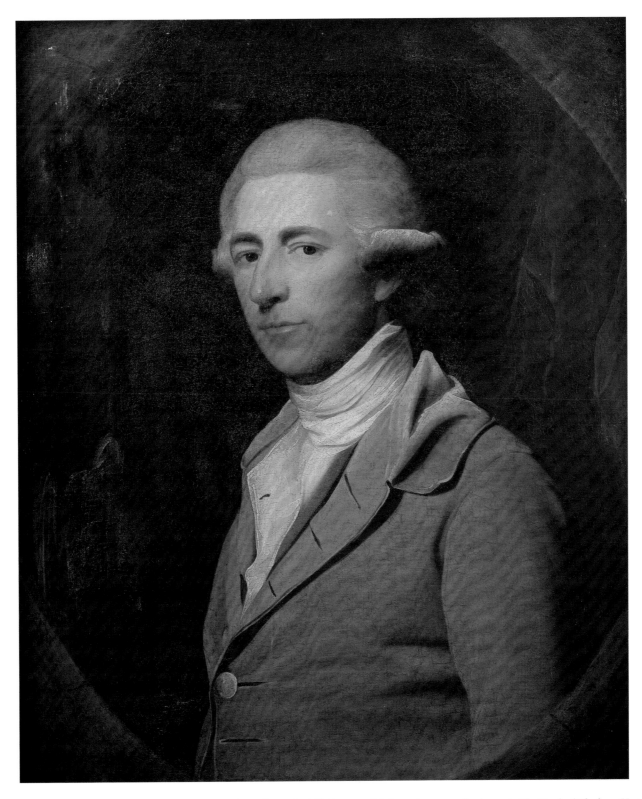

BORN AT Boston, Massachusetts of Irish parents, John Singleton Copley was self-taught as an artist but by the late 1750s had established himself as a portraitist in his native city. A small painting of a boy with a squirrel was exhibited at the Royal Society of Arts in London 1760 and helped to spread his reputation across the Atlantic. In 1774 he visited Italy, and arrived in England just as the American War of Independence was erupting. Consequently he settled in London, became an associate of the Royal Academy in 1777 and an academician in 1783 following the exhibition of his best-known work, the dramatic *The Death of Chatham*. He is esteemed on both sides of the Atlantic, for his portraits of the British royal family and for his studies of the leading political and military figures in Boston society in the late-colonial period.

Henry Fuseli (Johann Heinrich Füssli) The Birth of Sin

Born 1741 Switzerland Painted in England, Italy, Switzerland and Germany Died 1825

MOVEMENT: Romanticism **OTHER WORKS:** *Titania's Awakening, The Ladies of Hastings* **INFLUENCES:** Michelangelo, William Blake, Sir Joshua Reynolds

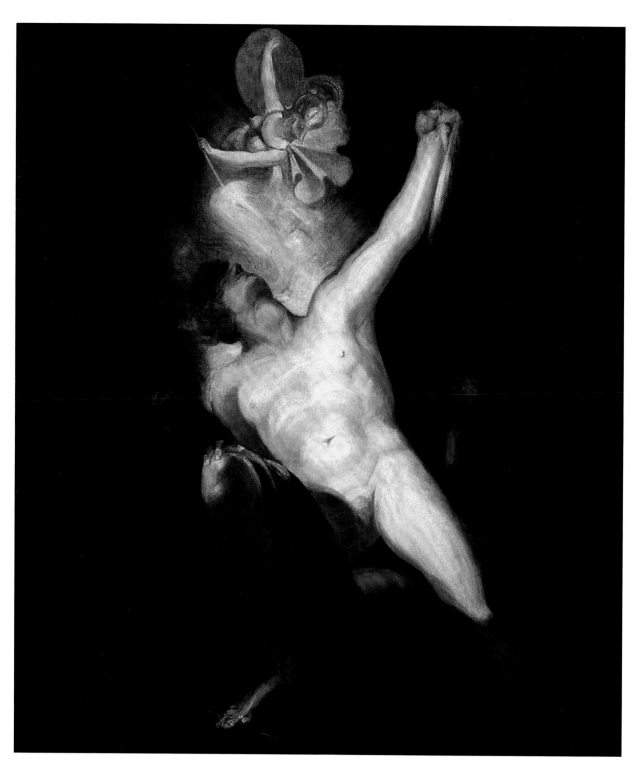

SWISS PAINTER and graphic artist; a key figure in the English Romantic movement. Born in Zurich, the son of a town clerk and amateur painter, Fuseli trained as a minister in the Swiss Reformed Church. He was ordained in 1761, but turned to art in 1768, after receiving encouragement from Sir Joshua Reynolds. Pursuing this ambition, he spent several years in Italy (1770–78), where he was impressed, above all, by

Michelangelo's vision of the Sublime – a mood which he tried to capture in many of his own paintings. In 1778, Fuseli moved to London, making this his principal artistic base. He cemented his reputation with *The Nightmare*, which was exhibited at the Royal Academy in 1782. Fuseli made several versions of this haunting image, which is undoubtedly his most famous work. Although the picture may have had a purely

personal meaning for him – the expression of his unrequited passion for a Swiss girl – it has become one of the landmarks of Romanticism. In it, as in his other works, the artist focused on the darker side of the imagination, weaving together elements of horror, fantasy and eroticism.

Kitagawa Utamaro Act IX of Chusugiwa (detail)

Born 1753 Kawayoye near Edo (now Tokyo), Japan   Painted in Edo   Died 1806 Edo

MOVEMENT: Ukiyo-e **OTHER WORKS:** *Lovers, Girl Playing Glass Flute, Women Working in the Kitchen* **INFLUENCES:** Hishikawa Moronobu, Ando Hiroshige

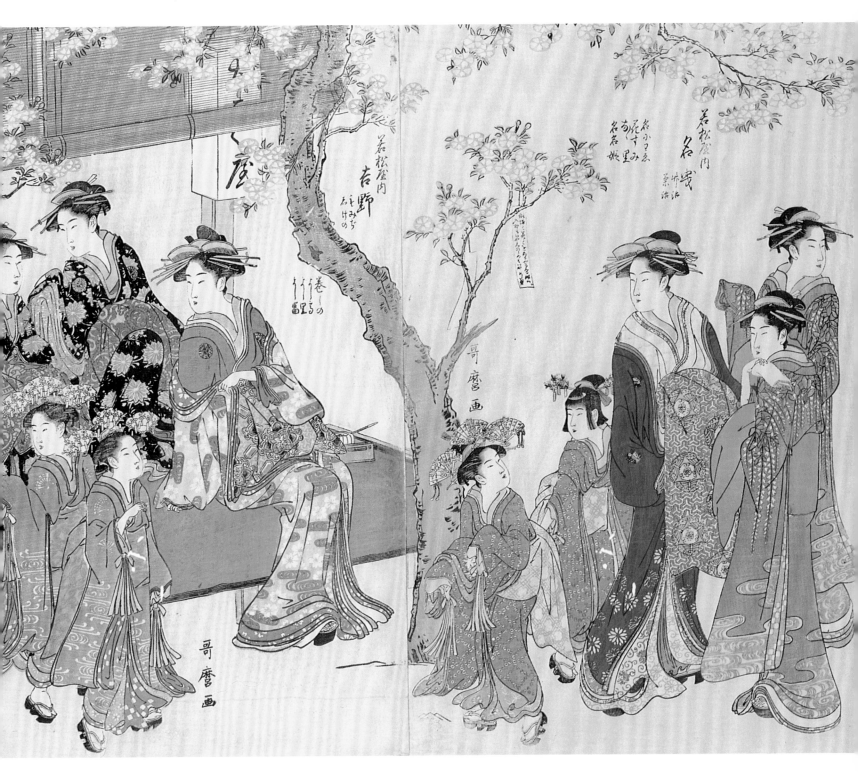

KITAGAWA NEBSUYOSHI received a conventional art training but raised it to an entirely new level, earning for him the epithet of *Ukiyo-ye Chuko-no-so* ('great master of the popular school'). A versatile artist who painted flowers, birds, fish and insects in meticulous detail as well as great sweeping landscapes, he specialized in portraits and genre scenes involving the ladies of the court. No one ever surpassed him in the precise delineation of faces, figures and flowing robes that capture the gracefulness and elegance of the courtesans and professional beauties of the Shogunate at the height of its prestige. Though he painted in oils, his fame rests mainly on the colour prints, which had immense appeal not only for the Japanese but also for the Dutch community at Nagasaki, whence his work was brought to Europe and had a tremendous influence on many artists of the nineteenth century.

Sir Henry Raeburn   The Reverend Robert Walker skating on Duddington Loch, 1784

Born 1756 Scotland   Painted in Edinburgh and Rome   Died 1823 Edinburgh

MOVEMENT: British School of Portraiture **OTHER WORKS:** *Self-Portrait, Sir Walter Scott, Mrs Robert Bell* **INFLUENCES:** Allan Ramsay, Pompeo Batoni, Sir Joshua Reynolds

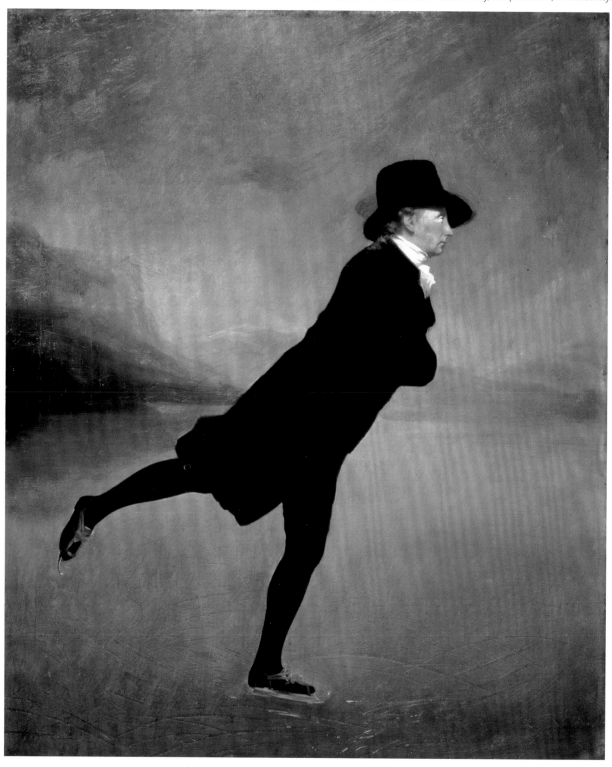

HENRY RAEBURN was originally apprenticed to a goldsmith but began painting portrait miniatures and soon expanded to full-scale oil paintings, though entirely self-taught. After marrying one of his sitters, a wealthy widow, he was enabled to travel to Italy to study for two years, mainly under Pompeo Batoni. He returned to Edinburgh in 1787 and established himself as the most fashionable portraitist of his generation. Unlike Ramsay, he spent most of his life in Edinburgh and seldom visited London. He became a full member of the Royal Academy in 1815. In 1823 he was appointed His Majesty's Limner for Scotland and was knighted the same year. Although his contemporaries judged him less successful in his female subjects, his portraits of both men and women are full of vigour and liveliness and had a profound influence on the development of Scottish art in the nineteenth century.

Torii Kiyonaga   Viewing the Cherry Blossom at Asukayama, *c.*1785

Born 1752 Edo (now Tokyo) Japan   Painted in Edo   Died 1815 Edo
MOVEMENT: Ukiyo-e **OTHER WORKS:** *Kabuki Scene, Ladies and Young Man Walking* **INFLUENCES:** Kiyomitsu

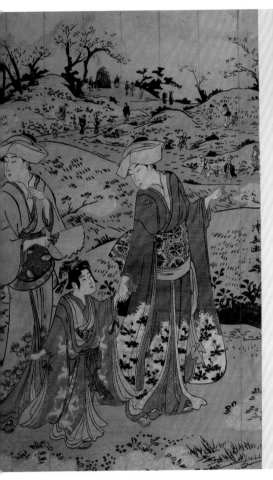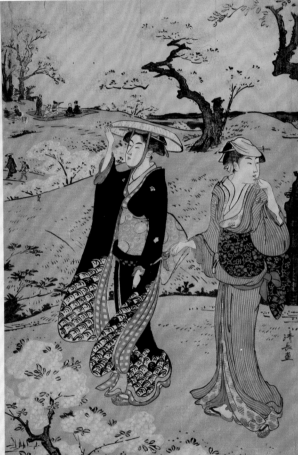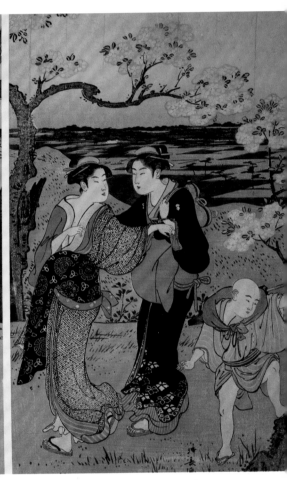

THE SON of an Edo (Tokyo) bookseller, Kiyonaga was the star pupil of Kiyomitsu, last of great masters of the Torii line. In due course he succeeded as head of the Torii school, his adopted names reflecting the great influences on him. A very large part of his prolific output consisted of prints of the Kabuki theatre but he also painted genre subjects of everyday life in the capital. Kiyonaga introduced a note of greater realism and less idealism which revolutionized *ukiyo-e* ('pictures of the passing world') and paved the way for the mordant style of Sharaku and his followers. By the late 1770s Kiyonaga was spearheading the movement for a more naturalistic approach, with figures that were much more fully rounded and better proportioned than previously. It was Kiyonaga's style that influenced Utamaro, but when the latter overtook him in the 1790s Kiyonaga returned to Kabuki paintings and produced very few prints in his later years.

George Romney   Portrait of Emma, Lady Hamilton, 1786

Born 1734 England   Painted in England and Italy   Died 1802
MOVEMENTS: Neoclassicism, Romanticism **OTHER WORKS**: *The Parson's Daughter, The Beaumont Family, Lady Rodbard* **INFLUENCES**: Sir Joshua Reynolds, Henry Fuseli, Joseph Highmore

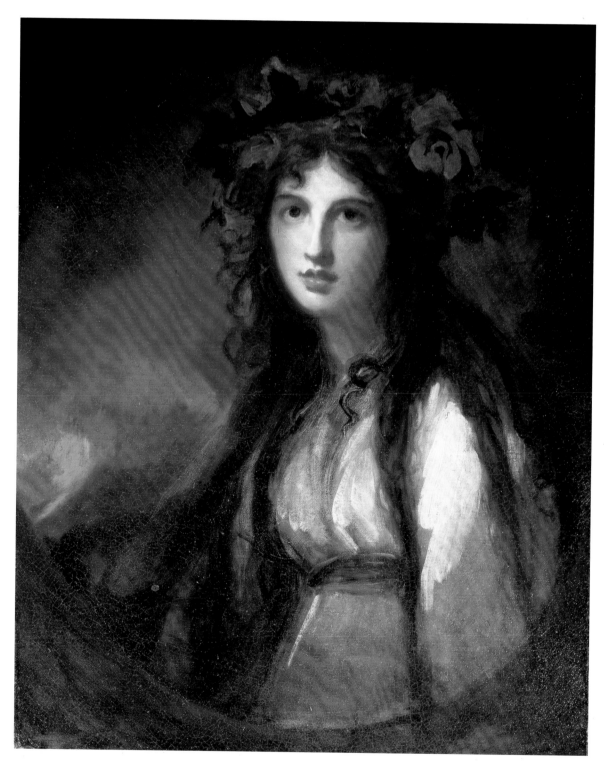

ENGLISH PAINTER, specializing in portraits. Romney was born in Lancashire, the son of a cabinet maker, and trained under an itinerant portraitist named Christopher Steele. For a time, he picked up commissions by travelling from town to town, before making his base in Kendal. Moving to London in 1762, he established a reputation as a fashionable portrait painter, although his style did not really mature until after his tour of Italy (1773–75). There, his study of Classical and Renaissance art paid huge dividends, and most of his best paintings were produced in the decade after his return to England. Romney, like Gainsborough, was deeply dissatisfied with portraiture. His ambition of becoming a history painter was never fulfilled, perhaps partly because of his nervous, introspective character, and partly because of his reluctance to exhibit. His later career was marred by his obsession with Emma Hart (later Lady Hamilton, Nelson's mistress). Romney met her in 1781 and, in the years which followed, produced dozens of pictures of her, usually masquerading as a character from mythology. As his reputation began to wane, the artist returned to Kendal, where he suffered a serious mental decline.

Louise Elisabeth Vigée-Lebrun   Marie Antoinette and her Four Children, 1787

Elisabeth Vigée-Lebrun Born 1755 France   Painted in France, England and Europe   Died 1842 Paris

MOVEMENT: French School **OTHER WORKS:** *Portrait of the Artist and her Daughter* **INFLUENCES:** Joseph Vernet, Jean Baptiste Grueze, Jean Baptiste Lebrun

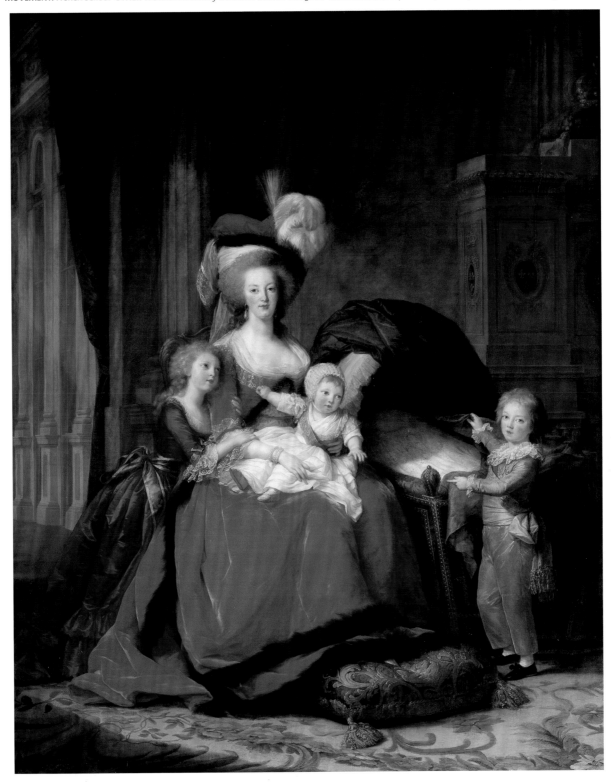

MARIE LOUISE Elisabeth Vigée-Lebrun was the daughter of an artist from whom she received her early training, but later benefited from the help of several fellow-painters. By the age of 20 she had already made her mark with portraits of Count Orloff and the Duchess of Orleans. In 1783 she was admitted to the Academy on the strength of her allegorical masterpiece *Peace Bringing Back Abundance*. Following the outbreak of the Revolution she fled to Italy and worked in Rome and Naples, later visiting Vienna, Berlin and St Petersburg. She returned briefly to Paris in 1802 but went to London the same year, where she painted the Prince of Wales and Lord Byron. She was a prolific portraitist, and a score of her paintings portray Marie-Antoinette alone.

John Robert Cozens   Cetaro, Gulf of Salerno, 1790

Born 1752 London, England   Painted in England, Switzerland, Italy   Died 1797, London
MOVEMENT: English Landscape School   **OTHER WORKS:** *Landscape with Hannibal on his March over the Alps*   **INFLUENCES:** Alexander Cozens

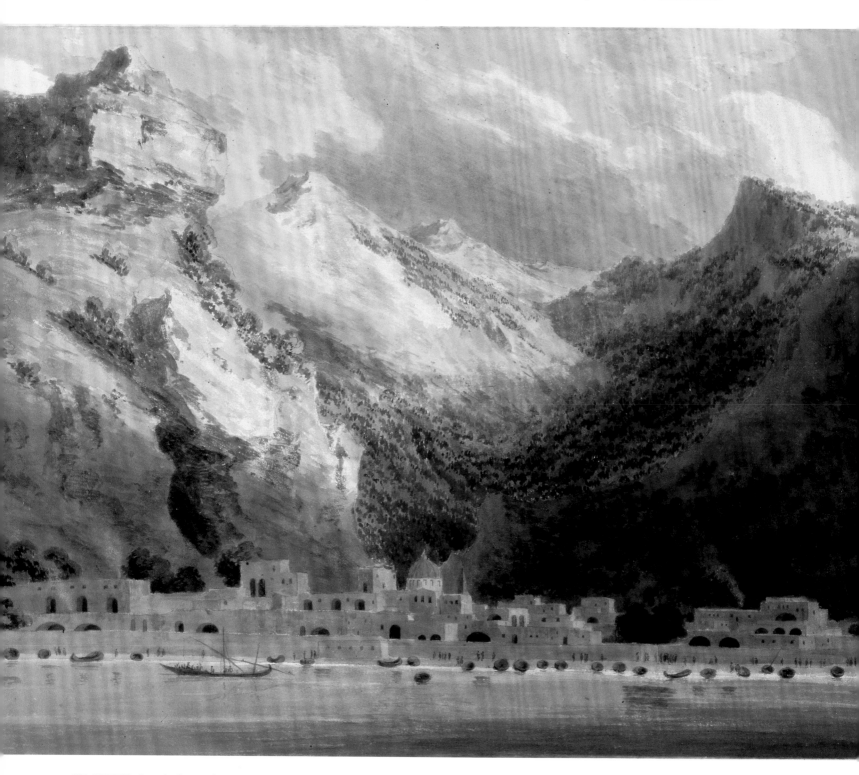

AN ARTIST whose background was more colourful than his paintings (Cozens' artist father Alexander is believed to have been the illegitimate son of Peter the Great by an English girl while the Tsar was learning the shipbuilding trade at Deptford). John Robert Cozens studied under his father, the drawing master at Eton who wrote treatises on watercolours and is best remembered for his technique of incorporating accidental blots into his landscapes. In turn, his son evolved a style of watercolour painting that departed from his predecessors: impressionistic and decidedly atmospheric. He was thus the forerunner of Girtin and Turner, the latter freely admitting his indebtedness to Cozens, while Constable's regard for his talent was effusive: 'the greatest genius that ever touched landscape.' In 1776 and 1782 Cozens travelled overland to Italy, sketching and painting prolifically en route, and providing the basis for his great landscapes and historical works. His colours were muted, often somber, and there is a dark, foreboding element in his paintings which reflect the severe depressive illness which led to his incarcer-ation in a lunatic asylum in the last years of his relatively short life.

William Blake   Ancient of Days, 1794

Born 1757 London, England   Painted in England   Died 1827

MOVEMENT: Romanticism, Neoclassicism **OTHER WORKS:** *Glad Day, God Judging Adam, God Creating the Universe* **INFLUENCES:** Michelangelo, Henry Fuseli, John Flaxman

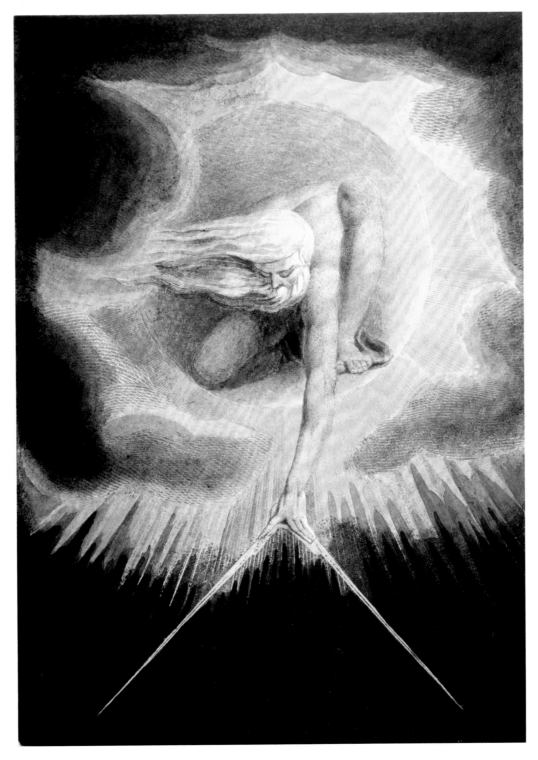

VISIONARY POET and painter, one of the most individual talents to emerge from the Romantic movement. Blake lived in London for most of his life. He trained as a commercial engraver and briefly attended the Royal Academy Schools, although he soon felt stifled by the life classes; for him, the imagination was always far more important than the imitation of nature. Stylistically, Blake's art bore some of the hallmarks of Neoclassicism – particularly in its linear approach and its dramatic intent – but a classical sense of restraint was notably absent. His figures, meanwhile, owed much to the inspiration of Michelangelo.

Blake's technique was highly inventive. He devised a system of 'illuminated printing', which enabled him to produce lavish editions of his books of poetry, and pioneered a form of tempera painting, in place of oils. His subject matter was largely drawn from the complex, personal mythology outlined in his verses. This baffled many of his contemporaries, who regarded him as an eccentric. Blake did have his admirers however, which included the group of young artists known as the Ancients.

Jacques–Louis David   The Death of Marat, 1793

Born 1748 France   Painted in France, Italy and Belgium (then Holland)   Died 1825

MOVEMENT: Neoclassicism   **OTHER WORKS:** *Madame Récamier, Brutus and his Dead Sons*   **INFLUENCES:** Gavin Hamilton, Joseph-Marie Vien, Anton Raffael Mengs

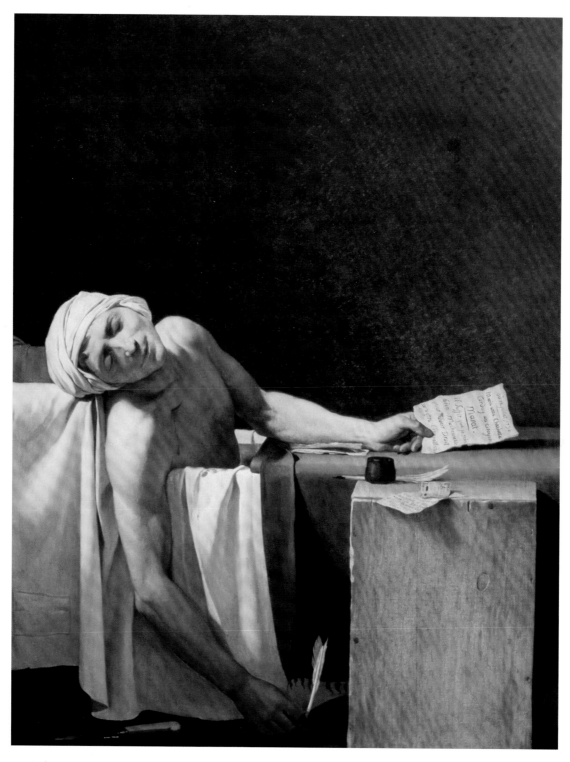

FRENCH PAINTER, the leader of the Neoclassical revival. In both his art and his life, David displayed a tempestuous nature, possibly inherited from his father, who was killed in a duel in 1757. He trained under Vien, and his early paintings featured the same uncomfortable blend of Rococo sweetness and antique trappings as those of his master. After winning the Prix de Rome, however, David spent an extended study period in Italy (1775–80), where his art acquired a new dignity and grandeur. With their fiery patriotism and stern morality, David's paintings of the 1780s captured the rebellious mood of the times. Indeed, his greatest picture, *The Oath of the Horatii*, has often been seen as a visual call to arms. During the Revolution, David was swept up in politics, joining the National Convention, where he became associated with Robespierre and Marat. After their fall, he was imprisoned and was only saved from the guillotine by his royalist wife. This experience did nothing to quell the artist's spirit, however, for he became equally involved with Napoleon. After the latter's defeat, David fled to Brussels, where he remained in exile for the rest of his days.

Toshusai Sharaku   Portrait of Sakata Hangoro III as Fujikawa Mizuema, 1794

Born *c.* 1750 Edo (now Tokyo), Japan   Painted in Edo   Died 1801 Edo

MOVEMENT: Ukiyo-e **OTHER WORKS:** *Otani Oniji III as Edohei, Iwai Hanshiro IV as Shigenoi* **INFLUENCES:** Kitagawa Utamaro, Suzuki Harunobu

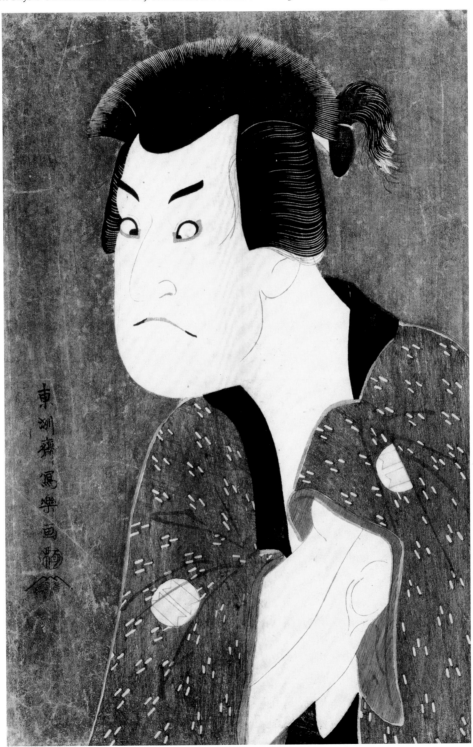

NOTHING APPEARS to be known regarding the origins or early career of Toshusai Sharaku, other than that he came from a noble family and had been an actor in the Kabuki theater before taking up art. In the brief period of only 10 months in 1794–95 he produced some 159 caricatures and portraits of Kabuki actors, drawn with extraordinary power and originality, coupled with savage satirical qualities which had not been witnessed in Japanese art since the Kamakura period (1185–1333). Sharaku mastered the new technique of tinted mica backgrounds extremely effectively, so that the silhouettes of the posturing actors almost jump out at the spectator. Sharaku's harsh, uncompromising pictures shocked the public, more accustomed to the simpering beauties of Masanobu or Utamaro, and not surprisingly they were unpopular. The exaggerated features of the subjects may have given offence to the actors themselves and perhaps concerted action on their part helped bring Sharaku's enterprise to an abrupt end.

Thomas Girtin   Dunstanborough Castle, *c.*1797

Born 1775 London, England   Painted in London   Died 1802 London
MOVEMENT: English School   **OTHER WORKS:** *A Winding Estuary, Porte St Denis*   **INFLUENCES:** Turner

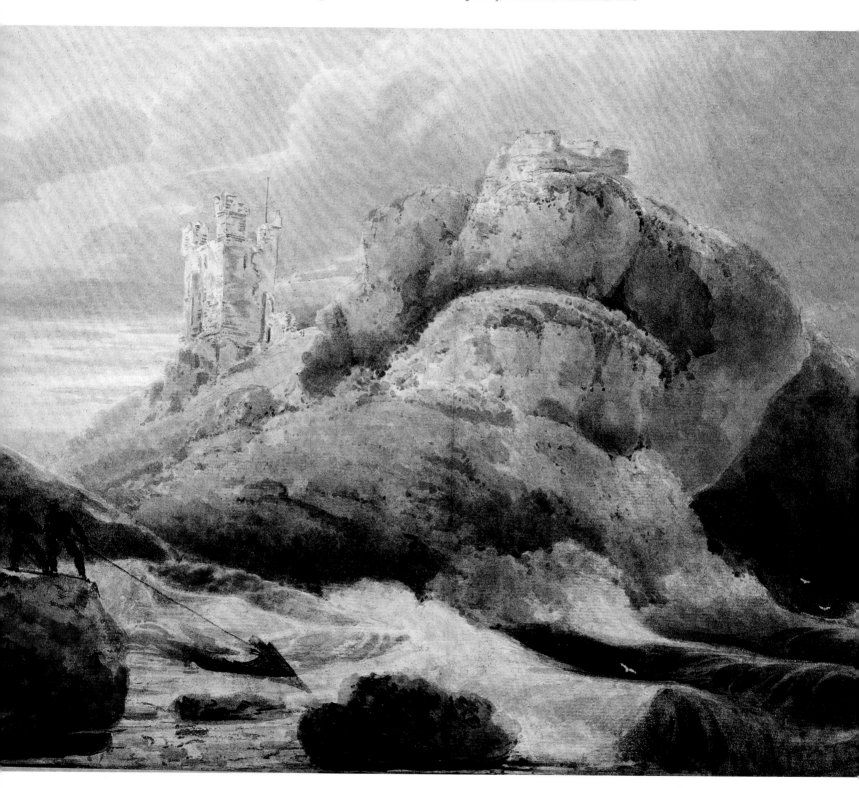

THOMAS GIRTIN served his apprenticeship in London as a mezzotint engraver under Edward Dayes, through whom he made the acquaintance of J. M. W. Turner who, being shown Girtin's architectural and topographical sketches, encouraged him to develop his talents as a landscape painter. His early death from tuberculosis brought a very promising career to an untimely end, but even by that date he had established a high reputation as an etcher. Hitherto watercolours had been used almost entirely for tinting engravings, but to Girtin goes the credit for establishing watercolour painting as a major art form in its own right. From 1794 onwards he exhibited his great watercolour landscapes at the annual Royal Academy exhibitions and this helped to develop the fashion for this medium from the beginning of the nineteenth century. Girtin collaborated with Turner in making a series of copies of architectural paintings for Dr Monro, notably works by Canaletto.

Marie–Guillemine Benoist   Portrait of a Negress, 1799–1800

Born 1768 Paris   Painted in Paris   Died 1826 Paris

MOVEMENT: French Romantic School   **OTHER WORKS:** *Napoleon Bonaparte, The Imperial Family*   **INFLUENCES:** Marie Vigée-Lebrun, David

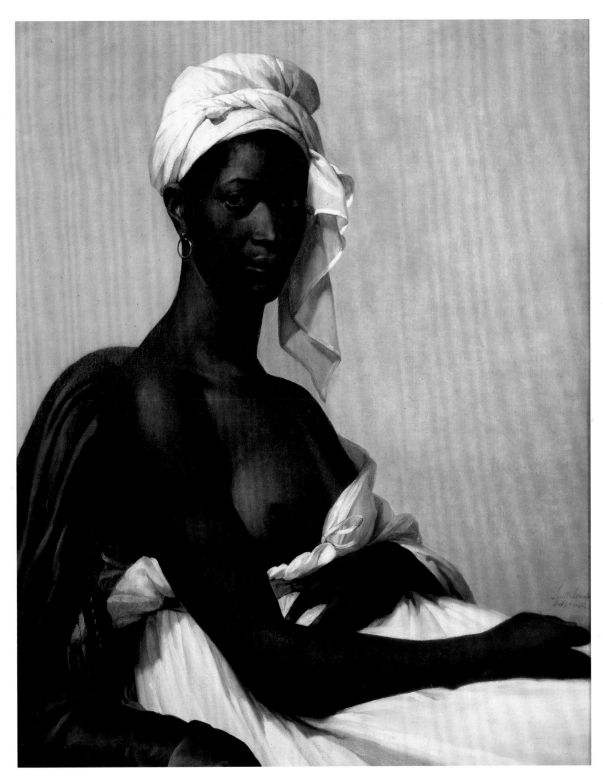

MARIE-GUILLEMINE Benoist was the daughter of a govern-ment official who recognized her talent and enrolled her as a pupil of Vigée-Lebrun in 1791; the latter's influence is very evident in Benoist's early works, mainly portraits done in pastels. Later she studied under Jacques-Louis David and as a result she began producing more ambitious works in oils. She made her debut at the Salon with two historical scenes and thereafter painted both portraits and historical subjects. She achieved a high reputation and received a gold medal and an annual government grant. Napoleon commissioned portraits of himself and his family from her. In the early 1800s she switched to painting genre subjects and sentimental domestic scenes which were immensely popular. Her best-known painting, a remarkable portrait of a young black woman painted in 1800, is believed to have been inspired by the decree of 1794 abolishing slavery.

Antoine–Jean Gros Napoleon Bonaparte Visiting the Plague Stricken of Jaffa, 1799

Born 1771 Paris, France Painted in France and Italy Died 1835 Bas-Meudon, France
MOVEMENT: French Classicism **OTHER WORKS:** *The Departure of Louis XVIII* **INFLUENCES:** David

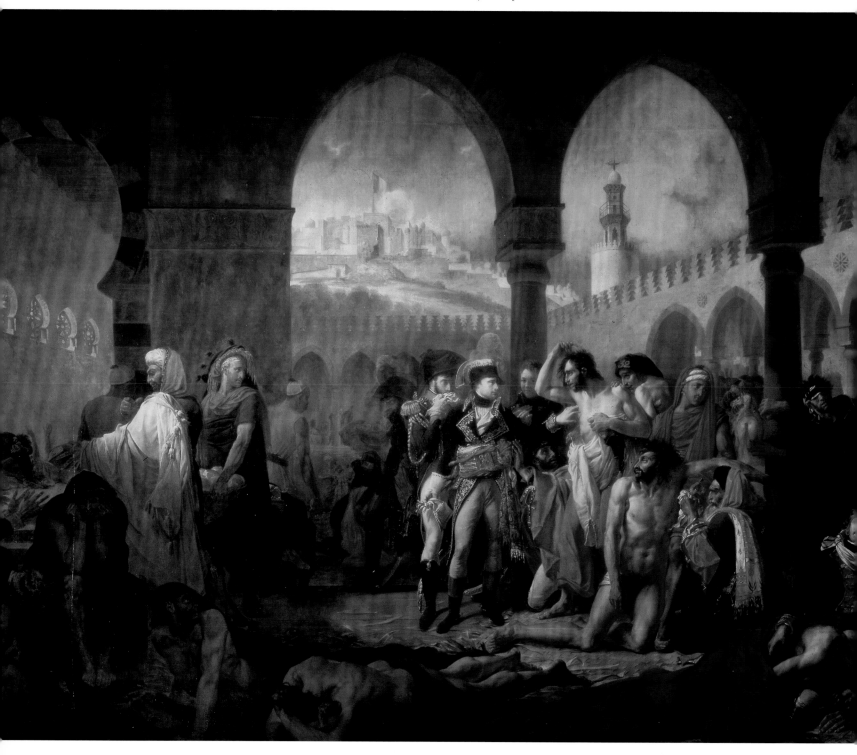

THE SON of a miniature painter, Antoine-Jean Gros studied under Jacques-Louis David. Following the death of his father in 1791 he went to Italy and it was there that he met Josephine Beauharnais, who introduced him to Napoleon, whom he accompanied on his Italian campaign. He was an eye-witness of the dramatic scene when Bonaparte planted the Tricolour on the bridge at Arcole in November 1796 and the dramatic painting that recorded this incident gave Gros a sense of purpose. Thereafter, as a war artist, he chronicled on canvas the exploits of the Napoleonic arms down to the campaign of 1811, and it is on these heroic paintings that his reputation is largely based, earning him the Napoleonic title of Baron in the process. The downfall of Napoleon robbed Gros of his true vocation. In the aftermath of Waterloo he returned to his classicist roots and concentrated on such works as *Hercules and Diomedes*, but by now he was fighting a losing battle against the rising tide of Romanticism.

Farrukh Beg   Humayun Hunting near Kabul, (copy) *c.*1800

Born *c.* 1550 Qalmakia, Persia   Painted in India   Died *c.* 1610 Delhi, India

MOVEMENT: Mughal or Indo-Persian School   **OTHER WORKS:** *Akbar Nama, Babur Nama, Sufi Pir at the Tavern Door*   **INFLUENCES:** Mir Sayyid Ali, Abdus Samad

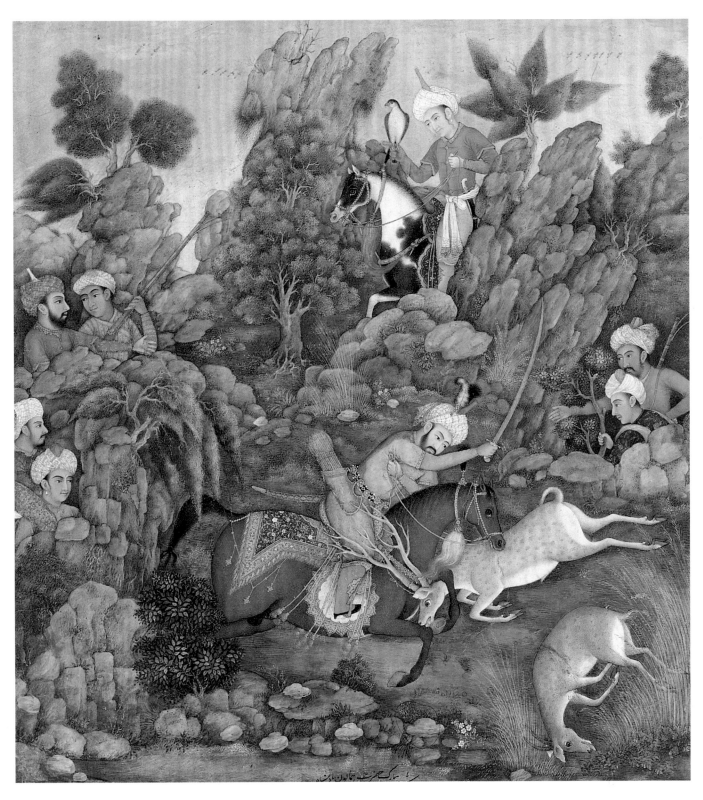

FARUKH BEG is often referred to as Farukh the Qalmak (Kalmuck), which suggests that he hailed from that region of the Mughal Empire. Like other painters of the Indo-Persian School, little is known of his life, but he was one of the four Muslim artists named by Abul Fazl in the list of 17 court painters. Farukh

contributed excellent miniature paintings to the Akbar Nama and was the author of a remarkable painting in three scenes, occupying a full page on the reverse of a folio in the Oriental collection at the British Library. He painted in the Persian manner, characterized by flatness and a fondness for surface patterns, extreme

elegance in line and decorative detail. Farukh excelled in portraiture, reflecting the Emperor Akbar's total disregard of orthodox Muslim teaching, which forbade representation of living creatures, human or animal.

John Crome Gibraltar Watering Place, Heigham

Born 1768 Painted in England Died 1821

MOVEMENT: Romanticism, Norwich School **OTHER WORKS:** *Yarmouth Jetty, Mousehold Heath: Mill and Donkeys* **INFLUENCES:** Richard Wilson, Gainsborough, Hobbema

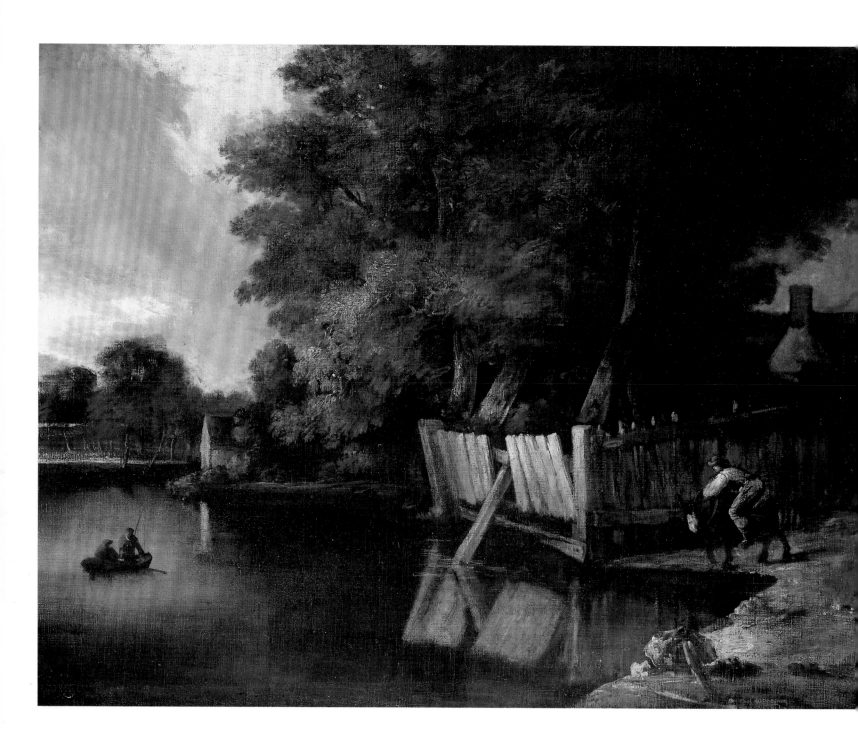

ENGLISH LANDSCAPE PAINTER, a leading member of the Norwich School. Crome was apprenticed to a coach-and-sign painter at the age of 15, before moving to London in 1790. There he learned his trade by copying pictures in the collection of his patron, Thomas Harvey. These included British artists Wilson and Gainsborough and the Dutch landscapists Ruisdael and Hobbema.

Crome travelled to Paris in 1814 to view the artworks looted by Napoleon, but the greater part of his career was spent in East Anglia. In 1803, he became one of the founder members of the Norwich Society of Artists, serving as its President for many years. Despite his growing reputation, however, Crome still had to rely on teaching for much of his income. Stylistically, he was a transitional artist.

Paintings such as his *Old Houses at Norwich* were still very much in the Picturesque tradition, though he also produced lyrical, moonlit scenes, which displayed a budding Romantic sensibility. He was often known to his contemporaries as Old Crome, to distinguish him from his son – another John – who was also an artist.

Francisco Goya   The Clothed Maja, *c.*1800–05

Born 1746 Fuendetodos, Spain   Painted in Madrid and Bordeaux   Died 1828 Bordeaux
MOVEMENT: Spanish School   **OTHER WORKS:** *Execution of the Defenders of Madrid, The Naked Maja*   **INFLUENCES:** Anton Raphael Mengs, Tiepolo

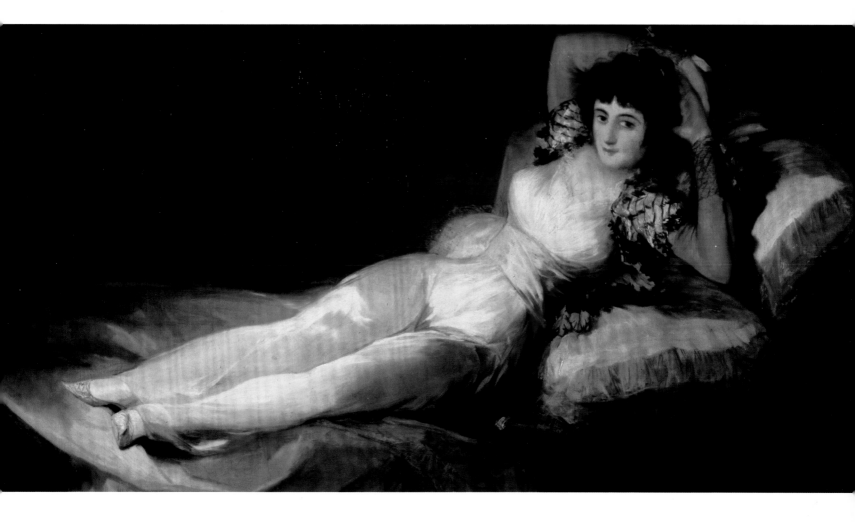

FRANCISCO JOSÉ de Goya y Lucientes was raised in the small town of Fuendetodos near Saragossa, Spain. Frequently involved in parochial gang fights, he fled to Madrid in 1765 after a brawl in which three youths were killed. As a result of continued sparring he left Madrid precipitately, joining a troupe of itinerant bull-fighters and eventually reaching Rome, where he resumed his studies in art. In 1798 he returned to Spain as a designer for the royal tapestry factory and executed a number of frescoes drawn from contemporary life, as well as a series of satirical etchings. In 1799 he was appointed court painter to Charles IV, which resulted in some of his most notable portraits. After the French invasion (1808) he sided at first with the invaders, but secretly sketched their atrocities, which resulted in both full-scale canvasses and numerous etchings. In 1824 he moved to Bordeaux where, in old age, he produced some of his finest genre paintings.

Sir Thomas Lawrence Portrait of Mrs Robert Burne–Jones

Born 1769 Bristol, England   Painted in England and Europe   Died 1830 London, England
MOVEMENT: British School **OTHER WORKS:** *The Duke of Wellington, Pinkie, Mrs Siddons, Princess Lieven* **INFLUENCES:** Sir Joshua Reynolds

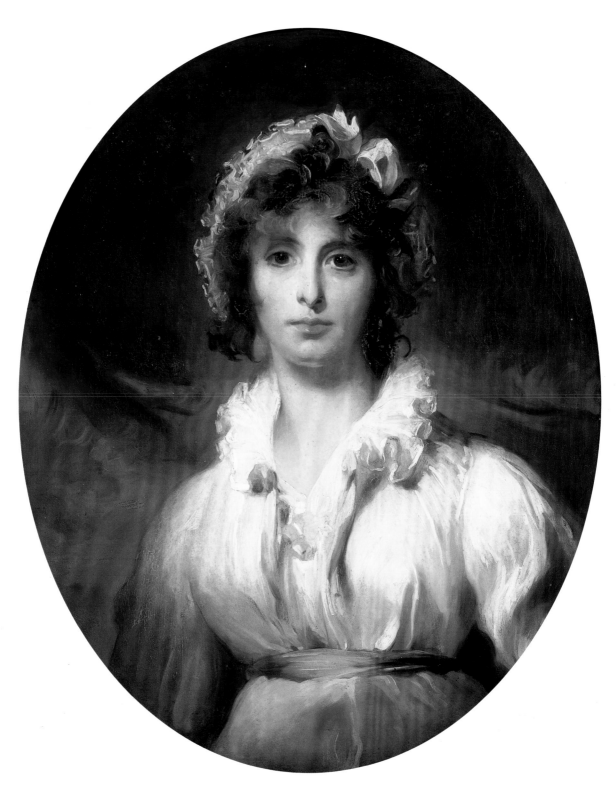

THE SON of an innkeeper, Thomas Lawrence amazed and amused guests from the age of six by sketching their portraits. When his father became bankrupt four years later, it was the infant prodigy who became the family's breadwinner. At the age of 18, he went to London to study at the Royal Academy and exhibited almost immediately. On the death of Reynolds in 1792 he was appointed Painter-in-Ordinary to King George III and became the most fashionable portrait painter of the ensuing decades. He was knighted in 1815 and embarked on a European career, during which he painted all the royalty and most of the nobility of the Continent. As President of the Royal Academy (1820–30) he was the leader of the British art establishment. Ironically, he was no better a businessman than his father, and his prolific output barely kept pace with his immense debts.

John Constable   Lock on the Stour

Born 1776 Suffolk, England   Painted in England   Died 1837

MOVEMENT: Romanticism **OTHER WORKS:** *The Hay Wain, Flatford Mill, Salisbury Cathedral* **INFLUENCES:** Thomas Gainsborough, Jacob van Ruisdael, Claude Lorrain

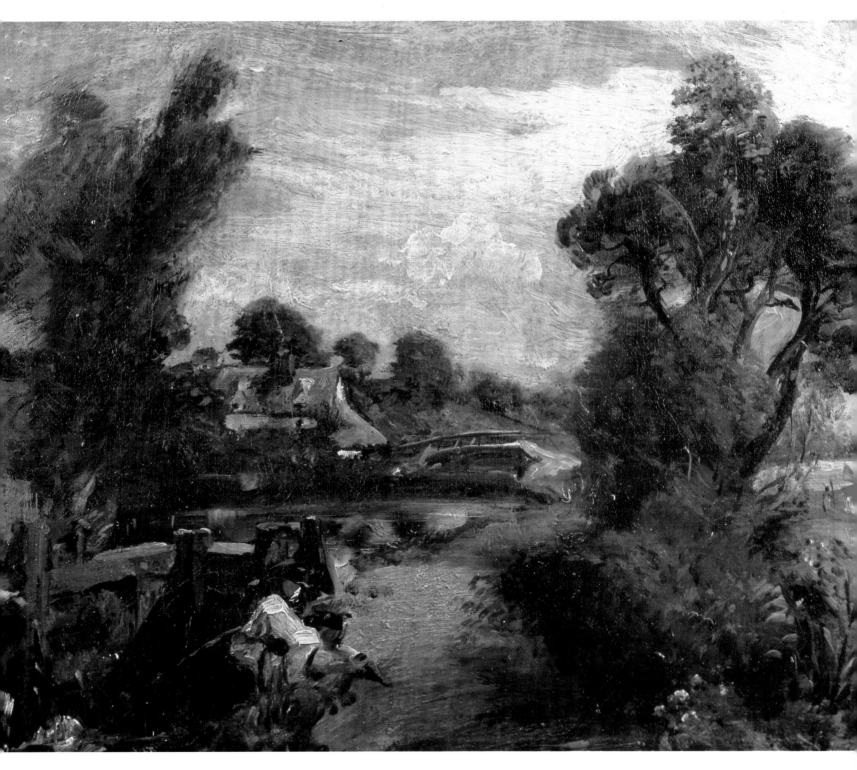

A PIONEERING British artist who, together with Turner, raised the status of landscape painting in England. Constable enjoyed a happy childhood in his native Suffolk, and this region became the focus for most of his paintings. In Constable's day, however, landscape painting was a poorly paid profession and both his family and that of his lover, Maria Bicknell, were appalled by his choice of career. For many years, the couple were forced to meet in secret, until they eventually married in 1816. Constable's struggle for success was as difficult as his father had feared and, for a time, he was obliged to paint portraits for a living. In part, this was because he did not seek out romantic or picturesque views, but preferred to paint his local area, even though many regarded it as dull, agricultural land. He also paid unprecedented attention to atmospheric conditions, making copious sketches of individual clouds. These were so realistic that one critic joked that Constable's paintings always made him want to reach for his umbrella. Eventually, he found success with his 'six-footers' (i.e. six foot wide), gaining membership of the Royal Academy and winning a gold medal at the Paris Salon.

Jean–Auguste–Dominique Ingres   Jupiter & Thetis, 1811

Born 1780   Painted in France and Italy   Died 1867

MOVEMENT: Neoclassicism, Romanticism **OTHER WORKS:** *Madame Moitessier, The Apotheosis of Homer* **INFLUENCES:** David, Raphael, John Flaxman

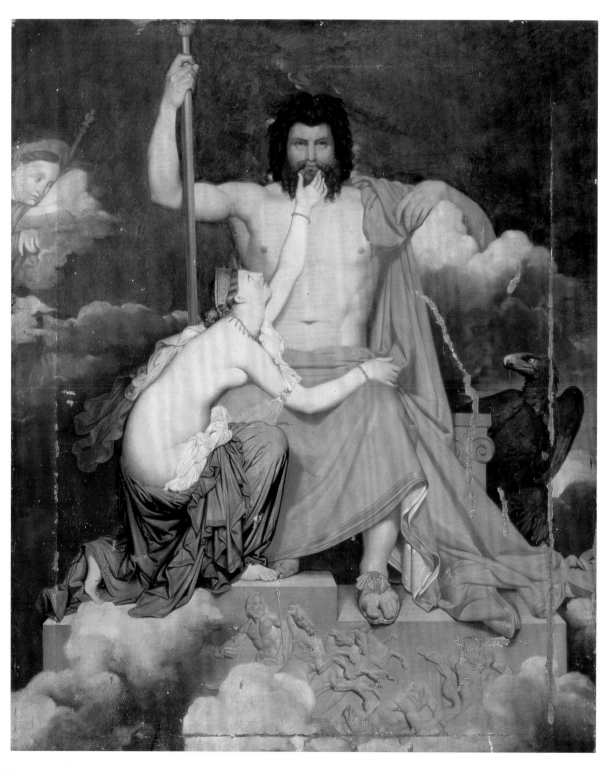

FRENCH PAINTER and draughtsman, a champion of academic art. Ingres' father was a minor painter and sculptor and, with parental encouragement, he displayed a talent for both drawing and music at a very early age. Opting for the former, he moved to Paris in 1797 and entered David's studio. There, inspired by his teacher and by Flaxman's engravings of antique vases, Ingres developed a meticulous neoclassical style, notable for impeccable draughtsmanship and a smooth, enamel-like finish. This helped him to win the Prix de Rome in 1801, and brought him a succession of lucrative portrait commissions.

Ingres worked extensively in Italy after 1806, although he continued to exhibit at the Salon and rapidly became the epitome of the academic establishment. This was most obvious in the 1820s, when his pictures were contrasted with those of Delacroix, in the 'battle' between Classicism and Romanticism. While his style was a model of classical correctness, however, Ingres' subject matter was often distinctly Romantic. This is particularly evident in the exotic eroticism of Oriental scenes, such as *La Grande Odalisque* and *The Turkish Bath*.

John Sell Cotman   Fishing Boats off Yarmouth

Born 1782 Norfolk, England   Painted in Norwich and London   Died 1842 London
MOVEMENT: English Landscape School **OTHER WORKS:** *Greta Bridge, Chirk Aqueduct, Duncombe Park* **INFLUENCES:** Thomas Girtin, Turner

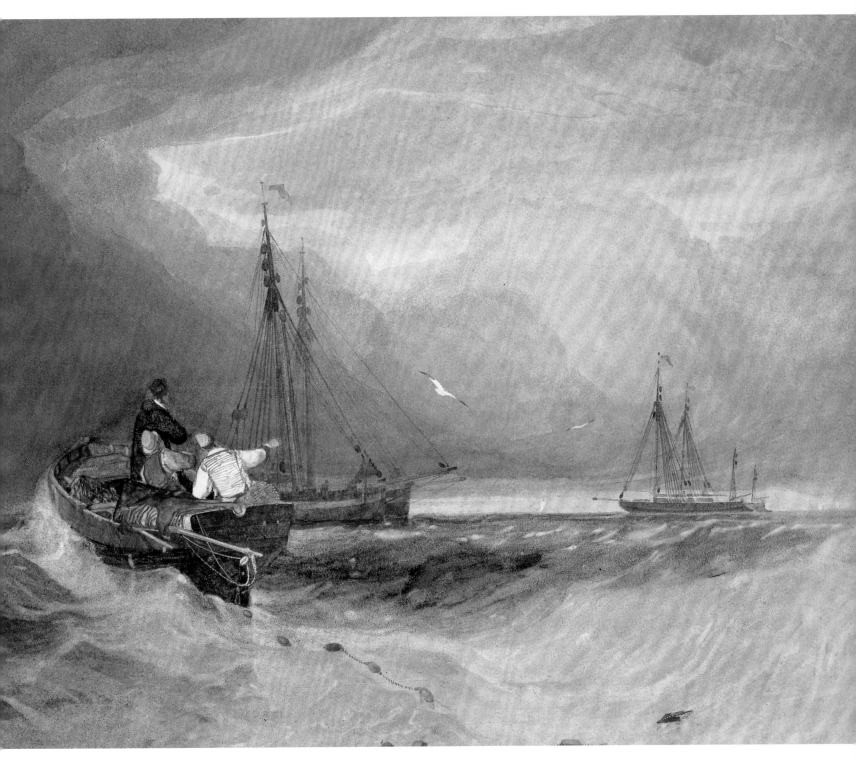

JOHN SELL Cotman received his art training in London before returning to his native Norwich in 1806, where he became the foremost watercolourist among the group of East Anglian artists who came to be known as the Norwich School. In the early years of the nineteenth century he travelled extensively in England and Wales and his best work belongs to this period. Although chiefly remembered for his work in this medium he also executed a number of fine oil paintings during the time when he resided at Great Yarmouth (1811–23). Failing in business, however, he was forced to sell all his paintings and etchings and return to London, where he obtained a position as drawing master at King's College. There is an uncompromisingly austere character to his landscapes, very much ahead of his time and not at all in step with the fashions prevailing in Regency England, but his handling of light and shade was to have a profound influence on his followers.

J.M.W. Turner The Fighting Temeraire Tugged to her Last Berth to be Broken up, before 1839 (detail)

Born 1755 London, England Painted in England Died London 1851
MOVEMENT: Romantic **OTHER WORKS:** *Rain, Steam and Speed, The Great Western Railway, The Thames above Waterloo Bridge* **INFLUENCES:** Claude Lorrain, Nicolas Poussin

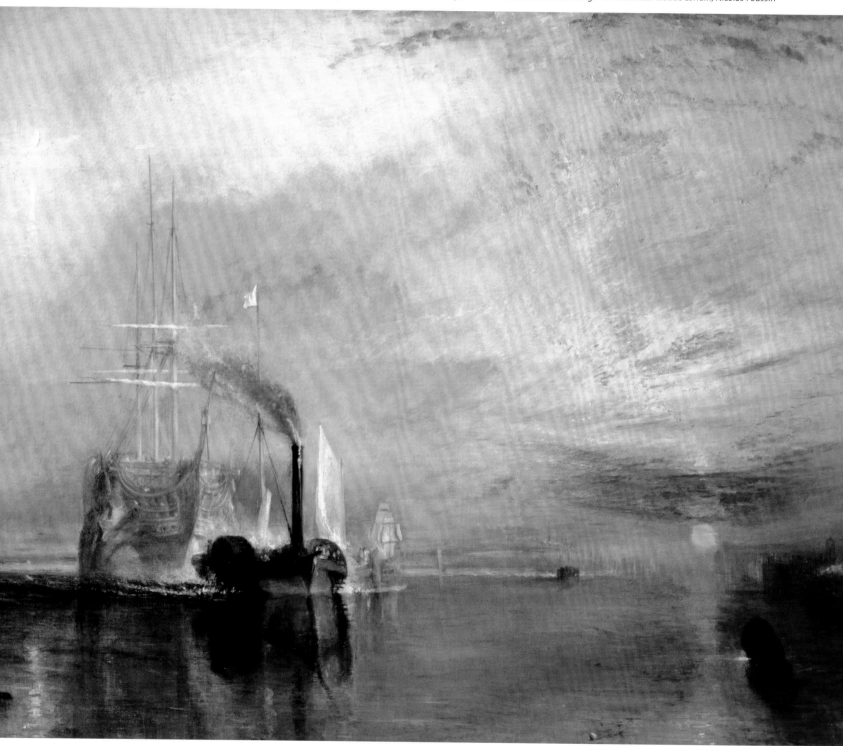

JOSEPH MALLORD William Turner entered the Royal Academy School in 1789 and began exhibiting the following year. He travelled all over England, filling sketch-books with drawings of scenery and landmarks which would later provide the raw material for his oils and watercolours. He collaborated with Girtin on a three-year watercolour project but later turned to oils. After his first trip to Italy (1819) his paintings showed a marked Classical influence and following his second (1829) his art entered its greatest phase with works such as *Rain, Steam and Speed* (1844) – the precursors of Impressionism. A solitary, rather reclusive man, Turner bequeathed over 300 oils and some 20,000 watercolours and drawings to the nation. A prolific artist, he ranks with Constable as one of the greatest British landscape painters of all time and his career marks a turning-point in the development of modern British art.

In this painting Turner commemorates the final journey of the *Fighting Temeraire* – an old warship that had accompanied Nelson's ship *Victory* at the Battle of Trafalgar – as she is towed up the Thames to be broken up. The use of the evocative setting sun strongly symbolizes both the decline of Britain's mercantile power and the demise of the ship.

Caspar David Friedrich   The Wanderer above the Sea of Clouds, 1818

Born 1774 Germany   Painted in Dresden, Germany   Died 1840 Dresden

MOVEMENT: Romanticism **OTHER WORKS:** *The Wreck of the Hope, The Stages of Life, Graveyard in Snow* **INFLUENCES:** Albrecht Altdorfer, Turner

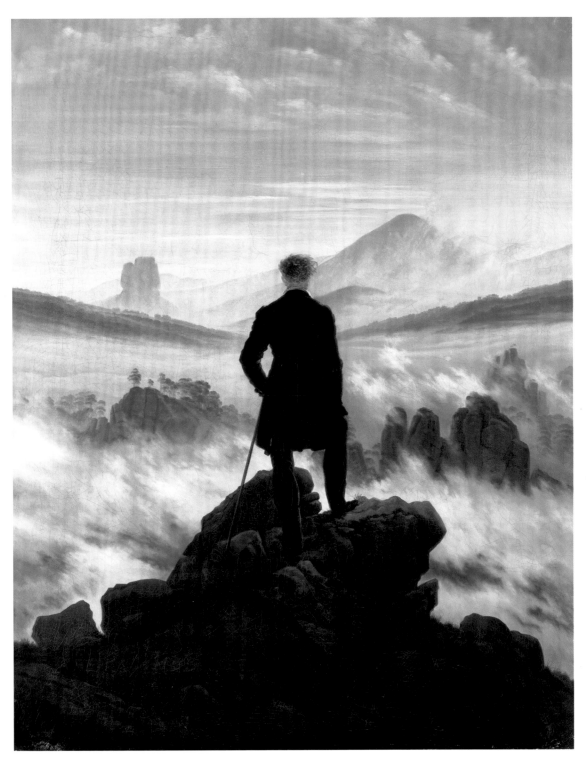

CASPAR DAVID Friedrich studied drawing under J.G. Quistorp in Greifswald before going to the Copenhagen Academy between 1794–98. On his return to Germany he settled in Dresden, where he spent the rest of his life. His drawings in pen and ink were admired by Goethe and won him a Weimar Art Society prize in 1805. His first major commission came two years later in the form of an altarpiece for Count Thun's castle in Teschen, Silesia, entitled *Crucifixion in Mountain Scenery.* This set the tone of many later works, in which dramatic landscapes expressed moods, emotions and atmosphere. Appointed a professor of the Dresden Academy in 1824, he influenced many of the young German and Scandinavian artists of the mid nineteenth century and as a result he ranks high among the formative figures of the Romantic movement. For many years his works were neglected, but in the early 1900s they were rediscovered and revived.

Anne-Louis Girodet de Roussy-Trioson   Portrait of Mustapha, 1819

Born 1767   Painted in France and Italy   Died 1824

MOVEMENT: Neoclassicism, Romanticism **OTHER WORKS:** *The Entombment of Atala, Mlle Lange as Danaë* **INFLUENCES:** David, Prud'hon, Correggio, Primaticcio

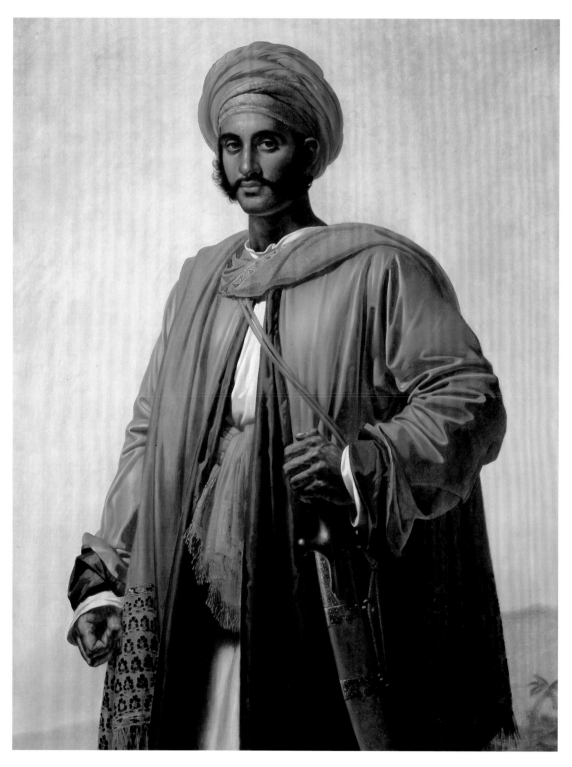

VERSATILE FRENCH painter and illustrator. Girodet was probably the illegitimate son of Dr Trioson, adopting his surname in 1806. After a false start in architecture, he trained as a painter under David, rapidly becoming one of his most talented followers. Girodet won the Prix de Rome in 1789, working in Italy until 1795. His smooth, sculptural finish linked him with Neoclassicism, but his choice of subject matter became increasingly Romantic. He often opted for poetic, nocturnal themes or for literary subjects, such as Chateaubriand's story of Atala. More Romantic still was his most famous picture *Ossian*, which was commissioned for Bonaparte's country retreat at Malmaison. This exploited the contemporary craze for Celtic matters, and depicted a misty scene with a bard-like figure welcoming Napoleon's generals into paradise. Girodet also produced coolly erotic nudes, which betrayed his fondness for Mannerist artists such as Correggio. Girodet had a waspish personality, which occasionally landed him in trouble. There were frequent clashes with David and his scurrilous portrait of Mademoiselle Lange created a public scandal. In later life, he inherited a considerable fortune and his artistic output diminished.

Théodore Géricault   Homme Nu a Mi–Corps (Man Naked to the Waist)

Born 1791 Rouen, France   Painted in Paris   Died 1824 Rouen

MOVEMENT: Romanticism   **OTHER WORKS:** *Officer of the Hussars, Coirse des Chevaux Libres*   **INFLUENCES:** Carle Vernet, Pierre Narcisse Guérin

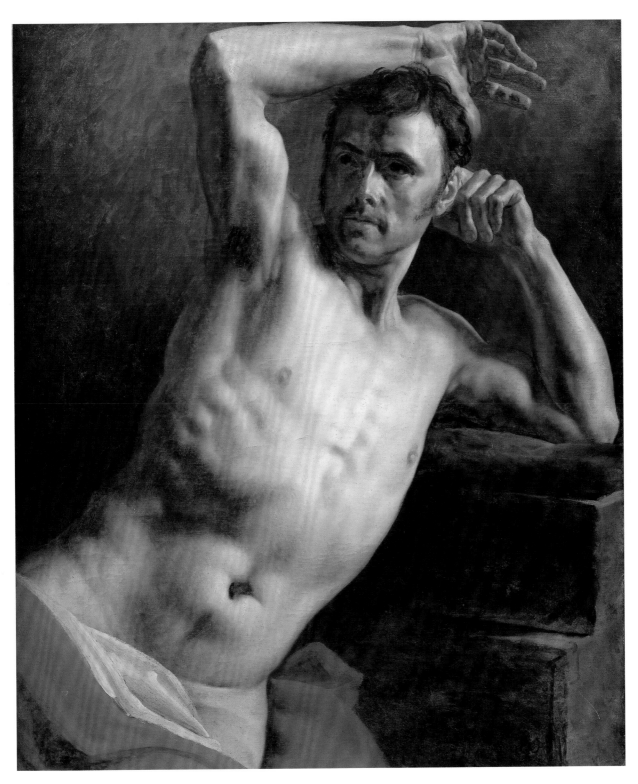

JEAN LOUIS André Théodore Géricault studied under Carle Vernet and Pierre Narcisse Guérin, although he was frequently at odds with the latter because of his passion for Rubens and his unconventional approach in interpreting nature. He made his debut at the Salon of 1812 with his spirited portrait of a cavalry officer on horseback,

and followed this with the *Wounded Cuirassier* (1814), subjects which were immensely popular at the height of the Napoleonic Empire. During the Hundred Days, he served as a volunteer in a Royalist regiment, witnessing soldiers and horses at close quarters. He travelled and studied in Italy in 1816–19, and on his return to Paris embarked on the large-scale works

which established his reputation as one of the leading French Romantics. For an artist renowned for his equestrian subjects it is ironic that he died as the result of a fall from his horse.

Katsushika Hokusai   In the Well of the Great Wave, 1823–29

Born 1760 Edo (now Tokyo), Japan   Painted in Edo   Died 1849 Edo
MOVEMENT: Ukiyo-e **OTHER WORKS:** *The Dream of the Fisherman's Wife* **INFLUENCES:** Hishikawa Moronobu, Ando Hiroshige

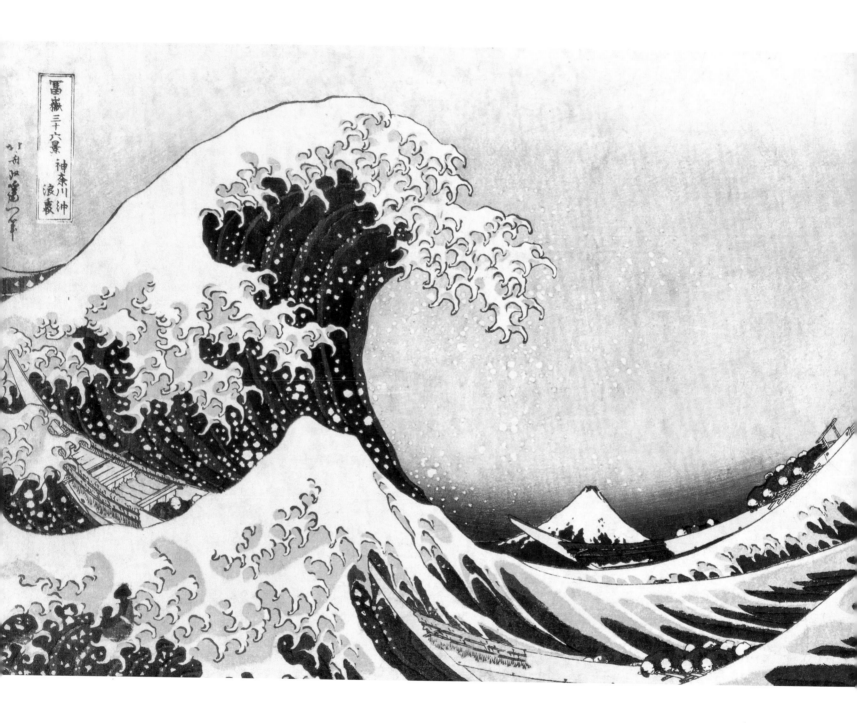

BORN AT Edo (modern Tokyo), the son of a mirror-maker, Hokusai learned the craft of wood-engraving before entering the studio of the painter Katsugawa Shunsho. Disagreement with his master over artistic techniques and principles resulted in his dismissal in 1785. Thereafter he worked on his own as a book illustrator and print-maker, using the Japanese techniques of block printing. His illustrations of everyday life executed for the encyclopaedic Mangwa established his reputation as the leading exponent of ukiyo-e ('pictures of the passing world') whose charm is exceeded only by their technical accomplishment. Of his prolific series of colour prints, the best known are *Thirty-six Views of Mount Fuji* (1823–29) and *Hundred Views of Mount Fuji* (1834–35), but he also produced several shorter sets and individual works. His prints had a tremendous impact on the Western world. Quite by chance, some of his prints were used as packing material for some china sent to Felix Bracquemond in 1856, triggering off the enthusiasm for Japanese art which strongly influenced the Impressionists.

Richard Parkes Bonington   Cottages by a Stream

Born 1802   Painted in France, England, Italy and the Low Countries   Died 1828

MOVEMENT: Romanticism **OTHER WORKS:** *Fish Market near Boulogne, Scene on the Coast of Picardy* **INFLUENCES:** Louis Francia, Eugene Delacroix, John Constable

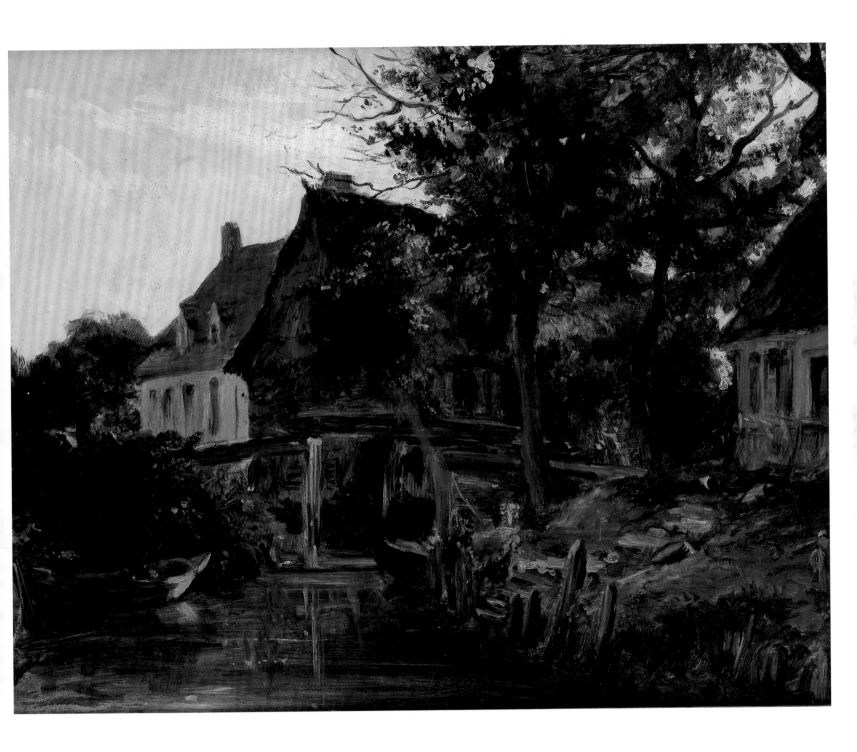

ENGLISH ROMANTIC artist, mainly active in France. Born near Nottingham, Bonington migrated to France with his family in 1817. He learned watercolour techniques from Louis Francia before completing his training under Antoine-Jean Gros at the École des Beaux-Arts. While in Paris, he met Eugene Delacroix, with whom he later shared a studio. Both men were greatly impressed by John Constable's exhibits at the 1824 Salon, and they travelled together to England in the following year. By this stage, Bonington had already made his mark at the Salon, where he won a gold medal for his landscapes. These were acclaimed for their freshness, spontaneity and feeling for atmospheric effects – qualities which the artist had developed by making copious *pochades* (outdoor oil sketches). In addition to his landscapes, Bonington also produced a series of costume paintings, illustrating picturesque anecdotes from British history.

Bonington's promising career was cut short by ill health. He contracted tuberculosis and died in London, shortly before his twenty-sixth birthday.

Thomas Cole   Mountain Sunrise, 1826

Born 1801, Lancashire, England   Painted in North America and Europe   Died 1848 Catskill, New York, USA
MOVEMENT: Hudson River School   **OTHER WORKS:** *Expulsion from the Garden of Eden, The Course of Empire*   **INFLUENCES:** Washington Alliston

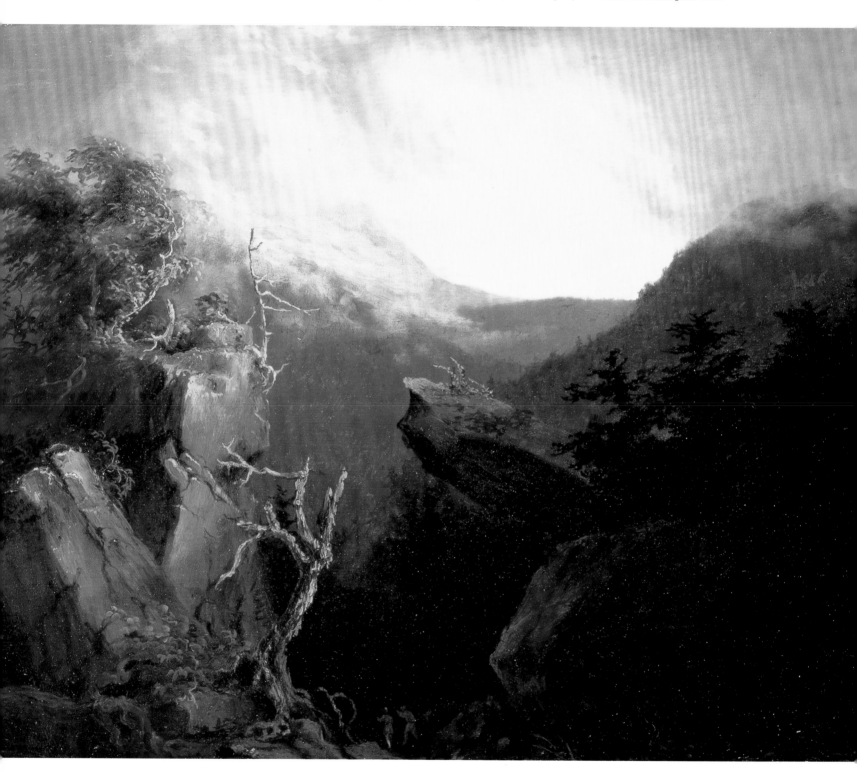

BORN IN Lancashire, England, Thomas Cole served his apprenticeship as an engraver of textile designs for calico printing. He emigrated with his family in 1818 and worked briefly as an engraver in Philadelphia before settling in Steubenville, Ohio, where he took lessons from an unknown travelling artist. In 1823 he returned to Philadelphia and enrolled at the Pennsylvania Academy of Fine Arts, then moved to New York in 1825. He began sketching along the Hudson River and through the Catskill Mountains, and his paintings of the American wilderness brought him fame and fortune. In 1829–32 he travelled all over Europe painting landscapes and classical ruins. On his return to New York he embarked on a colossal project – a series of large paintings that would chronicle the rise and fall of civilization. He took immense pride in his allegories and deprecated the landscapes which made his fortune and on which his reputation still rests.

Ando Hiroshige   Nagakubo, *c.*1830s

Born 1797 Edo Japan   Painted in Edo and Kyoto, Japan   Died 1858
MOVEMENT: Ukiyo-e **OTHER WORKS:** *Moonlight at Nagakubo, Fifty-Three Stages of the Tokaido* **INFLUENCES:** Hokusai

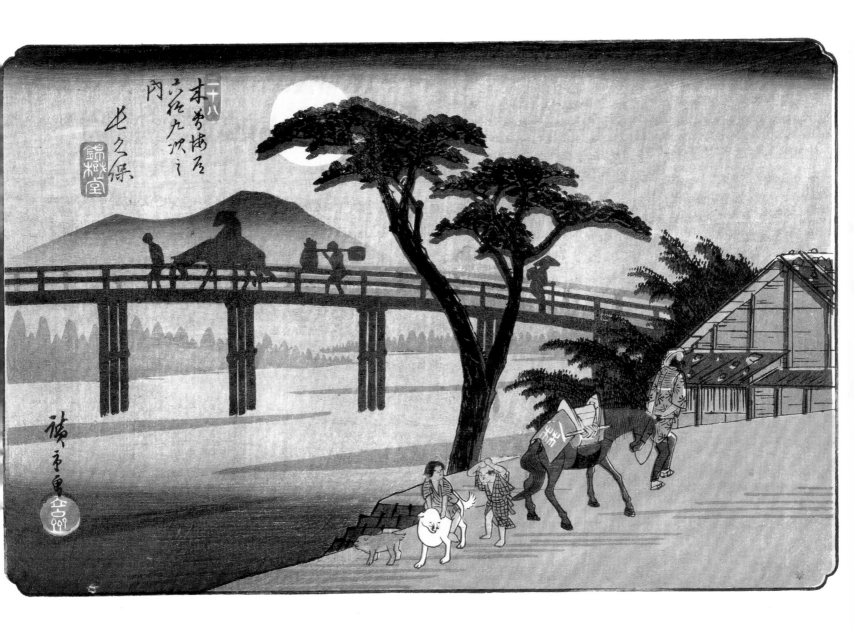

HIROSHIGE'S FAMILY name was Ando Tokitaro, but according to the custom of the time, his professional name was derived from the fact that he was a pupil of Toyohiro. He was a child prodigy, whose sketch of a procession, drawn at the age of 10, was regarded as one of the marvels of the Japanese capital in the early nineteenth century. On the death of his master in 1828, Hiroshige established his own studio, but discouraged by the lack of custom he moved to Kyoto where he produced a series of landscapes. Returning to Edo (now Tokyo) he became immensely popular and widely imitated. His landscapes in the style of Hokusai (whom he greatly admired) were executed as prints with clearly incised lines and solid blocks of colour which featured every aspect of the scenery along the Tokaido road linking Edo to Kyoto, as well as landmarks in and around the cities where he worked.

John Martin   Sunset over Rocky Bay, 1830

Born 1789 Northumberland, England   Painted in Northumberland and Isle of Man   Died 1854 Douglas, Isle of Man
MOVEMENT: English Romantic School   **OTHER WORKS:** *The Great Day of His Wrath, Eve of the Deluge, Belshazzar's Feast*   **INFLUENCES:** Hieronymus Bosch

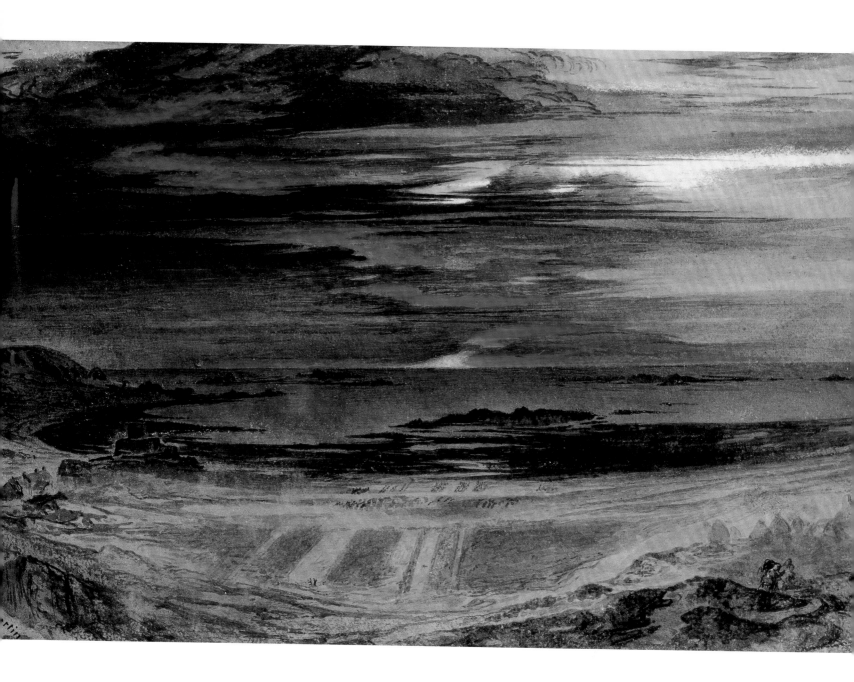

JOHN MARTIN trained as a heraldic painter in Newcastle, producing coats of arms for the nobility and gentry, and mainly worked in enamels to decorate their coach panels. Influenced by the flaming sunsets of his native Northumberland and inspired by the Book of Revelations and the apocalyptic poetry of John Milton, he began creating vast paintings which captured the end of the world and earned for him the nickname of Mad Martin. He made his debut at the Royal Academy annual exhibition in 1812 with *Sadak in Search of the Waters of Oblivion* in which the hero appeared as a tiny figure at the foot of the canvas, overwhelmed by mountains and beetling crags suffused with fiery light. His later paintings have all the qualities of some Hollywood epic and had immense appeal to the English Romantics. He also illustrated editions of Milton and produced a series of biblical illustrations.

Eugène Delacroix   Le Puits de la Casbah Tanger (detail)

Born 1798   Painted in France, England, Morocco, Spain, Algeria   Died 1863

MOVEMENT: Romanticism **OTHER WORKS:** *The Massacre at Chios, Women of Algiers, The Death of Sardanapalus* **INFLUENCES:** Rubens, Géricault, Constable

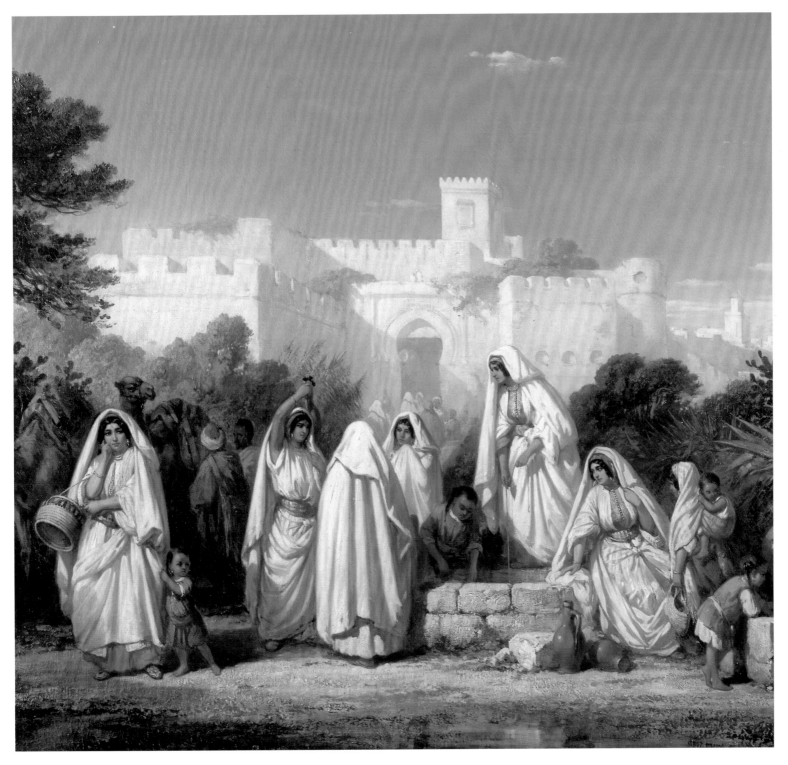

A CHAMPION of the Romantic cause, legally Delacroix was the son of a politician but in reality he was probably the illegitimate child of Talleyrand, a celebrated diplomat. He trained under Guérin, a respected Neoclassical painter, but the dominant influence on his style came from Géricault, a fellow pupil. Delacroix watched the latter creating *The Raft of the Medusa*, one of the seminal works of the Romantic movement, and was overwhelmed by its raw, emotional power. He swiftly began to emulate this in his own canvasses, achieving his breakthrough with *The Massacre of Chios*.

Critics attacked Delacroix for his apparent fixation with violence and his lack of finish. They accused him of wallowing in scenes of brutality, rather than acts of heroism. In addition, they denounced his pictures as 'sketches', because he abandoned the smooth, linear finish of the Neoclassical style, preferring to build up his compositions with small dabs of colour.

Like most Romantics, Delacroix was fascinated with the exotic but, unusually, he actually visited the Arab world. As a result, his Orientalist paintings were more sober and realistic than most European fantasies.

Sir Edwin Landseer   St Bernard Dogs

Born 1802 London   Painted in London   Died 1873 London

MOVEMENT: English School   **OTHER WORKS:** *Monarch of the Glen, The Old Shepherd's Chief Mourner*   **INFLUENCES:** George Stubbs

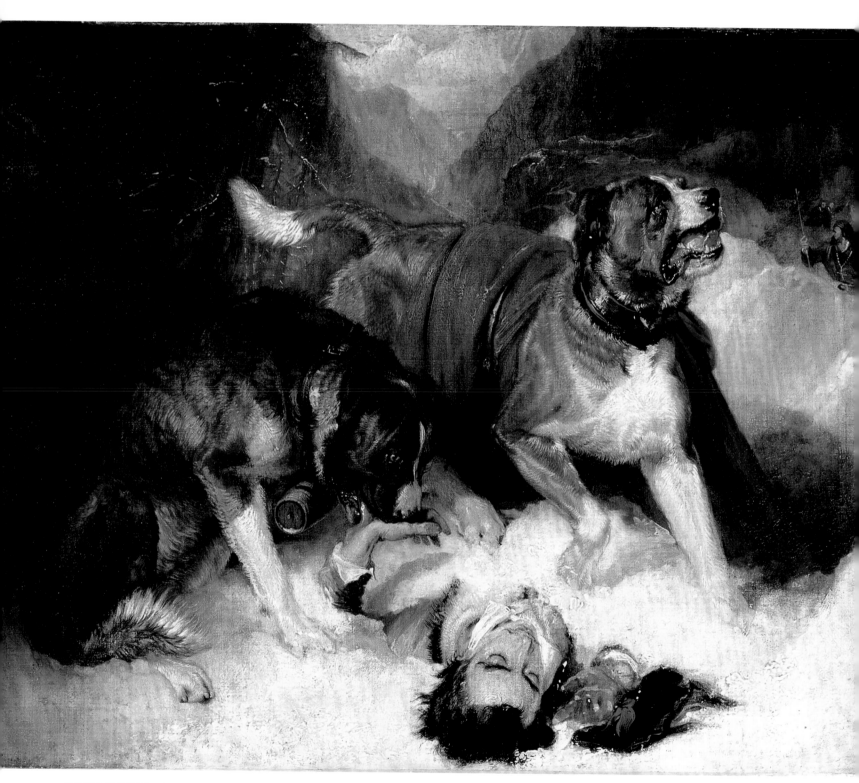

EDWIN HENRY Landseer was taught by his father to sketch animals from life. From the age of 13 he exhibited at the Royal Academy and became one of the most fashionable painters of the mid-Victorian period, specializing in pictures of dogs with humanoid expressions and deer, usually set in misty, romantic Highland glens or moorland made popular by the

novels of Scott and Queen Victoria's passion for Balmoral. Landseer's paintings attained even wider prominence as a result of the fine engravings of them produced by his brother Thomas. One of the Queen's favourite artists, he was knighted in 1850. He modelled the four lions, cast in bronze, which sit at the foot of Nelson's Column in Trafalgar Square, London,

unveiled in 1867. Landseer's posthumous reputation was dented by accusations of sentimentalizing animals and, in more recent years, of political incorrectness in glorifying blood sports, but he wielded enormous influence on a later generation of British artists.

Joshua Johnston   Portrait of Henry Long, c.1814–16

Born c. 1770   Painted in Maryland, USA   Died 1832 Baltimore, Maryland

MOVEMENT: American School of Portraiture **OTHER WORKS:** *Letitia Grace McCurdy, The Westwood Children* **INFLUENCES:** Charles Peale Polk, Charles Wilson Peale, Rembrandt

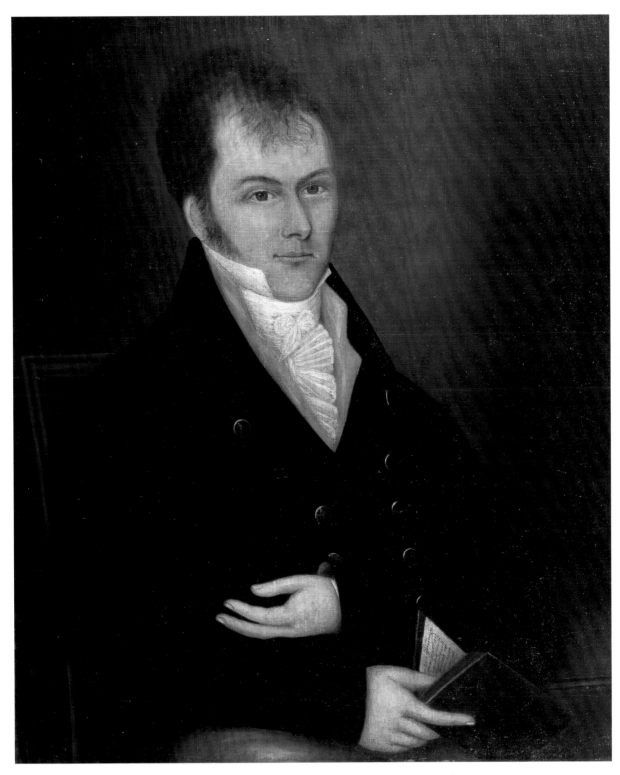

NOTHING IS known of the birth or origins of Joshua Johnston and it is likely that he was born into slavery. He may have been a slave owned by the Peale family and perhaps received his artistic training from Charles Peale Polk, whose style he closely resembles. He first appears in the Baltimore directories in 1796, and by that time must have purchased his freedom. From then until 1824 he is listed as a limner or portrait painter, and many of his paintings are still in the possession of Baltimore's oldest families. He is regarded as the first African American to become a professional artist. The portraits have a curiously naive appearance, the figures very rigid, the faces expressionless with eyes staring straight off the canvas and tightly-pursed lips. What Johnston lacked in conveying the expression of his figures was compensated in the detail of clothing and furniture in the background, and the resulting portraits and groups have a definite charm.

191

George Caleb Bingham   Fur Traders Descending the Missouri, 1845

Born 1811 Augusta, USA   Painted in Missouri, USA   Died 1879 Kansas City, USA
MOVEMENT: North American Frontier style   **OTHER WORKS:** *Raftsmen Playing Cards, The Country Election*   **INFLUENCES:** George Catlin, Seth Eastman

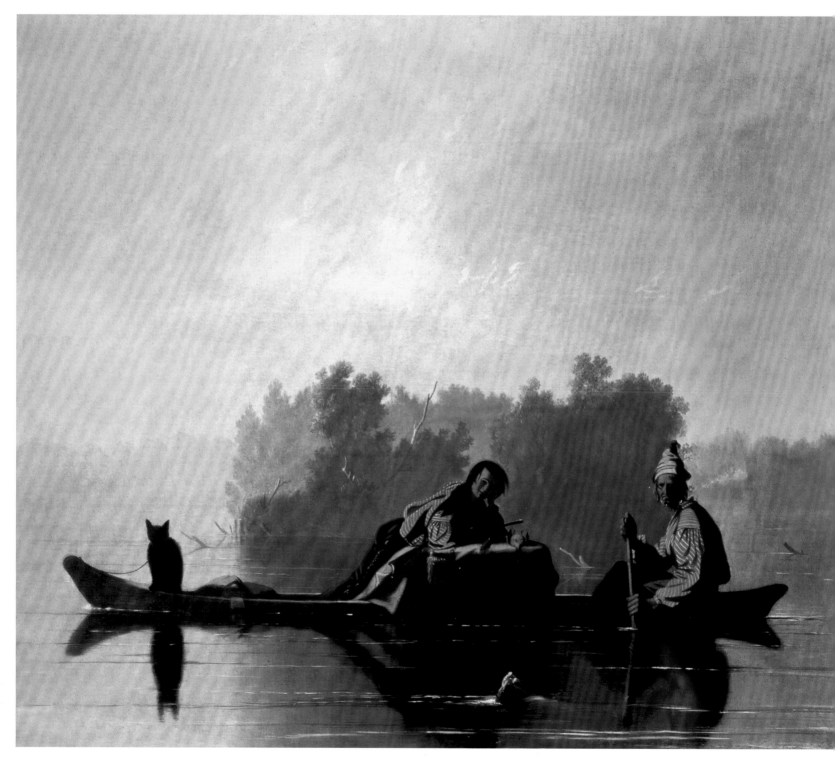

ONE OF the leading artists of the American West, George Caleb Bingham trained at the Pennsylvania Academy of Fine Arts in Philadelphia. His education was rounded off by a trip to Europe, followed by extensive travel round North America before he settled in Missouri, then on the western frontier. From here he explored the wilderness, recording landscape, sights and scenes of a rapidly vanishing way of life, although he is best remembered for his genre scenes of boatmen and trappers in Missouri. Regrettably he returned to Europe to improve his style, but the time spent in Düsseldorf had the opposite effect, stifling the homespun character of his painting with the rather stereotyped academicism of mid-nineteenth century Germany. As far back as 1848 he had been elected to the state legislature and by the time of the American Civil War he abandoned his palette altogether to concentrate on politics.

Théodore Rousseau   A Wooded Landscape at Sunset with a Faggot Gatherer

Born 1812 Paris, France   Painted in France   Died 1867 Paris

MOVEMENT: Barbizon School   **OTHER WORKS:** *Edge of a Forest – Sunset, Farm in the Landes*   **INFLUENCES:** Jacob van Ruisdael, Constable

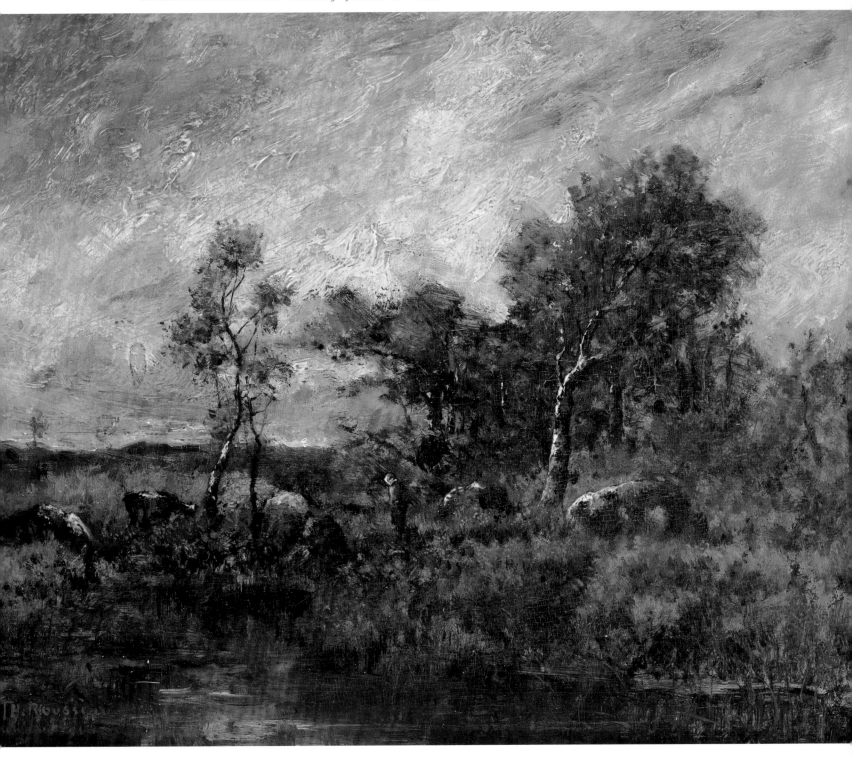

FRENCH LANDSCAPE painter, hailed as the leader of the Barbizon School. The son of a clothier, Rousseau developed a deep love of the countryside at an early age. After working briefly in a sawmill, he decided to take up landscape painting and trained with Joseph Rémond. The latter produced classical landscapes, however, and Rousseau's naturalistic tendencies were better served by the study of foreign artists, such as Ruisdael and

Constable. He adopted the practice of making sketches outdoor - a foretaste of Impressionism - although he still preferred to finish his paintings in the studio.

Rousseau's favourite location was the Barbizon region, at the edge of the Forest of Fontainebleau. By the late 1840s, this area had become the focus for a group of like-minded artists known as the Barbizon School. Headed by Rousseau, this circle included

Corot, Daubigny, Diaz and Millet. In the 1850s, Rousseau's work achieved widespread recognition, fetching high prices, but he preferred to remain in Barbizon, campaigning to preserve the character of the forest. He died in his cottage, in the arms of fellow landscapist Jean-François Millet.

Robert Duncanson   Fruit Piece, 1849

Born c. 1817 New York, USA   Painted in Cincinnati   Died 1872 Cincinnati
MOVEMENT: American School   **OTHER WORKS:** *Mount Healthy, Ohio, Belmont Murals*   **INFLUENCES:** Thomas Cole

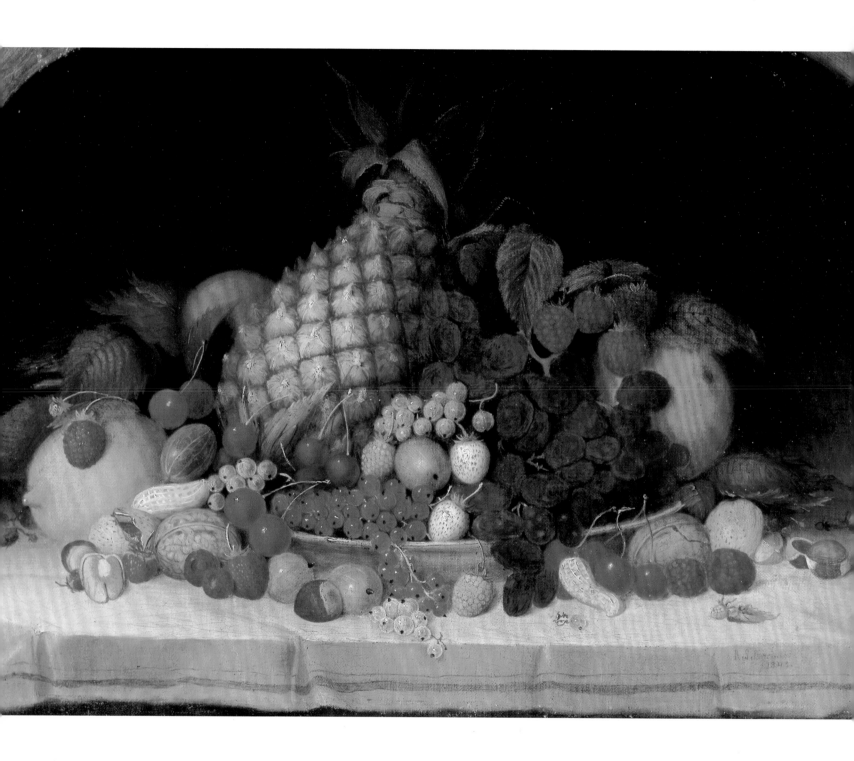

BORN IN upstate New York, the son of a Canadian Scot and a black mother, Robert Stuart Duncanson was taken to Canada as a boy and raised there by his father. It is believed that he received part of his education in Scotland before returning to America in 1841, when he went to live with his mother in Cincinnati. He was by that time an accomplished artist who showed three of his paintings in the art exhibition of 1842. He was a skilled and versatile artist, equally proficient in portraits as in the landscapes for which he is famous. He was the first black American to become a professional painter, producing a wide range of work, from still life to genre subjects. A grant from the Anti-Slavery League enabled him to travel to Italy, France and England in 1853 to further his studies. He was also an early exponent of photography, which he used as an aid to his landscapes.

Paul Delaroche Napoleon Crossing the Alps, 1850

Born 1797 France Painted in France and Italy Died 1856

MOVEMENT: Romanticism **OTHER WORKS:** *The Death of Queen Elizabeth, The Princes in the Tower* **INFLUENCES:** Antoine-Jean Gros, Richard Parkes Bonington

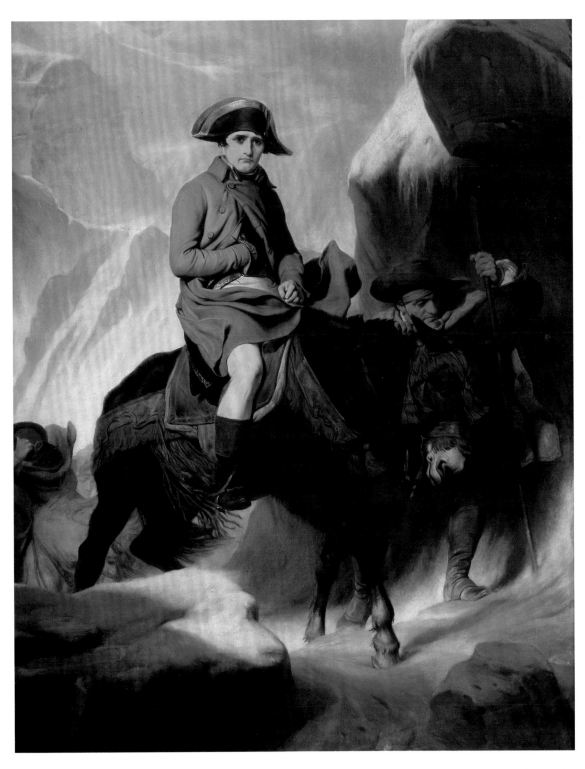

FRENCH PAINTER and sculptor, specializing in historical scenes. Delaroche trained initially as a landscapist, but turned to figure painting in 1817 after failing to win the Prix de Rome. He entered the studio of Gros and began exhibiting at the Salon in the early 1820s – at the very time when the rivalry between Romanticism and Classicism was at its fiercest. Delaroche steered a middle course between these two extremes. His historical subjects, which aimed at poignancy rather than grandeur, were typical of the Romantics, but were handled in a bland academic manner.

Neoclassical painters had taken their historical themes from ancient Greece and Rome, but for the Romantics British subjects were more appealing. This was largely due to the popularity of the novels of Sir Walter Scott. Certain themes also had a particular resonance for French spectators. Cromwell was often seen as a forerunner of Napoleon, while the beheading of Lady Jane Grey evoked memories of the French Revolution. After Delaroche's death, his melodramatic style fell completely out of favour although, in recent years, his reputation has undergone a minor revival.

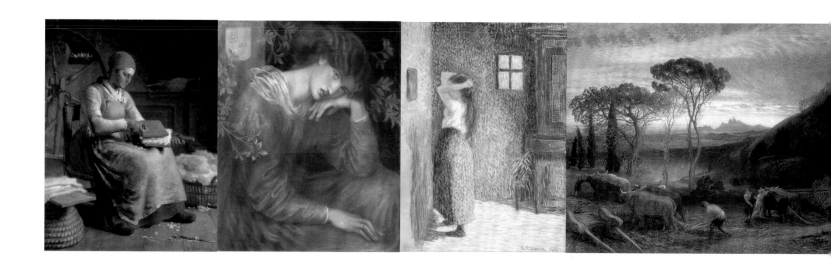

The Era of Impressionism

The Era of Impressionism
The Era of Impressionism
The Era of Impressionism
The Era of Impressionism
The Era of Impressionism
The Era of Impressionism
The Era of Impressionism
The Era of Impressionism
The Era of Impressionism
The Era of Impressionism
The Era of Impressionism
The Era of Impressionism
The Era of Impressionism
The Era of Impressionism
The Era of Impressionism

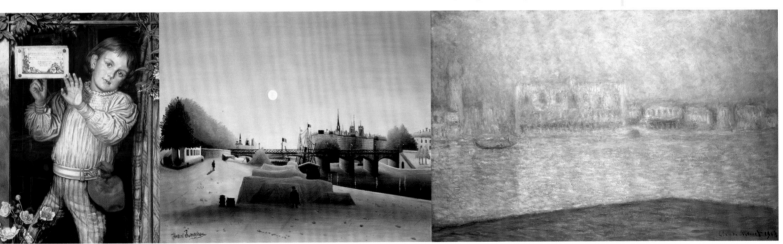

The Era of Impressionism
The Era of Impressionism
The Era of Impressionism
The Era of Impressionism
The Era of Impressionism
The Era of Impressionism
The Era of Impressionism
The Era of Impressionism
The Era of Impressionism

Cornelius Krieghoff   Indian Hunter in the Snow, 1850s

Born 1815 Holland   Painted in Canada and USA   Died 1872 Chicago, Illinois, USA

MOVEMENT: Nineteenth Century Canadian School   **OTHER WORKS:** *Merrymaking, Gentlemen's Sleigh, Lorette Falls near Quebec*   **INFLUENCES:** Jacob van Ruysdael, Gerrit van Honthorst

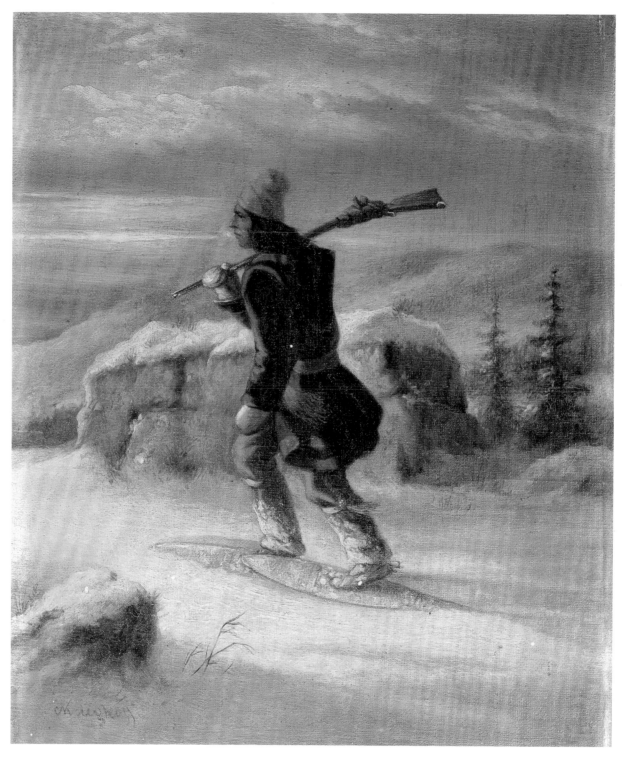

CORNELIUS DAVID Krieghoff was taught by his father, but in around 1830 he enrolled at the Academy of Fine Arts in Düsseldorf, Germany. Five years later he immigrated to the USA and joined the army, but in 1840 he settled in Montreal as a painter and musician. He later worked in Rochester, New York (1842–43) and studied in Paris (1844–45) before returning to Canada, where he worked at various times in Toronto, Montreal and Quebec City. From 1864 to 1867 he was in Paris and Munich, but continued to paint Canadian scenes there. Subsequently he worked in Quebec, concentrating on genre subjects. Though chiefly renowned for his landscapes (notably the panoramic murals in the Quebec Parliament building), he produced lively and colourful paintings of French-Canadian and Native American life in a style reminiscent of the seventeenth century Dutch masters, imparting a romantic flavor which has never been equalled. He also painted portraits of leading Canadian figures.

Gustave Courbet Bonjour Monsieur Courbet, 1854

Born 1819 France   Painted in France, Switzerland and Germany   Died 1877
MOVEMENT: Realism **OTHER WORKS:** *The Painter's Studio, The Bathers* **INFLUENCES:** Le Nain brothers, Velázquez, Millet

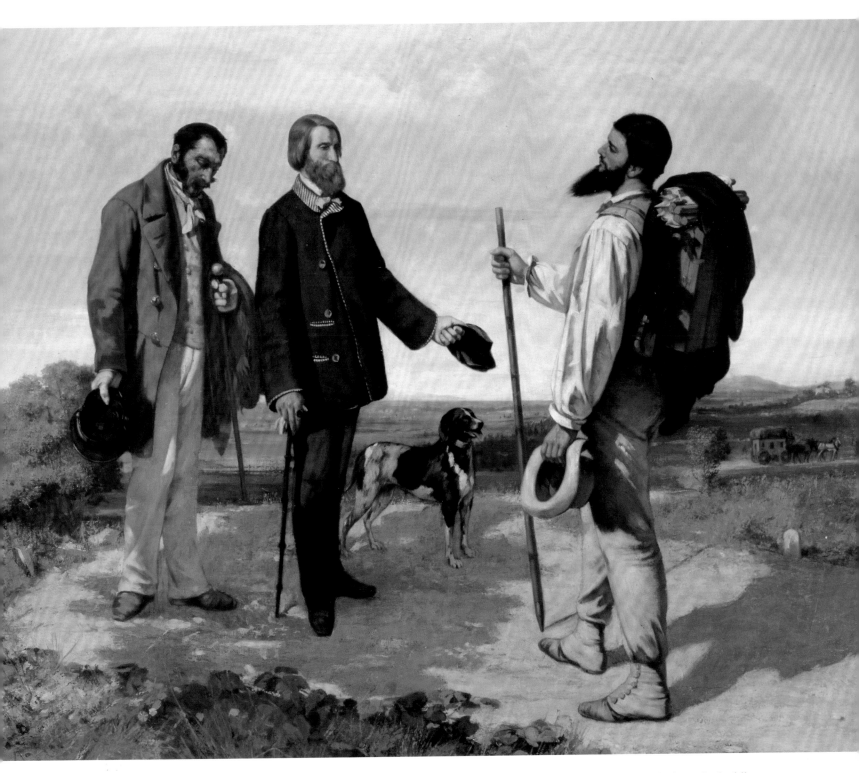

FRENCH PAINTER, the leader of the Realist movement. Courbet was born at Ornans in the Jura region, and remained fiercely loyal to this area throughout his life, featuring it prominently in his paintings. Although he later claimed to be self-taught, he actually studied under a succession of minor artists, but learned more from copying Old Masters in the Louvre. Initially, Courbet aimed for conventional success by exhibiting at the Salon, even winning a gold medal for his 1849 entry. After he showed *The Burial at Ornans*, however, official approval evaporated. Instead, this landmark realist picture was savagely criticized for being too large, too ugly and too meaningless. Worse still, in the light of the recent 1848 Revolution, the artist was suspected of having a political agenda.

Courbet revelled in the furore. In the following years, he gained greater recognition abroad, but remained antagonistic towards the French Establishment. He refused to exhibit at the 1855 World Fair, turned down the offer of a Legion of Honor, and served as a Councillor in the Paris Commune. The latter proved his undoing and he was forced to spend his final years exiled in Switzerland.

Jean–Baptiste–Camille Corot   Un Moulin à Vent, Etretat, 1855

Born 1796   Painted in France, Italy, Switzerland, England and Low Countries   Died 1875
MOVEMENT: Romanticism, Barbizon School   **OTHER WORKS:** *The Bridge at Narni, Gust of Wind, Recollection of Mortefontaine*   **INFLUENCES:** Achille-Etna Michallon, Claude Lorrain, Constable

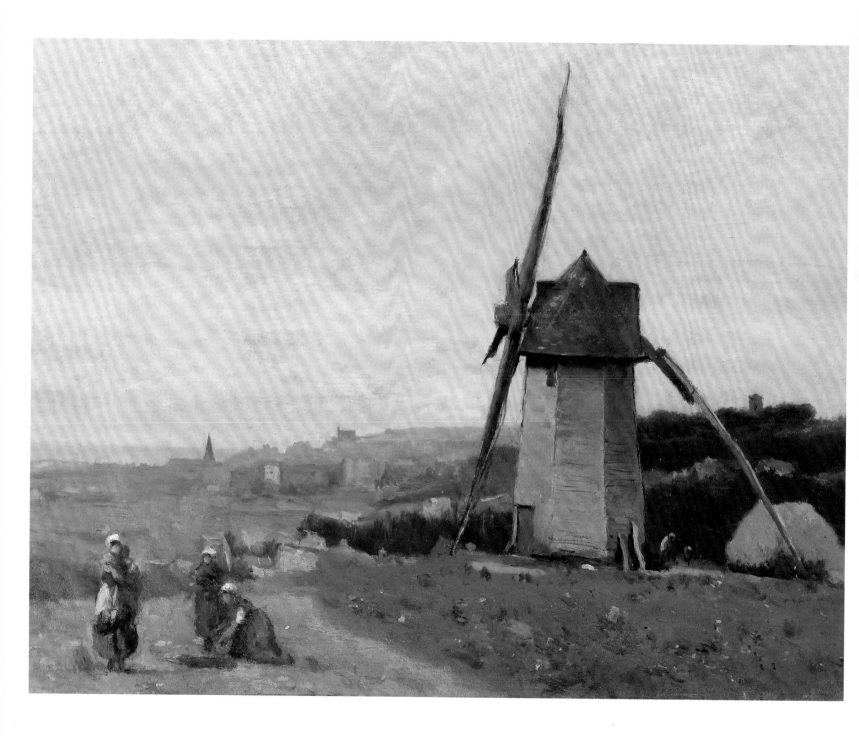

FRENCH PAINTER, specializing in landscapes in the classical tradition. Born in Paris, Corot was the son of a cloth merchant and initially followed his father's trade. For a time, he worked at The Caliph of Bagdad, a luxury fabric shop. Turning to art, he trained under Michallon and Bertin, both of whom were renowned for their classical landscapes. Indeed, Michallon was the first winner of the Historical Landscape category in the

Prix de Rome, when it was introduced in 1817. This genre, which Corot was to make his own, consisted of idealized views, set in the ancient, classical world, and was inspired by the 17th-century paintings of Poussin and Claude Lorrain.

Corot's distinctive style stemmed from his unique blend of modern and traditional techniques. Each summer, he made lengthy sketching trips around

Europe, working these studies up into paintings in the winter, in his Paris studio. He combined this traditional practice with a fascination for the latest developments in photography. The shimmering appearance of his foliage, for example, was inspired by the *halation* or blurring effects, which could be found in contemporary photos.

Honoré Daumier   Deux Buveurs, c.1857–60

Born 1808 France   Painted in France   Died 1879

MOVEMENT: Realism   **OTHER WORKS:** *The Refugees, Chess Players, Ecce Homo*   **INFLUENCES:** Charles Philipon, Gustave Courbet, Rembrandt

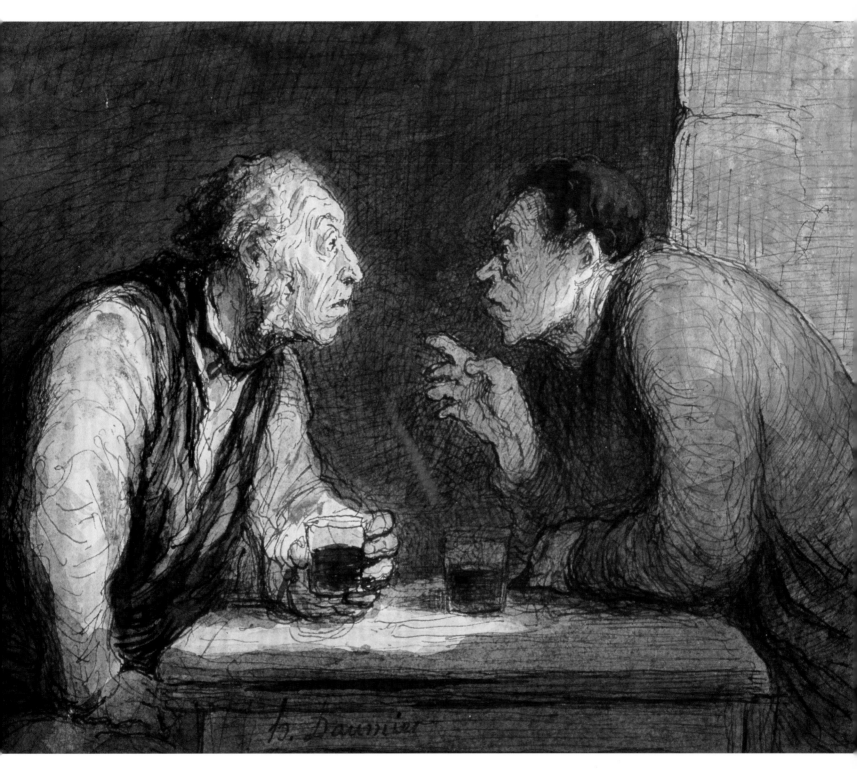

FRENCH GRAPHIC ARTIST, painter and sculptor, noted above all for his stinging caricatures. Daumier had a deprived childhood, which fuelled the campaigning nature of much of his art. His first job, in a bailiff's office, also left him with a permanent loathing for lawyers and bureaucrats. After learning lithography, however, he was soon in great demand as a political cartoonist, working principally for *Le Charivari* and *La Caricature*. A scurrilous drawing of Louis-Philippe in the guise of Gargantua made Daumier notorious, but also earned him a spell of imprisonment. Undaunted, he branched out into social satire, illustrating the foibles of contemporary society. During his lifetime, Daumier's paintings were virtually unknown and never provided him with a viable living. In their general outlook, as objective depictions of modern Parisian life, they can be linked with Courbet's Realist movement. Stylistically, however, Daumier was an isolated figure. His paintings were shaped by his graphic work, displaying a bold economy of form, subtle characterization and an overall lack of finish. In later years, his eyesight failed and he was only saved from absolute penury by the generosity of fellow painter, Corot.

Gustave Doré The Beggar Children

Born 1832, France   Painted in France and England   Died 1883
MOVEMENT: Romanticism **OTHER WORKS:** *London: A Pilgrimage* **INFLUENCES:** Charles Meryon, Grandville, Charles Philipon

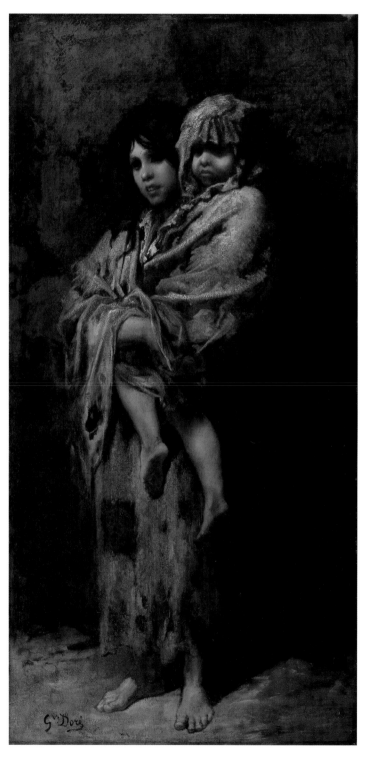

DORÉ WAS the most prolific and successful French illustrator of his age. Initially, he was drawn to caricature, spurred on by the encouragement of Philipon. As a teenager, Doré visited the Paris shop of this noted cartoonist and was briefly employed by him. He also began producing humorous drawings for *Le Journal pour Rire*. These precocious skills proved invaluable, when, following the death of his father in 1849 he became the family's main breadwinner.

Doré soon progressed to book illustrations. During the 1860s, his wood engravings for Dante's *Inferno* and Cervantes' *Don Quixote* made him famous. Stylistically, he owed much to the Romantics, excelling at depictions of the exotic and the macabre. This is particularly evident from his strange, glacial landscapes in the *Rime of the Ancient Mariner* and the grotesque beasts in the *Inferno*. Yet Doré could also be brutally realistic. His unflinching portrayal of the London slums attracted widespread praise and captured the imagination of the young Van Gogh. In later life, Doré produced some paintings and sculpture, but these are less highly regarded. His most successful venture in this field was the monument to his friend, the novelist Alexandre Dumas.

Jean–François Millet La Cardeuse, *c.*1858

Born 1814 France   Painted in France   Died 1875 France

MOVEMENTS: Naturalism, Barbizon School **OTHER WORKS:** *The Winnower, Man with a Hoe* **INFLUENCES:** Rousseau, the Le Nain brothers, Gustave Courbert

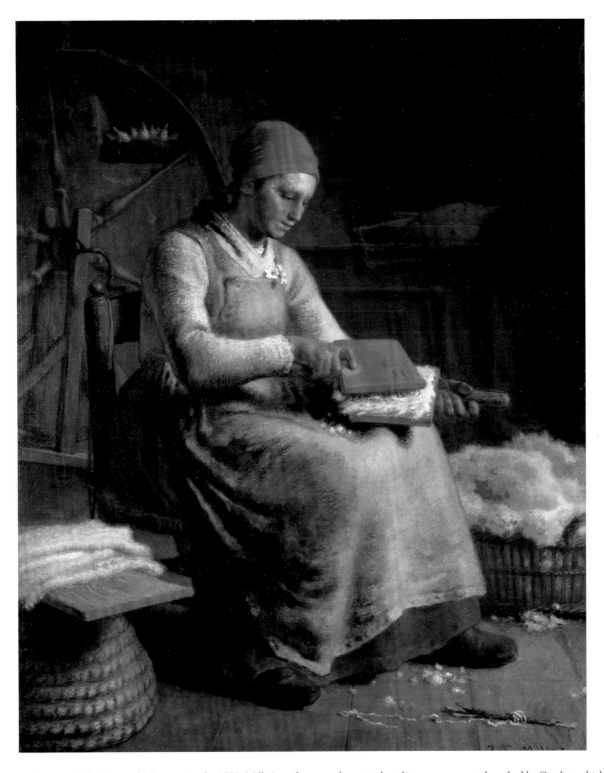

MILLET WAS born near the city of Cherbourg, which granted him a scholarship to train in Paris, under Delaroche. His early paintings were mainly portraits or pastoral idylls, but by the 1840s he was producing more naturalistic scenes of the countryside. These drew on his own experience, since he came from peasant stock, but the pictures disturbed some critics, because of their unglamorous view of rustic life.

In the 1850s Millet's work attracted genuine hostility. In part, this was due to fears that his paintings were political. Memories of the 1848 Revolution were still very fresh, and the authorities were nervous about any images with socialist overtones. Millet declined to express his political views, but *The Gleaners*, for example, was a compelling portrait of rural poverty. Some critics also linked his work with the Realist

movement, launched by Courbet, which was widely seen as an attack on the academic establishment.

After 1849, Millet was mainly based at Barbizon, where he befriended Rousseau and other members of the Barbizon School. Under their influence, he devoted the latter part of his career to landscape painting.

Grafton Tyler Brown   (after) Gold Mining in California, 1861

Born 1841 Harrisburg, USA   Painted in San Francisco and St Paul, USA   Died 1918 St Paul
MOVEMENT: American Realism **OTHER WORKS:** *San Francisco* **INFLUENCES:** Northern Sung landscape artists of China

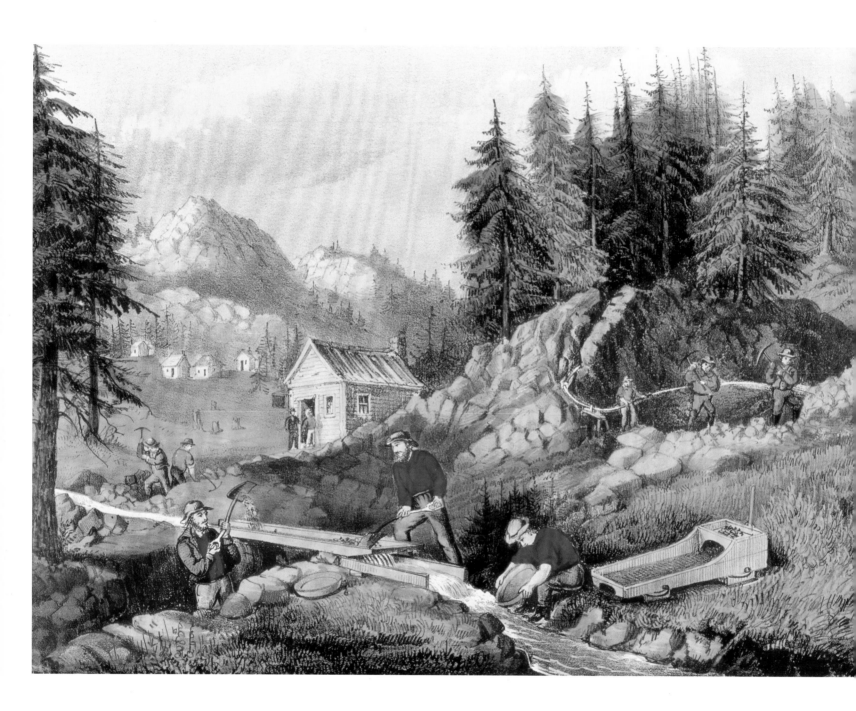

GRAFTON TYLER BROWN was the first African American to work as a professional artist in California, where he settled in the 1850s. He worked as a draughtsman and later a lithographer for Kuchel & Dressel of San Francisco, but established his own company in 1867, producing lithographic views of buildings and landmarks, many of which appeared in stock certificates. In 1882 he took part in the Bowman geological survey of British Columbia, producing numerous sketches which he later reworked as watercolours. He lived in Portland, Oregon (1886–90) and from 1892 to 1897 was employed as a draughtsman by the United States Army Engineers in St Paul, Minnesota, where he died in 1918. His landscapes are very realistic and packed with detail, well deserving the comment by one early critic that he was 'the originator of intellectual and refined art'.

Samuel Palmer   Illustrations to Milton's Lycidas, c.1864

Born 1805 London, England   Painted in England and Italy   Died 1881
MOVEMENTS: Romanticism, the Ancients **OTHER WORKS**: *The Sleeping Shepherd, Coming from Evening Church* **INFLUENCES**: William Blake, John Linnell, Edward Calvert

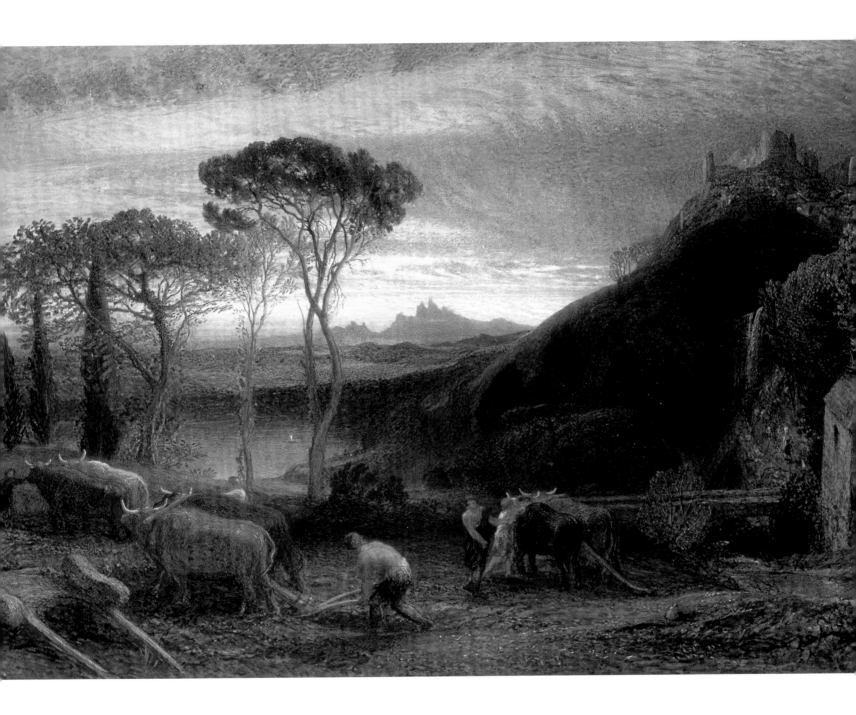

BORN IN London, the son of an eccentric bookseller, Palmer revealed his artistic talent at a very early stage. In 1819, aged just 14, he exhibited at the Royal Academy and the British Institution, selling a painting at the latter. Three years later he met the painter John Linnell, who gave him some instruction. More importantly, perhaps, Linnell also introduced Palmer to William Blake – a meeting which only served to intensify the youngster's mystical outlook.

In 1824, the same year as his encounter with Blake, Palmer started painting at Shoreham, in Kent. In this rural retreat, he began to produce the strange, pastoral idylls, which made his name. Using nothing more than ink and a sepia wash, he conjured up a worldly paradise, stocked with dozing shepherds, carefree animals and luxuriant foliage. In 1826, Palmer settled in Shoreham, where he was soon joined by a group of like-minded artists, who came to be known as the Ancients. Sadly, Palmer's period of poetic inspiration was short-lived. By the mid-1830s, his paintings had become disappointingly conventional, although his etchings retained some of his earlier, lyrical power.

Dante Gabriel Rossetti Reverie, 1868

Born 1828 Painted in England Died 1882

MOVEMENT: Pre-Raphaelite Brotherhood **OTHER WORKS:** *Beata Beatrix, Proserpine* **INFLUENCES:** Ford Madox Brown, William Bell Scott

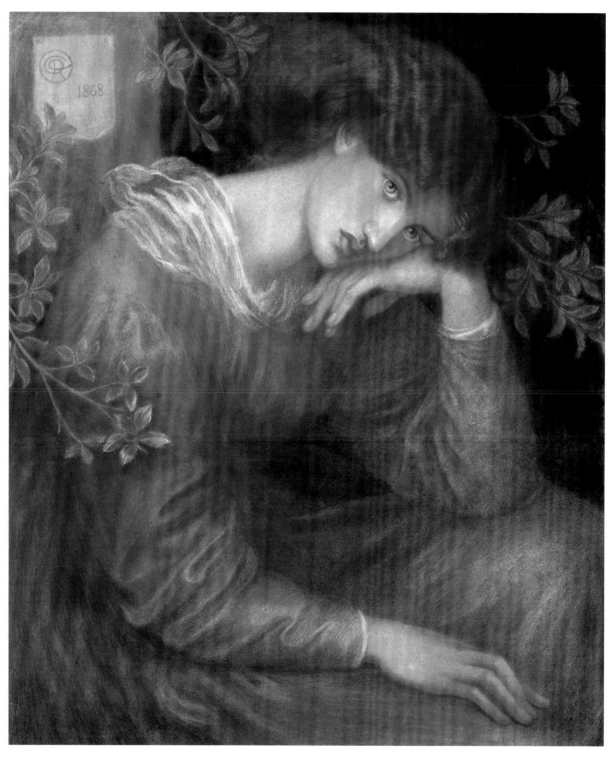

ROSSETTI CAME from a hugely talented family. His father was a noted scholar while his sister Christina became a celebrated poet. For years Dante wavered between a career in art or literature, before devoting himself to painting. While still only 20, he helped to found the Pre-Raphaelite Brotherhood, the radical group that shook the Victorian art world with their controversial exhibits at the Royal Academy in 1848. The Pre-Raphaelites were appalled by the dominant influence of sterile, academic art, which they linked with the teachings of Raphael – then regarded as the greatest Western painter. In its place, they called for a return to the purity and simplicity of medieval and early Renaissance art.

Although championed by the critic Ruskin the Pre-Raphaelites' efforts were greeted with derision and this discouraged Rossetti from exhibiting again. During the 1850s, he concentrated largely on watercolours, but in the following decade he began producing sensuous oils of women. These were given exotic and mysterious titles, such as *Monna Vanna* and were effectively the precursors of the femmes fatales, which were so admired by the Symbolists.

Sir Edward Burne–Jones   The Prince Enters the Briar Wood, 1869

Born 1833 Birmingham, England   Painted in England   Died 1898 London, England
MOVEMENT: Romanticism and Mannerism   **OTHER WORKS:** *King Cophetua and the Beggar Maid, The Beguiling of Merlin*   **INFLUENCES:** Botticelli, Mantegna, Pre-Raphaelites

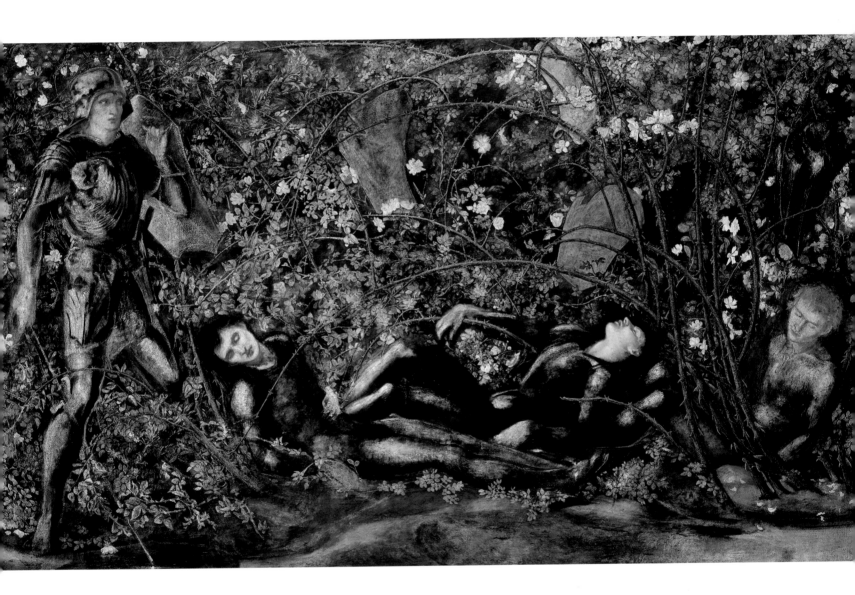

EDWARD COLEY BURNE-JONES studied at Oxford where he met William Morris and Dante Gabriel Rossetti, who persuaded him to give up his original intention of entering holy orders and concentrate on painting instead. He was also heavily influenced by the art critic John Ruskin, who introduced him to the paintings of the Pre-Raphaelites and with whom he travelled to Italy in 1862. On his return to England he embarked on a series of canvasses that echoed the styles of Botticelli and Mantegna, adapted to his own brand of dreamy mysticism in subjects derived from Greek mythology, Arthurian legend and medieval romance. Burne-Jones, made a baronet in 1894, was closely associated with the Arts and Crafts movement, designing tapestries and stained glass for William Morris, as well as being a prolific book illustrator.

James Whistler   Arrangement in Grey and Black No. 1,
Portrait of the Artist's Mother, 1871

Born 1834 Massachusetts, USA   Painted in London   Died London 1903

MOVEMENT: Realism **OTHER WORKS:** *Nocturne in Blue and Gold, Old Battersea Bridge* **INFLUENCES:** Gustave Courbet, Oriental art, Henri Fantin-Latour

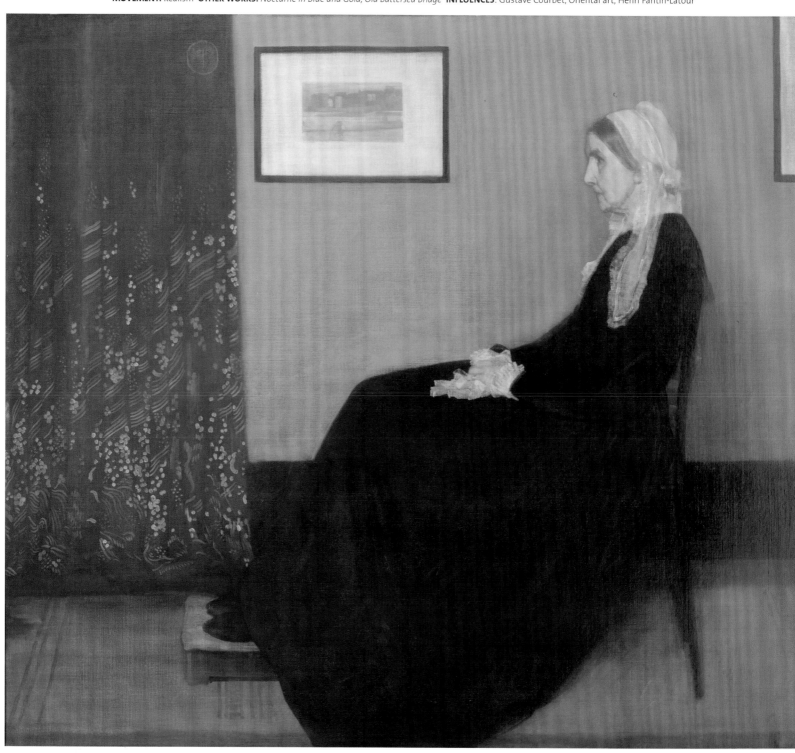

JAMES ABBOTT McNeill Whistler was originally intended for a career in the army and studied at West Point from 1851 to 1854, then worked for a year as a Navy map-maker before going to Paris to take up art instead. He met Courbet and Fantin-Latour, and joined their group of Realist painters. He copied paintings in the Louvre and fell in love with Japanese art, which was then a novelty. In 1859 he settled in London, where he began painting in a style which combined these influences rather than following the English narrative convention. He strove to present a harmonious composition of tone and colour, doing in paint what a composer might do in music. This analogy was evident in the titles of these paintings, which Whistler called *Nocturnes*. Not surprisingly, his work – including the piece shown here – got a very mixed reception, John Ruskin being his most vociferous critic and accusing him of 'flinging a pot of paint in the public's face'. Nevertheless his views gradually gained ground and influenced the next generation of British artists.

This painting has become one of Whistler's best-known and reproduced, balancing colour and form while capturing the essence of his subject.

Winslow Homer   Driftwood, 1909

Born 1836 Boston, Massachusetts, USA   Painted in USA and England   Died 1910 Maine, USA
MOVEMENT: American School   **OTHER WORKS:** *The Gulf Stream, Fishing Boats at Key West, Bearing Up, Picking Flowers*   **INFLUENCES:** John Frederick Kensett, Fitz Hugh Lane

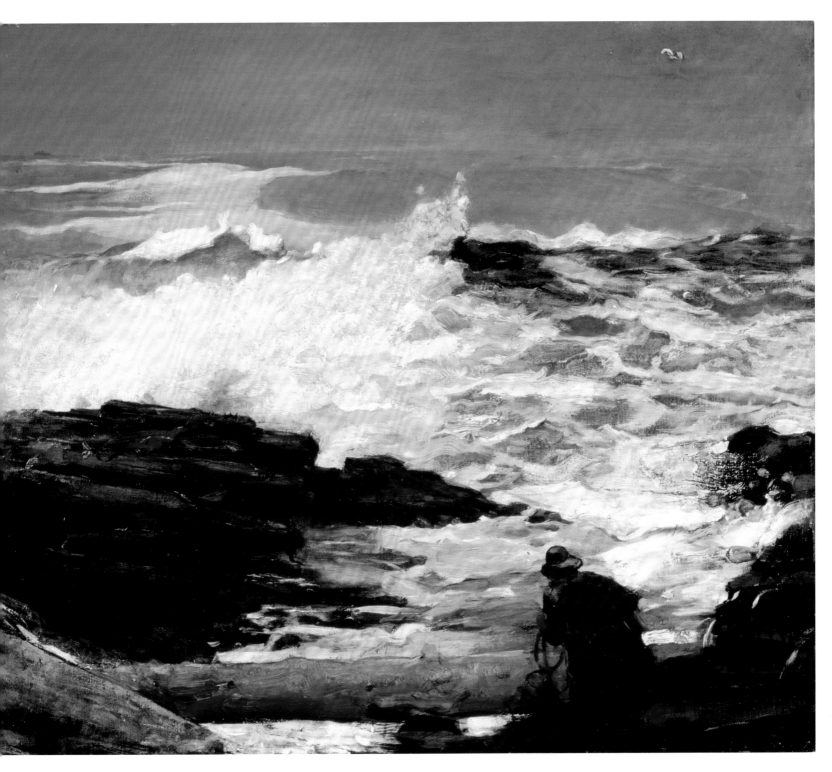

BORN IN Boston, Massachusetts, Winslow Homer served his apprenticeship there as a lithographer, but following the outbreak of the American Civil War he accompanied the Union forces and contributed sketches from the battlefront to Harper's Weekly as well as executing his earliest full-scale paintings, *Home Sweet Home* and *Prisoners from the Front*. He spent two years (1881–83) in England, mainly at Tynemouth, painting nautical subjects. Following his return to the USA he continued to paint the sea – apart from occasional genre subjects such as *The Fox Hunt*. During the last two decades of his life he lived at Prout's Neck on the coast of Maine, where he concentrated on watercolours of fishermen in the eternal struggle against the elements. Occasional forays to Florida, the Bahamas and Bermuda provided more exotic material but invariably with a maritime theme: he is perhaps best known for his dramatic views of the rugged coastline of New England, as depicted here in *Driftwood*. Here the sea itself is the main subject, and Homer successfully conveys the sheer force of nature with its potentially devastating impact upon frail humanity. In these seascapes the influence of J.M.W. Turner (1775–1851) can be seen.

Berthe Morisot   Enfant dans les Roses Trémières, 1881

Born 1841   Painted in France and England   Died 1895

MOVEMENT: Impressionism   **OTHER WORKS:** *Summer's Day, The Lake in the Bois de Boulogne*   **INFLUENCES:** Manet, Renoir, Corot

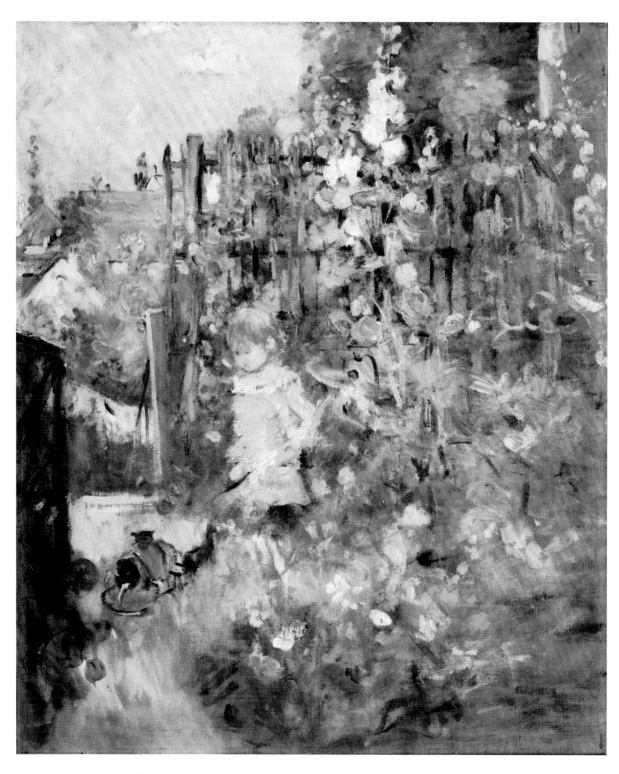

ONE OF the leading female Impressionists. The daughter of a high-ranking civil servant, Morisot received art lessons from Corot. Then in 1859, she met Fantin-Latour, who would later introduce her to future members of the Impressionist circle. Before this, she had already made her mark at the Salon, winning favourable reviews for two landscapes shown at the 1864 exhibition. Conventional success beckoned, but a meeting with Manet in 1868 altered the course of Morisot's career. She was strongly influenced by his radical style, and appeared as a model in several of his paintings. For her part, she also had an impact on Manet's art, by persuading him to experiment with *plein-air* painting. The close links between the two artists were further reinforced when Morisot married Manet's brother in 1874.

Morisot proved to be one of the most committed members of the Impressionist group, exhibiting in all but one of their shows. She concentrated principally on quiet, domestic scenes, typified by *The Cradle*, which depicts her sister Edma with her newborn child. These canvasses displayed Morisot's gift for spontaneous brushwork and her feeling for the different nuances of light.

Thomas Eakins   The Gross Clinic, 1875

Born 1844 Philadelphia, USA   Painted in Philadelphia and France   Died 1916

MOVEMENT: American School **OTHER WORKS:** *The Swimming Hole, Max Schmitt in a Single Scull* **INFLUENCES:** Jean Léon Gérôme, Léon Bonnat

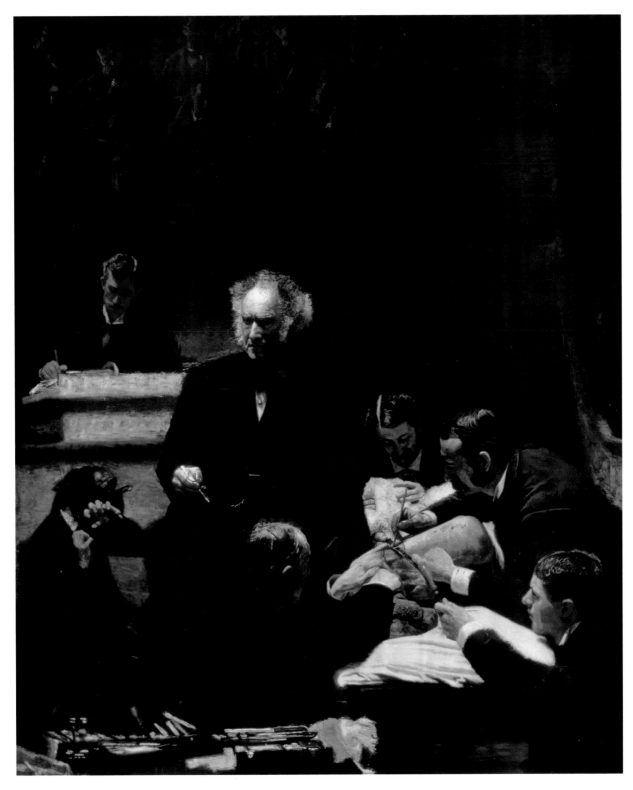

THOMAS EAKINS studied at the Pennsylvania Academy of Fine Arts and took anatomy at Jefferson Medical College before going to Paris to study under J.L. Gérôme and Léon Bonnat at the École des Beaux-Arts. On his return to Philadelphia in 1870 he established his studio, later working as Professor of Anatomy at the Pennsylvania Academy of Fine Arts. In addition to figures, he painted numerous genre scenes, such as *Chess Players*, which was critically acclaimed when exhibited at the Centennial Exposition of 1876. His greatest masterpiece, illustrated here, shows his mastery of portraiture and anatomy as the eminent surgeon Professor Gross demonstrates an operation to a group of medical students. Eakins also excelled as a sculptor and many of his paintings have a sculptural quality. He painted athletes and sportsmen, black Americans and rural subjects.

Edward M. Bannister   Oak Trees, 1876

Born 1828 Canada   Painted in Boston, Providence and Rhode Island, USA   Died 1901 Providence

MOVEMENT: American School **OTHER WORKS:** *Seaweed Gatherers, Dorchester, Massachusetts* **INFLUENCES:** Corot, Millet

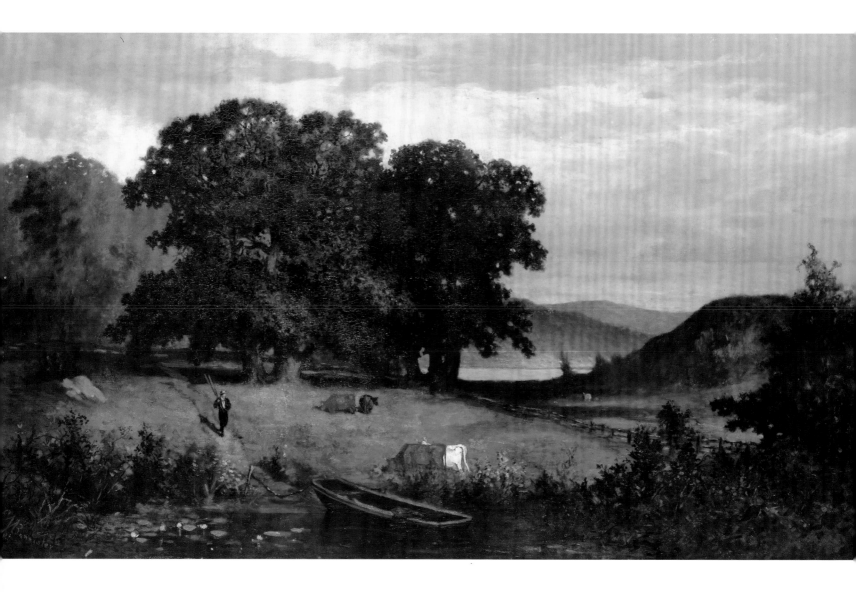

THE SON of a West Indian and a woman from Canada's Maritime provinces, Edward Mitchell Bannister moved to Boston in 1848, working as a ship's cook and then as a barber. In the 1850s he joined the Crispus Attucks Choir and the Histrionics Club, a black drama group. His marriage to Christiana Carteaux, who owned a chain of high-class hair salons, gave him the financial freedom to pursue his artistic interests and he became the first black to attend art classes at the Lowell Institute. In 1870 the Bannisters moved to Providence, Rhode Island, where Bannister took a prominent role in the circle of artists influenced by the Barbizon School. He regarded the rural landscape as an affirmation of harmony and spirituality, although he did not cavil at the advances of industrialization and painted such subjects with equal enthusiasm. In the last years of his life he produced a number of paintings of rural scenes and genre subjects.

Henri Rousseau   Vue de L'Isle Saint–Louis, Prise du Port Saint–Nicolas Le

Born 1844 France   Painted in France   Died 1910 Paris, France
MOVEMENT: Naive Art **OTHER WORKS:** *Surprised! (Tropical Storm with a Tiger), The Sleeping Gypsy* **INFLUENCES:** Jean-Léon Gérôme, Félix Clément

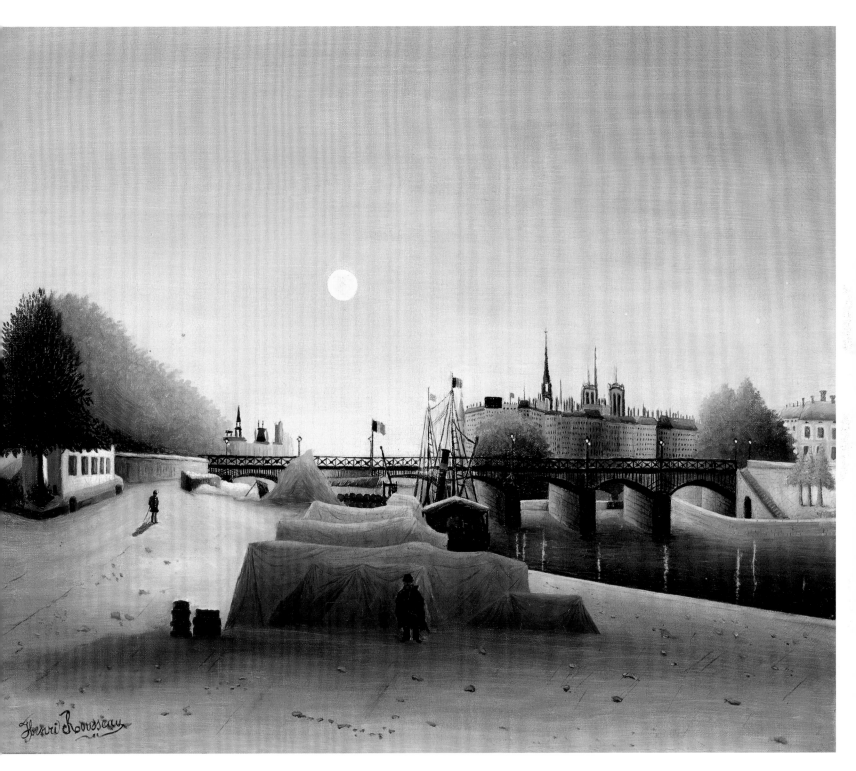

FRENCH PAINTER, perhaps the most famous of all Naive artists. Rousseau came from a poor background and he went through a succession of menial jobs, before turning to art late in life. Among other things he was a clerk, a soldier and a toll-collector. While working as the latter, he began painting as a hobby and, in 1893, he took early retirement, in order to pursue his artistic ambitions.

Rousseau was entirely self-taught, although he did take advice from academic artists such as Clément and Gérôme. He copied many of the individual elements in his pictures from book illustrations, using a mechanical device called a pantograph. But it was his dreamlike combination of images and his intuitive sense of colour which gave his art its unique appeal.

Rousseau began exhibiting his paintings from the mid-1880s, using avant-garde bodies such as the Salon des Indépendants, for the simple reason that they had no selection committee. He never achieved great success, but his guileless personality won him many friends in the art world, among them Picasso, Apollinaire and Delaunay. Posthumously, his work was an important influence on the Surrealists.

Edgar Degas   Danseuses Vertes, 1878

Born 1834 France   Painted in France, USA and Italy   Died 1917

MOVEMENT: Impressionism **OTHER WORKS:** *The Dancing Class, Carriage at the Races, Absinthe* **INFLUENCES:** Jean-Auguste-Dominique Ingres, Edouard Manet

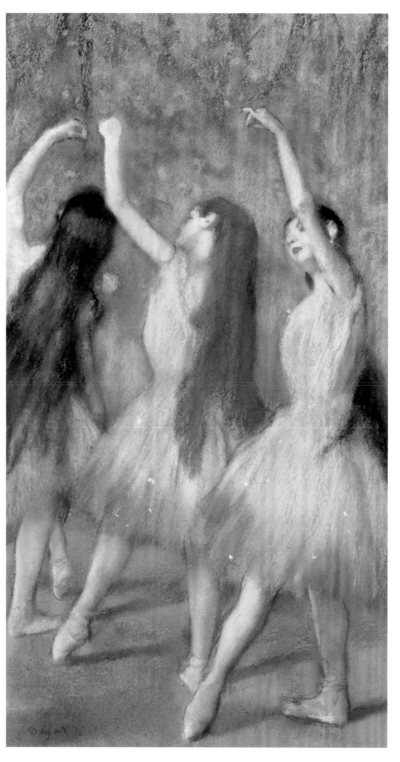

FRENCH PAINTER and graphic artist, one of the leading members of the Impressionist circle. Originally destined for the law, Degas' early artistic inspiration came from the Neoclassical painter Ingres – who taught him the value of sound draughtsmanship – and from his study of the Old Masters. However, he changed direction dramatically after a chance meeting with Manet in 1861. Manet introduced him to the Impressionist circle and, in spite of his somewhat aloof manner, Degas was welcomed into the group, participating in most of their shows.

Degas was not a typical Impressionist, having little enthusiasm for either landscape or *plein-air* painting but he was, nevertheless, extremely interested in capturing the spontaneity of a momentary image. Where most artists sought to present a well-constructed composition, Degas wanted his pictures to look like an uncomposed snapshot; he often showed figures from behind or bisected by the picture frame. Similarly, when using models, he tried to avoid aesthetic, classical poses, preferring to show them yawning, stretching or carrying out mundane tasks. These techniques are seen to best effect in Degas' two favourite subjects: scenes from the ballet and horse-racing.

Edouard Manet   La Rue Mosnier aux Drapeaux, 1878

Born 1832 France   Painted in France   Died 1883 France
MOVEMENTS: Realism, Impressionism   **OTHER WORKS:** *A Bar at the Folies-Bergère*   **INFLUENCES:** Velázquez, Gustave Courbet

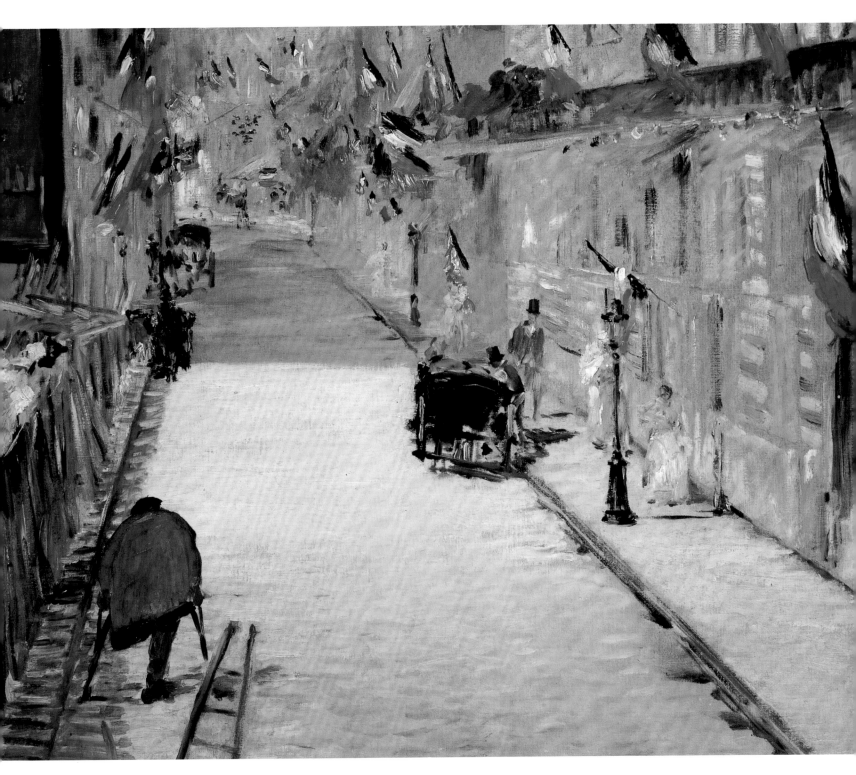

INFLUENTIAL FRENCH painter, regarded by many as the inspirational force behind the Impressionist movement. Coming from a wealthy family, Manet trained under the history painter Couture, but was chiefly influenced by his study of the Old Masters, particularly Velázquez. His aim was to achieve conventional success through the Salon, but ironically two controversial pictures cast him in the role of artistic rebel. *Le Déjeuner sur l'Herbe* and *Olympia* were both updated versions of Renaissance masterpieces, but the combination of classical nudes and a modern context scandalized Parisian critics. This very modernity, however, appealed strongly to a group of younger artists, who were determined to paint scenes of modern life, rather than subjects from the past. This circle of friends who gathered round Manet at the Café Guerbois were to become the Impressionists.

Manet was equivocal about the new movement. He enjoyed the attention of his protégés, but still hoped for official success and, as a result, did not participate in the Impressionist exhibitions. Even so, he was eventually persuaded to try open-air painting, and his later pictures display a lighter palette and a freer touch.

Pierre–Auguste Renoir   Les Baigneuses, 1892

Born 1841 France   Painted in France   Died 1919

MOVEMENT: Impressionism   **OTHER WORKS:** *The Luncheon of the Boating Party, The Bathers, The Umbrellas,*   **INFLUENCES:** Monet, François Boucher, Rubens

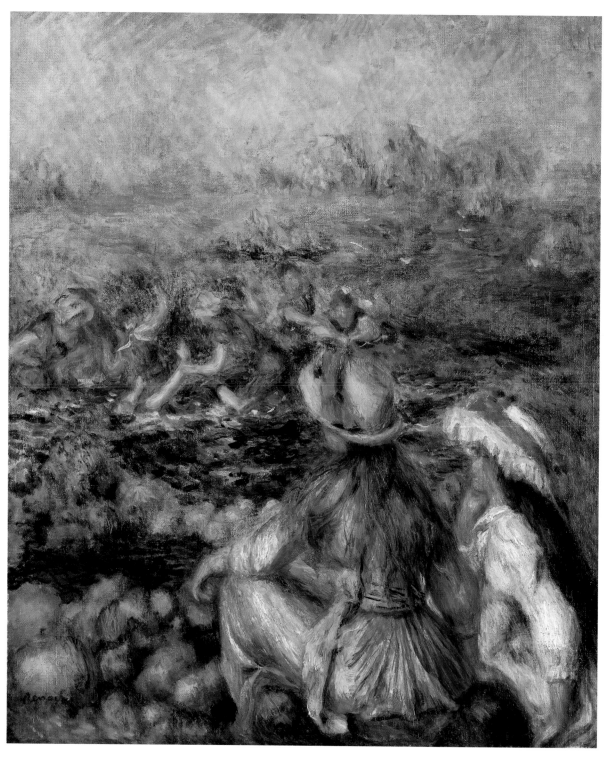

FRENCH IMPRESSIONIST. Born in Limoges, Renoir trained as a porcelain-painter before entering the studio of Gleyre in 1862. He learnt little from this master, but did meet future members of the Impressionist circle who were fellow-pupils. Together they attended the meetings at the Café Guerbois, where Manet held court. Initially, Renoir was particularly close to Monet, and the pair often painted side by side on the River Seine. Although both were desperately poor, these early, apparently carefree pictures are often cited as the purest distillation of Impressionist principles.

Renoir participated at four of the Impressionist shows, but gradually distanced himself from the movement. This was partly because of his growing success as a portraitist, and partly because he had never lost his affection for Old Masters such as Rubens and Boucher. In the early 1880s, he reached a watershed in his career. He married Aline Charigot, one of his models, and travelled widely in Europe and North Africa, reaffirming his taste for the art of the past. In his subsequent work, he moved away from traditional Impressionist themes, concentrating instead on sumptuous nudes.

Albert Pinkham Ryder   Sundown, 1880

Born 1847 USA   Painted in New Bedford and New York, USA   Died 1917 New Bedford
MOVEMENT: American Expressionism   **OTHER WORKS:** *The Watering Place*   **INFLUENCES:** William Edgar Marshall

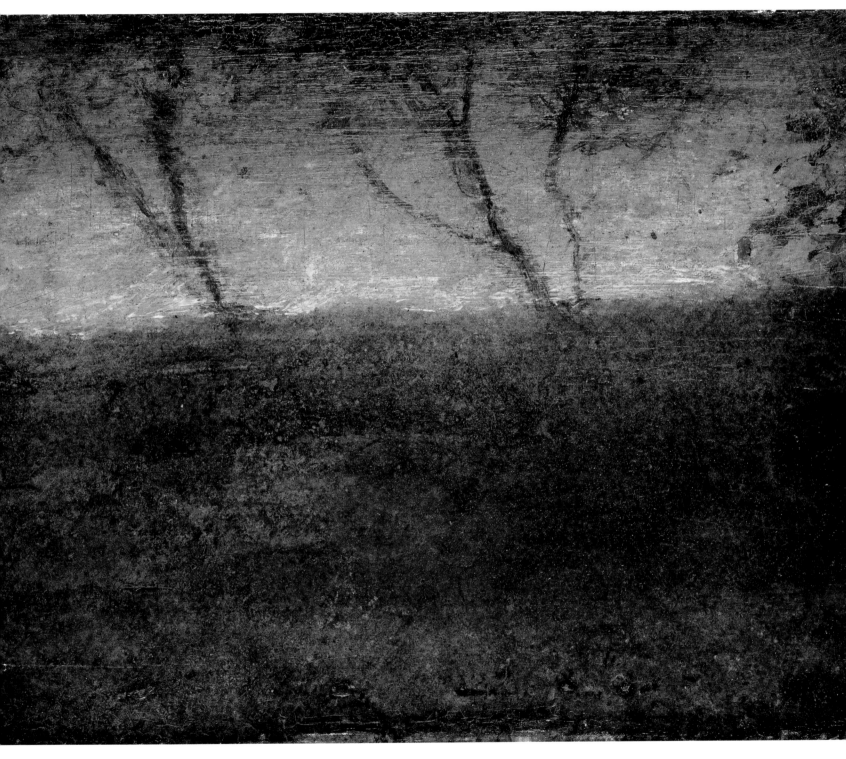

ALBERT PINKHAM RYDER came from a long line of seafarers and whalers, but his formal education was terminated as a result of an illness which gravely affected his eyesight, and it has been suggested that his dark, moonlit pictures and vague forms may have resulted from his impaired vision. To while away the time his father bought him paints and a few lessons from a local amateur got him started. Not until he moved to New York in 1867 was he able to improve his skills under William Edgar Marshall and four years later he succeeded at the second attempt in enrolling at the National Academy of Design. Although he visited Europe several times, neither the Old Masters nor contemporary artists had any influence on his work, which consisted mostly of small landscapes. In the 1880s he turned to more metaphysical paintings inspired by poetry and the Bible, becoming a recluse in his last years.

Alfred Sisley   Le Barrage de Saint Mammes, 1885

Born 1839, Paris, France   Painted in France and England   Died 1899 Moret-sur-Loing, France
MOVEMENT: Impressionism **OTHER WORKS:** *Wooden Bridge at Argenteuil, Snow at Veneux-Nadon* **INFLUENCES:** Corot, Paul Renoir, Monet, Charles Gleyre

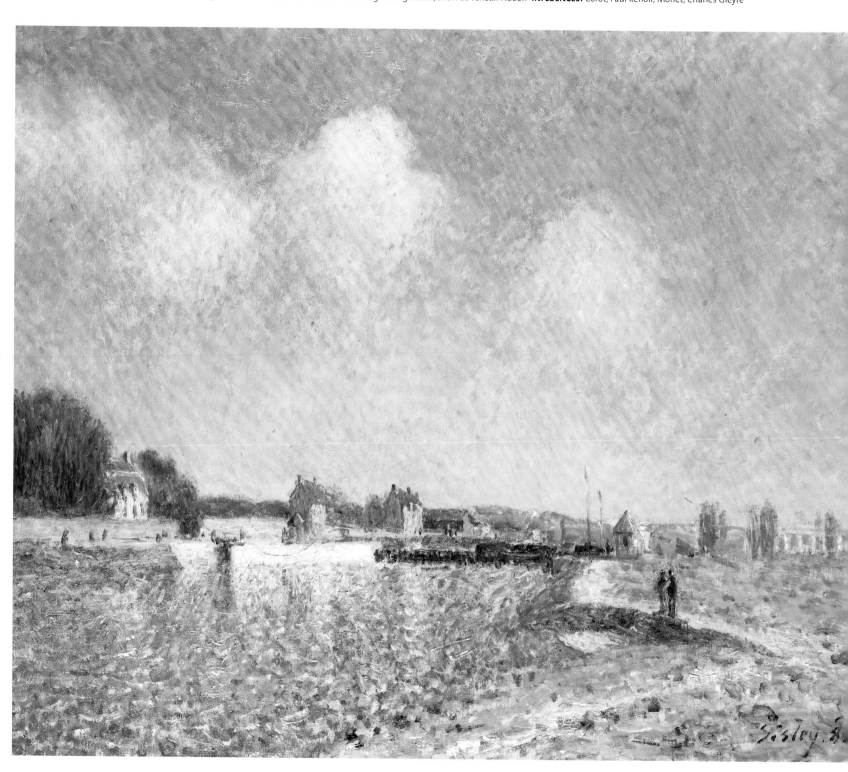

BORN IN Paris of English parents, Alfred Sisley had a conventional art education in Paris and at first was strongly influenced by Corot. In 1862 he entered the studio of Charles Gleyre, where he was a fellow pupil with Monet and Renoir, whom he joined on sketching and painting expeditions to Fontainebleau. The range of colours employed by Sisley lightened significantly under the influence of his companions.

From 1874 onwards he exhibited regularly with the Impressionists and is regarded as the painter who remained most steadfast to the aims and ideals of that movement. The vast majority of his works are landscapes, drawing on the valleys of the Loire, Seine and Thames for most of his subjects. Sisley revelled in the subtleties of cloud formations and the effects of light, especially in the darting reflection of water.

Hopeless at the business aspects of his art and largely dependent on his father for money, Sisley spent his last years in great poverty. Like Van Gogh, interest in his paintings only developed after his death.

Sir Lawrence Alma–Tadema   Roses of Heliogabalus, 1888

Born 1836 Dronrijp, Holland   Painted in Holland, England   Died 1912 Wiesbaden, Germany
MOVEMENT: Neoclassical **OTHER WORKS:** *The Finding of Moses, The Conversion of Paula* **INFLUENCES:** Baron Hendryk Leys

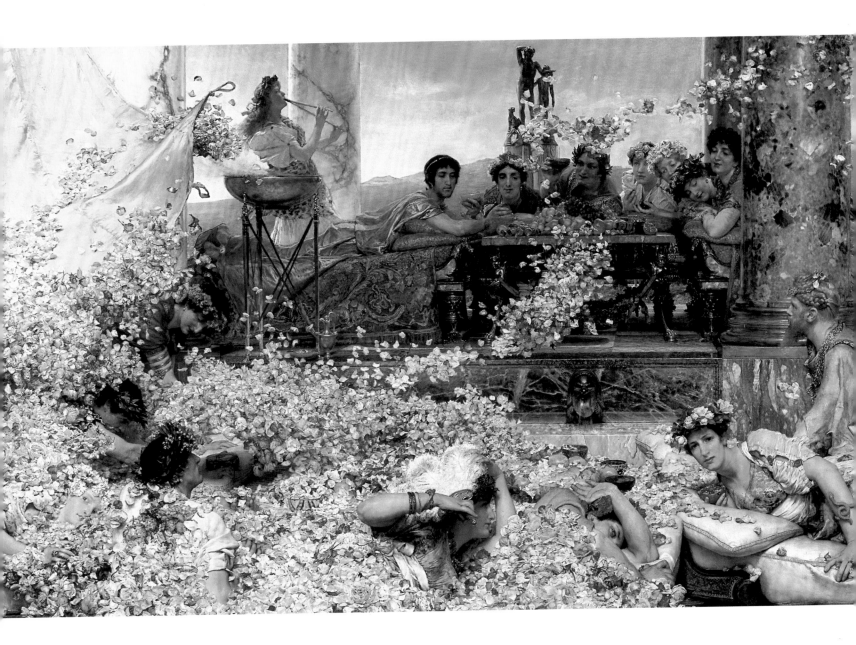

LAWRENCE ALMA-TADEMA trained at the Antwerp Academy of Art and later studied under Baron Hendryk Leys, an artist noted for his large historical paintings. In 1863 Alma-Tadema went to Italy, whose classical remains, notably at Pompeii, exerted a great influence on him. He moved to England in 1870, where he built up a reputation for narrative paintings in the Classical style. He was knighted in 1899. Three years later he visited Egypt and the impact of Pharaonic civilization had a major impact on the works of his last years. His large paintings brought everyday scenes of long-dead civilizations vividly to life through his extraordinary master of detail. He amassed a vast collection of ancient artefacts, photographs and sketches from his travels; the visual aids that enabled him to recreate the ancient world.

Camille Pissarro   Jeune Paysanne à sa Toilette, 1888

Born 1830   Painted in France, England and Venezuela   Died 1903
MOVEMENT: Impressionism **OTHER WORKS:** *View of Pontoise, A Road in Louveciennes, Red Roofs* **INFLUENCES:** Corot, Monet, Seurat

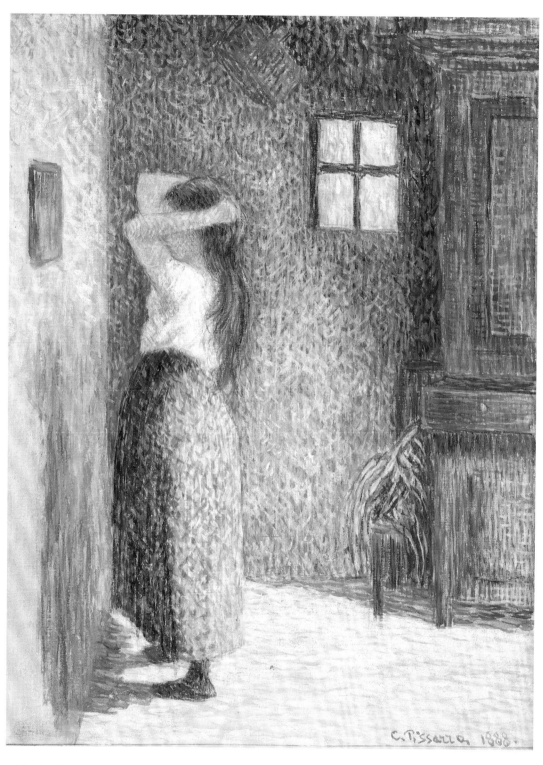

FRENCH PAINTER, one of the founding fathers of Impressionism. Born at St Thomas in the West Indies, Pissarro was schooled in Paris and enjoyed a brief interlude in Venezuela, before eventually settling in France in 1855. There, he was initially influenced by Corot, whose landscapes he admired at the Universal Exhibition. He also studied at the Académie Suisse, where he met Monet, who introduced him to the future Impressionist circle at the Café Guerbois. Pissarro remained in close contact with Monet in 1870–71, when both men took refuge in London during the Franco-Prussian War.

Pissarro was slightly older than the other Impressionists and this, together with his ability as a teacher, enabled him to assume a guru-like authority within the group. In the mid-1880s, Pissarro flirted briefly with Seurat's Neo-Impressionist techniques, before reverting to his traditional style. In later years, he had increasing trouble with his eyesight and could no longer paint out of doors. Instead, he took to painting lively street scenes from rented hotel rooms. His son Lucien also became a successful artist.

John Singer Sargent Women at Work, *c.*1910

Born 1856 Florence, Italy Painted in France, England and USA Died 1925 London, England
MOVEMENT: Anglo-American School **OTHER WORKS:** *The Lady of the Rose, Carmencita, Gassed* **INFLUENCES:** Carolus-Duran, Frans Hals, Velázquez

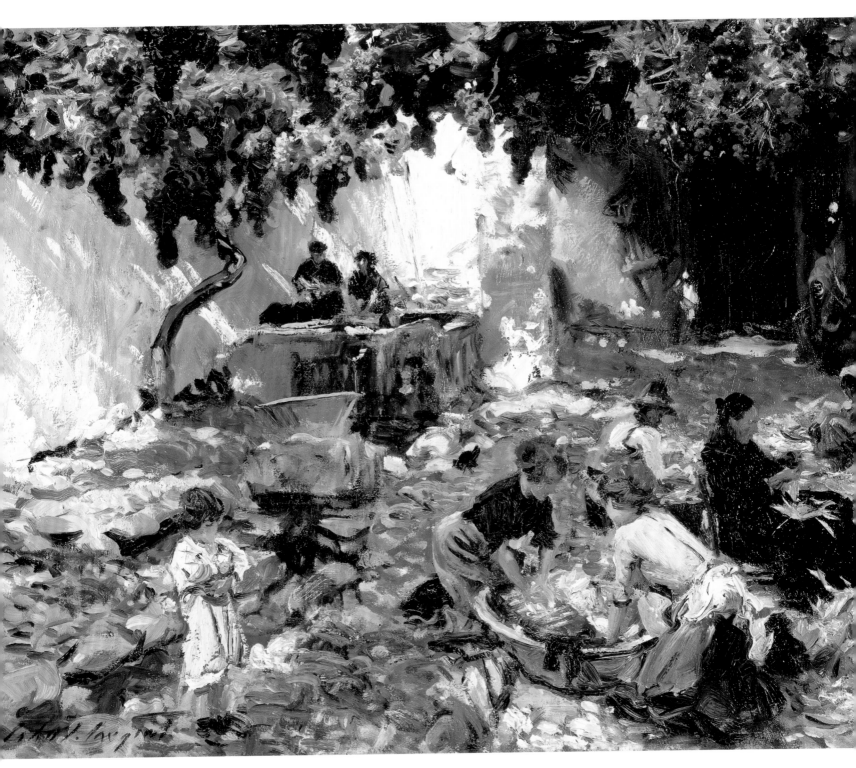

BORN OF American parents in Florence, Italy, John Singer Sargent was brought up in Nice, Rome and Dresden – giving him a rather sporadic education but a very cosmopolitan outlook. He studied painting and drawing in each of these cities, but his only formal schooling came at the Accademia in Florence, where he won a prize in 1873, and in the studio of Carolus-Duran in Paris (1874). In 1876 he paid the

first of many trips to the USA, re-affirming his American citizenship in that Centennial year. He painted landscapes, but it was his early portraits that earned him acclaim. However, the scurrilous treatment of him by the French press over a décolleté portrait of Madame Gautreau induced him to leave France in 1885 and settle in London, where he spent most of his life. As well as portraits he produced large

decorative works for public buildings from 1910 onwards. Some of his most evocative paintings were produced as a war artist in 1914–18.

Sir John Everett Millais   Sweet Emma Morland, 1892

Born 1829, England   Painted in England and Scotland   Died 1896 London, England

MOVEMENT: Pre-Raphaelite Brotherhood   **OTHER WORKS:** *Ophelia, Sir Isumbras at the Ford, Bubbles*   **INFLUENCES:** William Holman Hunt, Dante Gabriel Rossetti

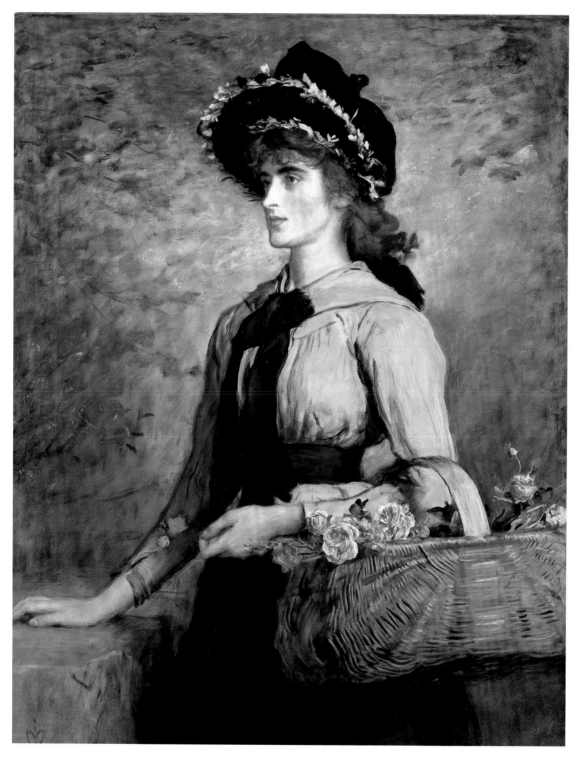

ENGLISH PAINTER and illustrator, a founding member of the Pre-Raphaelite Brotherhood. Born in Southampton, Millais was a child prodigy and, at the age of 11 became the youngest-ever pupil at the Royal Academy Schools. With Rossetti and Hunt, he formed the nucleus of the Pre-Raphaelite Brotherhood. His *Christ in the Carpenter's Shop* was pilloried by the critics, although his work was vigorously defended by John Ruskin. Millais' relations with this influential critic were initially very cordial, until he fell in love with Ruskin's wife, Effie.

Millais' rift with the art establishment did not last long. He continued painting dreamy Pre-Raphaelite themes until around 1860, but found that they did not sell well and took too long to complete. So gradually he adopted a more commercial style and subject matter, specializing in imposing portraits, sentimental narrative pictures, and mawkish studies of children. He also became a prolific book illustrator. This approach won Millais many honors – he was raised to the peerage and became President of the Royal Academy – but damaged his long-term artistic reputation.

Adolph Von Menzel   Auf der Fahrt durch Schone Natur, 1892

Born 1815 Breslau, Germany (now Wroclaw, Poland)   Painted in Berlin   Died 1905 Berlin

MOVEMENT: German Romanticism   **OTHER WORKS:** *Chess Players, Coronation of Wilhelm I in Königsberg*   **INFLUENCES:** Claude Monet

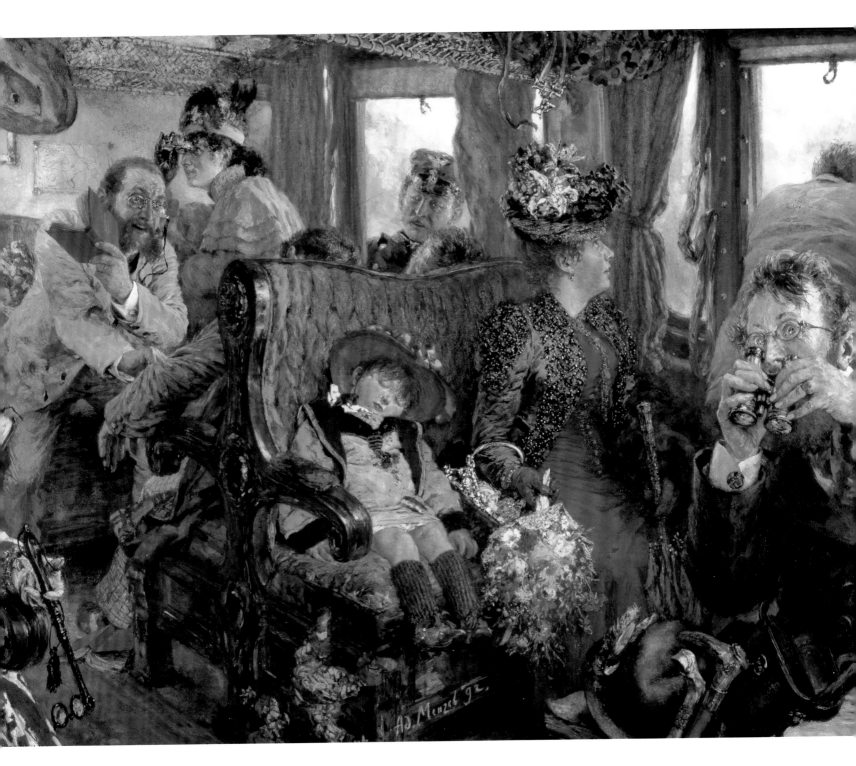

THE SON of a schoolmaster and lithographer, Adolph von Menzel was taught by his father and made his debut at an exhibition in Breslau in 1828 with a drawing of a tigress. The family moved to Berlin in 1830, where Adolph was employed in his father's business as a draughtsman and book illustrator. At the Berlin Academy show (1833) he exhibited illustrations for the works of Goethe. Later he produced a series showing the uniforms of the Prussian Army and woodcut engravings of historical subjects. Inspired by the Revolution of 1848 he painted his first great historic work, *The Lying in State of the March Fallen* – the first German political painting. Later he produced numerous portraits and historical scenes, and was employed as a war artist during the Seven Weeks' War (1866) and the Franco-German War (1870–71), for which he was awarded the Ordre Pour le Mérite, Prussia's highest decoration. A pillar of the establishment, he influenced the heroic style of German painting in the late nineteenth century.

John William Waterhouse Ophelia, *c.*1894

Born 1849   Painted in England and Italy   Died 1917

MOVEMENTS: Late Romantic, Symbolism **OTHER WORKS:** *Hylas and the Nymphs, St Eulalia, Echo and Narcissus* **INFLUENCES:** Frederic Leighton, Alma-Tadema, Sir Edward Burne-Jones

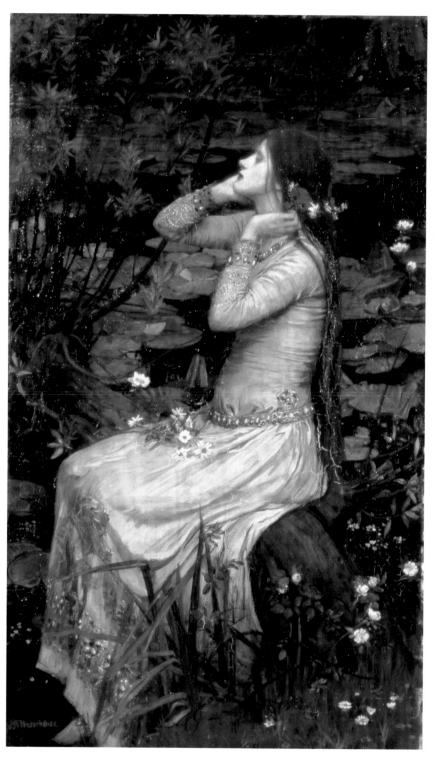

ENGLISH PAINTER, whose dreamy mythological paintings represent one of the last flowerings of Romanticism in Britain. Born in Rome, the son of a minor artist, Waterhouse moved to England with his family in 1854. He trained at the Royal Academy Schools and began exhibiting there in 1874. Initially, he painted in a traditional, academic vein, specializing in decorative, classical themes, which recall the work of Alma-Tadema and Leighton. By the late 1880s, however, elements of Symbolism and *plein-air* painting began to enter his work.

The pivotal work in Waterhouse's career was *The Lady of Shalott*. Painted in 1888, this was a typically Pre-Raphaelite subject – the kind of theme which he favoured increasingly, in his later years. The style, however, was more modern. The landscape background, in particular, displays a freshness and a robust handling, which underlines Waterhouse's links with the Newlyn School and his debt to continental, *plein-air* painting. During the same period, he also began to paint sirens, mermaids and other *femmes fatales*, drawing his inspiration from the French Symbolists.

Max Liebermann   Bathers on the Beach at Scheveningen, *c.*1897–98

Born 1847 Berlin, Germany   Painted in France, Holland and Germany   Died 1935 Berlin
MOVEMENT: German Impressionism   **OTHER WORKS:** *The Parrot Keeper, Haarlem Pig Market*   **INFLUENCES:** Courbet, Millet

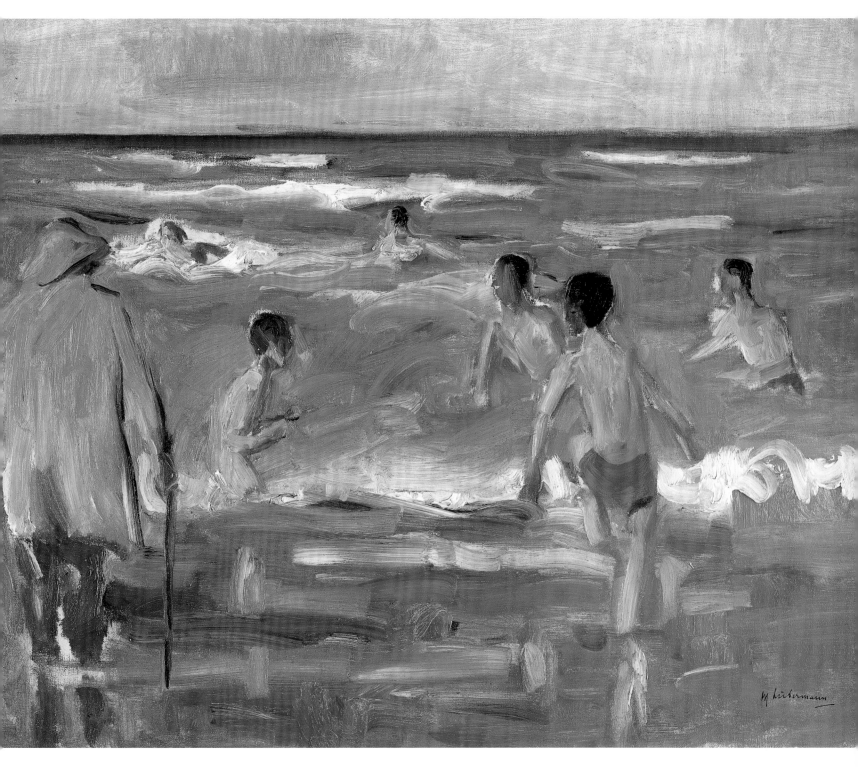

AFTER HIS early training in Weimar, Germany, Max Liebermann continued his studies in Amsterdam and Paris, one of the first German artists of his generation to go abroad and come under the influence of foreign painters – in his case Courbet, Millet and the Barbizon School. Returning to Germany in 1878 Liebermann quickly established himself as the leading Impressionist, noted for his canvasses of mundane subjects in which elderly people and peasants predominate, although he also produced some noteworthy paintings of more sophisticated subjects, especially the outdoor cafés.

Liebermann played a major role in the establishment of the Berlin Secession in 1899. A major innovator in his heyday, he failed to move with the times and was later eclipsed by the younger avant-garde artists, led by Emil Nolde. Nevertheless, he remained a highly influential figure in German art, where the fashion for the heroic and romantic assured his works a substantial following.

Henry Ossawa Tanner Moroccan Man

Born 1859 USA   Painted in USA, France and Middle East   Died 1937 Paris, France

MOVEMENT: Modern American School **OTHER WORKS:** *Daniel in the Lions' Den, The Disciples of Emmaus* **INFLUENCES:** Thomas Eakins, Benjamin Constant, Jean-Paul Laurens

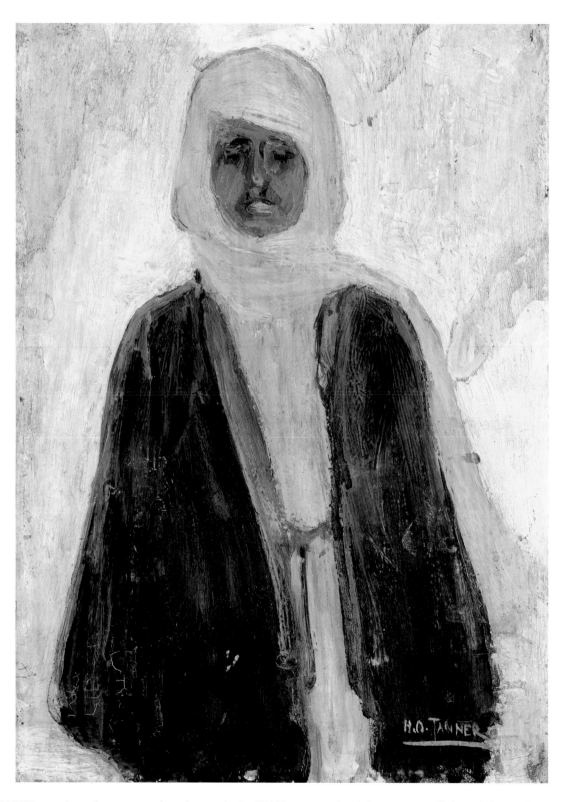

HENRY OSSAWA TANNER was educated in Philadelphia, where his father was bishop of the African Methodist Church. Against strong parental opposition he decided to pursue a career in art, enrolling at the Pennsylvania Academy of Fine Arts and studying under Thomas Eakins, who also taught him photography. In 1888 Tanner moved to Atlanta, Georgia and opened a photographic studio, but the business failed and he scraped a living as a part-time art teacher, supplementing his meagre salary by painting portraits. In 1891 he moved to Paris where he continued his studies at the Académie Julien, and later travelled round the Middle East, gaining material for his religious paintings. He continued to live mainly in Paris, working for the Red Cross in World War I and becoming a Chevalier of the Legion d'Honneur.

Mary Cassatt   The Young Mother, 1900

Born 1844 Pennsylvania, USA   Painted in USA and France   Died 1926 Paris, France
MOVEMENT: Impressionism   **OTHER WORKS:** *Mother and Child, Woman Sewing*   **INFLUENCES:** Thomas Eakins, Degas

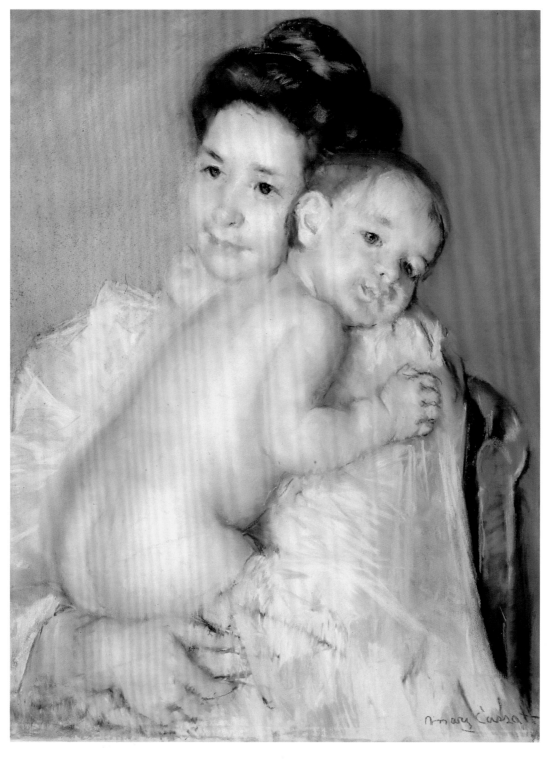

MARY CASSATT studied art at the Pennsylvania Academy of Art in Philadelphia from 1861 to 1865, but after the American Civil War she travelled to Europe, continuing her studies in Spain, Italy and the Netherlands before settling in Paris, where she became a pupil of Edgar Degas. Her main work consisted of lithographs, etchings and drypoint studies of genre and domestic subjects which often reflect her interest in Japanese prints; but her reputation now rests on her larger works, executed in pastels or oils, which explore the tender relationship between mother and child, although her mastery of technique (which owed much to her original teacher, Thomas Eakins) prevented her from descending into the banal or mawkish. After her death in Paris in 1926 her work was for some time neglected, but in more recent years it has been the subject of re-appraisal and her realistic but sensitive portraiture of women, girls and young children is now more fully appreciated.

William Holman Hunt   Master Hilary – The Tracer, 1900

Born 1827   Painted in England, Egypt and the Holy Land   Died 1910
MOVEMENT: Pre-Raphaelite Brotherhood **OTHER WORKS:** *The Hireling Shepherd, The Light of the World* **INFLUENCES:** Dante Gabriel Rossetti, Augustus Egg, John Everett Millais

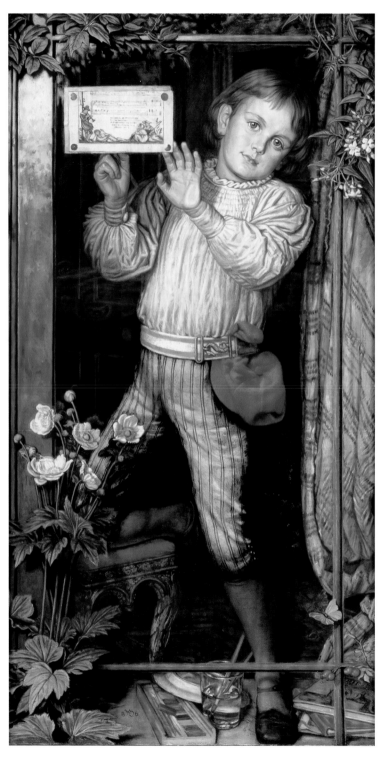

ENGLISH PAINTER; one of the founders of the Pre-Raphaelite movement. Born in London, the son of a warehouse manager, Hunt worked as a clerk before entering the Royal Academy School in 1844. There, he met Millais and, together with Rossetti, they formed the core of the Pre-Raphaelite Brotherhood. Hunt's meticulous attention to detail and his fondness for symbolism accorded well with the aims of the group, but his deeply felt religious convictions led him away from the British art scene. In January 1854, he embarked on a two-year expedition to Egypt and the Holy Land, believing that this was the only way to produce realistic images of biblical themes.

The critical response to this enterprise was mixed. *The Scapegoat* was greeted with puzzlement, but *The Finding of the Saviour in the Temple* was received far more enthusiastically, securing Hunt's reputation as a religious painter. Further trips to the East followed, although these were not always happy affairs. In 1866, his wife died in Florence, shortly after giving birth to their son. Hunt later married her sister. In 1905, he wrote his memoirs, which have become a primary source document for the Pre-Raphaelite movement.

Claude Monet   Nympheas, 1907

Born 1840 Paris, France   Painted in France, England and Italy   Died 1926
MOVEMENT: Impressionism   **OTHER WORKS:** *Waterlilies, Wild Poppies, Rouen Cathedral*   **INFLUENCES:** Eugène Boudin, Johan Barthold Jongkind, Renoir

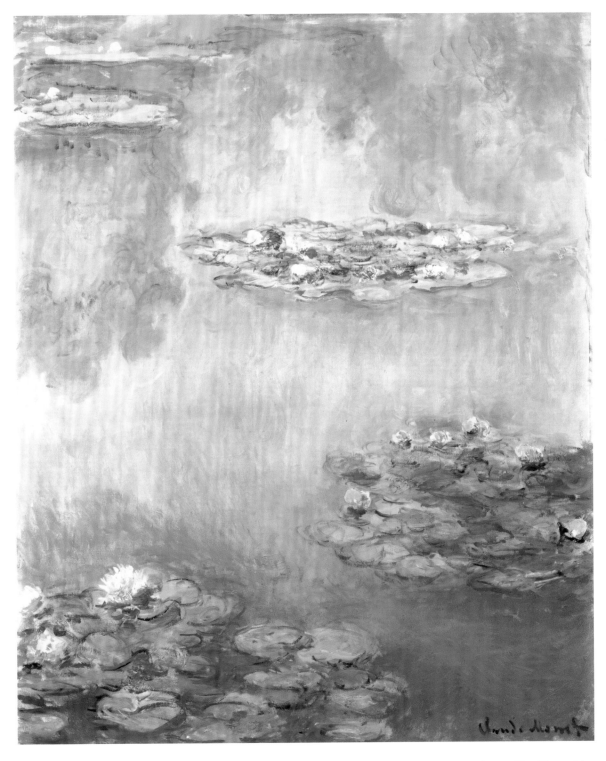

CLAUDE MONET was a key founding member of the Impressionist circle – in fact one of his paintings, *Impression: Sunrise* was to give the group its name (albeit coined pejoratively by the journalist Louis Leroy in response to the painting). He was born in Paris, but grew up on the Normandy coast, where he developed an early interest in landscape painting. His early mentors were Jongkind and Boudin, and the latter encouraged Claude to paint outdoors rather than in the studio. This was to be one of the key principles of Impressionism.

While a student in Paris, he met Pissarro, Renoir and Sisley, and together they formulated the basic ideas of the movement. They staged their own shows, holding eight exhibitions between 1874 and 1886. Initially these attracted savage criticism, causing genuine financial hardship to Monet and his friends. His most distinctive innovation was the 'series' painting. Here, Monet depicted the same subject again and again, at different times of the day or in different seasons. In these pictures, his real aim was not to portray a physical object – whether a row of poplars or the façade of Rouen cathedral – but to capture the changing light and atmospheric conditions.

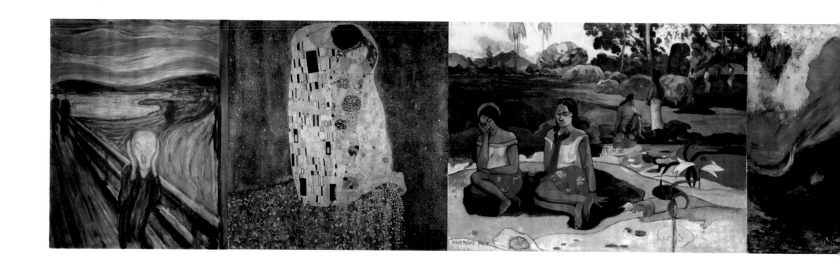

The Era of Post–Impressionism
The Era of Post–Impressionism
The Era of Post–Impressionism
The Era of Post–Impressionism
The Era of Post–Impressionism
The Era of Post–Impressionism
The Era of Post–Impressionism
The Era of Post–Impressionism
The Era of Post–Impressionism
The Era of Post–Impressionism
The Era of Post–Impressionism
The Era of Post–Impressionism
The Era of Post–Impressionism
The Era of Post–Impressionism

The Era of Post–Impressionism

The Era of Post–Impressionism

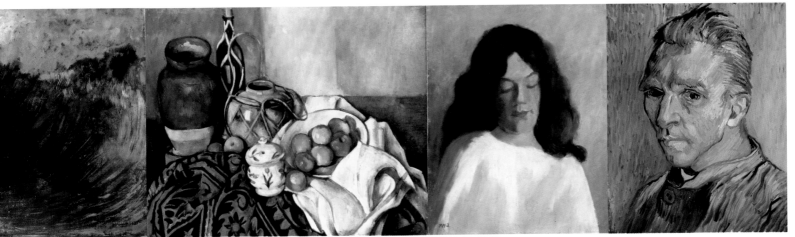

The Era of Post–Impressionism
The Era of Post–Impressionism
The Era of Post–Impressionism
The Era of Post–Impressionism
The Era of Post–Impressionism
The Era of Post–Impressionism
The Era of Post–Impressionism
The Era of Post–Impressionism

Georges Seurat Les Poseuses, 1887–88

Born 1859 Paris, France Painted in France Died 1891 Paris
MOVEMENT: French Impressionism **OTHER WORKS:** *The Can-Can, Sunday Afternoon on the Island of the Grande Jatte* **INFLUENCES:** Ingres, Eugène Chevreul

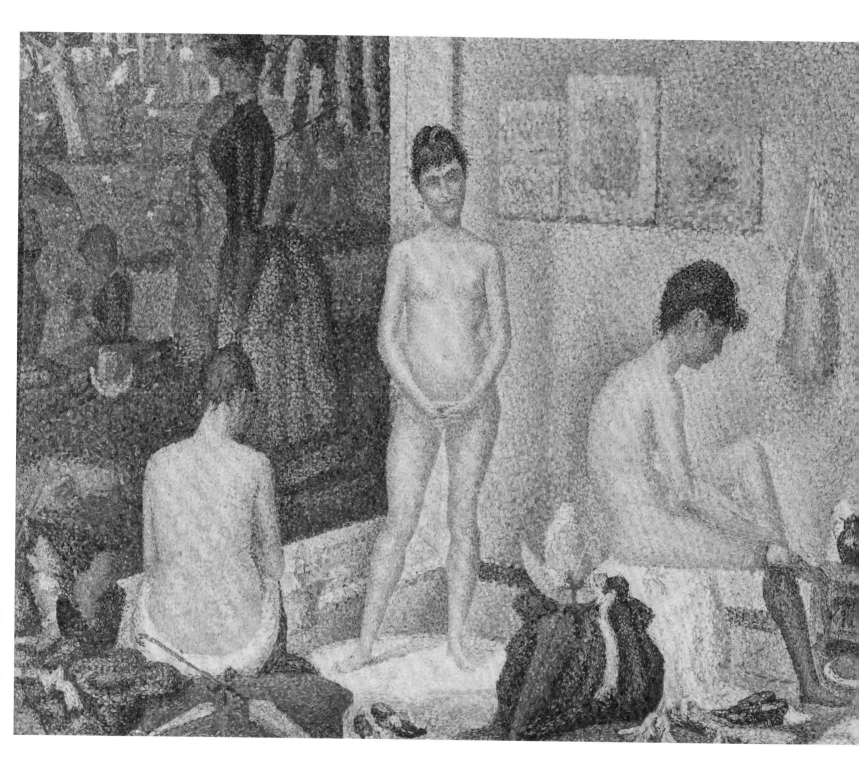

GEORGES PIERRE SEURAT studied at the École des Beaux-Arts and was influenced by the precise draughtsmanship of Ingres, as well as with Chevreul's theories on colour. He combined the Classicist tradition with the newer ideas of the Impressionists. In particular, he painted in a very distinctive style using a multitude of different-coloured dots to build up the impression of the subject, much as the half-tone process or multicolour photogravure use a screen of dots of varying intensity and depth to achieve the overall image. This extremely precise method he termed Divisionism, and it was instrumental in the subsequent development of Pointillism. There is not much evidence of this technique, however, in his first major work depicting bathers at Asnières (1884), but it became almost a trademark in his later paintings.

Always meticulous in the execution of his work, Seurat was also painstaking in the preparation, often spending months on preliminary sketches for each canvas.

Vincent van Gogh   Portrait de L'artiste sans Barbe, 1889

Born 1853   Painted in France, Holland and Belgium   Died 1890

MOVEMENT: Post-Impressionism   **OTHER WORKS:** *Starry Night, Sunflowers, The Potato Eaters*   **INFLUENCES:** Jean-François Millet, Louis Anquetin, Gauguin

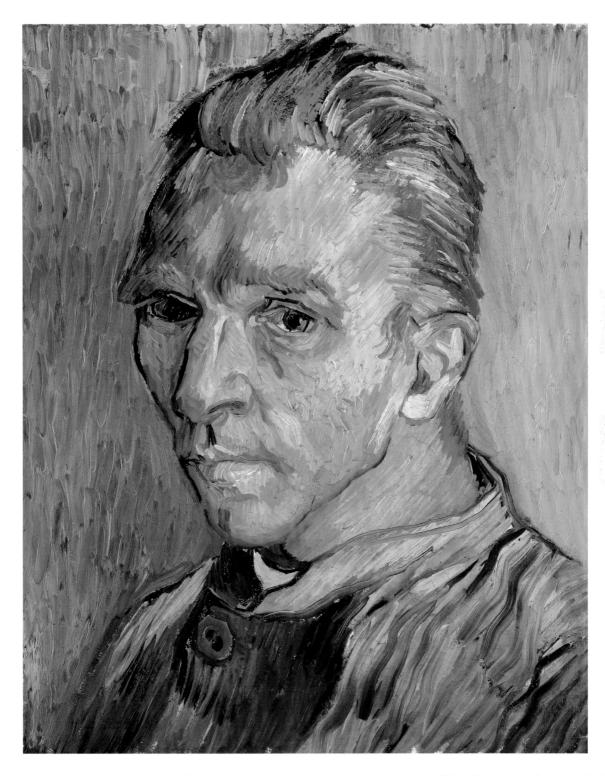

A LEADING Post-Impressionist and forerunner of Expressionism. Vincent's first job was for a firm of art dealers, but he was sacked after a failed affair affected his ability to work. After a brief stint as a teacher, he became a lay preacher in a Belgian mining district. Here again he was fired when the Church became concerned at his over-zealous attempts to help the poor. Vincent had at least found his true vocation:

illustrating the plight of the local peasantry.

Previously influenced by Millet, in 1886 Van Gogh went to Paris where his style changed dramatically. Under the combined impact of Impressionism and Japanese prints, his palette lightened and he began to employ bold simplifications of form. Like Gauguin, he also used colours symbolically, rather than naturalistically. With financial help from his brother,

Theo, Vincent moved to the south of France. Gauguin joined him but the pair soon clashed, hastening Van Gogh's mental collapse. Despite his illness he continued working at a frenzied pace until his suicide in July 1890. Van Gogh sold only one painting in his lifetime, but his work has since become the most popular and sought-after of any modern artist.

Henri de Toulouse–Lautrec   Moulin Rouge – La Gouloue, 1891

Born 1864 France   Painted in Paris   Died 1901 Paris
MOVEMENT: Post-Impressionism **OTHER WORKS:** *At the Moulin Rouge, The Bar, At the Races, Jane Avril* **INFLUENCES:** Degas

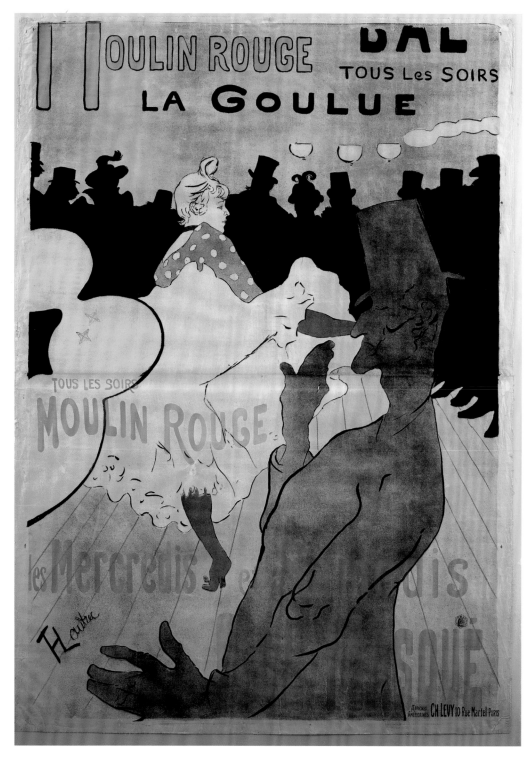

HENRI MARIE RAYMOND de Toulouse-Lautrec-Monfa was the scion of one of France's oldest noble families who had been rulers of Navarre in the Middle Ages. Henri was a chronically sick child whose legs, broken at the age of 14, stopped growing and left him physically deformed. In 1882 he went to Paris to study art and settled in Montmartre, where he sketched and painted the cabaret performers, can-can dancers,

clowns, barmaids and prostitutes, although occasionally he painted more conventional subjects as well. He played a prominent part in raising the lithographic poster to a recognized art form. He worked rapidly and feverishly from life, seldom using posed models. He belonged to the artistic milieu in which Impressionists and Post-Impressionists mingled and both schools left their mark on his work. Alcoholism led to a complete

breakdown and confinement in a sanatorium (1899) but he recovered sufficiently for a last frenzied bout of hard work.

Paul Cézanne   Still Life With Apples, 1893–94

Born 1839 France   Painted in France   Died 1906

MOVEMENT: Post-Impressionism **OTHER WORKS:** *Mont Sainte-Victoire, Apples and Oranges, The Card Players* **INFLUENCES:** Delacroix, Courbet, Pissarro

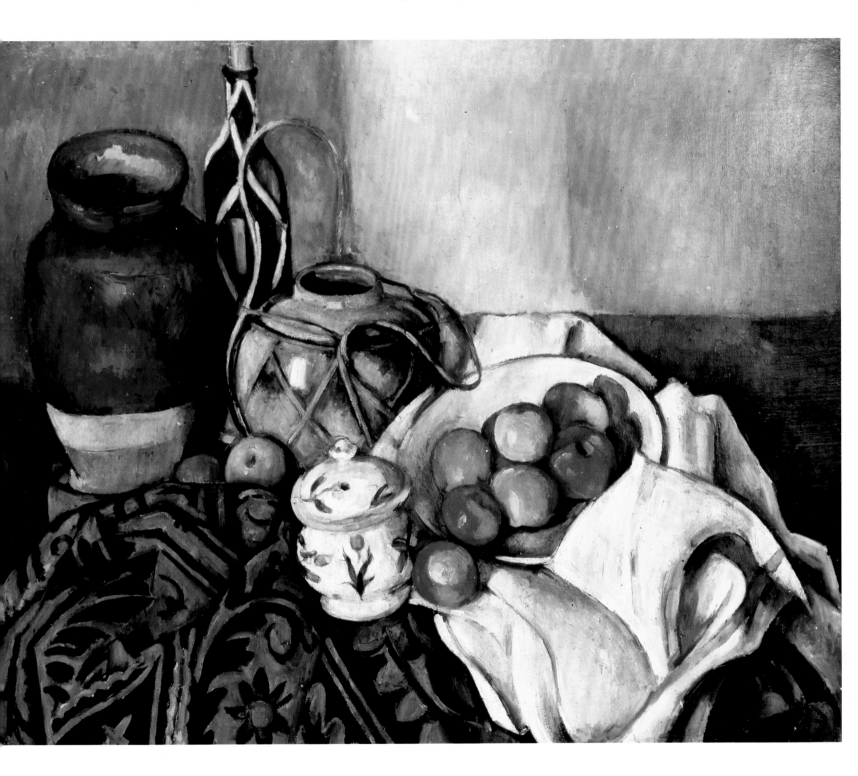

FRENCH PAINTER, a leading member of the Post-Impressionists. Born in Aix-en-Provence, the son of a banker, Cézanne's prosperous background enabled him to endure the long struggle for recognition. He studied in Paris, where he met the future members of the Impressionist circle, although his own work at this time was full of violent, Romantic imagery. Cézanne did not mix easily with the group; he was withdrawn,

suspicious and prey to sudden rages. Gradually, with Pissarro's encouragement, he tried *plein-air* painting and participated at two of the Impressionist exhibitions. But, in art as in life, Cézanne was a solitary figure and he soon found the principles of the movement too restricting.

After his father's death in 1886, Cézanne returned to Aix, where he brought his style to maturity. His

aim was to produce 'constructions after nature'. He followed the Impressionist practice of painting outdoors but, instead of the transient effects which they sought, he tried to capture the underlying geometry of the natural world. This was to make him a fertile source of inspiration for the Cubists.

Edvard Munch   The Scream, 1893

Born 1863 Loten, Norway   Painted in Oslo, Norway   Died 1944 Oslo

MOVEMENT: Expressionism   **OTHER WORKS:** *Puberty, The Dance of Life, The Madonna, Ashes*   **INFLUENCES:** Gauguin, Van Gogh

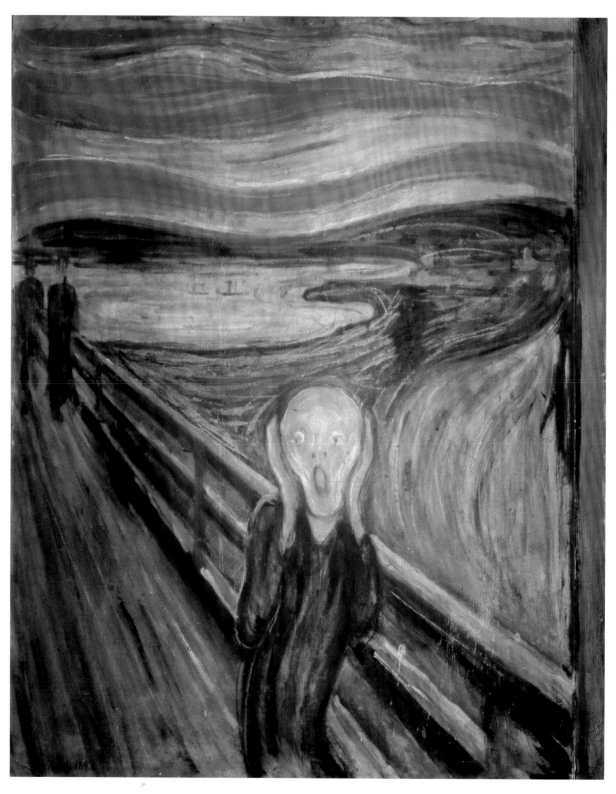

EDVARD MUNCH studied in Christiania (now Oslo) and travelled in Germany, Italy and France before settling in Oslo. During his time in Paris (1908) he came under the influence of Gauguin and had immense sympathy for Van Gogh due to the bouts of mental illness which both of them suffered.

In fact, this would have a profound effect on the development of Munch as an artist and explains the extraordinary passion that pervades his work. Life, love and death are the themes that he endlessly explored in his paintings, rendered in an Expressionist symbolic style. His use of swirling lines and strident colours emphasize the angst that lies behind his paintings. He also produced etchings, lithographs and woodcut engravings which influenced the German artists of the movement known as Die Brücke.

Aubrey Beardsley The Peacock Skirt, Illustration for Oscar Wilde's play, 'Salome' 1894

Born 1872, Brighton Worked in England and France Died 1898

MOVEMENT: Symbolism, Decadence, Art Nouveau **OTHER WORKS:** *The Toilet of Salome, How King Arthur saw the Questing Beast*

INFLUENCES: Sir Edward Burne-Jones, Kitagawa Utamaro, Toulouse-Lautrec

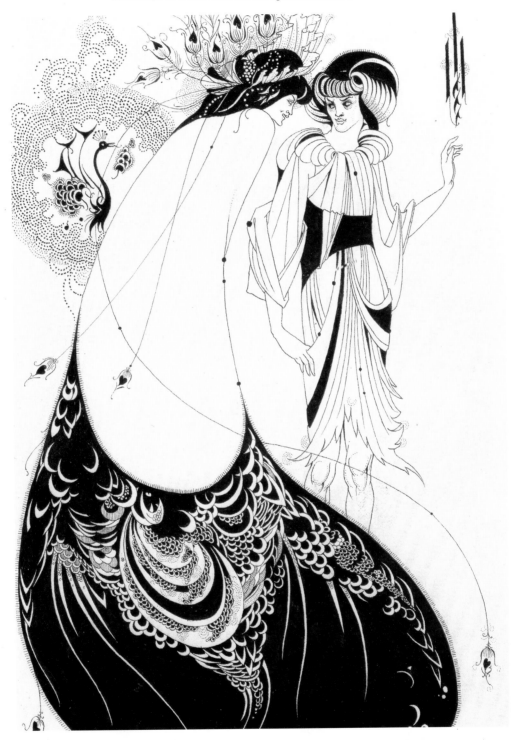

ENGLISH GRAPHIC ARTIST, the epitome of fin-de-siècle decadence. Born in Brighton, Beardsley was a frail child and suffered his first attack of tuberculosis in 1879. He left for London at the age of 16, working initially in an insurance office, while attending art classes in the evening. In 1891 Edward Burne-Jones persuaded him to become a professional artist and, two years later, Beardsley received his first major commission, when J.M. Dent engaged him to illustrate Malory's *Morte d'Arthur*. The success of this venture gave him the opportunity to work on an even more prestigious project, the illustration of Wilde's 'Salome', while also producing images for a new journal, *The Yellow Book*.

Soon Beardsley developed a unique style, combining the bold compositional devices used in Japanese prints; the erotic, sometimes perverse imagery of the Symbolists; and an effortless mastery of sinuous, linear design, which prefigured Art Nouveau. A glittering career seemed to beckon, but in 1895 the scandal surrounding the Wilde trial led to his sacking from *The Yellow Book*. His tubercular condition flared up again and within three years he was dead.

Paul Gauguin Nave Nave Moe, 1894

Born 1848 Paris, France Painted in France, Denmark, Martinique, Tahiti Died 1903

MOVEMENT: Post-Impressionism, Impressionism, Symbolism **OTHER WORKS:** *Where Do We Come From? What Are We? Where Are We Going To?*

INFLUENCES: Camille Pissarro, Emile Bernard, Vincent Van Gogh

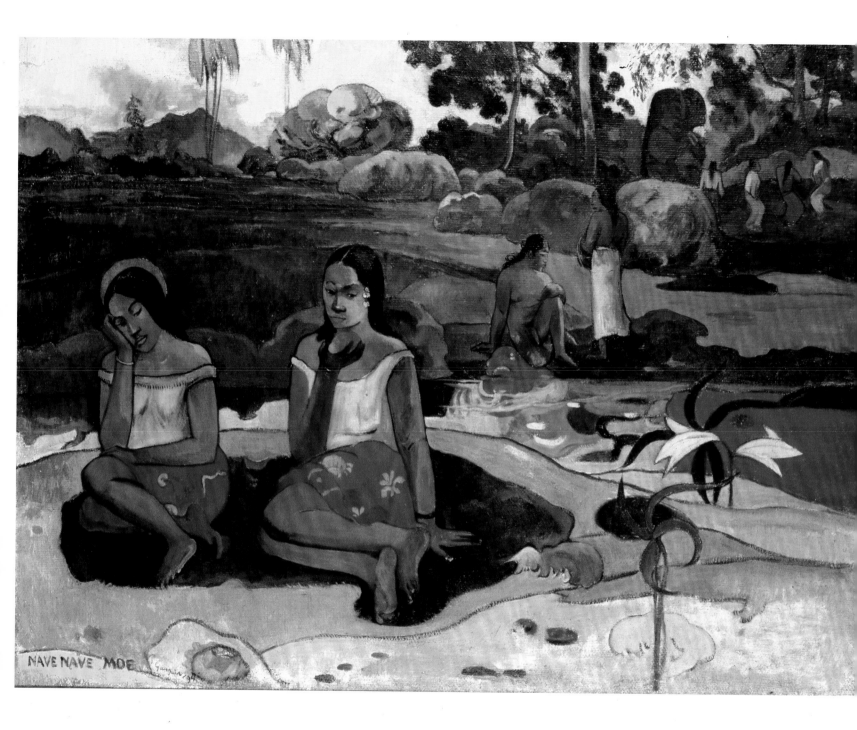

NAVE NAVE MOE

ALTHOUGH HE was born in Paris, Gauguin spent his early childhood in Peru, returning to France in 1855. He worked for a time as a stockbroker, painting only as a hobby, until the stock market crash of 1882 prompted a dramatic change of career. His first pictures were in the Impressionist style, influenced in particular by his friend, Camille Pissarro. Increasingly, though, Gauguin became dissatisfied with the purely visual emphasis of the movement, and tried to introduce a greater degree of symbolism and spirituality into his work. Inspired by Japanese prints, he also developed a new style, coupling bold splashes of bright, unmixed colour with simplified, linear designs. At the same time, haunted by memories of his Peruvian childhood, Gauguin developed a growing fascination for exotic and 'primitive' cultures. Initially, he was able to satisfy this need in Brittany where, inspired by the region's distinctive Celtic traditions, he produced *The Vision after the Sermon*, his first great masterpiece. Then in 1891, he moved to the French colony of Tahiti. Dogged by poverty and ill health, he spent most of his later life in this area, producing the paintings for which he is best known today.

Walter Sickert   L'Hotel Royal Dieppe, *c.*1894

Born 1860 Munich, Germany   Painted in London, Dieppe, and Venice   Died 1942 Bathampton, Avon, England
MOVEMENT: British Impressionism   **OTHER WORKS:** *Mornington Crescent Nude, La Hollandaise Nude*   **INFLUENCES:** James McNeill Whistler, Degas

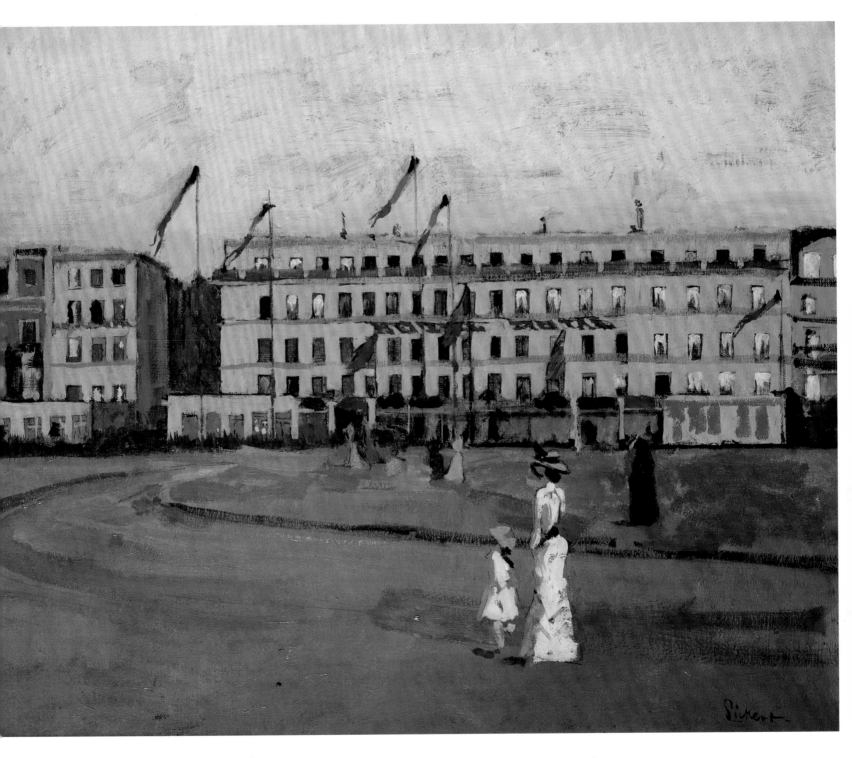

BORN IN Munich, Bavaria, Walter Richard Sickert was the son of the painter Oswald Adalbert Sickert and grandson of the painter and lithographer Johannes Sickert. With such an artistic pedigree it was almost inevitable that he should follow the family tradition. In 1868 his parents moved to London, where he later studied at the Slade School of Art and took lessons from Whistler, whose limited tonal range is reflected in much of Sickert's work. On the advice of Degas – whom he met while studying in Paris – he made detailed preliminary drawings for his paintings rather than paint from life. As a youth, Sickert had been an actor and he had a lifelong interest in the theater, reflected in many of his paintings. He was a competent all-rounder, painting portraits, rather seedy genre subjects and murky landscapes, and as a teacher he wielded enormous influence on the British artists of the early twentieth century.

Odilon Redon   La Mort D'Ophelie, 1900–05

Born 1840 Bordeaux, France   Painted in Paris   Died 1916 Paris
MOVEMENTS: Symbolism, Surrealism   **OTHER WORKS:** *Portrait of Gauguin, The Marsh Flower, The Red Sphinx*   **INFLUENCES:** Rodolphe Bresdin, Gauguin, Gustave Moreau

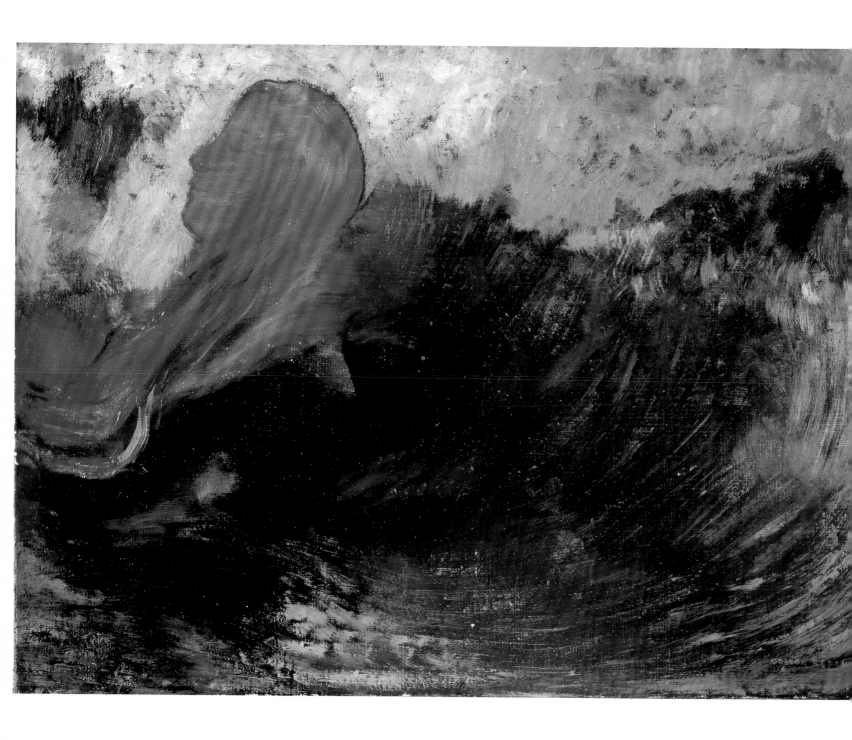

ODILON REDON'S ambitions to become an architect were thwarted by ill health; instead he became apprenticed to Rodolphe Bresdin, a master lithographer and engraver. The first 20 years of Redon's career were almost entirely devoted to working in monochrome, producing a vast number of charcoal drawings and lithographs, and it was not until the late 1870s that he turned to colour, mainly using pastels. He was very friendly with a botanist named Clavand, whose microscopic researches on plant structures fired his imagination and encouraged him to explore their artistic potential. These Redon later utilized in his Symbolist paintings. From about 1900 these developed a dreamlike quality, which is regarded as a precursor of the Surrealists. In his later years Redon also produced portraits that were a riot of colour. A recluse who shunned the limelight, Redon nevertheless became a role model for the next generation of French artists.

Edouard Vuillard   Causerie chez les Fontaines

Born 1868 Cuiseaux, France   Painted in France   Died 1940 La Baule, France

MOVEMENT: Les Nabis **OTHER WORKS:** *Femme Lisant, Le Soir, Two Schoolboys, Mother and Child* **INFLUENCES:** Paul Sérusier, Gauguin

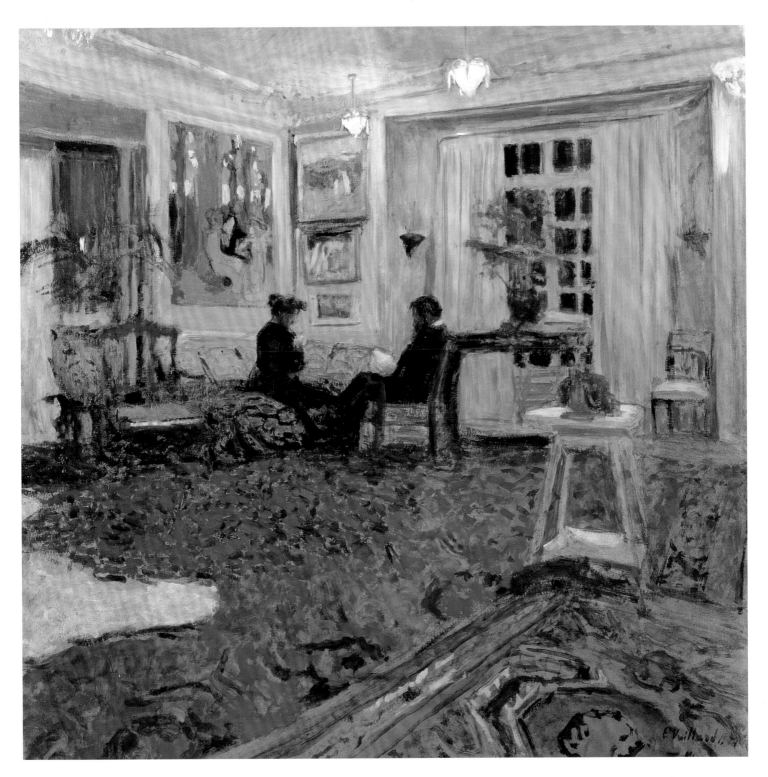

JEAN EDOUARD VUILLARD studied at the Académie Julien in Paris and shared a studio with Pierre Bonnard. Both artists were inspired by Sérusier's theories derived from the works of Gauguin and became founder members of the Nabis in 1889. Vuillard was also influenced by the fashion for Japanese prints and this was reflected in his paintings of flowers and domestic interiors, executed with a keen sense of tone, colour and light. He was also a prolific designer of textiles, wallpaper and decorative features for public buildings. His paintings of cozy domestic subjects show a tremendous feeling for texture and patterning, a skill he picked up from his mother, who was a dressmaker. The bolts of brightly coloured cloth that surrounded him as a child found an echo in his own textile designs. His later paintings were more naturalistic, aided by photography, which he employed to capture the fleeting moment.

Gustav Klimt   The Kiss, 1907–08

Born 1862, Vienna, Austria   Painted in Austria-Hungary, Belgium   Died 1918
MOVEMENT: Vienna Sezession   **OTHER WORKS:** *The Kiss, Judith I, The Beethoven Frieze*   **INFLUENCES:** Hans Makart, Edvard Munch, Franz von Stuck

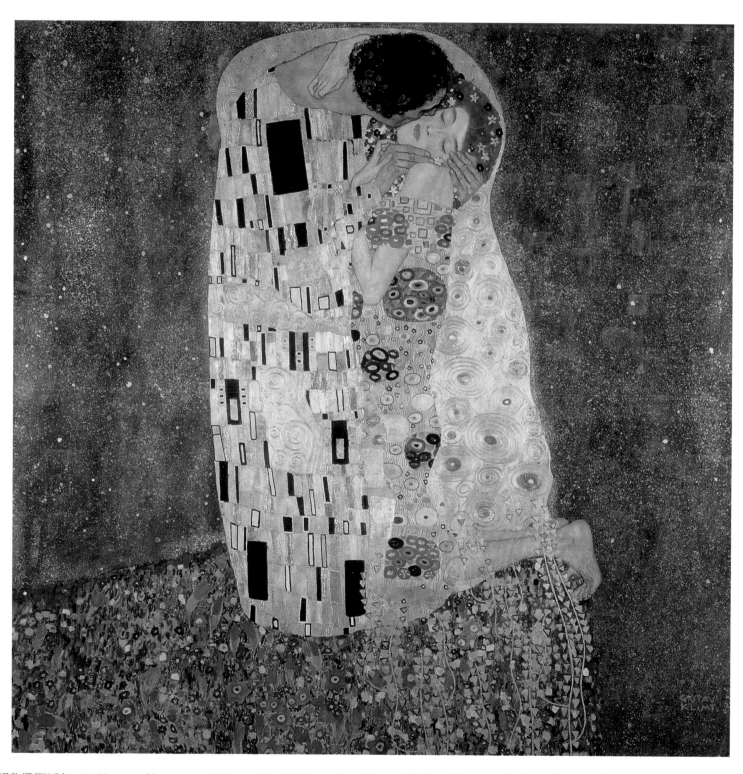

KLIMT WAS born in Vienna and became one of the leading lights in the city's most dazzling, artistic period. The son of a goldsmith, he trained at the School of Applied Arts and started work as a decorative painter. He achieved early success with the schemes at the Burgtheater and the Kunsthistorisches Museum, but future commissions were threatened by his growing fascination with avant-garde art. Faced with official opposition, Klimt resigned from the Viennese Artists' Association in 1897 and founded the Vienna Sezession, becoming its first president. This coincided with protracted disputes about his decorations for the university, a project that he abandoned in 1905.

Klimt's style was a compelling blend of Art Nouveau and Symbolist elements. From the former, he derived his taste for sinuous, decorative lines, while from the latter he borrowed his erotic subject matter and, in particular, his interest in the theme of the *femme fatale*. It was this blatant eroticism which troubled the authorities, though it did not seriously damage Klimt's career. He was always in great demand as a portraitist, and he continued to receive private commissions for decorative schemes.

Paula Modersohn–Becker   Brustbild einer Jungen Frau mit offenem Haar

Born 1876 Germany   Painted in Dresden, Berlin and Worpswede   Died 1907 Wopswede, Germany

MOVEMENT: German Expressionism   **OTHER WORKS:** *Old Poorhouse Woman with a Glass Bottle*   **INFLUENCES:** Cézanne, Gauguin, Van Gogh

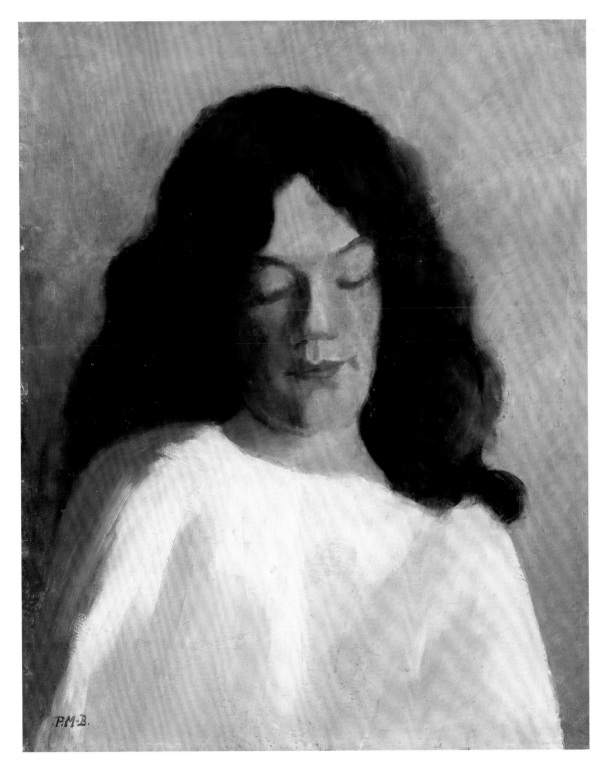

BORN PAULA BECKER, she was largely self-taught, although she was encouraged by her parents to develop her art by sending her to Paris on several occasions, during which she became familiar with the works of Cézanne, Gauguin and Van Gogh. What formal training she had she received at the classes held by the Association of Berlin Women Artists in 1893–95, but three years later she joined the artists' colony at Worpswede, where she spent most of the last nine years of her short life. Her early paintings concentrated largely on landscapes and peasant genre subjects. In 1901 she married Otto Modersohn, a widower 11 years her senior, and the more mature style of her later paintings may owe something to his advice and example. To her last years belong a number of portraits which reflect the influence of the Expressionists. Unable to cope with her domineering husband she fled to Paris in 1906 and died early the following year while giving birth to her daughter Mathilde.

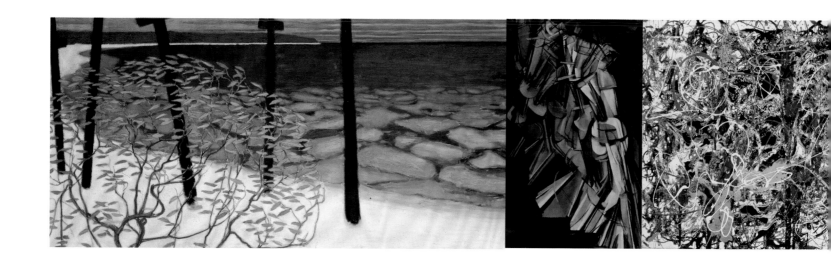

The Modern Era
The Modern Era
The Modern Era
The Modern Era
The Modern Era
The Modern Era
The Modern Era
The Modern Era
The Modern Era
The Modern Era
The Modern Era
The Modern Era
The Modern Era
The Modern Era
The Modern Era

The Modern Era

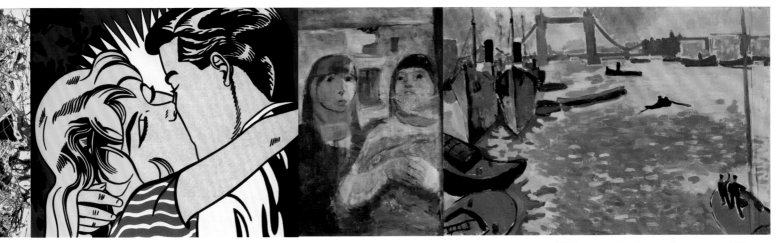

The Modern Era
The Modern Era
The Modern Era
The Modern Era
The Modern Era
The Modern Era
The Modern Era
The Modern Era
The Modern Era

Robert Henri Grace – Chinese Girl, 1917

Born 1865 Cincinnati, Ohio, USA Painted in Paris, Philadelphia and New York, USA Died 1929 New York
MOVEMENT: American Realism **OTHER WORKS:** *La Neige, The Equestrian, Young Woman in Black* **INFLUENCES:** Manet, Renoir

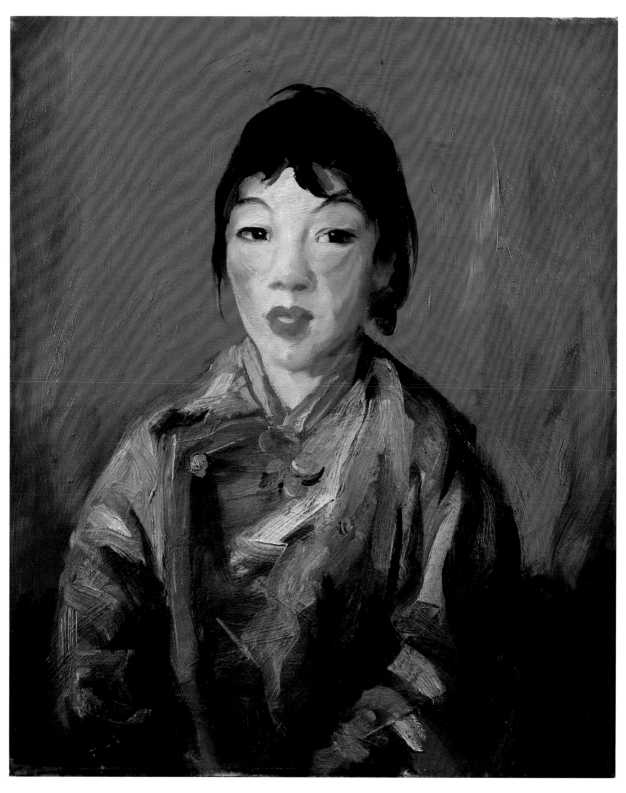

BORN IN Cincinnati, Ohio in 1865, Robert Henri enrolled at the Pennsylvania Academy of Fine Arts, Philadelphia, in 1886 and two years later went to Paris where he studied at the École des Beaux Arts. His formal training was rounded off by extensive travels in Italy and Spain. On his return to the USA in 1891 he became a teacher at the Women's School of Design, Philadelphia. He worked in Paris again from 1896 to 1901, but later settled in New York where he taught at the Art Students' League. He was a fervent believer in realism, which led critics to deride his 'Ashcan School', but he wielded enormous influence on the next generation of American artists. Despite his teaching commitments he was a prolific artist. In 1908 he founded his own art school in New York and formed the group known as 'The Eight'.

Akseli Gallen–Kallela   Autumn, the Five Crosses

Born 1865 Pori, Finland   Painted in France and Finland   Died 1931 Helsinki, Finland

MOVEMENT: Finnish School **OTHER WORKS:** *Head of a Young Girl, The Fratricide, Peace* **INFLUENCES:** August Ahlstedt, Karl Peter Mazer, Gustaf Albert Edelfelt

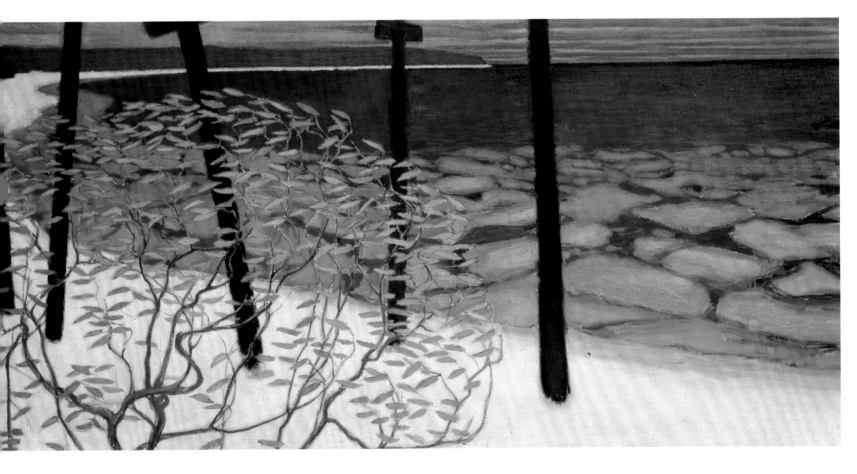

IN THE period before Finland gained its independence at the end of World War I, Akseli Valdemar Gallen-Kallela played a major role in the revival of the national spirit, especially among the Finnish-speaking population. Hitherto the art establishment of the Grand Duchy was predominantly Swedish speaking and culturally oriented to Sweden. Gallen-Kallela studied in Paris from 1884 onwards and spent much of his life there prior to 1920, but throughout this period took a keen interest in the rebirth of Finnish culture. Although he is best known for his paintings of scenes from the great epic poem *Kalevala*, he produced numerous landscapes, the most evocative being of the lakes and forests of Finland in winter. He was also an accomplished portraitist and painted one of the best likenesses of Maxim Gorky.

The disparate strands of his artistry came together in his great masterpiece, the triptych telling the story of Aino and Väinämöinen from Finnish mythology. He executed works in black and white, notably the sensitive and lively illustrations for the writings of Aleksis Kivi (1906–07).

Anders Zorn   Nudes, 1902

Born 1860, Mora, Sweden   Painted in Sweden, England, Spain, Algiers and USA   Died 1920 Mora
MOVEMENT: Modern Swedish School   **OTHER WORKS:** *Our Daily Bread, Mona, Self-Portrait, Dagmar, By Lake Siljan*   **INFLUENCES:** *Max Liebermann*

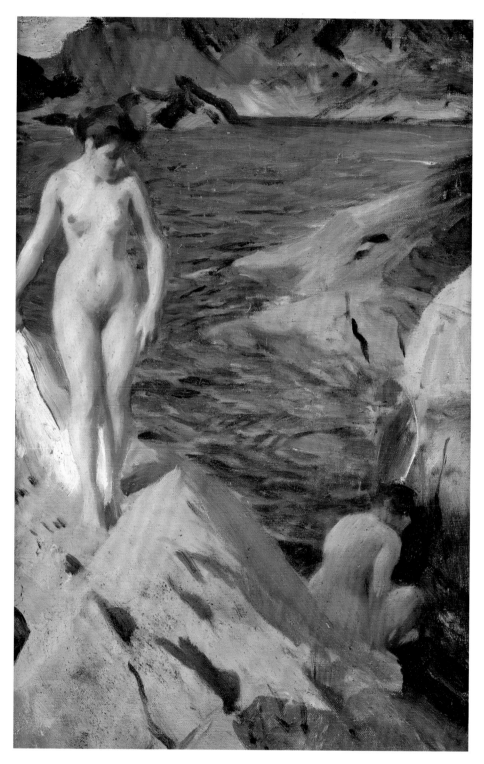

ANDERS LEONHARD Zorn began as a watercolourist in the manner of Egron Lundgren, under whom he studied. He achieved instant fame with the portrait of a girl entitled *Mourning*, which was exhibited in 1880, after which he received numerous commissions for portraits. His fortune assured, he travelled widely, studying the art of England, Spain, Eastern Europe and North Africa – experiences which resulted in some of his finest landscapes and genre paintings. He resided in Paris from 1887 to 1893 and switched direction by taking up oil painting and rejecting his early realism in favour of Impressionism. From 1893 onwards he made frequent trips to the United States and specialized in portraits of American tycoons and leading political figures. In his later years he spent more time in the Swedish countryside concentrating on landscapes and genre scenes. He was also one of the most accomplished etchers of the turn of the century, as well as a fine sculptor.

Wassily Kandinsky   Composition No. 7, 1913

Born 1866 Moscow, Russia   Painted in Russia, Germany, France and Holland   Died 1944

MOVEMENT: Expressionism, Abstract Art   **OTHER WORKS:** *Swinging, Composition IV (Battle), Cossacks*   **INFLUENCES:** Claude Monet, Paul Klee, Franz Marc

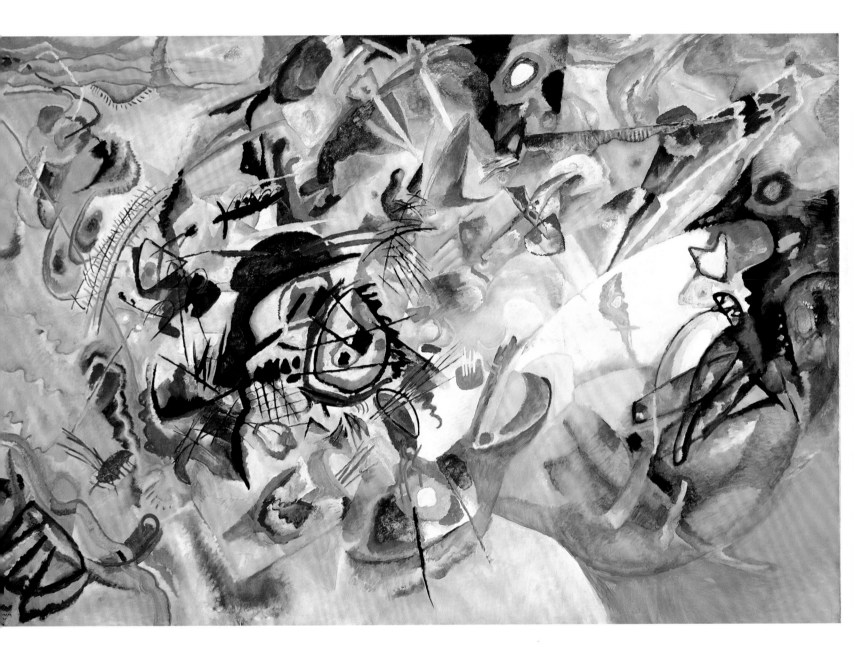

BORN IN Moscow, Kandinsky trained as a lawyer, but turned to art after visiting an exhibition of Monet's work. He moved to Munich, where he studied under Franz von Stuck. Here, he demonstrated his talent for organizing groups of artists, when he founded influential Der Blaue Reiter ('The Blue Rider'), which included Franz Marc, August Macke and Paul Klee – all Expressionist yet very distinct from each other in terms of technique.

Kandinsky's personal style went through many phases, ranging from Jugenstil (the German equivalent of Art Nouveau) to Fauvism and Expressionism. He is most celebrated, however, for his advances towards abstraction. This came about after he returned to his studio one evening, and was enchanted by a picture he did not recognize. It turned out to be one of his own paintings lying on its side. Kandinsky immediately realized that subject matter lessened the impact of his pictures, and he strove to remove this from future compositions.

In later life, Kandinsky taught at the Bauhaus, until it was closed down by the Nazis in 1933. He spent his final years in France, becoming a French citizen in 1939.

Sir Arthur Streeton   Buffalo Mountains, *c.*1913

Born 1867 Australia   Painted in Australia and Europe   Died 1943 Olinda, Victoria, Australia
MOVEMENT: Modern Australian School **OTHER WORKS:** *Still Glides the Stream, Fire's On* **INFLUENCES:** Turner, Constable, Philip Wilson Steer

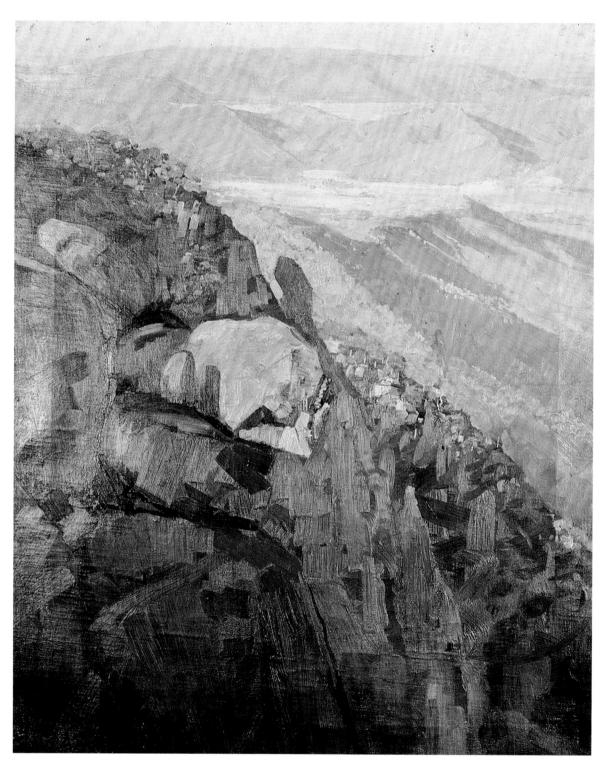

ARTHUR ERNEST Streeton studied at the National Gallery School in Melbourne and worked as a lithographer. In 1885 Tom Roberts returned from Europe and together with Frederick McCubbin and Streeton, founded the Heidelberg School of artists, who painted from nature. Later Streeton founded a permanent artists' colony at Eaglemont, where he perfected his techniques of landscape painting, noted for its realism and sense of atmosphere. He travelled extensively in Egypt and Europe and worked in London (1898–1906), where he studied the works of Turner and Constable and exhibited at the Royal Academy. He was back in Australia in 1906–07, then worked in England and became a war artist on the Western Front. From 1919 onwards he lived mainly in Australia, travelling all over the country and painting prolifically.

He was knighted in 1937. As well as landscapes he painted powerful scenes of men at work, making a major contribution to the art of social realism.

André Derain   La Tamise et Tower Bridge, 1906

Born 1880 Chatou, France   Painted in France and England   Died 1954

MOVEMENT: Fauvism **OTHER WORKS:** *Houses of Parliament, Barges on the Thames, The Pool of London* **INFLUENCES:** Vlaminck, Matisse, Cézanne

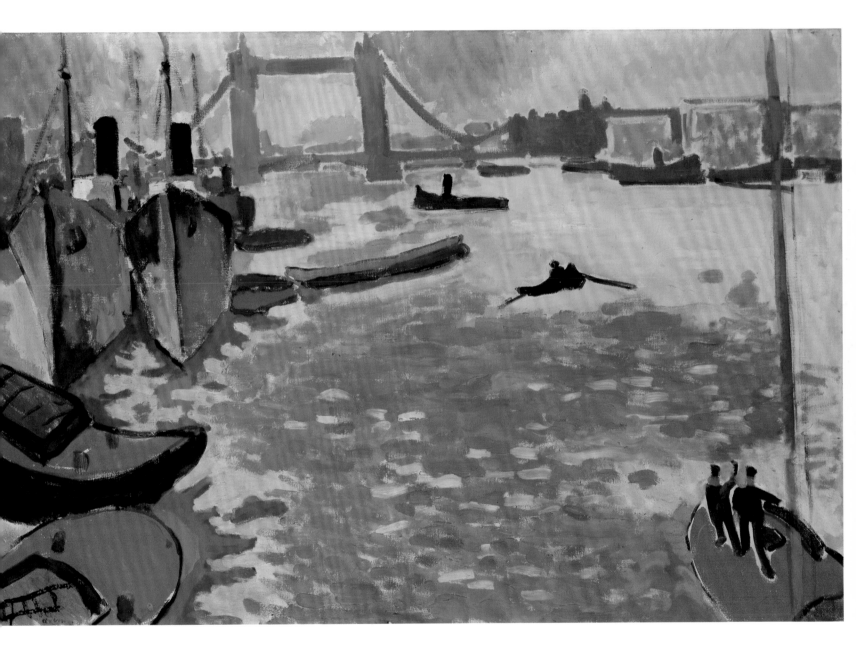

WHILE STUDYING art in Paris, André Derain teamed up with fellow student Maurice de Vlaminck with whom he shared a studio. Although very different in temperament they sparked radical ideas off each other regarding the use of colour and, encouraged by Matisse whom they met in 1899, they gradually evolved the style known as Fauvism, distinguished by its often violent and savage use of contrasting colours. In 1905 Ambroise Vollard, a prominent art dealer, encouraged Derain to travel to England and try to capture the strange lighting effects in the Pool of London. The results were startling but considered to be some of his greatest masterpieces. Later he toned down the adventurous use of colour and, under the influence of Cézanne, painted landscapes in a more Impressionist style. He also designed theatre sets, notably for Diaghilev, as well as working as a book illustrator.

Gwen John   A Corner of the Artist's Room in Paris, *c.*1907

Born 1876   Painted in England and France   Died 1939

MOVEMENT: Intimisme **OTHER WORKS:** *The Convalescent, Girl Reading at the Window, Nude Girl* **INFLUENCES:** Whistler, Henry Tonks

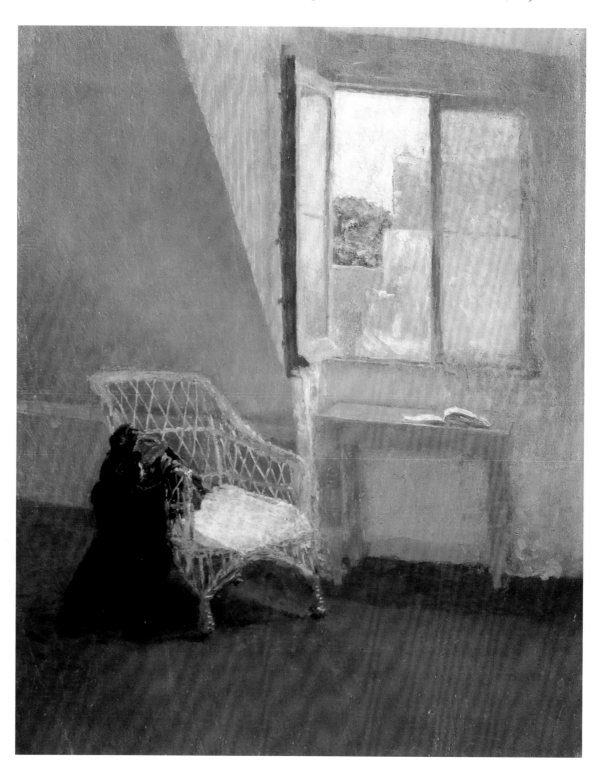

WELSH PAINTER, the greatest female artist of her age. John trained at the Slade School in London, together with her brother Augustus, who also went on to become a famous artist. She then moved to Paris to study under Whistler, from whom she derived her delicate sense of tonality. In 1903, John planned to walk to Rome with a friend, but they only got as far as France, where she decided to settle. For a time she worked as a model in Paris and, through this, met the sculptor Rodin, who became her lover. He urged her to paint more, but John's output was small and it was only through the generosity of her chief patron, an American lawyer named John Quinn, that she was able to give up modelling and devote herself to her art.

Quiet and retiring, John lived alone and rarely exhibited her work. In her solitude, she developed a unique style, painting intimate, small-scale subjects – usually female portraits or corners of her studio – in thin layers of exquisitely muted colours. At first glance, these often appear frail and insubstantial but, like the artist herself, they also exude an inner calm and strength.

Maurice Utrillo   Bancs à Montmagny (Val d'Oise), c.1906–7

Born 1883 Paris, France   Painted in Paris   Died 1955 Dax, France

MOVEMENT: Impressionism **OTHER WORKS:** *La Place du Tertre, Street in a Paris Suburb with Trees* **INFLUENCES:** Suzanne Valadon, Camille Pissarro

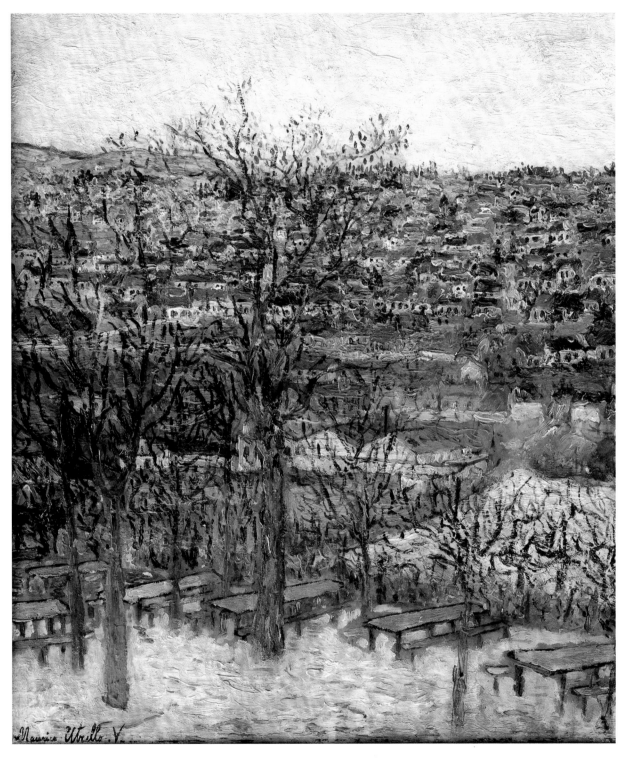

THE ILLEGIMITATE son of the painter Suzanne Valadon, Maurice Utrillo led an extremely Bohemian life. Despite alcoholism and drug addiction, however, he was a prolific painter, turning out vast numbers of Parisian street scenes, especially in and around Montmartre, where he lived. Except what he learned from his mother, he had no formal art training and, in fact, only took up painting as a form of therapy during one of his periodic spells in a detoxification clinic. He started off by making copies of Parisian picture postcards and this is reflected in the meticulous, almost photographic, quality of all his work. He began exhibiting in 1909 and thereafter was closely associated with the Impressionists, especially Camille Pissarro, although Utrillo left his own indelible mark – 'a wild thirst for reality' was how he succinctly described it himself. In his 'white period' (1909–16) his palette consisted of very light colours, but thereafter they became much deeper and richer in tone. A reformed alcoholic, Utrillo became extremely devout in old age.

James Ensor   La Mangeuse D'Huitres, 1908

Born 1860 Ostend, Belgium   Painted in Ostend and Brussels   Died 1949 Ostend
MOVEMENT: Expressionism   **OTHER WORKS:** *Death and the Masks, Entry of Christ into Brussels*   **INFLUENCES:** Odilon Redon

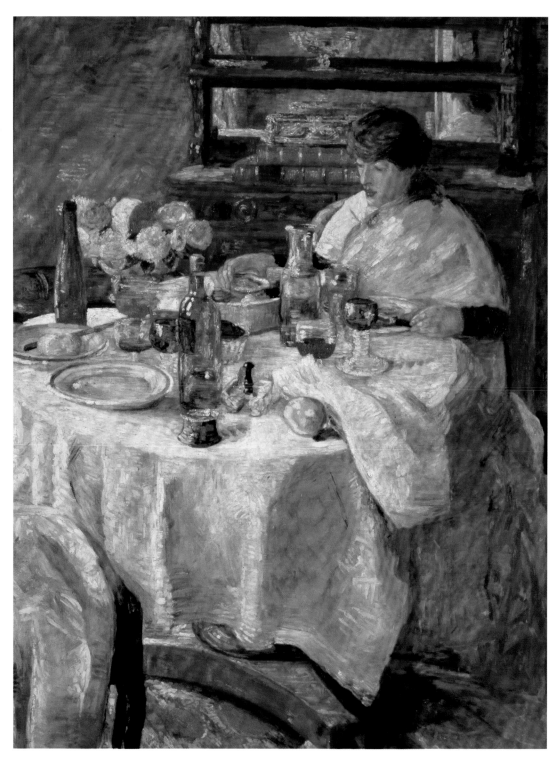

BORN IN Ostend, Belgium, of English parents, James Sydney Ensor is one of those painters whose art seems to have been wholly his own, with very little discernible influence from his contemporaries or predecessors, apart from some slight echoes of the Symbolists. In 1884 he founded the group known as Les Vingt ('The Twenty'), but he soon broke away from them. Essentially a loner, he reacted violently to the comments of art critics and the general public alike, who regarded his pictures as disturbed and macabre. Their obsession with corpses, grotesque masks and skeletons painted in garish colours, symbolized the corruption of society and the world around him. From about 1900, when he was no longer an 'angry young man', his paintings mellowed and became more conventional, and eventually he was back in the mainstream of Belgian art, recognized by his peerage in 1929 shortly after taking Belgian nationality. Nevertheless, it is for his satirical painting that he is remembered today, marking the transition from Symbolism to Expressionism and anticipating the Surrealism of Magritte.

Frances Mary Hodgkins A Peasant Family

Born 1869 New Zealand   Painted in New Zealand, France and England   Died 1947 London, England

MOVEMENT: Romanticism **OTHER WORKS:** *Maori Woman and Child, Hilltop, Barn in Picardy* **INFLUENCES:** Matisse

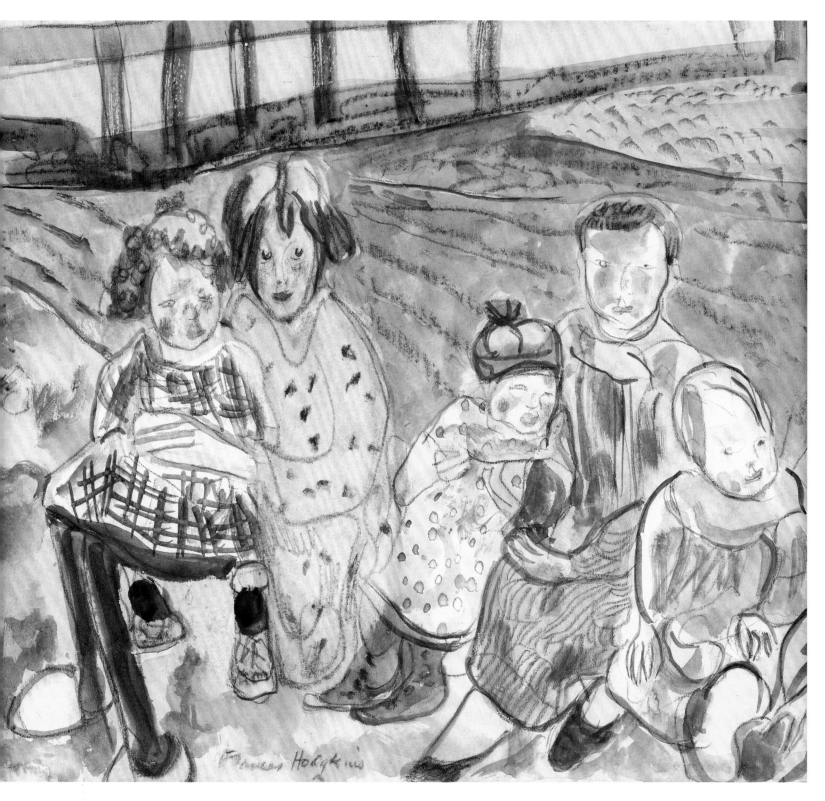

FRANCES MARY Hodgkins studied art in Dunedin, New Zealand and achieved a high reputation in her native country with charming genre studies of Maori life as well as landscapes and still- life studies. Her early success enabled her to travel all over the world, especially throughout Europe, spending considerable periods furthering her studies and perfecting her technique in Paris and London, where she eventually settled. At the beginning of the twentieth century she came under the influence of Henri Matisse in his Impressionistic period and this is reflected in her paintings which explored the harmonious use of flat colours. Although much older than most of her contemporaries in English art circles between the World Wars she was regarded as one of the leading figures in the Romanticism of that period.

Erich Heckel   Windmill, Dangast, 1909

Born 1883 Döbeln, Germany   Painted in Dresden, Berlin and Karlsruhe   Died 1970 Hemmenhofen, Switzerland
MOVEMENT: German Expressionism   **OTHER WORKS:** *Bathers, Sleeping Negress, Landscape in Thunderstorm*   **INFLUENCES:** Ernst Ludwig Kirchner, Edvard Munch

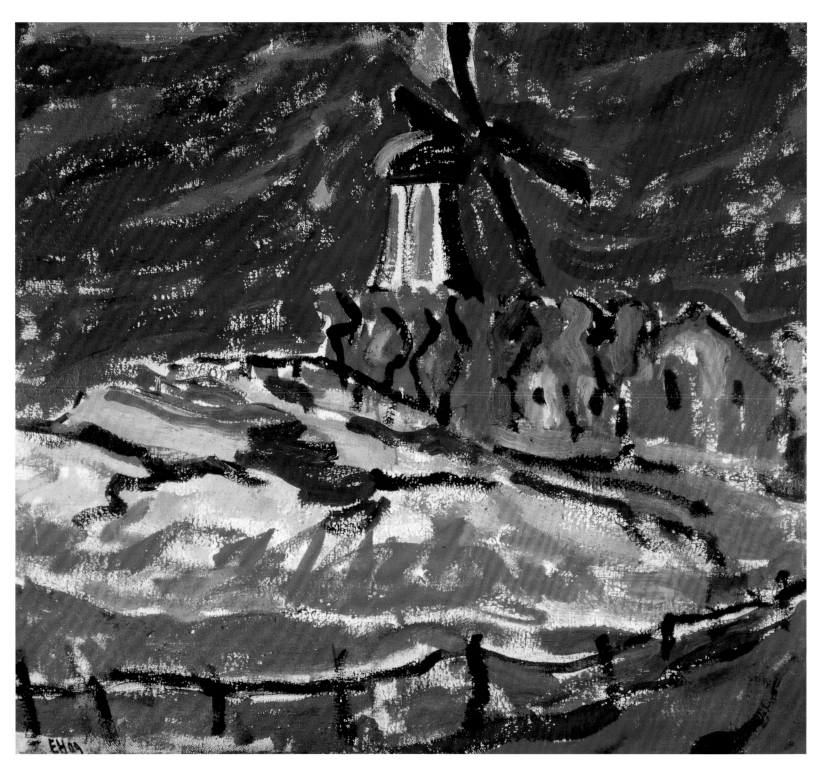

ERICH HECKEL studied architecture in Dresden from 1904 to 1906 and it was during this period that he met Ernst Ludwig Kirchner and Karl Schmidt-Rottluf, with whom he formed the avant-garde group known as Die Brücke ('The Bridge'). They were strongly influenced by Edvard Munch, Cézanne and Van Gogh, and this was reflected in the vigorous quasi-primitive approach which they adopted in their paintings and prints – well suited to works which invariably had a strongly radical character. The group was dissolved in 1913 and the following year Heckel was drafted into the German Army, serving as a medical orderly throughout the war. Like many of his contemporaries, his wartime experiences influenced his paintings in the postwar period. Vilified by the Nazis when they came to power, he continued to live in Berlin but from 1949 to 1956 he was professor at the Karlsruhe Academy of Art. He was noted for his nudes, his style mellowing and becoming more decorative in his later years.

Käthe Kollwitz   Mother and Child, 1910

Born 1867 Königsberg, East Prussia   Painted in Berlin, Germany   Died 1945 Berlin
MOVEMENT: German Realism   **OTHER WORKS:** *Weavers' Revolt, No More War*   **INFLUENCES:** Otto Nagel

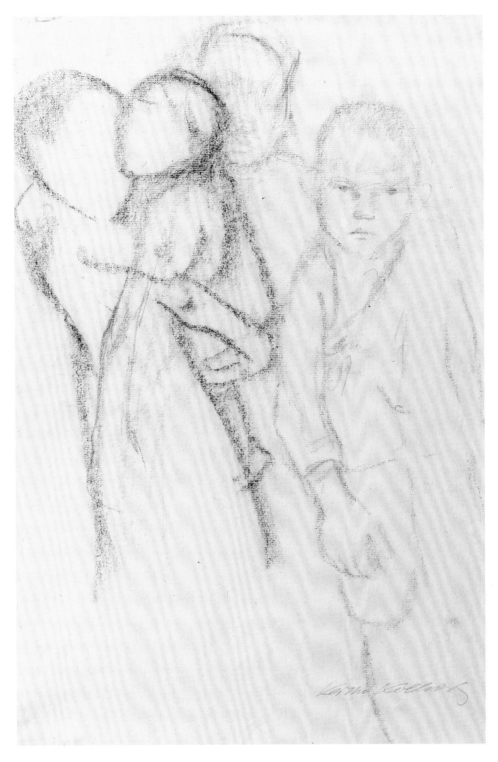

BORN KÄTHE Schmidt at Königsberg, East Prussia (now Kaliningrad, Russia), she studied there and later in Berlin, where she married Karl Kollwitz, a doctor who ran a children's clinic in a slum district. Through this connection the artist witnessed at close quarters the poverty and deprivation of the Berlin poor at the turn of the century, and this influenced her painting and sculpture, in which she concentrated on subjects with a strong social message. After her youngest son was killed in World War I she sculpted a large granite memorial, later erected at Dixmuiden in Flanders as a monument to all the young men who fell in battle. In 1928 she became the first woman elected to the Prussian Academy of Arts, but she was expelled by the Nazis in 1933. Her home, studio and most of her works were destroyed in an air raid in 1943. Although best known for her stone carvings and bronze sculptures, she also produced paintings, posters and lithographs with a powerful social message.

J.E.H. MacDonald   Clearing after Rain, Maganatawan River, Ontario, 1910

Born 1873 London, England   Painted in Canada   Died 1932 Toronto, Ontario, Canada
MOVEMENT: Modern Canadian School   **OTHER WORKS:** *Mist Fantasy, Autumn, Algoma*   **INFLUENCES:** Henry Thoreau, Walt Whitman

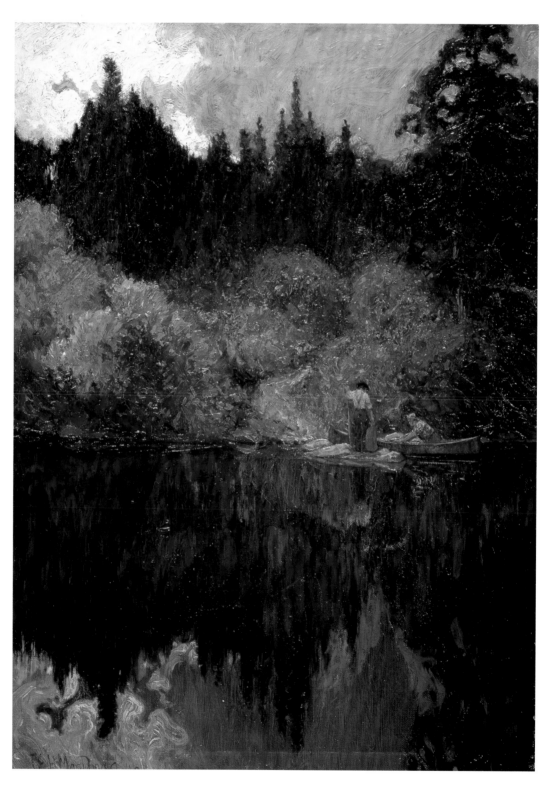

JAMES EDWARD Hervey macdonald was born in England of Scottish-Canadian parents, and at the age of 14 he settled with them in Hamilton, Ontario. He studied art there and later in Toronto, and in 1894 joined the leading Toronto graphic art company Grip, where he remained until 1912. He was the doyen of the extremely talented group of artists working for this firm, including Tom Thomson, Arthur Lismer, Frederick Varley and Franklin Carmichael. MacDonald was a founder member of the Arts and Letters Club (1908) which, under his leadership rapidly became the forum for Canadian avant-garde artists. Notoriety came his way in 1916 when he exhibited seven paintings at the Toronto annual show; his painting *The Tangled Garden* was ferociously attacked by the newspaper critics. After Thomson's untimely death in 1917, MacDonald continued to be the guiding light and the prime mover in establishing the Group of Seven in 1920. Significantly, the Group broke up after his death.

Kasimir Malevich   Suprematist Composition, 1915

Born 1878 Kiev, Ukraine   Painted in Moscow, Russia   Died 1935 Leningrad (now St Petersburg), Russia
MOVEMENTS: Cubism, Suprematism   **OTHER WORKS:** *Dynamic Suprematism, Woman with Buckets*   **INFLUENCES:** Mikhail Larionov, Picasso

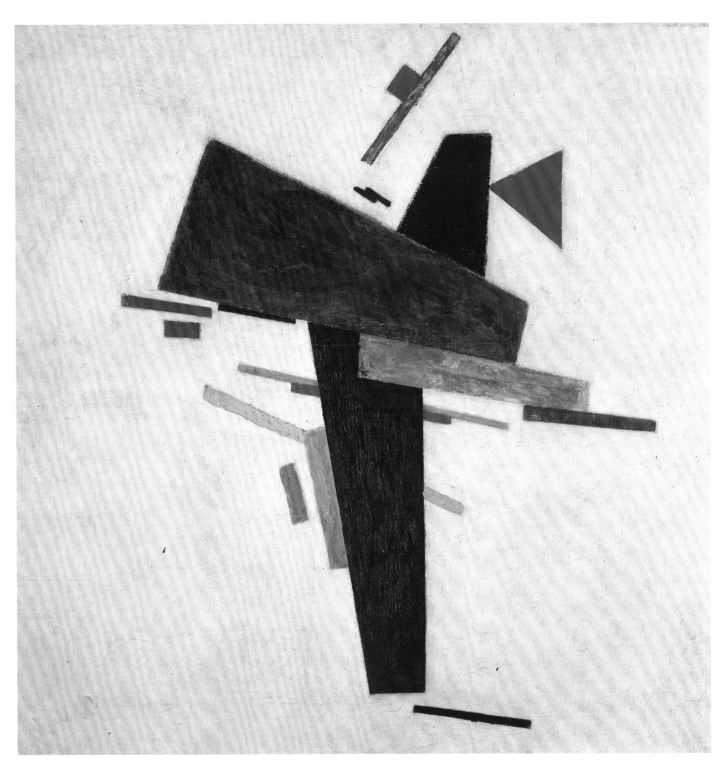

KASIMIR SEVERINOVICH Malevich studied in Moscow from 1902 to 1905 and came under the influence of the French Impressionists. In 1912 Mikhail Larionov invited him to take part in the inaugural Knave of Diamonds exhibition. Later the same year he visited Paris and immediately converted to Cubism, attacking this new style with zeal and improving and refining it in a style which he called

Suprematism. 'Under Suprematism', said Malevich, 'I understand the supremacy of pure feeling in creative art.' A pure black square was, he insisted, the true 'zero of form', the white space that stretched away behind it the empty void.

His exhibition of Suprematist art in 1915 gained a mixed reception and he subsequently modified his style, rejecting the stark minimalism of such works as *Black*

Square and injecting a great deal of colour. But he reverted to his ideals in 1918 with a series of paintings entitled *White on White*, the ultimate example of minimalism. Thereafter he abandoned painting and concentrated on sculpture, becoming one of the leading Constructivists of the early Soviet era.

John Marin   Brooklyn Bridge Series, 1910

Born 1870 New York, USA   Painted in USA   Died 1953 Addison, Maine, USA
MOVEMENTS: Fauvism, Cubism **OTHER WORKS:** *Maine Islands, Four-Master off the Cape Maine Coast* **INFLUENCES:** James McNeill Whistler, Raoul Dufy, Emil Nolde

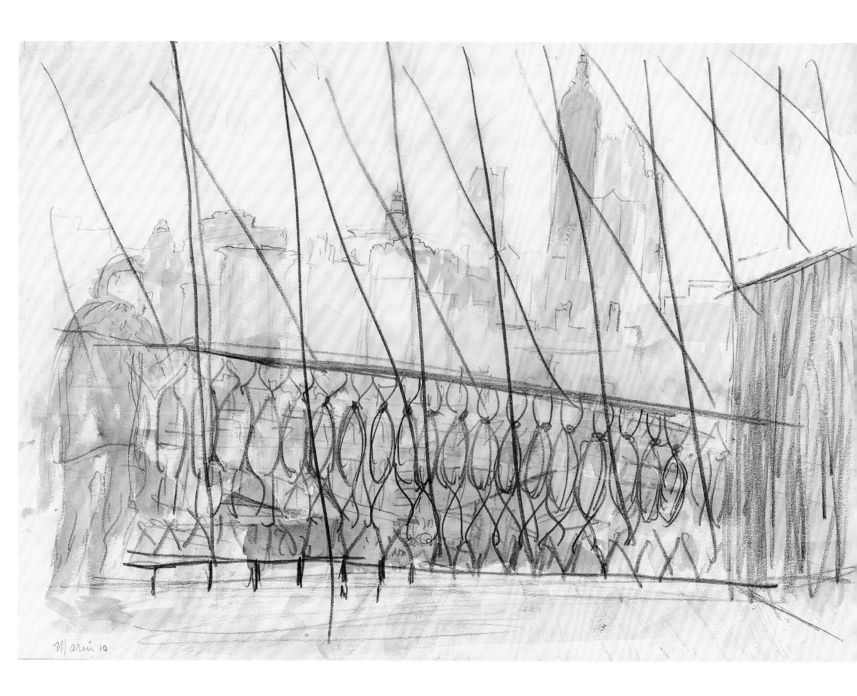

JOHN MARIN studied architecture at the Pennsylvania Academy in Philadelphia and the Art Students' League of New York and subsequently pursued this profession, while gradually becoming involved in painting under the influence of James McNeill Whistler. Between 1905 and 1910 he travelled extensively in Europe, continuing his art studies in Paris, Rome and London. In 1909

he exhibited his work for the first time at the 291 Gallery in New York – run by Alfred Stieglitz – and as a result he came into contact with the Stieglitz Circle, an avant-garde group. Subsequently he went through phases of flirting with Fauvism and Cubism, both of which left their mark on his later paintings, although interpreted from a purely American standpoint. Although he occasionally worked in

oils on canvas his preferred medium was watercolours. He was also a prolific etcher, his landscapes rendered in a highly individualistic style.

Egon Schiele   Liegender Halbakt Mit Rolem, 1910

Born 1890 Tulln, Austria   Painted in Vienna, Austria   Died 1918 Vienna
MOVEMENT: Austrian Expressionism **OTHER WORKS:** *The Embrace, Recumbent Female Nude with Legs Apart* **INFLUENCES:** Klimt

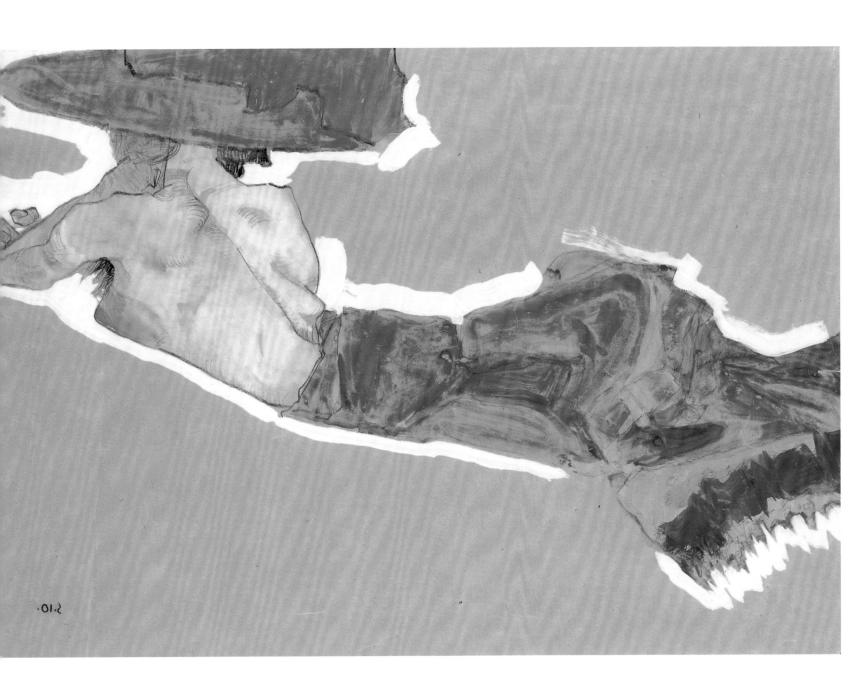

EGON SCHIELE studied at the Vienna Academy of Fine Arts in 1906 and the following year he met Gustave Klimt, whose Vienna Sezession movement he joined in 1908. A disciple of Sigmund Freud, Schiele sought to explore the deeper recesses of the human psyche, especially the sexual aspects. He developed a particularly stark style of Expressionism – distinguished by figures, often naked and usually emaciated – with harsh outlines, filling the canvas with contorted limbs and anguished features. Long before the Nazis were denouncing his paintings as degenerate art, the Austrian authorities were confiscating and destroying his works. In 1912 he was actually arrested, convicted of offences against public morals and briefly imprisoned. After his marriage in 1915 his art mellowed, taking on a brighter and more sensuous form, and it is interesting to conjecture how this trend might have developed had he not died in the influenza pandemic of 1918.

Max Pechstein   Rote Kirche, 1911

Born 1881 Zwickau, Germany   Painted in Dresden and Berlin   Died 1955 Berlin, Germany

MOVEMENT: German Expressionism   **OTHER WORKS:** *Meadow at Moritzburg, Tale of the Sea, Seated Female Nude*   **INFLUENCES:** Van Gogh, Matisse

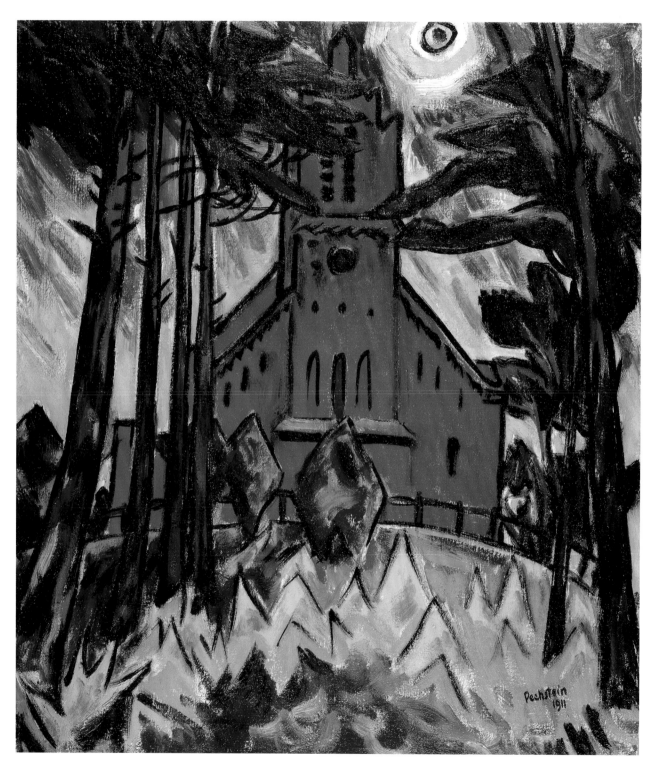

MAX HERMANN Pechstein studied art in Dresden, where he joined Die Brücke ('The Bridge') in 1906. The only member of this avant-garde group to have received a formal art education, he had a formulative influence on his contemporaries. Later he co-founded the Neue Sezession in Berlin and was the first of that group to achieve widespread popularity, mainly because his paintings were more decorative than those of his fellow artists. He was profoundly influenced by Van Gogh, Matisse and the Fauves, reflected in his vibrant colours and dramatic composition. Later he was also attracted to primitive art, evident in the greater angularity of his figures in the 1920s and 1930s. Bright, contrasting colours are emphasized by thick black lines creating an almost stained-glass effect. Pechstein taught at the Berlin Academy from 1923 until 1933, when he was dismissed by the Nazis, but he survived the Third Reich and was reinstated in 1945.

Marcel Duchamp   Nude Descending a Staircase, No 2, 1912

Born 1887 Normandy   Painted in France and the USA   Died 1968

MOVEMENT: Cubism, Dada, Conceptual Art   **OTHER WORKS:** *Fountain, The Bride Stripped Bare by her Bachelors Even*   **INFLUENCES:** Francis Picabia, Paul Cézanne, Man Ray

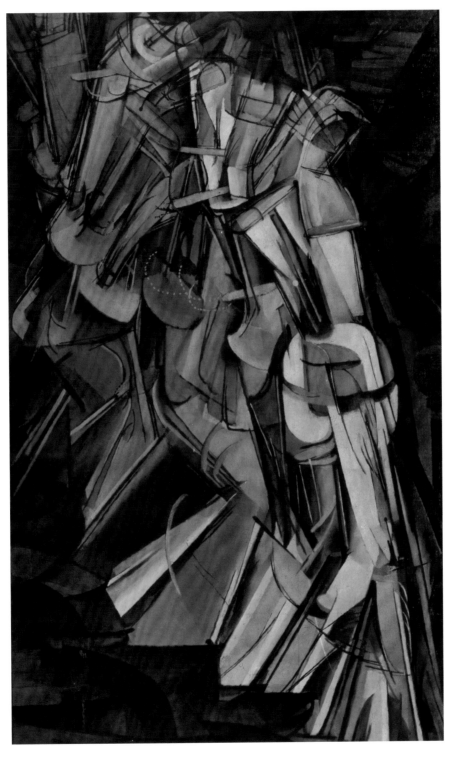

ALTHOUGH HE produced relatively few artworks, Duchamp was a key figure in twentieth century art, playing a seminal role in the development of several different movements. Duchamp trained in Paris, and was briefly influenced by Cézanne and the Fauves. His first real masterpiece – *Nude Descending a Staircase* – was a potent blend of Cubism and Futurism, In 1913 he invented the ready-made – an everyday object, divorced from its normal context and presented as a work of art in its own right. Two years later, Duchamp moved to the USA, where he became a leading light of the New York Dada movement. His work from this period displayed a mischievous sense of humour, whilst also challenging existing preconceptions about the nature of art. In *L.H.O.O.Q.*, for example, he added a moustache and a smutty inscription to the *Mona Lisa*. His most notorious ready-made was a urinal, which he exhibited under the title of *Fountain*. After receiving a legacy, Duchamp's output slowed dramatically but his later work has been seen as a foretaste of Kinetic art and Conceptual art.

Alexei Jawlensky   Spaneteru mit Roten Schal, 1912

Born 1864 Kuslovo, Russia   Painted in Russia, France and Germany   Died 1941 Wiesbaden, Germany
MOVEMENT: Fauvism, Cubism   **OTHER WORKS:** *The White Feather, Abstract Head*   **INFLUENCES:** Kandinsky, Matisse, Paul Klee

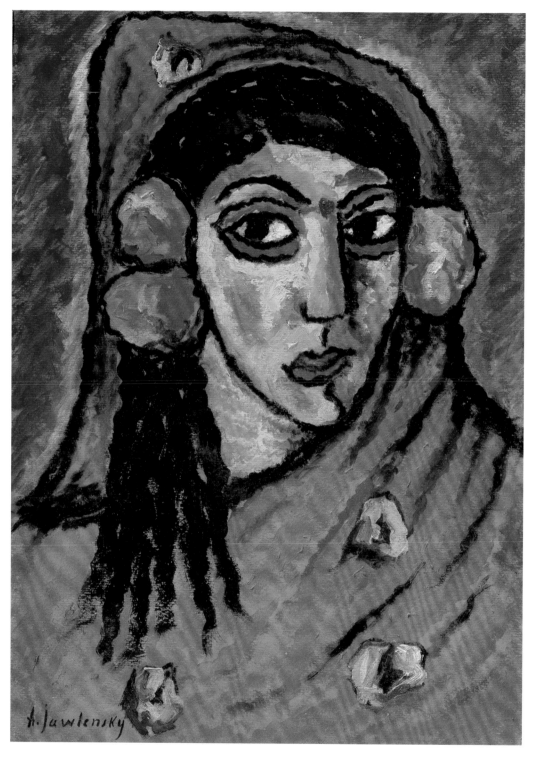

THE SCION of a Russian aristocratic family, Alexei Jawlensky served as an officer in the Imperial Guard before abandoning a military career in favour of art. He enrolled at the St Petersburg Academy and then moved to Germany in 1896, completing his education in Munich, where he met fellow Russian Wassily Kandinsky; under his guidance evolved his own highly distinctive brand of Fauvism. He spent some time painting in Brittany and Provence in about 1905. During a visit to Paris in 1913, however, he came under the influence of Matisse and Picasso and embraced Cubism, initially adapting it to his style of portraiture, which owed much to the religious icons of his native country. Later, however, his paintings became much less figurative and gradually switched to a more overtly abstract character, relying on simple geometric patterns in more muted colours than those that had been the hallmark of his Fauvist period. After World War I he settled in Wiesbaden, Germany, where he joined the group known as the Blaue Vier ('Blue Four') with Kandinsky, Klee and Feininger. Jawlensky used colour in a lyrical sense, believing that tones and shades corresponded to notes and chords.

Pierre Bonnard   Interieur, 1913

Born 1867 Fontena-aux-Roses, France   Painted in Paris, France   Died 1947 Le Cannet, France

MOVEMENTS: Les Nabis, Intimism, Fauvism   **OTHER WORKS:** *Mirror on the Washstand, The Open Window, The Table*   **INFLUENCES:** Gauguin, Van Gogh

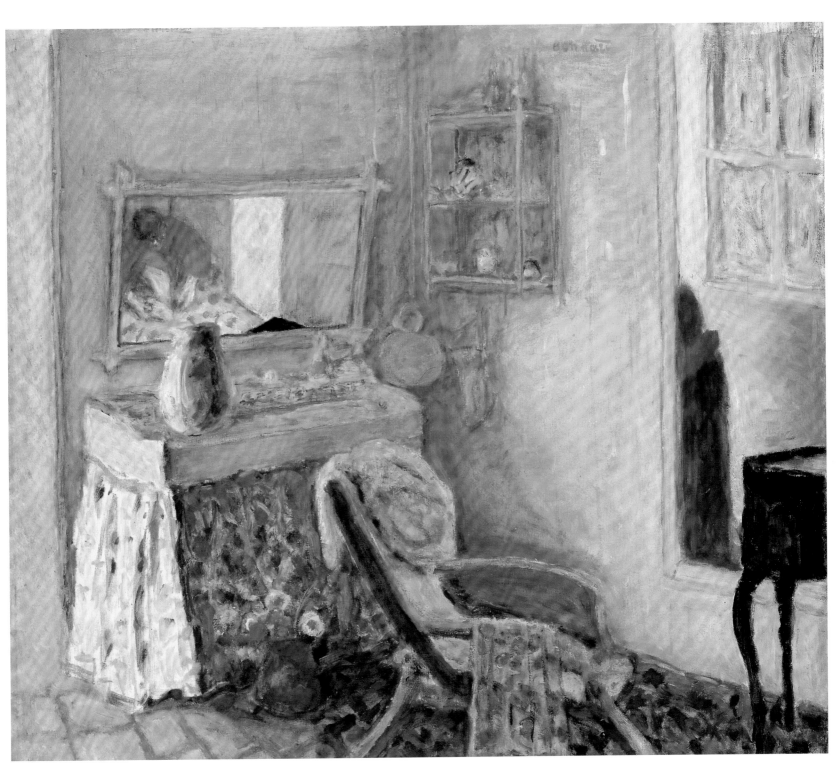

PIERRE BONNARD settled in Paris in 1888, where he studied at the Académie Julien and the Ecole des Beaux-Arts. With Maurice Denis and Edouard Vuillard (with whom he shared a studio) he was influenced by Paul Gauguin's expressive use of colour and formed the group known as Les Nabis (from the Hebrew word for prophet) and later the Intimists. While other artists at the end of the nineteenth century were tending towards abstraction, Bonnard was influenced by Japanese prints and concentrated on landscapes and interiors which strove after subtle effects in light and colour at the expense of perspective. At the turn of the century he was moved by the intensity and passion in the paintings of Van Gogh and this led him to become a founder member of the Salon d'Automne in 1903. Thereafter he was influenced by Les Fauves (literally 'the wild beasts'), whose strident colours and distorted images he tamed and harnessed to his own style.

Franz Marc   Spingendes Pferd, 1913

Born 1880 Munich, Germany   Painted in Munich and Paris   Died 1916 Verdun, France
MOVEMENTS: Impressionism, Expressionism **OTHER WORKS:** *Tiger, Deer in Wood, Foxes, Tower of the Blue Horses* **INFLUENCES:** August Macke, Kandinsky

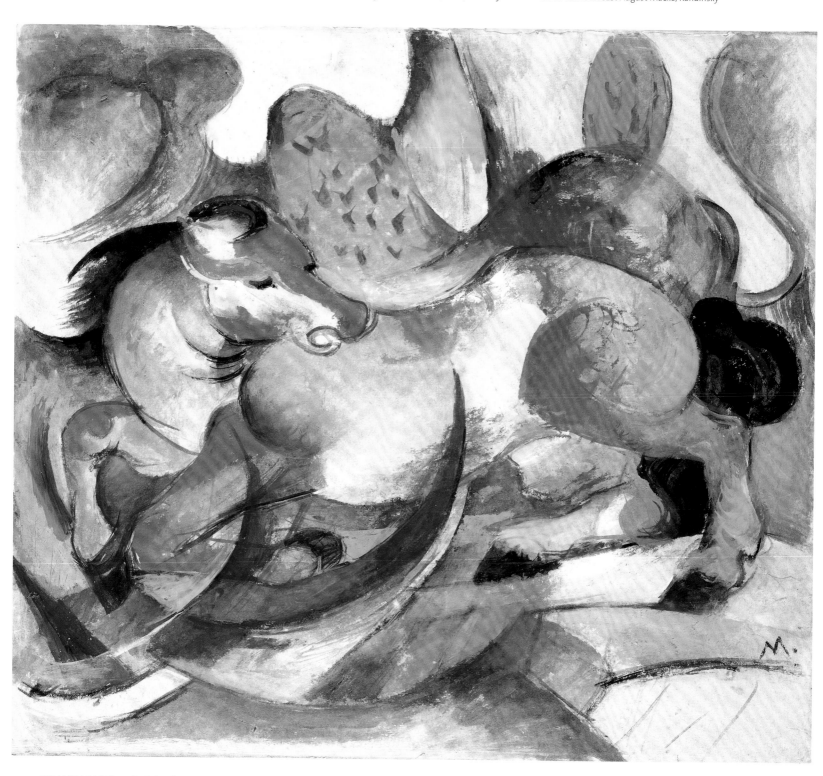

FRANZ MARC studied theology in Munich, intending to enter the Church, but switched to art, which he regarded as an intensely spiritual activity. He studied painting in Italy and France before returning to Munich where, with Kandinsky, he founded the Blaue Reiter group in 1911. An intensely religious man, he believed that animals were more in harmony with nature than human beings and therefore he concentrated on paintings in which animals, notably horses and foxes, featured prominently. In his earlier works the animals form the dominant subject but later they merged into the landscape as though an integral part of it. He speculated on how animals perceived the world and this influenced his later Expressionist work, which was almost devoid of figural motifs and explored the emotional potential of colour. He returned to Germany on the outbreak of World War I; his death in action brought to an abrupt end one of the most promising artists of the early twentieth century.

Giacomo Balla   Grand Fiore Futurista

Born 1871 Turin, Italy   Painted in Italy   Died 1958 Rome, Italy
MOVEMENT: Futurism **OTHER WORKS:** *Girl Running on the Balcony, Dog on a Leash, Flight of Swallows* **INFLUENCES:** Umberto Boccioni, Carlo Carrà

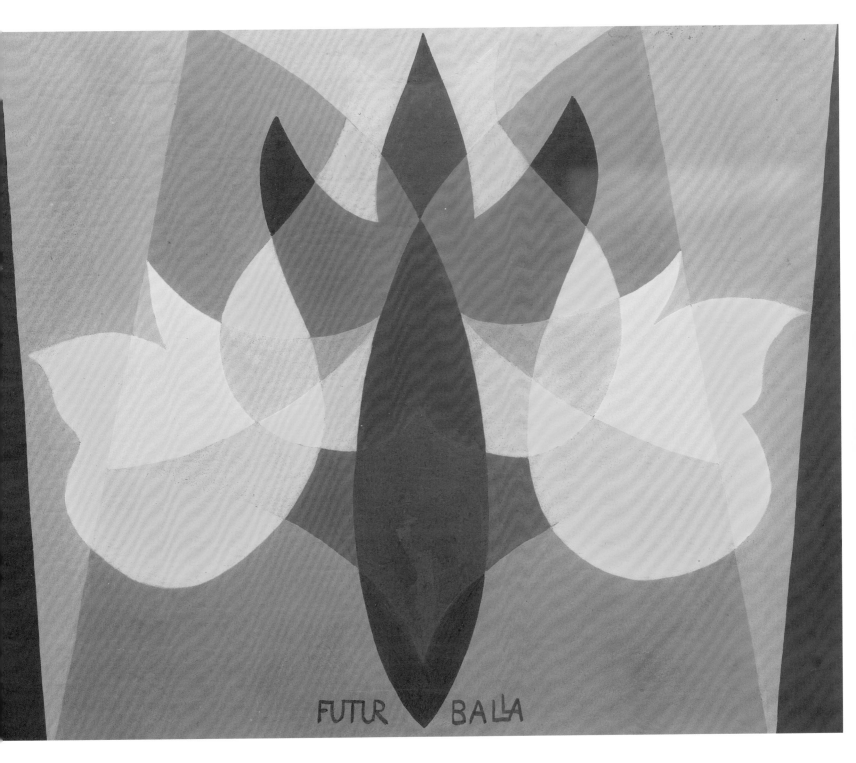

AFTER A CONVENTIONAL art training in his native Turin, Giacomo Balla went to Paris in 1901, where he was strongly influenced by Impressionism and Divisionism. In 1910 he signed the Futurist Manifesto, publicizing his commitment to a form of art that would express the vibrant dynamism of the twentieth century. In his paintings Balla tried to convey the impression of speed through the use of overlapping images, comparable to time-lapse photographs. Futurism lost its freshness and idealism during World War I and in the 1920s it became increasingly stereotyped and associated with Fascism. As a result, Balla turned to more abstract forms and from 1930 onwards tended to return to the more mainstream styles of figural painting. Nevertheless, echoes of Balla's technique may be found in many works of the late twentieth century which use blurred or overlapping images to suggest rapid movement.

Giorgio de Chirico Piazza d'Italia, *c.*1915

Born 1888 Volo, Greece   Painted in France and Italy   Died 1978 Rome
MOVEMENT: Metaphysical painting, Surrealism **OTHER WORKS:** *The Uncertainty of the Poet, The Archaeologists* **INFLUENCES:** Carlo Carrà

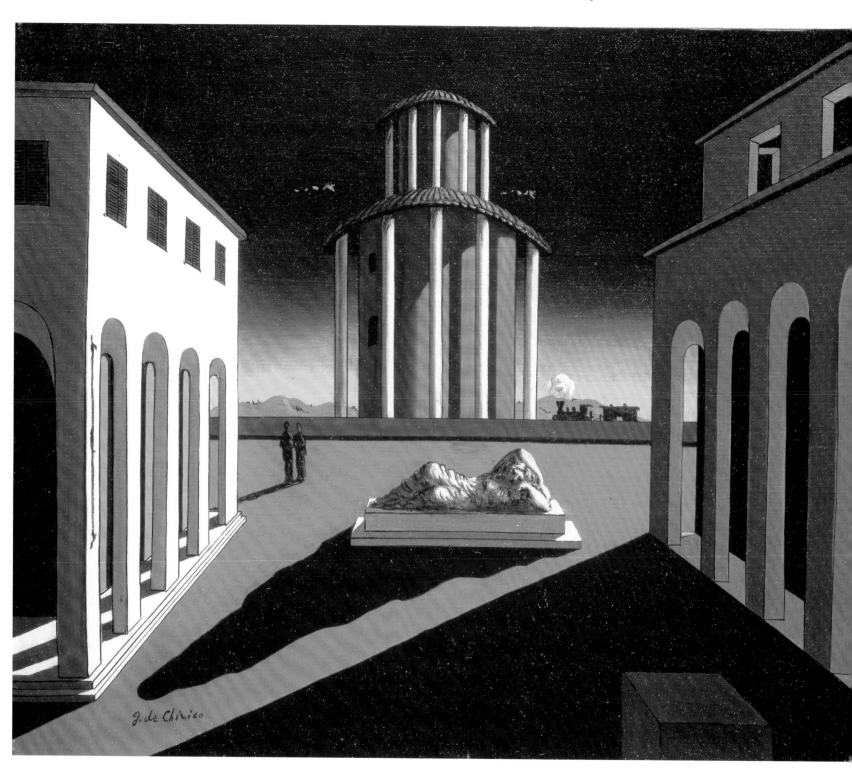

BORN IN north-western Greece of Venetian descent, Giorgio de Chirico studied in Athens and Munich, then worked in Paris and finally collaborated with Carrà in Italy, founding *Pittura Metaphisica*. About 1910 he began painting a series of pictures of deserted town squares, imbued with a dreamlike quality, characterized by incongruous figures and strange shadows which anticipated the style of the Surrealists, on whom he exerted tremendous influence. After suffering a breakdown during World War I he developed his metaphysical style of paintings, which conveyed an intensely claustrophobic impression. In the 1920s, however, his paintings often verged on the abstract before he returned to a more traditional style shortly before World War II – the complete antithesis of all he had done up to that time. He continued to embrace academic naturalism in the postwar period.

Amedeo Modigliani   Beatrice Hastings Assise, 1915

Born 1884, Italy   Painted in Italy and France   Died 1920 Paris, France
MOVEMENT: School of Paris **OTHER WORKS:** *Seated Nude, The Little Peasant, Portrait of Jeanne Hébuterne* **INFLUENCES:** Botticelli, Cézanne, Brancusi

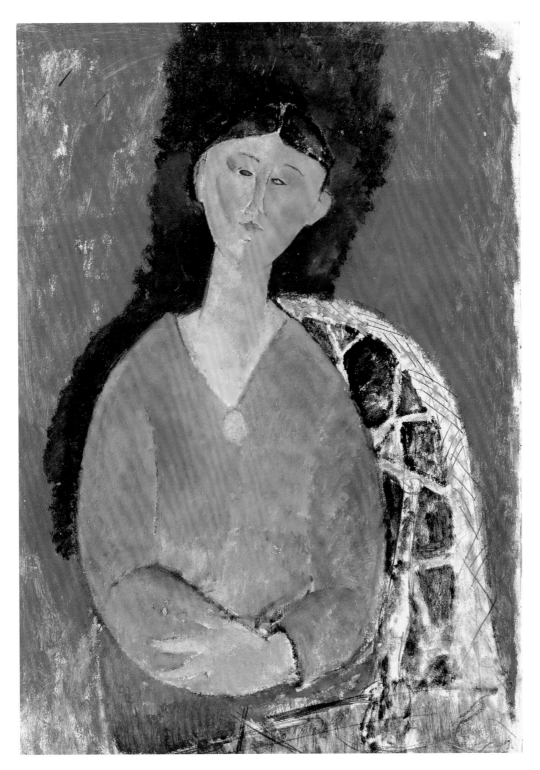

MODIGLIANI WAS born into a Jewish family in Livorno, Italy. Although educated in Florence and Venice he spent most of his career in France. His highly individual style combined the linear elegance of Botticelli, whose work he had studied in Italy, with the avant-garde ideas that were circulating in pre-war Paris. The key influence was the Romanian sculptor Brancusi, whom he met in 1909. Under his guidance,

Modigliani produced an impressive series of African-influenced stone figures.

After the outbreak of war, the raw materials for sculpture became scarce, so Modigliani turned to painting. Most of his subjects were sensual nudes or portraits, featuring slender, elongated figures. These received little attention from the critics; he was better known for his self-destructive, bohemian

lifestyle, a lifestyle which caused the breakdown of his health. Modigliani died of tuberculosis at the age of 35. Tragically, Jeanne Hébuterne, his mistress and favourite model, committed suicide on the following day, while pregnant with the artist's child. Modigliani's reputation was only secured posthumously, through a retrospective exhibition in Paris in 1922.

Ernst Ludwig Kirchner   Königstein Mit Roter Kirche, 1916

Born 1880 Germany   Painted in Germany and Switzerland   Died 1938 Davos, Switzerland

MOVEMENTS: Die Brücke, Expressionism **OTHER WORKS:** *Striding Into the Sea, Berlin Street Scene, The Red Tower in Halle* **INFLUENCES:** Van Gogh, Edvard Munch, Gauguin

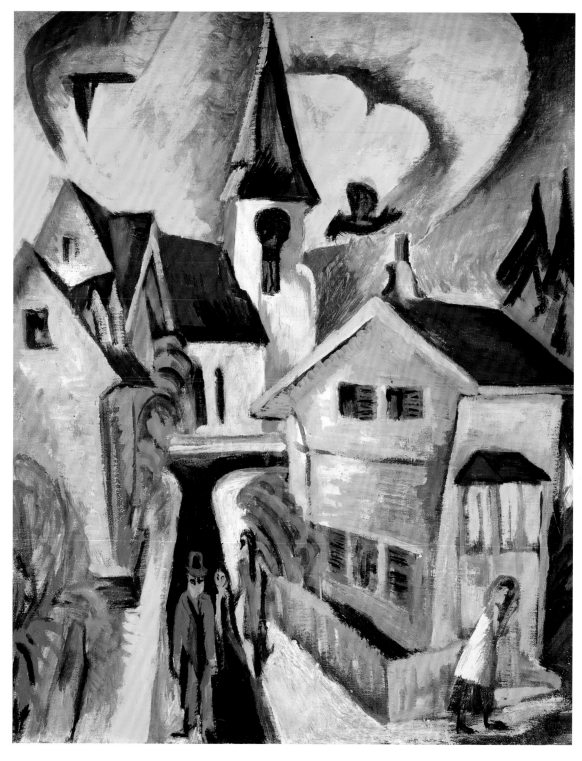

BORN IN Aschaffenburg, Germany in 1880, Kirchner studied architecture in Dresden before turning to painting as a result of encouragement from fellow students Erich Heckel and Karl Schmidt-Ruttluf. In 1905 these three artists formed the movement known as Die Brücke ('the Bridge'), which continued until 1913. The name signified the fact that they spanned the art of the past and present,

and derived inspiration from a variety of disparate sources, from primitive tribal art to Van Gogh. Kirchner was the dominant personality in this group, which sought to give direct expression to human feelings. Kirchner evolved a distinctly angular style highlighted by bold, contrasting colours. Like so many other artists drafted into the infantry, Kirchner suffered a severe nervous breakdown and while

convalescing in Switzerland he concentrated on Alpine landscapes as an antidote to the horrors of trench warfare. His postwar paintings grew more abstract in the time leading up to his suicide in 1938.

José Clemente Orozco   Caballo Salvajes

Born 1883 Mexico   Painted in Mexico and USA   Died 1949 Mexico City
MOVEMENTS: Expressionism, Social Realism   **OTHER WORKS:** *Table of Universal Brotherhood, Modern Migration of the Spirit*   **INFLUENCES:** Diego Rivera

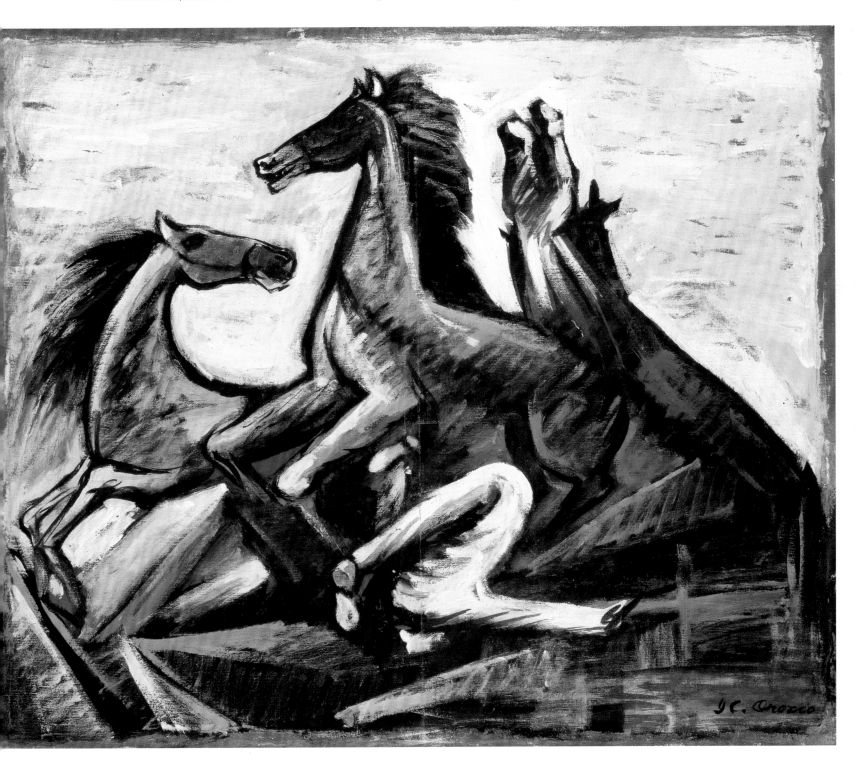

JOSÉ CLEMENTE Orozco studied engineering and archi-tecture in Mexico City and later art at the Academia San Carlos. Although schooled in the Spanish classical tradition, Orozco was strongly influenced by his studies of the art and architecture of the Toltecs and Mayas and this was reflected in his paintings, which also imbibed much from the European Expressionists. At the same time, he was an ardent revolutionary and a lifelong political activist, and as a result his canvasses often have an emphatic social message. Many of his paintings deal with dramatic events in Mexico's turbulent history – the revolution of 1911 and the subsequent civil war providing a fertile source of material. Orozco's passion for the sweeping social and economic changes wrought in the 1920s and 1930s also comes across very vividly in his work. He worked at various times between 1917 and 1934 in the United States and painted the murals and other decorations for several public buildings.

Tom Thomson   The Jack Pine, 1916–17

Born 1877 Ontario, Canada   Painted in Canada   Died 1917 Wapomeo Island and Canoe Lake, Ontario
MOVEMENT: Modern Canadian School **OTHER WORKS:** *Pine Island, Snow in the Woods, Sunrise* **INFLUENCES:** A.Y. Jackson, J.E.H. MacDonald, Arthur Lismer

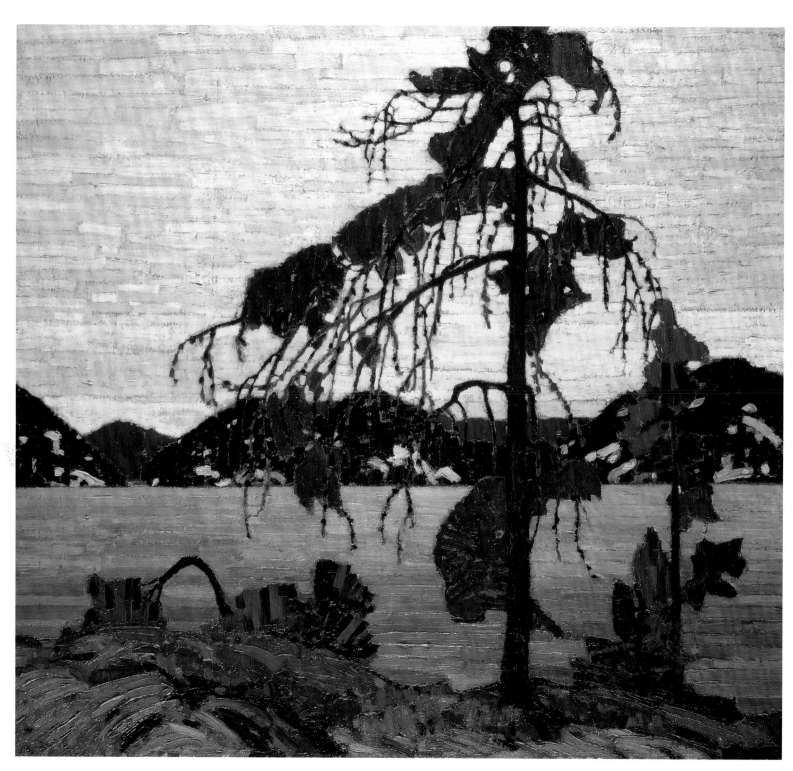

THOMAS JOHN THOMSON originally worked as an engraver and draughtsman at Grip Limited in Toronto, illustrating books and periodicals, and it was not until 1906 that he took up painting seriously. While working at Grip he was encouraged by co-workers J.E.H. MacDonald and Arthur Lismer to develop his painting. Other artists who were subsequently employed as graphic designers at Grip included Frederick Varley, Frank Johnston and Franklin Carmichael, who all made their name as painters; never before or since has any commercial firm employed such a talented group. While many of his younger colleagues became official war artists, Thomson remained behind, but it was his tragic death in mysterious circumstances – drowned near Wapomeo island in Canoe Lake in 1917 – which had a major impact on the post-war development of Canadian art. His death shocked his friends but increased their determination to paint Canada their way. A.Y. Jackson summed this up when he wrote, 'he was the guide, the interpreter, and we the guests partaking of his hospitality so generously given'.

Georges Braque   Verre et as de Trefle, 1917

Born 1882, France   Painted in France   Died 1963

MOVEMENT: Cubism **OTHER WORKS:** *The Round Table, Guitar and Fruit Dish, Still Life with Violin* **INFLUENCES:** Picasso, Cézanne, Juan Gris

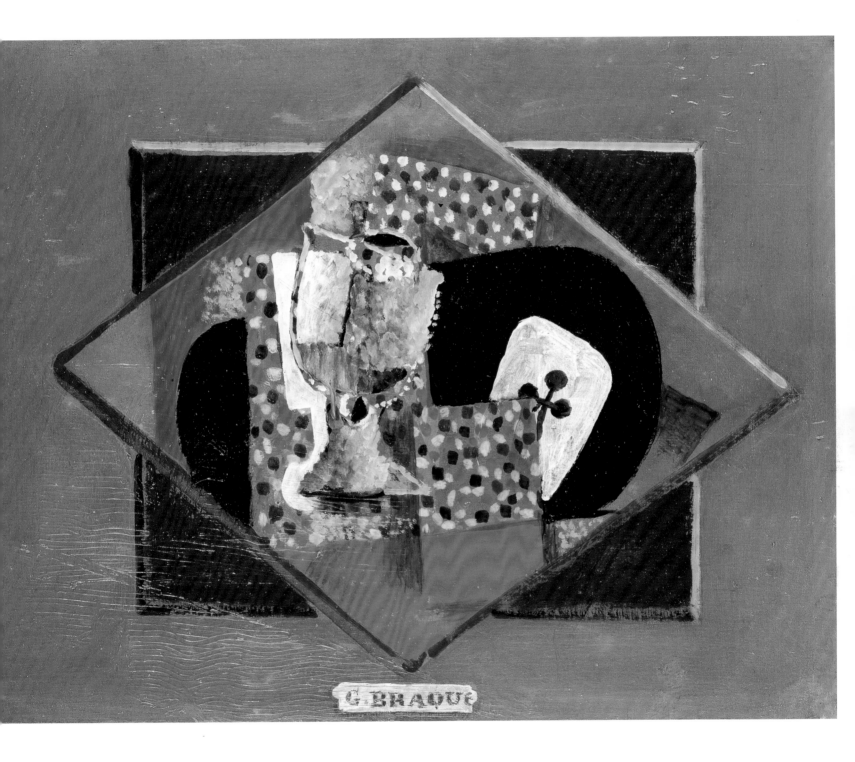

BORN IN Argenteuil, the son of a house-painter, Braque was initially trained to carry on the family business. In 1902 he switched to art, but retained a profound respect for craftsmanship and always ground his own pigments. Initially, he joined the Fauvist group, but his style altered radically after two key events in 1907. Firstly he was overwhelmed by an exhibition of Cézanne's work, then, later in the year, he saw *Les Demoiselles d'Avignon* in Picasso's studio and embarked on a unique collaboration with the Spaniard. Working, in Braque's words, 'like two mountaineers roped together', they created Cubism. This artistic partnership was halted by the war, when Braque was called to the Front. He was decorated for bravery before being discharged with serious wounds in 1916. Unlike Picasso, who changed direction completely, Braque spent the remainder of his career refining his experiments with Cubism. These culminated in a magnificent cycle of paintings on *The Studio*, which he began in 1947. Braque also diversified into design work, producing ballet décors, stained-glass windows, book illustrations and, most notable of all, a ceiling for the Etruscan Gallery in the Louvre.

Maurice de Vlaminck   Paysage

Born 1876 Paris, France   Painted in France   Died 1958 Rueil-la-Gadelière, France
MOVEMENT: Fauvism, Realism   **OTHER WORKS:** *Landscape with Red Trees, The River, Summer Landscape*   **INFLUENCES:** André Derain, Matisse, Cézanne

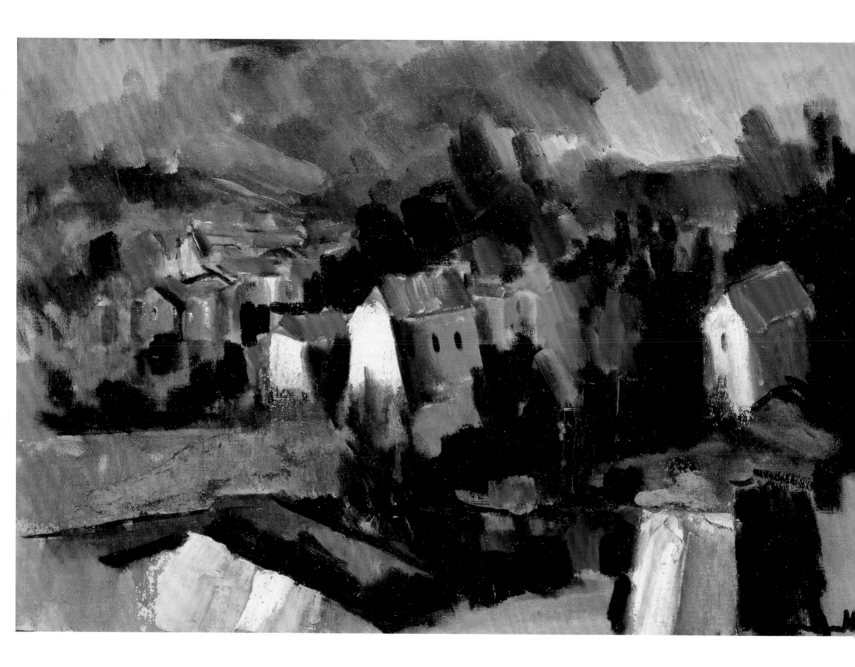

ALTHOUGH LARGELY self-taught, this exuberant, highly extrovert artist wielded a considerable influence over the development of avant-garde styles at the beginning of the twentieth century. Influenced by the expressive quality in the paintings of Van Gogh and Gauguin, he was later closely associated with André Derain and Henri Matisse, with whom he established Fauvism, painting flat patterns in the most extravagantly brilliant colours. Subsequently he came under the influence of Paul Cézanne and between 1908 and World War I produced landscapes that were more in the mainstream Realist manner and much more restrained in their use of colour. War service left its mark on him and in his later years he withdrew to a remote part of the country, where he developed a form of brooding Expressionism characterized by more sombre colours.

Liubov Popova   Pictorial Architectonic, 1918

Born 1889 Moscow, Russia   Painted in Moscow   Died 1924 Moscow
MOVEMENT: Constructivism **OTHER WORKS:** *Space-Force Construction, Cubist Nude* **INFLUENCES:** Vladimir Tatlin, Alexander Archipenko

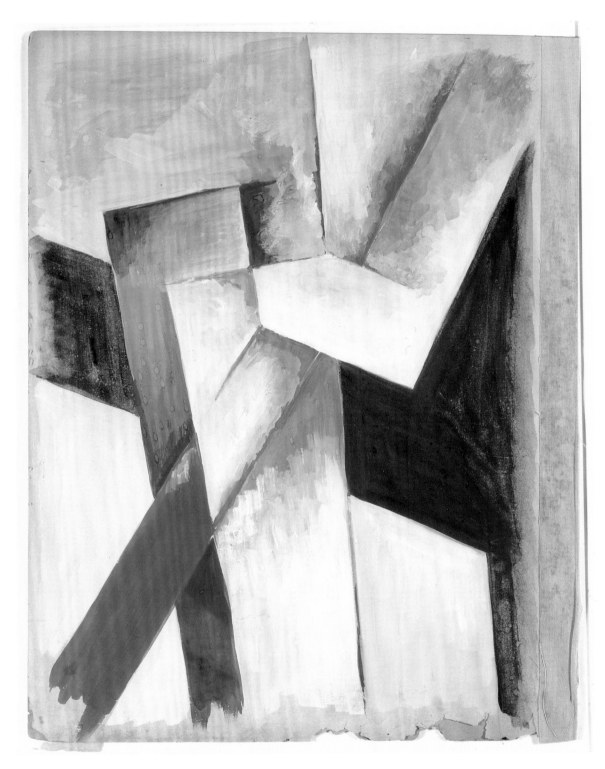

BORN LIUBOV Sergeyevna Eding on the outskirts of Moscow, Popova studied in Paris shortly before the outbreak of World War I. On her return to Russia in 1914 she met Vladimir Tatlin, who would later become the founder of Soviet Constructivism, and whose principles are very evident in her paintings immediately after the Revolution. In the last years of her life she designed costumes and sets for the theater as well as patterns for the First State Textile Factory in Moscow, which put on a major retrospective exhibition of her works shortly after her sudden death from scarlet fever in 1924. Her paintings broke new ground in their exploration of spatial possibilities and in their colour values, characterized by overlapping circles, curved, diagonal lines and geometric shapes in which the colours merge or contrast sharply. She fervently believed that art should not be merely decorative but should serve some useful purpose, and but for her untimely death she would undoubtedly have become one of the major forces in Soviet art.

Paul Klee   Moonshine, 1919

Born 1879 Münchenbuschsee, Switzerland   Painted in Berne and Munich   Died 1940 Muralto-Locarno, Switzerland
MOVEMENTS: Expressionism, Cubism   **OTHER WORKS:** *The Castle in a Garden, At the Sign of the Hunter's Tree*   **INFLUENCES:** August Macke, Robert Delaunay

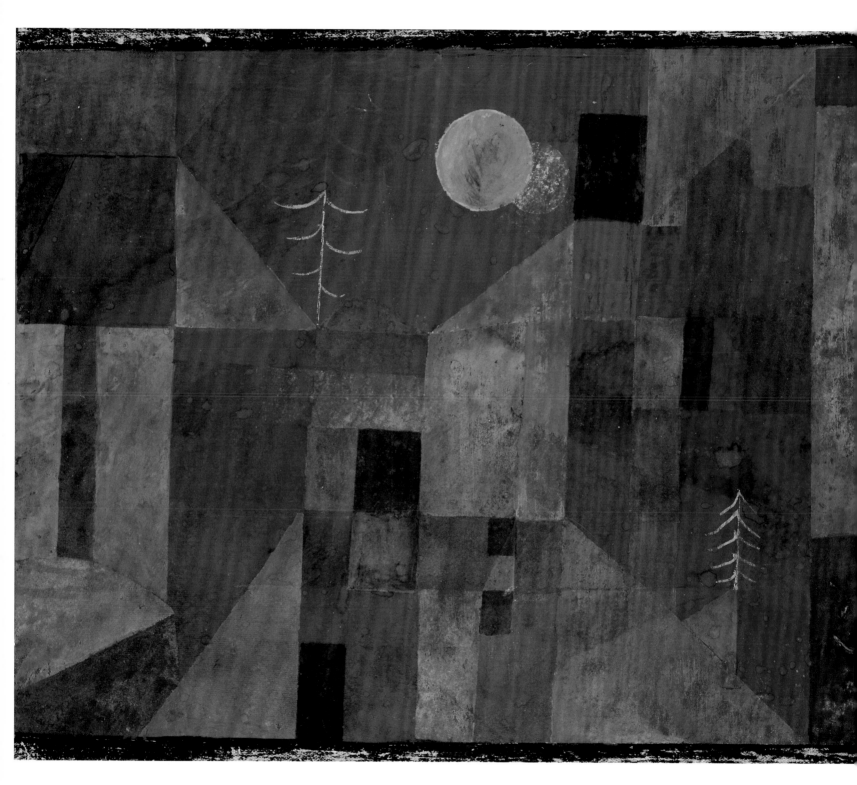

PAUL KLEE studied in Munich and worked there as an etcher. In 1911 he joined with Feininger, Kandinsky and Jawlensky in the Blaue Reiter group founded by August Macke; up to that time he had worked mainly in watercolours, painting in an Expressionist manner with overtones of Blake and Beardsley, but subsequently he veered towards Cubism under the influence of Robert Delaunay and from 1919 onwards painted mostly in oils. In 1920 he became a teacher at the Bauhaus and in the ensuing period his paintings mingled the figural with the abstract as he explored subtle combinations of colours and shapes, often deriving elements from folk art and even children's drawings. He severed his connections with the Bauhaus and returned to Switzerland when the Nazis came to power in 1933 and condemned his works as degenerate art.

Augustus John   Meditation at Ischia, Portrait of Thomas Earp

Born 1878 Wales   Painted in England   Died 1961 Hampshire, England
MOVEMENT: English School   **OTHER WORKS:** *Canadians Opposite Lens, The Smiling Woman*   **INFLUENCES:** Rembrandt, El Greco

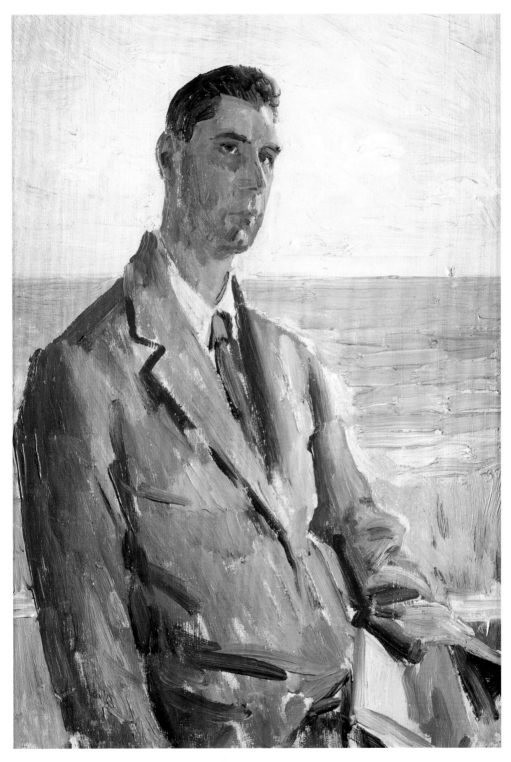

AUGUSTUS EDWIN John studied at the Slade School of Art and the University of London under Fred Brown and Henry Tonks, winning a scholarship with his *Moses and the Brazen Serpent* (1896). He went to Paris in 1900 and later travelled in the Netherlands, Belgium and Provence. His early work was influenced by Rembrandt, El Greco and the Post-Impressionists. A colourful, larger-than-life character,

John hit the headlines when he roamed around England in a horse and cart, painting gypsy scenes. His later style was marked by the use of bold, bright colours, his first major oil being *The Smiling Woman* (1908) the first of many paintings in which his wife Dorelia was the model. During World War I he served as a war artist with the Canadians. From the 1920s onwards he painted numerous portraits.

He became a member of the Royal Academy in 1928, resigned in protest in 1938, was re-elected in 1940 and in 1942 was awarded the Order of Merit. His genre scenes are full of wry humor.

Stanton MacDonald–Wright   Synchromy No. 3, 1917

Born 1890 Charlottesville, Virginia, USA   Painted in New York   Died 1973
MOVEMENT: Synchromist **OTHER WORKS:** *Airplane Synchromy in Yellow-Orange* **INFLUENCES:** Frantisek Kupka, Robert Delaunay

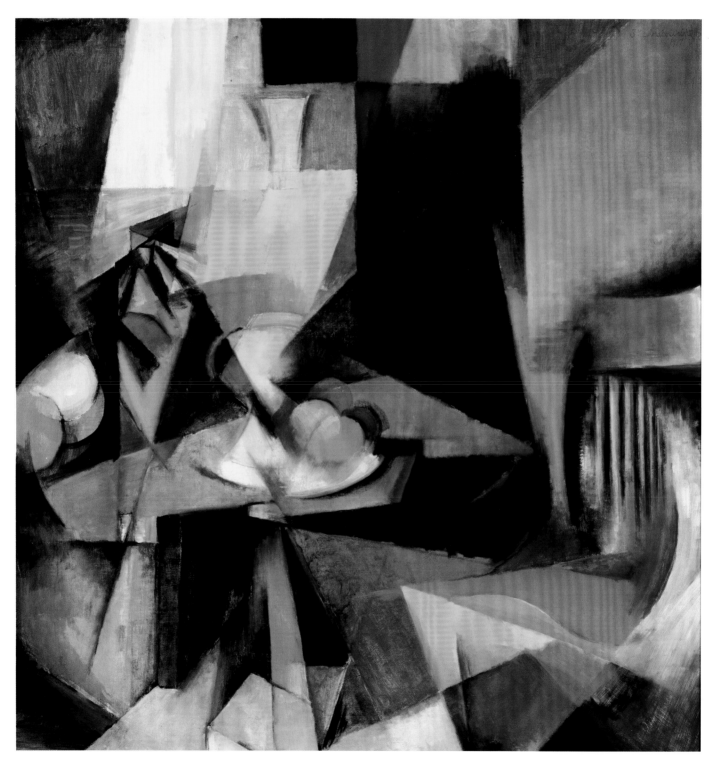

THROUGHOUT THE first decade of the twentieth century many American artists travelled to Europe, and particularly Paris, to experience first-hand developments in what was widely recognized as the art capital of the world. Among these was the painter Stanton MacDonald-Wright who, along with Morgan Russell (1886–1953), is recognized as the founder of the movement known as

Synchromism, meaning literally 'with colour'. MacDonald-Wright moved to Paris in 1907 and, over the next few years, acquired a familiarity with the works of key avant-garde artists, including Frantisek Kupka (1871–1957) and Robert Delaunay (1885–1941). Like these artists, MacDonald-Wright explored the possibilities of an art that was entirely non-representational and that strove to link the

visual experience of colour to the aural experience of music. In this way, many of MacDonald-Wright's paintings were given titles similar to musical compositions, such as *Synchromy No. 3*. Although many of his *Synchromies* were produced in Paris, MacDonald-Wright returned to the United States in 1916, where he continued to develop his particular form of abstract painting.

George Wesley Bellows   Stag at Sharkey's, 1917

Born 1882 Columbus, Ohio, USA   Painted in New York   Died 1925
MOVEMENT: Ashcan School   **OTHER WORKS:** *Between Rounds*   **INFLUENCES:** Thomas Eakins

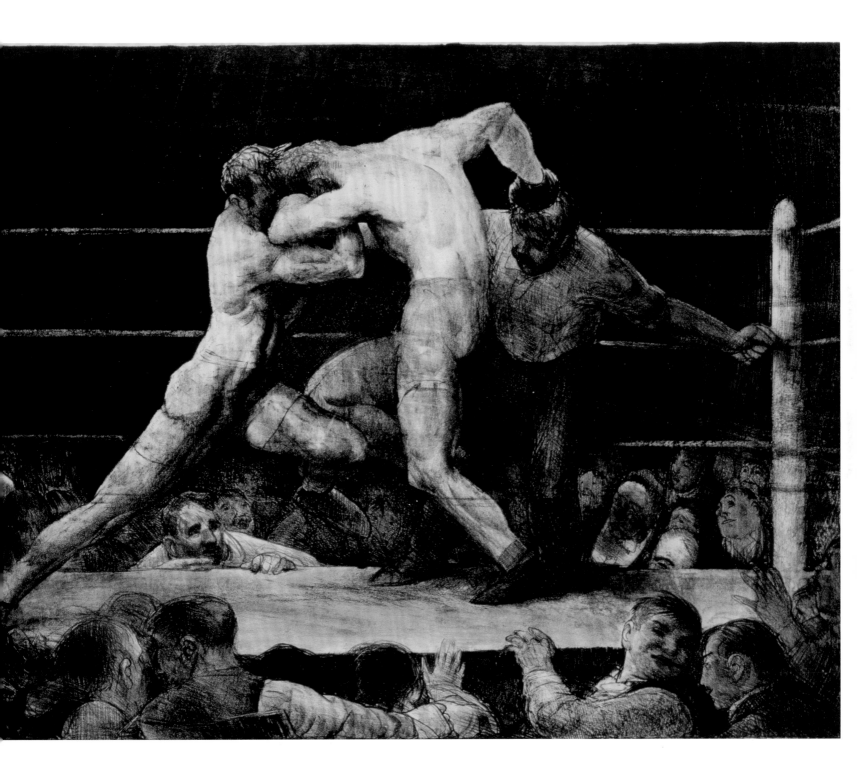

THROUGHOUT HIS career, the Ashcan School artist George Bellows was always attracted to the darker, grittier aspects of city life. He developed a particular fascination for boxing, and regularly attended fights at a local saloon run by an Irishman by the name of Tom Sharkey. Here he witnessed the sheer brutality of the sport as it was practised in the early twentieth century. In 1909 Bellows produced several boxing paintings, including one entitled *Stag at Sharkey's*. This later lithograph replicates the original composition. Here Bellows places the spectator in the thick of the action, at ringside amongst a motley crowd whose faces appear twisted and contorted in the low light of the boxing ring. The fighters themselves – anonymous, faceless combatants – are loosely executed with rapidly applied marks, thus capturing the immense physical effort of the battle. The rawness of their flesh resembles meat in a packing factory and Bellows abandons any sense of grace or dignity in this grim contest. For Bellows this Darwinian struggle for the survival of the fittest acted as an appropriate metaphor for the everyday struggle for survival among the often poverty-stricken inhabitants of early twentieth-century New York.

Joseph Stella   The Bridge, 1920–22

Born 1877 near Naples, Italy   Painted in New York   Died 1946

MOVEMENT: Futurism **OTHER WORKS:** *Battle of Lights, Mardi Gras, Coney Island* **INFLUENCES:** Giacomo Balla and the Futurists

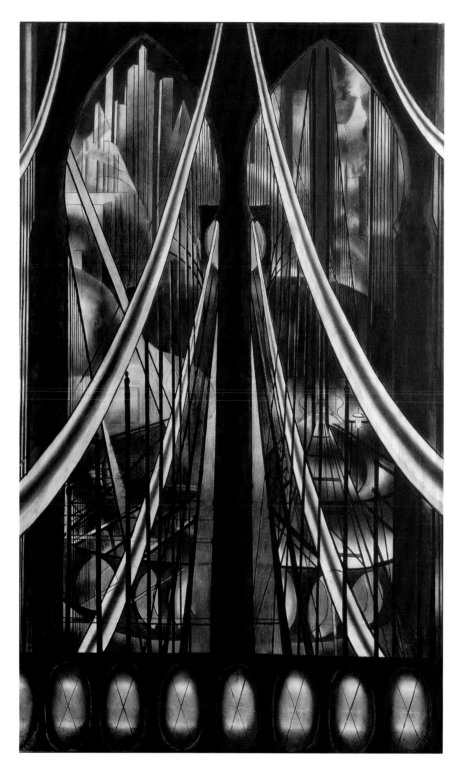

FOR THE Italian-born artist Joseph Stella, the vision of New York at night was nothing short of a religious experience. Between 1920 and 1922 Stella produced a series of five paintings entitled *The Voice of the City of New York Interpreted*, which set out to encapsulate his sense of awe when confronted with nocturnal New York, the city that never sleeps. One work from this series, *The Bridge*, aptly explores the sacred nature of Stella's vision. Here the artist represents the towers and cables of the Brooklyn Bridge, first completed in 1883. Much emphasis is placed upon the gothic arches of the bridge tower, through which are seen the skyscrapers of Wall Street framed against a dark night sky. Despite the overt modernity of the work, however, Stella's work notably recalls medieval stained-glass windows, whilst the view of the tunnels running beneath the bridge, seen at the bottom of the image, also recalls the predella panels of early Renaissance altar panels. Here both the past and the present, the sacred and the secular are conjoined to celebrate the sheer richness and diversity of New York City.

Fernand Léger   Le Petit Dejeuner, 1921–22

Born 1881 Argentan, France   Painted in France and USA   Died 1955 Gif-sur-Yvette, France

MOVEMENT: Cubism   **OTHER WORKS:** *The Construction Workers, The Builders, Still Life with a Beer Mug*   **INFLUENCES:** Georges Braque, Picasso

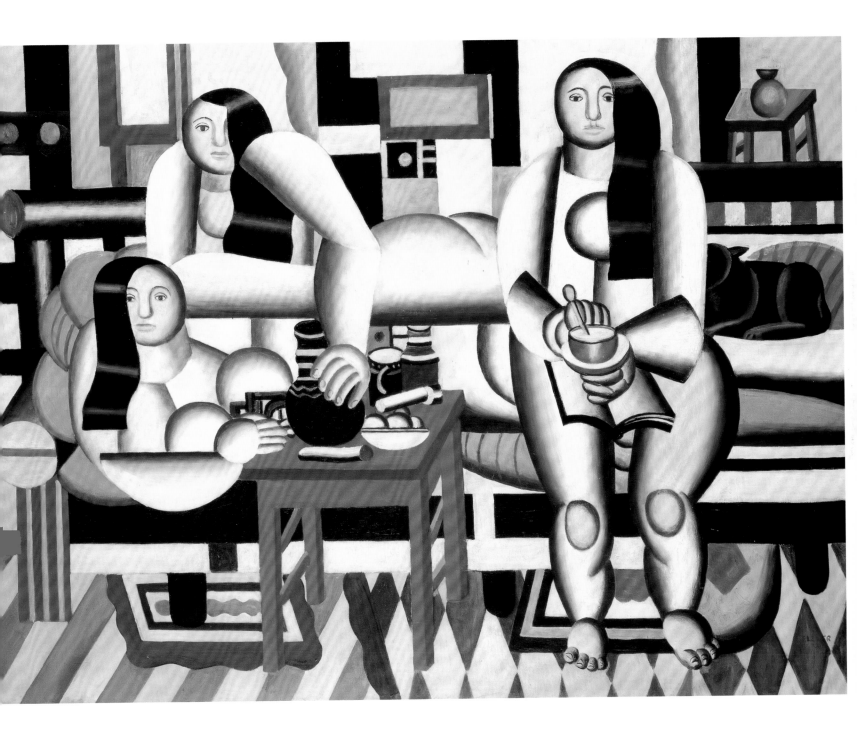

FERNAND LÉGER studied architecture in Caen and painting at the Académie Julien in Paris from 1903. Through Braque and Picasso he was introduced to Cubism in around 1910, but he soon developed his own distinctive brand of art described as the 'aesthetic of the machine', already evident in his work by 1913 but more fully developed after World War I. In this period he designed costumes and sets for the Swedish Ballet and collaborated with Man Ray on the first abstract film, *Le Ballet Mécanique* (1924). During World War II he lived in the USA where he taught at Yale and painted mainly acrobats and cyclists as well as working on the murals for the UN headquarters building in New York. After returning to France he concentrated on large paintings of men and machinery, earning the epithet of the 'Primitive of the Machine Age'.

Natalia Gontcharova   Le Printemps

Born 1881 Russia   Painted in Moscow and Paris   Died 1962 Paris

MOVEMENT: Der Blaue Reiter   **OTHER WORKS:** *The Cyclist, The Ice Cutters*   **INFLUENCES:** Mikhail Larionov, Picasso

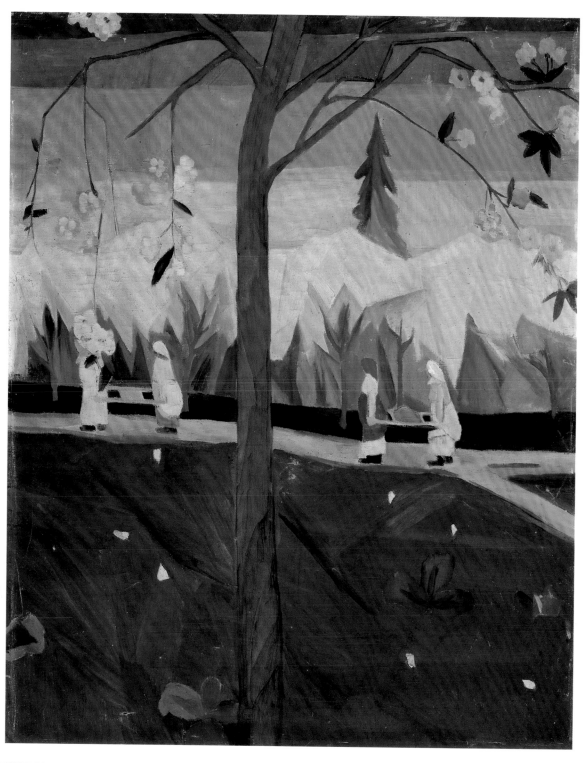

NATALIA GONTCHAROVA originally studied science but later changed direction and enrolled at the Moscow Academy of Art and trained as a sculptor. She turned to painting in 1904, attracted to the naive folk art of Russia and emulating the flat colours and primitive forms in which these paintings were expressed, combined with concepts borrowed from the Fauves and Cubists. All the elements in these pictures were reduced to simple circles and rectangles or flat shapes that complemented each other (as, for example, the woman's hat and the back of the carriage in her most famous painting). From 1911 she was a member of the German avant-garde movement known as Der Blaue Reiter. In 1915 she and her husband Mikhail Larionov moved to Geneva in order to design ballet costumes and sets for Diaghilev and never returned to Russia after the Revolution. Instead, she settled in Paris in 1921 where she continued to work mainly as a designer, and became a naturalized French citizen in 1938.

Lawren Harris   Above Lake Superior, *c.*1922

Born 1885, Ontario, Canada   Painted in Canada   Died 1970 Toronto, Ontario
MOVEMENT: Modern Canadian School   **OTHER WORKS:** *Northern Lake, Kempenfelt Bay, Early Houses*   **INFLUENCES**: J.E.H. MacDonald, Tom Thomson

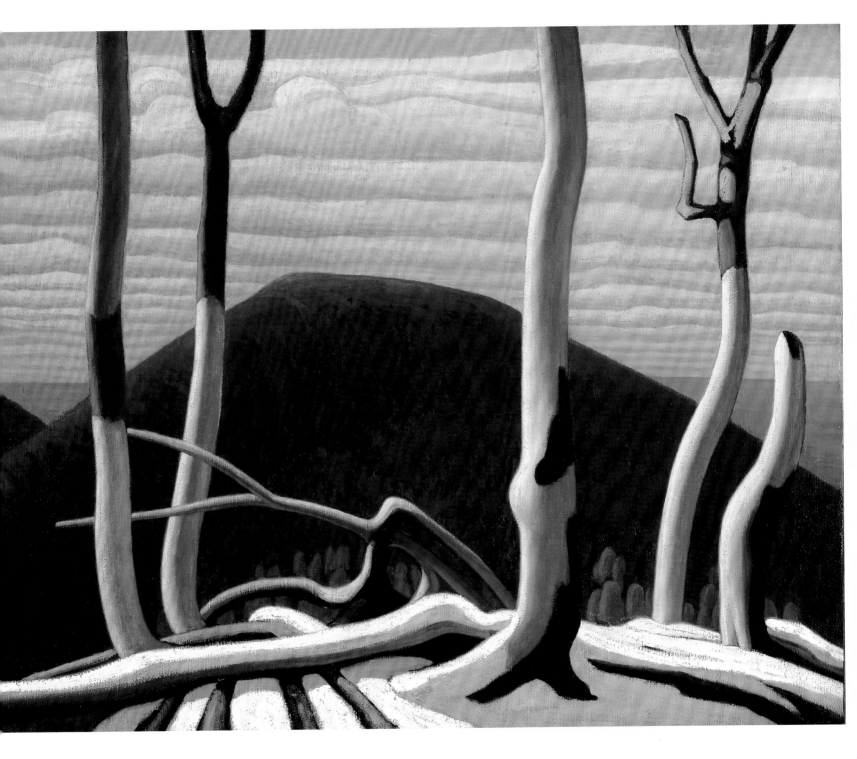

ONE OF the leaders of the modern Canadian movement, Lawren Harris worked as a commercial artist in Toronto. In 1908 he joined the newly formed Arts and Letters Club, which brought him into contact with other graphic designers and would-be artists, such as Arthur Lismer, Tom Thomson and J.E.H. MacDonald. But it was Harris who apparently took the lead in proposing that they should adopt a distinctive Canadian style – abandoning preconceived ideas, especially the classicism of English and European art – and paint nature as they found it. With the help of an art patron, Dr James McCallum, Harris founded the Studio Building for Canadian Art, to encourage graphic artists to concentrate on landscape painting. He also organized painting expeditions to Algonquin Park, Georgian Bay and the Laurentian Highlands. Though derided as the 'Hot Mush School', out of this eventually emerged the Group of Seven which revolutionized Canadian art. Later he joined the Theosophical Society, believing that art must express spiritual values as well as depicting the visual world.

Otto Dix   Kupplerin – A Woman Smoking, 1923

Born 1891 Gera-Unternhaus, Germany   Painted in Dresden, Germany   Died 1969 Konstanz, Germany
MOVEMENT: New Objectivity, Expressionism **OTHER WORKS:** *Die Grosstadt, Homage to Beauty, The War* **INFLUENCES:** George Grosz, Max Beckmann

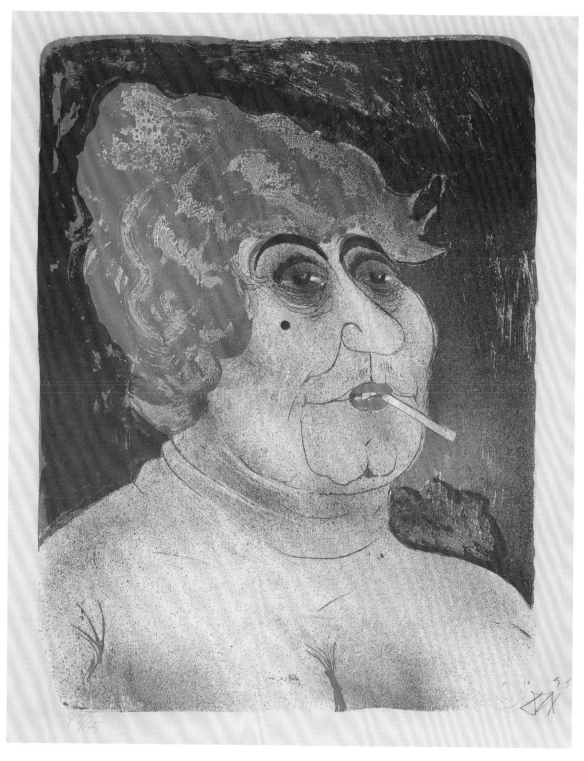

OTTO DIX studied art in Dresden, where he developed an intense interest in realism. Drafted into the infantry on the outbreak of World War I he experienced at first hand the horrors of trench warfare, and this was to have a profound effect on his work. After the war he continued his studies at Dresden and Düsseldorf, producing grimly shocking collages and etchings. In around 1925 he turned from these strident anti-war messages to social realism, producing paintings of beggars, the war-maimed and prostitutes, which earned him his place in the New Objectivity. Brilliant but devastating in his merciless criticism of the Weimar Republic's social and political shortcomings, he was intensely reviled by the Nazis, who dismissed him from his teaching post and condemned his works as degenerate. Persecuted by the Gestapo, he turned to romanticism and religious art and in his later years painted in an Expressionist style.

Tarsila do Amaral   Central Railroad of Brazil, 1924

Born 1886 Sao Paulo, Brazil   Painted in São Paulo, Rio de Janeiro, Paris   Died 1973 São Paulo, Brazil
MOVEMENT: Modern Brazilian School **OTHER WORKS:** *A Negra (The Black Woman)* **INFLUENCES:** Albert Gleizes, Picasso, Fernand Léger, Giorgio de Chirico

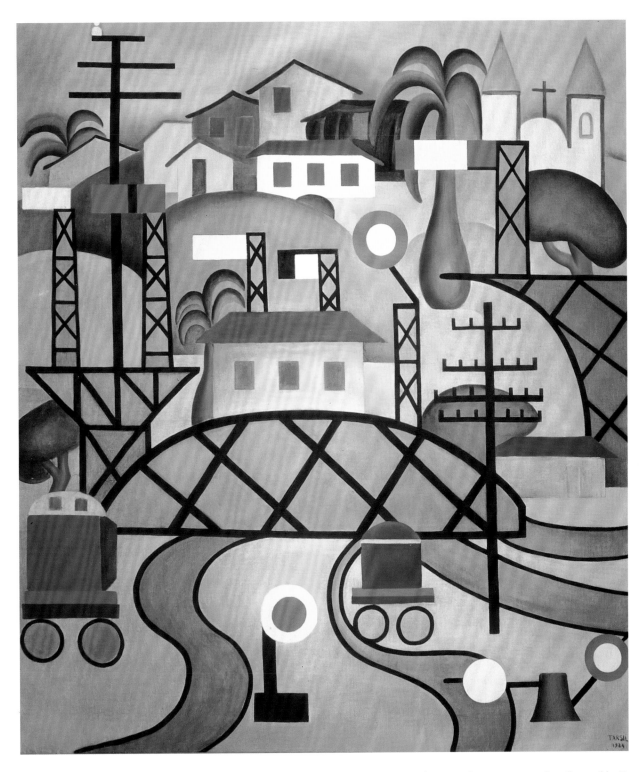

BORN NEAR CAPIVARI, São Paulo State, Brazil in 1886, Tarsilo do Amaral was the daughter of a wealthy businessman and travelled to Europe several times in childhood. She began studying art in São Paulo in 1916 under Pedro Alexandrino and Fischer Elpons. She studied at the Académie Julien in Paris (1920–22) and on her return to Brazil became a prominent member of the short-lived art circle known as the Grupo dos Cinco. She then returned to Paris with Oswald de Andrade, where they were influenced by Picasso and Chirico. She later divided her time between Paris and Rio de Janeiro, bringing Brazilian art to Europe and taking Modernist ideas back to Brazil. Her paintings, in a style she dubbed 'Pau-Brazil', are an unusual blend of native Brazilian art forms, notably from the Tupi-Guarani tradition, with a geometric style influenced by Fernand Léger. Later she created a movement known as Antropofagia, which sought to replace the Portuguese colonial tradition with an indigenous style that was primitive and earthy.

Carlo Carrà   Lot's Daughters

Born 1881 Quargnento, Italy   Painted in Milan, Italy   Died 1966 Milan
MOVEMENT: Futurism, Metaphysical Painting   **OTHER WORKS:** *Le Canal, Lot's Daughters*   **INFLUENCES:** Giacoma Balla, Giorgio de Chirico, Giorgio Morandi

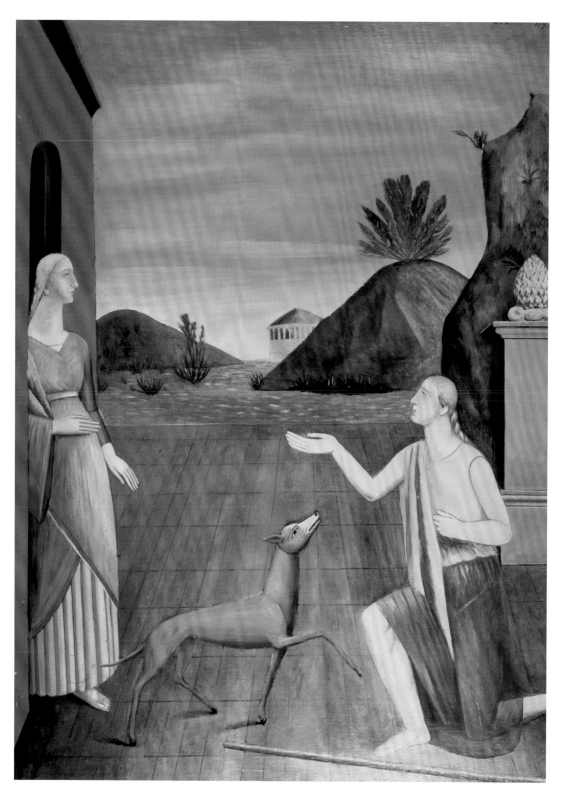

CARLO CARRÀ was largely self-taught, but at the beginning of the twentieth century he came under the influence of Giacomo Balla and signed the Futurist Manifesto of 1910. His paintings of this period show the futurist preoccupation with speed and movement. For a time, however, he also studied the works of Giotto. He served in the Italian army during World War I and while recuperating in a military hospital in 1917 he met Giorgio de Chirico, with whom he evolved a metaphysical style which in fact bordered on Surrealism. From 1921 onwards, however, he switched to a more reflective mode into which he injected notions of heightened realism which he imbibed from his friend Giorgio Morandi. Back in the mainstream of Italian art, he taught at the Milan Academy and influenced the interwar generation of painters.

George Grosz   Amor, Lichtspiele, 1924

Born 1893 Berlin, Germany   Painted in Berlin and USA   Died 1959 Berlin
MOVEMENT: Dada **OTHER WORKS:** *Pillars of Society, Suicide* **INFLUENCES:** Giorgio de Chirico, Carlo Carrà

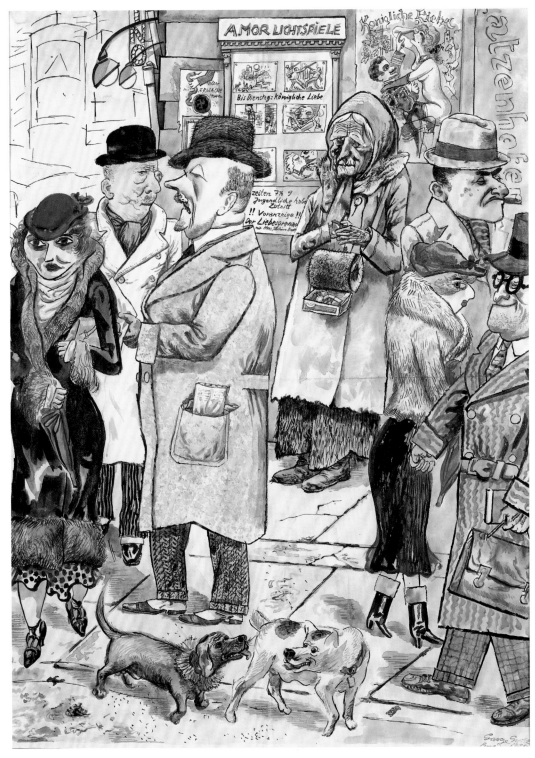

GEORGE GROSZ studied in Dresden and Berlin before being drafted into the army at the outbreak of World War I. In 1917 he was discharged as permanently unfit for service, traumatized by the horrors of trench warfare. In the same year he became associated with the German Dadaists and was an eye-witness of the moral disintegration of Germany through the Spartakist uprising of 1918–19 and the violent street battles between Communists and Nazis in the 1920s. These events, combined with the corruption of the Weimar Republic, provided Grosz with endless material for his ruthlessly satirical and savage attacks on German militarism and the decadence of the middle classes. Garish colours and grossly distorted images, especially faces, were his main weapons. Grosz left Germany in 1932 and settled in the USA where he became naturalized in 1938. In his American period he concentrated on paintings of a more symbolic, less strident, nature. He returned to Germany in 1959, shortly before his death.

Juan Gris   La Grappe de Raisins, 1925

Born 1887 Madrid, Spain   Painted in Paris and Boulogne   Died 1927 Paris
MOVEMENT: Synthetic Cubism   **OTHER WORKS:** *Glasses, Newspaper and a Bottle of Wine, The Bay*   **INFLUENCES:** Matisse, Picasso

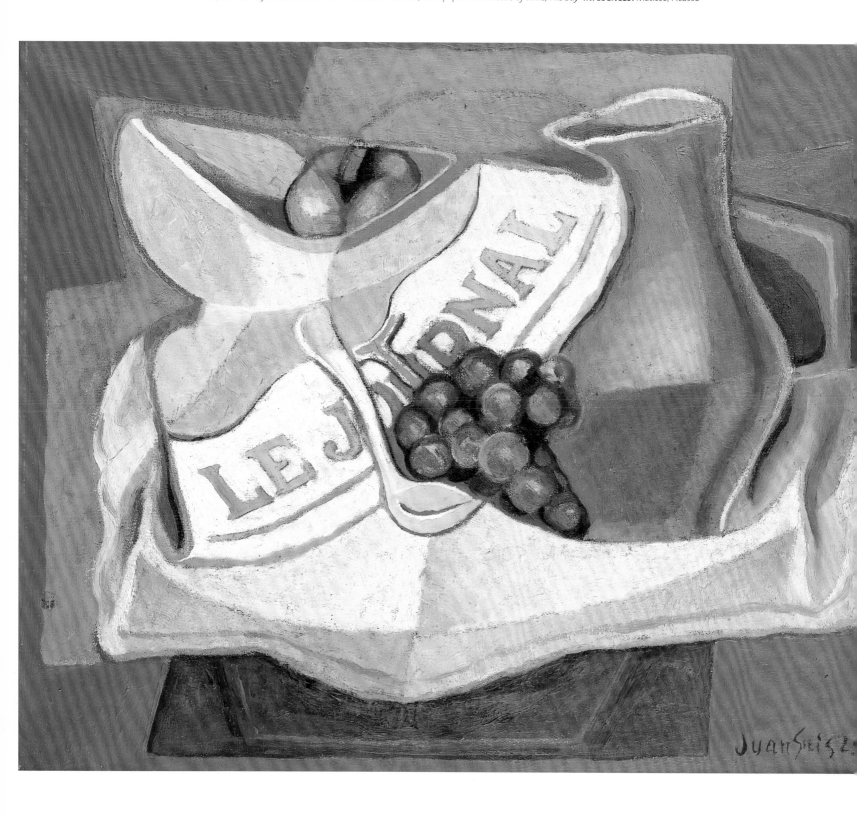

BORN JOSÉ Victoriano Gonzalez, Gris began his art studies in Madrid before going to Paris in 1906 to work as a magazine illustrator. An early associate of Picasso and Matisse, he became one of the leading exponents of Synthetic Cubism from 1912 onwards, the majority of his paintings involving the deliberate distortion and rearrangement of the elements. He also made extensive use of collage, such as strips of newspaper cut up and rearranged. He moved to Boulogne after World War I and in the 1920s designed costumes and sets for several of Diaghilev's Ballets Russes as well as working as a book illustrator. In his later years he experimented with brighter, contrasting colours and also produced a number of multicoloured sculptures.

László Moholy–Nagy   CH Beata 2

Born 1895 Hungary   Painted in Vienna, Berlin, Weimar, London and Chicago   Died 1946 Chicago, USA
MOVEMENT: Constructivism **OTHER WORKS:** *CHX, Composition A II, Jealousy* **INFLUENCES:** Naum Gabo, Kasimir Malevich

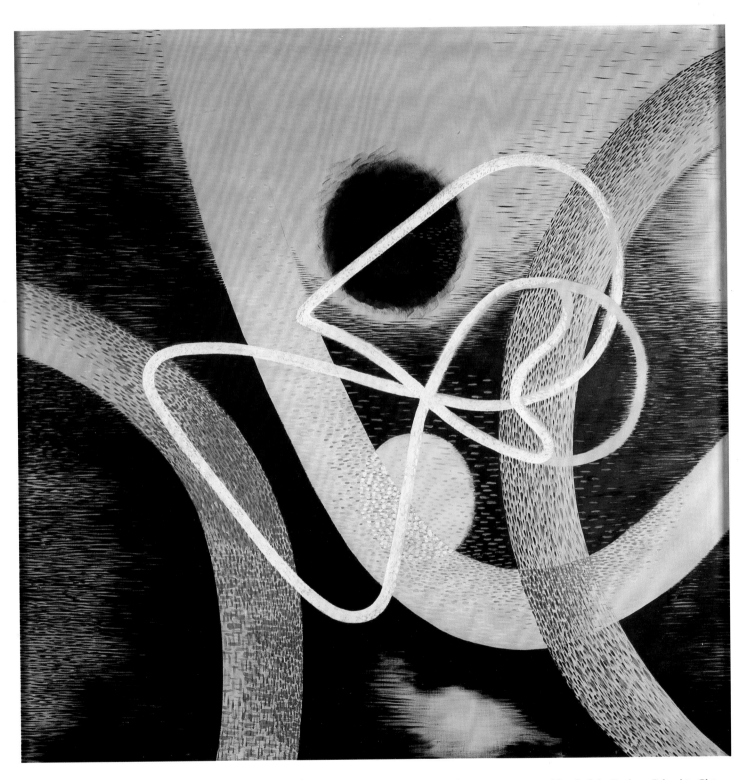

LÁSZLÓ MOHOLY-NAGY studied law in Budapest, but never practiced. Instead he dabbled in photography and turned to painting after World War I, associating with Dadaists and Constructivists in Vienna and Berlin and constructing what he termed 'photograms': non-representational photographic images made directly from the subject without a camera. In 1925 he joined the Bauhaus under Gropius and established his reputation in the ensuing decade as the foremost exponent of the New Photographers' movement. In 1935 he moved to London, where he designed the futuristic sets for fellow-Hungarian Alexander Korda's film, *Things to Come*. In 1937 he went to the USA where he was appointed head of the Bauhaus School in Chicago, later renamed the Institute of Design. He became an American citizen at the end of World War II. Although primarily associated with photography, he also worked as a sculptor, designer and painter, often using collage and photo-montage.

Amédée Ozenfant   Nature Morte aux Verres, Bouteilles et Pot Blanc

Born 1886 France   Painted in France   Died 1966 Cannes, France
MOVEMENT: Purism **OTHER WORKS:** *Smoking Room* **INFLUENCES:** Le Corbusier

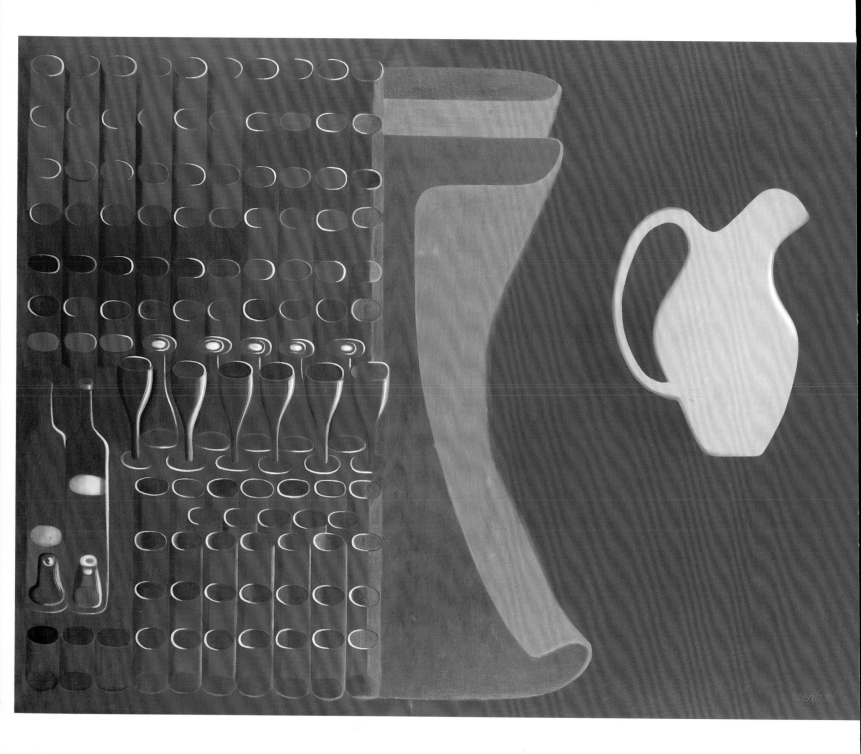

AMÉDÉE OZENFANT was not only a painter, but also a very articulate propagandist for modern art and a prolific writer on the subject. After a conventional art education he collaborated in Paris with Le Corbusier in the development of a post-Cubist style known as Purism, and together they published the Purist manifesto entitled *Après le*

Cubisme ('After Cubism') in 1919. Later they published an avant-garde art periodical *Esprit nouveau* ('New Spirit') from 1921 to 1925 and co-authored *La Peinture moderne* in 1925. An English translation under the title *Foundations of Modern Art* appeared in 1931 and was widely acclaimed as an imaginative account by a practicing artist.

Ozenfant spread the gospel of Purism abroad, founding art schools in London (1935) and New York (1938) for this purpose. His paintings were mainly of still life, characterized by sinuous curvilinear elements reduced to their bare essentials, revealing his gradual departure from an early decorative style to the clear-cut forms of Purism.

Laura Wheeler Waring   Anna Washington Derry, 1927

Born 1887 USA   Painted in Pennsylvania and Paris   Died 1948 Philadelphia, Pennsylvania, USA
MOVEMENT: African American School   **OTHER WORKS:** *Portrait of a Child, Frankie*   **INFLUENCES:** Henry Ossawa Tanner

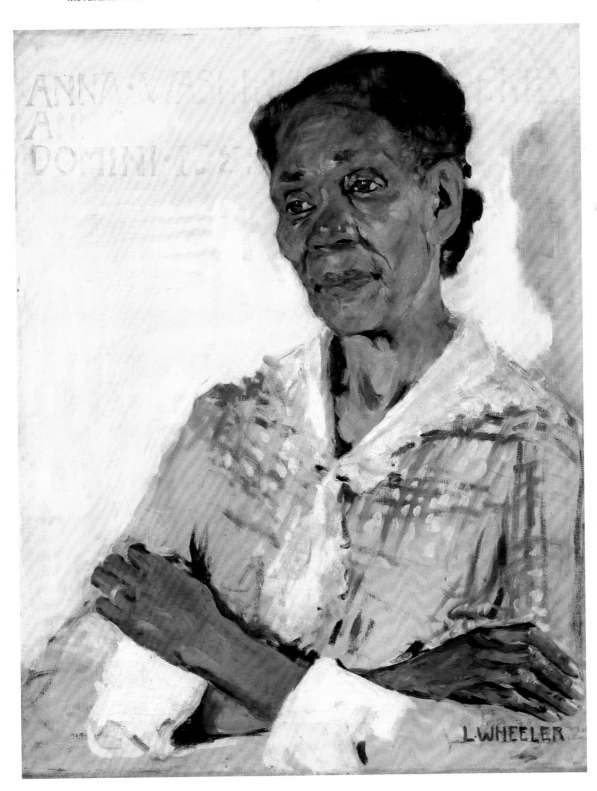

A NATIVE of Connecticut, Laura Wheeler Waring attended the art school in Hartford before going to the Pennsylvania Academy of Fine Arts in Philadelphia from which she won a travelling scholarship in 1914. Her studies were interrupted by World War I, but in 1924–25 she attended classes at the Académie de la Grande Chaumière in Paris. Later she taught art in the Cheney State Teachers College, Pennsylvania. Her portraiture contained elements of Expressionism but she was also influenced by the Romantics, resulting in an unusual blend of the two styles, which had a much livelier appearance than normally associated with wholly representational portraits of the interwar period. At the same time, although her portraits are sensitive, they manage to avoid the cloying sentimentality often associated with the Romantics. She also worked as an illustrator.

Robert Delaunay Triomphe de Paris, 1928–29

Born 1885 Paris, France   Painted in Paris   Died 1941 Montpellier, France
MOVEMENT: Orphism   **OTHER WORKS:** *Eiffel Tower, Sainte Severin, Political Drama*   **INFLUENCES:** Picasso, Otto Freundlich, Franz Marc, Kandinsky

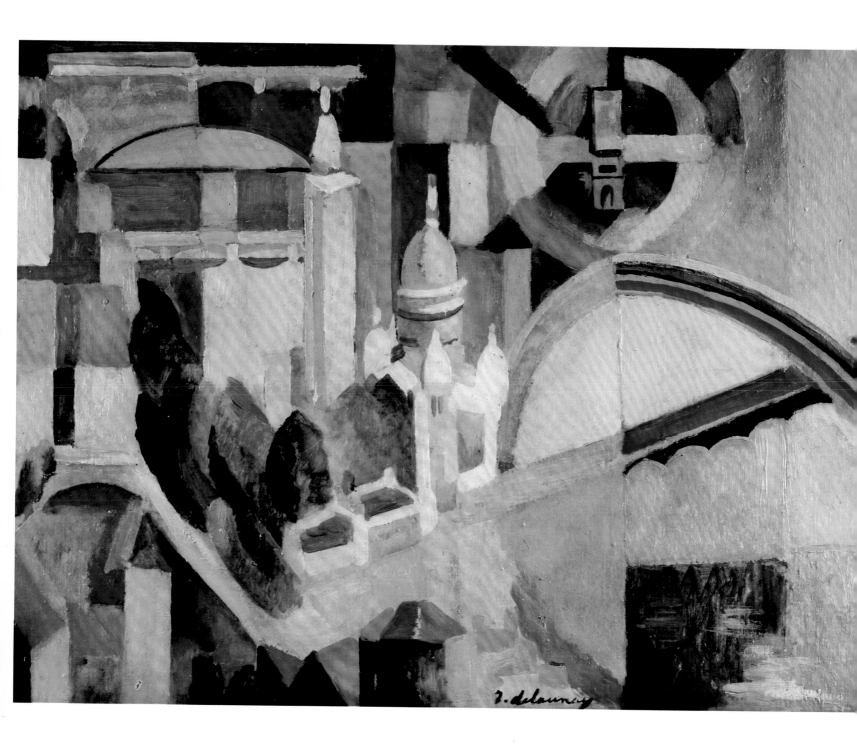

AFTER A conventional art training in Paris, Robert Delaunay worked as a designer of sets for the theater and did not take up painting seriously until 1905–06, when he came under the influence of the Neo-Impressionists. Over the ensuing decade he was also closely associated in turn with the Fauves, the Cubists and especially Der Blaue Reiter in 1911–12. In the latter years, however, his experimentation with contrasting colour patterns resulted in the development of a distinctive style which his friend, the poet Guillaume Apollinaire, dubbed Orphism because of its lyrical, almost musical, harmony. In his initial period, Delaunay painted numerous landscapes in and around Paris – the Eiffel Tower being a favourite subject – but gradually he moved towards a more non-figurative style, and in his organization of contrasting colours he had a profound influence on the development of Abstract art in the 1920s. He collaborated with his wife Sonia, especially from 1918 onwards when he returned mainly to stage design.

Tamara de Lempicka   Les Deux Amies, *c.*1928

Born 1898 Warsaw, Poland   Painted in Paris and Mexico   Died 1980 Cuernavaca, Mexico
MOVEMENT: Cubism **OTHER WORKS:** *The Two Friends* **INFLUENCES:** Cézanne, Fernand Léger

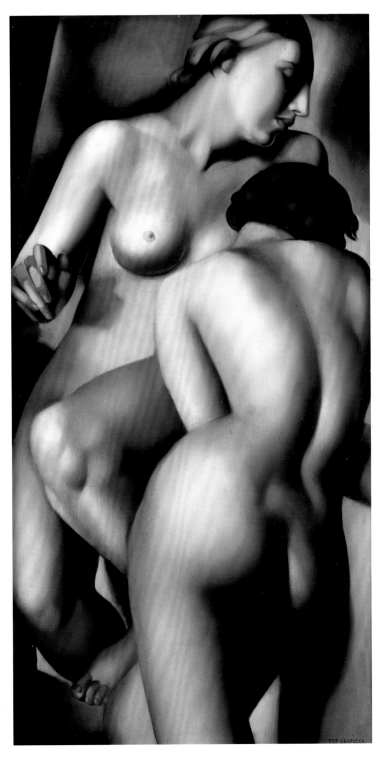

TAMARA DE Lempicka came from a Polish upper-class family, which gave her an excellent all-round international education. In 1918 she and her Russian husband fled the Russian Revolution to Paris. Here Lempicka came under the influence of the avant-garde artists, notably Fernand Léger. However, the painter whose work most impressed her and whose style is reflected in her own female nudes was Paul

Cézanne, then near the end of his long career. Lempicka became one of the most fashionable portrait painters in Paris in the interwar period, her work emphasizing the glamour and ostentatious wealth of her patrons, idealizing their beauty and elegance. The other side of Lempicka, however, was her homosexuality – which was reflected in her extraordinary studies of female nudes, always fully

representational (and often devastatingly so) yet with overtones of Cubism in the use of simplified anatomy and the geometric patterns of the background. The result was electrifying and highly distinctive.

Georgia O'Keeffe   Red Gladiola in White Vase, 1928

Born 1887 Wisconsin, USA   Painted in USA   Died 1986 Santa Fé, New Mexico, USA
MOVEMENT: Modern American School   **OTHER WORKS:** *Radiator Building, Cow's Skull with Calico Roses*   **INFLUENCES:** Alfred Stieglitz

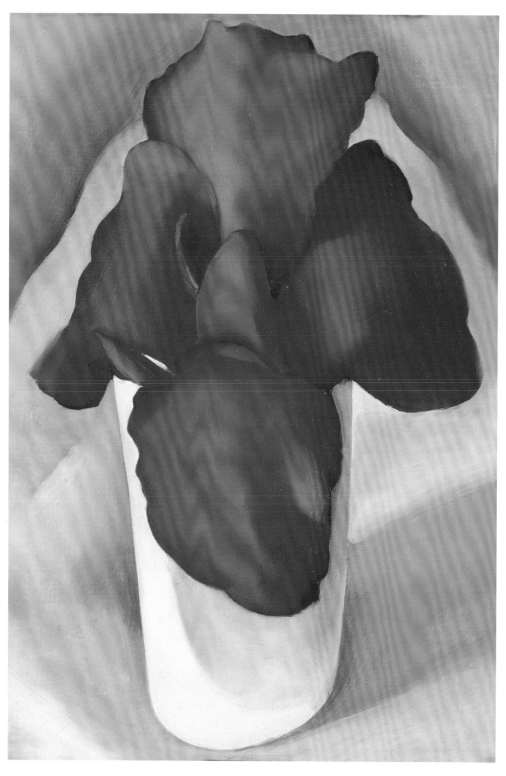

GEORGIA O'KEEFFE studied at the Art Institute of Chicago in 1905–06 and then the Art Students' League in New York City (1907–08), where she met her future husband Alfred Stieglitz, the founder of the avant-garde circle that bears his name. She was an early convert to Abstract Art and, with Stieglitz, did much to spread the gospel among American artists from 1915 onwards. In the 1920s, however, she developed a more figurative style, concentrating on architectural or floral motifs but injecting a note of Surrealism into her paintings. Her work was characterized by sharply defined images that explored geometric patterns and earned for her work the epithet of Precisionism. She travelled all over the world, drawing on her experiences in many of her later works. In her last years she resided in New Mexico, whose monumental scenery found expression in a number of her landscapes.

Charles Demuth   I Saw the Figure 5 in Gold, 1928

Born 1883 Lancaster, Pennsylvania, USA   Painted in Pennsylvania   Died 1935
MOVEMENT: Precisionism **OTHER WORKS:** *Buildings Abstraction – Lancaster* **INFLUENCES:** Cubism, Futurism, William Carlos Williams

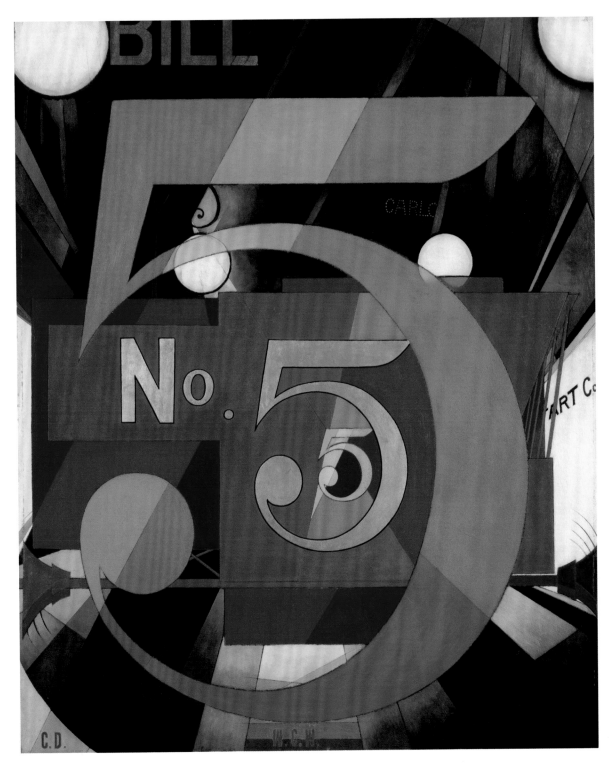

CHARLES DEMUTH was one of the key figures in the American Precisionist movement. Precisionism's main themes included industrialization and the modernization of the American landscape, and Demuth's *I Saw the Figure 5 in Gold* is a fine example. One of America's most famous and familiar icons, the work is based on an Imagist poem by Demuth's close friend, William Carlos Williams. The poem, using terse, precise, staccato phrases (Among the rain/ and lights/I saw the figure 5/in gold), describes the experience of seeing, and indeed hearing, a fire truck screaming through the streets of New York. Demuth attempted to produce a visual analogue to Williams' poem, adopting a similarly terse, precise and staccato vocabulary. In place of the truck itself, Demuth presents fragmented views of the vehicle and focuses his attention on the gold-emblazoned number 5, seen three times as it recedes down a street, past glaring electric lights and neon signs, several of which (BILL, CARLO, and W.C.W.) refer explicitly to Williams. Demuth's use of fragmentation and multiple viewpoints was clearly influenced by Cubism, but is here deployed to express the energy, excitement and sheer cacophony of New York in the 1920s.

Edward Hopper   Chop Suey, 1929

Born 1882 New York, USA   Painted in New York   Died 1967 New York

MOVEMENT: American School   **OTHER WORKS:** *Room in New York, People in the Sun*   **INFLUENCES:** Robert Henri

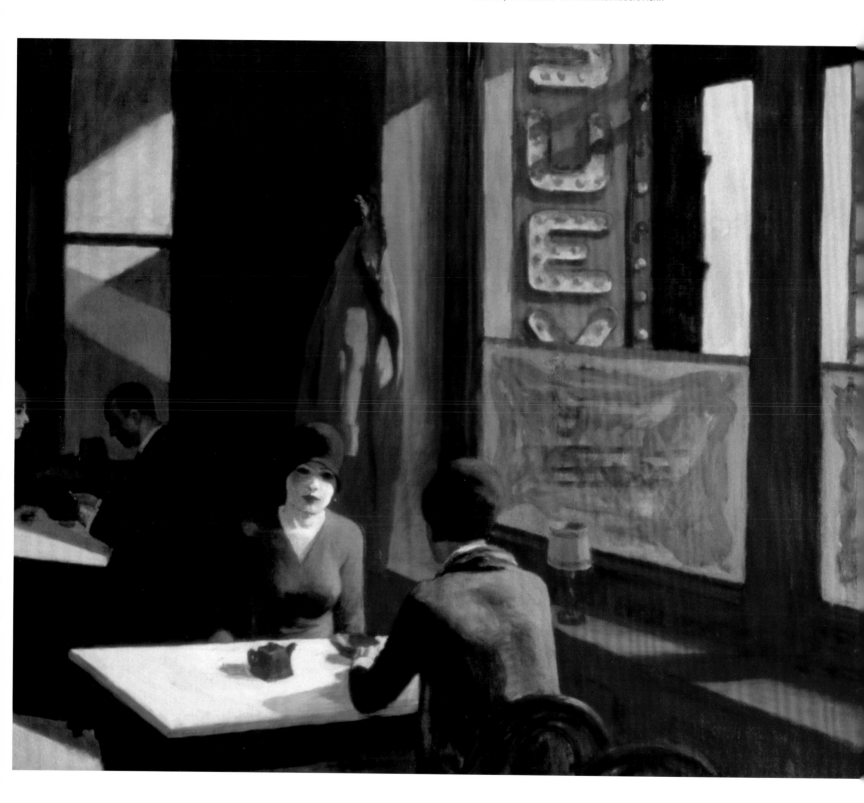

EDWARD HOPPER studied in New York City under Robert Henri between 1900 and 1906 and then travelled in Europe over the ensuing four years. The artistic atmosphere in Paris (1909–10) had a major impact on him and his paintings up to the mid-1920s reflect the influence of the French Impressionists. In this period he worked mainly as an illustrator, but from 1924 he concentrated on large-scale works which drew upon contemporary American life for their inspiration, from diners and gas stations to hotel lobbies and late-night bars. This emphasis on scenes which were instantly recognizable, coupled with the strong interplay of light and shadow, left an indelible impression – so much so that Hopper's art has come to represent urban America of the interwar years and had a major impact on the Pop Art of more recent years.

Georges Roualt   Danseuse, 1929

Born 1871 Paris, France   Painted in Paris   Died 1958 Paris
MOVEMENT: French Expressionism   **OTHER WORKS**: *Bust of a Woman Wearing a Necklace, The Three Judges*   **INFLUENCES**: Gustave Moreau, Matisse

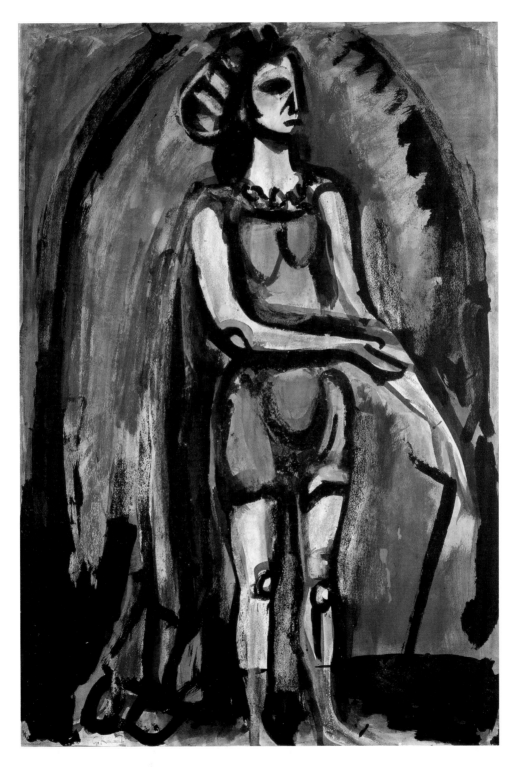

GEORGES HENRI Roualt was originally apprenticed to a stained-glass designer and the vivid colours of this material left their mark on his later work as a painter, in which forms and shapes were sharply outlined in black, rather like leaded windows. In 1892 he took up painting, studying under Gustave Moreau at the École des Beaux-Arts, where he met Matisse. About 1904 he joined the Fauves, but their violent colours were at odds with Roualt's preference for strong, dark shades. He had his first one-man show six years later. Apart from painting, he designed ballet sets and costumes and textiles, notably tapestry. Brought up in a staunchly Catholic environment, Roualt had a crisis of faith in about 1902, which led him to paint somber pictures with harsh motifs that symbolized man's fall from grace. He returned to a much purer form of religious art during World War I and this dominated his output during the global conflict of the 1940s. A prolific artist, he also illustrated books and designed ceramics.

Thomas Hart Benton   The Steel Mill, 1930

Born 1889 Neosha, Missouri, USA   Painted in New York and Kansas City, Missouri   Died 1975
MOVEMENT: Regionalism, Depression Era **OTHER WORKS:** *July Hay* **INFLUENCES:** Stanton MacDonald-Wright

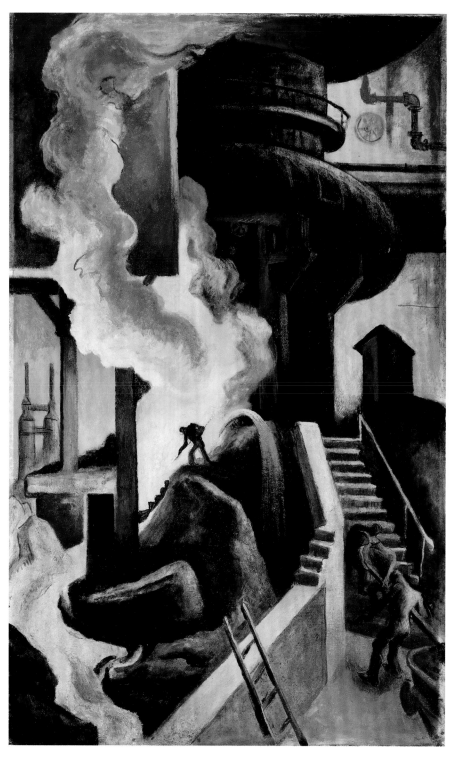

THOMAS HART Benton was originally a supporter of the avant-garde and a follower of MacDonald-Wright's Synchromism, before abandoning New York in the mid-1930s and spending the rest of his life in Kansas City, Missouri, where he was to adopt the realist, narrative style of Regionalism. Benton epitomized this new art which embraced isolationist themes of the American people and history, often based in the heartland of the rural Midwest.

This painting precedes the development of Benton's Regionalism. The Wall Street Crash of 1929 had brought much of America's industry and prosperity to an end, leading to the Great Depression. By 1932 steel production had dropped to a mere fraction of its pre-1929 volume. In this context, Benton's depiction of a steel mill working at full tilt carried strong political resonances. His work is neither a celebration nor a condemnation of American industry. While ignoring the reality of closing factories and the subsequent social destitution, Benton's work extols the sheer energy and force of industry. Yet his diminutive workers appear as little more than anonymous minions, mere cogs in the wheels of powerful industry.

Raoul Dufy   Large Blue Nude, 1930

Born 1877 Le Havre, France   Painted in Paris and the French Riviera   Died 1953 Forcalquier, France
MOVEMENT: Modern French School   **OTHER WORKS:** *The Paddock, The Pier and Promenade at Nice*   **INFLUENCES:** Matisse, André Derain, Vlaminck

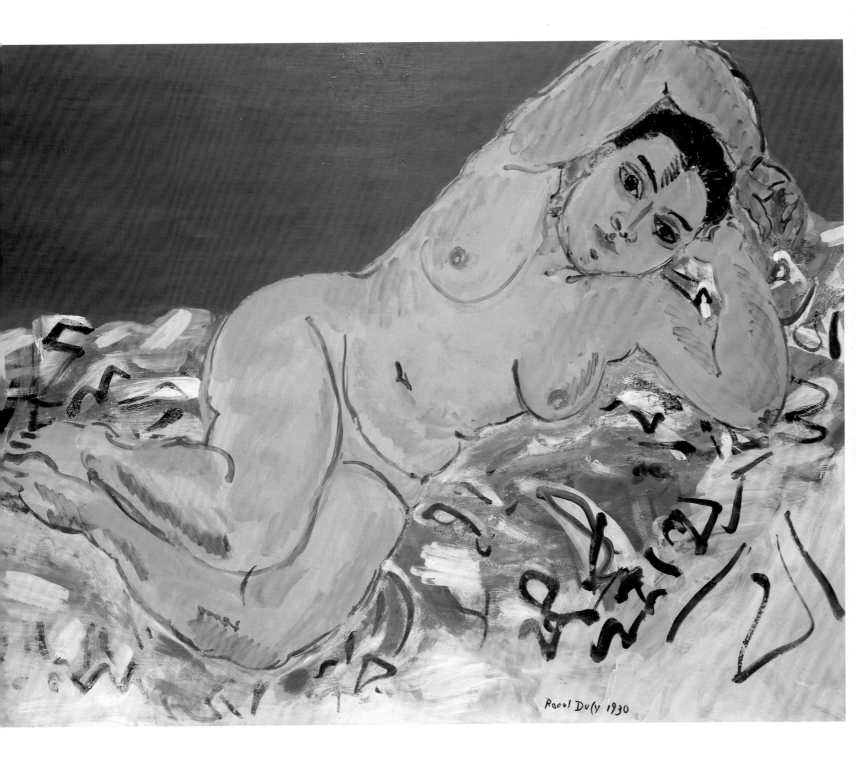

Raoul Dufy 1930

ALTHOUGH HE had a conventional training at the École des Beaux Arts in Paris, Raoul Dufy was attracted to the radical ideas of Matisse and Derain and for some time flirted with Impressionism, Cubism and Fauvism. In 1907 he turned away from painting to concentrate on textile patterns, graphic design and book illustrations, but in 1919 he took up painting again and settled on the French Riviera. There he was encouraged by his friend, the couturier Paul Poiret, to embark on a prolific series of paintings executed swiftly, characterized by large areas of flat colour and sharply incised black lines after the manner of the Chinese calligraphic artists. He created a kind of *ukiyo-e*, pictures of transient scenes, on promenades and beaches, at regattas and race meetings. His greatest masterpiece was the vast mural for the Exposition Universelle in Paris, 1938, one of the largest works ever painted.

Piet Mondrian   Composition with Red, Blue and Yellow, 1930

Born 1872 Amersfoot, Holland   Painted in Holland, London, England and New York   Died 1944 New York
MOVEMENTS: De Stijl, Neoplasticism **OTHER WORKS:** *Composition with Red, Yellow and Blue, Broadway Boogie Woogie* **INFLUENCES:** Henri Matisse

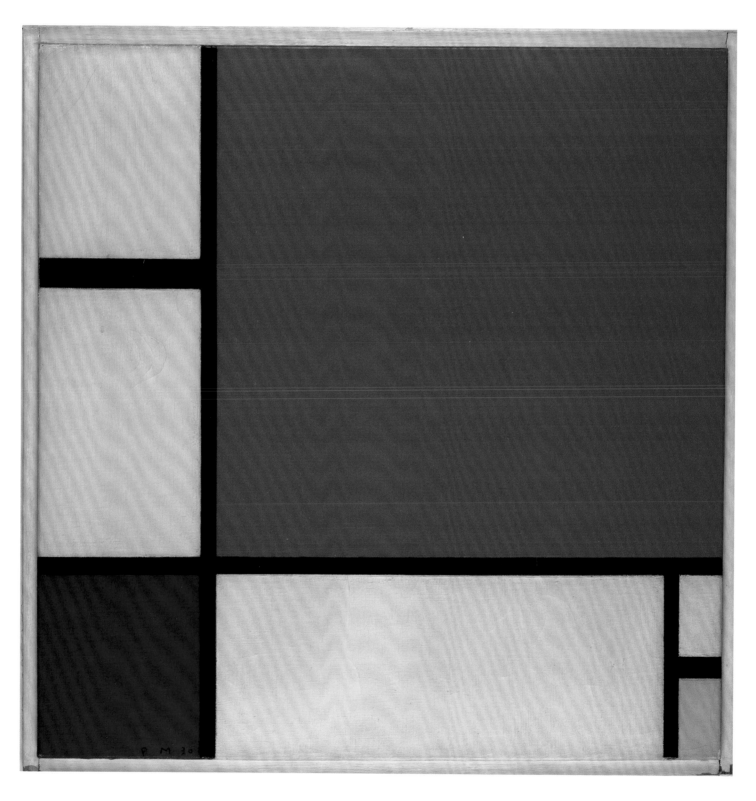

BORN PIETER Cornelis Mondriaan, he simplified his name in 1909 when he moved to Paris, where he came under the influence of the Cubists, notably Henri Matisse. From still life, his work became progressively more abstract, his paintings distinguished by tightly regimented geometric shape and contrasting bright colours. In 1917 he became a founder member of De Stijl, the movement which derived its name from the journal which provided a forum for the Dutch avant-garde artists. Through this medium he propounded the theories which had a profound effect on a later generation as well as his contemporaries, and led to the development of the movement known as Neoplasticism. Mondrian was the arch-apostle of the abstract in its purest, simplest form. He moved to London in 1938, but after his studio was destroyed in the Blitz he settled in New York.

Emily Carr   Western Forest, c.1931

Born 1871 Victoria, British Columbia, Canada   Painted in British Columbia   Died 1945 Victoria, British Columbia
MOVEMENT: Modern Canadian School   **OTHER WORKS:** *Skidegate, British Columbian Indian Village*   **INFLUENCES:** A.Y. Jackson, Lawren Harris

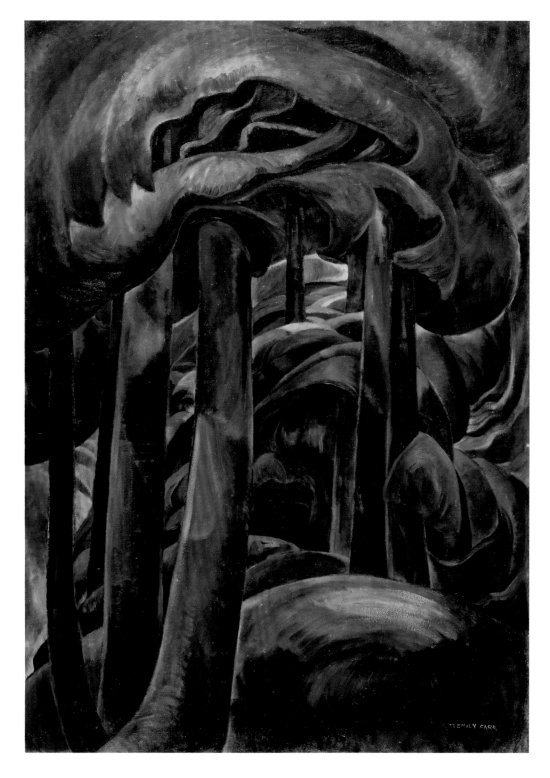

EMILY CARR received her art education at the California School of Design in San Francisco (1891–94) and then went to England where she continued her studies at the Westminster School of Art (1899). She returned to Vancouver in 1904 to explore Indian sites in British Columbia, but a period in Paris (1910–11) had a profound effect on her art.

She exhibited at the Salon d'Automne of 1911 and studied the works of the Impressionists, Post-Impressionists and Fauvists in particular. On her return to Vancouver she resumed her study of the art of the Indian communities of the north-west Pacific Coast and devoted much of her life to salvaging the remnants of their civilization, which permeated her

later paintings. She painted nothing from 1912 until 1927 when she met the Group of Seven artists in Ottawa and was inspired by them to resume her artistic career. Her best work belonged to the ensuing decade. Following a heart attack in 1937 she spent the last years of her life mainly writing books.

Rabindranath Tagore   Head of a Woman, 1931

Born 1861 Calcutta, India   Painted in Bengal, India   Died 1941 Calcutta

MOVEMENT: Symbolism **OTHER WORKS:** *Untitled Portraits* **INFLUENCES:** Bengali art

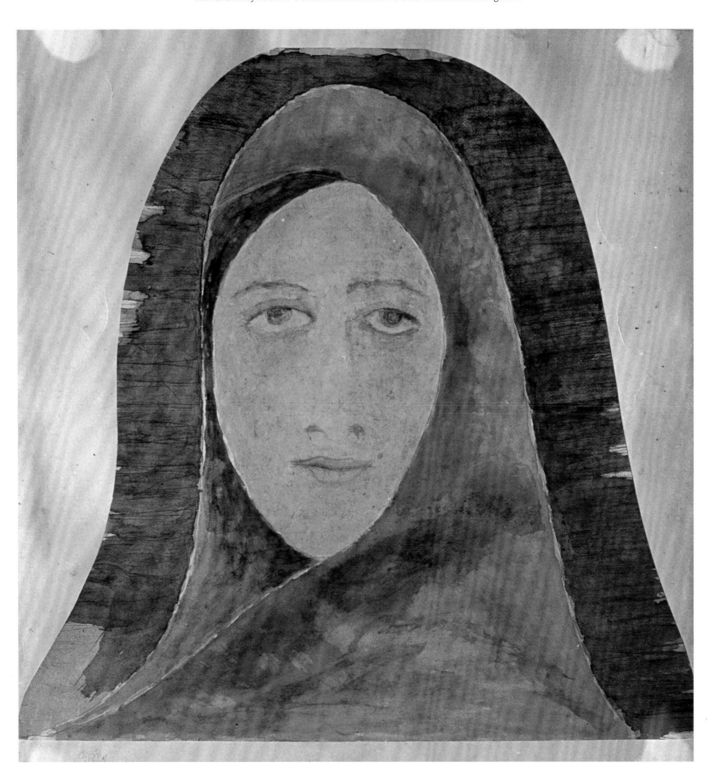

BORN AT Calcutta of a princely family, Rabindranath Tagore was educated privately in India, then sent to England to study law, but before 1900 he began writing poetry and essays for Bengali periodicals. In 1901 he established the Santineketan at Bolpur, an unconventional educational institute. A prolific writer of poetry, novels and plays, he was awarded the Nobel Prize for literature in 1913 and was knighted in 1915. Tagore took up painting in 1929, but in the decade preceding his death he produced a number of major works which influenced a later generation of Indian artists. Like his writings, his paintings are suffused by a visionary quality. Although his work is executed in a Western style, it contains elements derived from Bengali art, a delicate blend of East and West. He worked mainly in ink on paper, building up an image from lines, doodles, smudges and blots with minimal use of secondary colours. His work suggests the influence of Symbolism.

Ben Shahn   Sacco and Vanzetti, 1931–32

Born 1898 Kovno, Lithuania   Painted in New York, USA   Died 1969
MOVEMENT: Social Realist **OTHER WORKS:** *This is Nazi Brutality* **INFLUENCES:** Expressionism, Typograhpy

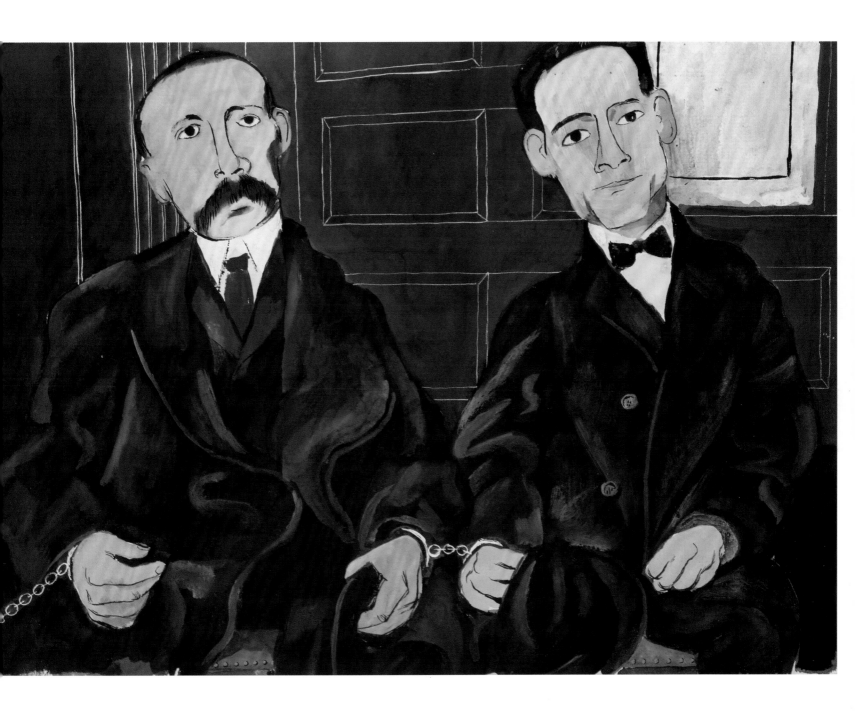

LITHUANIAN-BORN Ben Shahn emmigrated to America with his family in 1906, and the influence of Shahn's early training as a typographer in New York can be seen in his later works, which often include text.

After the Wall Street Crash of 1929, which had a devastating effect upon the art market, a large number of artists were forced to join the ranks of the unemployed. In response to these desperate circumstances, many painters abandoned the avant-garde experimentalism of the early twentieth century in favour of a more realist-inspired art addressing the social concerns of the day. Ben Shahn was one of the most prominent left-wing artists to emerge at this time. Obsessed with exposing injustice, Shahn produced over two-dozen works in the early 1930s representing the two Italian-Americans Nicola Sacco and Bartolomeo Vanzetti, who in 1920 had been tried and found guilty of murder following a robbery at a Massachusetts shoe factory. They were executed in 1927, despite being widely believed to be innocent and arrested because of their left-wing political beliefs. Shahn's works set out to promote their cause, presenting them as martyrs and victims of the political oppression of the American justice system.

Frida Kahlo   Autoretrato en la Frontera entre Mexico y los Estados, 1932

Born 1907 Coyoicoan, Mexico   Painted in Mexico City   Died 1954 Mexico City
MOVEMENT: Surrealism   **OTHER WORKS:** *Self-Portrait with Cropped Hair, Self-Portrait with Monkey*   **INFLUENCES:** Diego Rivera

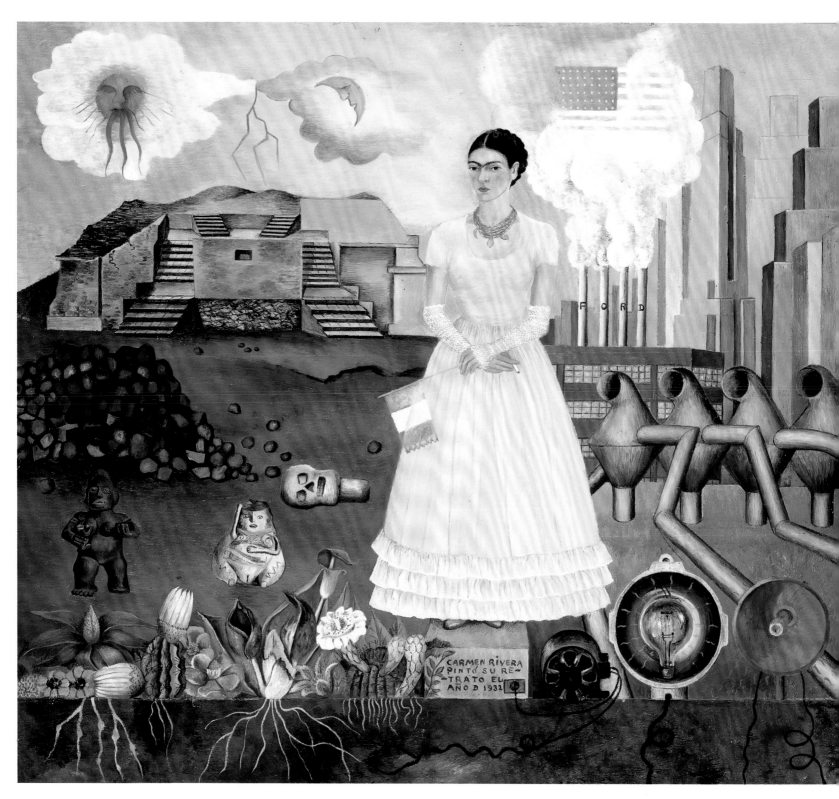

BORN AT Coyoicoan near Mexico City, Frida Kahlo had the misfortune to be in a streetcar crash at the age of 15. During the long convalescence from her terrible injuries she took up painting and submitted samples of her work to Diego Rivera, whom she married in 1928. Artistic temperament resulted in a stormy relationship that ended in divorce in 1939, and many of Kahlo's self-portraits in this period are wracked with the pain she suffered all her adult life, as well as reflecting anger at her husband's numerous infidelities. Indeed, pain and the suffering of women in general were dominant features of her paintings, endlessly explored and revisited in canvasses that verge on the surreal and often shock with their savage intensity. André Breton, the arch-apostle of Surrealism, neatly described her art as 'like a ribbon tied around a bomb'.

Pablo Picasso   Les Demoiselles d'Avignon, 1907

Born 1881 Málaga, Spain   Painted in Spain, France and Italy   Died 1973
MOVEMENT: Cubism, Surrealism, Classical Revival **OTHER WORKS:** *Three Musicians, Le Repos* **INFLUENCES:** Cézanne, Georges Braque, Toulouse-Lautrec

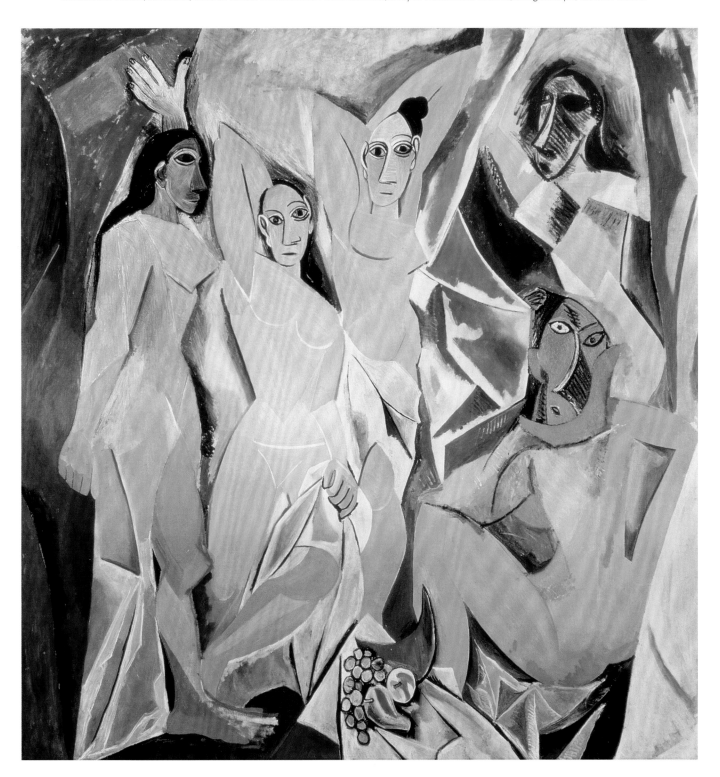

SPANISH PAINTER, sculptor, draughtsman and ceramicist; the most versatile and influential artist of the twentieth century. Having studied in Barcelona, Picasso finally settled in Paris in 1904. His Blue (1901–04) and Rose (1904–06) periods produced his popular scenes of vagrants and circus performers, which were loosely inspired by Puvis and the Symbolists. Then, in 1907, he produced *Les*

Demoiselles d'Avignon, the most influential painting of the twentieth century. Named after Avignon Street, the red-light district in Barcelona, and drawing inspiration from African sculpture, it opened the way for the Cubist movement, which Picasso spearheaded with Braque.

In the 1920s he ushered in a Classical revival, while also being hailed as an inspiration by the

Surrealists. Increasingly, though, his paintings displayed a pessimistic strain, brought on by the collapse of his marriage and the deteriorating political situation. This culminated in his most celebrated picture, *Guernica*, which commemorated an atrocity in the Spanish Civil War. Picasso's ongoing hostility to the Franco regime led him to make France, rather than Spain, the base for his later artistic activities.

Ian Fairweather   Roi Soleil or Sun King, c.1956–57

Born 1891 Scotland   Painted in Australia   Died 1974 Brisbane, Australia
MOVEMENT: Australian School   **OTHER WORKS:** *Kite Flying, Monastery, Monsoon, Bathing Scene Bali*   **INFLUENCES:** Chinese traditional art

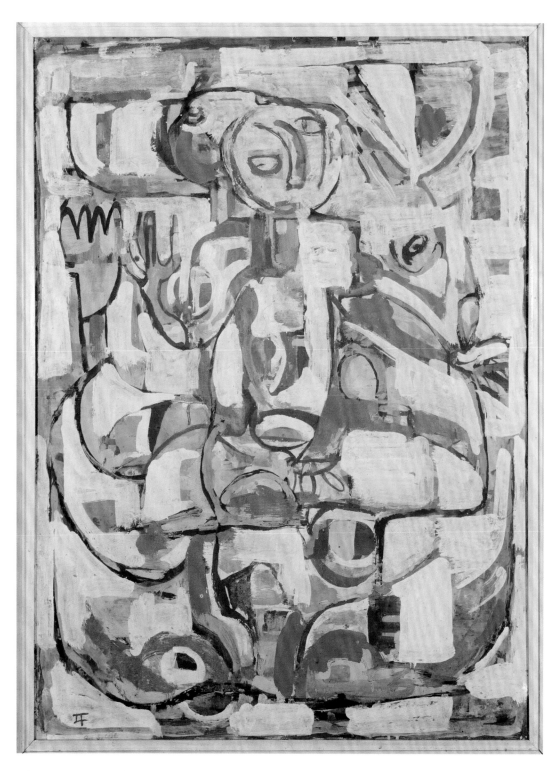

REGARDED AS an Australian painter of Scottish birth, Ian Fairweather trained at the Slade School of Art in London. In 1924 he began wandering nomadically all over the world, living and working in Germany, Canada, India, China and Japan before settling in Australia. During World War II he served as a captain with the British Army in India, but returned to his adopted land in 1943 after being invalided out. An eccentric loner, in 1952 he hit the headlines when he sailed from Darwin to Indonesia on a home-made raft and a year later settled on Bribie Island in northern Australia. His paintings range from portraits to landscapes but he is particularly noted for genre subjects. Relatively few of his paintings have an Australian theme – the majority of his works being Chinese scenes decorated with calligraphy in the Oriental manner. After World War II he worked mainly in gouache before turning to synthetic polymers in 1958. His best work consists of the virtually monochrome abstracts of 1959–61.

A.Y. Jackson   Winter, Charlevoix County, 1933

Born 1882 Montreal, Canada   Painted in Canada and France   Died 1974 Kleinburg, Ontario, Canada
MOVEMENT: Modern Canadian School **OTHER WORKS:** *Terre Sauvage, Springtime in Picardy, First Snow* **INFLUENCES:** Jean-Paul Lauren, Lawren Harris, Tom Thomson

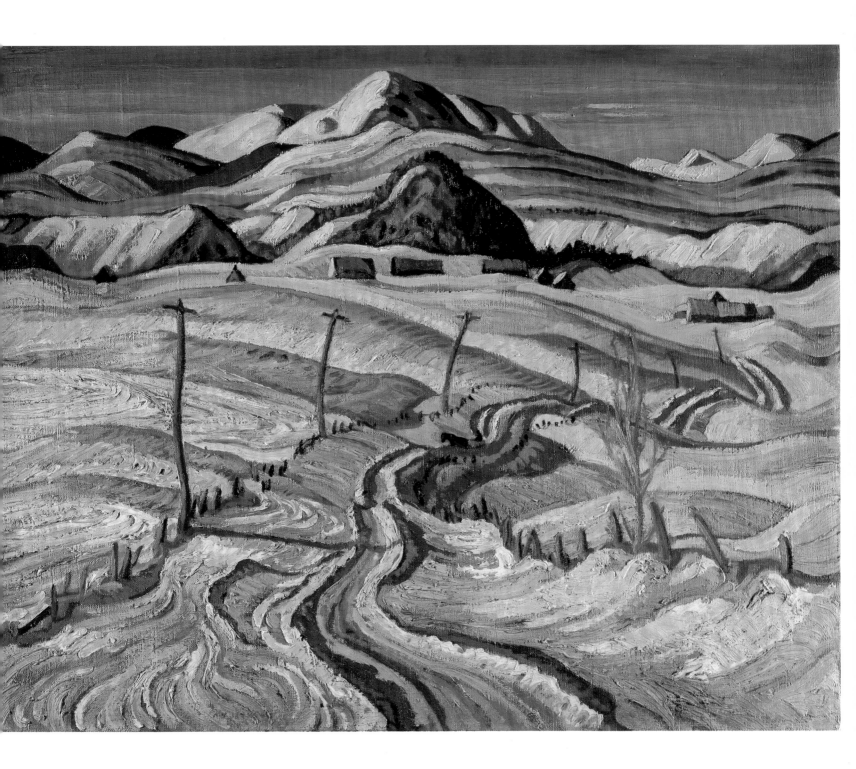

ONE OF the most influential Canadian artists of the twentieth century, Alexander Young Jackson originally worked as a commercial artist in Montreal (1895–1906), before moving to Chicago. While continuing in the same profession, he attended classes at the Art Institute of Chicago and then went to Paris in 1907, where he studied under Jean-Paul Laurens at the Académie Julian. He returned to Canada in 1909 and settled in Toronto in 1913, where he became one of the leaders of the Group of Seven, founded in 1920. In World War I he was wounded in action but later became a war artist. He resumed his work as a landscape painter in 1919, becoming the leading advocate for a distinctive Canadian style of painting, his words as eloquent as his paintings were striking. He travelled to every part of Canada, including the Arctic, to record the rich variety of landscape.

René Magritte   Le Chef D'Oeuvre ou Les Mysteres de L'Horizon

Born 1898 Lessines, Belgium   Painted in Belgium   Died 1967 Brussels, Belgium
MOVEMENT: Surrealism   **OTHER WORKS:** *Rape, The Reckless Sleeper, The Treachery of Images*   **INFLUENCES:** Giorgio de Chirico

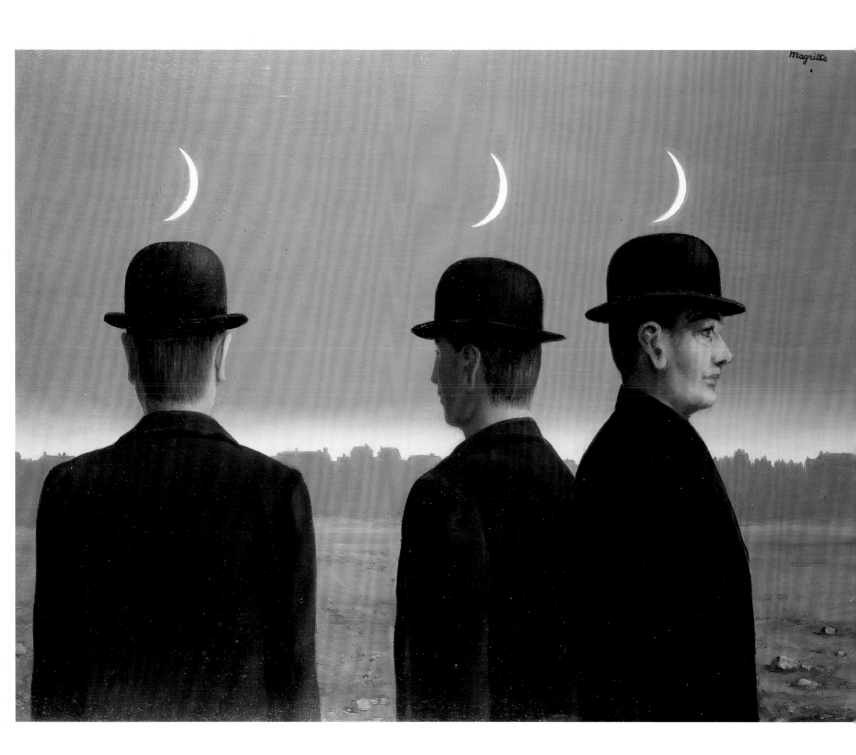

THE GREAT Surrealist master René François Ghislain Magritte studied at the Académie Royale des Beaux-Arts in Brussels (1916–18) and became a commercial artist for fashion magazines and a designer of wallpaper. His paintings were initially influenced by Futurism and Cubism, but later he was attracted to the work of Giorgio de Chirico. In 1924 he became a founder member of the Belgian Surrealist group, which provided an escape from the dull routine of his everyday work. From 1927 to 1930 he lived in Paris to better continue his study of the Surrealists, then returned to Brussels where he built his reputation for paintings of dreamlike incongruity, in which themes and objects are jumbled in bizarre, nonsensical situations, often showing paintings within paintings. He is regarded in the United States as a forerunner of Pop Art.

Chaim Soutine   Les Escaliers à Chartres, *c.*1933

Born 1893 Smilovich, Russia   Painted in Paris   Died 1943 Paris

MOVEMENT: French Expressionism   **OTHER WORKS:** *The Boy in Black, Pageboy at Maxim's, Portrait of Modigliani*   **INFLUENCES:** Emil Nolde, Matisse, Chagall

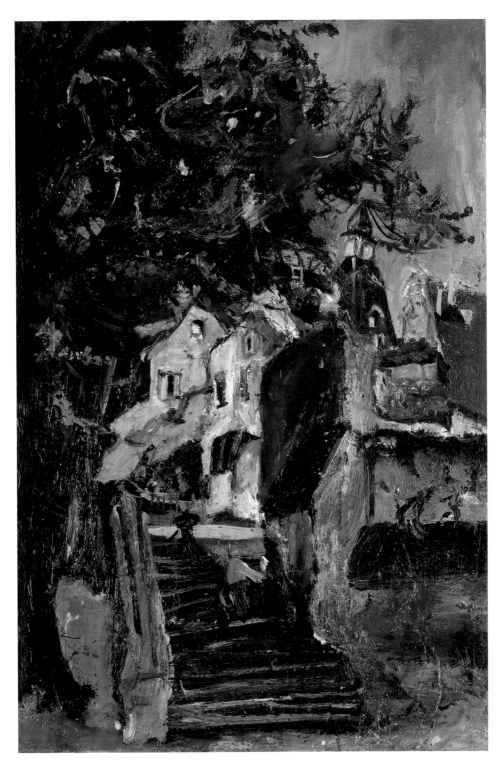

BORN AT Smilovich, Russian Poland (now Belarus), Chaim Soutine studied in Vilnius and travelled to Paris in 1911, where he was befriended by fellow Russian Jew Marc Chagall. Modigliani introduced him to the Expressionist school in Paris and he, in turn, exerted an exotic influence on its development, adding a dash of Fauvism and the German approach to Expressionism. Soutine delighted in painting the carcasses of animals, much to the disgust and annoyance of neighbours, who habitually complained of the stench of rotting flesh that emanated from his studio. Apart from studies of dead birds and decomposing sides of beef, Soutine painted portraits whose emaciated features and deathly expression bear a gruesome resemblance to the living dead of Belsen and Auschwitz. Soutine, who continued to live in Paris after the fall of France, managed to evade deportation to the camps and died in Paris in 1943.

Grant Wood   Parson Weems' Fable, 1939

Born 1892 near Anamosa, Iowa, USA   Painted in Iowa   Died 1942 Anamosa
MOVEMENT: Regionalism **OTHER WORKS:** *Haying, Adolescence* **INFLUENCES:** Van Eyck, Rogier van der Weyden

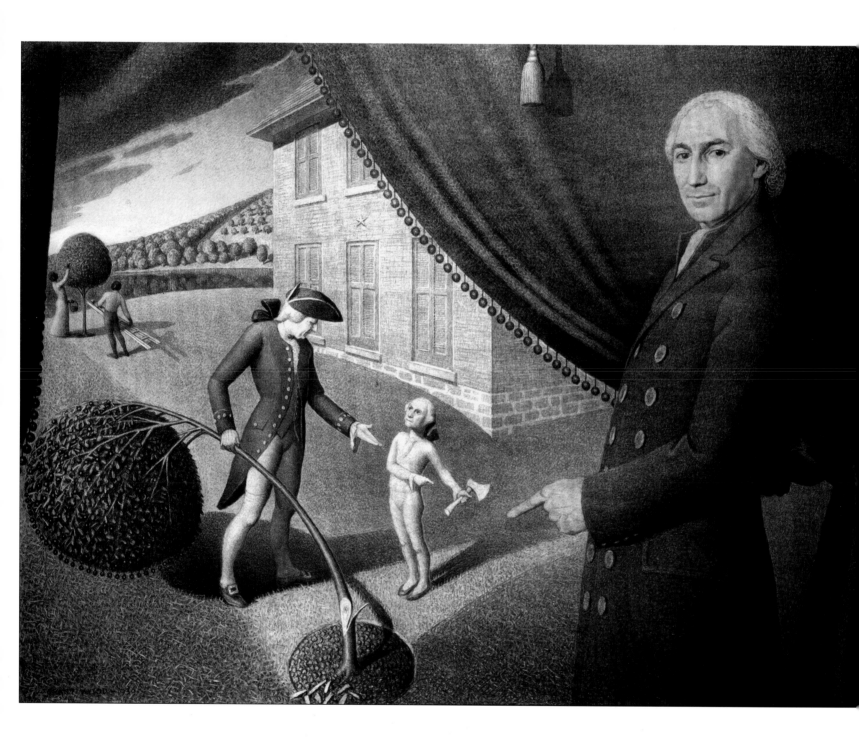

BORN IN Anamosa, Iowa, Grant Wood spent his entire life in this small town in the American Midwest. In the 1920s, however, he travelled to France and the Netherlands where he studied the works of the Old Masters, especially the Gothic, Romanesque, Renaissance and Flemish School, all of which had a strong influence on his own work. His best-known painting, *American Gothic*, depicts a cottage in Wood's home town whose Gothic window appealed to him, while in the foreground stands a typical Midwestern farmer and his wife. Severely criticized at the time for lampooning the values of Middle America, he defended himself insisting that the painting was intended as a sincere tribute to the simple dignity of rural communities. Likewise, the painting shown here depicts the popular myth of Washington confessing to a childhood crime, an apocryphal story designed to act as a parable extolling the virtues of honesty and fortitude. For Wood, this was a perfect vehicle for celebrating his own particular vision of traditional American values – typical of the foremost artist of the Regionalists, a group of American artists who rejected the abstract in favour of the realism of ordinary people and their locale.

Aaron Douglas   Aspects of Negro Life: Song of the Towers, 1934

Born 1899 Topeka, Kansas, USA   Painted in New York, Nashville and Paris   Died 1979 Nashville, Tennessee
MOVEMENT: Modern American School   **OTHER WORKS:** *Aspects of Negro Life, From Slavery through Reconstruction*   **INFLUENCES:** Winold Reiss, Charles Despiau

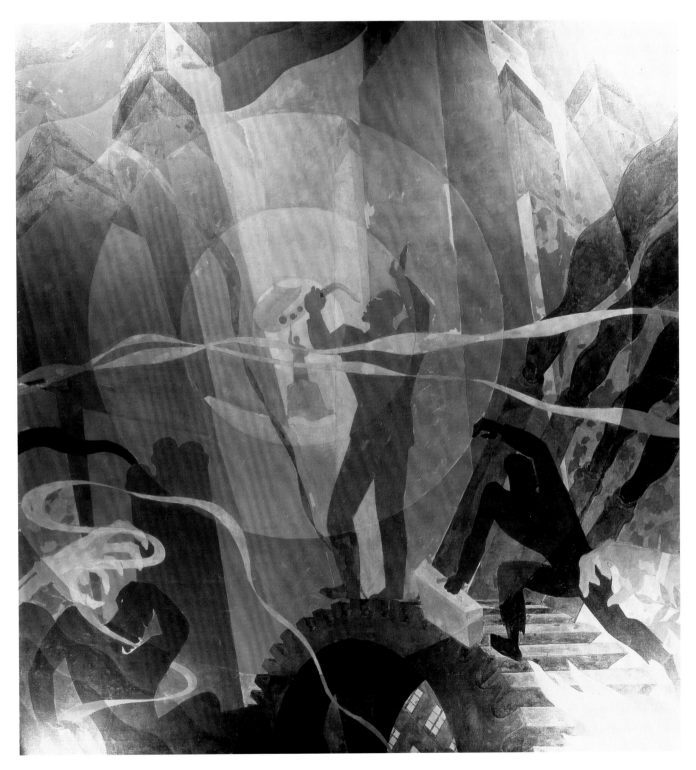

THE LEADING exponent of the Harlem Renaissance, Aaron Douglas studied at the University of Kansas and from 1925 to 1927 studied art in New York under Winold Reiss, who encouraged him to accept and celebrate his black heritage. Throughout the 1920s he illustrated a number of books by emerging black authors, while drawings contributed to a number of magazines of the period show the influence of African art forms, putting Douglas in the forefront of the Harlem Renaissance. In 1931 he went to Paris and studied at the Académie Scandinave under Despiau, and in 1938 he travelled all over the American South and Haiti. He later taught at Fisk University in Nashville, Tennessee. In the 1930s he executed a number of large murals for public buildings in Nashville and New York which drew on the black cultural tradition and history. He played a prominent role in the development of modern black consciousness.

Oskar Kokoschka Zwei Madchen, 1934

Born 1886 Pöchlarn, Austria   Painted in Vienna, Dresden, Prague and London   Died 1980 Montreux, Switzerland
MOVEMENT: Expressionism **OTHER WORKS:** *Portrait of a 'Degenerate Artist', Children Playing* **INFLUENCES:** Klimt, Max Beckmann

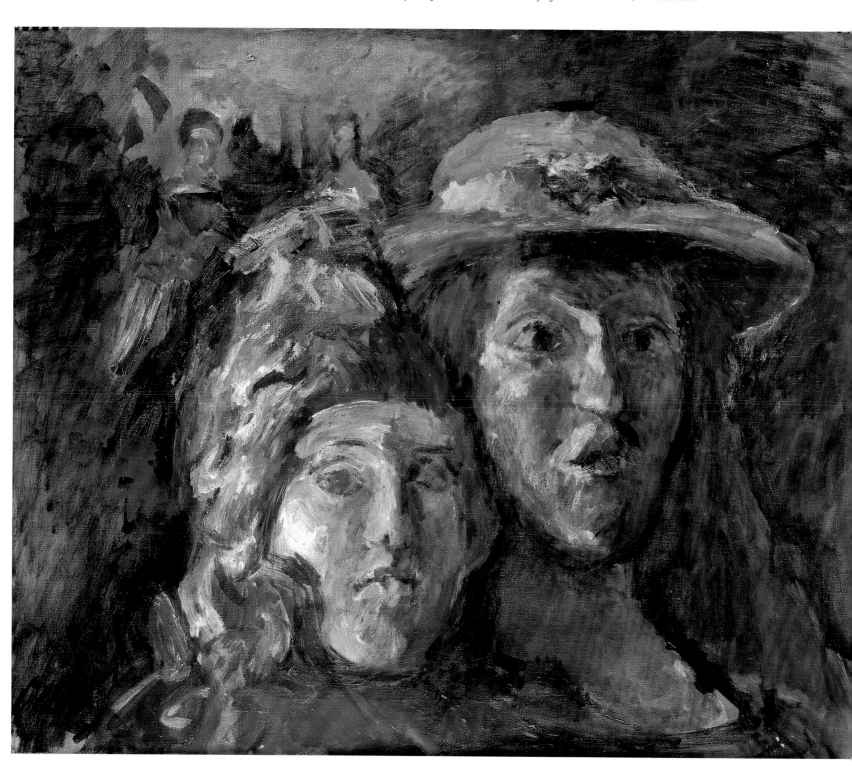

OSKAR KOKOSCHKA studied at the Vienna School of Arts and Crafts (1905–09) and joined the Wiener Werkstätte, where he produced lithographs distinguished by their strong graphic sense. His drawings contributed to the German avant-garde magazine *Der Sturm* reveal a highly original approach to Expressionism. After military service in World War I, in which he was seriously wounded, he taught at the Dresden Academy of Art from 1919 until 1924 but subsequently he travelled extensively in Europe and North America before settling in Prague. When the Nazis dismembered Czechos-lovakia in 1938 he moved to England, becoming naturalized in 1947, but six years later he settled in Switzerland, where he died in 1980. A versatile artist, he painted landscapes and urban scenes but it is for his very expressive portraits, in which disparate colours bring out the psychological profile of the sitter, that he will be remembered.

Charles Sheeler   City Interior, 1935

Born 1883 Philadelphia, Pennsylvania, USA   Painted in New York and Detroit, USA   Died 1965
MOVEMENT: Precisionism **OTHER WORKS:** *Upper Deck, Convergence II* **INFLUENCES:** Cubism

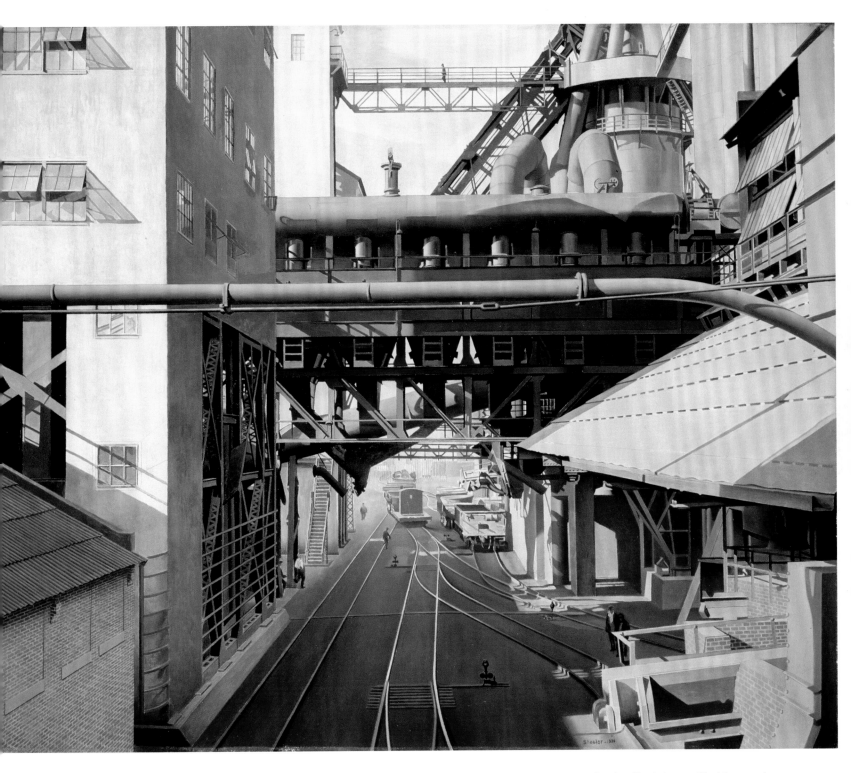

CHARLES SHEELER was a major figure of the Precisionist movement, and is also recognized as one of the founders of American modernism and one of the master photographers of the 20th century. Having experienced Cubsim at its height on a visit to Paris in 1909, he developed his precise linear style in his painting as well as his photographs, depicting the products of America's mass industrialization.

In the mid 1930s the city of Detroit was at the very heart of American industry. Shortly after Henry Ford's new car factory outside Detroit, the River Rouge, opened in 1927, Ford invited Sheeler to visit. Over the next six weeks Sheeler took hundreds of photographs. He also used these as source material for a series of paintings of the factory, including *American Landscape* (1930), *Classic Landscape* (1931) and *City*

Interior. Produced in Sheeler's typical highly meticulous style, these works extol the virtues of Ford's achievements with respect and reverence. As Sheeler himself stated, 'Our factories are our substitute for religious expression'. For all their wonder, however, Sheeler's works noticeably exclude the presence of the workers themselves, whose labour had built not only Ford's factories and cars, but also his fortune.

David Alfaro Siqueiros   El Botero

Born 1896 Mexico   Painted in Mexico, USA, Uruguay and Chile   Died 1974 Mexico City

MOVEMENT: Mexican Muralists   **OTHER WORKS:** *Portrait of the Bourgeoisie, The Victory of Science over Cancer*   **INFLUENCES:** Diego Rivera, Amado de la Cueva

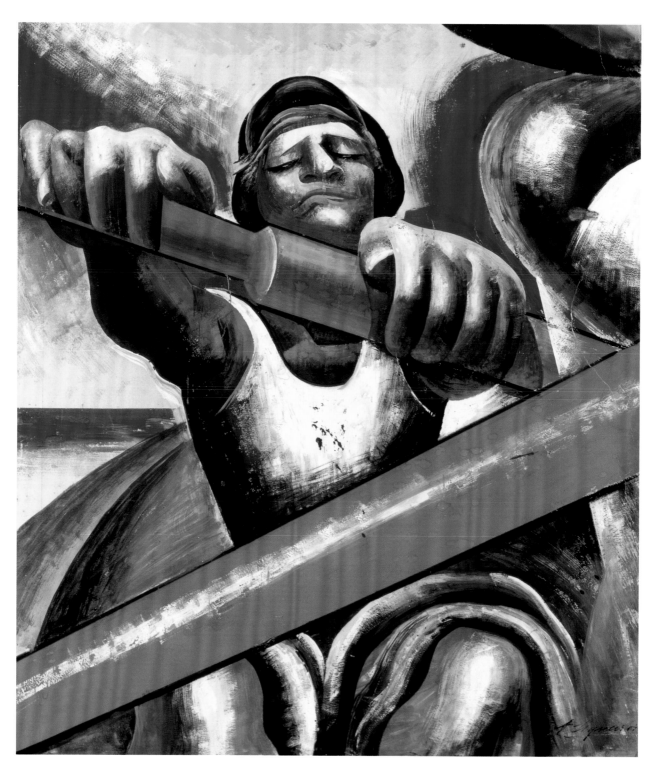

MEXICAN PAINTER and political activist, best known for his murals. Siqueiros was born in Chihuahua, the son of a lawyer. In his youth, he became involved in the Mexican Revolution and, as a reward, was given a scholarship to study in Europe (1919–22). There he met Rivera, a fellow muralist and future rival. The revival of mural-painting was deliberate government policy, aimed at bringing art to the people. Siqueiros received a commission to decorate the Preparatoria, but work was halted by student riots and, in fact, he did not complete a mural in his homeland until 1939.

Although a late developer, Siqueiros proved hugely influential as a teacher. In 1936, he ran an experimental workshop in New York, which did much to shape the Abstract Expressionism of Jackson Pollock. The latter was particularly impressed by Siqueiros's theories about the potential of 'pictorial accidents' and his use of industrial materials. These included spray-guns, blow-torches and the pyroxylin paints used in car manufacture. In the artist's own work, these were seen to best effect in the massive *March of Humanity in Latin America* and his extraordinary, multimedia creation the *Polyforum Siqueiros*.

Percy Wyndham Lewis   Sheik's Wife, 1936

Born 1882 Canada   Painted in England, Canada and USA   Died 1957 London, England
MOVEMENT: Vorticism   **OTHER WORKS:** *The Dancers, A Battery Shelled, A Reading of Ovid*   **INFLUENCES:** Albert Gleizes, George Grosz

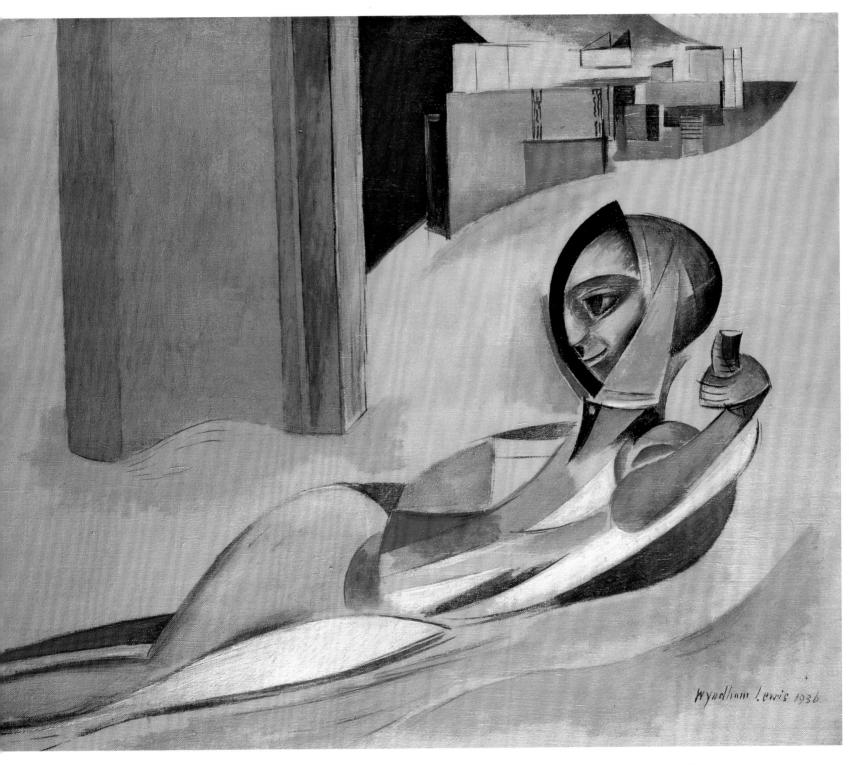

PERCY WYNDHAM LEWIS was born in Canada, but following the break-up of his parents' marriage when he was 10 years old he moved with his mother to England, where he enrolled at the Slade School of Art (1898–1901). For six years he travelled extensively in Europe, painting and continuing his studies before settling in London, where he joined the Camden Group of avant-garde artists in 1911 and the Omega Workshops in 1913. One of the most articulate and intellectual painters of his group, he edited their magazine *Blast*, in which he published his Vorticist Manifesto in 1914. This, the only distinctively British art movement to emerge in the early twentieth century, was short-lived. Lewis volunteered for active service on the outbreak of World War I and subsequently became an official war artist.

Nevertheless, there are echoes of Vorticism in his powerful war paintings as well as in the great series of canvasses in the postwar period inspired by characters from classicalmythology. In 1939 he returned to Canada and also worked for a time in the USA before going back to England in the last years of his life. Although blind in his old age he continued to teach and write.

Salvador Dalí   Le Sommeil, 1937

Born 1904 Catalonia, Spain   Painted in Spain, France, USA and Italy   Died 1989

MOVEMENT: Surrealism **OTHER WORKS:** *The Metamorphosis of Narcissus, The Persistence of Memory* **INFLUENCES:** Pablo Picasso, Giorgio de Chirico, Yves Tanguy

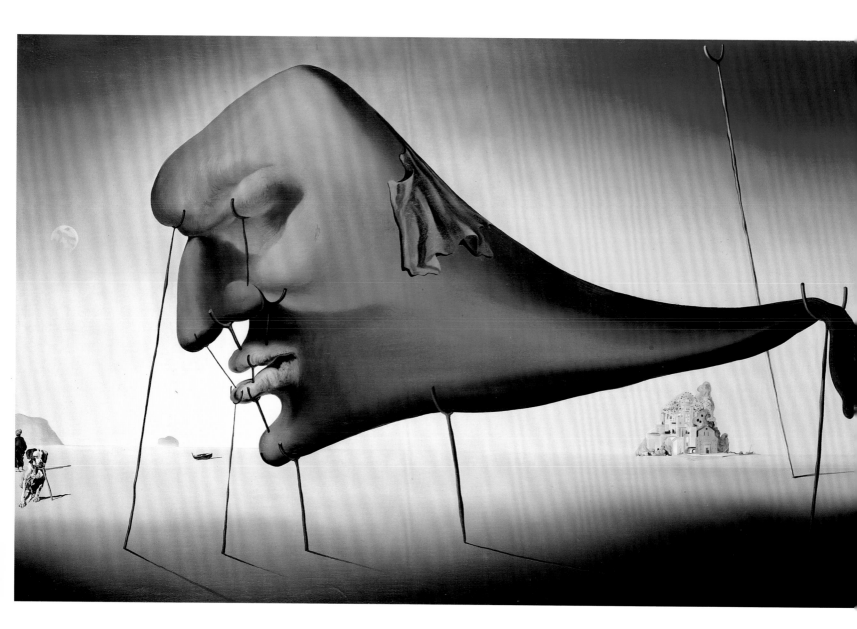

SPANISH PAINTER, graphic artist and film-maker – the most controversial member of the Surrealists. Dalí was born in Catalonia and studied at the Academy of Fine Arts in Madrid, until his outrageous behaviour caused his expulsion. Before this, he had already made contact with the poet Lorca and the film-director Buñuel. In the early 1920s, he dabbled in a variety of styles, including Futurism and Cubism, although it was the metaphysical paintings of De Chirico which made the deepest impact on him.

The key stage in Dalí's career came in 1929, when he made *Un Chien Andalou* with Buñuel, met his future wife Gala, and allied himself with the Surrealists. His relationship with the latter was rarely smooth and, after several clashes with Breton, he was forced out of the group in 1939. In the interim, he produced some of the most memorable and hallucinatory images associated with the movement, describing them as 'hand-painted dream photographs'. Dalí remained very much in the public eye in later years, gaining great celebrity and wealth in the US, but for many critics his showmanship overshadowed his art.

Lyonel Feininger   Four–Masted Barque, 1937

Born 1871 New York, USA   Painted in Paris, Weimar, Dessau, Germany, Chicago and New York   Died 1956 New York

MOVEMENT: Cubism, Orphism, Bauhaus   **OTHER WORKS:** *Sailing Boats, Village Church, Gelmeroda*   **INFLUENCES:** Picasso, Juan Gris, Robert Delaunay, Kandinsky, Giacomo Balla

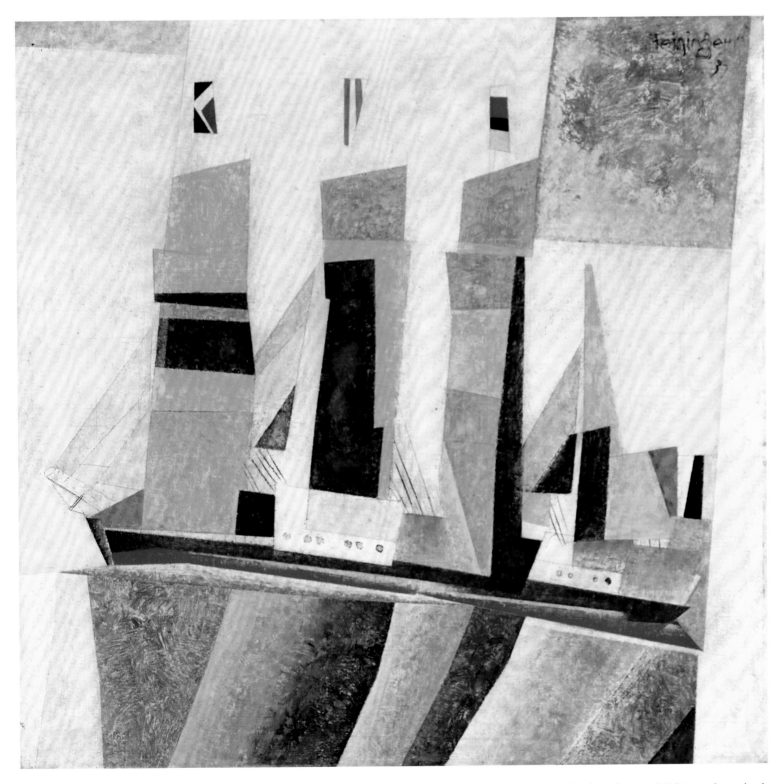

LYONEL CHARLES Adrian Feininger was born and died in New York City, but he is regarded more as a European than as an American artist. The son of German Jewish parents, he was educated in Germany and studied art in Munich, where he joined the Blaue Reiter group in 1913 and associated with Wassily Kandinsky, with whom he worked at the Bauhaus in Weimar and later Dessau. Following the advent of the Nazi regime he returned to the United States in 1935 and there helped establish the New Bauhaus in Chicago. His artistic career was very varied. Having started as a political cartoonist in the 1890s, he only turned to painting in 1907 when he moved to Paris. There he came under the influence of Cubism and was closely associated with Robert Delaunay, whose Orphism is reflected in Feininger's intense interest in the emotional qualities of colour.

Yves Tanguy   Paysage Surrealiste, 1937

Born 1900 Paris, France   Painted in Paris, France and Woodbury, Connecticut, USA   Died 1955, Woodbury
MOVEMENT: Biomorphism, Surrealism   **OTHER WORKS:** *Dehors, The Invisible, The Rapidity of Sleep*   **INFLUENCES:** Giorgio de Chirico, Salvador Dal´

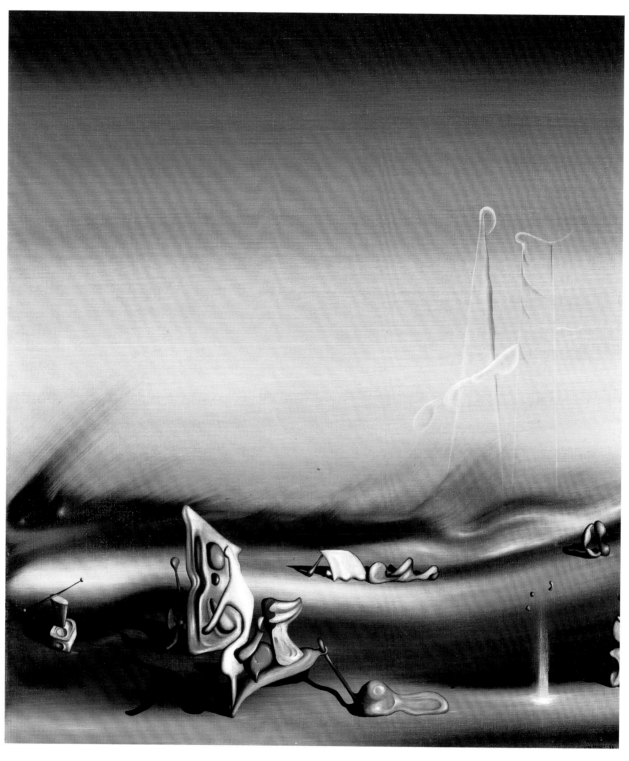

GOING TO sea as a teenager, and later serving in the French Army, Yves Tanguy did not take up painting until his return to Paris in 1922. Without any formal training, he was influenced by the work of Giorgio de Chirico and joined the Surrealists in 1925, subsequently concentrating on that style known as Biomorphism because its images were derived from living organisms. Inevitably, Tanguy's paintings in the ensuing period drew heavily on memories of naval and military service. In 1939 he immigrated to the United States, where he married fellow-artist Kay Sage and settled in Woodbury, Connecticut. In his last years his work took on a darker character, suggestive of dream sequences which reflected his fascination with the Freudian theories of psychoanalysis. His paintings were non-figurative, inhabited by small objects, often boney-like but defying description and suggestive of some other world.

Max Ernst   Foret et Soleil, 1938

Born 1891 Colgne, Germany   Painted in Germany, France and the USA   Died 1976

MOVEMENT: Surrealism, Dada **OTHER WORKS:** *The Robing of the Bride, Europe after the Rain* **INFLUENCES:** August Macke, Hans Arp, Giorgio de Chirico

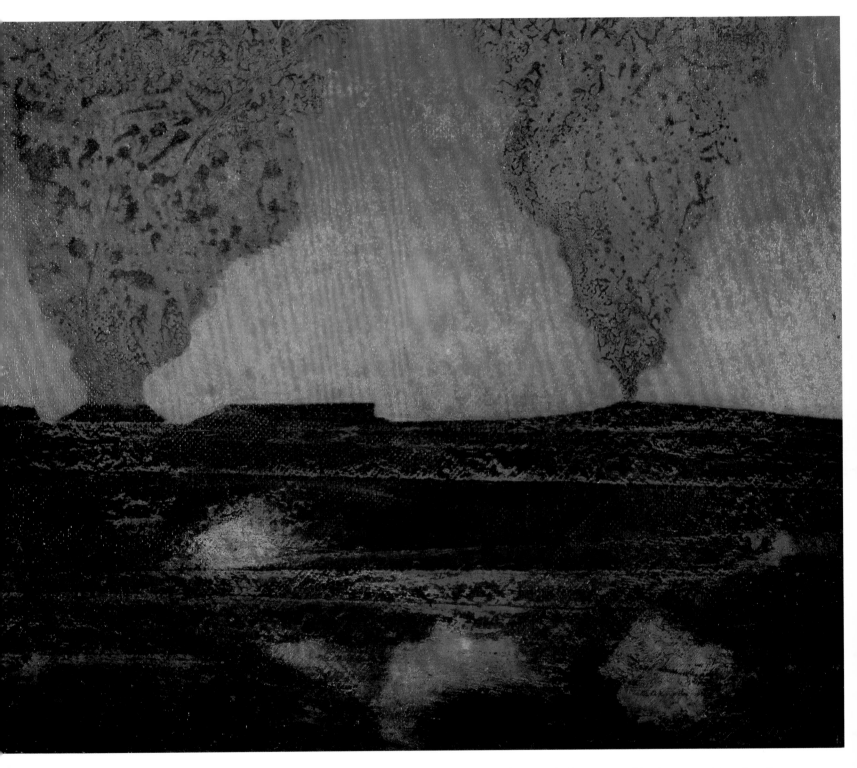

GERMAN PAINTER and a leading Surrealist. Born near Cologne, Ernst studied psychology at Bonn University, taking a particular interest in the art of the insane. Before the war he befriended Arp and Macke, and mixed with the Blaue Reiter ('Blue Rider') group. Then, in 1919, he staged the first Dada exhibition in Cologne. Typically for this movement, visitors had to enter the show through a public urinal and were handed axes, in case they wished to destroy any of the exhibits. In 1922, Ernst moved to Paris and joined the Surrealist circle. His work in this style was incredibly varied. He made considerable use of the chance images, which were suggested by automatic techniques, such as *frottage* (rubbings of textured surfaces). At the same time, he exploited the 'poetic sparks', which were created by the juxtaposition of totally unrelated objects. These sometimes took the form of paintings, but were also produced as collages, drawn from popular magazines.

Ernst was interned during World War II and spent much of his later career in America.

Jacob Lawrence   The Diner, 1938

Born 1917 New Jersey, USA   Painted in New York and Seattle   Died2000 Seattle
MOVEMENT: American Modernism   **OTHER WORKS:** *The Migration of the Negro*   **INFLUENCES:** Charles Alston, Augusta Savage, Orozco, Giotto, Cimabue

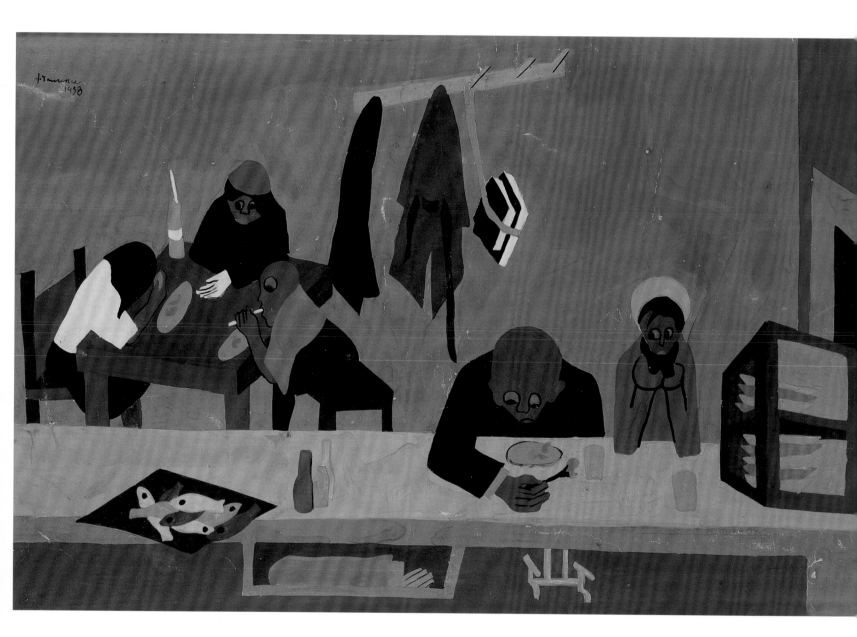

JACOB LAWRENCE was brought up in Harlem, New York City, where he attended the Harlem Art Workshop and studied under Charles Alston. In 1937 he went to the American Artists' School and the following year became a painter in the WPA Federal Art Project. In the 1930s and 1940s Lawrence painted a series of portraits of historical scenes illustrating the lives of black personalities such as Frederick Douglass and Harriet Tubman, and traced the migration northward of African Americans after the Civil War. Wartime service in the Coast Guard provided material for paintings in the late 1940s, but in the ensuing decades he has dedicated his art to the civil rights movement and such causes as the desegregation of the South. A visit to Nigeria in 1964 enabled him to explore a purely African idiom. His late work was less explicit in its social commentary and more engaged with universal concerns and abstract ideals.

Seison Maeda   Wild Goose Calling its Mate

Born 1901 Gifu, Japan   Painted in Japan   Died 1977 Kanagawa, Japan

MOVEMENT: Modern Japanese School   **OTHER WORKS:** *Yoritomo in the Cave, Awaiting the Outset*   **INFLUENCES:** Hank Kajita, Kokei Kobayashi, Masaccio, Fra Angelico

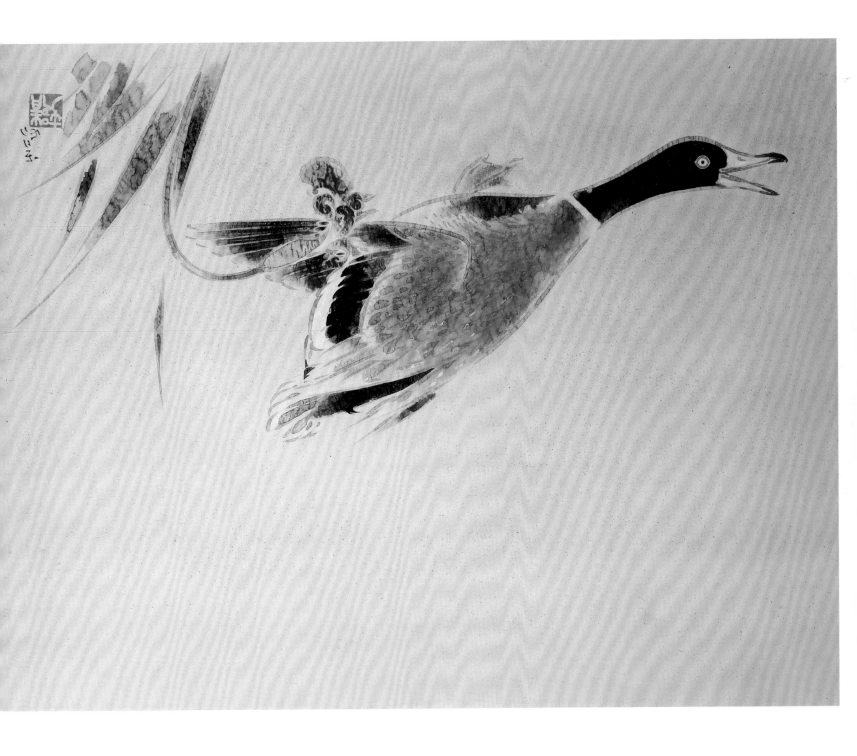

AFTER A CONVENTIONAL education Seison Maeda went to Tokyo in 1901, where he enrolled at the art school run by Hanko Kajita and formed a close friendship with Kokei Kobayashi, whose style influenced his own painting. From 1914 onwards Maeda was a prominent figure in the Inten (Japan Art Institute exhibitions). In 1922 he travelled to Italy where he was fascinated by the frescoes of the Early Renaissance which left an indelible mark on his later work, although Maeda continued to paint in the traditional Japanese style. He was a prolific and versatile artist, excelling in landscapes and genre scenes, although his reputation rests mainly on his mastery of figures. He was very highly regarded by his contemporaries, being appointed to the Imperial Art Academy in 1935 and awarded the Order of Cultural Merit in 1955. He published his autobiography in 1969.

Palmer Hayden   The Janitor Who Paints, 1939–40

Born 1890 Wide Water, Virginia, USA   Painted in France and New York   Died 1973
MOVEMENT: Harlem Renaissance   **OTHER WORKS:** *John Henry* series, *Just Back from Washington*   **INFLUENCES:** Alain Locke (Harlem Renaissance literature)

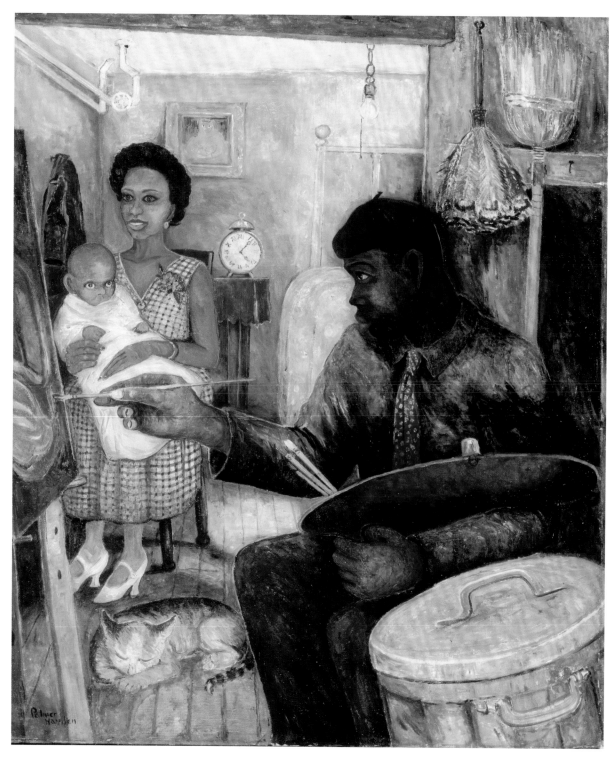

PEYTON HEDGEMAN acquired the name Palmer Hayden during the First World War, when the sergeant in his regiment was reputedly 'unable' to pronounce his real name. Under this name, however, he established a reputation as one of the pre-eminent African-American artists of the twentieth century. After the war, Hayden participated in the great African-American cultural awakening known as the Harlem Renaissance. In 1927 he travelled to Paris, where his work was exhibited at the prestigious Bernheim-Jeune Gallery. Hayden's pieces frequently incorporate African cultural artefacts. However, he is best known for his depiction of African-American subjects and experiences, as can be seen in the autobiographical work, *The Janitor Who Paints*. Here, Hayden emphasizes his status as an artist painting a portrait of a mother and child in a domestic interior. However, he also incorporates a bin, a mop and a duster – an indication of how he was forced to support his art throughout his early career by undertaking a series of low-paid jobs. Hayden's works have sometimes been criticized for pandering to racial stereotypes, but this painting – later reworked – captures the artist's dignity.

Bill Traylor   Untitled (pig with corkscrew tail), *c.*1939–42

Born *c.* 1854 Benton, Alabama, USA   Painted in Montgomery, Alabama   Died 1946 Montgomery, Alabama
MOVEMENT: American Vernacular and Outsider School   **OTHER WORKS:** *Fish, Cat, Man, Plant Pot, Dog and Figures*   **INFLUENCES:** None

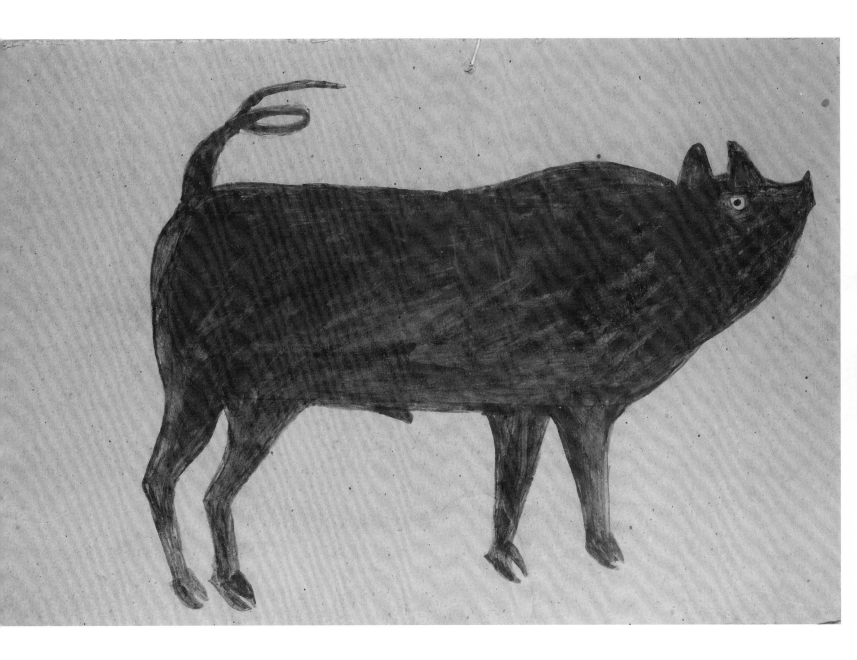

ONE OF the earliest artists belonging to the American Vernacular and Outsider tradition, without any training or outside influences whatsoever, Bill Traylor was born a slave and for many years after Emancipation continued to work as a field hand on a plantation in rural Alabama. Later he moved to Montgomery as an unskilled factory worker and latterly was a homeless down-and-out, an outsider both artistically and in reality, sleeping rough and existing on welfare hand-outs. He took up drawing and painting in 1939 and in three years he produced over 1,800 pictures, executed on cardboard. His technique developed rapidly from simple geometric shapes to complex abstract constructions inhabited by tiny moving figures. He drew on his memories and imagination as well as keenly observing the people and scenes around him.

Although his work had come to the notice of the Museum of Modern Art in 1941, it is only within more recent years that it has been recognized as one of the major triumphs of self-taught art.

William H. Johnson Going to Church, *c.*1940–01

Born 1901 South Carolina, USA   Painted in Denmark, Norway and USA   Died 1970 Long Island, New York

MOVEMENT: African-American School **OTHER WORKS:** *Lamentation, Cagnes-sur-Mer, Minnie, Jacobia Hotel, Jitterbugs* **INFLUENCES:** Van Gogh, Kasimir Malevich

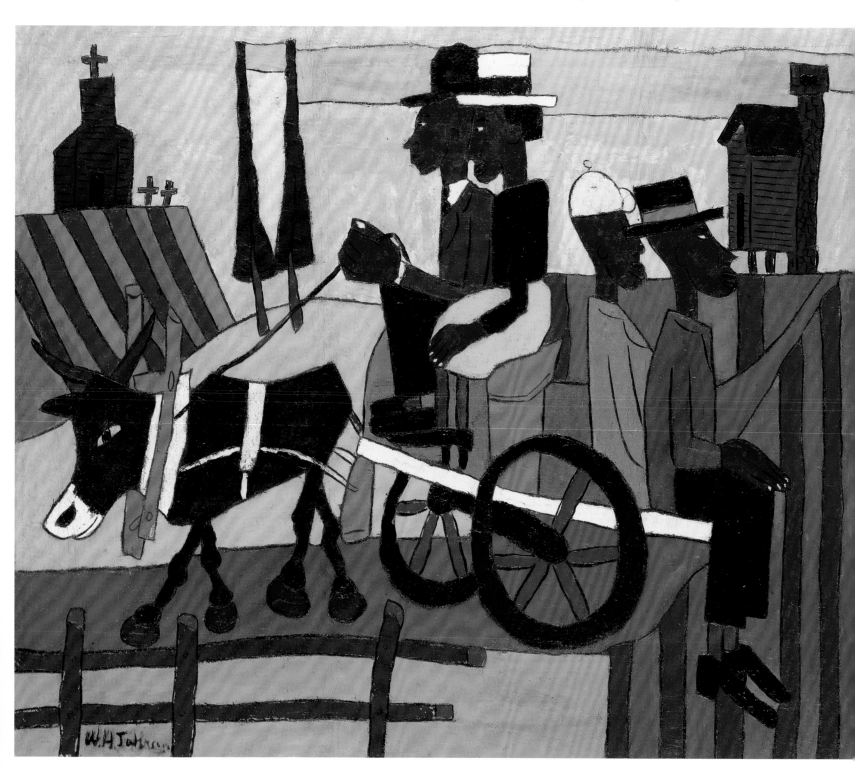

BORN IN South Carolina in 1901, William Henry Johnson migrated to New York in 1918 and settled in Harlem. For five years he studied art at the National Academy of Design and later moved to Denmark, after marrying the Danish weaver and potter Holche Krake in 1930. He later spent some time in Norway before returning to the USA shortly before World War II. In 1943 they lost everything as a result of a house fire, and soon afterwards his wife died. Johnson had a mental breakdown and by 1947 had to be committed to an institution. In 1967 he gave his collected works, amounting to some 800 oils and watercolours and about 400 sketches and drawings, to the National Museum of American Art. He died three years later, and it is only since the 1970s that his achievement has been fully recognized and his importance in the development of contemporary American art fully appreciated. His paintings are characterized by their passion and exuberance, with echoes of Van Gogh and the Constructivists as well as the influence of African tribal sculpture and textile patterns.

Horace Pippin   Giving Thanks, 1942

Born 1888 West Chester, Pennsylvania, USA   Painted in West Chester   Died 1946 West Chester
MOVEMENT: African American School   **OTHER WORKS:** *The End of War: Starting Home, Night Call, Buffalo Hunt*   **INFLUENCES:** Henri Rousseau, Renoir

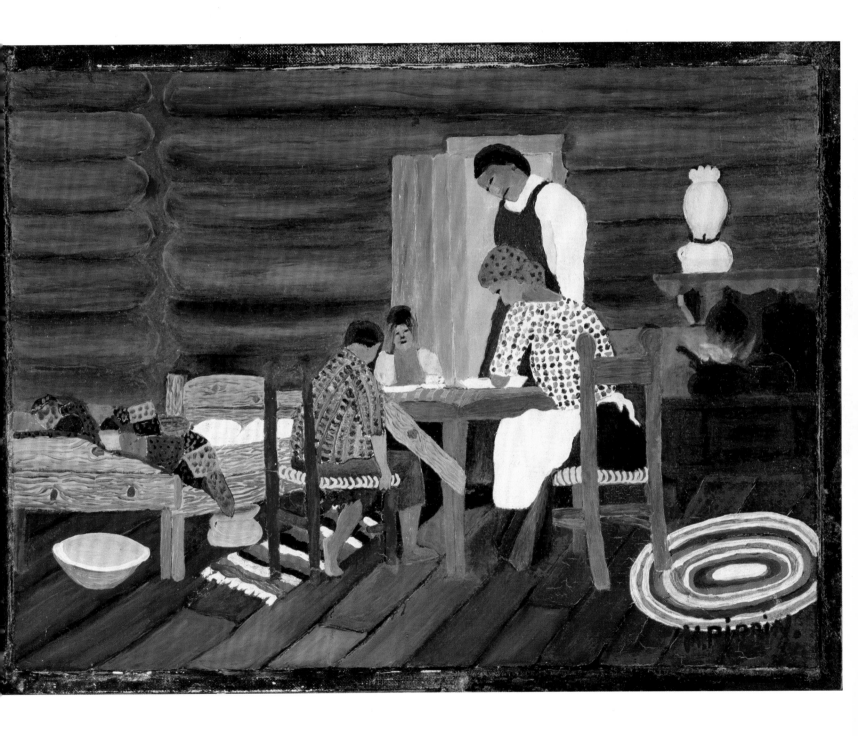

HORACE PIPPIN began drawing at the age of seven, but in his youth he held a variety of menial jobs before joining the army in 1917. He returned to West Chester in 1920, his right arm badly damaged by a sniper's bullet, and as part of his therapy he began executing pictures in pokerwork on wood panels. In 1929 he took up painting and without any formal training developed into one of America's leading primitive painters. He started by painting the grim scenes from his experiences on the Western Front, vividly conveying the psychological trauma of trench warfare. Later he turned to historic events, biblical subjects, genre paintings derived from childhood incidents and domestic interiors, as seen here. Pippin's work was first widely exhibited at the Museum of Modern Art in New York at the 1938 exhibition entitled 'Masters of Popular Painting: Modern Primitives of Europe and America'.

Pippin's works, such as *Giving Thanks*, were executed in bright colours with flat forms, reminiscent of the French 'naïve' painter Henri Rousseau (1844–1910). A recurring feature of his work is his own highly personal interpretation of events and personalities. His last paintings were the *Holy Mountain* series from 1944.

Edward Burra   Salome

Born 1905 London, England   Painted in London   Died 1976 Rye, Sussex, England
MOVEMENT: Surrealism   **OTHER WORKS:** *The Snack Bar, Harlem, Soldiers*   **INFLUENCES:** George Grosz, Dadaism, Surrealism

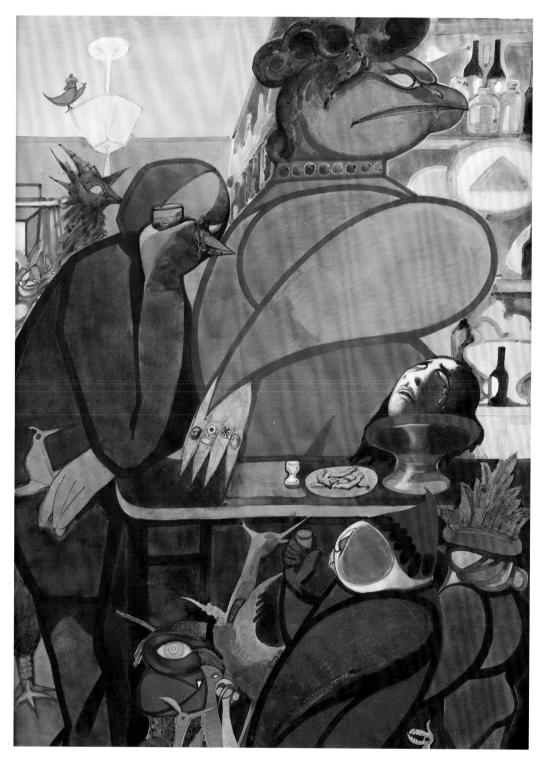

EDWARD BURRA was mainly educated at home on account of chronic ill health as a child, but in 1921 he enrolled at the Chelsea Polytechnic and later studied at the Royal College of Art. Later he travelled widely in Europe and America where he imbibed the ideas and techniques of the Surrealists and Dadaists, as well as German painters such as George Grosz. Bouts of ill health dogged him throughout his career and may explain the frenetic activity in his paintings and the exceptionally vivid colours, often placing his figures against exotic backgrounds. He had a keen eye for the absurd, the offbeat and the louche, and delighted in recreating scenes of low life in bars, brothels and nightclubs. By contrast, his pictures relating to the Spanish Civil War (1936–9) are stark and sombre, a prelude to his grim paintings of World War II. In the postwar period he turned to landscapes and still-life compositions. Burra also designed sets for ballet.

Paul Delvaux   La Ville Inquiete, 1941

Born 1894 Antheit-lez-Huy, Belgium   Painted in Brussels, Belgium   Died 1994 Knokke-Heist, Belgium
MOVEMENT: Surrealism **OTHER WORKS:** *The Sleeping Town, The Call of the Night* **INFLUENCES:** Giorgio de Chirico, Magritte

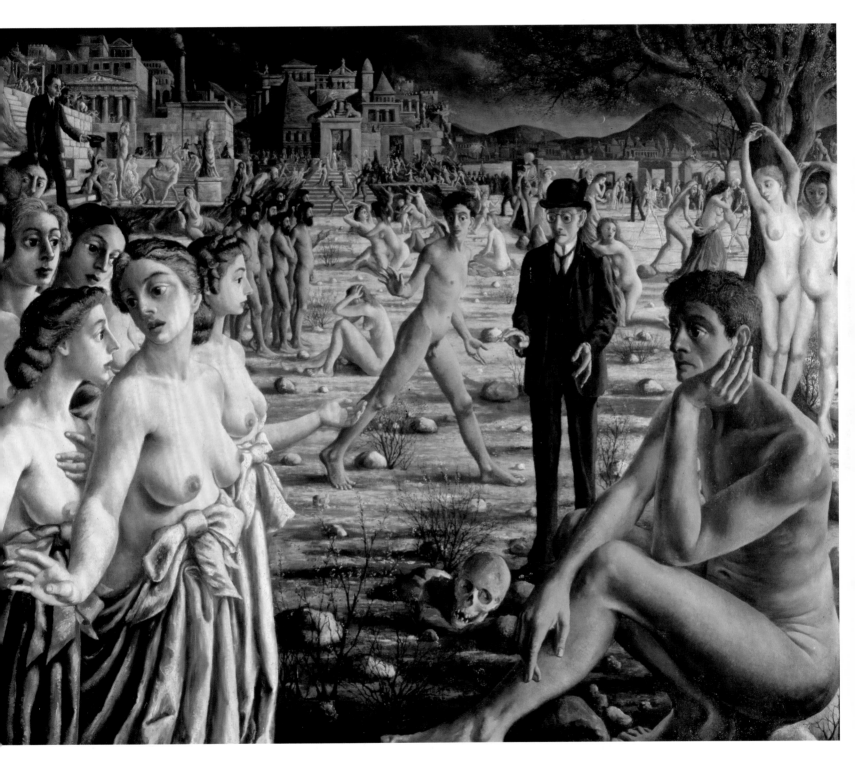

BORN NEAR Liège in Belgium Delvaux studied architecture then painting in Brussels, where he established his studio. In his early career he dabbled in Expressionism and Impressionism but later came under the influence of Giorgio de Chirico and especially his fellow-countryman René Magritte. He evolved his own distinctive style of Surrealism in which somnambulatory nudes and doe-eyed semi-nude figures are set alongside skeletons amid classical ruins while the artist, in conventional modern dress, looks on. This largest and most ambitious painting features the arrival of the artist, alighting from a ghostly train in silent cities in the dead of night, illumined only by the Moon, in which bodies sleep-walk or flit languorously. This combination of the classical and the contemporary gives these dreamlike paintings a timeless quality. Between 1950 and 1962 he was professor of painting at the École Nationale Supérieure d'Art et d'Architecture in Brussels. In 1982 the Paul Delvaux Museum was established at Sint-Idesbald.

Diego Rivera   Vendedora de Flores, 1942

Born 1886 Guanajuato, Mexico   Painted in Mexico and USA   Died 1957 Mexico City
MOVEMENT: Mexican Modernism   **OTHER WORKS:** *Court of the Inquisition, Workers of the Revolution*   **INFLUENCES:** Juan Gris, Georges Braque

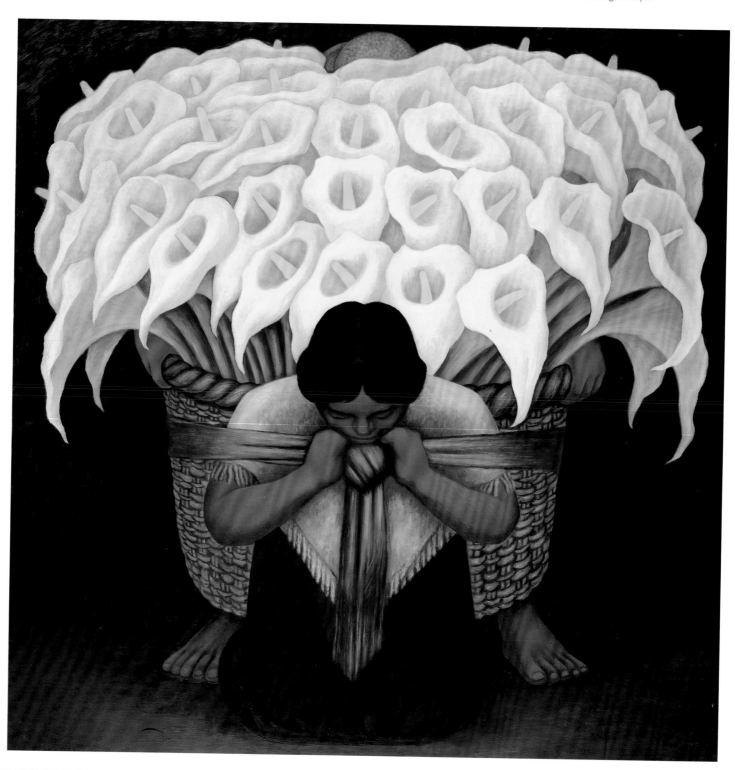

THE OUTSTANDING muralist of Latin America, Diego Rivera studied art in Mexico City and Madrid; he went to Paris in 1911, where he met Picasso and began painting Cubist works, which were strongly influenced by Gris and Braque. By contrast, a sojourn in Italy studying the frescoes of the Renaissance Masters made such an impact on him that, on his return to Mexico in 1921, he concentrated on large murals decorating the walls of public buildings. These depicted every aspect of life in Mexico and drew on the turbulent history of its people. Rivera's best work was carried out during a period when Mexico was dominated by left-wing, anti-clerical governments, which regarded Rivera as the leading revolutionary artist. He also worked in the USA where he painted murals extolling the industrial proletariat and preaching social messages. He evolved his own brand of folk art with overtones of such disparate elements as Aztec symbolism and Byzantine icons.

Kurt Schwitters   Roter Kreis, 1942

Born 1887 Hanover, Germany   Painted in Germany, Norway and England   Died 1948 Ambleside, Cumbria, England
MOVEMENT: Dada   **OTHER WORKS:** *Chocolate, Spring Picture, Circle*   **INFLUENCES:** Jean Arp, Marcel Duchamp, Raoul Hausmann

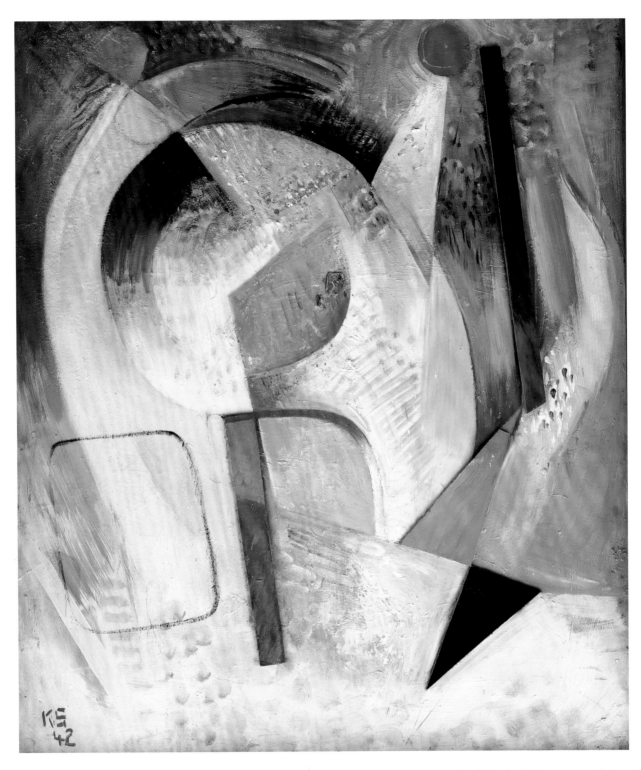

KURT SCHWITTERS studied at the Dresden Academy and worked as a painter, designer, architect, typographer, writer and publisher, disparate occupations and disciplines which he combined with remarkable flair. He was intrigued by Cubism very early on and produced a number of abstract paintings in this style, but was then attracted to Dadaism and strongly influenced by Hausmann, Arp and other leading exponents. During this phase he produced montages of totally unrelated objects and incongruous fragments of junk and ephemera, such as discarded leaflets, bus tickets and used stamps torn off envelopes. After 1920 he took this notion a step further, incorporating street rubbish in enormous three-dimensional collages which he termed Merzbau ('cast-off construction').

This led to the Dadaist magazine *Merz*, which he ran from 1923 until 1932. When the Nazis came to power he fled to Norway and from there moved in 1940 to England, where he died in 1948.

Wifredo Lam   Foret Tropicale, 1943

Born 1902 Sagua la Granda, Cuba   Painted in Cuba, France and Spain   Died 1992 Havana, Cuba
MOVEMENT: Surrealism   **OTHER WORKS:** *All Souls*   **INFLUENCES:** Picasso, Michel Leiris, André Breton

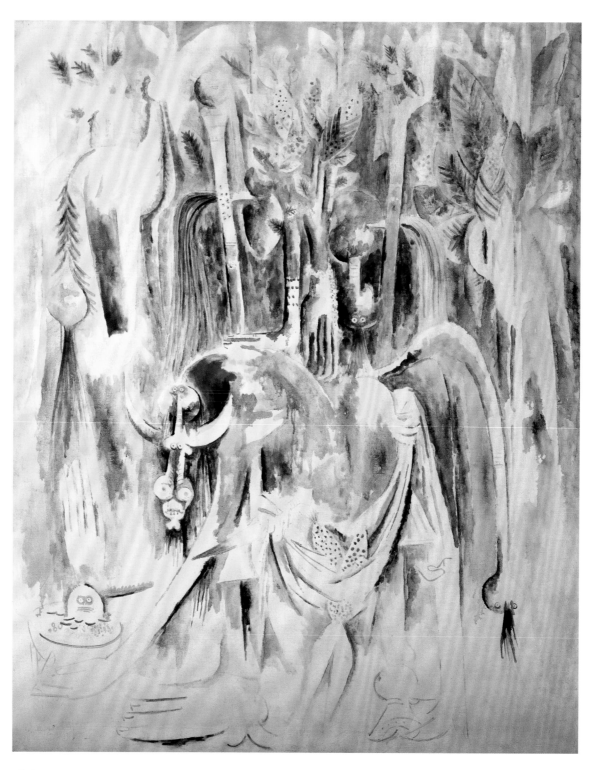

WIFREDO OSCAR de la Concepcion Lam y Castilla was the son of a Chinese immigrant and a woman of Afro-Cuban origin. In his art he strove to combine the disparate elements in the artistic traditions of these three different cultures. He enrolled at the Escuela de Bellas Artes in Havana and went to Madrid in 1923, where he studied under Fernandez Alvarez de Sotomayor and at the Academia Libre.

Caught up in the Spanish Civil War, Lam fought with the Republicans in the defence of Madrid (1937). Escaping to Paris, he met Picasso and joined the Surrealists in 1940. On his return to Cuba in 1942 he began painting pictures that combined the dreamlike qualities of Surrealism with elements derived from Cubism and indigenous Afro-Cuban art. For a time he lived in Haiti before settling in Paris again in

1952, though continuing to travel back and forth between Europe and the Caribbean. His greatest masterpiece, *The Jungle* (1943) draws on Afro-Cuban myth and ritual, sugar cane stalks merging with human limbs in a hallucinatory effect.

Archibald Motley Jr   Nightlife, 1943

Born 1891 USA   Painted in Chicago, USA   Died 1980 Chicago

MOVEMENT: Modern American School   **OTHER WORKS:** *Old Snuff Dipper, The Picnic in the Green, Chicken Shack*   **INFLUENCES:** Ashcan School

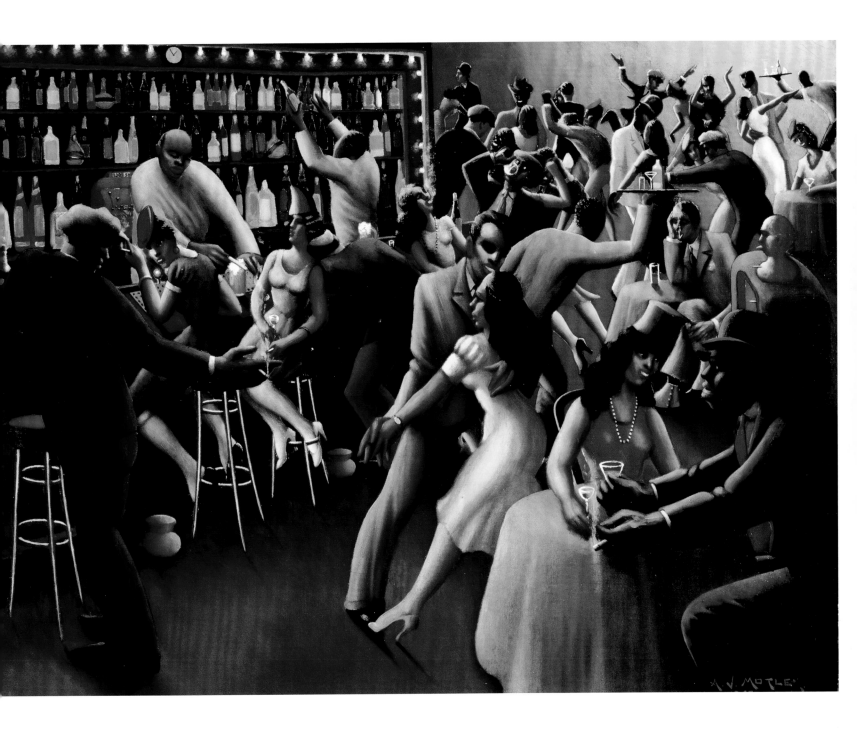

ARCHIBALD MOTLEY Jr moved from New Orleans to Chicago in his youth and took various labouring occupations. Largely self-taught, he won a Guggenheim Fellowship in 1929 which enabled him to travel and study in Paris, where he also produced a number of paintings of the lively black music scene. A one-man show in New York in 1928 showed his deep interest in African-American culture, tinged with mysticism, voodoo and the spirit world, but after his Paris sojourn he concentrated on living subjects and genre scenes crammed with figures, full of action and movement, with a lively portrayal of the gambling and illegal drinking in the Prohibition era. Unlike many other African-American artists, Motley was not concerned so much with the racial consciousness of the Harlem Renaissance, but belonged more to the Ashcan School in his depiction of ordinary, often seedy, activities of people regardless of ethnic origin.

L.S. (Laurence Stephen) Lowry   Industrial Landscape, 1944

Born 1887 Manchester, England   Painted in England   Died 1976 Glossop, England

MOVEMENT: Naive Art   **OTHER WORKS:** *Our Town, Man Lying on a Wall, Sudden Illness, The Pond* **INFLUENCES:** Adolphe Valette, Camden Town School

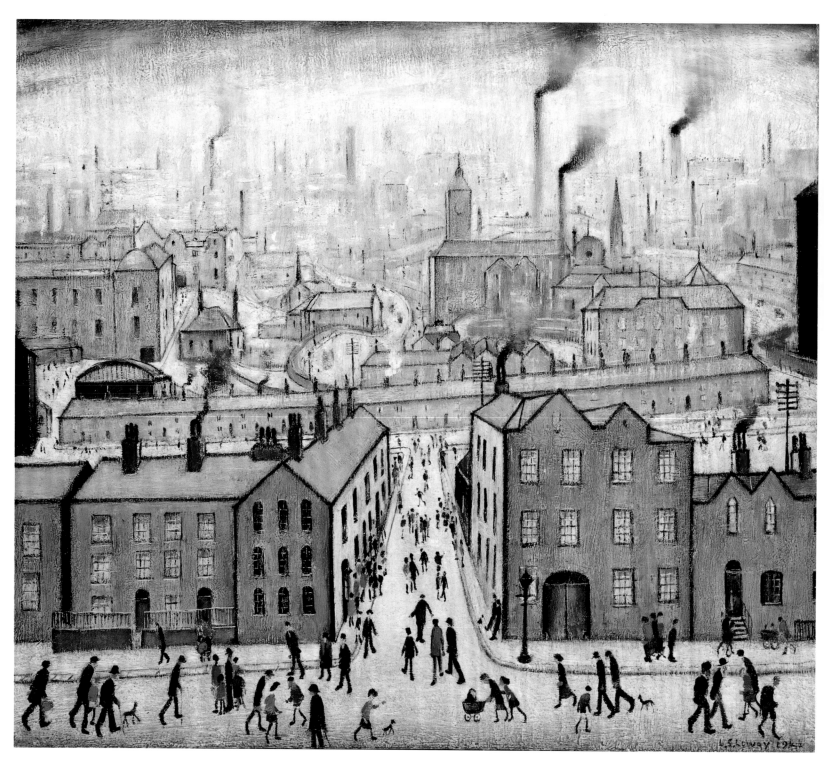

DISTINCTIVE BRITISH painter, famous for his pictures of 'matchstick men'. Lowry was born in Old Trafford, Manchester, and lived in or near the city throughout his life. He failed to gain entry to the local art school and, instead, took on office work and painted in the evenings. Initially, he was employed by an insurance company and, after 1910, as a rent collector for a property firm. In later years, much of his time was also devoted to the care of his invalid mother. They were very close and Lowry was devastated when she died in 1939.

The childlike qualities of Lowry art have often been classified as naive, but technically this is untrue, since he had a succession of teachers at evening school. The most significant of these was Adolphe Valette, who also painted urban townscapes. From an early stage, Lowry began producing unglamorous views of the local, industrial scene, focusing in particular on details of everyday life. These ranged from the grotesque to the humorous. Lowry's style baffled the art establishment – he was conspicuously omitted from the Royal Academy's survey of twentieth century British art – but his paintings sold well and he has remained unfailingly popular with the public.

Clyfford Still   1955–D, 1955

Born 1904 Grandin, North Dakota, USA   Painted in Spokane, Washington, San Francisco, California, USA   Died 1980 New Windsor, Maryland, USA
MOVEMENT: Abstract Expressionism/Colour Field Painting   **OTHER WORKS:** *Jamais, Untitled No.1, Untitled 1953*   **INFLUENCES:** Barnett Newman, Mark Rothko

RAISED IN the American Midwest, Clyfford Still studied art at Spokane University, Washington, graduating in 1933 when the United States was still recovering from the Depression. Eschewing the social realism of his contemporaries, he strove to evolve his own distinctive style, embracing elements of Biomorphism in which organic forms predominated. In 1941 he settled in San Francisco and subsequently taught at the California School of Fine Arts (1946–50). During this period he emerged as one of the leading exponents of Abstract Expressionism. Heavily influenced by Barnett Newman and Mark Rothko, he favoured large canvasses in which a single colour predominated; the variations in colour, form and content being largely confined to the periphery. Interest and variety in the principal colour was imparted by its rich texture and brushwork. Many of his works were either completely untitled or only given the most cryptic of titles. Thus it was mainly left to the viewer to divine the significance of the detail at the edges of his canvas, although Still himself was a past-master in the art of making pretentious statements that allegedly explained the metaphor of his work.

Ben Nicholson   1945 (Airmail Letter)

Born 1894   Painted in England, France and Switzerland   Died 1982 London

MOVEMENT: Abstract Art, Cubism, St Ives School   **OTHER WORKS:** *1928 (Cornwall), 1933 (milk and plain chocolate)*   **INFLUENCES:** Sir William Nicholson, Piet Mondrian, Georges Braque

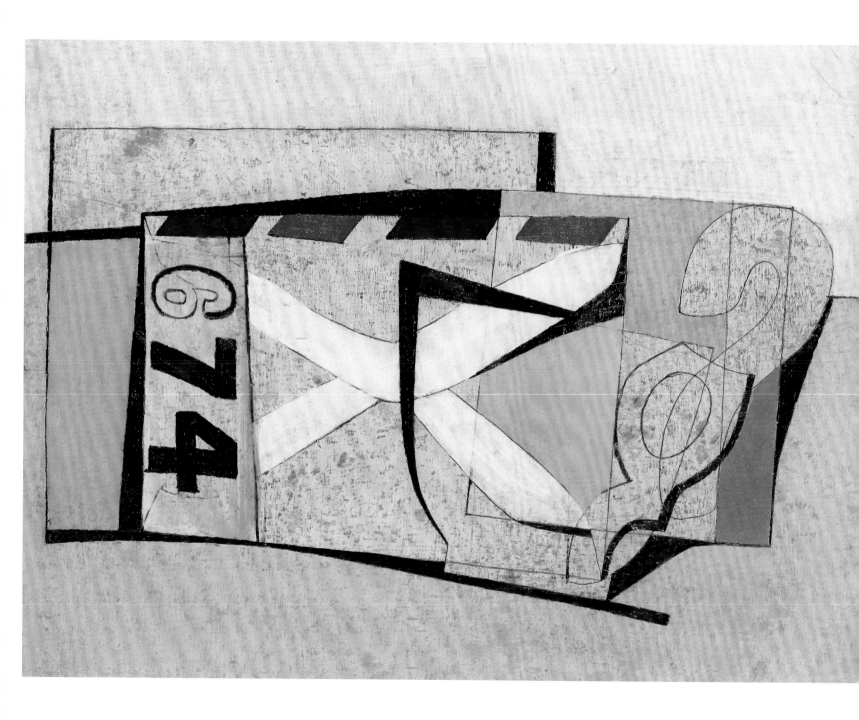

A PIONEERING figure in the development of British Abstract Art. Both of Nicholson's parents were artists, but he was slow to discover his own vocation. He studied briefly at the Slade School, but did not begin painting seriously until 1920. Initially, he painted naive landscapes and sturdy still lifes, which were reminiscent of his father's work. Increasingly, though, he turned to abstraction, joining a number of avant-garde groups.

These included the Seven & Five Society, Unit One and the Abstraction-Création circle.

The primary influence on Nicholson's abstracts came from Cubism. Early examples featured motifs – guitars, jars, glasses – used by Picasso and Braque. After visiting Mondrian's studio in Paris, however, he began to banish figurative objects from his pictures, echoing the austere, geometric style favoured by the Dutchman.

Nicholson married three times, and two of his wives – Winifred Nicholson and Barbara Hepworth – were distinguished artists in their own right. With the latter, he moved down to St Ives in Cornwall in 1939, where they became the focus of a famous artists' colony, until 1958 when he left for Switzerland.

Dorothea Tanning   The Truth about Comets and Little Girls

Born 1910 Galesburg, Illinois, USA   Painted in Chicago, New York and Paris
MOVEMENT: Surrealism **OTHER WORKS:** *Born A Little Night Music, A Very Happy Picture, A Family Portrait* **INFLUENCES:** Max Ernst

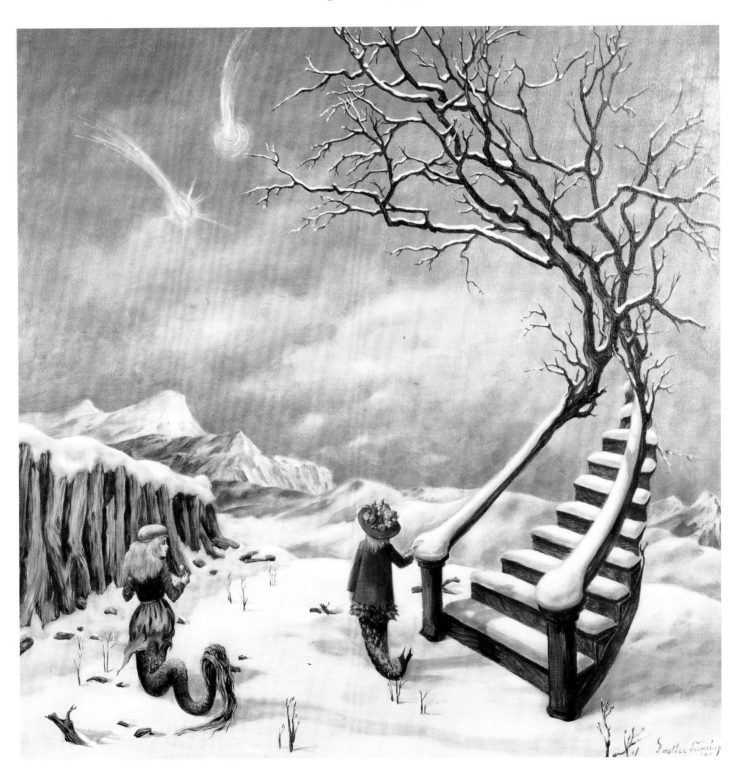

DOROTHEA TANNING worked as a librarian in her home town of Galesburg, Illinois. In 1930 she went to work in Chicago and attended a two-week course of evening classes in art at the Academy of Fine Art, before going to New York in 1936, where she found employment as a commercial artist. Her earliest paintings drew on childhood nostalgia interpreted in a surreal manner, and this brought her to the attention of the American Surrealists. In 1946 she married Max Ernst, the German Dadaist then living in exile in the USA, and together they settled in France, where she worked as a painter, graphic artist and designer of theatrical sets and costumes. Tanning's later work has a more fully rounded character but still essentially explores the female psyche and sexuality through the medium of dreams. Her paintings often combine a superficial childhood innocence with rather disturbing sexual undertones and morbid symbolism.

335

Alex Colville   The Horses, 1946

Born 1920 Toronto, Ontario, Canada   Painted in Amherst and Wolfville, Nova Scotia
MOVEMENT: Modern Canadian School **OTHER WORKS:** *Horse and Train* **INFLUENCES:** Camille Pissarro, Seurat

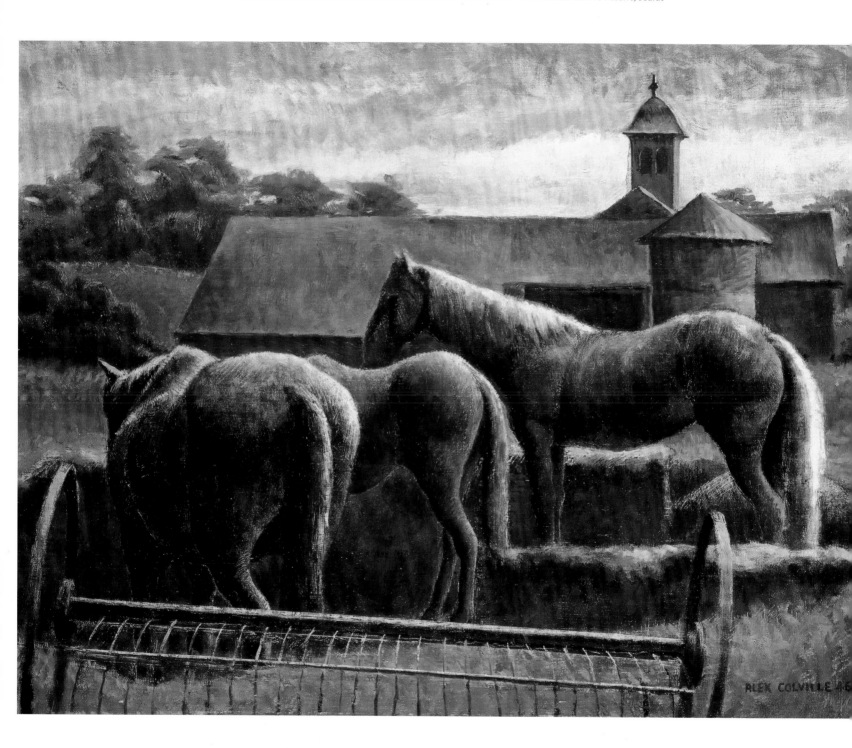

ALTHOUGH BORN in Toronto, David Alexander Colville was raised in Amherst, Nova Scotia. At the age of nine he suffered a bout of pneumonia and during a long convalescence was encouraged to draw and paint. Later he studied under Stanley Royle, who persuaded him to abandon his plans for a career in law and politics and concentrate on art. In 1942 he was one of the first graduates in Fine Arts anywhere in Canada, and spent three years as an official war artist, an experience that shaped his later career. After the war he taught art at Mount Allison University until 1963, when he retired to paint full-time. A versatile artist, he has designed everything from Canadian coins and medals to album sleeves for folk singers. His realist style is executed in the manner of the French pointillists, using thousands of tiny brushstrokes to create an almost sculptural effect.

Roberto Matta   Abstracto

Born 1911 Santiago, Chile   Painted in Chile and USA   Died 2002 Civitavecchia, Italy

MOVEMENTS: Surrealism, Abstract Expressionism   **OTHER WORKS:** *Invasion of the Night, Disasters of Mysticism, Abstraction, Untitled*   **INFLUENCES:** Hans Bellmer

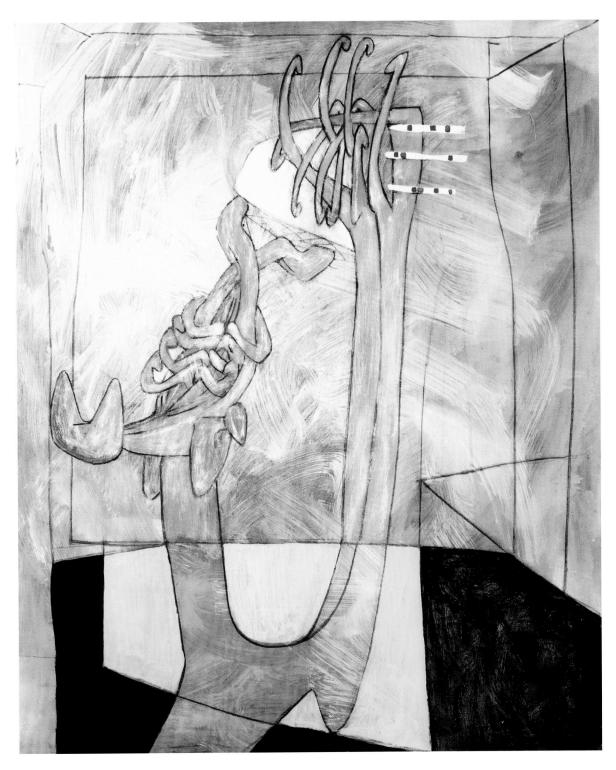

BORN ROBERTO Sebastian Matta Echaurren, Matta trained as an architect in his native city of Santiago and continued his studies under Le Corbusier in Paris. He took up painting in 1937 and was immediately attracted to Surrealism, of which he became one of the outstanding figures over the ensuing decade. He moved to the United States in 1939 and made his debut at the Julien Levy Gallery the following year. His work had an enormous impact on the younger generation of American artists, his approach to Surrealism being markedly different from that of Dalí and the other main European exponents. His technique of apparently random brushstrokes without rational control influenced such painters as Arshile Gorky and Jackson Pollock. From Abstract Expressionism he gradually moved towards what he termed as 'transparent Cubism' in the late 1940s, bringing back figural elements.

Jackson Pollock Number 6, 1948

Born 1912 Cody, Wyoming, USA Painted in USA Died 1956

MOVEMENT: Abstract Expressionism **OTHER WORKS:** *Convergence, Autumn Rhythm, Lavendar Mist* **INFLUENCES:** André Masson, Thomas Hart Benton, David Siqueiros

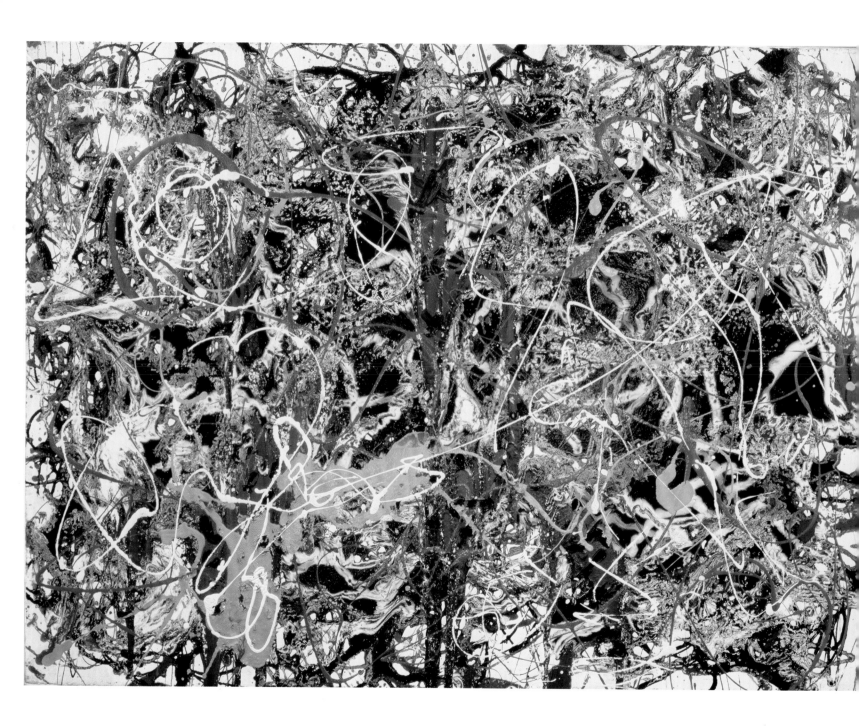

Pollock grew up in the American West, becoming familiar with Native American art at an early age. He was briefly influenced by Benton and the Regionalists, but learned more from Siqueiros and the Mexican muralists. He was impressed by their expressive, almost violent use of paint. Pollock also began to explore the possibilities of Jungian psychology. This started as an aspect of his private life – psychotherapy

was one of the many treatments he tried for his long-term alcoholism – but it also fuelled his art. For, like the Surrealists, he adopted the idea of automatic painting, as a mirror of the subconscious.

After years of isolation and critical neglect, Pollock's experiments bore fruit in the late 1940s. By 1947, he had perfected the 'drip' technique which made him famous. He placed his canvas on the floor

and covered it in trails of paint, poured directly from the can. This process was carried out in an artistic frenzy of 'Action Painting', comparable with the Indian ritual dances which he had witnessed as a boy. His paintings offer no *articulate* meaning, but they are fraught with energy, tension, passion and drama. Pollock's output slowed in the 1950s, and he was killed in a car crash in 1956.

Leonora Carrington   The Temptation of Saint Anthony, 1947

Born 1917 Clayton Green, Lancashire, England   Painted in England and Mexico
MOVEMENT: Surrealism **OTHER WORKS:** *Baby Giant, The Magic Works of the Mayas* **INFLUENCES:** Hieronymus Bosch, Dal`

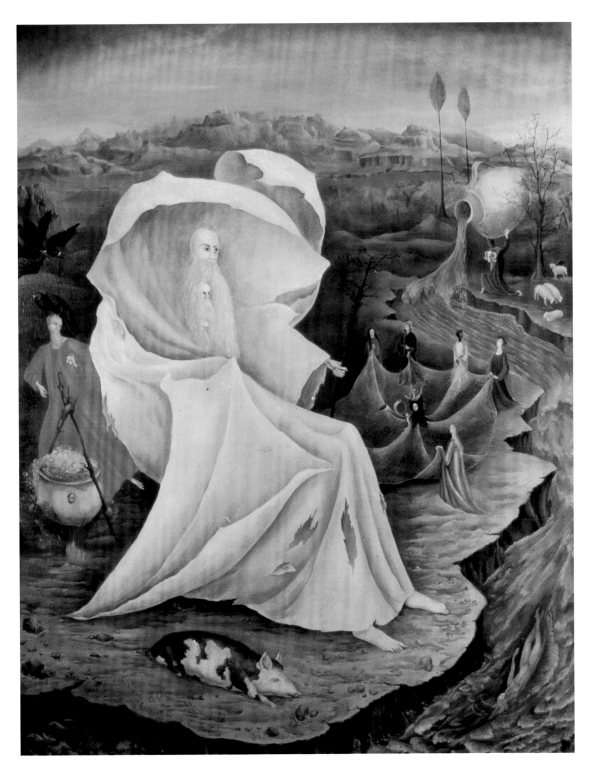

BORN IN Lancashire but brought up in London, Leonora Carrington came under the influence of the Surrealists in the 1930s and produced a number of paintings which combined scenes and images from her childhood with mystical and fairytale themes. In 1942 she crossed the Atlantic and settled in Mexico, where she shared a studio with Remedios Varo, a Spanish female painter of similar outlook, who shared her enthusiasm for the occult, alchemy and other magical subjects.

A feminist ahead of her time, Carrington attempted to explore and analyse the female psyche through the medium of painting. A recurring theme was woman as the life force at the heart of all creativity contrasted by malign forces in nature, which often gives her paintings a rather sinister undertone. There are echoes of the early Renaissance religious artists in her work, especially in the use of allegory and mythology, but these are often mingled with weird and bizarre elements that owe more to the Surrealists.

Sir George Russell Drysdale   Bob & Mandie

Born 1912 Sussex, England   Painted in Australia   Died 1981 Sydney, Australia
MOVEMENT: Modern Australian School   **OTHER WORKS**: *Back Verandah, The Walls of China*   **INFLUENCES**: Surrealism

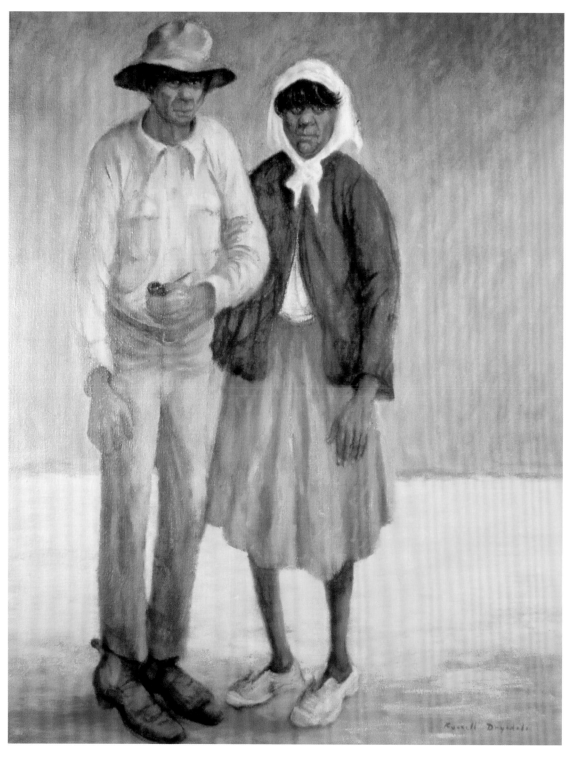

BORN AT Bognor, Sussex, where he received his early education, George Russell Drysdale emigrated with his parents to Australia in 1923 and settled in Melbourne, Victoria. He took up sketching while recovering from an eye operation as a boy and this led him to enrol at the George Bell Art School. He continued his studies at the Royal Academy School in London and then went to Paris, where he came under the influence of the Surrealists. On his return to Australia he began painting and drawing the desolate scenes of the Outback, drawing upon the styles and techniques of contemporary British artists in depicting the Australian wilderness with a rugged realism. His work was first exhibited in London in 1950 and immediately established him as one of the most promising Australian artists of his generation.

Over the ensuing three decades he was the most influential figure in Australian art. He was knighted in 1969 and became a Companion of the Order of Australia in 1980.

Arshile Gorky   Year after Year, 1947

Born 1904 Khorkom Vari, Turkey   Painted in USA   Died 1948 Sherman, Connecticut, USA

MOVEMENT: Abstract Expressionism **OTHER WORKS:** *Agony, Waterfall* **INFLUENCES:** Joan Miró, Picasso, Cézanne

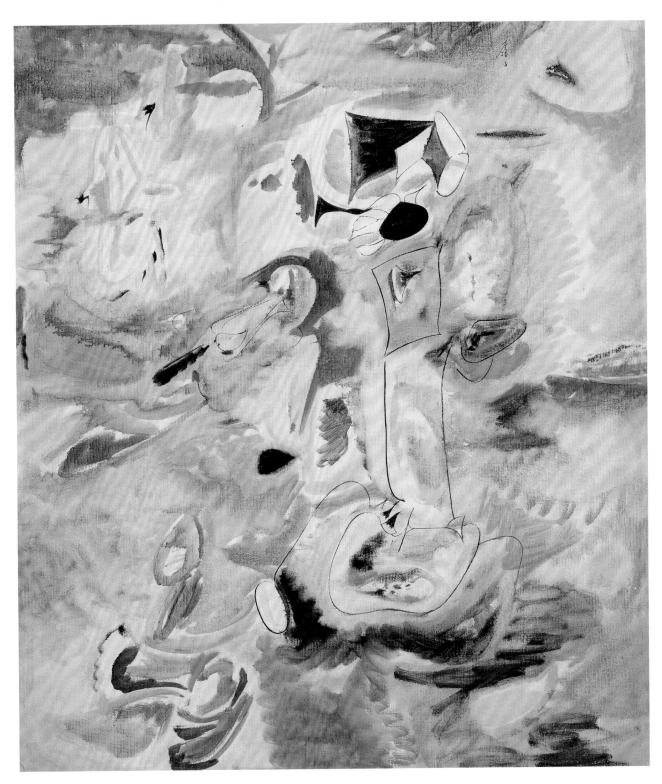

ORIGINALLY NAMED Vosdanig Manoog Adoian, Gorky was born at Khorkom Vari in Turkish Armenia. He survived the genocide perpetrated on the Armenians by the Turks during World War I and escaped to the West, settling in the USA in 1920. The death of his mother during one of the Turkish atrocities had a profound influence on his art. It was at this time that he adopted his new name, taking the surname from the celebrated Russian writer Maxim Gorky. In America he trained at the Rhode Island School of Design and continued his studies in Boston. For several years his style was a heady but eclectic mixture of elements drawn from Miró, Cezanne, Picasso, Motta and André Breton, and it was from the latter that he was attracted to Surrealism, concentrating on biomorphism (the creation of organic abstracts), but later he developed his own distinctive style which promoted Abstract Expressionism.

Henri Matisse   Jazz, 1947

Born 1869 France   Painted in France and Morocco   Died 1954
MOVEMENT: Fauvism **OTHER WORKS:** *The Dance, Luxe, Calme et Volupte, The Blue Window* **INFLUENCES:** Paul Signac, Henri-Edmond Cross, Gustave Moreau, Cézanne

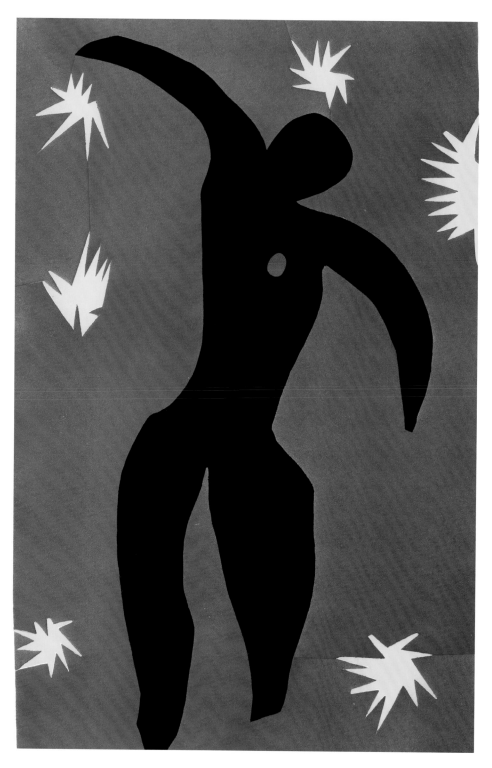

FRENCH PAINTER, printmaker and designer; the dominant figure in the Fauvist movement. Initially a lawyer's clerk, Matisse turned to art in 1890. His first teacher, Bouguereau, was a disappointment, but he learned a great deal from his second master, Gustave Moreau, a Symbolist painter with a taste for exotic colouring. Matisse's early works were mainly Impressionist or Neo-Impressionist in character but, after painting trips to the Mediterranean, he began to employ more vivid colours; using them to create an emotional impact, rather than simply to transcribe nature.

After years of failure, Matisse and his friends made their breakthrough at the Salon d'Automne of 1905. Critics were overwhelmed by the dazzling canvasses on display and dubbed the group *Les Fauves* ('the wild beasts').

Matisse continued to find his greatest inspiration from painting on the Riviera, but he also travelled widely, visiting Morocco, America and Spain. He decorated a chapel in Vence in southern France, in gratitude for a nun who had nursed him, and experimented with 'cut-outs' (pictures formed from coloured paper shapes, rather than paint).

Emil Nolde   Lichtzauber, 1947

Born 1867 Nolde, Germany   Painted in Germany   Died 1956 Seebüll, Germany
MOVEMENT: Expressionism **OTHER WORKS:** *The Life of Christ, Meeting on the Beach, Red Poppies* **INFLUENCES:** James Ensor, Vlaminck

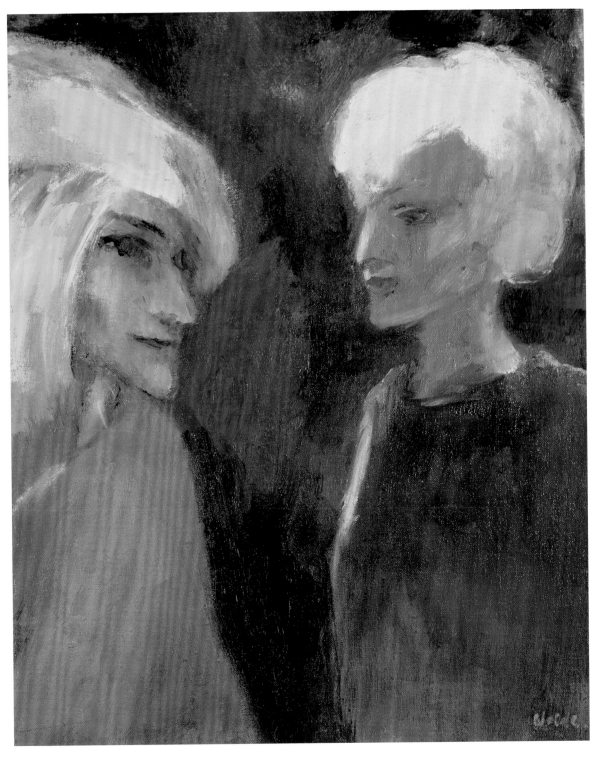

BORN EMIL Hansen in Nolde, Germany, he later adopted the name of his birthplace. He trained as a wood-carver but later studied painting in Munich, where he was briefly a member of the Expressionist group known as Die Brücke ('The Bridge') in 1906–07 as well as Die Blaue Reiter ('the Blue Rider'). He was, however far too rugged an individualist ever to conform too closely to any particular movement, and developed his own distinctive Blut und Boden ('blood and soil') style of painting, originally confined largely to religious themes expressed with distorted images and violent brushstrokes, but later extended to landscapes, seascapes, still life and flowers. Most of his work was done in a remote area of the German North Sea coast where he lived increasingly as a recluse. His last work, a series entitled *Unpainted Pictures*, was completed in secrecy as he suffered the delusion of still being harassed by the Nazis. He was also a prolific producer of etchings, lithographs and woodcuts.

343

Jack B. Yeats   The Race, 1947

Born 1871 London, England   Painted in Ireland   Died 1957 Dublin, Ireland
MOVEMENT: Modern Irish School   **OTHER WORKS:** *Waiting for the Long Car, The Rogues' March*   **INFLUENCES:** Oskar Kokoschka

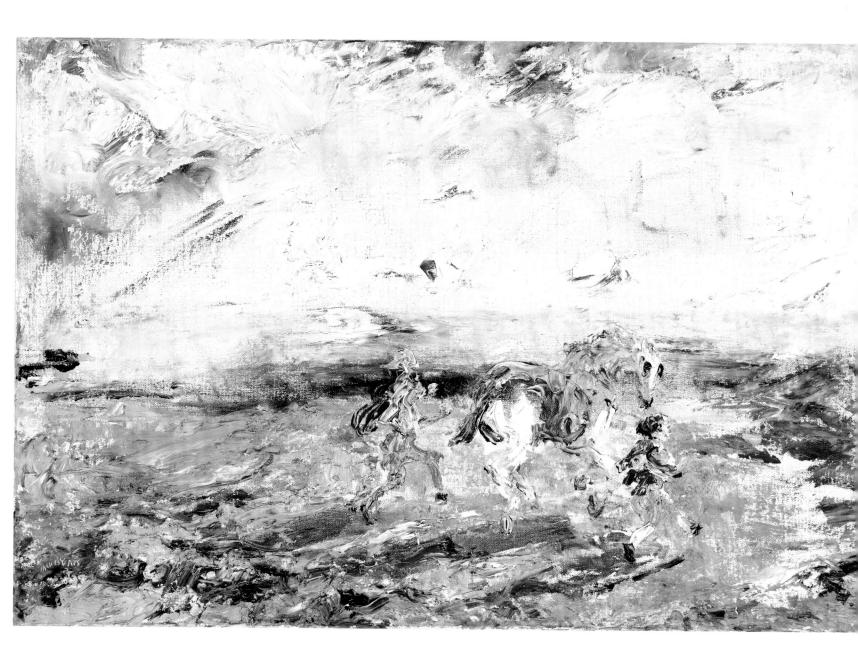

JOHN BUTLER Yeats was the son of an Irish painter and younger brother of the celebrated Irish poet and playwright William Butler Yeats. Though born in London, he was raised in Co. Sligo and spent most of his life in Ireland. His earliest artistic efforts were strip cartoons and illustrations for children's comics, but he did not turn to painting until 1915. In the aftermath of the Easter Rising the following year, his art took on a much more serious tone; his style became increasingly violent and revelling in strident colours as he strove to give an Expressionist interpretation to the Irish Troubles, often using religious metaphors. Unlike his brother, he did not involve himself in Irish politics, but his passionate loyalty to his country leaps off the canvas. Later he adapted his Expressionism to mellower subjects that chronicled life in rural Ireland, and he also went back to the roots of Irish culture, exploring scenes from Celtic myths and legends.

Max Beckmann   Seated Women by Water, 1948

Born 1884 Leipzig, Germany   Painted in Germany, Holland and USA   Died 1950 New York, USA
MOVEMENT: Expressionism   **OTHER WORKS:** *Departure, Quappi with Parrot, The Night*   **INFLUENCES:** George Grosz

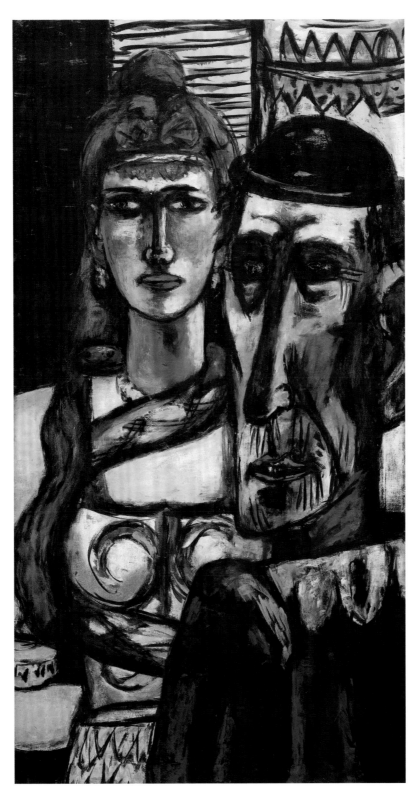

MAX BECKMANN is regarded as one of the greatest figurative artists of the twentieth century. He studied in Weimar and worked as a draughtsman and print-maker before moving to Berlin in 1904, where he embarked on large-scale paintings. During World War I he worked as a hospital orderly – a terrifying experience that shaped his subsequent art. There are Gothic overtones in his canvasses which starkly depict the hopeless struggle of the individual against evil. Not surprisingly, his work was dismissed by the Nazis as degenerate. In 1937 he fled to Holland and spent the last years of his life in the USA, a period in which his paintings expressed a new hope for the world. He was both prolific and versatile, his work ranging from still life and formal portraits to landscapes, abstracts and symbolic compositions, often bizarre and monstrous but always thought-provoking.

Barnett Newman   Untitled, 1948

Born 1905 New York, USA   Painted in New York   Died 1970 New York

MOVEMENT: Abstract Expressionism   **OTHER WORKS:** *Moment, Adam, Covenant, Onement III*   **INFLUENCES:** Piet Mondrian, Mark Rothko

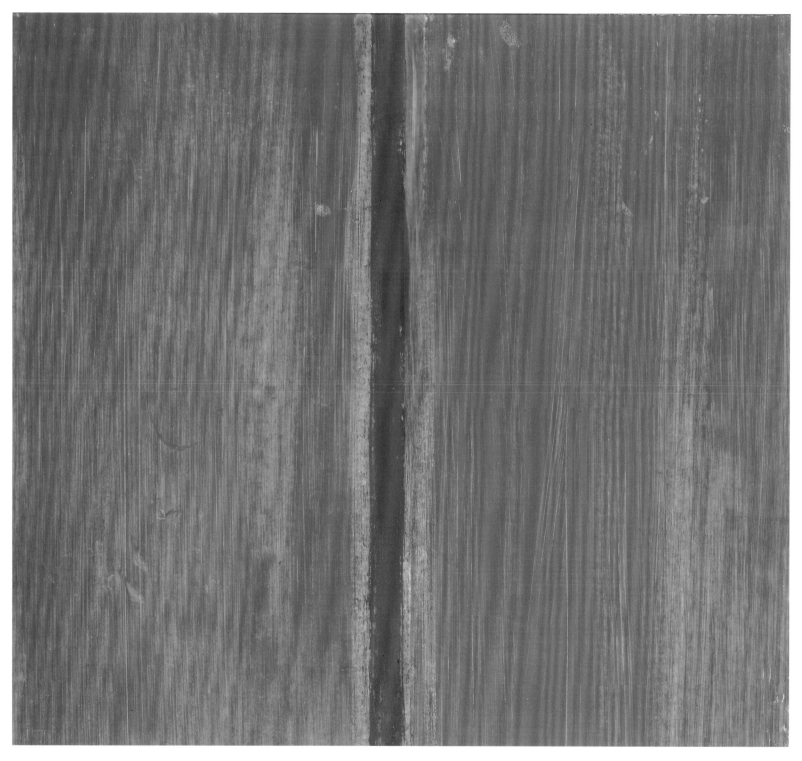

BARNETT NEWMAN trained at the Art Students' League in New York City while also studying at the City College in the early 1920s. Many years later, in the last decade of his life, he taught at the universities of Saskatchewan and Pennsylvania. In between he began his professional career as an Abstract Expressionist about 1930, but gradually developed his own highly distinctive style which eschewed the loose techniques of Expressionism for a more disciplined, rigorous approach. At the same time, the range of his palette gradually decreased as he moved towards a more monochrome treatment, relieved only by one or two vertical bands of contrasting colour which Newman styled as 'zips' from their resemblance to zip-fasteners on clothing. Ultimately, between 1952 and 1962, Newman painted in black and white, the minimalism of his pictures relieved only by the subtleties of shade and density, but in his last years he utilized colours of extraordinary depth and tone. From about 1965 he also produced a number of steel sculptures.

John Piper   Palazzo in Vicenza

Born 1903 Surrey, England   Painted in England, Wales, Italy and France   Died 1992
MOVEMENT: Neo-Romanticism   **OTHER WORKS:** *Forms on Dark Blue, Seaton Delaval, The Gothic Archway*   **INFLUENCES:** Turner, Georges Braque, Picasso, John Sell Cotman

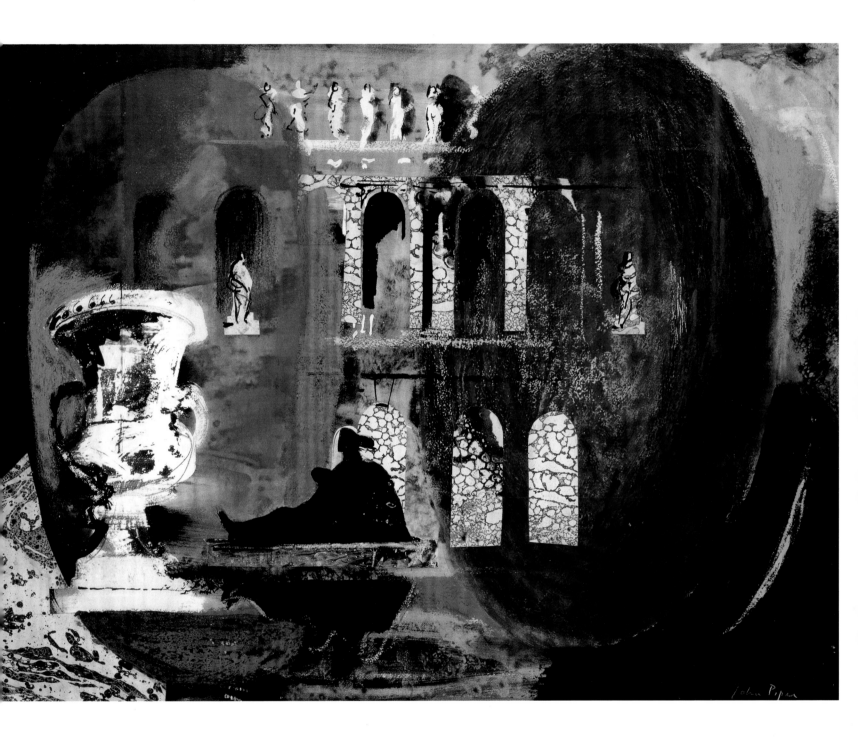

ENGLISH PAINTER, graphic artist, writer and designer. The son of a solicitor, Piper only turned to art after his father's death in 1926. After training at the Royal College of Art, his early work was predominantly abstract. He joined the London Group (1933) and the Seven & Five Society (1934), while also working on the avant-garde journal *Axis* with his future wife, Myfanwy Evans. But, in common with other Neo-Romantic painters, Piper found abstraction an artistic cul-de-sac. Instead, inspired by the late works of Turner, he began to celebrate the glories of the English countryside and its architecture.

In part, the visionary landscapes produced by Piper and his Neo-Romantic colleagues were prompted by the threat of wartime destruction. Accordingly, Piper became a war artist and contributed to the 'Recording Britain' scheme by painting war-damaged buildings. He also produced marvellous, brooding studies of Renishaw and Windsor Castle. In later years, Piper's interests diversified. He designed stained-glass windows for Coventry Cathedral, devised stage sets for Benjamin Britten and created a notable tapestry for Chichester Cathedral.

Ad Reinhardt Untitled Gouache on Paper 1949

Born 1913 New York, USA   Painted in New York   Died 1967 New York

MOVEMENT: Minimalism **OTHER WORKS:** *Painting, Abstract Painting, Black Painting No 34* **INFLUENCES:** Mark Rothko, Barnett Newman, Constantin Brancusi

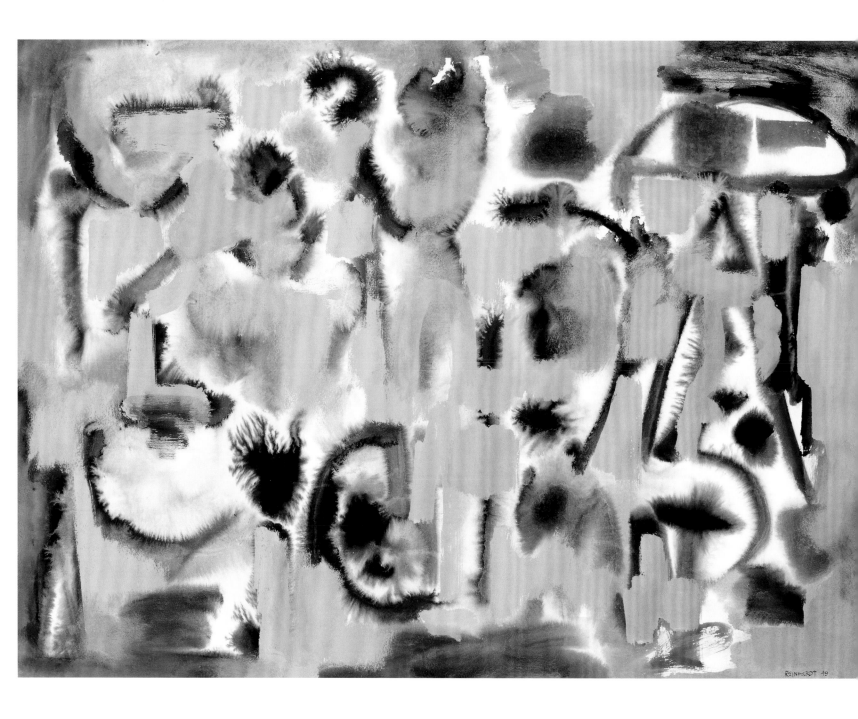

BORN ADOLPH Frederick Reinhardt, he studied at the National Academy of Design in New York City (1936) before joining the American Abstract Artists, an avant-garde group which advocated hard-edged abstraction. He soon broke away from this New York group, whose brand of Abstract Expressionism he found alien to him. Instead he was attracted to the art of India, seeking to develop a style that would be 'breathless, timeless, styleless, lifeless, deathless, endless'. To his way of thinking, Oriental art rejected anything that was 'irrational, momentary, spontaneous, primitive, expressionist…' Consequently he developed a geometric form of abstraction, but contact with Rothko and Newman in the 1940s led him to concentrate on canvasses covered with paint on which he worked up rectangles of different sizes. Out of this arose his Minimalist art, which would be highly influential in the 1960s.

Sir Stanley Spencer Angels of the Apocalypse, 1949

Born 1891 England   Painted in Cookham and Port Glasgow, Scotland   Died 1959 Cookham
MOVEMENT: Modern English School   **OTHER WORKS:** *The Resurrection, The Crucifixion, Self-Portrait with Patricia* **INFLUENCES:** Pre-Raphaelites

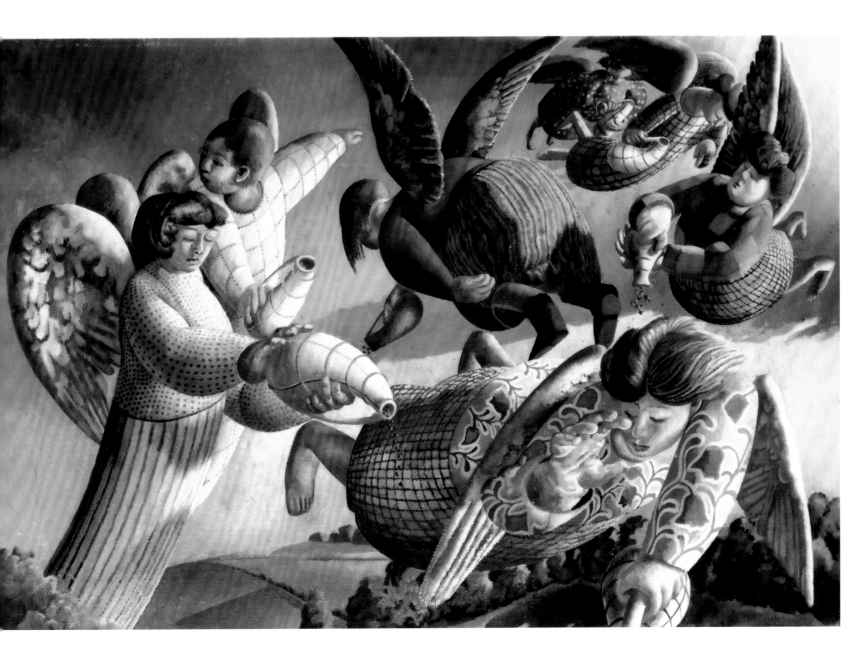

STANLEY SPENCER spent most of his life in the Berkshire village of Cookham, which provided him with most of his inspiration. He studied at the Slade School of Art in London from 1909 to 1912 but appears not to have been affected by any of the avant-garde developments in that period. Apart from military service in World War I, and a period during World War II spent on Clydeside recording the toil of shipyards, he remained very close to his roots – a familiar sight in Cookham, painting or sketching. Often dismissed as an eccentric, he worked outside the artistic mainstream, but inevitably some trends in art found a reflection in his paintings, notably his use of distorted anatomy and space. A profoundly religious man, his paintings often have biblical connotations, although events such as the Resurrection are placed in the context of Cookham or Clydeside. He covered his enormous canvasses with drawings of the subjects, which were then painted over. He was knighted shortly before he died.

Lucio Fontana   Spatial Concept, 1950

Born 1899 Argentina   Painted in Italy   Died 1968 Varese, Italy
MOVEMENT: Italian Abstract School   **OTHER WORKS:** *Spatial Concept, New York 15, The End of God*   **INFLUENCES:** Yves Klein, Mark Rothko

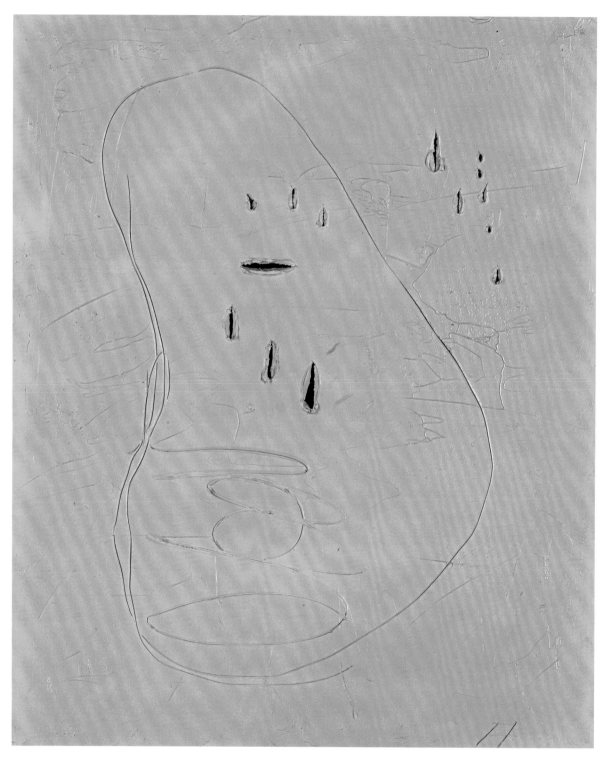

BORN IN Argentina of Italian parents, Lucio Fontana was raised in Milan, where he studied art at the Brera Academy from 1927 to 1930. Five years later he was a signatory of the First Manifesto of Italian Abstract Artists. In the early part of his artistic career he concentrated on sculpture and did not turn to painting until after World War II, when he began producing canvasses in which he used a very restricted range of colours, verging on monochrome effects. In 1946 he produced his White Manifesto, launching a series of paintings in shades of white. He really came to prominence a year later when he developed a style which he called Spatialism, in which cuts and slashes in the canvas were combined with a plain painted surface, bringing a new dimension to bear on Minimal Art. The apparent simplicity of his paintings was deceptive and they had a profound influence on a later generation of conceptual artists.

Willem De Kooning   Woman, 1950

Born 1904 Holland   Painted in New York, USA   Died 1997 New York
MOVEMENT: Abstract Expressionism   **OTHER WORKS:** *The Visit, Marilyn Monroe*   **INFLUENCES:** Arshile Gorky, Adolph Gottlieb

BORN IN the Netherlands, Willem de Kooning was apprenticed to a firm of commercial artists at the tender age of 12 but shortly after receiving his diploma from the Rotterdam Academy of Fine Arts in 1925 he emigrated to the United States and settled in New York, where he worked as a house painter and commercial artist. From the early 1930s he shared a studio with Arshile Gorky and made painting a full-time career from about 1936. Through Gorky he was introduced to Surrealism, reflected in the predominantly black and white paintings of his early period. In the immediate postwar period, under the influence of Adolph Gottlieb, he turned to colour and painted female figures, tending towards Abstract Expressionism. He became one of the foremost exponents of this movement, especially as expressed in his action paintings. In the last years of his long life, however, he turned to modelling figures in clay.

Hale Woodruff   Afro Emblems, 1950

Born 1900 Cairo, Illinois, USA   Painted in Alabama, Georgia and Tennessee   Died 1980 USA
MOVEMENT: African American School   **OTHER WORKS:** *The Mutiny Aboard the Amistad, Leda, Landscape with Green Sun*   **INFLUENCES:** Diego Rivera, José Clemente Orozco

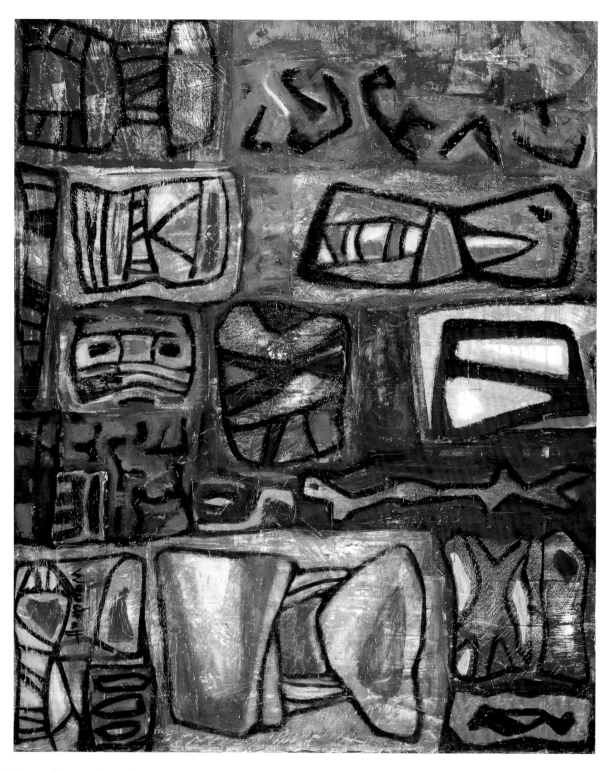

ALTHOUGH BORN IN Illinois, Hale Woodruff was raised in Tennessee and witnessed the persecution of African Americans at close quarters. He studied at the John Herron Art Institute in Indianapolis and won a Harmon scholarship that enabled him to continue his studies at the Académie de la Grande Chaumière in Paris (1927–31). His later Expressionist paintings reflect the influence of this period. On his return to America he taught at Atlanta and New York Universities. He was one of the foremost creators of large murals on an epic scale, illustrating episodes in the history of African Americans, notably the Amistad Mutiny panels for the Savery Library of Talladega College, Alabama. The Amistad mutiny was a defining moment in the history of Black Americans and it was the turning point in Woodruff's career. Subsequent murals were commissioned for Atlanta University but in the latter part of his working life Woodruff turned from representational painting to Abstract Expressionism.

Norman Rockwell   Saying Grace, 1951

Born 1894 New York, USA   Painted in USA   Died 1978

MOVEMENT: Realist **OTHER WORKS:** *Are We Downhearted?* **INFLUENCES:** N.C. Wyeth, J.C. Leyendecker and Howard Pyle

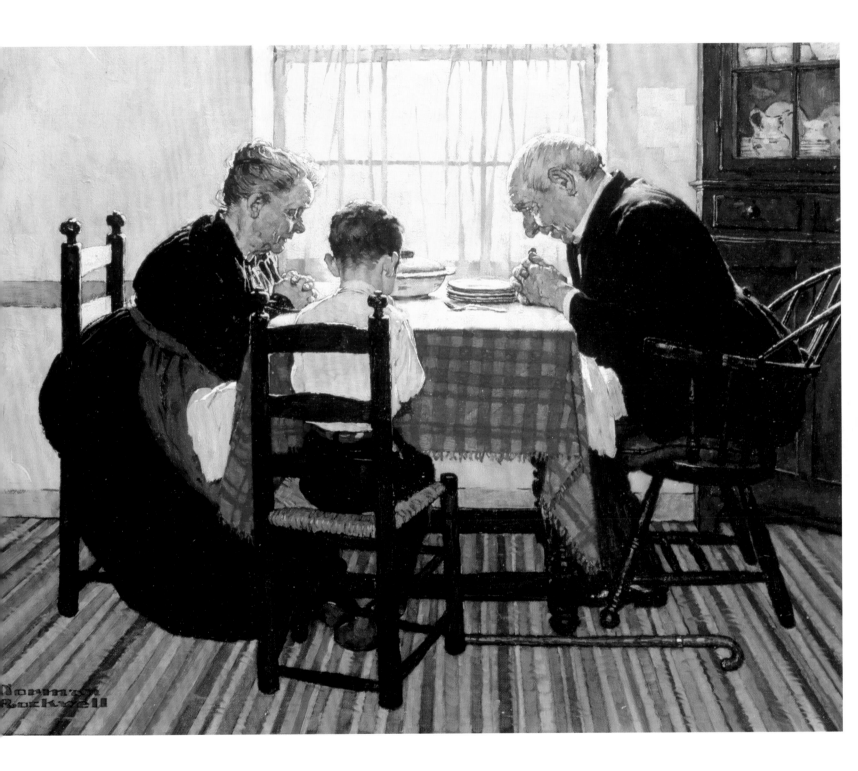

WHILE JACKSON Pollock and Abstract Expressionism gained wide press coverage in the late 1940s and early 1950s, Norman Rockwell remained for many Americans the quintessential American artist. Having started his career as an illustrator for the *Saturday Evening Post* in 1916, Rockwell continued to produce countless cover illustrations, charting the changing mood and society in the United States. *Saying Grace* shows Rockwell's meticulously detailed Realist style, representing a family at table, saying a prayer before the evening meal. It is a scene of quiet contemplation and spiritual reverie that extols the virtues of piety and family life. However, it also gently implies that all may not be quite as perfect as it first seems. The youngster is notably dining with his grandparents, raising the question of where his parents might be. Were they victims of the Second World War, when so many American servicemen and women lost their lives? Or did the constant anxieties, long absences and changing standards of social behaviour lead to the break-up of their marriage, as it did for so many at this time? Rockwell offers no answers, but his image certainly encourages us to ask the question.

Hans Hofmann   The Veil in the Mirror, 1952

Born 1880 Weissenburg, Germany   Painted in Munich, Paris and New York   Died 1966, New York

MOVEMENT: Abstract Expressionism   **OTHER WORKS:** *Apparition, Nulli Secundus, The Prey, Exuberance*   **INFLUENCES:** Matisse, Picasso

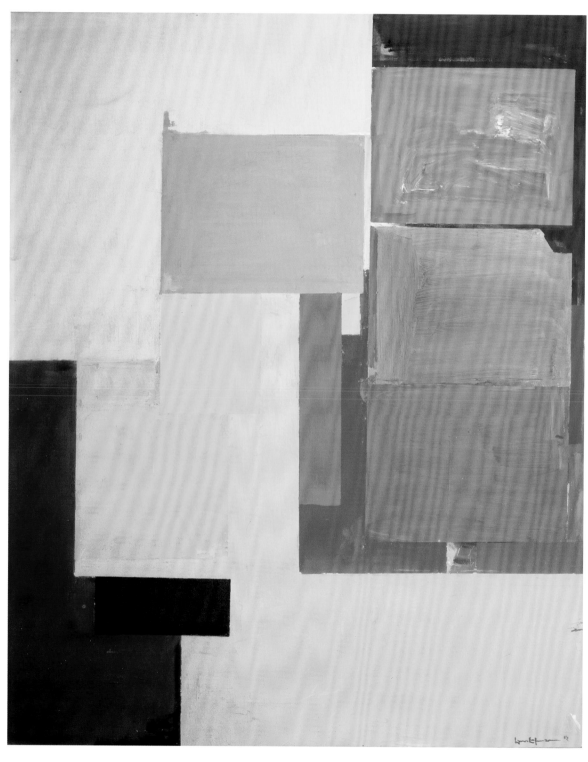

HANS HOFMANN studied art in Munich before settling in Paris at the beginning of the twentieth century. Here he came under the influence of the Impressionists, Fauves and Cubists in turn, imbibing their ideas and selecting the aspects of their art which suited him best. On the outbreak of World War I he returned to Munich, where he established his own art school in 1915. In 1930 he emigrated to the United States where, the following year, he opened the Hofmann School of Fine Art in New York City. He introduced to America the techniques of improvisation, which he had pioneered in Germany. He strove to translate the feelings of the artist into light, colour and form; texture was of major importance and he revelled in exploring this aspect of painting. These experiments conducted over many years finally evolved in the distinctive style which he practiced in America and was to have a profound influence on the development of Abstract Expressionism in his adopted country.

Andrew Wyeth   Christina's World, 1948

Born 1917 Chadds Ford, Pennsylvania, USA   Painted in Pennsylvania and Maine
MOVEMENT: Regionalism   **OTHER WORKS:** *In the Sauna, Up in the Studio, Field Hand, That Gentleman*   **INFLUENCES:** Winslow Homer, Thomas Eakins, Grant Wood

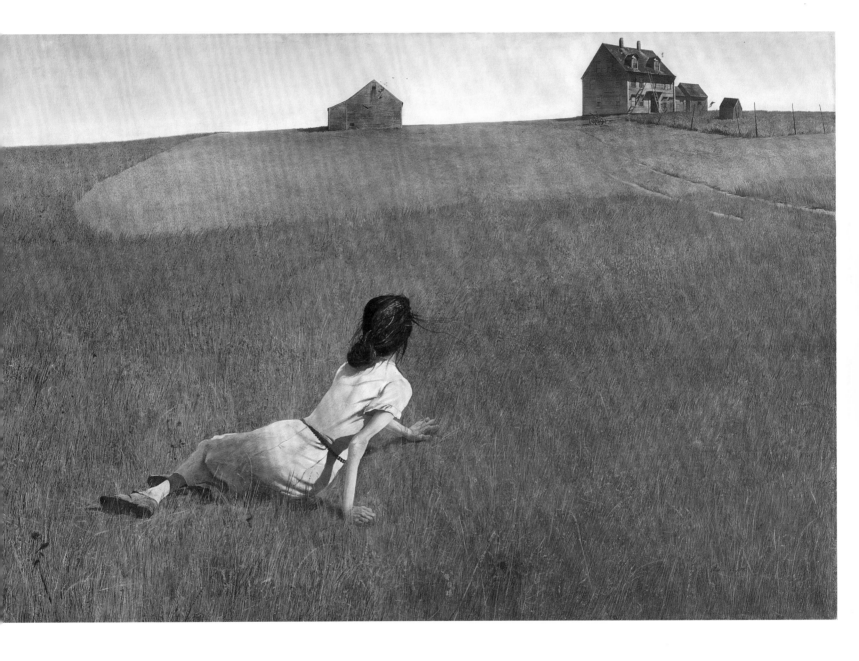

ANDREW NEWEL Wyeth studied under his father, the book illustrator Newel Convers Wyeth, closely following his style until 1945, when his father was killed in a level-crossing accident. The sense of bereavement led Wyeth to change his artistic direction and concentrate on landscapes, executed mainly in drybrush watercolours or tempera rather than oils. Both methods are slow and laborious and

Wyeth even went to the length of mixing his own pigments, often combining them with earth to achieve the special subdued tones that are characteristic of his pictures. Like Grant Wood and other Regionalists, he was concerned to depict the ordinary people and scenes of rural America, particularly in Pennsylvania and Maine. His landscapes often pose a solitary figure against a vast

expanse, conveying an uneasy sense of desolation and pathos. His paintings have a compelling realism, almost photographic in their painstaking detail.

Christina's World empathetically depicts Wyeth's friend Christina Olson. Crippled with polio, she is shown dragging herself along towards the house on the distant horizon. The work is one of the best-known and widely reproduced of all American paintings.

Josef Albers Homage, 1954

Born 1888 Bottrup, Germany   Painted in Germany, USA   Died 1976 New Haven, Connecticut, USA

MOVEMENT: Abstract Expressionism **OTHER WORKS:** *Skyscrapers, Homage to the Square: Blue Climate, Apparition* **INFLUENCES:** Walter Gropius, Kandinsky

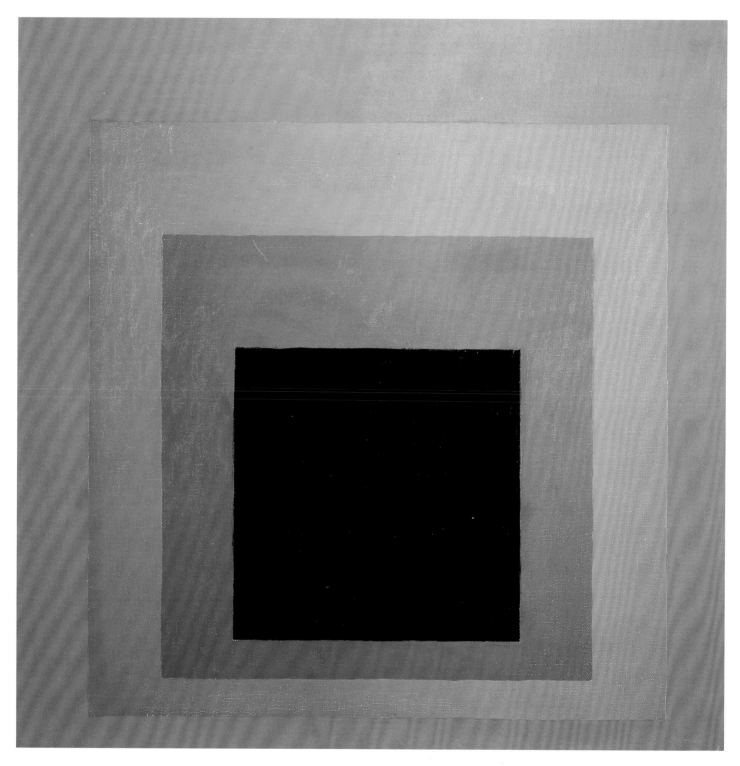

ALBERS TRAINED in the prevailing German academic tradition, at the art schools of Berlin, Essen and Munich. He combined their discipline in draughtsmanship with his own imaginative flair and innovative approach when he continued his studies at the Bauhaus in Weimar, subsequently working as an abstract painter and furniture designer. The advent of the Nazi regime forced him to leave Germany and settle in the United States, where he developed a style that gave free rein to the exploration of colours and their relationship to each other. He held a series of important academic appointments, at the avant-garde Black Mountain College, North Carolina (1933–49) and at Yale University (1950–60). His work became increasingly non-figurative, and in the 1950s culminated in purely geometric canvasses, notably in his series entitled *Homage to the Square*. He was also one of the foremost colour theorists of the immediate post-war period, publishing a seminal work on the subject in 1963 which was influential in the subsequent rise of geometric abstract painting.

Alberto Giacometti Annette Assise, 1954

Born 1901 Switzerland Painted in Paris Died 1966 Chur, Switzerland

MOVEMENT: Surrealism **OTHER WORKS:** *Jean Genet, Portrait of Yanaihara* **INFLUENCES:** Bourdelle, Antoine, Andre Breton

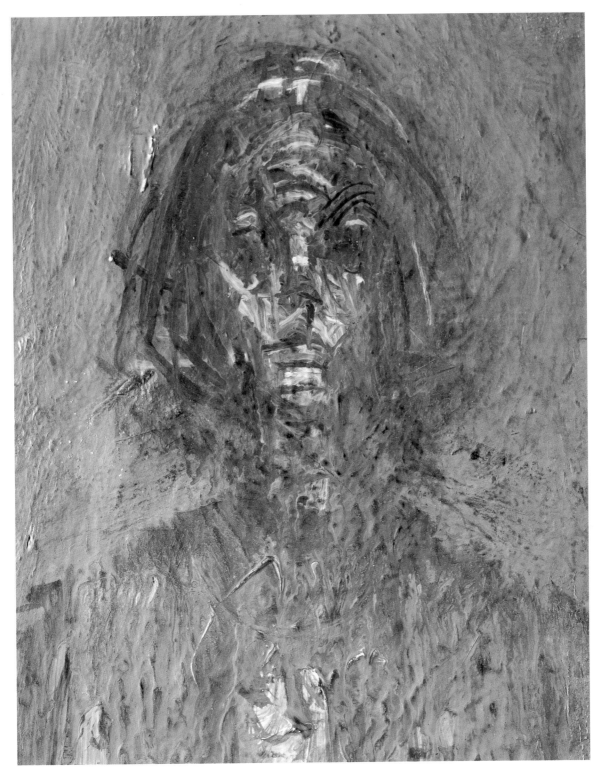

ALBERTO GIACOMETTI studied in Geneva but worked mostly in Paris, where he settled in 1922, working for some time primarily as a sculptor with Antoine Bourdelle. He moved in the intellectual circle dominated by Jean-Paul Sartre and was an enthusiastic disciple of Existentialism. In his painting he was originally drawn to the Cubists but in 1930 he embraced Surrealism as preached by André Breton, although he was expelled from the movement five years later. This was a defining moment, which resulted in a radical departure from previous styles and the evolution of strange, wraith-like figures. Although he is best remembered as a sculptor for his semi-abstract bronzes such as the *Thin Man* series and even more skeletal, spidery figures of the immediate postwar period, the same qualities are evident in his paintings – mostly portraits of real people executed in an abstract fashion.

Sir Sidney Nolan   Ned Kelly, 1955

Born 1917 Australia   Painted in Australia, Greece, North Africa and England   Died 1992 London, England
MOVEMENT: Modern Australian School   **OTHER WORKS:** *Burke and Wills Expedition 'Gray Sick', The Leda Suite*   **INFLUENCES:** R.B. Kitaj, Arthur Boyd

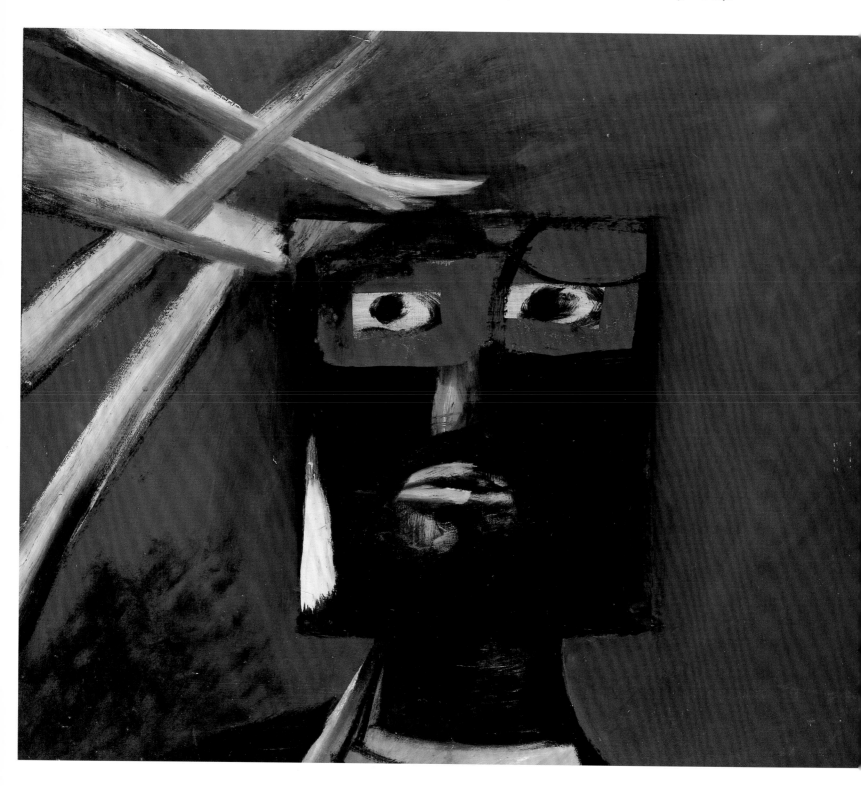

SIDNEY ROBERT Nolan had no formal art training. A self-taught amateur, he took up full-time professional painting in 1938, experimenting with abstract forms before turning in the early 1940s to the subject which would make him famous, the exploits of the bush-ranger Ned Kelly and his gang. This series of paintings, executed in a naive style, was followed by canvasses charting the exploits of the explorers Burke and Wills in the mid-nineteenth century. He travelled to Europe in 1950, studying the art of Italy and working in Greece and North Africa before settling in London where he continued to paint, developing a more mature style which combined figuration with the abstract. He designed sets for a number of Covent Garden operas and ballets from 1962 onwards. He also worked as a book illustrator and in 1972 published a volume of his own poetry illustrated with drawings and paintings. He was knighted in 1981.

Antonio Berni   Los Emigrantes, 1956

Born 1907 Buenos Aires, Argentina   Painted in France and Argentina   Died 1981 Buenos Aires

MOVEMENT: Modern Latin American School   **OTHER WORKS:** *Desocupados (Unemployed), Manifestación (Demonstration)*   **INFLUENCES:** Giorgio de Chirico, Surrealism

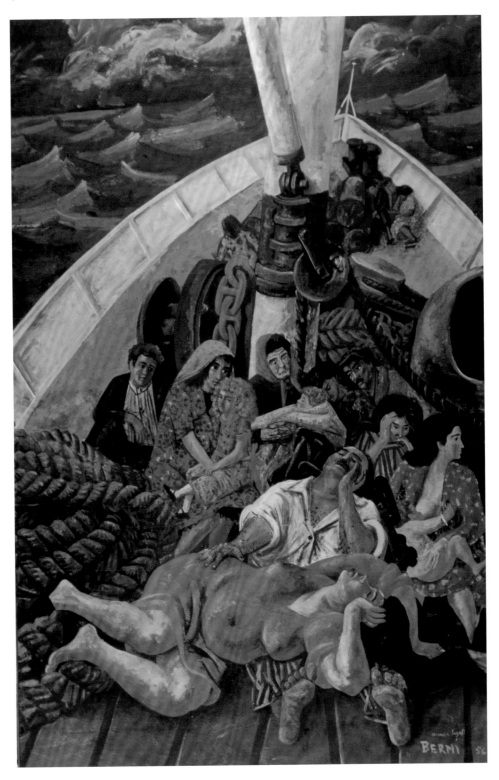

AFTER A CONVENTIONAL art training in Buenos Aires, Antonio Berni travelled to Paris, where he continued his studies under Othon Friesz and André Lhote. With a number of other young Argentinian artists in the late 1920s formed the Grupo de Paris, through whom he also came under the influence of the Surrealists, De Chirico's Pittura Metafisica and the Italian muralists of the fifteenth century. More importantly, perhaps, he also imbibed the Marxist politics of the inter-war period and the course of the Spanish Civil War left a deep impression on him. On his return to Argentina he embarked on Surrealist works that concentrated on social themes ideally suited to the rugged material and technique. For these he used burlap (rough canvas) painted with distemper. The unusual perspective, foreshortened figures and a technique borrowed from film stills and religious icons combined to make his paintings truly distinctive.

Fateh Moudarres Prayer for the Rain

Born 1922 Aleppo, Syria Painted in Damascus, Rome and Paris
MOVEMENT: Modern Syrian School **OTHER WORKS:** *Christ the Child of Palestine* **INFLUENCES:** Salvador Dali

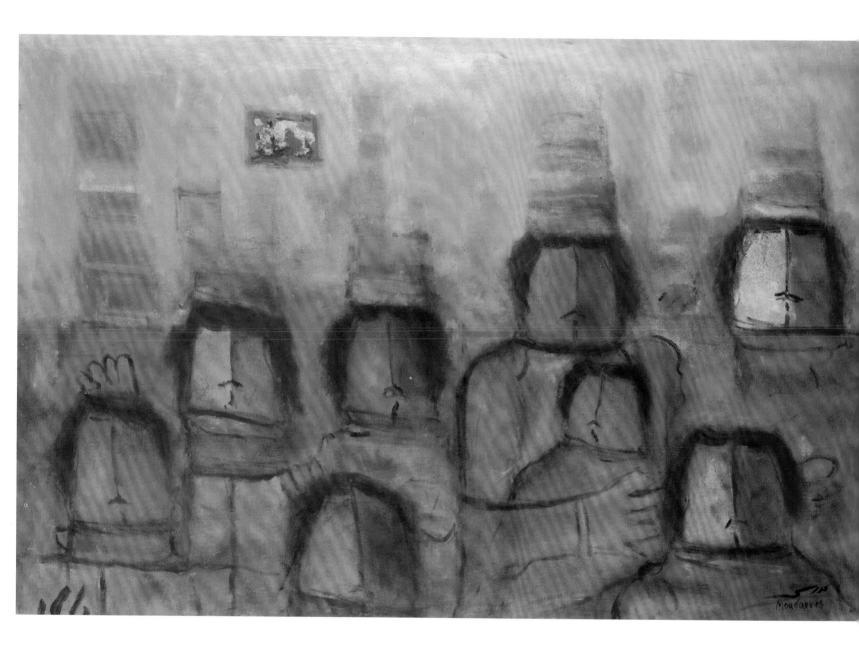

ORIGINALLY A self-taught painter working in a realistic style, Fateh Moudarres subsequently came under the spell of the Surrealists and took part in public exhibitions, at which he explained his paintings in verse. Between 1954 and 1960 he studied at the Accademia di Belle Arti in Rome and on returning to Syria he developed a style which he describes as 'surrealistic and figurative with a strong element of abstraction'. Powerful influences in his work are the icons of the Orthodox Church and Syriac art, but from the early 1960s onwards his painting became increasingly abstract. Due to contemporary events, however, he returned to a more representational style from 1967 onwards, painting works with a strong political theme. A period in Paris (1969–72) studying at the École des Beaux Arts has resulted in a much more confident touch, with greater technical mastery of composition and colour. As Professor of Fine Arts in the University of Damascus, Moudarres has been a major influence over the rising generation of Syrian artists.

Jean–Paul Riopelle Composition (non–representational), 1958

Born 1923 Montreal, Quebec, Canada   Painted in Canada and France   Died 2002 Île-aux-Grues, Quebec
MOVEMENT: Modern Canadian School **OTHER WORKS:** *Green Parrot, Composition, Blue Night, Pavane* **INFLUENCES:** Paul-Emile Borduas, Marcel Duchamp

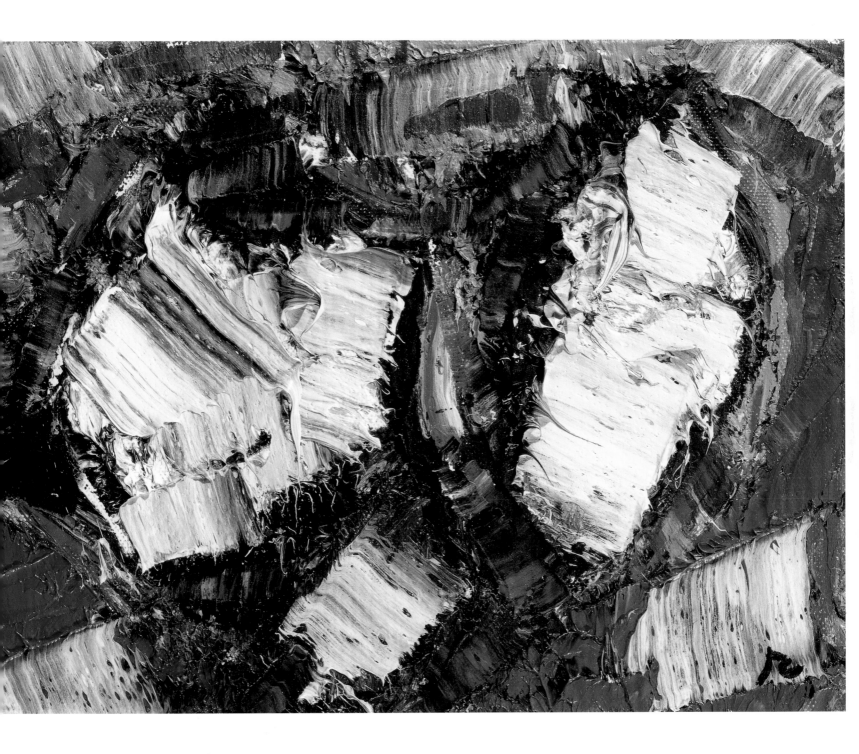

ALTHOUGH HE painted landscapes from early childhood, Riopelle studied at the Montreal Polytechnic (1939–41), but later concentrated for some time on architecture. In 1943 he resumed his art studies at the Montreal École des Beaux Arts and the École du Meuble, where he studied furniture design. Under the influence of Paul-Emile Borduas he developed an interest in Abstraction, Surrealism and mechanical techniques used by the group of French-Canadian artists known as Les Automatistes. In 1947 he settled in Paris, where he came into close contact with Duchamp and the other Surrealists. For a time he painted in the tachiste manner, but after 1950 he evolved a technique in which blobs of paint were squeezed direct from the tube on to the canvas, then about 1953 he turned to the palette knife to create almost sculptural effects. In turn this was followed by a fragmented, mosaic effect, which eventually gave way to a more representational style. From 1958 onwards he also modelled figures, cast in bronze. From 1970 he experimented with collages, employing a wide range of materials and techniques.

Francisco Amighetti   El Monge, c.1960s

Born 1907 San José, Costa Rica   Painted in Costa Rica
MOVEMENT: Modern Latin American School   **OTHER WORKS:** *Toro y Gente (Bull and People)*   **INFLUENCES:** Japanese ukiyo-e prints

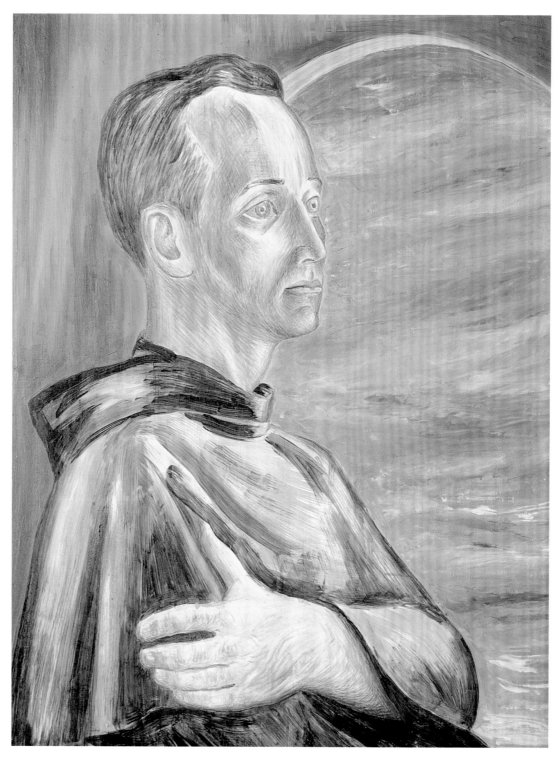

COSTA RICA was not a country with a rich artistic tradition, and something like a national school did not emerge till the end of the nineteenth century, when the development of the coffee trade gave rise to an affluent middle class, stimulated by contact with North America and Europe. At first painting tended to follow Neoclassicist lines, influenced by Spanish and German artists who taught in San José. The dead hand of the stereotyped Classicism was not removed until the 1920s when the so-called 'nationalist generation' of artists received their training at the Escuela de Bellas Artes. Amighetti, however, is largely self-taught but absorbed the stylistic development from Mexico, the United States and Europe (notably German Expressionism) as well as Japanese prints, evolving his own regional brand of painting to chronicle the everyday life of the Costa Rican peasantry in a luminous style which has been dubbed Creole Impressionism. Figures, animals and colourful adobe houses are painted in a style that mirrors his preoccupation with social problems.

Francis Bacon Seated Figure (Red Cardinal), 1960

Born 1909 Dublin Painted in Britain, France and South Africa Died 1992

MOVEMENT: School of London **OTHER WORKS:** *Sleeping Figure, Man with Dog* **INFLUENCES:** Picasso, Velázquez, Mathis Grünewald, Eadweard Muybridge

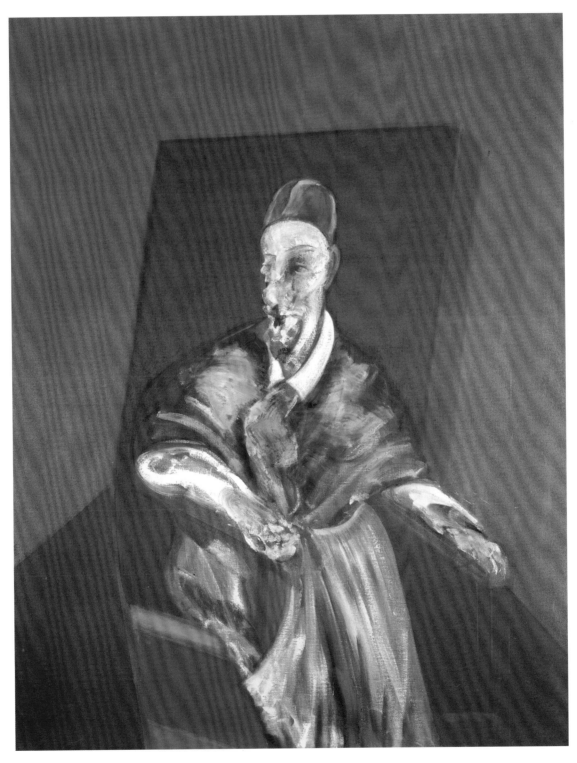

BORN IN Dublin of English parents, Bacon left home at the age of 15, travelling to London, Berlin and Paris. In Paris he visited a Picasso exhibition, which inspired him to paint. In 1929, Bacon settled in London, where he designed Bauhaus-style furnishings and later, during wartime, joined the Civil Defence. His breakthrough as an artist came in 1945, when his *Three Studies for Figures at the Base of a Crucifixion*

caused a sensation at the Lefevre Gallery. In this, as in many of his future works, elements of mutilation, pain and claustrophobia combined to create a highly disturbing effect.

From 1946 to 1950, Bacon resided in Monte Carlo, partly to satisfy his passion for gambling. His international reputation growing, he returned to London. His source material was very diverse, ranging

from the work of other artists (Velázquez, Van Gogh) to films and photographs (Muybridge, Eisenstein) and autobiographical details. His studies of caged, screaming figures, for example, are often viewed as a reference to his asthma. Bacon's prevailing theme, however, is the vulnerability and solitude of the human condition.

Arthur Boyd   Expulsion 1960

Born 1920 Victoria, Australia   Painted in Australia and England   Died 1999
MOVEMENT: Australian Realism **OTHER WORKS:** *Shearers Playing for a Bride, The Mockers* **INFLUENCES:** Van Gogh, Oskar Kokoschka, Brueghel

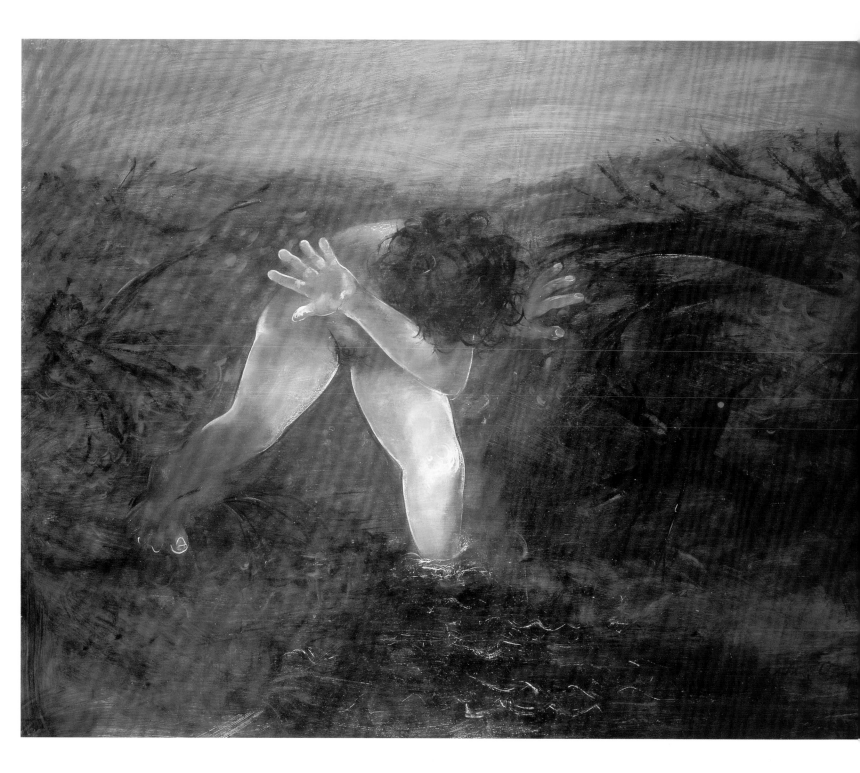

ARTHUR MERRIC Bloomfield Boyd was born at Murrumbeena, Victoria, the younger son of the New Zealand-born painter Merric Boyd (1862-1940). He studied at the National Gallery of Victoria Art School, Melbourne, and at the Rosebud, Victoria. After war service he returned to Murrumbeena to work with his father and brother-in-law, John Perceval. From 1959 to 1972 he worked in London before becoming Fellow in Creative Arts at the University of Canberra. Although schooled in the Australian tradition, he came under European influence at an early age, both Van Gogh and Kokoschka being major sources of inspiration, which have given Boyd's paintings a more cosmopolitan character. Some of his more radical, avant-garde paintings were even confiscated by the Australian authorities during World War II. Later he concentrated on religious works, mixing the landscapes of Victoria with the imagery of Brueghel, Bosch and Stanley Spencer.

Roy Lichtenstein   Kiss II, 1962

Born 1923 New York, USA   Painted in USA   Died 1997 New York
MOVEMENT: Pop Art   **OTHER WORKS:** *In the Car, M-Maybe, Whaam!* **INFLUENCES:** Allan Kaprow

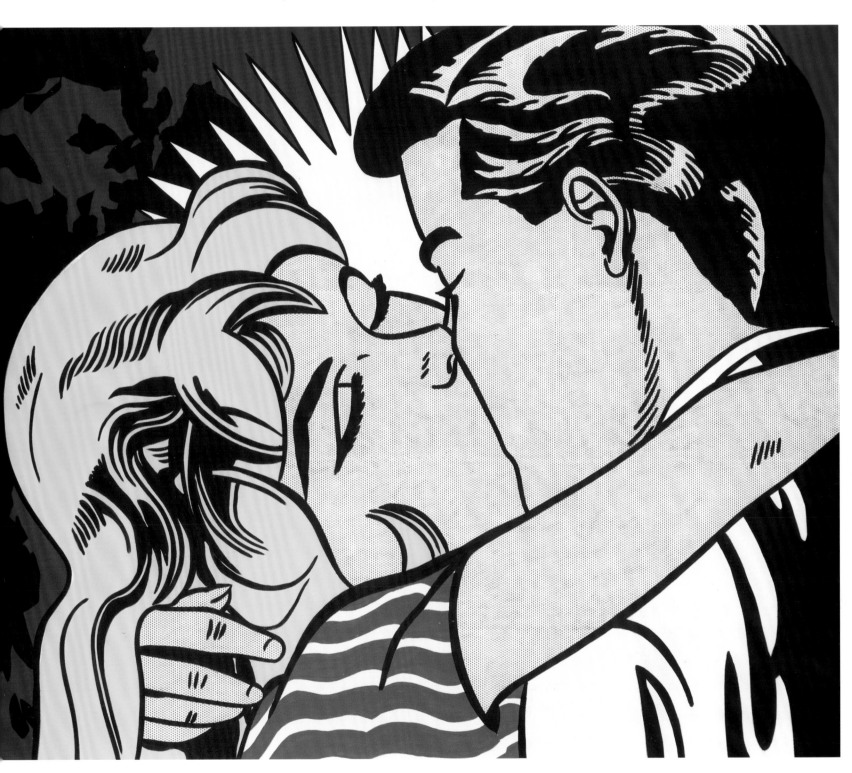

ROY LICHTENSTEIN enrolled at the Art Students' League (1939) and later studied at Ohio State College. After military service (1943–46) he returned to Ohio State as a teacher, and later taught at New York State and Rutgers Universities. He began exhibiting in 1949, his early works inspired by aspects of American history, strongly influenced by Cubism, though later he tended towards Abstract Expressionism. While teaching at Rutgers he met Allan Kaprow, who opened his eyes to the artistic possibilities inherent in consumerism and from about 1960 he developed what later came to be known as Pop Art, in which images are painted in the style of the comic strip. Even the dots of the screening process used in the production of comic books is meticulously reproduced in Lichtenstein's highly stylized paintings.

Antoni Tàpies   Black with Four Grey Corners, 1960

Born 1923 Barcelona, Spain   Painted in Barcelona

MOVEMENT: Modern Spanish School **OTHER WORKS:** *Violet Grey with Wrinkles, Perforated Body, Peintre Grise et Verte* **INFLUENCES:** Alberto Burri, Robert Motherwell, Miró, Jean Fautrier

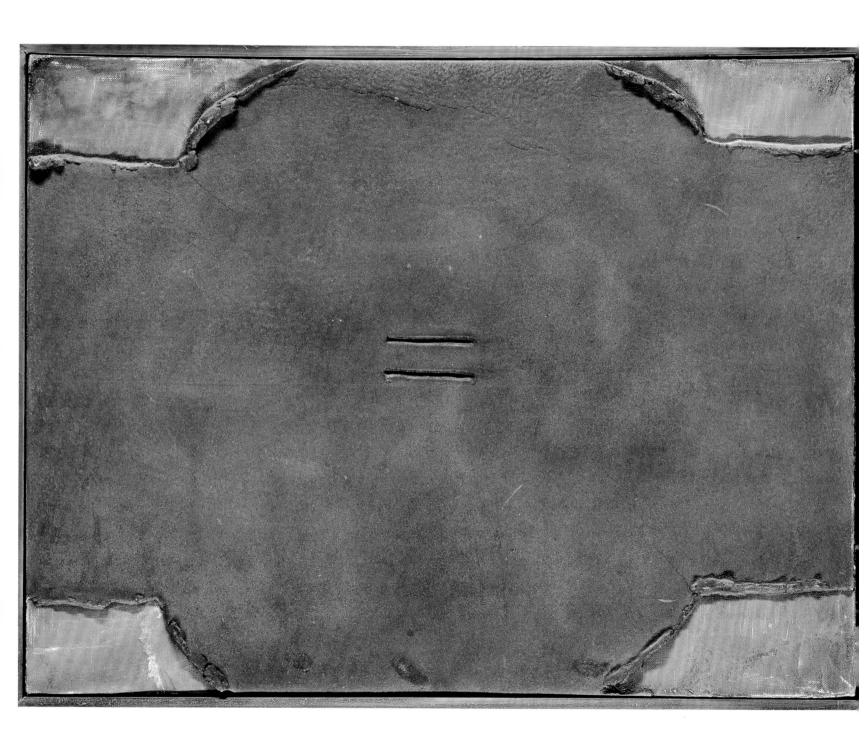

ANTONI TÀPIES studied law in Barcelona in 1943–46 but then gave up his studies to concentrate on painting, in which he was almost entirely self-taught. He became a founder member of the Catalan group of avant-garde writers and artists known as Dau al Set ('Seven on the Die'). His paintings reflect a diversity of influences, from the abstract radicalism of Catalonia in the Civil War period to the philosophy of the Surrealists and the lyrical qualities of Robert Motherwell and Joan Miro. He had his first one-man show in America in 1953 and thereafter made an impact on the international scene, winning many prizes. Since 1955 he has concentrated on 'matter' painting, influenced by such French artists as Fautrier. At first this consisted of mixing paints and varnish with unusual substances such as marble dust, pieces of cloth, straw and strips of metal. Taking this to its logical conclusion he eventually replaced canvas with solid objects, as in his 'Desk with Straw'.

Sonia Delaunay   Rythme Couleur, 1961

Born 1885 Gradizhsk, Ukraine   Painted in France   Died 1979 Paris, France
MOVEMENT: Orphism, Cubism   **OTHER WORKS:** *Girls in Swimming Costumes*   **INFLUENCES:** Robert Delaunay, Kandinsky

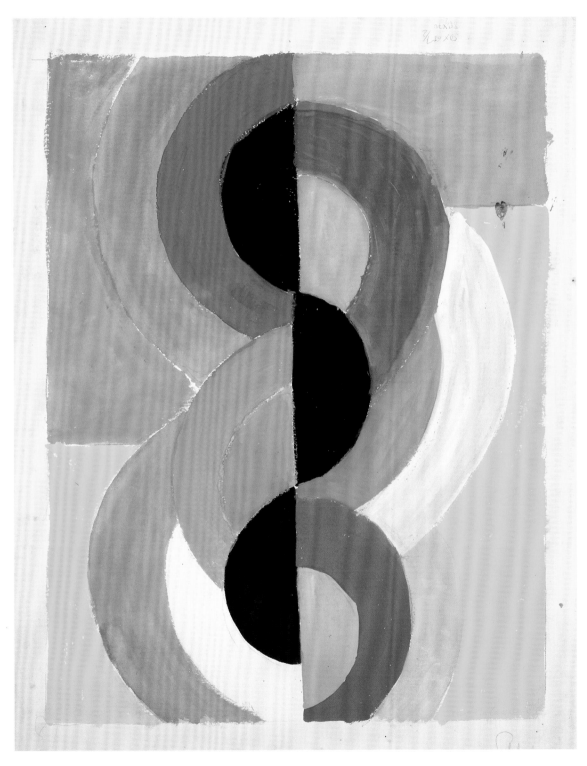

BORN SONIA Terk Stern at Gradizhsk in the Ukraine, she was raised in St Petersburg and studied art in Karlsruhe, Germany and then, in 1905, attended the Académie de la Palette in Paris. In order to remain in France, in 1909 she contracted a marriage of convenience with the art critic Wilhelm Uhde but it was dissolved after a few months. In 1910 she married the French painter Robert Delaunay (1885–1941) with whom she founded the movement known as Orphism. Together they designed and painted sets and costumes for Diaghilev's Ballets Russes. Robert is chiefly remembered for his endless experiments in colour orchestration, which had a profound effect on abstract art, while Sonia concentrated on Art Deco textile designs. In the interwar period she also evolved a purity of expression using brightly contrasting colours in her paintings (mainly in watercolours) that influenced her textile designs and vice versa.

Richard Diebenkorn   Ocean Park No. 27, 1970

Born 1922 Portland, Oregon, USA   Painted in Oregon and California   Died 1993

MOVEMENT: Modern American School/Abstract Art   **OTHER WORKS:** *Seated Nude Black Background, Berkely series, City Scape*   **INFLUENCES:** Matisse, Willem de Kooning, Piet Mondrian

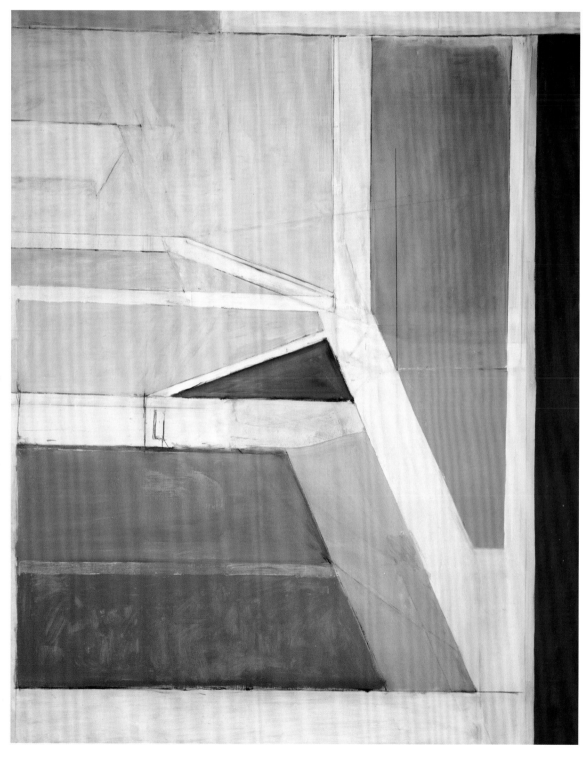

NO OTHER painter has so successfully created a body of work that is fundamentally abstract, yet simultaneously captures a sense of locale, as Richard Diebenkorn. Diebenkorn spent his entire life and career on the west coast of the United States. Whilst a student at the California School of Fine Arts he worked alongside the Abstract Expressionists Mark Rothko (1903–70) and Clyfford Still (1904–80), and his early works followed this Colour Field trend. In the late 1950s, however, he also produced a number of figurative works influenced by both Hopper and Henri Matisse (1869–1954). It was not until 1967 that he began to produce the *Ocean Park* series for which he is best known. In these works, Diebenkorn presents large, flat areas of colour that recall the hard-edged abstraction of Ellsworth Kelly (b. 1923). However, Diebenkorn softens this effect by using sun-bleached cobalt blues, greens and yellows, each colour gently modulated by his transparent brushwork. In this way, his works radiate warmth and invoke the Santa Monica coastline, with the sun setting over the Pacific.

Norman Lewis   Evening Rendezvous, 1962

Born 1909 New York, USA   Painted in New York   Died 1979 New York

MOVEMENT: Abstract Expressionism   **OTHER WORK:** *Yellow Hat, Ovum, Processional, Every Atom Glows*   **INFLUENCES:** Augusta Savage

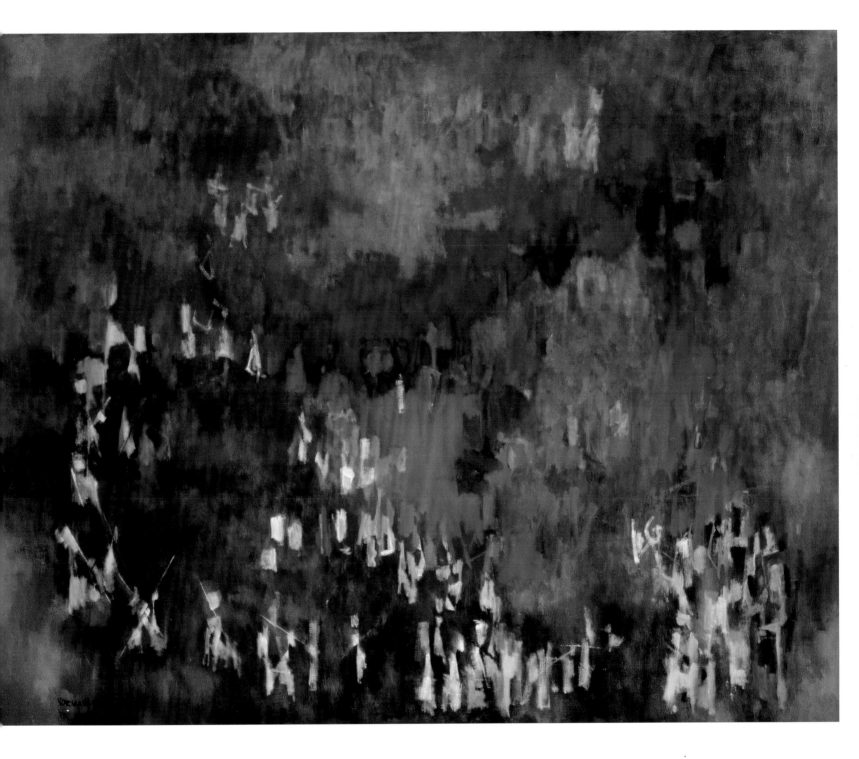

BORN IN New York Norman Lewis was one of the few natives of that city to gain early prominence as the artistic chronicler of African American life in Harlem. Under the WPA scheme of the 1930s, he was able to study at Columbia University and was later a pupil of Augusta Savage. His WPA assignment consisted of the decorations of the Harlem Art Centre, which put him in touch with other black American artists. In the late 1930s he began painting in a semi-abstract manner, reducing the human figure to geometric lines. Later he veered towards Abstract Expressionism. In the 1960s he belonged to the Spiral Group, which gave artistic interpretation to the civil rights movement. In 1971, while working at the Art Students' League, he formed the Cinque Gallery with Ernie Crichlow and Romare Bearden, with the aim of exhibiting the art of young people from ethnic minorities.

Andy Warhol   Shot Red Marilyn, 1964

Born 1928   Painted in USA   Died 1987
MOVEMENT: Pop Art   **OTHER WORKS:** *Campbell's Soup Can, Marilyn Monroe, Brillo*   **INFLUENCES:** Roy Lichtenstein, Jasper Johns

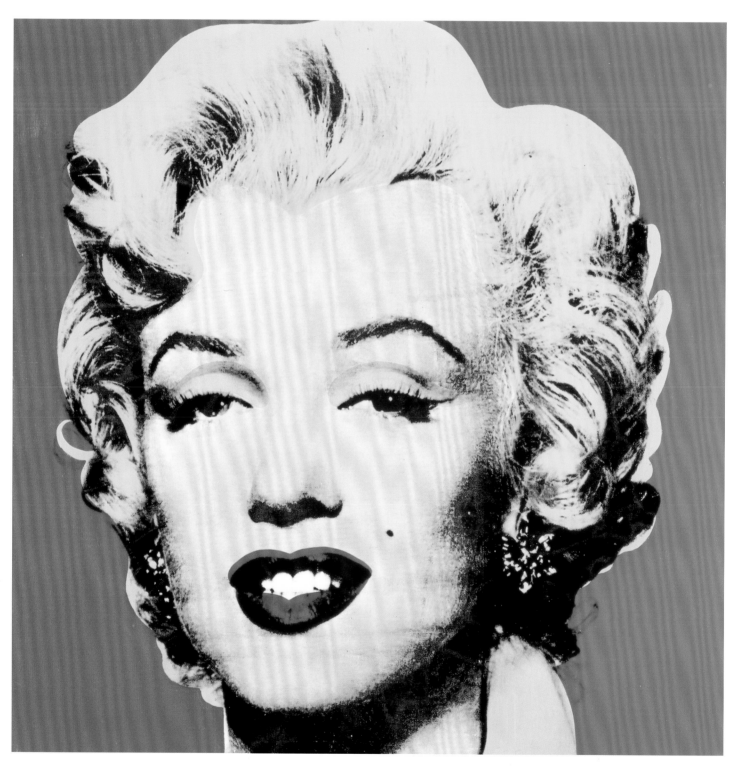

AMERICAN ARTIST specializing in printmaking and films. Warhol was born in Pittsburgh, the son of Czech immigrants. In 1949 he moved to New York, where he became a successful commercial artist. This gave him a solid grounding in silkscreen printing techniques and taught him the value of self-promotion – both of which were to feature heavily in his art. Warhol's breakthrough came when he began to make paintings of familiar, everyday objects, such as soup cans, dollar bills and brillo pads. Early examples were hand-painted, but Warhol soon decided to use mechanical processes as far as possible. His aim, in this respect, was to free the image from any connotations of craftsmanship, aesthetics or individuality. He further emphasized this by describing his studio as 'The Factory'.

Warhol rapidly extended his references to popular culture by portraying celebrities (Marilyn Monroe, Marlon Brando), as well as more sinister items, such as news clippings with car crashes or the electric chair. He also associated himself with other branches of the mass media, notably through his links with the rock band The Velvet Underground, and through his controversial films.

Jean Dubuffet Cortege, 1965

Born 1901 Le Havre, France   Painted in France   Died 1985 Paris, France
MOVEMENT: Abstract Expressionism   **OTHER WORKS:** *Man with a Hod, Villa sur la Route, Jazz Band*   **INFLUENCES:** Antoni Tapiès, Alberto Giacometti

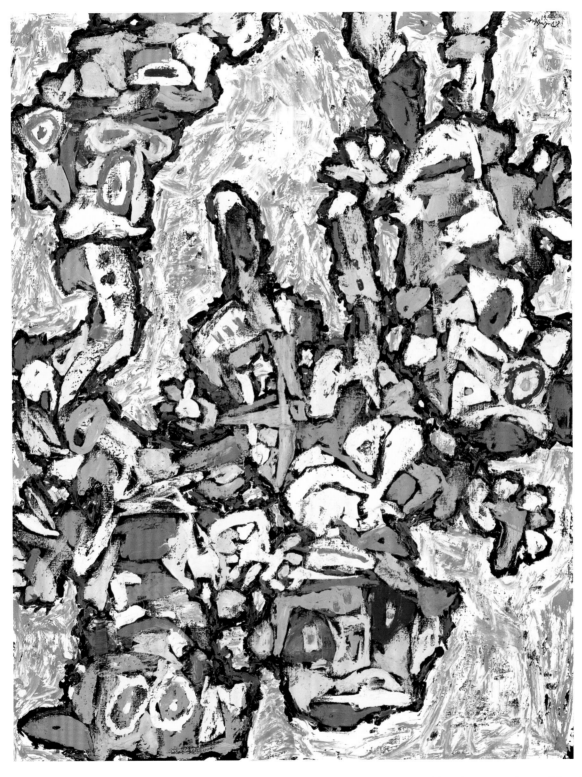

JEAN DUBUFFET studied at the Académie Julien in Paris but, dissatisfied with the styles in 'new art' then being taught, branched out on his own and began exploring unusual materials and the deliberate use of coarse canvas and paint applied roughly. He believed that there was more truth in the art produced by the untrained, the childish or the psychotic and strove to recreate such effects. The synthesis of rough materials with discarded rubbish such as pieces of old newspapers and broken glass resulted in what he termed Art Brut ('raw art'), which was the antithesis of painterly perfection and aesthetic sensitivity. By this means Dubuffet confronted the spectator with the seamier side of life and nature in the raw. Though often derided, he exerted a tremendous influence on the next generation of artists and anticipated the Pop Art and neo-Dadaism of the 1960s.

Jules Olitski   Non–Stop, 1965

Born 1922 Gomel, Russia   Painted in Paris and New York
MOVEMENT: Post-Painterly Abstraction **OTHER WORKS:** *Yaksi Juice, Thigh Smoke, Green Jazz* **INFLUENCES:** Hans Hoffman, Helen Frankenthaler

BORN IN Russia, Jules Olitski studied art in Paris before immigrating to the United States and continuing his studies in New York, where he subsequently taught and worked as a sculptor. By his background and training he thus combined elements of the avant-garde from both sides of the Atlantic. Originally he was strongly influenced by the colour-field painters and the vigorous abstracts of Hans Hoffman. In the 1960s, as many of his contemporaries were turning to Pop Art, he remained true to Abstract Expressionism while, along with Helen Frankenthaler, developing the style which came to be known as Post-Painterly Abstraction. This involved the staining of the canvas with paint in order to avoid brush-strokes. From this he moved on to spraying the canvas with acrylics to achieve a completely smooth surface with central abstract motifs of stridently contrasting colours, often with a narrow surround of bare canvas. Since the late 1970s, however, he has returned to the mainstream, producing thickly textured abstracts more reminiscent of the works of Hoffmann.

Kumi Sugai   Matin de L'Autoroute No 2, 1966

Born 1919 Kobe, Japan   Painted in Kobe, Tokyo, and Paris   Died 1996 Paris
MOVEMENT: Modern Japanese School   **OTHER WORKS:** *The Flying Deer, Devil's Chain, Alea, Printemps*   **INFLUENCES:** Ukiyo-e, Max Pechstein

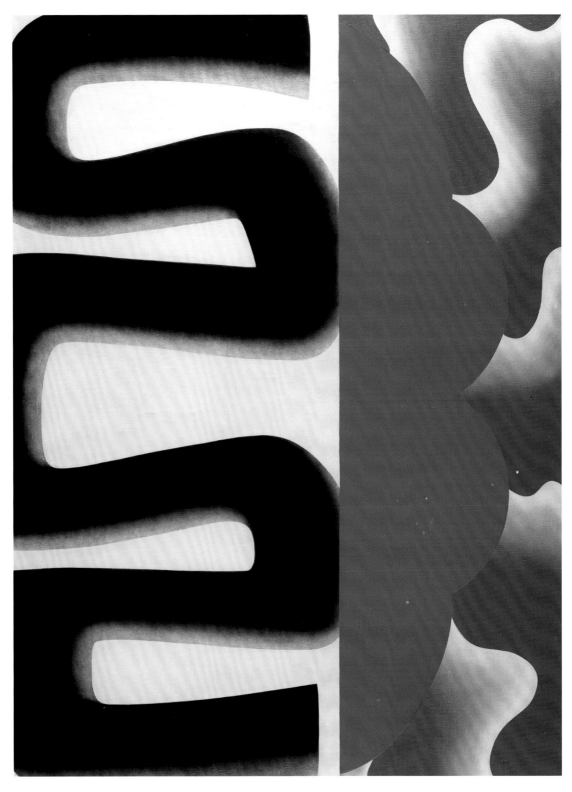

KUMI SUGAI received his early art education in his home town of Kobe, Japan, but after military service in World War II he resumed his studies and travelled to Europe, where he eventually settled in Paris and worked from 1952 onwards as a painter, print-maker and sculptor. After a period producing conventional oils on canvas he concentrated on prints, combining the traditional techniques of the *ukiyo-e* school of Japan with Western ideas and modern materials. Over a period of three decades he produced over 400 different prints. From about 1962 there was a noticeable change in his style, as he adopted the hard-edge geometric imagery of Max Pechstein, a marked contrast to the softer style of his earlier prints, reflecting the influence of the great Japanese masters of the eighteenth and nineteenth centuries.

Marc Chagall   Le Repos, 1967–8

Born 1887 Vitebsk, Russia   Painted in Russia, France and USA   Died 1985 Saint Paul-de-Vence, France
MOVEMENT: Surrealism **OTHER WORKS:** *Above the Town, I and the Village* **INFLUENCES:** Gauguin, The Fauves

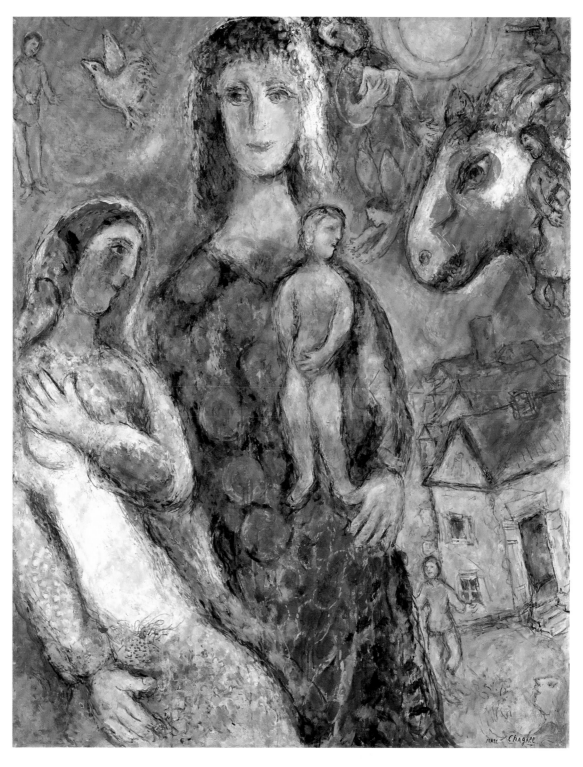

BORN INTO an Orthodox Jewish family in what was then known as Russian Poland, Marc Chagall studied in St Petersburg and Paris and returned to his native city on the eve of World War I. Initially he worked as a sign-writer but on his return to Russia he joined the Knave of Diamond group and participated in their 1917 exhibition, which was intended as an attack on the stuffy classicism of the Moscow School of Art. The Revolution broke out shortly afterwards and Chagall was appointed Director of the Vitebsk Art School before being summoned to Moscow to design sets for the Jewish Theatre. He left Russia in 1922 and settled near Paris. On the outbreak of World War II he moved to the USA where he designed sets and costumes for the ballet, as well as illustrating books and producing stained-glass windows, notably for the UN Building in New York and the Hadassah Hospital in Jerusalem. He also painted the murals for the Knesset (Israeli parliament). His paintings combine fantasy, folklore and biblical themes with an intensely surreal quality. Indeed, it is claimed that Guillaume Apollinaire originally coined the term 'Surrealist' to describe Chagall's paintings.

Hafiz Drubi   The Family, 1967

Born 1914 Baghdad, Iraq   Painted in Baghdad   Died 1991 Iraq

MOVEMENT: Modern Islamic Art   **OTHER WORKS:** *Still Life (oil on canvas, 1979)*   **INFLUENCES:** Picasso, Robert Delaunay, Max Beckmann

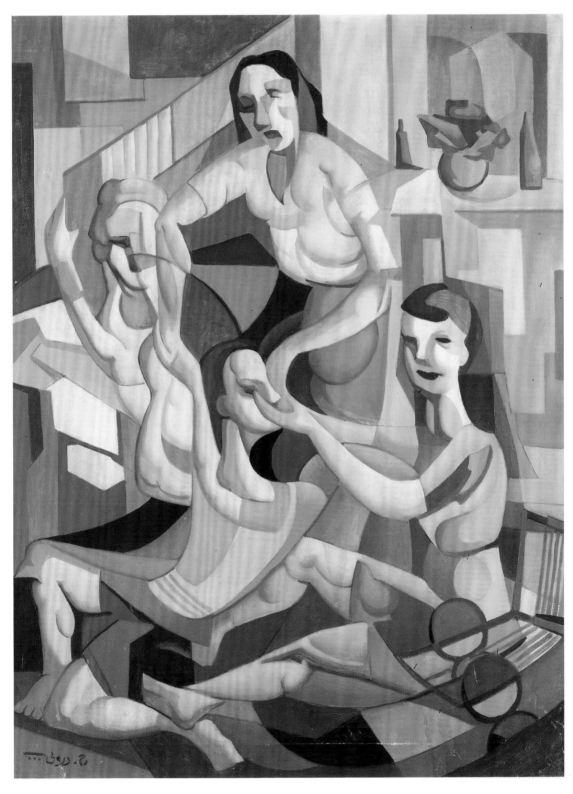

BORN INTO a mercantile family in what was then a provincial backwater of the crumbling Ottoman Empire, Hafiz Drubi had a conventional art education but later came under the influence of the European avant-garde artists of the 1930s and 1940s. He gradually developed his own distinctive style, showing the influence of the Cubists. His paintings reflect his cultural roots in the exuberant display of colour and tone, although the composition is usually in the Western idiom. Little-known outside Iraq, he came to international prominence in the early 1960s, when his paintings were exhibited at Gallery One in Beirut. This gallery, founded by the poet Yusuf al Khal and his Lebanese-American wife Helen, gave many Middle Eastern artists their first real break and established Beirut as the art centre of the Arab world.

Faik Hassan   Two Women, 1967

Born 1914 Baghdad, Iraq   Painted in Baghdad and Paris   Died 1992 Baghdad

MOVEMENT: Modern Iraqi School   **OTHER WORKS:** *Celebration of Victory (Mosaic mural in Baghdad)*   **INFLUENCES:** Picasso, Pierre Bonnard

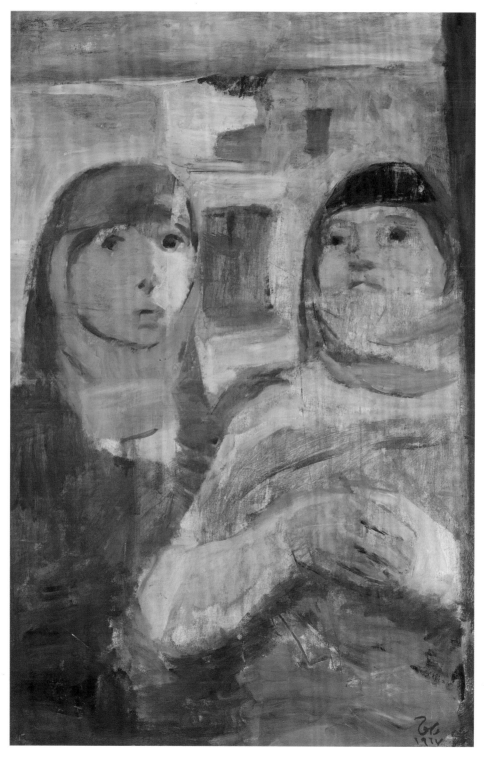

FAIK HASSAN studied at the Institute of Fine Arts in Baghdad, Iraq, then won a scholarship to the École des Beaux-Arts in Paris, from which he graduated in 1938. On his return to Iraq he established and directed the department of painting and sculpture at the Institute of Fine Arts. During his time in France he came under the influence of the Cubists and Impressionists, which are reflected in many of his own paintings, although he also explored abstract art and painted landscapes and genre scenes in a relatively conventional style. He established the Pioneers Group in 1950 but withdrew from it in 1962 and five years later formed the Corners Group (Al Zawiya), whose aim was to serve the nation through their art, hence his many pictures with a strong social or political theme. After Iraq became a republic in 1958 he created the colossal mosaic mural entitled *Celebration of Victory* located in Tiran Square. In the last decade of his life he resumed painting in the Impressionist style.

Fernando Botero   La Visita, 1968

Born 1932 Medellin, Colombia   Painted in Colombia

MOVEMENT: Modern Latin American School   **OTHER WORKS:** *Sunday Afternoon, Colombian Woman*   **INFLUENCES:** Paolo Uccello, Piero della Francesca, Velázquez, Rubens, Goya

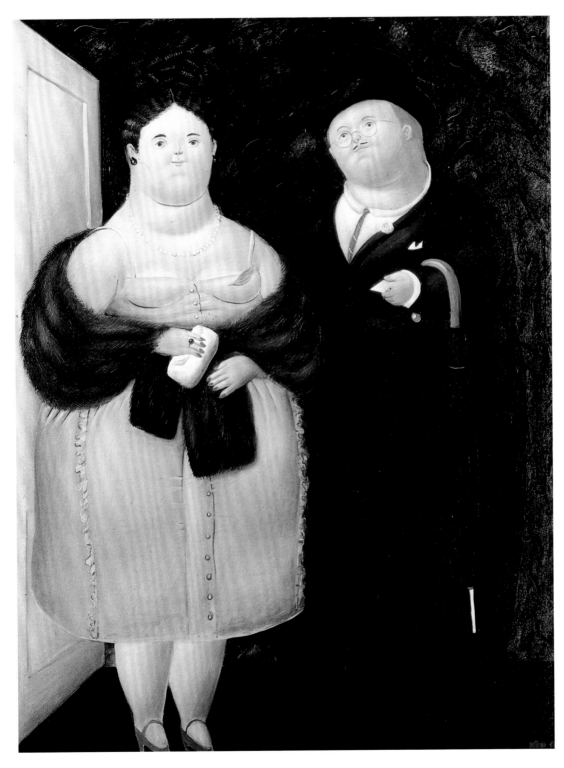

THE OUTSTANDING Colombian artist of the twentieth century is Fernando Botero, who has attained a universal reputation in recent years. He studied the Great Masters of European art and the influence of such disparate artists as Uccello, Piero della Francesca, Mantegna, Velázquez and Rubens is discernible in his work, which exalts form while exploring new realities. His work is by no means rigidly classicist, but he has combined his studies of the Old Masters with a detailed examination of the popular indigenous art of Colombia. The extraordinary range of his work, encompassing figures, portraits, landscapes and genre subjects, is characterized by ironic humour and warm humanity, coupled with wry, shrewd observation of the scenes and people around him. Figures are often depicted in a curious pneumatic fashion with fixed expressions on their grossly inflated faces, deliberately producing a naive style. Botero has also produced a number of monumental sculptures, chiefly of female nudes.

377

Mark Rothko   Untitled, 1968

Born 1903 Russia   Painted in USA   Died 1970 USA

MOVEMENT: Abstract Expressionism, Colour Field Painting   **OTHER WORKS:** *Central Green, Blue, Orange, Red, Number 118*   **INFLUENCES:** Henri Matisse, Arshile Gorky, Clyfford Still

BORN MARCUS Rothkovitch in Dvinsk, Russia, Rothko emigrated to the US in 1913. He studied briefly at Yale and in New York, although he considered this to have had little influence on his painting. Rothko's style took many years to evolve. His early figurative works included portraits and psychologically-infused urban scenes, which he exhibited with the American expressionist group,

The Ten. Rothko embraced ancient myth as he moved into a surrealist phase in the late 1930s, drawing on them as subjects for his increasingly abstract works. By 1946, he moved into pure abstraction, painting amorphous shapes(or 'Multiforms') that would coalesce into his familiar rectangles on fields of colour by 1949. Although the works were formally quite simple, Rothko executed

them with a meticulous eye for colour, balance and brushwork that give them a dramatic presence beyond their initial appearance. He was pleased that viewers often found looking at his paintings a deeply emotional experience. While he maintained the essential elements of his signature style, Rothko's paintings became generally larger, darker and more meditative in the last dozen years of his life.

Frank Stella   Agbatana II, 1968

Born 1936 Malden, Massachusetts, USA   Painted in New York

MOVEMENTS: Minimalism, Abstract Expressionism   **OTHER WORKS:** *Agbatana II, Tuxedo Park Junction, Harewa, Jarama II*   **INFLUENCES:** Josef Albers, Gwen John

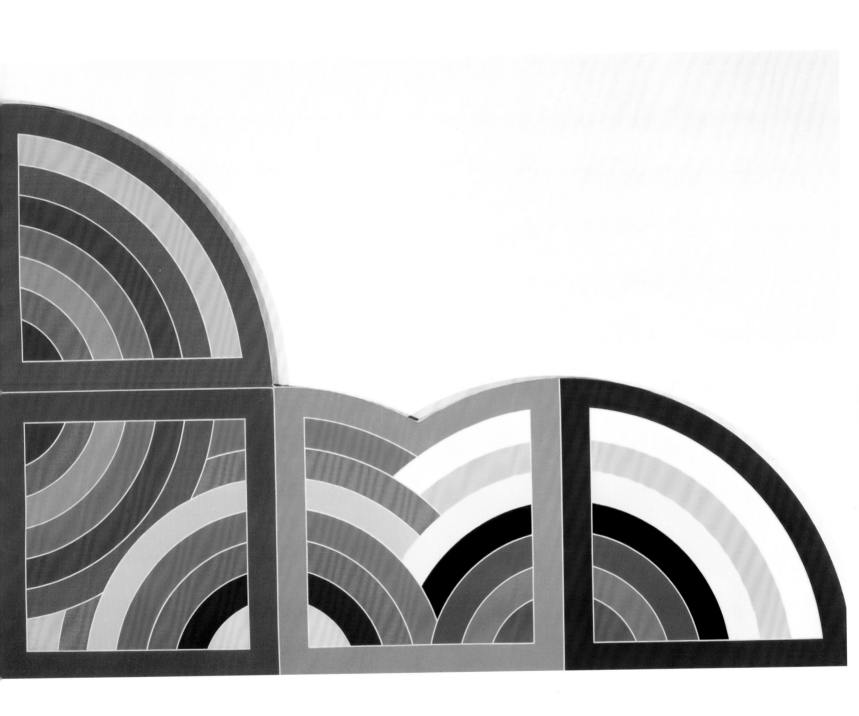

FRANK PHILIP Stella studied at Phillips Academy in Andover, Maine (1950–54) and Princeton University (1954–58). After university he went to New York City, where he worked as a house painter, an experience which influenced his art. He began painting in the Minimalist style in 1959, using a broad brush in order to eliminate the brushstrokes typical of art, and created works which were often virtually solid blocks of black, relieved only by a few contrasting stripes. Later he evolved polychrome patterns of straight lines or concentric rings and curves using the same technique of eliminating brushstrokes, which would have detracted from the overall effect. These paintings have a decidedly Art Deco character, reflecting Stella's admiration of the Bauhaus designs of the 1920s. His method is to cut templates and assemble them in reliefs painted in day-glo and metallic paints. His more recent work, in fact, verges on the sculptural, with its multicoloured, three-dimensional effects.

Romare H. Bearden   Sunday after the Sermon, 1969

Born 1914 Charlotte, North Carolina, USA   Painted in New York and Paris
MOVEMENT: Modern American School   **OTHER WORKS:** *Sunday After Sermon, Before the Dark, The Visitation*   **INFLUENCES:** George Grosz

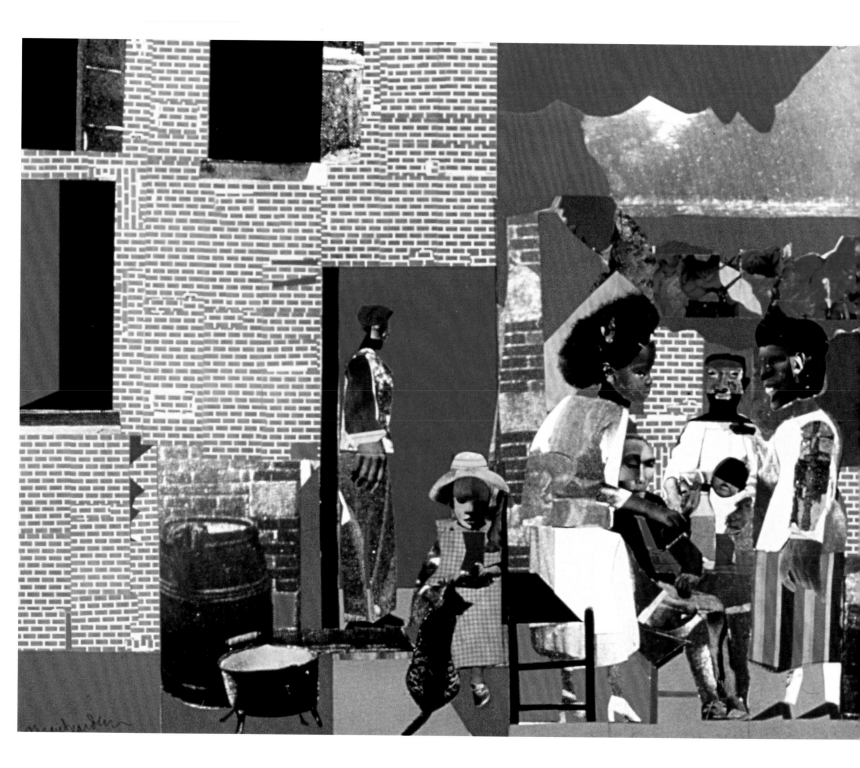

BORN IN Charlotte, North Carolina, in 1914, Romare Howard Bearden moved with his family to New York when he was three and eventually settled in Harlem. He began drawing cartoons at New York University, where he was also art editor of the student magazine *Medley*. Although originally intending a career in medicine, he switched to art and enrolled for evening classes at the Art Students' League where he studied under George Grosz. After military service in World War II the GI Bill enabled him to pursue his art studies at the Sorbonne, being particularly drawn to such masters as Duccio, De Hooch, Rembrandt and Manet. When he returned to the United States in 1952 he did not immediately take up creative painting, but from 1964 onwards he began producing collages. He is a versatile painter of landscapes and urban scenes, figures and abstracts, bringing to bear a highly intellectual approach in his work and drawing upon his southern roots for inspiration.

Meret Oppenheim   Blaues Auge, 1969

Born 1913 Berlin, Germany   Painted in Switzerland   Died 1985 Basle, Switzerland
MOVEMENT: Surrealism **OTHER WORKS:** *The Governess (My Nurse), Red Head, Blue Body,* **INFLUENCES:** Marcel Duchamp, Louise Bourgeois

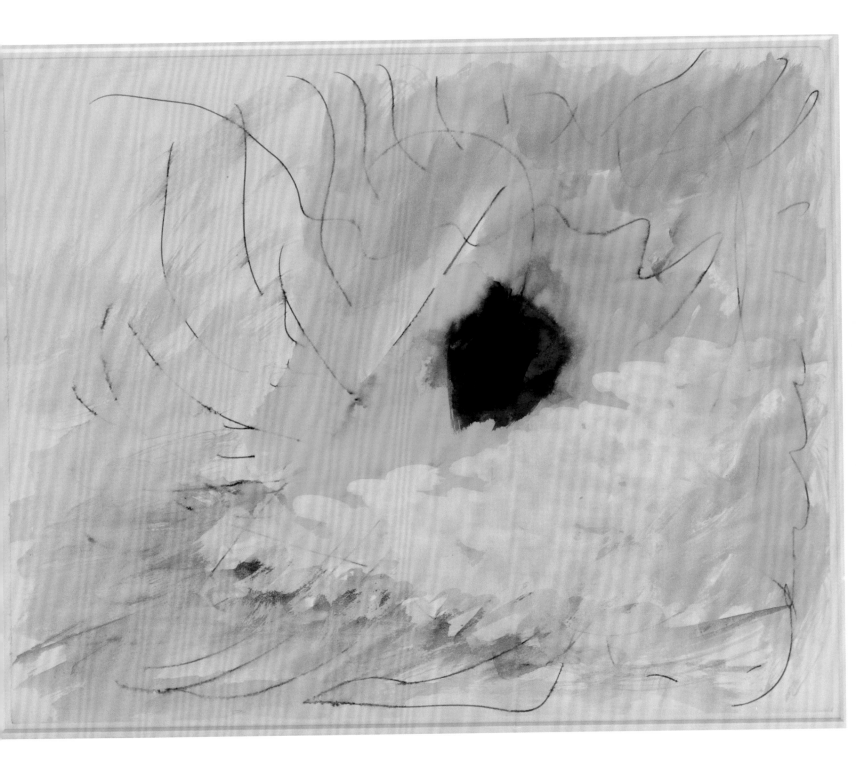

MERET OPPENHEIM was raised by her grandparents in Switzerland during World War I. At the age of 18 she went to Paris, where she enrolled at the Académie de la Grande Chaumière. She met Giacometti and Arp, who introduced her to Surrealism and she even modelled for Man Ray. Oppenheim began contributing her own three-dimensional objects to the Surrealist exhibitions in 1933 and achieved critical acclaim three years later with *Object, Fur Breakfast*: a cup, saucer and teaspoon covered with gazelle fur. This typified much of her later work, in which ordinary, everyday objects were transformed into articles with fetishistic or sado-masochistic undertones. In her paintings and sculptures she explored female sexuality and woman's role as a male sex object. One of the few female Surrealists, she was certainly the most highly original of them. On one occasion she even staged a banquet in which a nude female formed the centrepiece of the table decoration.

Robert Rauschenberg   Sky Garden (F74) Rocket Space

Born 1925 USA   Painted in France and USA

MOVEMENTS: American Abstract, Pop Art **OTHER WORKS:** *The Red Painting, Canyon, Bed, Reservoir* **INFLUENCES:** Joseph Albers, Marcel Duchamp

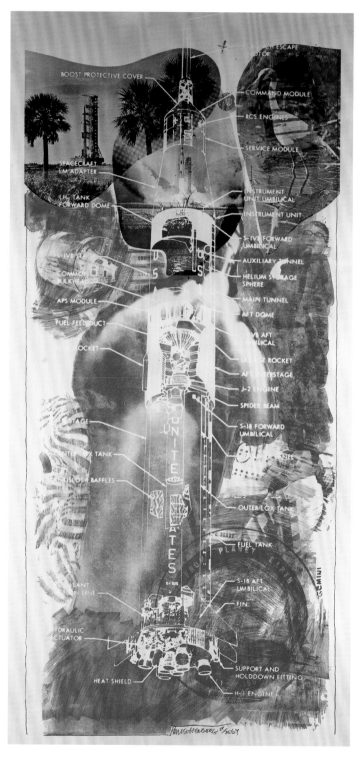

ROBERT RAUSCHENBERG studied at the Kansas City Art Institute and at Black Mountain College, North Carolina, where he was strongly influenced by Joseph Albers. In 1948 he crossed the Atlantic and enrolled at the Académie Julien in Paris (1948). His friendship with the avant-garde composer John Cage led to their collaboration in *Happenings*, in which Cage supplied the music and Rauschenberg

the visual entertainment, later extended from collages to painting entirely in one colour (black, white or red). From such minimalism in the early 1950s he moved on to highly controversial pictures, which were not only unusual in colour and surface treatment, but also incorporated scraps of ephemera and even three-dimensional objects such as stuffed birds, rusty metal, rubber tyres, pieces of discarded

clothing and any old junk, often dripping with paint. The results are unsettling and unnerving, but always thought-provoking.

Gerhard Richter   Wolken (Fenster), 1970

Born 1932 Dresden, Germany   Painted in Germany

MOVEMENT: Modern German   **OTHER WORKS:** *Abstraktes Bild, Stag, Betty, Colour Streaks, Townscape series* **INFLUENCES:** Otto Dix

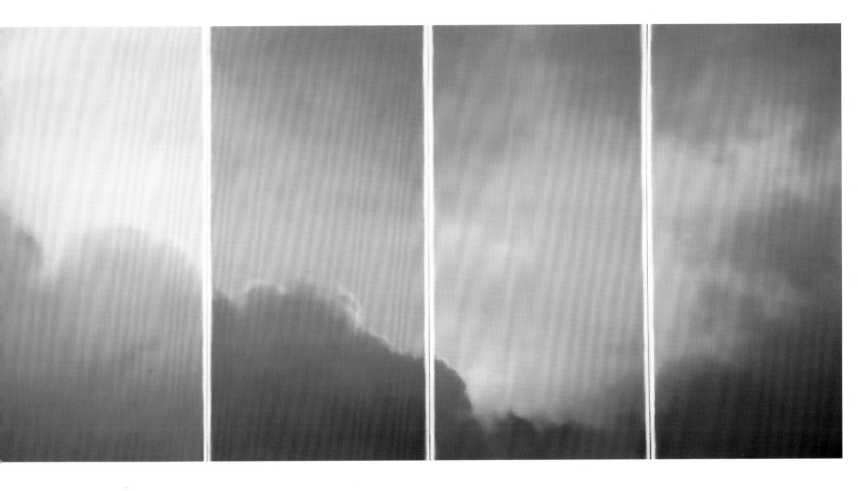

GERHARD RICHTER studied in his native city of Dresden and Düsseldorf before engaging in a career as a designer of sets for the stage and then working as a commercial artist in advertising. His early paintings were mostly figurative, but from 1962 onwards he produced paintings that were derived from blurred photographic images. Many of his paintings have been produced in series, exploring particular themes that continually flit back and forward between the camera and the canvas, and hover between figuration and the abstract. In particular, he painted a series of oils derived from aerial photographs of cities. His most recent work has consisted of enormous canvasses, more purely abstract in character, with emphasis on the artist rather than the subject. Noted for his range and versatility, coupled with absolute mastery of his technique, he has an infinite capacity to rediscover or reinvent the medium. A great innovator, he has had a tremendous influence on postwar German art.

Alma Thomas   Snoopy – Early Sun Display on Earth, 1970

Born 1891 Columbia, Georgia, USA   Painted in Washington, DC, USA   Died 1978 Washington, DC
MOVEMENT: Abstract Art   **OTHER WORKS:** *Pinks of Cherry Blossom, Light Blue Nursery*   **INFLUENCES:** Kandinsky

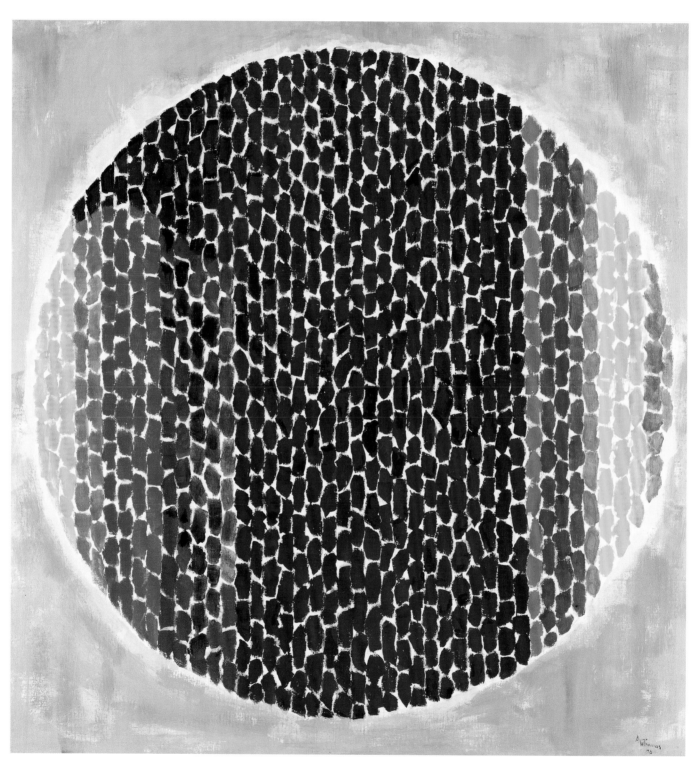

ALMA THOMAS moved with her family to Washington, DC in 1906 following race riots in the South. She came from a black professional, middle-class family and trained as a kindergarten teacher. After a spell in Wilmington, Delaware she returned to Washington in 1921 and became the first art graduate of Howard University. She taught art at Shaw Junior High School until her retirement in 1959. A spell in New York City, taking a teacher's postgraduate course at Columbia, brought her into contact with avant-garde art, but it was not until 1949 that she took a painting course at American University, and only when she retired in her sixties did she take up painting seriously. In the last decade of her life she painted prolifically in watercolours and acrylic, emerging as one of the greatest colourists of her generation. Always independent, she did not conform to any particular style but used colour in her own distinctive manner.

Shusaku Arakawa   War of the Worlds

Born 1936 Nagoya, Japan   Painted in Tokyo and New York

MOVEMENT: Dadaism **OTHER WORKS:** *Diagrams, Webster's Dictionary, The Mechanism of Meaning* **INFLUENCES:** Jean Arp, Kurt Schwitters, Man Ray

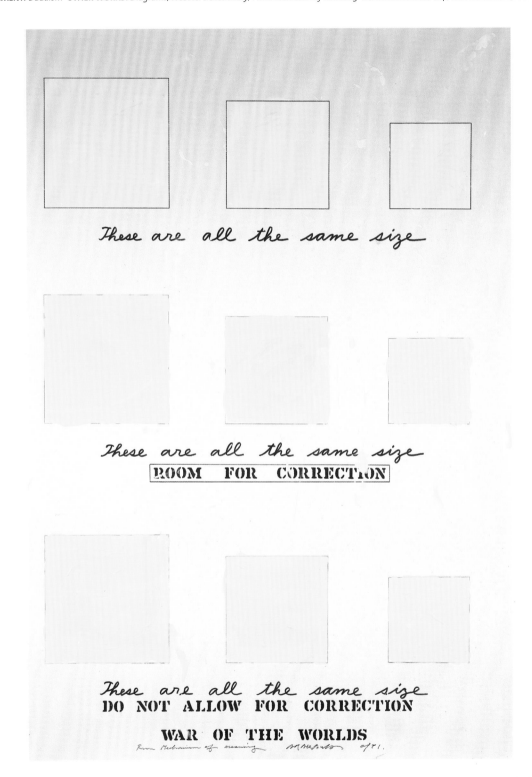

SHUSAKU ARAKAWA studied medicine and mathematics at Tokyo University but later switched to painting at the Musashino College of Art, and staged his first one-man show in the National Museum of Modern Art in 1958. Strongly influenced by the Dadaists of the early 1920s, he revived this movement in Japan and staged a number of 'happenings' from 1960 onwards to satirize the sickness and corruption in contemporary Japanese society. These activities caused a furore and Arakawa moved to the USA in 1961, settling in New York where he has lived ever since, working as a performance artist and film-maker as well as continuing to paint. Sending up those artists who produced works entitled *Untitled*, he produced a series under the name *Untitledness*, where blank spaces had pin marks where the object should be. A series entitled *Diagrams* consisted of spray-painted silhouettes of everyday objects. Later works explored the relationship between different forms of representation.

Sean Scully   Untitled, 1971

Born 1945 Dublin, Ireland   Painted in London and New York

MOVEMENT: Abstract Expressionism   **OTHER WORKS:** *Paul, The Fall, White Window, Why and What*   **INFLUENCES:** Noel Foster, Mark Rothko, Barnett Newman

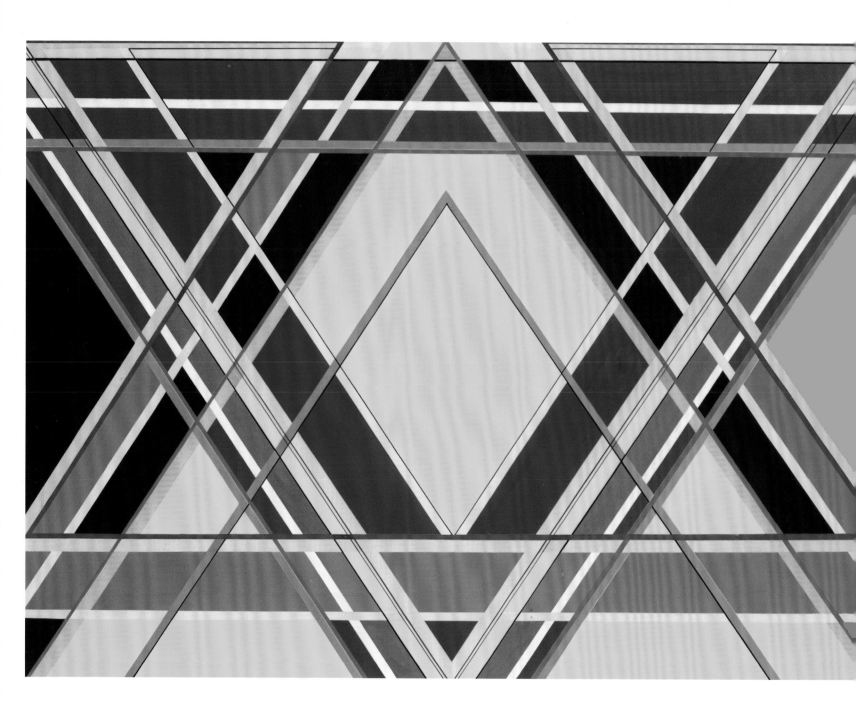

ALTHOUGH BORN in Dublin, Ireland, Sean Scully was raised in London, where he studied at the Croydon College of Art (1965–68) and Newcastle University (1968–72). He continued his art education at Harvard University before settling permanently in the United States in 1975. Such a rich and varied training is reflected in his paintings, which provide an interesting blend of elements derived from

Minimalism and Conceptual Art on the one hand and the Abstract Expressionism of his adopted country. This is manifest in his most characteristic works, in which the dominant features are vertical or horizontal bands of contrasting colours, generally muted shades of brown, beige and deep reds alternating with black. At first glance they may appear Minimal, but closer examination reveals the rich textures and

layers of colour. Scully styles these works triptychs, and this is true in so far as they comprise three pieces of canvas whose juxtaposition is deliberately uneven. The use of a term more commonly associated with medieval religious works is a reflection of Scully's regard for the spiritual qualities of abstract painting.

Graham Sutherland   Landscape Orange and Blue, 1971

Born 1903 England   Painted in England and Wales   Died 1980 London

MOVEMENT: Modern English Landscape School   **OTHER WORKS:** *Red Landscape, Entrance to a Lane, Devastation: House in Wales*   **INFLUENCES:** Samuel Palmer, Picasso, Odilon Redon

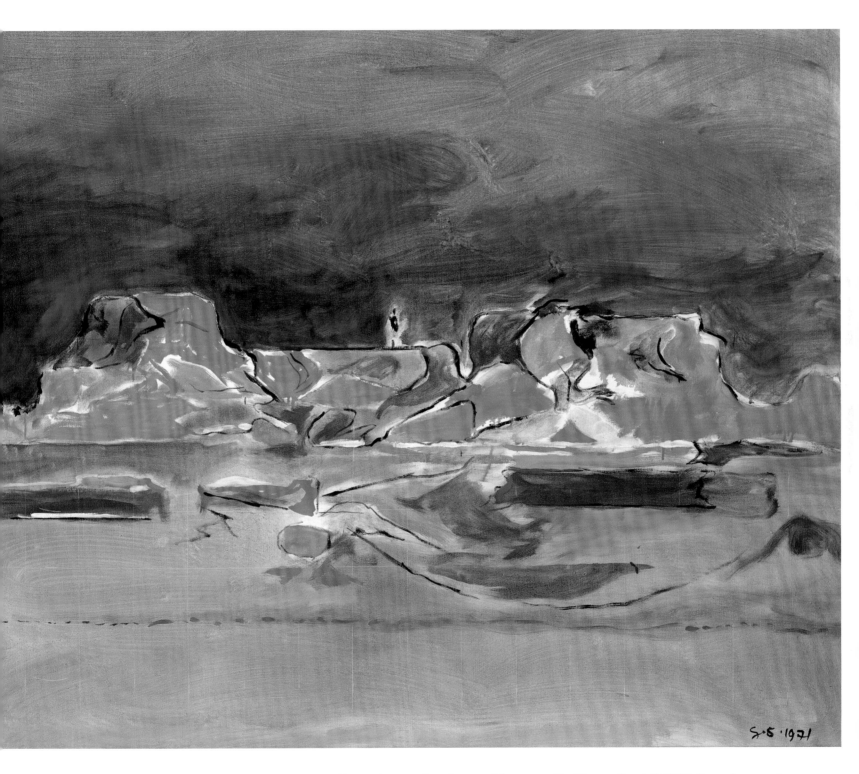

GRAHAM VIVIAN Sutherland originally intended to become a railway engineer, but switched courses and studied art at Goldsmiths College in London. Influenced by the visionary artist Samuel Palmer, he worked mainly as an etcher, but the market for prints collapsed in the aftermath of the stock-market crash of 1929, and as a result Sutherland took up painting instead. A visit to south-west Wales in 1934 introduced him to the astonishing diversity of the Pembrokeshire scenery which would provide endless subject matter for his later paintings. Sutherland's great landscapes combined elements of the romantic with the abstract. From 1941 until 1945 he was employed as an official war artist, and in the postwar period he produced a number of memorable (if occasionally controversial) portraits, including that of Sir Winston Churchill (1955). True to his original training, Sutherland also produced posters, ceramic designs and textiles, the best known being the extraordinary tapestry *Christ in Majesty*, which he executed for the new Coventry Cathedral in 1962.

David Hockney   'Sun' from The Weather Series, 1973

Born 1937 Yorkshire, England   Painted in Britain, USA and France
MOVEMENT: Pop Art, New Figuration **OTHER WORKS:** *A Bigger Splash, Mr. and Mrs. Clark and Percy* **INFLUENCES:** Picasso, Matisse, Jean Dubuffet

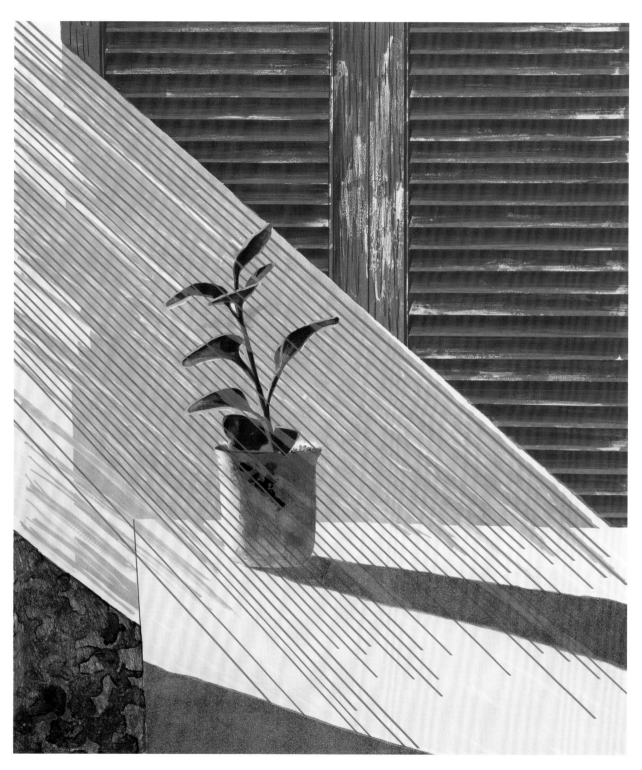

BRITISH PAINTER, photographer and designer.
Hockney was born in Bradford, Yorkshire, and trained
at the Royal College of Art. There, his fellow students
included Allen Jones, Derek Boshier and R.B. Kitaj,
and together they all exhibited at the Young
Contemporaries exhibition of 1961, a landmark show
which marked the arrival of British Pop Art. Hockney
himself denies belonging to this movement, even

though his early work contained many references to
popular culture. Instead, his style may be better
defined as New Figuration – a blanket term, relating
to the revival of figurative art in the 1960s.

Hockney has travelled widely in Europe, but his
main passion has been for the States, especially Los
Angeles where he settled in 1976. Throughout his
career, autobiographical subjects have featured heavily

in his paintings, ranging from friends, such as the
Clarks, lovers sunbathing by swimming pools, to an
entire book of pictures devoted to his dogs. Hockney
has also been a prolific stage designer, creating sets
and costumes for *The Rake's Progress, The Magic Flute*
and *Parade*. In recent years, he has also experimented
with photo-work, producing elaborate 'photocollages'
from hundreds of photographic prints.

Jasper Johns   Flags, 1973

Born 1930 Augusta, Georgia, USA   Painted in New York
MOVEMENT: Pop Art   **OTHER WORKS:** *Device, Zero Through Nine, Zone*   **INFLUENCES:** Marcel Duchamp

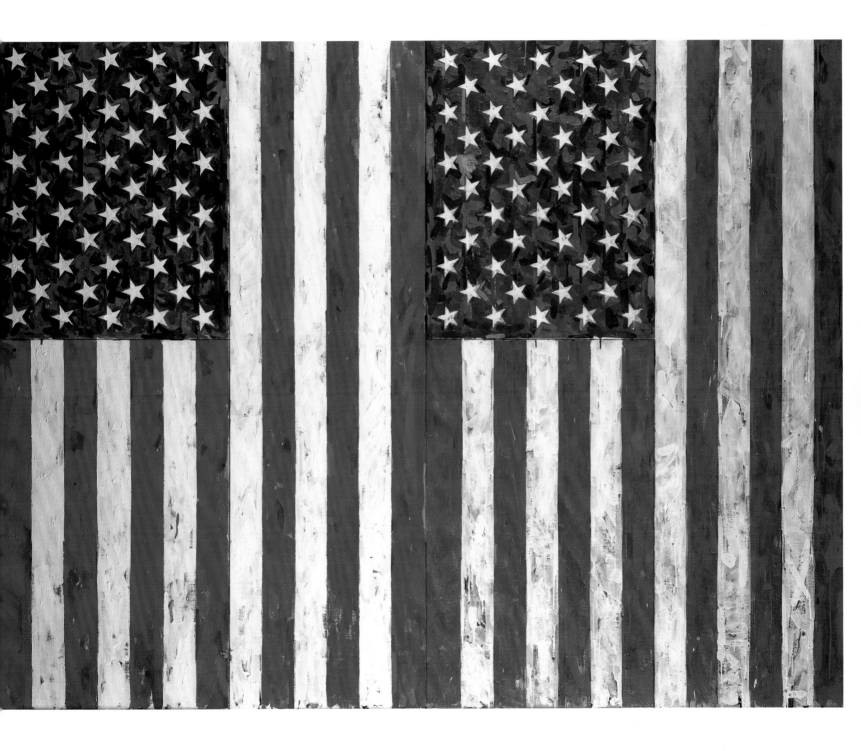

JASPER JOHNS studied at the University of South Carolina, Columbia. In 1952 he settled in New York City and there he met Robert Rauschenberg, who shared his views on the brash banality of contemporary culture, which they exploited in the development of Pop Art. By taking the familiar, the mundane and everyday icons such as the Stars and Stripes and the numerals on football jerseys he created works of art that put them in an entirely new light. The influence of Dada is evident as he deliberately set himself against the tenets of conventional art. Thus originality is eschewed by taking previously existing and immediately recognizable objects and emphasizing their very ordinariness. Johns is a versatile artist, working in oils, encaustic, plaster and other materials in various media.

Suad Al Attar   Paradise in Blue

Born 1942 Baghdad, Iraq   Painted in Iraq

MOVEMENT: Modern Iraqi School   **OTHER WORKS:** *Abacus, Birds of Paradise, Blue Sunset Birds, Bustan Guardian*   **INFLUENCES:** Classical Islamic art forms of the Middle East

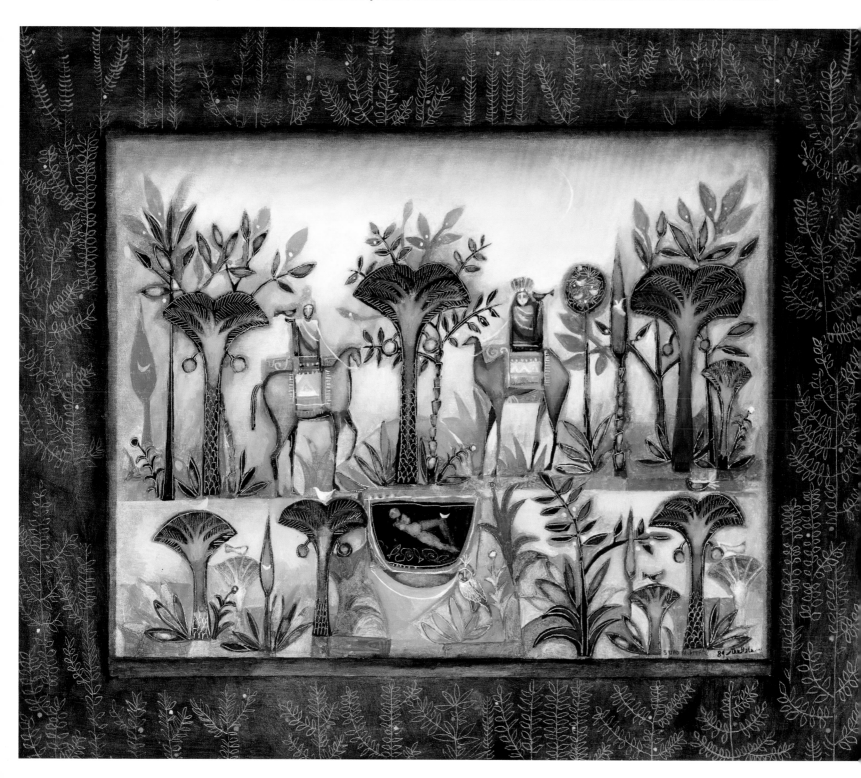

SUAD AL ATTAR studied at the University of Baghdad, the California Polytechnic State University in San Luis Obispo, the Wimbledon School of Art and the Central School of Art and Design, London (where she took a degree in print-making). In 1965 she became the first female Iraqi artist to have a solo exhibition in Baghdad and has since received numerous awards at international exhibitions in Cairo, Brazil, London, Madrid and Poland. She paints in oils on canvas or card laid down on board and her work ranges from figures and still life to landscapes and decorative works which combine the classical Islamic art forms of the Middle East with modern Western influences. In the past decade she has painted a number of semi-abstract works inspired by images in the love poems of Mahmoud Darwish. She also creates tapestries with traditional Arab motifs.

Helen Frankenthaler   Sundowner, 1974

Born 1928 New York, USA   Painted in New York

MOVEMENT: Abstract Expressionism   **OTHER WORKS:** *Black Frame, Door, The Other Side of the Moon*   **INFLUENCES:** Rufino Tamayo, Jackson Pollock, Robert Motherwell

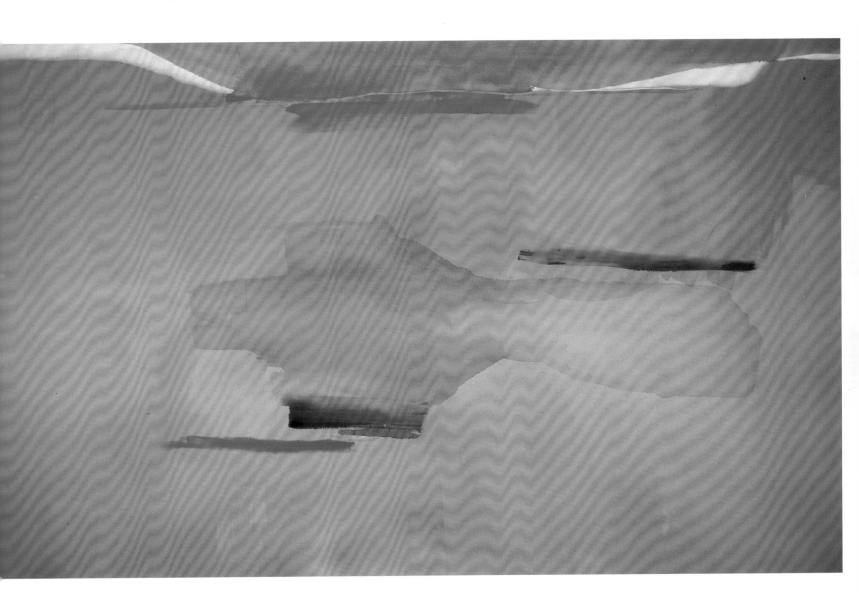

AFTER A college education at Bennington in Vermont, Helen Frankenthaler studied art under the abstract print-maker Hans Hoffman and the Mexican painter Rufino Tamayo. While still at Bennington, however, she evolved her own highly distinctive technique of applying very thin, diluted paint to the unprimed canvas so that it soaked right through. These 'stain-soak' paintings were created with a series of applications in different colours and consistencies, the canvasses being laid flat on the studio floor. This technique created an unusual atmospheric effect and the subtle blending of forms (not unlike that of certain watercolours, a medium in which she also worked) which form the basis for her large abstracts are vaguely suggestive of landscapes or the natural world. From 1958 to 1971 she was married to Robert Motherwell, whose influence can be discerned in her own brand of Abstract Expressionism. In her more recent paintings, acrylics have been applied to give greater depth to the principal details.

Joan Miró   Personnages, Oiseaux, Etoiles, 1974–6

Born 1893 Barcelona, Spain   Painted in Spain, France, USA and Holland   Died 1983
MOVEMENT: Surrealism   **OTHER WORKS:** *Dog Barking at the Moon, Aidez l'Espagne*   **INFLUENCES:** Picasso, Hans Arp, Paul Klee

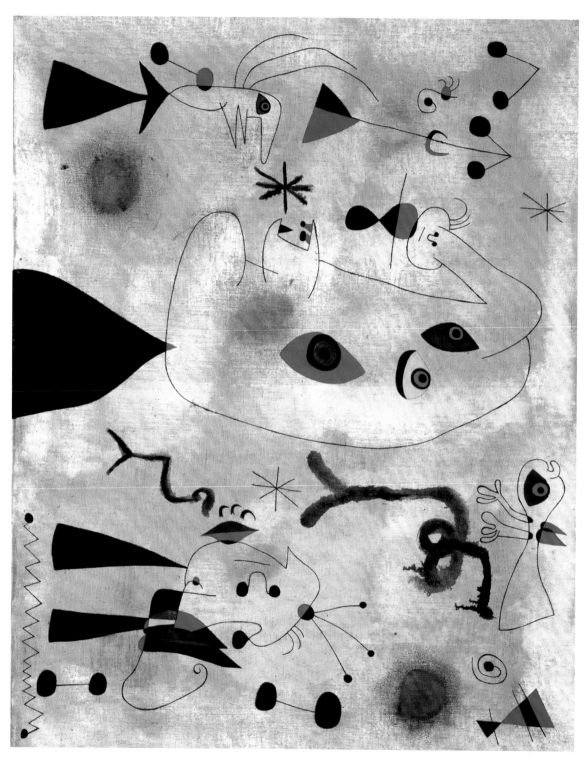

SPANISH PAINTER, ceramist and graphic artist; a key member of the Surrealists. Miró trained under Francisco Galí. His early work showed traces of Fauvism and Cubism, but his first one-man show was a disaster. Undeterred, Miró decided to travel to Paris, the acknow-ledged home of the avant-garde. There, he contacted Picasso, who introduced him to the most radical artists and poets of the day. These included the blossoming Surrealist group, which Miró joined in 1924.

Miró was fascinated by the challenge of using art as a channel to the subconscious and, from the mid-1920s, he began to fill his canvasses with biomorphic, semi-abstract forms. Nevertheless, he felt suspicious of some of the more outlandish, Surrealist doctrines and remained at the fringes of the group. He moved to France during the Spanish Civil War, producing patriotic material for the struggle against Franco, but was obliged to return south in 1940 after the Nazi invasion. By this stage, Miró's work was much in demand, particularly in the US, where he received commissions for large-scale murals. Increasingly, these featured ceramic elements, which played a growing part in the artist's later style.

Charles White   Mother Courage II, 1974

Born 1918 Chicago, Illinois, USA   Painted in Chicago and Los Angeles   Died 1979

MOVEMENT: African American School   **OTHER WORKS:** *Frederick Douglass, Booker T. Washington, In Memoriam*   **INFLUENCES:** Charles Alston, Hale Woodruff

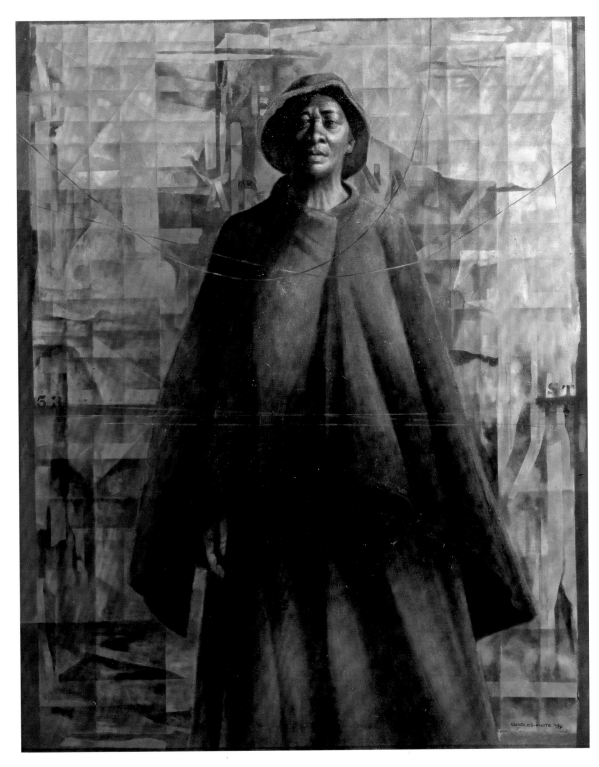

CHARLES WHITE was largely self-taught but from an early age he was imbued with the desire to depict the African American heroes whose exploits formed a large part of the folklore of the 1920s when he was growing up. His reputation was assured by one of his most ambitious early works, the mural entitled *Five Great American Negroes*, which was commissioned for the Chicago Public Library. In this great work can be seen the tension and emotion, the realistic depiction of persecution, injustice and struggle, that characterized much of his later work. The passion is more restrained in the tempera mural completed in 1943 for Hampton University illustrating the contribution of the Negro to American democracy – a mural whose vast expanse is crammed with portraits large and small. Features and forms are sharply outlined with a geometric, angular style that adds to their rugged character, and this intensely graphic quality came to fruition in White's later works, from murals to individual portraits.

Sir Howard Hodgkin   Dinner at the Grand Palais, 1975

Born 1932 London, England   Painted in London
MOVEMENT: Modern English   **OTHER WORKS:** *Lovers, Menswear, Interior at Oakwood Court*   **INFLUENCES:** William Scott, Mughal art

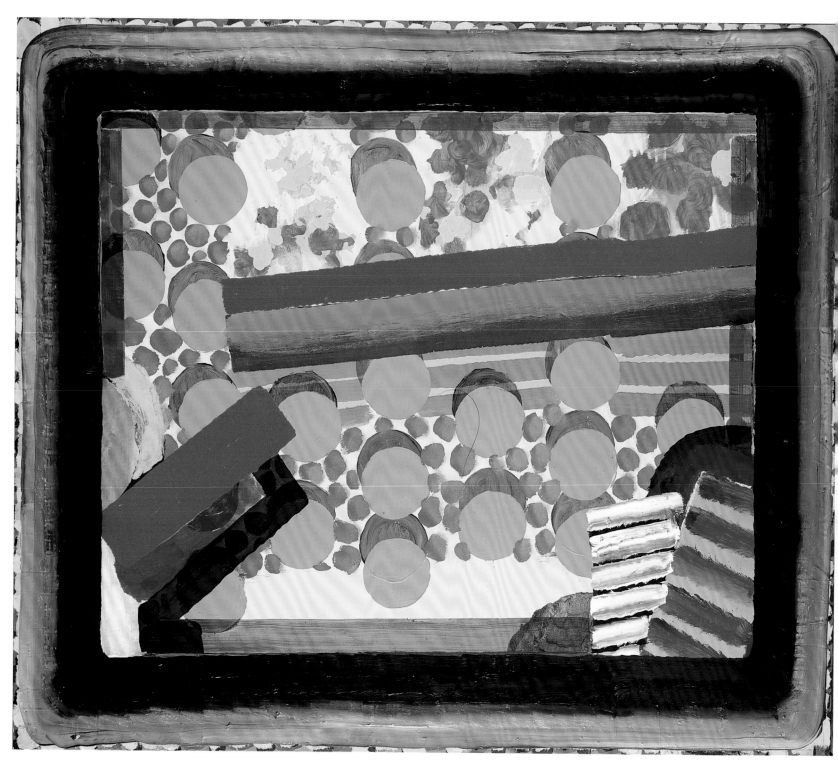

HOWARD HODGKIN studied at the Camberwell School of Art in London and then Bath Academy of Art, where he later taught (1956–66). Although his painting does not fit neatly into any particular movement he was influenced by William Scott, his teacher at Bath, to regard painting as a physical object. An early but lifelong attraction to the Mughal art of India is also evident in the range of brilliant, contrasting colour. His paintings have a superficial impression of being abstract, but a closer examination reveals that they are truly representational, mostly of interiors or encounters, with figures caught in a split second, and these qualities are evoked strongly in his masterpiece *Dinner at Smith Square*, painted in oil on wood between 1975 and 1979, now in the Tate Gallery. He was awarded the Turner Prize for contemporary British art in 1985 and was knighted in 1992.

Louis Khela Maqhubela   Untitled, 1975

Born 1939 Durban, Natal, South Africa   Painted in South Africa and England
MOVEMENT: Modern South African School   **OTHER WORKS:** *Equilibrium*   **INFLUENCES:** Douglas Portway, Cecil Skomes, Sydney Kumalo

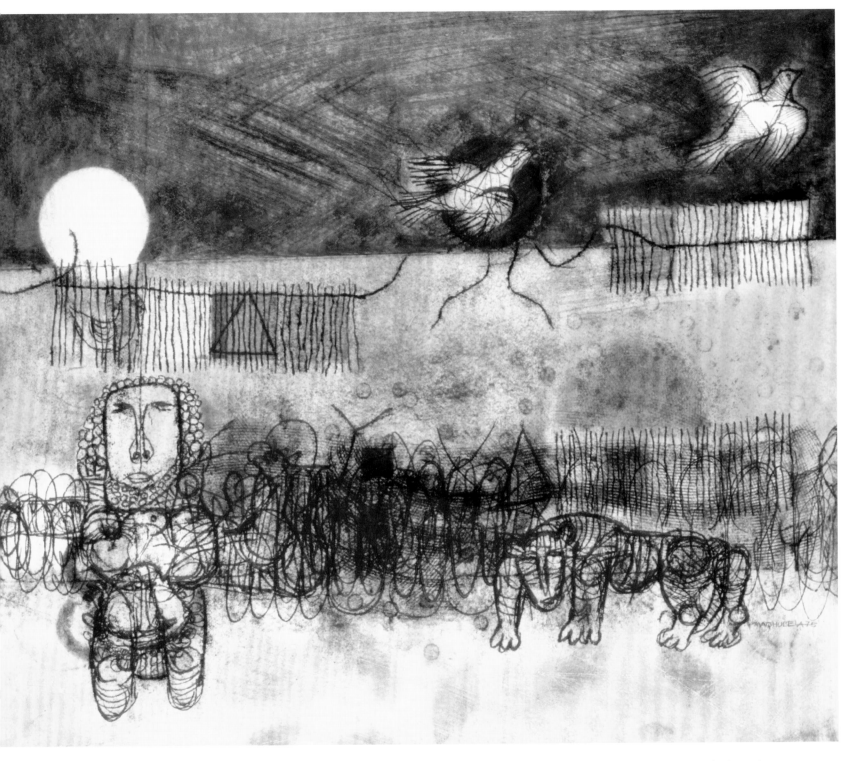

LOUIS KHELA Maqhubela studied at the Polly Street Art Centre in Durban under Cecil Skomes and Sydney Kumalo, imbibing the disparate strands of conventional genre painting and the more symbolic, abstract style which was becoming very fashionable in South Africa in the 1950s. These influences melded in Maqhubela's lively depiction of everyday life in the black townships, and the exhibition of his paintings in the Johannesburg galleries was a way of breaking through the barrier of apartheid in the 1960s. A prize as one of the most promising young artists of his time enabled him to travel to England to study under the South African abstract painter Douglas Portway. Maqhubela later studied at Goldsmiths College and the Slade School of Art (1985–87). Since then he has had a studio in London and now commutes between there and Johannesburg, a prominent figure in the modern movement since the downfall of the apartheid system.

Norval Morrisseau Ojibway Headdress, 1975

Born 1931 Painted in Canada, USA
MOVEMENT: Algonquian Legend Painters **OTHER WORKS:** *Thunderbird, Loon Totem and Evil Fish, The Creation of the Earth*
INFLUENCES: Midewiwin birchbark scrolls, aboriginal rock art, Ojibwa folklore

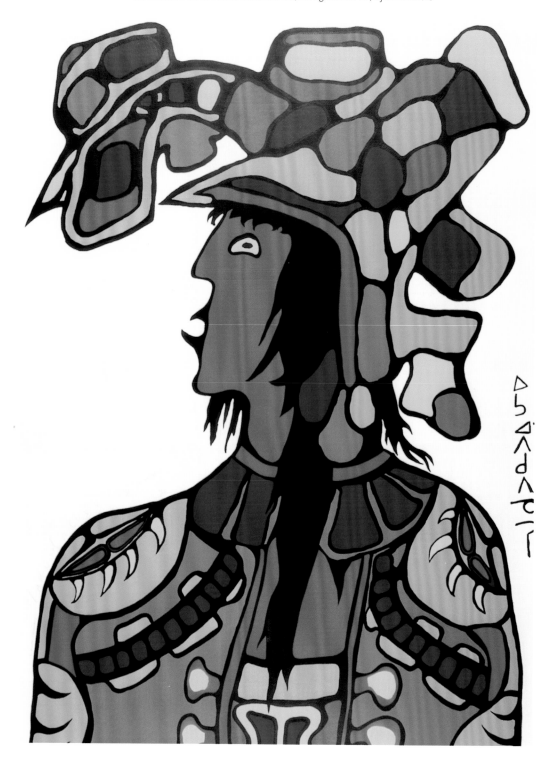

NATIVE NORTH American painter and graphic artist. Born in Fort William, Canada, Morrisseau hails from the Ojibwa tribe and has made this the focus of his art. Awareness of Native American traditions blossomed during the 1960s, as a by-product of the civil rights movement, and Morrisseau belonged to the generation that spearheaded this revival. He held his first one-man exhibition at the Pollock Gallery,

Toronto, in 1962, and the success of this show established him as the leader of a new school. This has been variously described as the Woodlands or Algonquian school of legend painting.

Morrisseau took his basic subject matter from Ojibwa folk traditions. Many of these had been preserved as pictographs on birchbark scrolls. Traditionally, non-Native Americans were not

permitted to see these images, but Morrisseau broke this taboo. He also combined the legends with more universal, Native American symbolism and European forms. Much of his work has a strong, spiritual basis, dealing with such themes as soul travel and self-transformation. It reached its widest audience in Montreal, when Morrisseau and Carl Ray designed the Indian Pavilion for Expo 67.

Otto Freundlich   Composition

Born 1878 Pomerania (now Poland)   Painted in Munich, Berlin, Paris, Pontoise and the Pyrenees   Died 1943 Majdanek, Lublin, Poland
MOVEMENTS: Abstract Art, Orphism   **OTHER WORKS:** *Diptych, La Rosace, Composition avec Trois Personnages*   **INFLUENCES:** Picasso, Kandinsky, Paul Klee, Robert Delaunay, Max Ernst

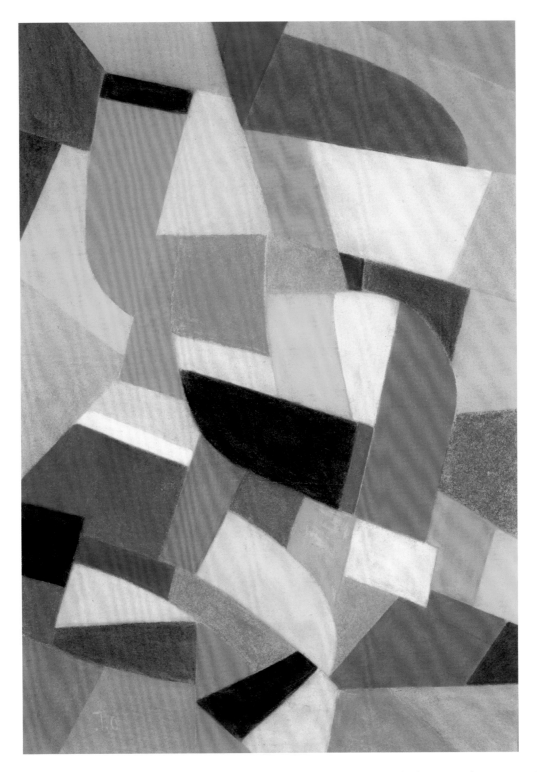

AFTER ART training in Munich and Berlin, Otto Freundlich settled in Paris in 1909, where he joined the avant-garde circle dominated by Picasso. In 1911 he exhibited at the Neue Sezession in Berlin, revealing the latest trends from France. He returned to Germany for military service in World War I, during which (1917) he joined the Aktion group of artists and between 1919–23 was associated with the Bauhaus.

He returned to Paris in 1924 and latterly worked in Pontoise as a painter, graphic artist and sculptor. In 1929 he commenced the magazine *A bis Z*; a prolific writer, he was the intellectual voice of the avant-garde. In 1939 he was interned as an enemy alien, released on the intervention of Picasso, and moved to the Pyrenees, where he spent the next two years repainting from memory all those works which had been destroyed

by the Nazis as degenerate art. Betrayed to the Gestapo in 1943, he was transported to Majdanek concentration camp where he died soon afterwards. Work on the restoration of the stained glass in Chartres Cathedral (1914) inspired his kaleidoscopic paintings which anticipated the Op Art of the 1960s.

Anselm Kiefer Noch Ist Poten Nicht Verloren IV, 1978

Born 1945 Donaueschingen, Germany Painted in Germany
MOVEMENT: Neo-Expressionism **OTHER WORKS:** *Spiritual Heroes of Germany, Parsifal series, Lilith* **INFLUENCES:** Joseph Beuys, Caspar David Friedrich

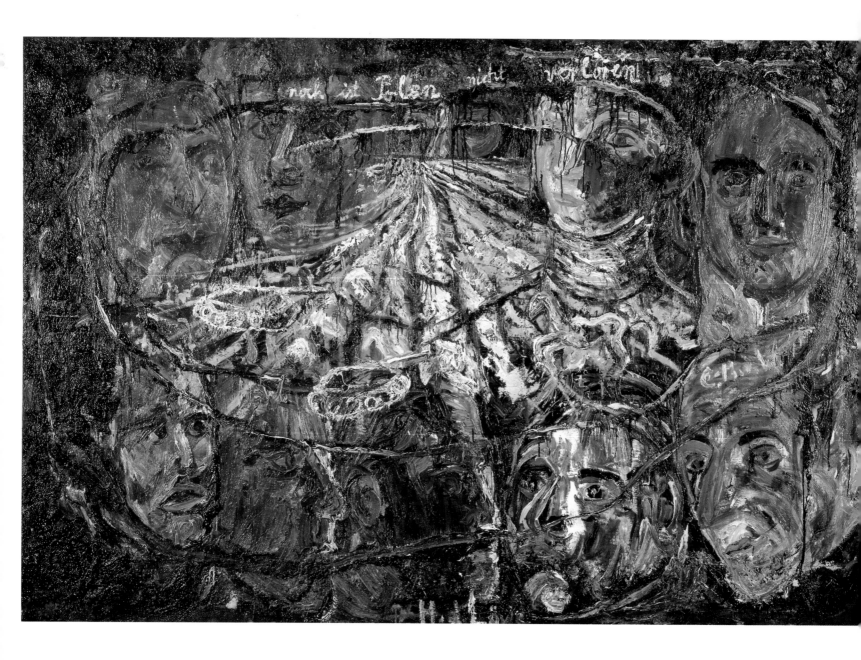

ONE OF the leading artists to emerge in Germany in recent years, Anselm Kiefer originally studied law, but switched to art around 1965 and had his first one-man show five years later. Between 1970 and 1972 he studied under Joseph Beuys, but did not embrace either Minimalism or Conceptual Art as did so many of his contemporaries. In subsequent years he developed large-scale paintings, executed on paper or burlap, mounted on canvas, and using charcoal or black paint to create a starkly etched effect with muted tones of yellow and brown, which drew upon the myths and legends of Germany. Although controversial (and sometimes accused of fascist overtones) Kiefer's monumental paintings are inspired by the works of Caspar David Friedrich and the operas of Wagner. In addition to his paintings, Kiefer has produced numerous drawings and etchings and well as massive 'books' in wood or lead, engraved and worked over.

Eric Fischl Love

Born 1948 New York, USA Painted in New York

MOVEMENT: Neo-Figurative School **OTHER WORKS:** *Bad Boy, Sleepwalker, Pizza Eater* **INFLUENCES:** Tamara de Lempicka, Norman Rockwell, Walter Sickert

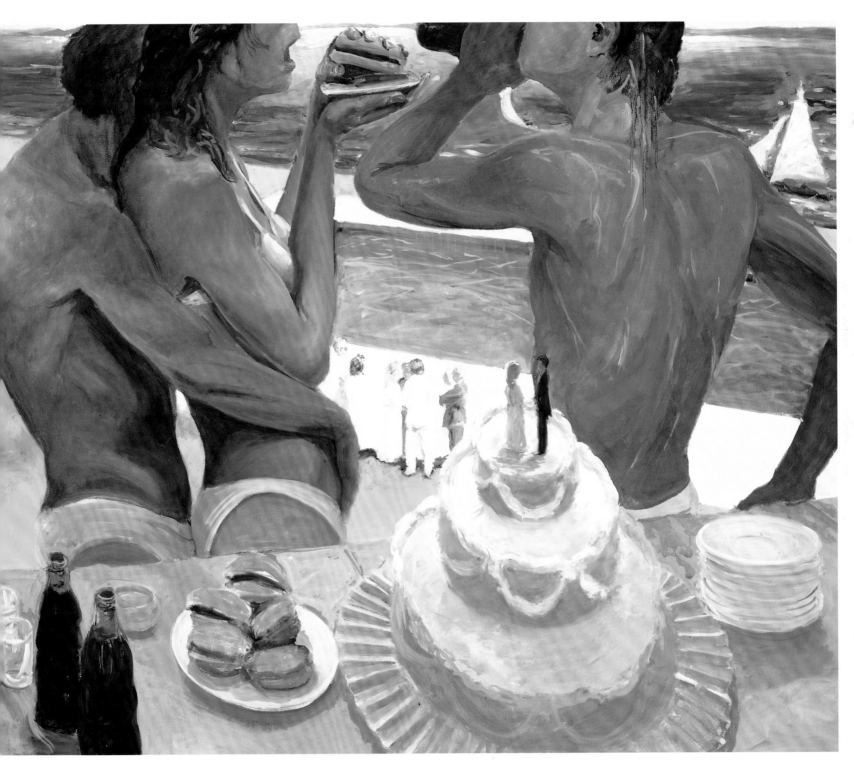

EDUCATED AT the California Institute of the Arts (1969–72), Eric Fischl led the reaction against Op Art and Minimalism in the late 1970s and 1980s, calling for a return to a more purely figurative and representational style of painting which had strong echoes of the Social Realism of the New Deal era. What has marked out his work from his predecessors of the 1930s, however, is the psycho-sexual undertones of his compositions, in which the spectator becomes a voyeur, looking at scenes which may appear relatively simple and straightforward on one level, but which reveal disturbing elements of anxieties, phobias, insecurities and a wide range of sexual hang-ups, invariably unexplained and thus open to individual interpretation. Although far less accomplished technically than the paintings of Tamara de Lempicka, for example, Fischl's sly exploration of repressed or ambivalent sexuality invites obvious comparison.

Gilbert and George   Helping Hands, 1982

Gilbert Proesch: Born 1942 Dolomites, Italy   Worked in Italy, Germany and England   George Pasmore: Born 1943 Devon, England   Worked in England
MOVEMENT: Modern British School **OTHER WORKS:** *Fear, Flying Shit, England, The Nature of Our Looking* **INFLUENCES:** Op Art, Performance Art

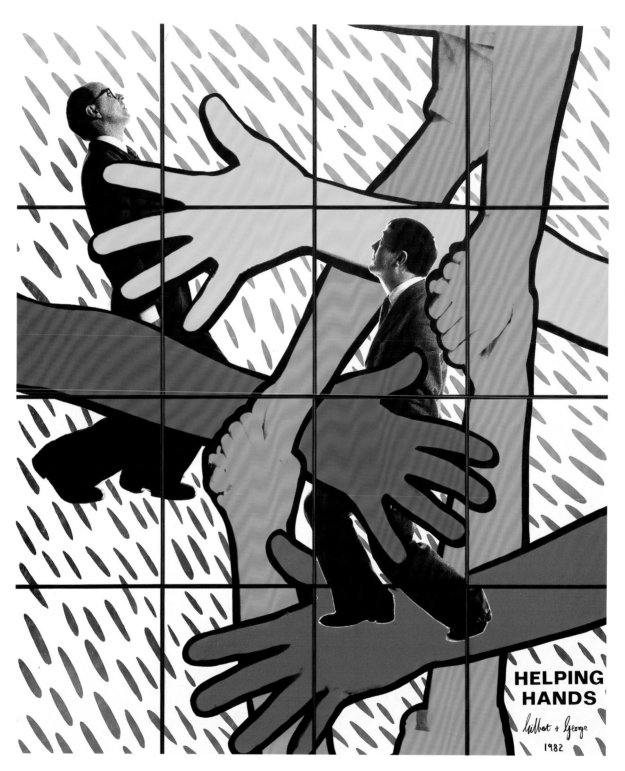

ITALIAN-BORN Gilbert Proesch first met George Pasmore when they were both students at St Martin's School of Art in London and have worked together since graduating in 1969. George had previously studied at Dartington Hall and the Oxford School of Art, while Gilbert had attended the Academy of Art in Munich. Since the late 1960s they have worked as performance artists, principally as living sculptures, their faces and hands covered with gold paint and holding the same pose for hours on end. Subsequently they developed two-dimensional art, often comprising a series of framed photographs which are integrated to form a single entity. Their very conservative images in these collaborative works often clash with the subject matter, in which bodily functions and overt references to homosexuality feature prominently. Controversy surrounds their work, which is often seen as promoting rather than condemning fascist or racist attitudes, although they claim to be attempting to define the 'new morality'.

Jean–Michel Basquiat   Profit I, 1982

Born 1960 Brooklyn, New York, USA   Painted in New York   Died 1988
MOVEMENT: Neo-Expressionist **OTHER WORKS:** *Skull*, *Florence* **INFLUENCES:** Picasso, Hitchcock films, Bebop jazz, Andy Warhol,

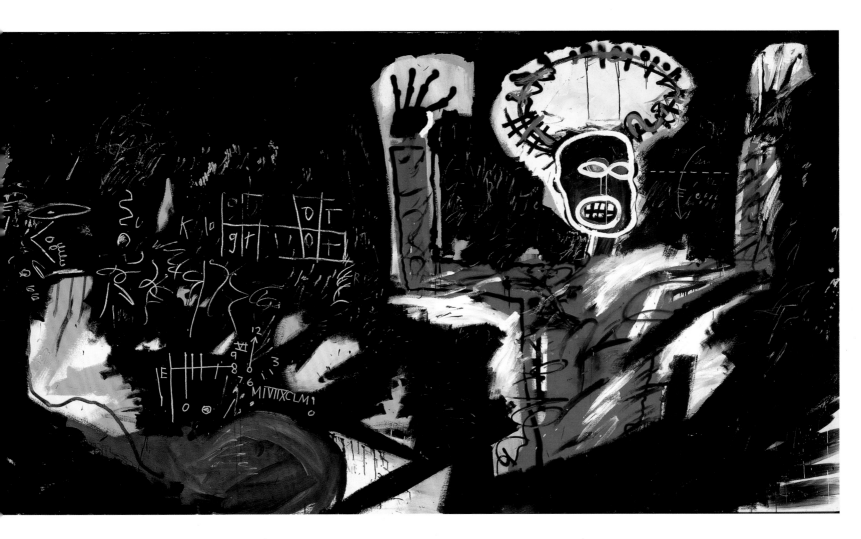

THE DOMINANCE of Conceptual and Performance Art in the 1970s led to a backlash in the 1980s, and the rise of a painterly movement called Neo-Expressionism, of which Jean-Michel Basquiat was one of the chief proponents. In an ironic reversal of the activities of many artists who had striven to take their works out of the gallery and into the streets, Basquiat's short career witnessed the opposite trajectory. His work first came to the public attention in an anonymous form when he participated in the graffiti craze that exploded in downtown Manhattan during the late 1970s. Together with his friend Al Diaz, he cultivated a pseudonymous character called SAMO and used the name to sign the public walls he spray-painted. In the heady economic boom of the 1980s, Basquiat's work was soon 'discovered' and his pieces, now executed in a studio and on canvas, were increasingly included in major exhibitions. They were celebrated for their immediacy, for the aggressive treatment of form and their starkly clashing colours. This was seen by some critics as capturing the dynamism and rawness of the street, and as an antidote to the control, precision and harmony of so-called museum art.

R.B. Kitaj   Golem, 1982–3

Born 1932 Cleveland, Ohio, USA   Painted in London, England

MOVEMENT: Pop Art **OTHER WORKS:** *If Not, Not* **INFLUENCES:** Arthur Boyd, Edward Burra

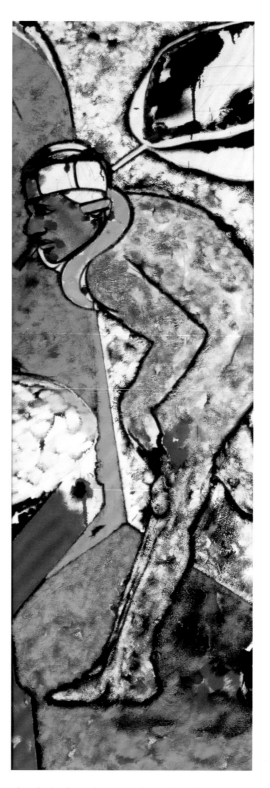

BORN IN Cleveland, Ohio, in 1932, Ronald Brooks Kitaj travelled the world as a merchant seaman (1951–55) but after service in the US Army he went to Oxford to study art. In 1960 he enrolled at the Royal College of Art in London. Older and infinitely more worldly wise that his fellow students, he was an outstanding figure with a charismatic personality who played a leading role in introducing Pop Art to Britain in the 1960s. An abiding friendship with David Hockney was forged in this period. The strident colours and brashness of Pop Art belie the intellectual depth of Kitaj's work, which draws on many disparate sources, from his Hungarian Jewish ancestry to the ethnic art of the countries he visited as a seaman. The result is often a riotously eclectic mixture of patterns and images. Most of his work up to 1975 was executed in oils but in more recent years he has concentrated on pastels, a trend encouraged by his second wife, Sandra Fisher. This is cleverly demonstrated in his masterpiece *The Wedding* which celebrates their marriage.

Julian Schnabel   Hamid in a Suit of Light, 1982

Born 1951 New York, USA   Painted in New York

MOVEMENT: Action Painting **OTHER WORKS:** *Blue Nude with Sword, Humanity Asleep, St Francis in Ecstasy* **INFLUENCES:** Robert Motherwell, Robert Rauschenberg

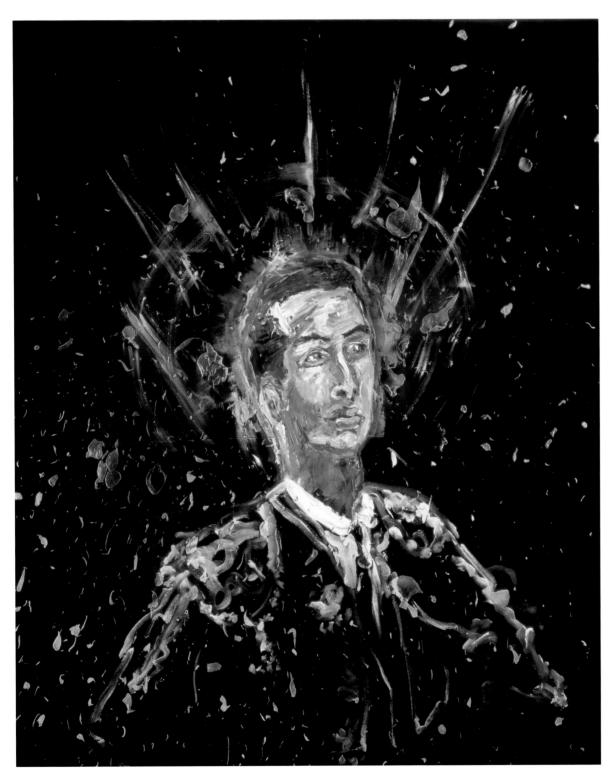

ALTHOUGH A NATIVE of New York City, Schnabel studied art at the University of Texas from 1969 to 1972. After moving back to New York, he began exhibiting in 1976, creating enormous canvasses in which layers of paint are applied in different ways in order to create interesting and unusual textures. A later development on these lines includes the use of shards of pottery to break up the surfaces and heighten dramatic effect. Unfortunately this combination of paint and crockery is friable and inherently unstable, creating numerous problems for curators and conservators of art galleries housing these monumental works. More recently he has also created paintings on velvet. Apart from re-inventing Action Painting, Schnabel has experimented with imagery on the grand scale, creating extraordinary works which incorporate numerous images and portraits mingled with allusions to history and emotions. Since the early 1980s he has enjoyed phenomenal commercial success.

Clifford Possum Tjapaltjarri   Water Dreaming, 1982

Born 1932 Nabberby Creek, Central Australia   Painted in Central Australia   Died 2002 Australia
MOVEMENT: Australian Aboriginal   **OTHER WORKS:** *Kangaroo Dreaming*   **INFLUENCES:** Tribal art

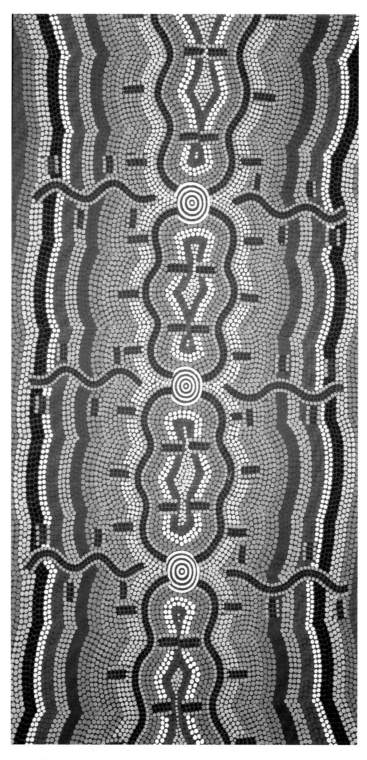

CLIFFORD POSSUM Tjapaltjarri had no formal art training in the conventional Western sense, but he inherited an Aboriginal artistic and spiritual tradition stretching back thousands of years. He belongs to the group of Aboriginal artists known as the Western Desert Painters, who have adapted their tribal art forms to the Western world only in so far as they use westernized materials and techniques, instead of wood, bark, sand or indigenous dyes. Tjapaltjarri works in acrylic paints on canvas, but otherwise much of his work clings steadfastly to the imagery and expression practiced by his ancestors. A large part of his oeuvre centres on the Dreamtime, the sacred world of the tribe's ancestral spirits, whom the Aborigines regard as the creators of all living things. Superficially, his paintings may seem abstract, but they are actually a carefully constructed and systematized map or chart of a particular tribal or community site.

Jim Dine   Townsend Monotype 1(Heart), 1983

Born 1935 Cincinnati, Ohio, USA   Painted in Cincinnati, Boston and New York

MOVEMENT: Performance Art, Pop Art   **OTHER WORKS:** *The Toaster, Wiring the Unfinished Bathroom*   **INFLUENCES:** Dadaism, Surrealism, Abstract Expressionism,

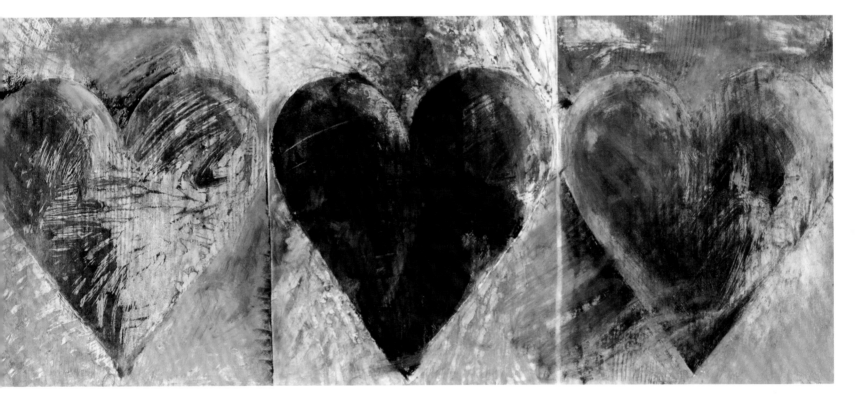

TRAINED AT the University of Cincinnati, the Boston Museum of Fine Arts School and the University of Ohio, Jim Dine was one of the foremost exponents of Pop Art. He held his first exhibition of objects as images in 1959, alongside Claes Oldenburg, with whom he subsequently collaborated on a number of projects. Like the Dadaists, he believed in the combination of many different media and the use of ready-made objects or fragments of them in creating his compositions. Taking this process to its logical conclusion in the late 1950s he began organizing a series of 'happenings', live performances which combined his art with his experience of life. These, in effect, were the forerunners of the Performance Art that came to fruition a few years later. In more recent years, however Dine has returned to a more representational and figurative style of painting. He has combined oils with collage, or etching and printing on hand-coloured paper.

Wayne Thiebaud   Free Way Traffic, 1983

Born 1920 Mesa, Arizona, USA   Painted in New York, Sacramento and San Francisco
MOVEMENT: Pop Art   **OTHER WORKS:** *Refrigerator Pies, Woman and Cosmetics, Various Cakes*   **INFLUENCES:** Pierre Bonnard, Man Ray, Edward Ruscha

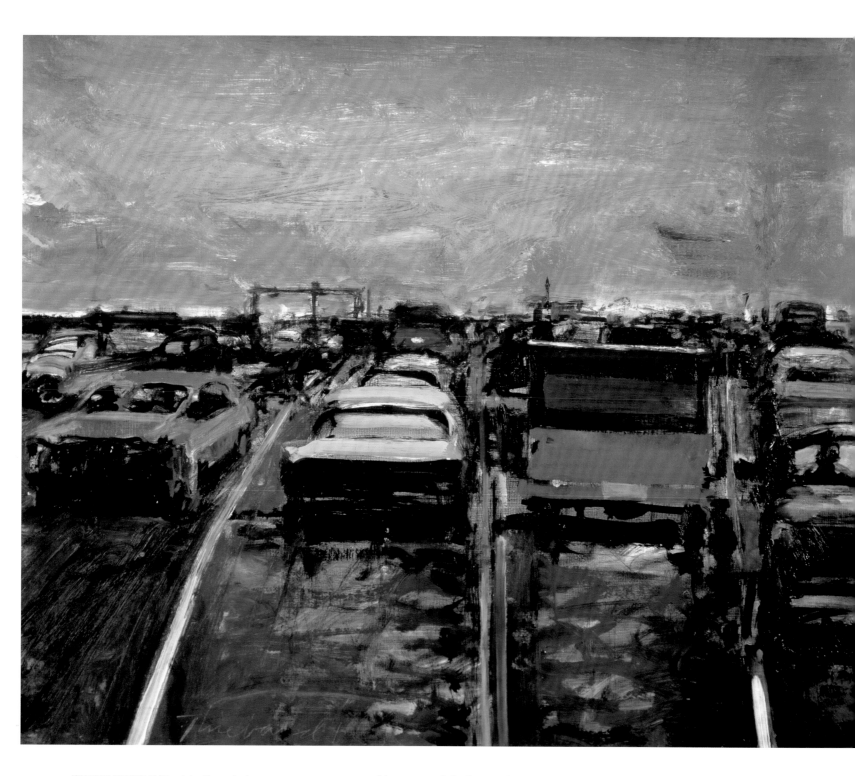

WAYNE THIEBAUD originally worked as a sign-painter and later a freelance cartoonist in New York before turning to fine art in 1949. His expertise in his earlier vocations stood him in good stead, for his paintings are both witty and executed with a clarity and deftness that make them instantly recognizable. His reputation has been built largely on the series of paintings of American junk food, pies, cakes, sweets, ice-cream and other delicacies, which often strike a nostalgic note but are invariably presented in a humorously deadpan manner. He injects realism by laying on the paint in thick slabs so that the icing or frosting on cakes looks good enough to eat. More recently he has painted figures of women, harshly lit in artificial light or the bright sunlight of California where he now lives, but here again he incorporates a wide range of minor objects, all painted against severely plain backgrounds.

Robert Motherwell   Chrome Yellow Elegy, 1984

Born 1915 USA   Painted in New York, USA   Died 1991 Cape Cod, Maine, USA

MOVEMENT: Abstract Expressionism   **OTHER WORKS:** *Elegies to the Spanish Republic, Bolton Landing Elegy*   **INFLUENCES:** Roberto Matta

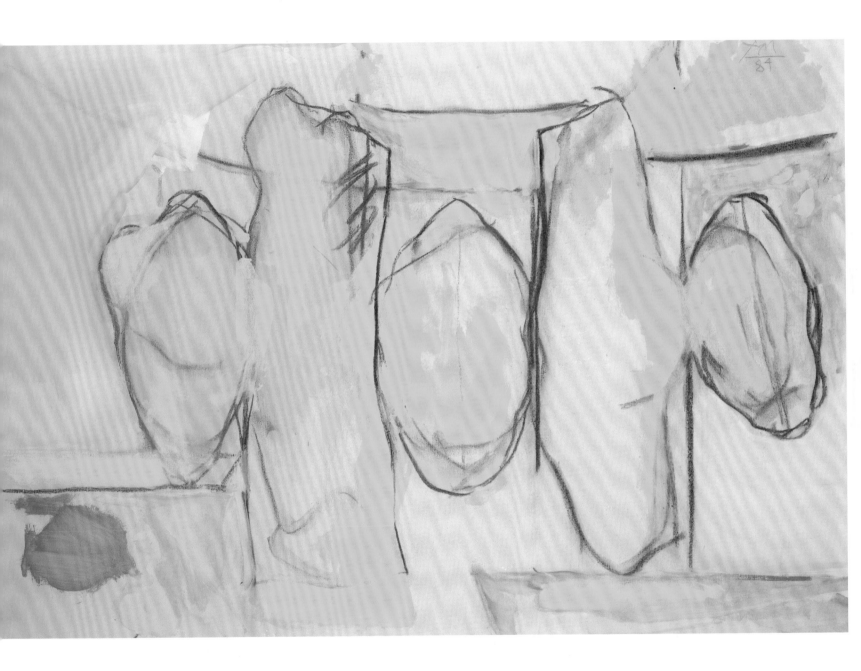

ROBERT BURNS MOTHERWELL briefly attended the California School of Fine Arts in San Francisco before studying philosophy at Stanford, Harvard, Grenoble and Columbia universities. This unusual combination of academic training enabled him to write authoritatively on various aspects and theories of modern art, more especially the American brand of Abstract Expressionism which he helped to formulate in the 1940s. He only took up painting professionally in 1941, due to the influence of Roberto Matta. Motherwell's large paintings were often characterized by unconscious doodles, a concept which arose from his interest in Freudian psychoanalysis and the interpretation of dreams.

With Mark Rothko and others he founded the Subjects of the Artist movement to encourage the development of the next generation, and was also preoccupied with aspects of Symbolism.

William Hawkins   Niagara Falls, 1986

Born 1895 Kentucky, USA   Painted in Columbus, Ohio   Died 1990 Columbus, Ohio
MOVEMENT: American Vernacular, Outsider School   **OTHER WORKS:** *Abstract, The Last Supper, Prancing Horse, Country House*   **INFLUENCES:** None

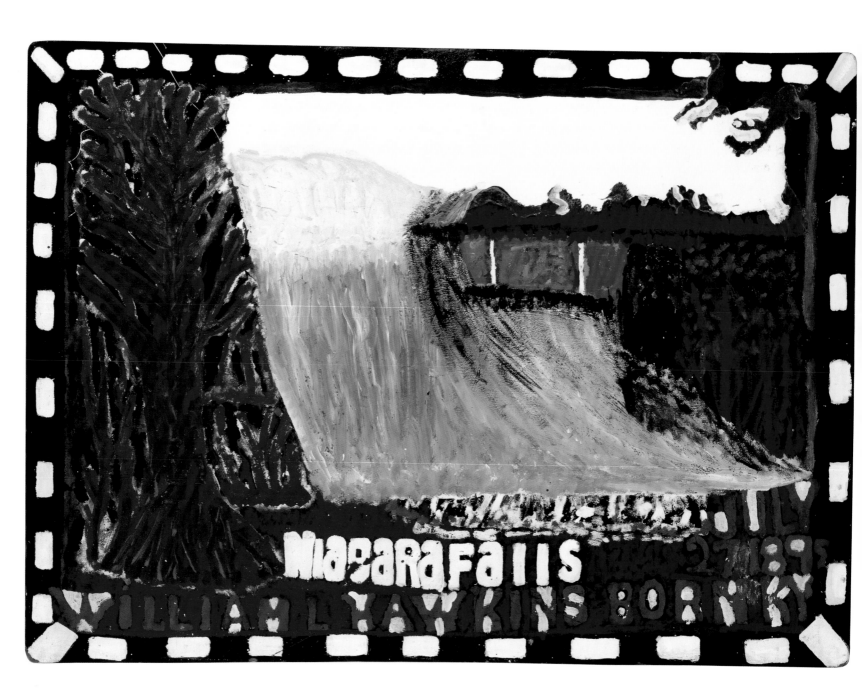

ONE OF the foremost practitioners of American Vernacular and Outsider Art to emerge in the late twentieth century, William Hawkins was barely able to read or write and had no art training at all. Despite this he produced an extraordinary range of paintings. He migrated to Columbus, Ohio in 1916, where he held a wide variety of jobs, from truck-driver to brothel-keeper. Although he began drawing in the 1930s, he did not begin painting in the style that made him famous until the late 1970s. His technique evolved naturally – dripping paint on to cardboard or plywood tilted to 'watch the painting make itself'. Vivid imagery combined motifs seen in newspapers with memories of his native Kentucky countryside. From his early years he had a deep knowledge of animals, an awareness that informs even his most fantastic dinosaur paintings. Latterly he combined paint with pieces of wood, gravel or found objects. His pictures often have elaborate borders including his full name with date and place of birth.

Keith Haring   Untitled

Born 1958 Pennsylvania, USA   Painted in New York   Died 1990 New York
MOVEMENT: Conceptualism **OTHER WORKS:** *Ignorance-Fear, Silence-Death, Untitled* **INFLUENCES:** Keith Sonnler, Joseph Kossuth

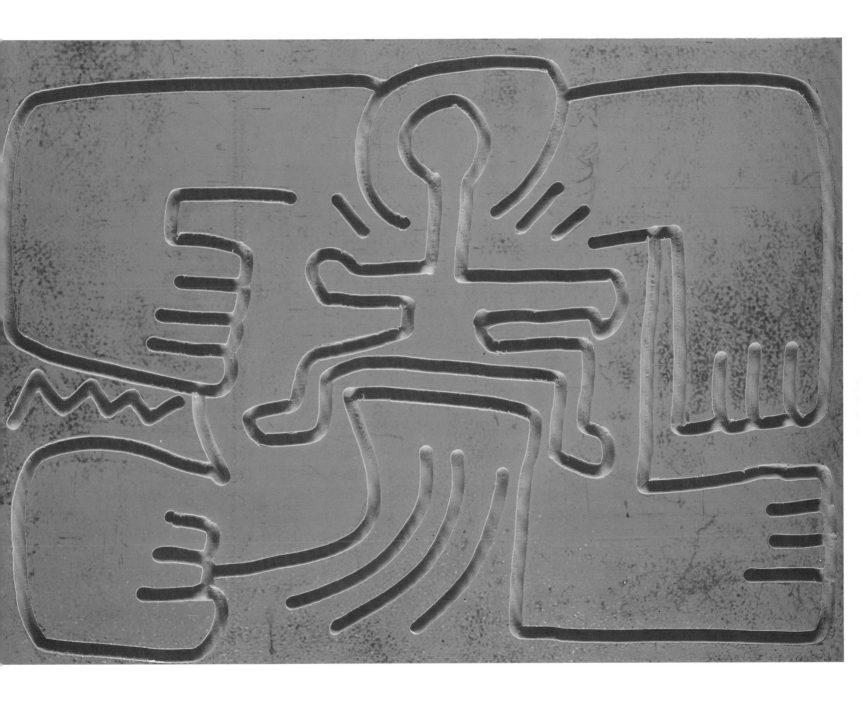

KEITH HARING received his formal training at the Ivy School of Art in Pittsburgh, followed in 1978 by a year at the New York School of Visual Arts. In this period he was influenced by Keith Sonnler and Joseph Kossuth, who encouraged him to experiment with form and colour, and to develop as a Conceptualist. His informal (though, in the long run the most influential) art education came through the medium of comic strips and television cartoons as well as the graffiti of the New York streets. He himself spent some time covering the commercial advertisements on the New York subway with flamboyant graffiti executed with coloured chalks and marker pens. Prolific and far-ranging, his work reflected the age in which he grew up. In the 1980s he graduated from the sidewalk to commercial art, producing motifs reproduced on T-shirts and badges, and then posters and murals, drawing on the fertile mix of cultures in his adopted city.

Avigdor Arikha   Alexander Frederick Douglas–Home, Lord Home of the Hirsel, 1988

Born 1929 Bukovina, Romania   Painted in Israel, France, England and USA

MOVEMENT: International School   **OTHER WORKS:** *Anne from the Back, 1973; The Square in June, 1983* **INFLUENCES:** Mondrian

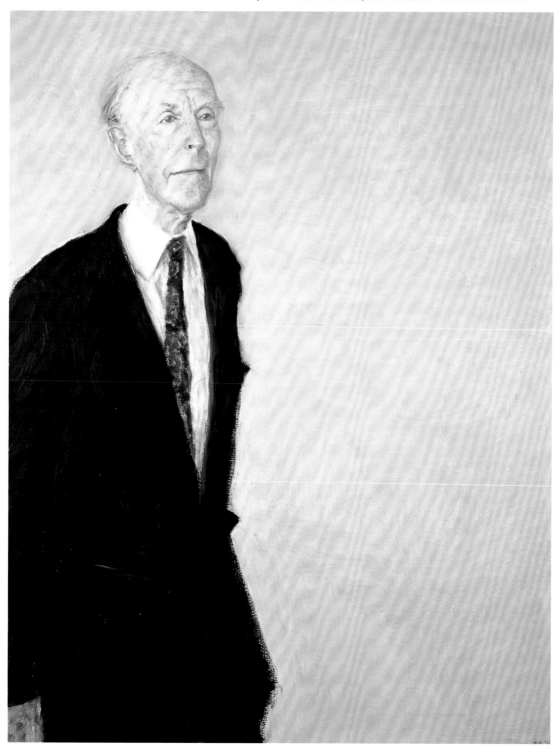

AVIGDOR ARIKHA was born in 1929 in Bukovina (Romania), and survived the Holocaust thanks to the boyhood drawings he had created in deportation. He arrived in Palestine in 1944 where he received a Bauhaus art-education at Bezalel, Jerusalem, (1946-1949), and where he was also severely wounded in Israel's war of Independence (1948). He continued his art studies at the Ecole des Beaux-Arts in Paris

(1949-1951) where he still mainly resides. His style, which was at first figurative, had evolved into abstraction in the late 1950s. He renounced abstraction in 1965 in favour of drawing and painting from observation, treating all subjects, whether they be still-lifes, landscapes, nudes or portraits (such as Lord Home and Queen Elizabeth the Queen Mother) in a single sitting. As an art historian, Arikha has

curated exhibitions at the Louvre (Poussin, 1979) and the Frick Collection in New York (Ingres, 1986), among others. His writings include: *Peinture et Regard*, Paris, 1991 and *On Depiction*, London, 1995. Books about him include *Arikha* by Samuel Beckett, Robert Hughes et al., London, 1985 and *Avigdor Arikha* by Monica Ferrando and Arturo Schwarz, Bergamo, 2001.

Chuck Close   Linda, 1975–76

Born 1940 Monroe, Washington State, USA Painted in New York, USA
MOVEMENT: Superrealism **OTHER WORKS:** *John, Cindy II* **INFLUENCES:** Claude Cahun

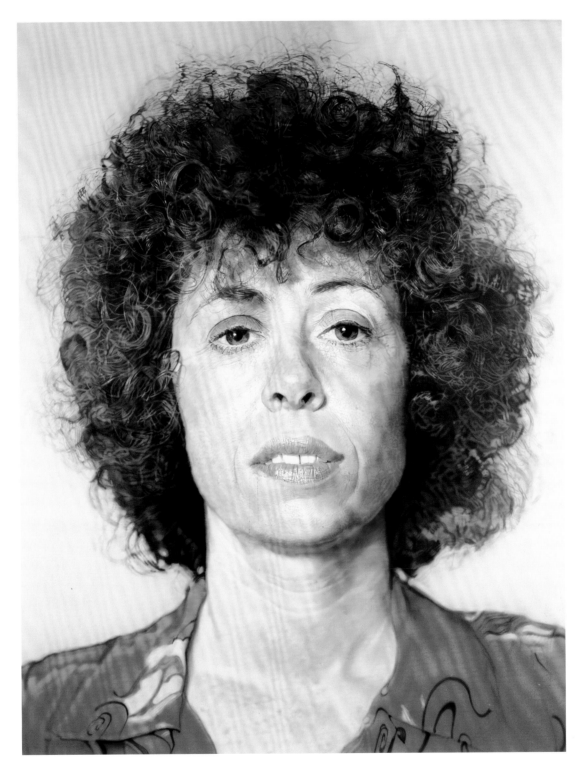

CHUCK CLOSE studied art at Yale from 1962 to 1964 and settled in New York City in 1967. In that year, influenced by the photographic self-portraits produced by Claude Cahun in the 1920s, he began painting photographs of portraits, meticulously reproducing the tiniest detail. Every line and wrinkle, every pore and individual strands of hair are carefully delineated. Close goes to enormous lengths to avoid any suggestion of painterly texture: he transfers a snapshot to a gigantic grid, then works with an airbrush to reproduce the sheer-smooth effects of the photographic original, and its flaws. Closer examination often reveals slight distortion or blurring around the ears or shoulders, which conveys the impression that the face is looming towards the viewer and duplicate's the shortcomings of the camera lens. Here, for example, the photograph's failure to cope with the stream of sunlight on the subject's hair, and the slight loss of focus about the shoulders, are both recreated by Close.

In more recent years he has taken this a stage further, combining this photo-realism with such techniques as finger-painting, a microscopic stippled effect reminiscent of pointillism and collages.

Paula Rego   The Cadet and his Sister, 1988

Born 1935 Lisbon, Portugal   Painted in Britain and Portugal

MOVEMENT: Symbolist Figuration **OTHER WORKS**: *Crivelli's Garden, The Policeman's Daughter* **INFLUENCES:** Jean Dubuffet, Picasso, Walt Disney, James Gillray

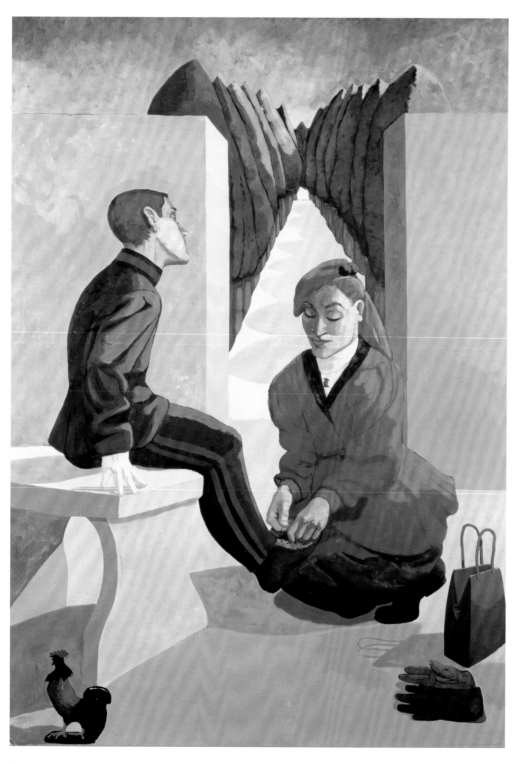

PAULA REGO was born in Lisbon, but her father worked for Marconi in Essex, and she was educated at an English school. In 1952, she entered the Slade School of Art, where she trained under Sir William Coldstream. There she met Victor Willing, a fellow painter, who became her husband in 1959. They lived in Portugal until 1963, after which they resided principally in England.

Rego's early work was strongly influenced by Dubuffet. She also produced semi-abstract collages, sometimes with political overtones. Increasingly, though, she turned to figurative painting, drawing much of her inspiration from children's illustration, nursery rhymes and her own memories of childhood. In mature works, such as The Maids, these playful elements are transposed into unsettling contexts,

hinting at games of a very sinister kind. Rego's paintings have brought her success, both in Portugal and the UK. She has twice represented her native land at the Bienal in São Paolo, and on one occasion for Britain. In 1990, she became the first Associate Artist of the National Gallery in London.

Chéri Samba   Mobali Ya Monyato, 1989

Born 1956 Kinto M'Vulia, Zaire (now Congo)   Painted in Congo
MOVEMENT: Modern African School   **OTHER WORKS:** *Mr Poor's Family*   **INFLUENCES:** Henri Rousseau, Gino Severini

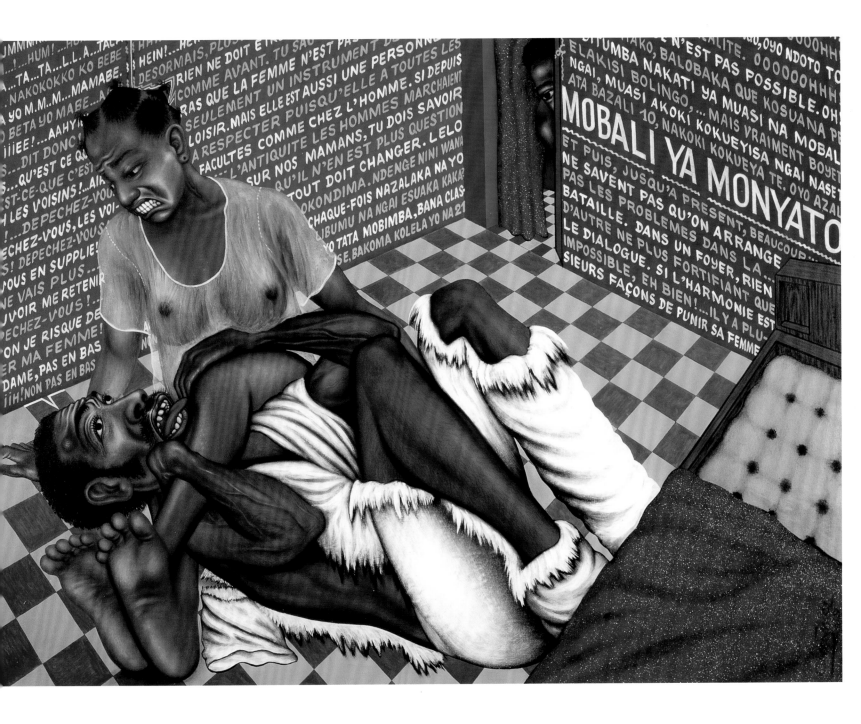

IN COLONIAL times it was axiomatic that aspiring African artists had to receive a good grounding in European styles and techniques, but gradually it dawned that such an influence was often negativeor counterproductive. Fortunately for Chéri Samba, he was entirely self-taught and if he had been influenced in any way by European art it was through the medium of the cartoons and graphic art in contemporary newspapers. In 1975 he graduated from drawing cartoons to painting them on canvas, but without compromising his direct, crystal-clear approach. Every painting tells a story, the images generally enhanced by words, an unconscious borrowing from the art of China and Japan. Detail is painstaking, brushwork is crisp and outlines are hard-edged, enhancing the impact of his work. One of the most prominent of the naive painters to emerge in post-colonial Africa, his paintings with their undertones of social realism are now in many international collections.

Ian Abdulla   Sowing Seeds at Nite, 1990

Born 1947 Swan Reach, South Australia   Painted in Australia

MOVEMENT: Modern Australian School   **OTHER WORKS:** *Tyerabarrbowaryaou, I Shall Never Become a White Man*   **INFLUENCES:** Aboriginal traditional art forms

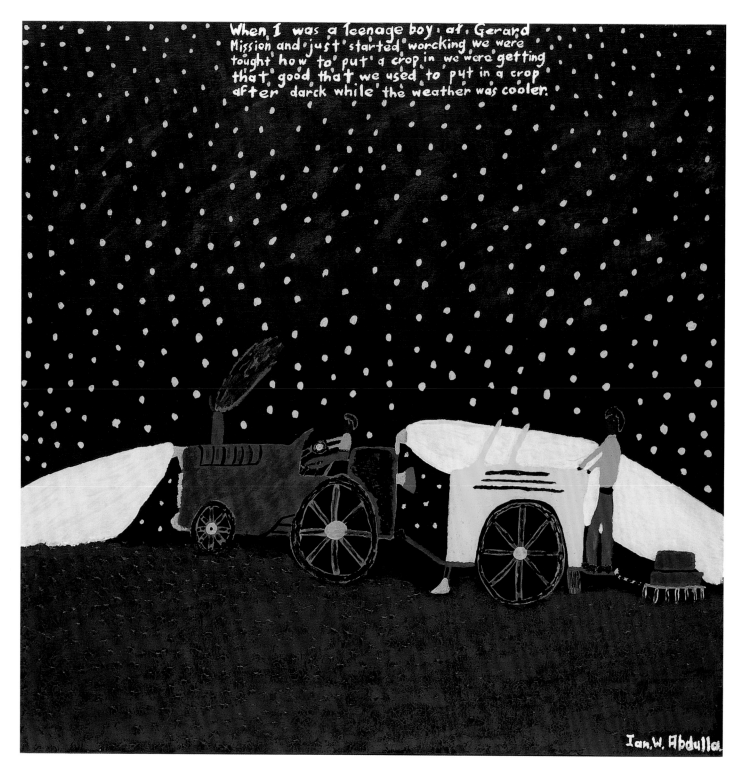

THIS ABORIGINAL artist spent his boyhood in an idyllic riverside setting in South Australia, and consequently the river in all its aspects is a recurring theme in his paintings. He studied art in Adelaide and had his first one-man show in the Tandanya National Aboriginal Culture Institute in that city in 1990. He has since had one-man shows in many other parts of Australia and was declared South Australian Aboriginal Artist of the Year in 1991, winning the National Aboriginal Award for best painting five years later. His paintings are in all the major Australian galleries, including the National Museum of Australia in Canberra. In more recent years he has achieved international fame with award-winning exhibits in Canada and Cuba. His paintings combine the traditional patterns and art forms of Aboriginal tribal culture stretching back thousands of years with Western techniques, creating both figurative and semi-abstract works in a highly distinctive style.

Lucian Freud   Annabel, 1990

Born 1922 Berlin, Germany   Painted in Britain

MOVEMENT: Realism, School of London **OTHER WORKS:** *Hotel Bedroom, Francis Bacon* **INFLUENCES:** Cedric Morris, Ingres, George Grosz

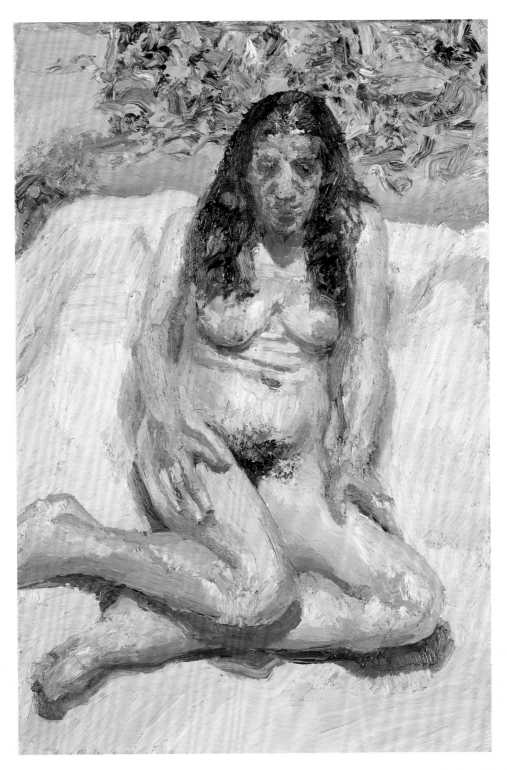

NATURALIZED BRITISH painter; a leading member of the school of London. Freud was born in Berlin, the grandson of the famous psychoanalyst Sigmund Freud. As a Jewish family living in the shadow of Nazism, the Freuds left Germany in the 1930s, settling in London. Lucian joined the Merchant Navy, becoming an artist after he was invalided out of the service in 1942. He trained under Cedric Morris, and the hallucinatory realism of his early style hints at an admiration for Surrealism and Neue Sachlichkeit. His greatest influence, however, was Ingres. Freud emulated the meticulous draughtsmanship of the Frenchman, apparently attempting to depict every strand of hair on his sitters. His virtuoso skill was recognized when in 1951, his remarkable *Interior at Paddington* won a prize at the Festival of Britain.

Freud's style changed in the late 1950s, when he replaced his fine sable brushes with stiffer, hog-hair ones which led to a more painterly approach, in which the artist conveyed his flesh-tones through thicker slabs of colour. Freud's favourite subject matter has been the 'naked portrait': starkly realistic nudes, devoid of any picturesque or idealizing elements.

Bridget Riley   Close by, 1992

Born 1931 London, England   Painted in London
MOVEMENT: Op Art **OTHER WORKS:** *Cataract I, In Attendance, Fission, Fall* **INFLUENCES:** Giacomo Balla, Umberto Boccioni, Joseph Albers

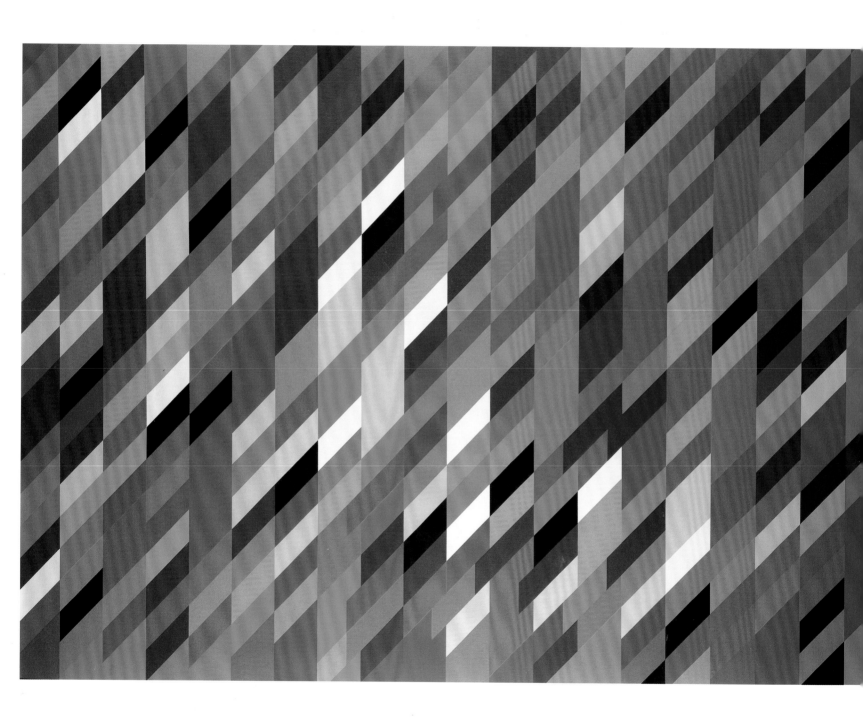

BRIDGET RILEY studied at Goldsmith's College of Art (1949–52) and the Royal College of Art (1952–55) in London. She had her first one-woman exhibition at Gallery One, London, in 1962 and has had many other shows all over the world in subsequent years. Influenced by the Futurists Giacomo Balla and Umberto Boccioni, she began to develop an optical style in the 1960s – now known as Op Art – in which hallucinatory images were created in black and white, in geometric or curvilinear patterns endlessly repeated to produce the illusion of rippling or undulating movement. By 1966 she had moved into colour, which enabled her to widen the scope of these images considerably; her colours vary in depth and tone and add subtlety to the overall pattern. Widely acclaimed in England, she made an impact on the international scene in 1968 when she became the first British artist to win the top award for painting at the Venice Biennale.

Jaune Quick–to–see Smith   Modern Times on the Rez, *c.*1992–93

Born 1940 St Ignatius Flathead Reservation, Montana, USA   Painted in New Mexico, USA
MOVEMENT: Native American School **OTHER WORKS:** *Ghost Dance Dress* **INFLUENCES:** Miró, Kandinsky, Paul Klee

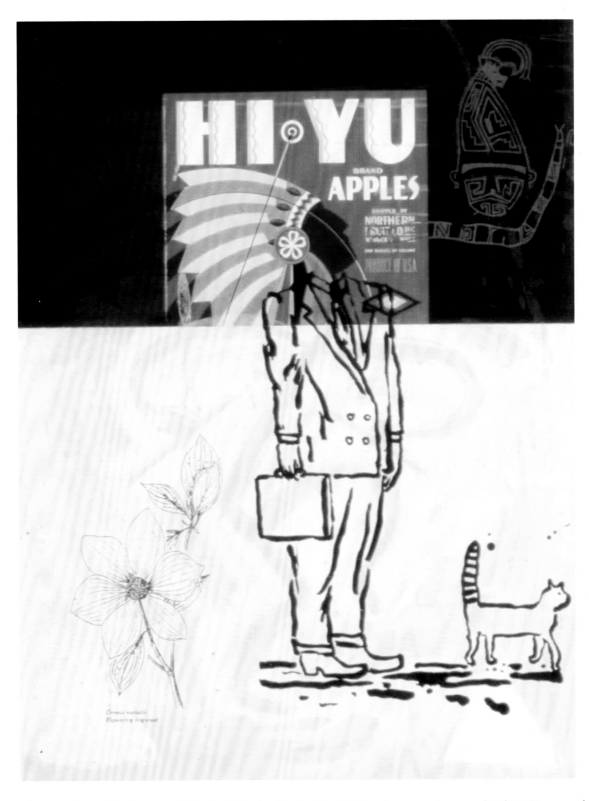

JAUNE SMITH derives her unusual name from her Shoshoni grandmother, being herself also of Cree and Métis descent. She followed the Famous American art course in high school then took degrees in fine art at Olympic College, Bremerton, Framingham State College and the University of New Mexico. Since the 1960s she has lived at Corrales, New Mexico, where she paints in a wide range of media, though preferring oils and acrylics. Her paintings, which she describes as 'nomad art' vary enormously in subject from figures and genre studies to landscapes and semi-abstract works. One of the most articulate of Native American artists, she emerged in the 1980s as one of the foremost Native American artists. Her paintings reflect a long-term commitment to feminist issues and the problems of the indigenous peoples of North America.

Peter Howson   Study for the Bestiary, Fieldmouse

Born 1958 London, England   Painted in England, Scotland and the Balkans
MOVEMENT: Modern British School   **OTHER WORKS:** *A Night That Never Ends, Plum Grove, Patriots*   **INFLUENCES:** Stanley Spencer

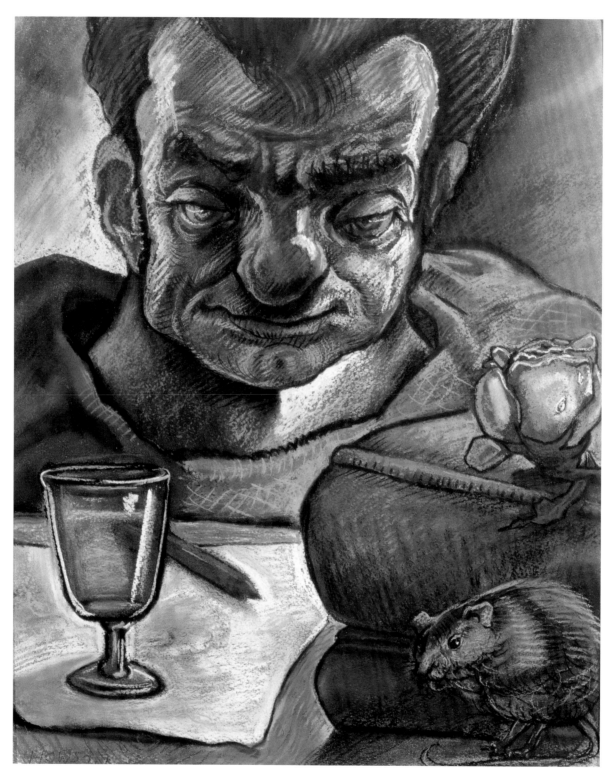

ALTHOUGH BORN in London, Peter Howson trained at the Glasgow School of Art from 1975 to 1981 and has since lived in Scotland, apart from forays abroad as an official war artist. His style is essentially figurative, but he took the lead in creating the New Image, which has had a tremendous impact on British art since the late 1980s. Living and working in Glasgow – a city which was then in the process of re-inventing itself in the aftermath of post-industrial decay – he was strongly influenced by the prevailing socio-economic conditions and his paintings have echoes of the Social Realism of the 1930s. His figures, though recognizable, are often monstrous in appearance, reflecting the harshness of living and working conditions. This stark realism came to fruition in his paintings from the Balkan conflicts of the 1990s when, as a war artist, he did not pull his punches on the atrocities and appalling hardships he witnessed. An uncompromising, often fearful, reality pervades his work.

Emily Kame Kngwarreye   Bush Yam Awelye, 1994

Born *c.* 1910 Northern Territory, Australia   Painted in Australia   Died 1996 Northern Territory, Australia
MOVEMENT: Utopia Australian School **OTHER WORKS:** *Emu Woman* **INFLUENCES:** Louie Pwerle

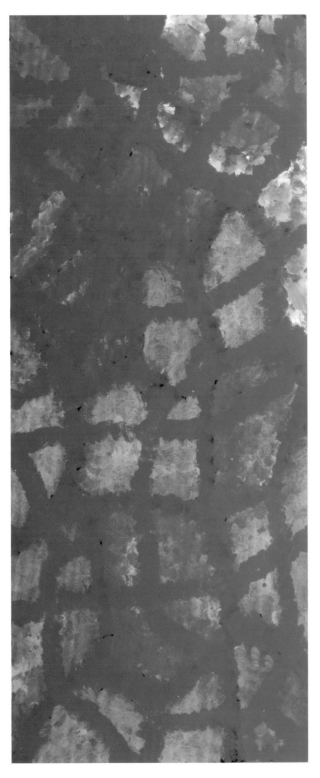

EMILY KAME Kngwarreye was an elder of the Alhalkere tribe and did not take up painting until her seventies. About 1977 she became a member of the Utopia Women's Batik group and showed artistic promise in her unusual treatment of traditional Aboriginal patterns. As a painter, she made her debut in the summer of 1988 with a series of pictures painted in acrylics on canvas and distinguished by their combination of traditional Amnatyerre ceremonial body designs and art forms. She used strong, linear designs, overlaid with fields of dots, in essence a miniaturization of the large ground paintings associated with tribal ceremonies. Although reduced to the confines of the canvas, however, her paintings possess great strength and vitality. Images are abstracted from several sources and coalesced in powerful motifs inspired by the mythological Aboriginal Dreamtime.

Joseph Matar   Glow of Morning, 2001

Born 1935 Ghadir, Lebanon   Painted in Lebanon, Spain, France and Italy

MOVEMENT: Modern Lebanese School **OTHER WORKS:** *Corner of the Galaxy, Marriage Feast at Cana, Harvest, Temple* **INFLUENCES:** Omar Onsi, Rachid Wehbe, George Corm

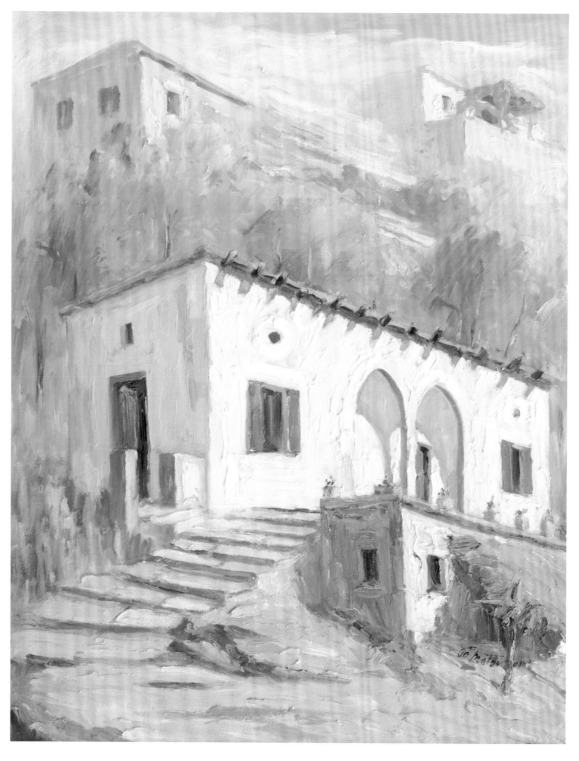

JOSEPH MATAR was educated at the Marist Brothers' School in Jounieh and began working as an artist in Beirut. He received his art training under Omar Onsi, Rachid Webbe and George Corm between 1951 and 1957, while studying at the Italian Cultural Centre in Beirut (1955–57) and anatomy at the Beirut Faculty of Medicine (1958). Travelling scholarships enabled him to continue his studies at the San Fernando School of Fine Arts in Madrid (1961–63), Rome (1973) and the University of Paris (1963 and 1985). He began teaching art in 1954 at both high-school and university levels and has held a number of professorships since 1980. He has had more than 60 one-man shows around the world and his paintings are in major collections in many countries. Matar paints in oils and watercolours, both abstracts and landscapes. In addition to being the Lebanon's foremost contemporary painter he is a poet of considerable merit, recognized by an award for outstanding achievement from the International Library of Poetry, 2001.

Kura Te Waru Rewiri I nga haerenga me nga hokinga mai (Coming and going), 2001

Born 1950 Painted in New Zealand

MOVEMENT: Modern Maori School, New Zealand **OTHER WORKS:** *Nga Tohu O Te Tiriti, Whenua Wahine Whenua* **INFLUENCES:** Rudolf Gopas

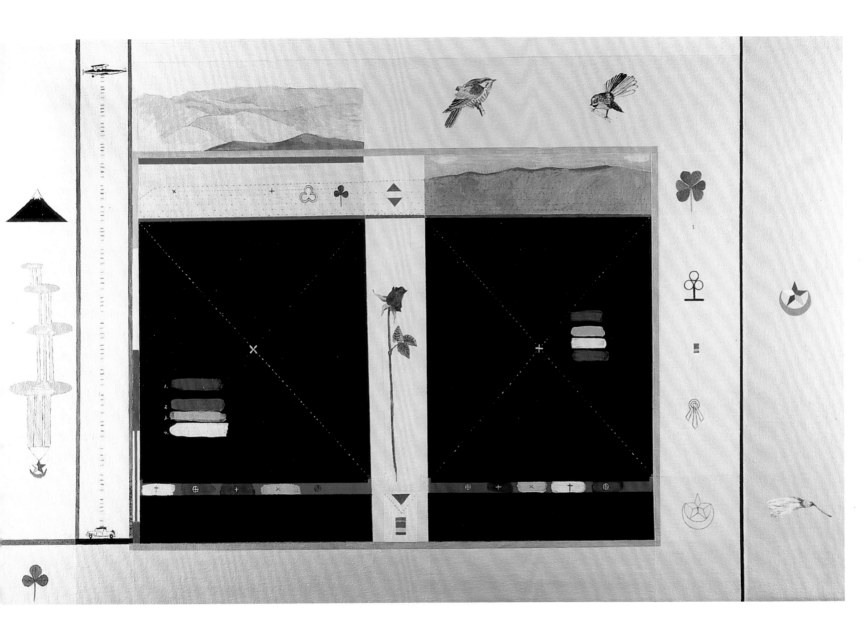

KURA TE Waru Rewiri studied at the Canterbury School of Fine Arts in Christchurch, from which she graduated in 1973. She had a conventional art training in Western Expressionism, but was strongly influenced by Rudolf Gopas, who told her that she should never forget that she was a Maori. This has shaped the pattern of her art in the subsequent period, both in subject matter and in the style of her painting. She uses strongly contrasting colours in vivid compositions which, while figural, have underlying symbolism and hidden meanings. A typical example of this is her great painting of the Treaty of Waitangi, negotiated between the British and the Maori chiefs in 1840. By placing the cross in the centre of the picture she suggests the sacrifice of her people and the role of the Christian missionaries in undermining Maori culture. In more recent years she has turned more and more to traditional art forms, notably godstick figures.

Painting Techniques

So often people look at a picture – the end-product of an artist's endeavour – for the form and content, and do not focus on the technicalities. What materials did he or she use and how were they applied? On what substance was the picture painted? A knowledge of the methods, techniques and materials and how they interact provides an invaluable insight into the art of different periods and styles as well as a better understanding of the individual artist. The materials available at different times and in different places have often had an important bearing on both the subject matter and the manner in which the work was painted.

To take one example (which, incidentally, spans the entire period of art in human history), for thousands of years Australian Aborigines have been employing the careful arrangement of soils and sands of different colours and textures to create pictures whose patterns and symbolism relate to the stories and myths of the ancestral Dreamtime and tribal history or customs. Today there are native Australian painters working with conventional Western materials such as oils or acrylics on canvas or board to produce stunning visual effects, in the very forefront of modern art, but which have adapted traditional, age-old imagery to contemporary techniques. This is, perhaps, an extreme case; but in the course of the past century alone it seems as if all the methods, techniques and materials from many different civilizations and periods have come together. In the never-ending search for something new, art has become more eclectic than ever.

By contrast, the art of the world up to the end of the nineteenth century followed fairly defined patterns and courses. There are many factors – aesthetic, social, economic and political – that have governed the various movements and styles in art through the ages, but many of them also evolved out of changes in technique and they, in turn, arose because of the introduction or invention of new materials. Although this survey is primarily concerned with methods and techniques it is essential that we also examine the materials available to artists at different times and in different parts of the world. These are the basic ingredients of a painting and they play an important part not only in what is possible or impossible but also in how the painter approaches the subject, or even what type of subject is available. There are other factors which, at various times in different places, have affected methods and techniques. Regional variations in climate should be obvious, yet their effects on how people painted, and in what media, have often been overlooked or ignored.

Paleolithic Techniques

The oldest forms of two-dimensional art (as opposed to sculpture) found in Europe are the paintings that have been discovered in caves from north-western Spain to southern Russia. These pictures, executed over thousands of years during the Old Stone Age (Paleolithic period) vary considerably in size and style. Some are very small while others are life-size representations of animals. What is more important in this context, however, is the manner in which these pictures were produced and the materials used.

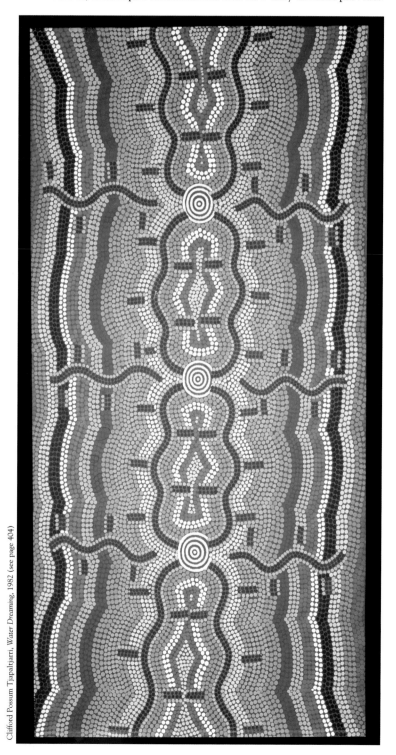

Clifford Possum Tjapaltjarri, *Water Dreaming*, 1982 (see page 404)

Many of these pictures on the walls and ceilings of caves were first engraved using a sharpened flint tool, rather like the burin used by etchers and engravers to this day. In the Trois Frères cave in southern France one such flint tool was discovered on a ledge below an engraving of a lion. One can imagine the artist putting it down while standing back to admire his handiwork, or perhaps he went off for the Stone Age equivalent of a lunch-break and forgot where he had left it. And there it would lie for perhaps 10,000 years until some pot-holer stumbled across it. Having created the outlines of the picture, the artist would then colour them in. The pigments used varied considerably from district to district, depending on what mineral oxides were available. Iron oxides produced a wide range of shades from bright red, through chestnut to darker brown, while manganese oxides provided the darker colours from blue to black. Iron carbonates yielded the yellows and vermilions. Carbon-dating has confirmed what early archaeologists could only surmise: that the greatest variety of different colours belong to the most recent period, around 10,000 BC. Burnt wood and bone produced primitive forms of charcoal pencil, which were also used to sketch the outline and sometimes to produce the effects of tones and shading. Although the black arising out of carbonized materials was less permanent than manganese oxides it has survived surprisingly well in those caves which were not exposed to the weather or climatic extremes. These oxides and carbonates were ground to a fine powder and then mixed with animal fat or oils. Tubes of paint fashioned from bones, and even palettes of slate or flat bones, have been discovered in these caves, showing how the paints were prepared and mixed. How they were applied is not known for certain, but they were probably laid on with the fingers and palms of the hands, although in some cases it appears that they were applied with sticks or pads made from pieces of fur or hide.

We tend to think of Stone Age painters merely adorning the walls of their living quarters, but many of these caves extend for considerable distances and it is astonishing that paintings have been discovered in extremely inaccessible places where the artist would have had to crawl through narrow spaces. Working in total darkness, illuminated only by some primitive stone lamp using animal oil and a moss wick, the Palaeolithic artists often created their masterpieces in extraordinary conditions. What drove them to do this is not known but we may speculate that their art had some mystical or quasi-religious significance.

What of the techniques employed by these cave dwellers? From the outset they strove to record their impressions of animals and hunting scenes. We can see the evolution of human figures, for example, from 'matchstick men' – not unlike the earliest attempts at drawings by little children to this day. In the most primitive works there was no correlation between the hunters and the hunted, but later some attempt was made to depict them in an appropriate scale, although these cave painters never seem to have progressed beyond the stage of creating images in direct proportions as if side by side. Movement is one illusion that they tried to recreate, although this never got beyond the simple convention of painting animal and human figures slanted upwards or downwards or, in the most sophisticated examples, by an attempt to convey such actions as running or jumping by the arrangement of the limbs.

Similar methods and techniques have been discovered in the cave paintings of primitive civilizations nearer the present time in many parts of the world, notably central Australia, where the Stone Age culture of the Aborigines has many affinities with that found in Paleolithic Europe. That there is a huge gap between the Old Stone Age and the art of the great civilizations of the Middle and Near East may be explained by the fact that paintings that were not preserved in remote and inaccessible caves would not have stood the test of time.

Fresco

Paintings dated to around 3,000 BC were used to decorate the walls of tombs and temples. Paint was probably also applied to the murals in palaces and villas as well, but none has survived. Like the earlier cave-paintings, tomb-paintings survived because they were not exposed to sunlight or weather. Similar paintings have been recorded in the Minoan civilization of Cyprus at a slightly later date and the same techniques continued through the Classical periods of Greece and Rome. The technique invented by the Egyptians and perfected by later civilizations is known as fresco (the Italian word for 'fresh'). It may be defined as painting on wet lime plaster using pigments mixed with water and lime. As the water evaporates, the setting of the lime binds the pigment to the plaster. The process is completed by chemical reaction: exposure to the air converts the lime to carbonate of lime and this has the effect of fixing the pigment, just as if the painting on a piece of pottery was glazed and fixed by firing in a kiln.

The pigments used by the earliest Egyptians were basically the same as those used by the prehistoric cave-dwellers, but gradually the range was extended to include ochre (reds and browns) and malachite (greens and blues). These minerals were ground to a very fine powder and mixed with water and lime, but the Greeks, and possibly also the Minoans of Knossos, gave body to their painting materials by adding egg yolk, size, gum arabic or beeswax. The earliest written account of the technique of fresco painting was given by Vitruvius, who stated that the Romans borrowed the practice from the Greeks. Immense care was taken in the preparation of Roman plaster, which was several inches thick. The basis was composed of the *arriccio*, a mixture of crumbled bricks, sand and lime, on top of which were several layers of lime and powdered marble, progressively finer and smoother and carefully applied with a trowel to create a highly polished surface. It has been argued that only the ground colouring was applied in a mixture of pigment and lime water, and that the final painting was executed in an emulsion, but it is impossible to say for certain. Roman painters also used a technique whereby colours with a wax base were applied by some kind of heat treatment, and there is some evidence to suggest that this refinement was used to create the astonishingly colourful frescoes at Pompeii.

This technique, however, seems to have been uncommon, and when fresco-painting was revived at Rome in the thirteenth century the usual method was either to apply the paint to the still-wet plaster or to dampen dry plaster immediately prior to painting. Whichever was the case, there was no way in which frescoes could be repainted and there was no margin for error on the part of the painter. This method of painting continued more or less unchanged until the fifteenth century and the great era of ecclesiastical decoration. By that time the Italian painters were distinguishing between *fresco secco*, the art of painting in watercolours on dry plaster, and *buon fresco*, the more traditional technique of mixing pigments with lime and water applied to fresh wet plaster. Because of the haste with which the painter had to work, he would plan the exact design in pencil on paper or parchment as a preliminary cartoon (from the Italian *cartone*, literally 'a little card') – long before this term took on the more specialized meaning of a satirical drawing. The cartoon was often overlaid with grid lines, corresponding, on a larger scale, to a pencil drawing on the plaster itself, known as the *sinopia* (from the Greek *synopsis*, meaning 'overview'). In the case of large murals a thin layer of wet plaster (*intonaco*) was applied to an area sufficient for each day's painting, working from the top left-hand corner to the bottom right-hand corner, in daily sections known as *giornate*. Whatever portion remained unpainted at the end of the day was carefully scraped away and the edges undercut, the process being repeated the following day. A careful examination of late medieval frescoes will often reveal the joins in the plasterwork. *Buon fresco* might be used for the principal subjects. Such features as the texture of clothing, hair and fur could be suggested with the point of a very fine hard brush.

Treatises on painting dating from the fifteenth century give various recipes for both lime and the mixture of pigments. The exact proportions of lime and sand (a ratio of 1:2) were just as important as the preparation of the lime itself, which could take years to mature correctly. White colouring was known as *bianco sangiovanni* ('St John's white') and was produced from little cakes of slaked lime exposed to air and sunlight for several months. To the basic pigments of the ancients, the Italians added raw or burnt sienna, *terra verte*, metallic oxides such as chrome yellow and the cobalt blues and greens. The Germans invented smalt (*Schmalte*), a deep blue pigment which revolutionized the appearance of stained glass and enamels, but which was also adapted to fresco painting. Previously the Italians had obtained this colour from ground azurite, which tended to turn green with exposure to the atmosphere and the carbonic acid in the lime. This chemical reaction was countered to some extent by mixing the powdered azurite with egg-yolk, but to achieve a true deep-blue effect only ultramarine (an expensive substance produced by grinding lapis lazuli) would suffice. Fresco painting has been revived in recent times; notable exponents include the Italian José Clemente Orozco (1883–1949) and the Mexican muralist Francesco Clemente (b. 1952).

Tempera

Broadly speaking tempera (Italian for 'temper') was a process that involved some sort of binding material (other than oil). Traditionally this was egg-yolk, a substance that was also extensively used in fresco painting, but any albuminous, gelatinous or colloidal material could be mixed with pigments to achieve similar results. The terms fresco and tempera are sometimes used as if they were synonymous, but the distinction lies not so much in the mixture but the material to which it was applied. Thus tempera is more commonly associated with the paintings on mummy cases and papyrus rolls in pharaonic Egypt, or medieval paintings on ivory or wood panels, although some wall paintings in ancient Egypt, Knossos, Mycenae and Classical Rome probably relied on this technique. Egg-yolk, sometimes diluted by a little vinegar, was the preferred medium, though a thin glue produced by boiling animal skins was also extremely effective, while Pliny mentions milk as a binding substance.

Although tempera is mainly associated with relatively small paintings executed on wood panels, the paint was not applied directly on to the wood. The surface had to be prepared and this entailed a process that was not unlike the plastering of walls, but on a much smaller scale. It was more refined than fresco and called for a greater degree of preparation. First of all, only certain types of close-grained timber were suitable for this purpose – lime, poplar and willow being preferred. Panels were carefully planed and any graining, knots or other blemishes filled with a mixture of size and sawdust and rubbed to a smooth surface. The panel was then covered with a piece of old linen affixed by glue. A material known as gesso (Italian for 'gypsum' or 'chalk', mixed with animal glue) was then added in up to eight layers. First came the *gesso grosso* ('heavy plaster'), evenly spread with a spatula or broad-bladed knife, and finally the *gesso sottile* ('subtle plaster'), diluted with water and mixed with size, was applied by means of a broad brush. When this surface was perfectly dry it could be painted with tempera paints.

Because the paints were readily absorbed by the gesso and dried rapidly, tempera was a technique that called for great skill and extreme rapidity on the part of the painter. In unskilled hands, tempera often appears as very flat, but the best practitioners were capable of amazing results. By the technique known as *chiaroscuro* (from the Italian words for 'light' and 'dark') tone and shade could be achieved, either by hatched strokes, as in fresco painting, or more usually by repeated coats of paint on the precise area until the desired depth and darkness was achieved. Tempera was a popular medium for icons and religious triptychs and looked particularly effective when the painted areas contrasted with gold surrounds. This called for a separate technique in which the areas to be gilded were given several coats of red bole to which the gold leaf was firmly affixed with egg white.

Egg tempera on wood was the preferred medium of such Renaissance artists as Cimabue, Duccio, Fra Lippo Lippi, Ghirlandajo and Botticelli, while others, such as Piero della Francesca, Titian and Tintoretto employed it in their underpainting, using oils for the final painting. Tempera was widely used before the advent of oil painting which spread from northern Europe, but though the Italian artists were the last to abandon it generally in favour of oils, paradoxically tempera continued for several generations among the primitive painters of Germany and the Low Countries.

Although largely superseded by oil painting, tempera survived fitfully over the years and enjoyed a new lease of life in the nineteenth century, as part of the general revival of interest in the arts and crafts of the late Middle Ages, and in more recent years the technique of tempera has been combined with oils. Dry colours with a tempera medium were also used extensively in commercial art from the early twentieth century, the pigments mixed with a compound of glycerine and gum arabic to produce colours of greater depth and intensity than was generally possible with watercolours. Like fresco, this modern version of tempera is a direct process which dries quickly and does not permit the artist second thoughts.

Oil Painting

Although the mixture of pigments with oil revolutionized the art of painting, the distinction between tempera and oil painting is not as clear-cut as is often stated, any more than it can positively be said that it was invented by any one man (although Jan Van Eyck generally gets the credit). There is ample evidence to suggest that oil-based paints were employed in the painting and preservation of timber in houses and boats long before the technique was applied to decorative painting. In paintings executed in tempera there are early examples in which portions of the panel were done in oils, either to enhance the central figure or, to paint the large surfaces of boats. In addition, it should be noted that some tempera paintings were subsequently given a thin coating of oil which not only enhanced the brilliance of the colours but made them more durable. Indeed, the principles of oil painting were first enunciated as early as 1100 by a German monk named Theophilus, a fact which implies that the technique, in various forms, was in use long before the 1420s when the brothers Hubert and Jan Van Eyck first employed it. It may be no accident that oil painting developed in northern Europe, where the climate was unsuitable for frescoes. For the same reason, painting in oils on canvas developed more rapidly in places – such as Venice – that had a damp climate unsuited to either frescoes or large wood panels. The chief drawback about oil paint was the inordinate time it took to dry, a point made by Theophilus himself, and it is now considered that over the ensuing three centuries artists experimented with oils and various materials in order to accelerate the drying process.

What is important is that oil paints freed artists from the limitations imposed by fresco and tempera painting for the simple reason that oil paints adhered more readily to a wide variety of surfaces and therefore did not require the costly and time-consuming preparation of these media. The most popular bases for oil painting have been wood and canvas, although other materials, including paper, pasteboard, ivory and metal (notably copper plates) have also been employed at various times right up to the present day. Until the end of the Renaissance period, wood was by far the most common support for oil painting. Although many different timbers have been recorded, the Italian artists preferred the white poplar whereas the Van Eycks and other members of the Flemish School used oak; from the seventeenth century onwards, however, hardwoods such as mahogany and lignum vitae were considered more desirable because they did not split or crack as thin panels of oak were prone to do.

Wood panels were suitable for small pictures but when larger works were contemplated this material was impractical unless (as in the case of the *Magi* by Rubens) it was possible to construct a huge surface

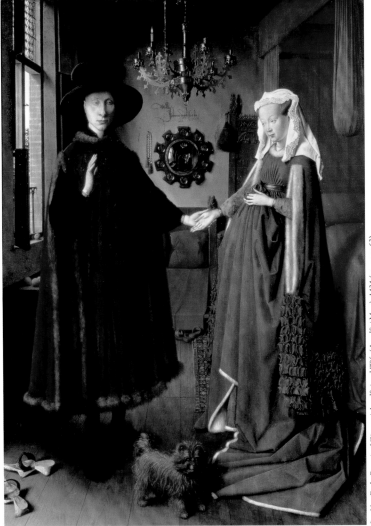

Jan Van Eyck, *Portrait of Giovanni Arnolfini and Wife (Arnolfini Marr)*, 1434 (see page 63)

from a number of transverse sections. For most practical purposes, however, canvas was, and still is, the preferred basis for oil paintings. Here again, the type and quality of canvas is very important. While there are examples of oil paintings on everything from sailcloth to old burlap sacks, the choice of the right materials is all-important, especially for the durability of the painting. In earlier centuries it was found that canvas of pure hemp was ideal, but by the eighteenth century linen canvas of unbleached flax fibre was widely regarded as the finest medium. Canvas that contained cotton fibres, on the other hand, was found to be much less suitable because of the tendency of cotton to expand and contract according to changes in temperature and relative humidity, thereby causing stresses which led to the priming of the paint flaking off and, in extreme cases, cracking the painting.

The surface of a wood panel or a canvas generally required some preparation, known as priming. In wood, for example, this entailed the application of an undercoat which would readily adhere to the wood and facilitate the application of oil paints. Early devotees of oil painting borrowed a practice from frescoes and applied a coating of carbonate of lime, but later a mixture called white lead (which might actually range from grey to brownish-red in colour) was used, either on its own or as a second coat over the lime. Jan Van Eyck, for example, favoured a ground composed of animal glue and chalk, completely

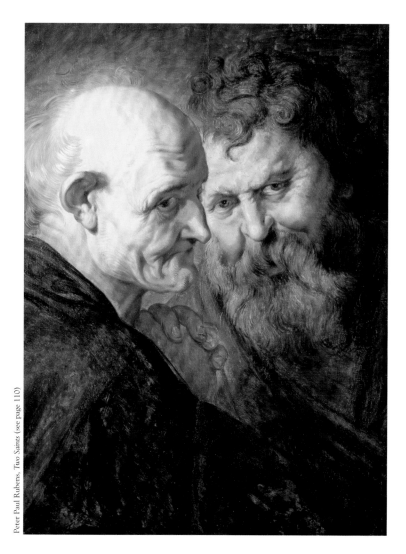

Peter Paul Rubens, *Two Saints* (see page 110)

bitumen (or rather bituminous pigments which included various hydrocarbons) was widely used, notably by Rubens, Rembrandt and other members of the Flemish and Dutch Schools, to produce those transparent shades of brown that characterize their paintings. But far too late in the day it was realized that bitumen never dries and thus is inherently unstable. When it came in contact with quick-drying varnishes the combination could be harmful.

The grinding of colours and mixing them with oil was a long and laborious task which was quite an art in itself. The degree of skill attained might make a considerable difference to the painting itself, and there have been numerous cases of beautiful paintings marred by inattention to this preparatory process. There was also considerable variation in the colours produced by mixing the pigments with different oils. Olive oil was extensively used in Italy chiefly because it was so cheap and readily available, but it fell into disfavour because it dried very slowly. Linseed oil, on the other hand, dried rapidly – perhaps too rapidly – and a happy medium was effected by the use of copal oil, although poppy oil, both light and almost colourless, has been preferred since the mid-nineteenth century. The practice of grinding and mixing colours by hand continued until the beginning of the twentieth century, when the supply of oil paints in tubes, ready-mixed, became prevalent.

Developments in Technique

Paint was generally applied by brushes. Until the nineteenth century these were rounded, but flat brushes were adopted at this time, being more suited to the technique of brushwork that was then coming into fashion, and enabling the artist to paint in separate touches with a full brush. Brushes composed of sable hairs were preferred for fine work while those made of hogs' bristles were more suitable for large expanses of the canvas requiring a broad and vigorous surface. Brushes of this type were first used in Venice because they were better adapted to the rather coarse canvasses popular there. Broad brushes with a rounded head were sometimes employed to blend paint when still wet and soften harsh outlines. Even at quite an early stage in the development of oil painting, artists frequently used their fingers and palms to achieve certain effects, especially in the underpainting. Finger painting was also used extensively in the nineteenth century. Many painters from El Greco onwards occasionally used a fine trowel or a knife with a very thin flexible blade to apply an even groundwork, although it seems to have been Gustave Courbet who took this a stage further and began laying on slabs of paint with a palette knife – a technique that has been applied by many modern painters to create an almost three-dimensional effect. Conversely Edouard Manet frequently scraped or pared away the thick impasto areas of his paintings with a knife before reworking them. Other techniques devised in relatively recent times include the saturation of the canvas with paint rather than sizing and priming it first, and even creating unusual effects by dripping paint on to the canvas or throwing paint at it apparently at random.

Considerable variation can be imparted to the canvas according to the fundamental colours chosen for the groundwork, on which the overall appearance of the finished painting may depend. Among the

covering the wood and rubbed down to produce a very smooth base. From the late seventeenth century, however, a couple of coats of white lead were regarded as the normal practice. The first coat would be applied quite thickly in order to fill up and conceal the weave of the fabric, followed by a thin coat to impart greater smoothness; some painters, however, preferred several fairly thin coats, with a period for thorough drying between each, to achieve the desired flexibility.

The actual pigments were derived from various mineral or vegetable substances and after the development of oil painting the range was infinitely extended. From the nineteenth century onwards scientific research into the properties of coal tar resulted in the vivid aniline colours as well as the combination of various substances such as sodium sulphide and alumina silicates to produce the vivid ultramarine so vital to Renaissance artists but so very expensive at that period.

Strangely enough, white was one of the most difficult colours to procure satisfactorily. Flake white, as it was called, was a lead carbonate, which had a distressing tendency to go yellow and, in extreme cases, turned black as a result of sulphur in the atmosphere. Other colours that were affected by oxidation or sulphurization included pigments from zinc, chromium and cadmium, which were particularly prone to atmospheric chemical reaction, changing colour, turning black or opaque. At one time a form of mineral tar known as

great masters, for example, there were those who had a preference for a particular shade, such as the distinctive grey used by Poussin or the warm pink favoured by Boucher. Rubens, on the other hand, used a groundwork of grey, yellow, brown or some greenish tint as well as plain white, at various times and to suit different circumstances. By contrast many of the paintings on a red or deep brown ground, or the sombre hues approaching black, have not worn well because whatever colours are painted over them have either faded or have been overcome by the dominance of these strong underlying tones. Conversely, pictures with a predominantly white groundwork have generally retained the freshness of their colour harmonies much better. Although oil painting has one obvious advantage over fresco and tempera painting, in that it is possible to paint over one's mistakes and even make quite radical alterations to the composition of a picture, there is always the possibility that in the fullness of time the original detail is going to rise to the surface because the colours have become transparent with the passage of time. There are numerous examples of what the French call *repentirs*, in which the artists' original thoughts prove unfortunately to be much stronger than their changes.

The only solution to this age-old problem was to sketch out on the canvas a fairly detailed outline, in pencil or charcoal, and then paint over it. This was particularly advisable in the case of large canvases and murals. A good example of this is provided by the enormous paintings by Stanley Spencer, where the drawings can still be seen in the unfinished areas of the canvas. Artists either prepared a cartoon to guide them, just as the fresco painters did in the Renaissance period, or prepared sheets of paper on which each of the squares from the cartoon was suitably enlarged. Then the details from the sheets were 'pounced' (pricked out) on to the canvas and the lines joined up.

In his great Arnolfini masterpiece, Jan Van Eyck sketched a detailed outline in watercolour which was then coated with drying oil. This fixed the drawing and provided an impervious basis for the actual painting. Other artists have sketched out a rough outline of the composition in a light monochrome wash, greatly diluted so that the form is barely discernible against the bare canvas but will never obtrude in the finished painting. This technique is extremely useful in landscapes where the large masses of light and shade in the sky, cloud formations, hills and fields, lakes and rivers, can be lightly sketched in and the principal lines mapped out before final and detailed painting takes place. Here again, great care has to be taken to ensure that the light monochrome wash does not clash with any of the colours of the final painting. The pitfalls that beset the artist in achieving the right combination of groundwork and final painting are too

numerous to elaborate here, and no amount of genius ever compensated for ignoring the basic rules. Moreover, painting over an area before it had sufficiently dried out caused cracking at a later date, and the same problem arose when the priming was too smooth.

A very important aspect of oil painting is the varnish applied to the finished canvas to protect the surface from atmospheric pollution and also to give the colours their sparkle and richness of tone. The varnish, in fact, compensates for the loss of oil in the original paintwork, either through natural evaporation as the picture proceeds or because some of the oil seeps through the layers of paint to the canvas. Ideally the varnish should be applied by the artist rather than be left to the art dealer (as was often the case). The varnish should be regarded as an integral part of the painting and deserves to be applied with as much care as the actual choice of colours or the brushwork. Unfortunately inadequate or far too lavish a coating of varnish, or perhaps application before the paint has sufficiently dried and hardened, has so often spoiled the final effect. Not all of the problems attributed to faulty varnish, however, are really due to this. Instead the fault may lie in the use of oil of the wrong consistency or the wrong proportion of oil to pigment. Delacroix and Prud'hon are always cited as examples of artists who paid insufficient attention to this matter, with the result that many of their paintings have suffered irremediable damage through cracks.

It was the Impressionists who began exploring new ways of working oils on canvas. Claude Monet was the arch exponent of this style, who succeeded in conveying the illusion of spontaneity, the image captured at a single moment in time. Obviously the actual execution of any painting, however rapidly it is carried out, takes more than a few moments. The secret lay in the preparation of the groundwork. Monet used a fine-weave canvas with a thin basic wash, on top of which he painted broad areas in two or three basic colours. Next he applied opaque paint in patches which allowed a glimpse of

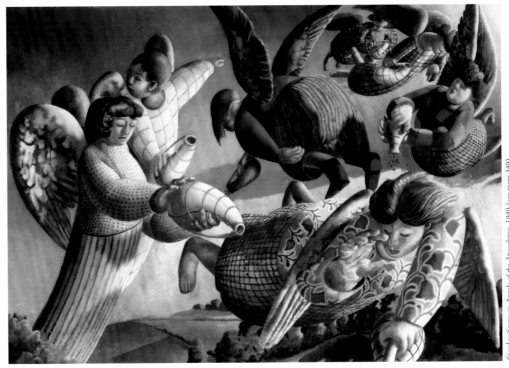

Stanley Spencer, Angels of the Apocalypse, 1949 (see page 349)

427

the underlying blocks and then used a wide variety of different brushwork, putting fresh paint on still-wet surfaces or dragging pure, almost dry paint, across the surface to create special effects and textures, often by using the wooden point of his brushes to let the pale ground show through. The resulting variety of colours and the scintillating play of light and reflection give his canvases their instantaneous character. The Impressionists in general made extensive use of wet-on-wet techniques to soften the edges of contrasting colours, or softened the lines by rubbing them or painting over them with a thin opaque coat of colour – a practice known as 'scumbling'.

Pierre-Auguste Renoir was the first painter of his generation to explore the potential of warm-cool colour contrasts which he used to great advantage in his nude studies. He also employed rubbing and staining to build up form, colour and depth. In the second half of the nineteenth century, scientists like James Clerk Maxwell studied the physical properties of light and colour and painters followed these developments closely. One of these was Georges Seurat who, in 1884, adopted a palette of 11 colours arranged in the sequence in which they appear across the spectrum, from raw sienna to yellow ochre, combined with white to enhance the effects of light. He strove for an opaque impression and deliberately left his paintings unvarnished to heighten the matt effect. Taking his interest in the composition of colour to its logical conclusion he began in 1885 to build up different hues using patterns of dots. Whereas traditionally artists had mixed

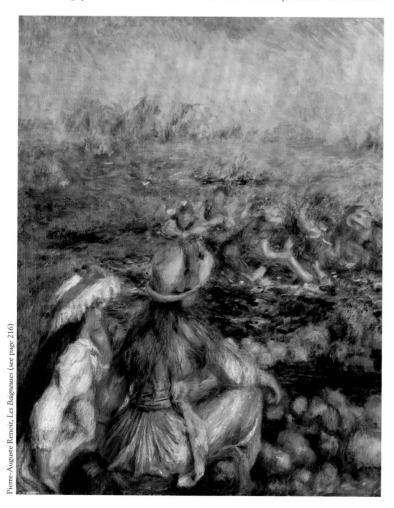

Pierre-Auguste Renoir, *Les Baigneuses* (see page 216)

yellow and blue pigments to produce shades of green, Seurat aimed at the same effect by placing dots of yellow and blue paint in close proximity, varying the intensity of the colour accordingly. The result, however, was seldom as he intended, for he failed to realize that the eye picked up the signal as a fusion of pigment rather than a blending of light. Camille Pissarro was the other ardent practitioner of Pointillism, but in his case it proved to be an extremely laborious way of achieving subtle shades. Paul Signac (1863–1935) modified this, using broader dabs of colour to achieve similar results. In the twentieth century Paul Klee was also preoccupied with the scientific theories of colour and used a mosaic or cloisonné technique, involving tiny cells of different pigments, to build up colour harmonies, which attained fruition in his painting entitled *Ad Parnassum* (1932).

Watercolour

Although sometimes looked down on as a minor art compared with oil painting, watercolour painting is one of the oldest techniques known to humankind. It was the medium used by the artists of China and Japan from the third century AD, if not earlier, and appears to have developed in India and Persia about five centuries later when the rulers of Turkestan began commissioning Chinese artists, from whom the technique spread further west and south. Interestingly, some of the earliest watercolours of China have an affinity to the tempera of the Mediterranean civilizations, although subsequently the Chinese preferred clear watercolour to the opaque forms associated with tempera. Just as the brushes used by European painters were made of sable or hogs' hair, depending on the quality of work desired, so too the Chinese used these materials in their brushes, but with the salient difference that the latter were infinitely finer as befitted the extremely delicate nature of their brushwork. By these means, Chinese painters and calligraphers achieved an extraordinary range of styles, from the most refined, almost microscopic styles to coarse, vigorous forms.

Another important difference between Chinese and Occidental painting was that the Chinese were primarily concerned with design, while colour was always of secondary importance. The versatility of watercolours was suited to the materials on which they were executed. Whereas Western artists relied on wood panels and canvasses, the Chinese preferred paper and silk panels from the outset. The earliest papers were relatively coarse, and were fashioned from the bark of certain trees. Later came a type of paper made from silk fibres and later still a very tough, hard rice-paper. Then sheets of silk were glued to layers of paper and this seems to have proved to be the most satisfactory medium, for it remained more or less constant for many centuries. Black ink was mainly employed although deep shades of sepia were also used, but under the influence of Buddhism sumptuous colours were introduced as well as a lavish use of gold leaf. Poetic suggestion rather than representation was the watchword of Chinese watercolour compositions in the Song dynasty. An interest in landscape also developed and would become the dominant feature of later Chinese art. Colours were now more subdued and used sparingly. Many artists were also poets who decorated their exquisite paintings with fine calligraphy. Having reached the acme of perfection around AD 1000, Chinese watercolour painting remained relatively static for centuries, and the hand-scrolls and wall-hangings executed in this medium continued with little stylistic difference until the influence of Western art began to make itself felt at the end of the nineteenth century.

Diffusion of the Chinese Style

The technique of watercolour painting spread to Japan in the middle of the sixth century and, until about AD 850, slavishly followed Chinese patterns and techniques; but then there began to develop a distinctly Japanese style which was encouraged by the establishment of a number of schools. There was a revival of the Chinese style from the fifteenth to the late seventeenth centuries, when a new popular style emerged. This gradually gave way to a more naturalistic style, influenced to some extent by ideas brought by the Portuguese and later the Dutch from Europe but harnessed to the particular parameters of Japanese watercolour painting. The heyday of the Japanese watercolour was from the late seventeenth century onwards, following the establishment of the art school founded by Hishigawa Moronobu (1646–1713). Landscapes, portraits of the actors of the Kabuki theatre, geishas and court scenes which make up the *Ukiyo-e* ('pictures of the floating world') formed the bulk of watercolour painting and inspired the production of block prints which were

hand-coloured. From about 1875, Western influences in watercolour painting can be detected in the greater use of *chiaroscuro* and linear perspective, as well as a greater concentration on the exact reproduction of form, a matter which had previously been of secondary importance.

The Persians learned the technique of watercolours via the Chinese artists who brought their craft to Turkestan, but very little appears to have survived from this early period. Even watercolour miniatures from the period of the Mongol invasions are very rare. At Herat, however, a great school of art was founded in the fourteenth century and from this developed the exquisitely jewelled manuscripts that reached their peak of perfection in the time of the Mughal emperors and accompanied them southwards to India. In the period from the sixteenth to eighteenth centuries Indian watercolour art expanded to include small-scale murals executed on paper and employing the techniques of fresco and tempera as well as clear colours. Various methods of treating or glazing the surface of the paper evolved, mainly in order to enhance the appearance of portraits.

Watercolour painting developed in Europe during the Middle Ages and was widely practised in monasteries and other religious foundations. The vast majority of these miniature paintings were executed on parchment, seldom as individual works and generally forming the embellishment of manuscript books. An offshoot of this was the development of the portrait miniature, done on smooth card or small ivory plates, watercolours being the preferred medium. The

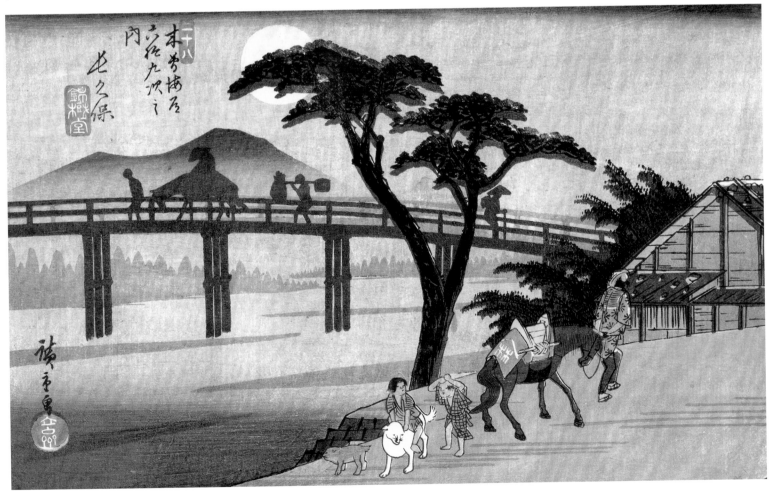

Ando Hiroshige, *Nagakubo*, c. 1830s (see page 187)

429

miniature continued in fashion until the 1840s, when it was ousted by the daguerreotype, one of the earliest photographic techniques.

Painting on silk, board, card or paper often includes fresco and tempera as well as clear colour and although the finished painting was left as it was, it was occasionally coated with shellac or some form of wax to give it greater permanence. Between the early sixteenth century, when illuminated manuscripts went out of fashion with the dissolution of the monasteries, the art of watercolour painting (apart from miniature portraits) virtually disappeared in Britain, but it was revived at the beginning of the eighteenth century. At first it was confined mainly to monochrome pictures, known as pen-and-wash, but soon browns and other colours came into use and by the end of the century the palette was greatly extended. Pigments in powdered or cake form were mixed with water and applied to paper, the form often being strengthened by pen drawing. Later watercolours took on greater depth following the introduction of opaque, gouache or body colour, although these techniques were difficult to master and the results were often harsh and raw, with uncomfortable ridges of colour. Making a virtue of necessity, however, artists exploited these qualities, painting on coarse paper or papers with a grey or tinted tone and sometimes combining watercolours with crayons or chalks for varied effect.

Watercolour sketches and preliminary cartoons are known to have been produced by some of the greatest masters, from Rubens and Rembrandt to Dürer and Daumier, but the watercolour as an art form in its own right only really came to prominence in the second half of the eighteenth century. What started as an amateur pastime was given a much higher status in the hands of such artists as Paul Sandby (1725–1809), Samuel Scott (1710–72) and Thomas Malton (1748–1804), the last-named producing some remarkable pictures of architectural subjects. The heyday of the English watercolour ran from 1780 until 1850, and produced some landscapists of the first rank, such as John Robert Cozens (1752–97), Peter de Wint (1784–1849), John Sell Cotman (1782–1842), Thomas Girtin (1775–1802) and Cornelius Varley (1781–1873).

Artists who worked in oils and other media, notably John Constable and William Blake, also produced outstanding watercolours, but the most prominent artist who may be said to have made the watercolour his very own medium was J. M. W. Turner, and it would be true to say that his exploration of the techniques of this medium considerably enhanced his work in oils. The range of his watercolours is incredible and reveals Turner as a bold and imaginative innovator. In the second half of the nineteenth century and the twentieth century, watercolour was an important aspect of British art in the hands of such painters as Sir William Orpen, Samuel Palmer, Sir Alfred Munnings, Wilson Steer, Frank Brangwyn and many others. Nor should it be forgotten that watercolour was extensively used by the Pre-Raphaelites and their successors, notably Sir Edward Burne-Jones, whose paintings in this medium have an exquisite jewelled quality.

Perhaps under English influence, watercolour painting also became extremely popular in the United States. Examples are known from pre-revolutionary times and consist mainly of rather naïve landscapes and still-lifes, but the movement received tremendous impetus during the Civil War, rivalling the new-fangled camera as a method of recording the scenes of battle and military life. An immediate outcome was the formation in 1866 of the American Water Color Society, based in New York, with separate groups arising in Boston and Philadelphia a few years later. Although this medium was regarded as more within the realm of the amateur and the dilettante, it should be noted that major artists such as Winslow Homer produced some excellent work in this medium. Early American watercolours tended to be rather dry and not particularly rich in colour, slavishly emulating their English counterparts, but in the last four decades of the nineteenth century a much freer, more colourful style developed.

Among the outstanding watercolourists of this period were John F. Kensett (1818–73), S. R. Gifford (1823–80) and Thomas Hicks (1823–90). They were followed by artists who appreciated that this medium could be used to convey rapid and dramatic work, full of pace and movement. First and foremost was John Singer Sargent (1856–1925) who was actually born in Italy and spent much of his life in England, but who exerted enormous influence in the United States, especially in raising the standard of watercolours. Other artists who excelled in this medium include John Ward Dunsmore (1856–1945) who concentrated on historical subjects, Henry B. Snell (1858–1943) who developed the so-called scrub method which gave his pictures a certain luminosity, Arthur B. Davies (1862–1928) whose paintings veered towards the mystical and fantastic, Dodge McKnight (1860–1950), the leading figure among the Boston watercolourists, and Rockwell Kent (1882–1971), one of America's latter-day Renaissance men who excelled as an engraver, lithographer, book designer, illustrator, explorer, sailor and writer as well as a watercolourist of note who advocated greater use of painting outdoors from life. Horatio Walker (1858–1938) was the prime exponent of watercolour painting in Canada, exhibiting an uncanny grasp of atmosphere in his quaint and romantic studies of the Canadian countryside.

Some artists started their careers in watercolours before moving on to oils. In this group may be named Norman Rockwell (1894–1978), who developed a realistic technique of idealizing small-town America, especially in his covers and illustrations for such periodicals as The Saturday Evening Post (1916–63). John Marin (1875–1953) branched out and created watercolours in a highly distinctive style before adapting the medium to Cubist concepts. Other European and American artists of more recent times who made extensive use of watercolours include Edward Burra, Mark Tobey, and Otto Dix. Gouache, a type of opaque watercolour thickened with gum, was employed by Joan Miró and Egon Schiele.

If watercolour lacks the lustrous depths and sumptuous colours of which oils are capable, it is a medium that is ideally suited to the lightning sketch and for that reason, if for no other, it would deserve notice for truly capturing the fleeting moment, a principle grasped by the Chinese and the Japanese so many centuries ago.

Miniatures

The word miniature has passed into the English language as a synonym for something tiny, or a representation of something on a much-reduced scale. In fact the word is derived from the Latin *minium*, which had nothing to do with size at all, but was the word used to describe cinnabar or red lead, used in the decoration of the borders of medieval manuscripts and the initial letters around which were woven tiny pictorial elements. Later the word miniature came to apply to these decorations rather than the red lines and, in turn, to signify any painting executed on a very small scale. In the sixteenth and seventeenth centuries such works were often described as 'paintings in little' or 'limnings' and the artists who practised this craft were known as limners, a corruption of the French *enluminer* and Latin *illuminare* (the verbs 'to paint'). The art of miniature painting has a long, if at times sketchy, history that stretches all the way back to the fragments of the Egyptian *Book of the Dead* and some scraps from Roman Imperial times – tantalizing glimpses of an accomplished art which perished because the materials used have themselves barely survived. Miniature paintings worked in tempera and watercolours but it was their skilful use of gold leaf (and more rarely silver foil) to embellish their illustrations that gave them their distinctly sumptuous qualities. The illuminated manuscripts of medieval Europe represent an astonishing range of styles and techniques. The manuscripts of the Irish monks, for example, exhibit a highly idiosyncratic blend of Celtic and Norse art, totally different from the Anglo-Saxon art practised in the monasteries of England. Out of the craft of the limners working in the Byzantine, Gothic and Romanesque traditions developed the art of painting which has already been noted. Persia, the Mughal Empire of India and Turkey were centres of miniature paintings, which could be wrapped up and transported easily by the substantial nomadic populations. The paintings were often produced as collections illustrating the lives and exploits of great rulers and bound in book form.

Content and the Miniature

Miniature painting for its own sake and not primarily as illustration to the written word developed in Europe in the sixteenth century at a time when the illuminated manuscript was nearing the end of its life. Most of the earliest practitioners of portrait miniatures probably learned their craft as limners, and merely adapted the techniques of tempera, watercolours and oils to the confines of these tiny portraits, executed on thin flakes of ivory and, later, highly glazed card. The earliest centres of European miniature paintings in this period were Ghent and Bruges in Flanders, Paris and Tours in France and Ferrara and Florence in Italy, but from these places the art spread rapidly to other parts of the continent. Although the traditional illumination of manuscripts lingered on for about a century after the introduction of the printed book, its exponents soon diversified from the sacred to the secular and created tiny portraits for patrons drawn from the rising middle classes as well as the royal court.

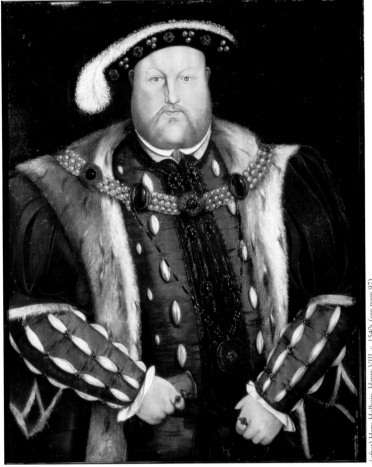

(after) Hans Holbein, *Henry VIII*, c. 1540s (see page 97)

Portraits of living persons may be found in illuminated manuscripts from the fourteenth century, gradually at first and later much more frequently, in copies of books commissioned by wealthy patrons. One of the greatest of the earliest miniaturists was Hans Holbein, who had already established his reputation for easel-paintings on wood panels. Between 1532, when he settled in England, and his death 11 years later he produced a number of these tiny masterpieces, although only a dozen or so of the 50 miniatures attributed to him are undoubtedly his work. Although his name is pre-eminent in this medium, he was by no means the only sixteenth-century artist who produced dainty little portraits of this type, and some of them – like Benninck and Teerlinc – also migrated from Flanders to England. Holbein worked in tempera, mixing his colours with both the white and yolk of eggs and giving them greater body with albumen mixed with a little vinegar.

Among Holbein's successors in England, Nicholas Hilliard (c. 1547–1619) provides an interesting insight into an art in transition, for his portraits, using opaque colours mixed with gum arabic or honey and a great deal of gold leaf, have a flatness and absence of shadows which place them firmly in the tradition of the illuminated manuscripts. The very fine work of this and later miniaturists was executed with a brush using squirrel hair. Isaac and Peter Oliver (father and son) carried on the tradition but during their working life it took on a new maturity. Isaac (c. 1567–1617) learned his craft from Hilliard himself, while Peter (1594–1647) was his father's pupil. They evolved the technique of imparting a roundness of form to the likenesses of their subjects and greatly enlivened the medium.

Whereas Holbein and Hilliard painted very small miniatures, suitable for mounting in jewellery, the Olivers literally expanded the miniature, often producing paintings that were the size of a book page. The miniatures of these early artists were truly two-dimensional but what they lacked in naturalism they made up in the astonishing attention to the minute details of jewellery, lacework or embroidery in the costume of their sitters – truly a triumph of technique over art.

John Hoskins (d. 1664) and his nephew Samuel Cooper (1609–1702) were the outstanding miniaturists of the next generation. The last of the original school of illuminators died out in the middle of the seventeenth century and this freed the portrait miniature from the stereotypes of that discipline. Hoskins pioneered the use of rich masses of colour, a greater and more intelligent approach to light and shade, and was probably the first miniaturist to capture the true flesh tints. Cooper trained under his uncle, but also spent some time in Holland and France perfecting his technique. His miniatures were true works of art, as accomplished as any full-scale painting but rendered exquisitely in a small format. He was also more adventurous than his predecessors in his use of colour.

The preferred medium for portrait miniatures until the middle of the eighteenth century was a glazed card – the plain backs of playing cards were often used for this purpose – but occasionally a very fine parchment made from the skin of chickens was employed. Cooper tried to find a more satisfactory but cheap substitute and experimented with painting on the flat bones of sheep, but early in the eighteenth century plaques of ivory came into fashion. This material was relatively expensive at first and it was a long time before it completely ousted the use of card or vellum. In the same period there was a certain vogue in Italy and the Netherlands for miniatures painted in oils on copper or silver plates, but these works were seldom, if ever, signed and very little is known about the artists who produced them. It should be noted that some miniaturists also painted in enamels on copper or porcelain, then fired or fused in a kiln and used in the manufacture of snuff-boxes and other objects of *vertu*, but these paintings belong more in the realm of the decorative arts than fine art. In the early 1760s there was a fashion for very small miniatures mounted as jewellery. The best of these microscopic miniatures – arguably fine art in its smallest form – were painted by Gervase Spencer (d. 1763).

The greater popularity of ivory more or less coincided with the development of transparent colours perfected in France. These materials eventually spread to England and triggered off a new and more sumptuous phase in miniature painting, given enormous impetus by the foundation of the Royal Academy in 1768. In the late eighteenth century the leading exponent of the art in Britain was Richard Cosway (1742–1821), whose miniatures were distinguished by the jewel-like brilliance of their colours. Andrew Plimer (1763–1857) produced many very engaging portraits, despite uneven draughtsmanship and attempts at *chiaroscuro* which did not always achieve the desired results. Probably the most successful, and certainly the most prolific, of the English miniaturists was George Engleheart (1750–1819), whose account books indicate that he painted almost 4,000 portraits. It should also be noted that Sir Thomas Lawrence and Sir Henry Raeburn both produced excellent miniatures in the early stages of their illustrious careers.

The heyday of this rather restricted medium was the eighteenth century, and by the 1770s every town in the British Isles of any importance had at least one studio catering to the needs of the rising middle classes, who might not be able to afford a full-scale oil painting, but for whom the miniature was an admirable substitute. This movement received tremendous impetus during the French Revolutionary and Napoleonic Wars, when it was customary for young officers to have their portrait painted before going off on campaign. The great garrison towns of England, Scotland and Ireland were the centres of the miniature industry. Often only the actual features of the sitter would be painted by the master, the uniform and other details being filled in by one of his numerous assistants. This technique carried on even after the Battle of Waterloo. Although this mass-production technique was detrimental to the miniature as a work of art, there were still artists of this period – incuding Ozias Humphrey, Nathaniel and Horace Hone, Peter Paillou and William Wood – who produced excellent individual pieces. The advent of photography in the middle of the nineteenth century rapidly led to the demise of the portrait miniature.

Samuel Cooper, Miniature of James II as the Duke of York, 1661 (see page 135)

The Growth of the Miniature

The artist Andrew Robinson realized that if the public regarded a studio photograph as a perfectly adequate substitute for a tiny miniature, the solution might be to give them something larger, if not a full-sized portrait. He pioneered miniatures which were similar to small oil paintings but were executed on stout cartridge paper using the new range of watercolours which were capable of a much darker, deeper and altogether more brilliant appearance than their predecessors, enhanced by setting the portrait against a very dark ground to give it greater dignity and force. The process of flattening out curved slices of ivory under hydraulic pressure enabled the new wave of miniature painters to combine the special qualities of ivory with the much larger format. Sir William Ross and Edward Chalon, among others, produced miniatures which ranged between octavo and quarto in size. While Chalon worked in broad masses of colour, Ross preferred a very laborious technique of microscopic detail which required special brushes and a high-powered magnifying glass.

Miniature painting also had immense appeal in North America. The pioneer of the portrait miniature in the American colonies was John Watson who, in about 1715, began producing some exquisite little works drawn in pencil and Indian ink. The leading exponent of the art was Charles Willson Peale (1741–1827), who seems to have been equally versatile in miniatures and life-size portraits. Many of his 17 children, all of whom were named after famous artists and, not surprisingly, followed their father's profession, also painted miniatures – the best of these being by the appropriately named Rembrandt Peale. Archibald and Alexander Robertson (both Scots) and Walter Robertson (an Irishman) settled in the United States and produced excellent miniatures as well as giving encouragement to artists of the next generation, including E. G. Malbone of Rhode Island, Benjamin Trott of Boston and Charles Fraser of Charleston. At the end of the eighteenth and beginning of the nineteenth centuries the foremost miniaturists included Alban Clark of Massachusetts and R. M. Staigg of Newport. Although the art of the miniature declined with the advent of photography, there were still artists producing excellent work in a dwindling market. As in Britain, there were artists who gained their reputations in full-scale painting but who also dabbled in miniatures.

If portrait miniatures found the greatest favour in the English-speaking world, they were by no means confined to it. The Flemish painter Jean Clouet (c.1485–1541), who settled in France, produced a number of miniatures painted on card or vellum. His son François (c.1516–72), who succeeded him as court painter, also excelled in this medium. Although both Clouets and Jean Fouquet made their reputations as painters of large-scale portraits they also helped to popularize the art of the miniature. In the time of Louis XV and XVI, with the exception of a few miniatures by Nicolas Lancret (1690–1743), François Boucher (1703–70) and Jean-Baptiste Greuze (1725–1805), French painters of the first rank showed little or no interest in this restrictive medium, and it is significant that many of the best French miniatures of that period were actually painted by Peter Adolf Hall (a Swede) and Heinrich Füger (an Austrian). To be sure, there was a handful of French artists who concentrated on miniatures and their works are very much sought-after nowadays. In this group must be named Jean-Baptiste-Jacques Augustin (1759–1832), François Dumont (1751–1831), Antoine Sergent (1751–1817) and especially Jean-Baptiste Isabey (1767–1855), who continued to produce first-class miniatures almost to the end of his long life. Elsewhere in Europe there was little interest in miniatures, far less the development of any national styles, though it should be noted that Rosalba Carriera (1675–1757), the celebrated Venetian pastellist was also a notable miniaturist, while the ever-versatile Francisco Goya of Spain included portrait miniatures in his vast repertory.

Pastel

Drawing in crayons or coloured chalks is the simplest method of putting colour on a surface, usually paper or cardboard. It has the advantage over other methods in that the artist can see immediately how the picture is progressing and how it will look when completed, whereas in those methods where pigments are mixed with oil or water, the end result is never obvious until the paint has dried. The chief drawback about pastel, however, is that the colour, essentially fine chalk dust, does not penetrate the medium but lies on the surface and is therefore easily disturbed. Lay one sheet on top of another and you will get an offsetting of the colours on the back of the top sheet. Pastels are prone to rubbing or surface disturbance unless carefully preserved under glass, and even then there is always a tendency for the colours to migrate. The fugitive nature of the chalk can be used to create subtle tones by gently rubbing with the fingers to blend one colour with another. In recent years, moreover, there have developed various types of soluble pencil which combine the control of a top-quality chalk with the natural fluidity of watercolour, releasing an infinite range of tonal variations. It is possible to create a picture with 'dry' pencils then go

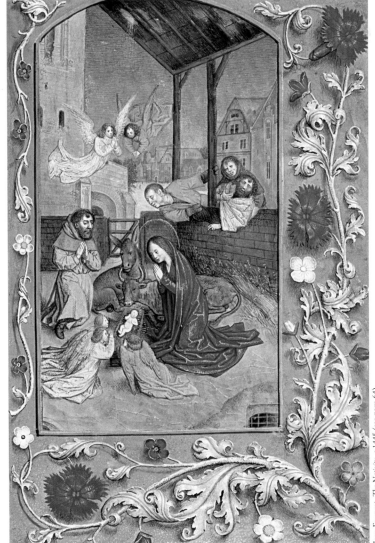

Jean Fouquet, *The Nativity*, c.1445 (see page 64)

433

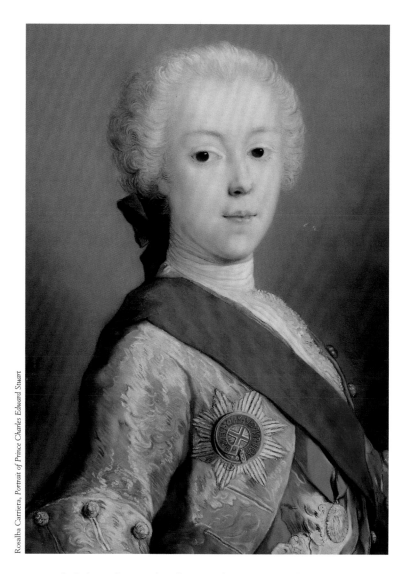

Rosalba Carriera, *Portrait of Prince Charles Edward Stuart*

other of these persons devised a method of producing coloured chalks in the form of sticks, but chalk drawing had certainly existed long before their time, for Hans Holbein (1497–1543) and Guido Reni (1575–1642) both created some portraits in this medium.

Whatever the precise origins of pastel, it triggered a distinctive movement in portraiture in France which, in the years leading up to the Revolution, enjoyed immense popularity and attracted the serious attention of many oil painters, notably Watteau, Boucher, Chardin and Greuze, although the leading artists in this medium were those who concentrated on it. The pastellists were led by Louis Tocque (1696–1772), the son-in-law of Nattier (1685–1766) who was one of the first artists to exhibit pastels at the Salon (in 1747). Another leading exponent was Hubert Drouais (1699–1767), who exhibited five pastel portraits at the Salon of 1746. However, the greatest French master of this medium was Maurice Quentin de la Tour (1704–88), who employed pastels very effectively in portraiture. He was, in fact, was a portraitist, first and foremost, for whom pastel was the ideal medium for capturing the fleeting expression of his sitters, and the results vividly bring to life the sparkle, wit and gaiety of French society of the Ancien Regime. In this regard the only artist who came close to him was Jean-Baptiste Perroneau (1715–83), who produced many pastels, remarkable for their use of colour. Pastel was virtually the closed preserve of the portraitist, although Simon Lantara (1729–78) pioneered the use of pastels in landscapes.

The Venetian artist Rosalba Carriera (1675–1757) was equally at home working in oils or pastels. During her time in Paris she was attracted to the freshness and lightness of the latter medium, and in her later career she produced a considerable number of quite remarkable portraits in pastels. During her extensive travels around Europe she did much to popularize the new medium. Indeed, her success encouraged other female artists to follow suit – the most notable being Vigée Le Brun, who executed many fine pastels in addition to her portraits in oils on canvas.

In Switzerland – where Moyer had led the way with his chalk drawings of the early seventeenth century – the principal exponent of pastels was Jean Étienne Liotard (1702–89), arguably one of the greatest pastellists of all time, whose portraits entitled *La Belle Chocolatière* (1745) and *La Belle Liseuse* (1746) established his reputation.

Painting with crayons was well established in England at an early date. John Riley (1646–91) produced numerous portraits in this medium, many of them formerly attributed to Sir Peter Lely. Francis Knapton (1698–1778) produced a prodigious quantity of pastel portraits, particularly of royalty and nobility. William Hoare of Bath (c. 1707–92) studied pastel in Paris and Rome and raised the English technique to new heights. Francis Cotes (c. 1725–70) studied under Rosalba Carriera and helped to develop a purely English style of pastel painting. This medium attained its peak in the hands of Cotes' pupil John Russell (1745–1806), who displayed an unsurpassed grace and elegance in his many fine portrait studies. Russell worked primarily in pastels and greatly extended the range of the medium, producing excellent groups as well as genre and historical subjects. There were many other artists working in pastels who demonstrated vividly that,

over it lightly with a wet brush to produce a watercolour effect which, because it penetrates the paper, becomes truly permanent. Or one can work with crayons dipped in water to produce a watercolour effect from the outset, or use a mixture of both techniques.

Although their composition is different, coloured wax crayons are used in the same manner as chalks to create pictures. The wax substances have a more adhesive quality than chalk but are less permanent than oil paints or watercolours, but the application of heat melts the wax so that it penetrates the paper and is thus fixed permanently, and the same heat treatment is used to merge the colours and soften the edges.

Just as the invention of oil painting is often credited to Jan Van Eyck, so also the invention of pastel or crayon has been attributed to various people, notably Johann Alexander Thiele (1685–1752), a landscape painter and etcher of note, or two ladies from Danzig (now Gdansk) named Vernerin and Heid who were exact contemporaries of Thiele. French art historians, on the other hand, credit the portraitist Robert Nanteuil with the invention. Dietrich Moyer of Switzerland (1572–1658) was a great innovator who experimented with various techniques, and these certainly included drawings in coloured chalks, though he is better remembered as the alleged inventor of soft-ground etching. It may well be the fact that one or

in skilled hands, this medium was the equal of oils. Richard Cosway (1742–1821) and his wife Maria (1759–1838) – though perhaps better known as miniaturists – were also masters of this technique.

Decline and Resurgence

Interest in pastels declined at the beginning of the nineteenth century. It continued to be practised by amateurs, but the only professional British artist of note to make a major contribution to the medium was Henry Bright (1814–73), who concentrated on landscapes. Interest revived in the 1860s and led to the foundation of the Société des Pastellistes at Paris in 1870. The medium attracted the serious attention of artists whose reputation in other fields was already assured. Foremost in this group were James McNeill Whistler, Jean François Millet and Edgar Degas. Indeed, Degas made pastels very much his own medium. Although he painted in oils on canvas, he explored colour and texture and in the course of his experiments he turned to pastels, developing his own highly distinctive technique which involved the application of fine chalk lines, criss-crossing like a woven fabric, often superimposing one colour on another in such a manner that the earlier colours peeped through. Degas experimented with a very fine spray of water covering the chalk that he then worked up into a paste which he could manipulate with his fingers or a brush with stiff bristles. He also experimented with steam or heat to melt the pigments and achieve similar effects. Ironically, Degas turned more and more to pastels as his eyesight failed, but his innovations helped to stimulate renewed interest in the medium and reveal exciting possibilities which were taken up by other artists.

By the end of the nineteenth century pastel-painting was well established once more and attracted the serious attention of many artists of the first rank who further extended the medium. There were artists, such as Odilon Redon in France, who applied pastels to vellum or parchment. Aristide Maillol was primarily a sculptor, but he used coloured wax crayons to sketch his ideas for those splendid nude figures he modelled, and nowadays these crayons are regarded as great artworks in their own right. Émile Wauters in Belgium achieved a notable success with his numerous life-size portraits whose strength, vitality and

sophistication had an immense impact at the turn of the century and in more recent years his fellow countryman Léon Spillaert has successfully combined pastels with watercolours. In Britain the leading pastellists of the modern movement include Henry Tonks, McLure Hamilton, Anning Bell, Walter Crane and William Rothenstein. The technique found an enthusiastic response in America, where excellent work in pastels was produced by Thomas Dewing, Robert Blum, Jerome Myers and James Alden Weir as well as Mary Cassatt, who is much better known for her oil paintings. Wifredo Lam combined chalks and oils on paper which was then pasted on to canvas.

Perspective

No account of methods and techniques would be complete without some reference to perspective – which is defined by the Oxford English Dictionary as, 'The art of representing three dimensional objects on a two dimensional surface, so as to convey the impression of height, width and relative distance.' Perspective was blithely ignored by the earliest primitives; even if Greek paintings of the sixth century BC are no longer extant, we have the startling example of Athenian coins in which the goddess Athena, depicted in profile, has an eye that stares straight out of the coin at us. This is decidedly disconcerting, and must have seemed so at the time; yet it remained unchanged throughout the Archaic period. Interestingly, this position of the eye was a characteristic of many of Picasso's Cubist paintings of the early twentieth century as he tried to show several different aspects of the subject simultaneously. In the art of the past two millennia artists were originally concerned with rhythm and harmony in composition, then changing from a static pose of figures (as shown on the friezes of Egypt and Greece) to an impression of movement when it was realized that the arrangement of figures within the confines of the picture could make a considerable difference to its overall appearance.

After the Romans, the problem of perspective was not confronted again until the Renaissance. Significantly the first painters to study this were those who had trained in a sculptural

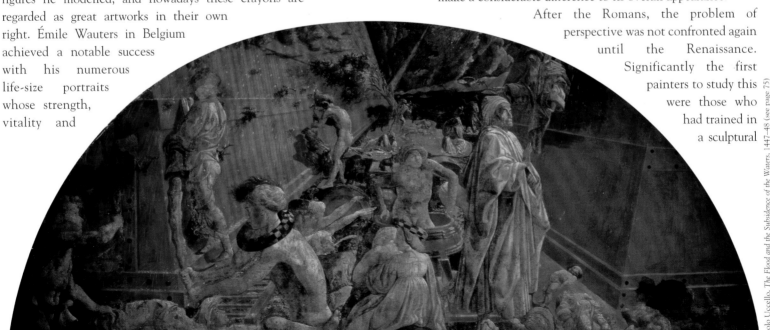

Paolo Uccello, *The Flood and the Subsidence of the Waters*, 1447–48 (see page 75)

435

medium and were primarily concerned to convey in the two dimensions of flat painting the impression of three dimensions. They knew that a straight road with parallel sides ran in a straight line and that at the end the sides were as far apart as ever; yet when they gazed along it they had the impression that the lines drew closer together and eventually reached a point at which they vanished altogether. Paolo Uccello (1397–1475) is credited with being the first painter to have grasped the basic principles of perspective and apply them successfully to his pictures. In the early part of his career he had worked with the sculptor Lorenzo Ghiberti, whose great bronze bas-reliefs exhibit an early and probably subconscious understanding of the concept of converging lines.

It should be emphasized that Uccello was by no means the first artist to make a successful attempt to convey perspective – Chinese artists had been doing just that for hundreds of years – but he was the first to explain and interpret it. The Florentine architect Filippo

Brunelleschi (1377–1446) exhibited a mastery of perspective in the design of the high-domed cupola of Florence Cathedral and wrote treatises on the subject. Other painters, such as Alberti and da Vinci, quickly developed the theories of Uccello and Brunelleschi, and it was Piero della Francesca who brought the concept to a triumphant conclusion by discovering the principle of the vanishing point, the point at which receding parallel lines appear to meet when represented in linear perspective. Uccello himself showed his understanding of this principle in his great panoramic view of *The Hunt in the Forest*, painted in the early 1460s.

Other notions, such as the apparent diminution in size of objects farther distant and foreshortening (the deliberate compacting of a detail to create the illusion of depth), were refined within a few years. Understandably the perspective of curves and circles took longer to grasp. Globes and balls, for example, may appear as ovals or even irregular shapes, depending on the angle from which they are

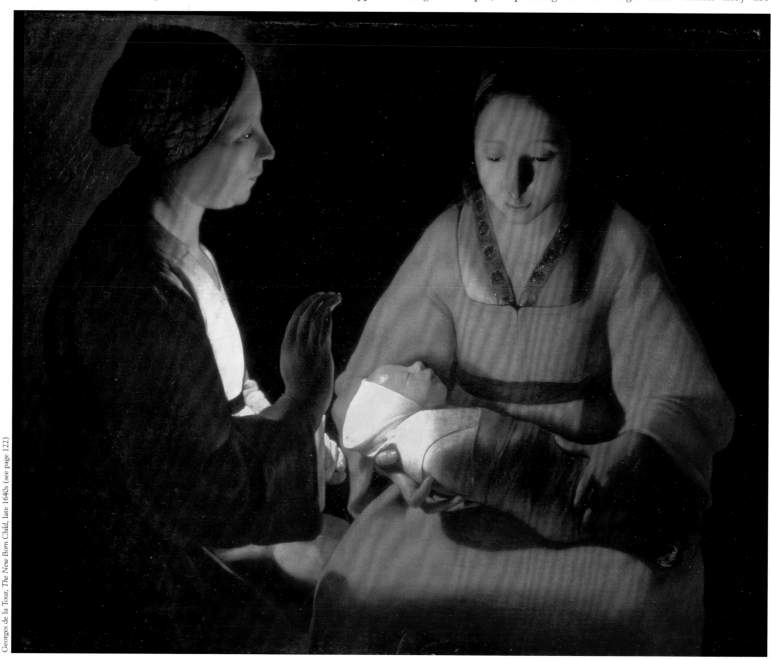

Georges de la Tour, *The New Born Child*, late 1640s (see page 122)

perceived. Subconsciously artists realized this, but without some knowledge of advanced geometry they did not understand why it should be so, and therefore the creation of the correct illusion was not always achieved. However, One artist, Masaccio (1401–28), showed an early and precocious understanding of the perspective of curves, triumphantly exhibited in his *Trinity* (1425), which inspired one of the most perceptive passages in the writings of Giorgio Vasari, describing the barrel vault 'drawn in perspective, and divided into squares with rosettes which diminish and are foreshortened so well that there seems to be a hole in the wall'.

Nevertheless, Uccello's discoveries were quite revolutionary. Suddenly artists realized that they could not just show the outline of a subject but depict it in the round. Hitherto this could only be hinted at by the adroit use of highlights and shadows, but until the geometry of perspective was understood paintings could not take on the illusion of three dimensions. From the time of Uccello and his colleagues onwards, however, people could not just look *at* a picture, they could now look *into* it as well.

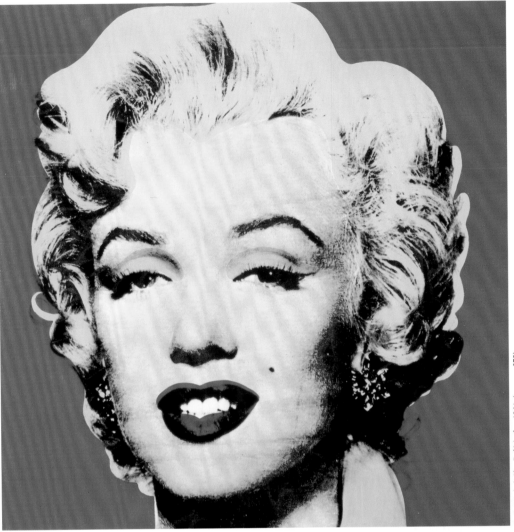

Andy Warhol, *Shot Red Marilyn*, 1964 (see page 370)

Later generations of painters would refine the principles of perspective by using light and shadow to give greater depths to their pictures, a notable exponent of light and darkness being Georges de la Tour (1593–1652). In general the scenes depicted were at the spectator's eye-level, but Rembrandt, in his great canvas *The Blinding of Samson* (1636), employed a very unusual angle, as if looking directly down on the scene, in order to heighten its dramatic effect.

Avant–garde Developments

The techniques and methods of painting evolved over hundreds of years; whatever the styles of painting at different periods, the techniques involved in their production followed clearly defined lines. All that had gone before would become liable to sudden, dramatic change, if not outright rejection, and over the past century artists have sought ways of breaking away from the rules and regulations that governed their predecessors. We find a hint of this in the paintings of Edouard Manet, who has been described as 'the father of modern art'. At first glance his great masterpiece, *The Picnic* (1863), seems technically conventional, even if his choice of subject-matter raised eyebrows at the time; but a closer look reveals flouting of the rules of perspective, with the female figure in the background of undiminished size.

Once the notion of the Post-Impressionists was accepted – that what we see depends on how we see it – the floodgates opened and artists exercised their prerogative to interpret everything in their own way. This paved the way for the multiplicity of psychological approaches of Surrealism, Futurisim, Dadaism and all the other 'isms' right up to the present day. In this free-for-all, methods and techniques have changed radically. There are probably more painters at work today than throughout all the ages from the Renaissance to the Impressionists put together, and we are confronted with a bewildering array of styles as artists of each decade strive to find something that has never been tried before. It is a veritable maelstrom and yet most artists are still governed by certain principles in laying paint on canvas, regardless of what they do with it or how they lay it out.

Nevertheless, there have been radical departures in the past 50 years. One of these relates to the use of photography to create fine art. Visual aids, such as the camera obscura, had been used by some painters for centuries, and from the 1840s many artists resorted to photography rather than the sketch-pad in generating the preliminary work for their paintings. The Scottish landscapist, David Octavius Hill was a prime exponent of this technique; today his paintings are all but forgotten but his place as one of the great pioneer photographers is assured. In more recent times Andy Warhol made extensive use of photographs or

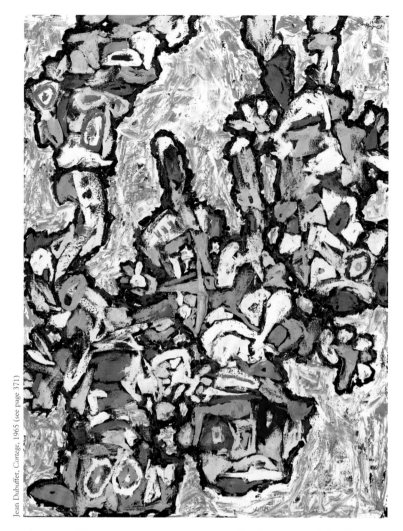

Jean Dubuffet, *Cortege*, 1965 (see page 371)

(1968) which consisted entirely of silver glue brushes mounted on polyester and Plexiglass, while Richard Hamilton (b. 1922) has made extremely effective use of plastic film combined with black ink, watercolour and graphite on paper. Roy Lichtenstein's paintings in oils and magna on canvas appear as blow-ups of strip cartoons, in which the original shading, composed of Ben Day dots, are meticulously reproduced.

Materials and the Fusion of Forms

Sometimes the boundaries between artistic media are blurred. Are the creations of Stanley William Hayter (1901–88) prints or paintings? They combine elements of both, in that they are basically combinations of engraving, soft-ground etching and scorper, often overlaid by paint. Increasingly also the lines between painting and sculpture are becoming blurred, as in the works of Eva Hesse (1936–70), which combined cheesecloth, fibreglass and latex to evoke metaphors for femininity. Yves Klein (1928–62) used broad swathes of oil paint on partially burned and charred paper to create his *Anthropometry* series. Piero Manzoni (1933–63) drenched pleated canvas in kaolin mud to produce his work entitled *Achrome* (literally 'uncoloured').

The Dadaists set the precedent for the technique of some modern artists in the accumulation of ordinary, everyday objects and even discarded refuse from which to create a montage or collage. *Sacking and Red* by Alberto Burri (1915-55) consists of scraps of old sacks glued to the canvas and surrounded by bright red slabs of vinyl paint, while Anselm Kiefer (b. 1945) has combined oil and charcoal worked on burlap which is then mounted on canvas. Serge Poliakoff (1906–69) was another painter who found the coarse texture of burlap well-suited to his brand of abstract painting. Jean Dubuffet's *Dimpled Cheeks* (1955) combined various media with a montage of butterfly wings. The ultimate materials in mixed media compositions designed primarily to shock the spectator are those in which the olfactory as well as the visual senses are involved. Pig's guts (Helen Chadwick), blood (Marc Quinn) and faeces, both animal and human, must surely represent the ultimate materials in the creation of works of art.

As its name suggests, collage (from the French verb *coller*, 'to stick') is a form of mixed media in which painting is combined with various objects that have been glued to the canvas or board. The German artist Kurt Schwitters (1887–1948) was a pioneer of this technique, producing severely geometric collages in the 1920s. One of the best-known examples of more recent years is *Flag*, which the American artist Jasper Johns (b. 1930) painted between 1954 and 1956 – the latter date is obvious since some of the pieces of newspaper which appear under the Stars and Stripes bear the date 15 February 1956, although Johns himself dated the painting to 1955. In his masterpiece *Smiling Landscape* of 1967, Jiri Kolá (b. 1914) took the *Mona Lisa* and a Dutch landscape, cut them into vertical strips, and then glued them together alternately so that both pictures are distorted yet retain their separate identity. The end result is not unlike those modern electrically powered billboards where the image is constantly changing. Other artists

photographic treatments to replicate endlessly images of the famous, of which his 1962 masterpiece portraying Marilyn Monroe is a good example. *Girlie Door* by Peter Blake (1959) is a collage of pin-up photographs and other objects mounted on a board painted to resemble a bright red door. Marlene Dumas is one of a number of contemporary artists who has used polaroid photographs in her compositions. Conversely, what appears to be a photograph in the work of Chuck Close is actually a meticulously painted image of photographic intensity.

The materials may change but the basic principles are still adhered to. Many painters work in acrylics and there are others who have achieved spectacular results with metallic paints, commercial paints normally employed in painting houses or bridges, enamels and Day-Glo or wax substances. Peter Halley (b. 1953) favours a combination of metallic and Day-Glo acrylics with a type of artificial stucco known as Roll-a-Tex applied to canvas, to give his paintings an unusual architectural texture. Lacquer, paper and acrylic on canvas has been the preferred combination of Sigmar Polke (b. 1941) in such works as *Opium Smoker* (1983). Niki de Saint-Phalle (1930–85) created very striking artworks in painted polyester. The paintbrush may give way to the paint-spray and the aerosol can, while traditional canvas may be supplanted by masonite or celotex panels and plywood boards. Arman (b. 1928) created a work entitled *Crusaders*

who have made very effective use of collage in their paintings include Jean Metzinger (1883–1956). The ultimate application of this technique seems to be the paintings of Robert Rauschenberg (b. 1925), who has made extensive use of pieces of magazines and all manner of objects apparently stuck at random on board. The American artists Tim and Kos Rollins used pages torn from a Czech novel as the basis for their *Amerika* series of paintings in the 1980s, adding a mixture of watercolours and acrylics with charcoal and pencil drawing. Frank Stella (b. 1936) has worked in mixed media on etched magnesium whereas the Australian Imants Tillers (b. 1950) prefers a mixture of oilstick, gouache and synthetic polymer paint on a number of small boards which combine to form a large work.

Most of the artists working in mixed media are highly individualistic and no two painters adopt the same technique. It is only when one examines the art being produced in the countries of the so-called Third World that one finds entire schools pursuing their own distinctive methods. Many of the Australian Aboriginal artists of the past 50 or 60 years have successfully combined not only the themes but the actual materials of their age-old traditions. Thus traditional sand painting, arguably the most ephemeral art form ever devised, has been transformed and made permanent by combining sand patterns with oils, acrylics and other substances laid on board or canvas. Interestingly, this technique was borrowed by Antoni Tàpies (b. 1923) in some of his paintings, which combine oils on canvas with sand and asphalt. Jessie Oonark is only the best-known of the Baker Lake Inuit artists of northern Canada, who create remarkable artworks using traditional skills in caribou hide decoration. Visually the most exciting of all these schools is the sequin painting of Haiti. Arguably the poorest and least-privileged country in the world, it has nevertheless produced a number of artists who, in recent years, have created dazzling pieces in which thousands of tiny sequins are built up, like mosaics, to create masterpieces of Voodoo art.

In many modern paintings, paint itself often assumes a secondary role. Jackson Pollock pioneered the vast canvas on which enormous swathes of paint were sloshed haphazardly, with buttons, nails and even cigarette butts embedded at random. Known as 'Jack the Dripper' from his custom of laying the canvas on the studio floor and then dripping the paint on to it, he has inspired many painters of a later generation to follow suit. Gillian Ayres (b. 1930), for example, has adapted Pollock's technique in her own huge abstracts, but going a step further by using her hands and knees to mould and knead the paint on unstretched canvas. Jean-Paul Riopelle's *Abstractions* are a positive riot of vibrant primary colours squirted straight from the tube on to the canvas in clusters and clumps which therefore take on a sculptural effect.

Mixed media open up seemingly limitless possibilities. Ashley Blickerton's *Le Art (Composition with Logos)* of 1987, a clever assemblage of modern brand logos sending up industrial design, was actually hand-crafted in silkscreen and acrylic with lacquer on plywood and aluminium. In *Wiring the Unfinished Bathroom* (1962) Jim Dine combines tiny metal lamps, toothbrushes and patches of paint on the canvas to make a very witty statement about DIY and the 'when I get round to it' syndrome. John Lennon's widow Yoko Ono (b. 1933) combined sumi ink, string, cloth, seeds and a bamboo screen to create her *Painting for the Wind* (1961). She has joined forces with other avant-garde artists such as Claes Oldenburg and Jim Dine in recent years in performance art, involving the burning of canvasses and jumping around on canvasses dripping with wet paint.

The Conceptual Art movement of the 1960s, whose fundamental premise was that the idea behind a work was of greater importance than the work itself, resulted in such very unusual combinations. Zvi Goldstein, for example, combined silkscreen with a painted aluminium relief in creating such works as *Future* (1985) depicting functionless objects. On Kawara, a Japanese Conceptualist, has used a substance called Liquitex on canvas to produce his 'date paintings' recording the passage of time. It has even reached the point at which art, such as Andy Goldsworthy's pictures created from flowers and leaves, has become a thing of the fleeting moment, but thanks to photography it can be recorded for posterity.

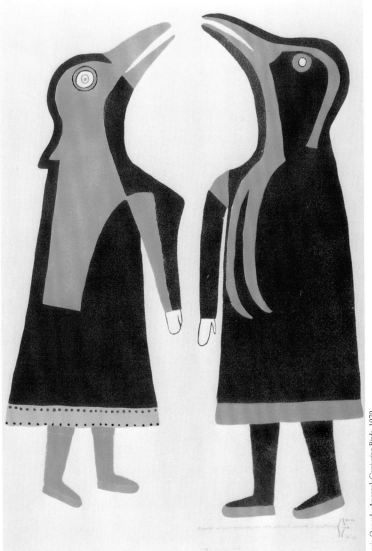

Jessie Oonark, *Anggegok Conjuring Birds*, 1979

Resources

Institutions and Museums

Africa
Johannesburg Art Gallery
King George Street
Joubert Park, South Africa
Tel: +27 11 725 3130/80/81

National Gallery of
Zimbabwe
Park Lane, Harare
Tel: +263 14 70 4666

Australia
Art Gallery of New
South Wales
Art Gallery Road
The Domain, Sydney
NSW 2000
Tel: +61 2 9225 1700

National Gallery of
Australia
Parkes Place, Canberra
ACT 2601
Tel: +61 2 6240 6502

National Gallery of Victoria
180 St Kilda Road
Melbourne
3004 Victoria
Tel: +61 3 627 411

Austria
Österrechische Galerie
Prinz Eugen-strasse 27
1037 Vienna
Tel: +43 1 7955 7134

Kunsthistorisches Museum
Burgring 5
1010 Vienna
Tel: +43 1 222 52177

Belgium
Koninklink Museum voor
Schone Kunsten
(Musée Royal des Beaux-
Arts)
Plaatnijdersstrasse 2
2000 Antwerp
Tel: +32 3 238 7809

Musée Royaux des
Beaux-Arts
(Musée d'Art Ancien)
Rue de la Régence 3
1000 Bruxelles
Tel: +32 2 508 3211

Brazil
Museo de Arte
Contemporaneo
Rua da Reitoria, 160
Cidade Universitária
05508-900 São Paulo
Tel: +55 11 3091 3039

Museu de Arte de Sao Paulo
'Assis Chateaubriand'
Avenida Paulista 1578
01310 Sao Paulo
Tel: +55 11 251 5644

Canada
National Gallery of Canada
380 Sussex Drive
Box 427, Station A
Ottawa
Ontario
K1N 9N4
Tel: +1 613 990-1985

Art Gallery of Ontario
317 Dundas Street W
Toronto
Ontario
M5T IG4
Tel: +1 416 977 0414

China/North Asia
Beijing Art Museum
Wanshou Temple,
North of West 3rd-ring
Road,
Beijing,
P.R. China
Tel: +86 10 68479391

Hong Kong Museum of Art
10 Salisbury Road,
Tsimshatsui,
Kowloon
Tel: +85 2 2721 0116

Taiwan Museum of Art
2, Sec. 1, Wu Chuan W. Rd.,
Taichung 403
Taiwan, R.O.C.
Tel: +88 6 4 23723552

Czech Republic
Národni Galerie v Praze
(National Gallery in Prague)
Hrad anské nám sti 15
Prague
Tel: +42 2 2451 0594

Denmark
Louisiana Museum of
Modern Art
Gl Standvej 13
3056 Humlebaek
Tel: +45 49 190 719

NY Carlsberg Glyptothek
Dantes Plads 7
1556 København
Tel: +45 33 418141

Finland
Finnish National Gallery
Kaivokatu 2
00100 Helsinki
Tel: +358 91 73361

France
Musée National Auguste
Rodin
77 Rue de Varenne
75007 Paris
Tel: +33 1 4705 0134

Musée National du Château
de Versailles
78000 Versailles
Tel: +33 1 3084 7400

Centre National d'Art et de
Culture Georges Pompidou
19 Rue de Renard
75191 Paris
Tel: +33 1 447 81233

National Museum of India
Janpath
New Delhi 110 011
Tel: +91 011 3018415

Musée d'Art Moderne de la
Ville de Paris
11 ave du President Wilson
751116 Paris
Tel: +33 1 472 36 127

Musée du Louvre
34–36 Quai du Louvre
75058 Paris
Tel: +33 1 402 05 009

Musée d'Orsay
62 rue de Lille
75007 Paris
Tel: +33 1 404 94814

Germany
Germanische
Nationalmuseum
Kartänsergasse I
90402 Nürn
Tel: +49 911 13310

Hamburg Kunsthalle
Glockengiesserwall
2000 Hamburg 1
Tel: +49 40 2486 2612

Alte Pinakothek
Barer Strasse 27
80333 München
Tel: +49 89 238 05216

Kunstammlung Nordrhein-
Westfalen
Grabbeplatz 5
40213 Düsseldorf
Tel: +49 211 83810

Ludwig Forum für
Internationale Kunst
Jülicher Strasse 97-109
52070 Aachen
Tel: +49 241 1807 104

Neue Nationalgalerie
Potsdamerstrasse 50
10785 Berlin
Tel: +49 30 266 2651

Holland
Rijksmuseum
Stadhouderskade 42
Postbus 74888
1070 DN
Amsterdam
Tel: +31 20 673 2121

Van Gogh Museum
Paulus Potterstraat 7
Postbus 75366
1070 AJ, Amsterdam
Tel: +31 20 570 5200

Stedelijk Museum of
Modern Art
Paulus Potterstraat 13
P.O. Box 75082
1070 AB, Amsterdam
Tel: +31 20 573 2911
[NB – temporary location
until 2008, located at the
2nd and 3rd floor of the
Post CS-building:
Oosterdokskade 5
1011 AD, Amsterdam
Tel: +31 20 5732 911

Hungary
Magyar Nemzeti Galéria
Szent György tér 2
Budavári Pálota Pf31 (1250)
Tel: +36 1 757 533

Indian Sub-Continent
National Gallery of
Modern Art
Jaipur House, near India
Gate, New Delhi
Tel: +91 11 3383032

Ireland
National Gallery of Ireland
Merrion Square West
Dublin 2
Tel: +353 1 661 5133

Italy
Galleria Borghese
Piazza Scipione Borghese 5
00197 Rome
Tel: +39 6 858 577

Galleria Degli Uffizi
Piazza degli Uffizi
50122 Florence
Tel: +39 55 238 8651

Museo Nazionale del
Bargello
Palazzo del Bargello
Via del Proconsolo 4
50122 Florence
Tel: +39 55 238 85

Pinacoteca di Brera
Via Brera 28
20121 Milan
Tel: +39 2 800 985

Vatican Museums and
Galleries
00120 Vatican City
(Rome)
Tel: +39 6 481 4430

Japan
National Museum of Art,
Osaka
10-4 Expo Park
Senri
Suita
565-0826
Tel: +81 6 6876 2481

National Museum of
Modern Art, Kyoto
Enshoji-cho
Okazaki
Sakyoto-ku
Kyoto
606-8344
Tel: +81 75 761 4111,
+81 75 761 9900

Mexico
Museo Nacional de Arte
Calle Tacuba 8
Mexico City
Tel: +52 5130 3400

Palacio de Bellas Artes
Avenida Juarez
Mexico City
P.O. Box 75082
Tel: +52 5512 2593,
+52 5521 9251

Middle East
Egyptian Museum
Tahrir Square
Maydan at-Tahrir
Cairo, 11557
Tel: +20 2 5742681

Egyptian Museum of
Modern Art
Gazirah Exibition Grounds
Cairo
Tel: +20 2 3416667

Israel Museum
Ruppin Blvd.
Jerusalem 91710
Tel: +97 2 2670 8811

New Zealand
Auckland Art Gallery
Corner of Wellesley and
Kitchener Streets
Auckland
Tel: +64 9 307 7700

Te Papa Tongarewa
Cable Street
Wellington
Tel: +64 4 381 7000

Norway
Nasjonalgalleriet
Universitetsgaten 13
0033 Oslo 1
Tel: +47 2 200 404

Poland
Muzeum Narodowe w
Warzawie
Al. Jerozolimski 3
00-495 Warsaw
Tel: +48 22 621 1031

Portugal
Musea Nacional de Arte
Antiga
Rua Das Janelas Verdes
1293 Lisbon
Tel: +351 1 397 6001

Romania
Muzeul de Art
Calea Unirii 15
1100 Craiova
Tel: +40 41 12342

Muzeul National de Art al
Romaniei
Calea Victoriei nr. 49-53
70101 Bucharest
Tel: +40 1 615 5193

Russia
Gosud Arstvennaja
Tretjakovskaja Galerija
Lavrushinskij Per 10
117049 Moscow
Tel: +7 095 230 7788

Hermitage Gosudarstvennij
Ermitaj
Dworcowaja Nabereshnaja
34-36
St Petersburgh 191065
Tel: +7 812 212 9545

Pushkin Museum
12 Volkhonka str
121019 Moscow
Tel: +7 095 203-79-98

Spain
Fundació Joan Miró
Barcelona
Tel: +34 93 329 1908

Museo Nacional del Prado
Paseo del Prado
28014 Madrid
Tel: +34 91 486 0950

Museu Nacional d'Art
de Catalunya
Palacio National
Parc de Montjuic
08038 Barcelona
Tel: +34 3 325 5635

South East Asia
Agung Rai Museum of Art
Ubud,
Bali, 80571
Tel: +62 361 974 228

Contempory Art Museum of
the Phillippines
Roxas Boulevard
1000 Manila
Philippines
Tel: +63 2 8321125

Malaysian National Art
Gallery
Pengarah Balai Seni Lukis
Negara Jalan Temerloh
Off Jalan Tun Razak
50400 Kuala Lumpur.
Tel: +60 3 425 4989

Thavibu Gallery
Silom Galleria Building,
3rd Floor
Suite 308, 919/1 Silom Rd.
Bangkok 10500, Thailand
Tel: +66 2 266 5454

Sweden
Göteborgs Konstmuseum
Göt aplatsen
41256 Göteborg
Tel: +46 31 612 980

Modern Museet
Birger Jarlsgatan 57
10327 Stockholm
Tel: +46 8 666 4250

Nationalmuseum
Södra Blasieholmshamnen
10324 Stockholm
Tel: +46 8 666 4250

Switzerland
Musée d'Art et d'Histoire
2 rue Charles Galland
1211 Geneva 3
Tel: +41 22 311 4340

Taiwan
Taiwan Museum of Art
2, Sec. 1,
Wu Chuan W. Rd.,
Taichung
403 Taiwan, R.O.C.
Tel: +886 4 23723552

United Kingdom
Ashmolean Museum
Beaumont Street
Oxford
Oxfordshire
OX1 2PH
Tel: +44 1865 278 000

Courtauld Institute of Art
Courtauld Gallery
Somerset House
Strand
London, WC2R 0RN
Tel: +44 20 7873 2526

Dulwich Picture Gallery
College Road
London
SE21 7AD
Tel: +44 20 8693 5254

National Gallery
Trafalgar Square
London, WC2N 5DN
Tel: +44 20 7839 3321

National Gallery of
Scotland
The Mound
Edinburgh
Scotland EH2 2EL
Tel: +44 131 624 6200

National Museum and
Gallery Cardiff
Cathays Park
Cardiff CF1 3NP
Tel: +44 1222 397 951

National Portrait Gallery
St Martin's Place
London
WC2H 0HE
Tel: +44 20 7306 0055

Royal Academy of Arts
Burlington House
Piccadilly
London
W1V 0DS
Tel: +44 20 7300 8000

School of Art Gallery
and Museum
University of Wales
Buarth Mawr, Aberystwyth
Ceredigion SY23 1NE
Tel: +44 1970 622 460

Scottish National Gallery
of Modern Art
Belford Road
Edinburgh
Scotland EH4 3DR
Tel: +44 131 624 6200

Scottish National Portrait
Gallery
1 Queen Street
Edinburgh
Scotland EH2 1JD
Tel: +44 131 642 6200

Tate Modern
Bankside
London SE1 9TG
Tel: +44 20 7887 8000

Victoria and Albert Museum
Cromwell Road
South Kensington
London
SW7 2RL
Tel: +44 20 7938 8500

United States
Albright Knox Art Gallery
1285 Elmwood Avenue
Buffalo
NY 14222
Tel: +1 716 882 8700

Art Institute of Chicago
111 Michigan Avenue
Chicago
IL 60603
Tel: +1 312 443 3600

Cleveland Museum of Art
University Circle
11150 E Boulevard
Cleveland
OH 44106-1797
Tel: +1 216 421 7340

Detroit Institute of Arts
5200 Woodward Avenue
Detroit, Michigan
MI 48202
Tel: +1 313 833 7900

J. Paul Getty Museum
17985 Pacific Coast
Highway
Malibu
CA 90265
Tel: +1 310 458 2003

Metropolitan Museum
of Art
1000 Fifth Avenue
NY 10028
New York
Tel: +1 212 879 5500

Museum of Fine Arts
465 Huntingdon Avenue
Boston
MA 02115
Tel: +1 617 267 9300

Museum of Modern Art
11 West 53rd Street
NY 10019
New York
Tel: +1 212 708 9480

National Gallery of Art
4th Street and Constitution
Avenue
Washington
DC 20565
Tel: +1 202 737 4215

National Museum of
American Art
Eighth and G Streets NW
Washington
DC 20560
Tel: +1 202 357 2700

Philadelphia Museum of Art
26th Street at Benjamin
Franklin Parkway
Philadelphia
PA 19130
Tel: +1 215 763 8100

Smithsonian Institute
1000 Jefferson Drive
Washington
DC 200009-1090
Tel: +1 202 357 2700

Whitney Museum
American Art
945 Madison Avenue
New York, NY 10021
Tel: +1 212 570 3600

BIBLIOGRAPHY

Adams, S., *The Barbizon School and the Origins of Impressionism*, Phaidon Press, 1994

Akurgal, E., *The Art of the Hittites*, Thames and Hudson, 1962

Aldred, C., *The Development of Ancient Egyptian Art from 3200 to 1315 BC*, 3 vols, Tiranti, 1973

Ames-Lewis, F. and Rogers, M. eds., *Concepts of Beauty in Renaissance Art*, Ashgate Publishing Limited, 1998

Amiet, P., *Art of the Ancient Near East*, New York, 1980

Archer, M., *Art since 1960*, Thames and Hudson, 1997

Arribas, A., *The Iberians*, Thames & Hudson, 1964

Atil, Ed., *Turkish Art*, Smithsonian Institute Press, Washington DC/New York, 1980

Barnhart, R.M. et al., *Three Thousand Years of Chinese Painting*, Yale University Press, 1997

Berenson, B., *The Italian Painters of the Renaissance 1894—1907*, Cornell University Press, 1980

Berger, J., *Ways of Seeing*, Penguin Books, 1990

Berlo, J.C. and Wilson L.A., *Arts of Africa, Oceania and the Americas*, Englewood Cliffs, NJ, 1993

Berrin, K. and Pasztory, E. eds., *Teotihuacán: Art from the City of the Gods*, San Francisco/London, 1993

Blurton, T.R., *Hindu Art*, British Museum Press, 1992

Boardman, J., *The Oxford History of Classical Art*, Oxford University Press, 1993

Boardman, J., *Greek Art*, Thames and Hudson, 1996

Boardman, J., *Pre-classical: From Crete to Archaic Greece*, Penguin Books, 1967

Boime, A., *Art in the Age of Revolution 1750—1800*, University of Chicago Press, 1987

Bomford, D. et al., *Impressionism*, National Gallery Company Ltd, 1990

Brilliant, R., *Roman Art from the Republic to Constantine*, Praeger Pub Text, 1974

Brown, J., *The Golden Age of Painting in Spain*, Yale University Press, 1991

Buckton, D. ed., *Byzantium*, London, 1994

Camille, M., *Gothic Art*, US Imports & PHIPEs, 1996

Campbell, L., *Renaissance Portraits*, Yale University Press, 1990

Canby, S.R., *Persian Painting*, British Museum Press, 1993

Carpenter, R., *Greek Art*, Philadelphia, 1962

Caruana, W., *Aboriginal Art*, Thames and Hudson, 1993

Charbonneaux, J., *Hellenistic Art*, George Braziller, 1973

Chastel, A., *French Art: The Renaissance 1430—1620*, Paris, 1995

Clarke, G., *The Photograph*, Oxford University Press, 1997

Clunas, C., *Art in China*, Oxford Paperbacks, 1997

Collon, D., *Ancient Near Eastern Art*, British Museum Press, 1995

Craven, R.C., *Indian Art* (1976) Thames and Hudson, 1997

Crichton, R.A., *The Floating World: Japanese Popular Prints 1700—1900*, London, 1973

Cumming, R., *Annotated Great Artist*, Dorling Kindersley, 1998

D'Alleva, A., *Art of the Pacific*, Weidenfeld Nicolson, London/New York, 1998

Davies, D. ed., *Harrap's Illustrated Dictionary of Art and Artists*, Harrap Books Ltd, 1990

Deepwell, K. ed., *Women Artists and Modernism*, Manchester/New York, 1998

de la Bédoyère, Camilla, *The World's Greatest Art: Art Deco*, Flame Tree Publishing, 2005; *The World's Greatest Art: Art Nouveau*, Flame Tree Publishing, 2005

Duro, P. and Greenhalgh, M., *Essential Art History*, Bloomsbury, 1992

Eisenman, S.E., *Nineteenth Century Art: A Critical History*, Thames and Hudson, 1994

Evans, H.C. and Wixom, W.D. eds., *The Glory of Byzantium*, Harry N. Abrams, Inc., 1997

Eyo, E. and Willett, F., *Treasures of Ancient Nigeria*, Collins, 1982

Fer, B., *On Abstract Art*, Yale University Press, 2000

Fong, Wen C., *Beyond Representation*, Yale University Press, 1992

Frankfort, H., *The Art and Architecture of the Ancient Orient*, Yale University Press, 1996

Fry, E.F., *Cubism*, Thames and Hudson, 1966

Gale, M., *Dada and Surrealism*, Phaidon Press, 1997

Gaze, D. ed., *Dictionary of Women Artists*, Fitzroy Dearborn, 1997

Geidion, S., *The Eternal Present: The Beginning of Art*, Oxford University Press, 1962

Gilbert, C., *History of Renaissance Art throughout Europe*, Abrams, 1973

Gillon, W., *A Short History of African Art*, Penguin Books, 1991

Godfrey, T., *Conceptual Art*, Phaidon Press, 1998

Gombrich, E.H., *Art and Illusion*, Phaidon Press, 2002

Goodman, C., *Digital Visions, Computers and Art*, Harry N. Abrams, 1987

Gordon, E.D., *Expressionism, Art and Idea* (1987) New Haven/London, 1991

Grabar, A., *Early Christian Art*, London, 1968

Hanfmann, G., *Roman Art*, W.W. Norton, 1975

Haskell, F., *History and its Images*, Yale University Press, 1993

Hauser, A., *The Social History of Art*, Routledge, 1985

Held, J. and Posner, D., *17th and 18th Century Art*, Harry N. Abrams, Inc, 1972

Henderson, G., *Early Medieval*, University of Toronto Press Inc, 1993

Hessel, I., *Inuit Art: An Introduction*, British Museum Press, 1998

Honour, H., *Neoclassicism*, Penguin, 1968

Honour, H., *Romanticism*, Viking, 1979

Howard, J., *Art Nouveau: International and National Styles in Europe*, Manchester University Press, 1996

Irwin, R., *Islamic Art*, Laurence King Publishing, 1997

James, T.G.H., *An Introduction to Ancient Egypt*, British Museum Publications, 1979

Jantzen, H., *High Gothic*, Princeton University Press, 1984

Kaplan, P. and Manso, S. eds., *Major European Art Movements 1900–1945*, E P Dutton, 1977

Keevill, Elizabeth, *The World's Greatest Art: Dalí*, Flame Tree Publishing, 2006

Kemp, M., *The Science of Art*, Yale University Press, 1990

Kennedy, Andrew, *The World's Greatest Art: Bauhaus*, Flame Tree Publishing, 2006

Kerrigan, Michael, *The World's Greatest Art: Asian Art*, Flame Tree Publishing, 2005; *The World's Greatest Art: Modern Art*, Flame Tree Publishing, 2005

Klindt-Jensen, O., *Viking Art*, University of Minnesota Press, 1980

Kramrisch, S., *The Art of India through the Ages*, Motilal Banarsidass, 2002

Kubler, G., *The Art and Architecture of Ancient America*, Yale University Press, 1992

Laing, L. and Laing, J., *Art of the Celts*, Thames and Hudson, 1992

Lee, S.E. and Richard, N., *A History of Far Eastern Art*, Thames and Hudson, 1997

Leroi-Gourhan, A., *The Art of Prehistoric Man in Western Europe*, Thames and Hudson, 1967

Leroi-Gourhan, A., *The Dawn of European Art*, Cambridge University Press, 1982

Levey, M., *High Renaissance*, Penguin, 1975

Levey, M., *The Early Renaissance*, Harmondsworth, 1967

Linn-William, Susan, *The World's Greatest Art: Folk Art*, Flame Tree Publishing, 2006

Livingstone, M. ed., *Pop Art: A Continuing History*, Harry N Abrams, 1990

Lodder, C., *Russian Constructivism*, Yale University Press, 1998

Loevren, S., *The Genesis of Modernism*, Hacker Art Books Inc, 1983

Lowden, J., *Early Christian and Byzantine Art*, Phaidon Press, 1997

Lynton, N., *The Story of Modern Art*, Phaidon Press, 1992

Martin, J.R., *Baroque*, Westview Press, 1977

Mason, P., *History of Japanese Art*, Harry N. Abrams, Inc., 1993

Miller, M.E., *The Art of Mesoamerica*, Thames and Hudson, 2001

Morphy, H., *Aboriginal Art*, Phaidon Press, 1998

Nochlin, L., *Realism*, Penguin Books, 1991

Noma, S., *The Arts of Japan*, Kodansha America, 1978

O'Mahony, Mike, *The World's Greatest Art: Picasso*, Flame Tree Publishing, 2006; *The World's Greatest Art: American Art*, Flame Tree Publishing, 2006

Osborne, R., *Archiac and Classical Greek Art*, Oxford University Press, 1998

Pächt, O. et al., *Book Illumination in the Middle Ages*, Harvey Miller Publishers, 1994

Panofsky, E., *Meaning in the Visual Arts*, Peter Smith Pub, 1988

Panofsky, E., *Renaissance and Renascences in Western Art*, Paladin, 1970

Partridge, L., *The Art of Renaissance Rome*, US Imports & PHIPEs, 1996

Phillips, P., *The Prehistory of Europe*, Viking, 1980

Phillips, T. ed., *Africa: The Art of a Continent*, Prestel Publishing Ltd, 1999

Pickeral, Tamsin, *The World's Greatest Art: Turner, Whistler, Monet*, Flame Tree Publishing, 2005; *The World's Greatest Art: Mackintosh*, Flame Tree Publishing, 2006

Piotrovsky, B. et al., *Scythian Art*, Phaidon Press, 1993

Pollitt, J.J., *Art and Experience in Classical Greece*, Cambridge University Press, 1972

Powell, R.J., *Black Art and Culture in the Twentieth Century*, Thames and Hudson, 1997

Rampage, N.H. & A., *The Cambridge Illustrated History of Roman Art*, Cambridge, 1991

Rawson, J., *The British Museum Book of Chinese Art*, British Museum Press, 1992

Rewald, J., *The History of Impressionism*, Secker & Warburg, 1980

Richter, G., *A Handbook of Greek Art*, Phaidon Press 1987

Robinson, Michael, *The World's Greatest Art: International Arts & Crafts*, Flame Tree Publishing, 2005; *The World's Greatest Art: Surrealism*, Flame Tree Publishing, 2005; *The World's Greatest Art: Kandinsky*, Flame Tree Publishing, 2006

Rosen, C. and Zerner, H., *Romanticism and Realism*, Faber and Faber, 1984

Rosen, R. et al., *Making Their Mark: Women Artists Move into the Mainstream*, Abbeville Press, 1991

Rosenblum, R. and Janson, H.W., *19th Century Art*, Thames and Hudson, 1984

Rosenblum, R., *Transformations in Late Eighteenth Century Art*, Princeton University Press, 1992

Roskill, M., *What is Art History?* University of Massachusetts Press, 1989

Rowland, B., *The Evolution of the Buddha Image*, Arno P, New York, 1976

Sandler, I., *Art of the Postmodern Era*, Icon Editions, 1996

Schäfer, H., *Principles of Egyptian Art*, Aris & Phillips, 1986

Schapiro, M., *Modern Art, 19th and 20th Centuries*, George Braziller, 1978

Singer, J.C. and Denwood, P. eds., *Tibetan Art: Towards a Definition of Style*, Laurence King, 1997

Spivey, N., *Etruscan Art*, Thames and Hudson, 1997

Stanley-Baker, J., *Japanese Art*, Thames and Hudson, 2000

Starzecka, D.C. ed., *Maori: Art and Culture*, British Museum Press, 1998

Stone-Miller, R., *Art of the Andes*, Thames and Hudson, 1995

Strong, D.E., *Roman Art*, Yale University Press, 1992

Ucko, P. and Rosenfeld, A., *Palaeolithic Cave Art*, Weidenfeld & Nicolson, 1967

Vermeule, C.V., *Roman Art: Early Republic to Late Empire*, Museum of Fine Arts, Boston, 1979

Watson, W., *The Arts of China to AD 900*, Yale University Press, 2000

Welch, S.C., *Art of Moghul India*, Arno P, NY, 1976

Whelte, K., *The Materials and Techniques of Painting*, Van Nost, Reinhold, New York, 1975

Willett, F., *African Art: An Introduction*, Harcourt School Pub, 1971

Wölfflin, H., *Principles of Art History*, G Bell, 1950

Wollheim, R., *Painting as an Art*, Thames and Hudson, 1990

Yonemura, A. et al., *Twelve Centuries of Japanese Art from the Imperial Collections*, Smithsonian Institution Press, 1998

Zarnecki, G., *Romanesque*, Herbert Press, 1989

WEBSITES

About.com (art history resources)
http://arthistory.about.com

Academic Info: Art and Art History
www.academicinfo.net/art.html

Art Channel
www.art4net.com

Art Daily.com
www.artdaily.com

Art History Network
www.arthistory.net

Art History: Resources on the Web
http://witcombe.sbc.edu/ARTHLinks.html

Art Museum Network
www.amn.org

Art Quest
www.artquest.com

Art Resources
www.geocities.com/rr17bb

Art-Search.com
www.art-search.com

Art Source
www.ilpi.com/artsource

Artchive
www.artchive.com

Artcyclopedia
www.artcyclopedia.com

Artlex Art Dictionary
www.artlex.com

Art World Dealers (directory)
www.artworlddealers.com

Bartleby.com (books online)
www.bartleby.com

BBC
www.bbc.co.uk/arts

Chinese Art Net
www.chineseartnet.com

Cornucopia (museum collections)
www.cornucopia.org.uk

Encyclopedia Britannica
www.britannica.com

Galleries Magazine (UK)
www.artefact.co.uk

Galleryguide.org
www.galleryguide.org

Hunt for: Art History
www.huntfor.com/arthistory

Internet Art Resources
www.artresources.com

Internet Public Library Reference Centre
www.ipl.org

Mother of all Art and Art History link pages
www.art-design.umich.edu/mother

Medieval Art History Resources
www.medievalarthistory.com

Refdesk.com (art resources)
www.refdesk.com/culture.html

The Gallery Channel
www.thegallerychannel.com

The World Wide Art Gallery
www.theartgallery.com.au

The World Wide Web Virtual Library: History of Art
www.chart.ac.uk/vlib

Guggenheim Museums
www.guggenheim.org

Virtual Library Museum Pages
http://vlmp.museophile.com

Worldwide Art Resources
http://wwar.com

Yahoo, Art History Resources
http://dir.yahoo.com/Arts/Art_History

Acknowledgements

Contributor Biographies

Dr Mike O'Mahony
A specialist in the twentieth-century art of Europe and the United States, Mike O'Mahony has lectured at the major London galleries and is founding editor of *Art on the Line*. His books include *American Art* and *Picasso* from the *World's Greatest Art* series, and he has contributed articles to many publications, including *The Atlas of World Art* and *The Oxford History of Western Art*.

Dr Robert Belton
Author of *The Beribboned Bomb: The Image of Women in Male Surrealist Art*, *Sights of Resistance* and *The Theatre of the Self: The Life and Art of William Ronald*, Dr Robert Belton is Dean and Associate Professor of Art History at Okanagan University College in Kelowna, British Columbia.

Tom Middlemost
Tom Middlemost is an art curator who specializes in Australian Art, and is passionate about making art accessible to people in country regions of Australia.

Dr James Mackay
James Mackay is a journalist, broadcaster, biographer and historian. He has written numerous books on art, sculpture, antiques and collectables, including *Dictionary of Sculptures in Bronze* and *Animaliers*.

Iain Zaczek
Educated at Oxford and the Courtauld Institute of Art in England, Ian Zaczek, has written numerous art books, some of which include *Lovers in Art*, *Impressionists*, *Celtic Art and Design* and *Women in Art*.

Dr Julia Kelly
Dr Julia Kelly is currently a lecturer at Manchester University. Educated at Oxford and the Courtauld Institute of Art in England, she specialises in twentieth-century art, with a particular interest in Surrealism and the inter-war period.

William Matar
The son of the famous Lebanese artist, Joseph Matar, William is the director of LebanonArt.net. He and his staff have provided invaluable help in choosing the Middle Eastern Art represented in this book.

Tamsin Pickeral
Author of *Mackintosh* and *Turner, Whistler, Monet* in the *World's Greatest Art* series, Tamsin Pickeral has a particular interest in art and design of the nineteenth and early twentieth centuries.

Michael Kerrigan
A wide-ranging author on history and literature, Michael Kerrigan also has a special interest in developments in art, literature and culture. His titles include *Greece and the Meditarranean*, *Shakespeare on Love*, and *Modern Art* in the *World's Greatest Art* series. He has also written for the *Times Literary Supplement* and in the *Guardian* and *Scotsman* newspapers.

Andrea Belloli
Writer and editor Andrea Belloli is the creator of *Make Your Own Museum: An Activity Package for Children*, and author of *Exploring World Art*.

Ihor Holubizky
One of Canada's most respected art critics, curators and authors, Ihor Holubizky now lives in Australia. He has written on a wide range of cultural topics over the years.

Picture Credits

(Page numbers follow source.)
Bridgeman Art Library: Courtesy of Private Collection, © Christie's Images/© Estate of Norman Rockwell 11 & 353; Courtesy of Private Collection/© Chuck Close 12 & 411; Courtesy of Galleria Degli Uffizi, Florence, Italy 16 & 60, 73, 74, 113; Courtesy of Musee d'Unterlinden, Colmar, France/Giraudon 20 & 69; Courtesy of Palazzo Barberini, Rome, Italy 26; Courtesy of Wallace Collection, London, UK 27; Courtesy of Louvre, Paris, France 29, 171, 172; Courtesy of Pushkin Museum, Moscow, Russia/Giraudon 35; Courtesy of Private Collection, Milan, Italy/Peter Willi/© DACS 2002 39; Courtesy of Private Collection/© ADAGP, Paris and DACS, London 2002 41, 46 & 357; Courtesy of Scrovegni (Arena) Chapel, Padua, Italy/Giraudon 61; Courtesy of National Gallery, London, UK 62, 63 & 425, 18 & 76, 78, 90, 30 &149, 180; Courtesy of British Library, London, UK 17, 64 & 433, 111, 112, 163; Courtesy of Prado, Madrid, Spain 65, 66, 68, 72, 91, 22 & 95; Courtesy of Kunsthistorisches Museum, Vienna, Austria 67, 86, 103; Courtesy of Santa Maria Novella, Florence, Italy 75 & 435; Courtesy of Ashmolean Museum, Oxford, UK 80; Courtesy of Dulwich Picture Gallery, London, UK 82, 23 &116, 142; Courtesy of Private Collection 85, 92, 204, 321, 364; Courtesy of Vatican Museums and Galleries, Vatican City, Italy 88; Courtesy of Kunsthistorisches Museum, Vienna, Austria/Ali Meyer 93; Courtesy of Muzeum Zamek, Lancut, Poland 99; Courtesy of Private Collection/Philip Mould, Historical Portraits Ltd, London, UK 24 & 118; Courtesy of Musee National d'Art Moderne, Paris/© DACS 2002 43; Courtesy of Johnny van Haeften Gallery, London, UK 120; Courtesy of Musee des Beaux-Arts, Rennes, France 122 & 436; Courtesy of Noortman, Maastricht, Netherlands 131, 132; Courtesy of Victoria & Albert Museum, London, UK 135 & 432, 173; Courtesy of Mauritshuis, The Hague, Netherlands 138; Courtesy of Church of St. Ignatius, Rome, Italy 141; Courtesy of Christie's Images, 158, 166, 179, 198, 247, 258, 340; Courtesy of National Gallery of Scotland, Edinburgh, Scotland 162; Courtesy of Philip Mould, Historical Portraits Ltd, London, UK 164; Courtesy of Chateau de Versailles, France 165; Courtesy of Musee des Beaux-Arts, Reims, France/ credit: Roger-Viollet, Paris 168; Courtesy of Hamburg Kunsthalle, Hamburg, Germany 181, 350; Courtesy of Musee Girodet, Montargis, France 182; Courtesy of Metropolitan Museum of Art, New York 192; Courtesy of The Detroit Institute of Arts, USA 194; Courtesy of Musee Fabre, Montpelier, France 199; © Musee d'Orsay, Paris, France, Giraudon 208; © Museum of Fine Arts, Boston, Massachusetts, USA, Henry H. and Zoe Oliver Sherman Fund and other funds 209; Courtesy of Jefferson College, Philadelphia, PA, USA 211; Courtesy of Fogg Art Museum, Harvard University Art Museums, USA 237; Courtesy of Hermitage, St Petersburg/Christie's Images 238; Osterreichische Galerie, Vienna, Austria 242; Courtesy of Wilhelm Lehmbruck Museum, Duisburg, Germany/© DACS 2002 256; Courtesy of State Russian Museum, St. Petersburg, Russia 259; Courtesy of Philadelphia Museum of Art, Pennsylvania, PA, USA/© Succession Marcel Duchamp/ADAGP, Paris and DACS, London 2002 263; Courtesy of Private Collection/Christie's Images/© DACS 2002 267; Courtesy of © Brooklyn Museum of Art, New York, USA, Bequest of Edith and Milton Lowenthal/© Estate of Stanton Macdonald-Wright 278; © Museum of Fine Arts, Houston, Texas, USA, Museum purchase funded by 'One Great Night in November 1988' 279; Courtesy of Art Gallery of Ontario, Toronto, Canada 283, 301, 307, 336; Courtesy of Museu de Arte Contemporaneo, São Paulo, Brazil/Index 285; Courtesy of Private Collection, Switzerland/© DACS 2002 286; Courtesy of Whitney Museum of American Art, New York, USA 296; Courtesy of Galerie Daniel Malingue, Paris, France/© ADAGP, Paris and DACS, London 2002 299; National Museum of India, New Delhi, India, Lauros/Giraudon 302; Courtesy of © Worcester Art Museum, Massachusetts, USA/© Estate of Charles Sheeler 313; Courtesy of © The Barnes Foundation, Merion, Pennsylvania, USA/© Estate of Horace Pippin 325; Courtesy of Peggy Guggenheim Foundation, Venice, Italy 333; Courtesy of Metropolitan Museum of Art, New York, USA/© ARS, NY and DACS, London 2002 354; Musee d'Art et d'Industrie, St. Etienne, France/Giraudon/ © ARS, NY and DACS, London 2002 379; Courtesy of National Academy of Design, New York, USA 393; Courtesy of Corbally Stourton Contemporary Art, London, UK/© Aborginal Artists Agency, Sydney 404 & 422; Courtesy of Private Collection/© The Artist 412; Courtesy of The Fleming-Wyfold Art Foundation/Courtesy of Angela Flowers Gallery 418; Courtesy of Private Collection/Dreamtime Gallery, London 419.

Christie's Images: 101, 126, 193, 206, 234, 386; Courtesy of Louvre, Paris/Bridgeman Art Library 8 & 84; Courtesy of Private Collection/© Succession H Matisse/DACS 2002 3 & 342; Courtesy of Nasjonal Galleriet, Oslo/Bridgeman Art Library/© Munch Museum/Munch – Ellingsen Group, BONO, Oslo, DACS, London 2002 13 & 236; Courtesy of Private Collection/© Kate Rothko Prizel and Christopher Rothko/DACS 2002 14 & 378; Courtesy of Private Collection 33, 34, 42, 81, 21 & 83, 89, 94, 96, 97 & 431, 98, 100, 105, 108, 109, 110 & 426, 114, 115, 117, 119, 121, 123, 124, 125, 129, 130, 134, 136, 137, 140, 143, 28 & 144, 145, 146, 147, 148, 150, 151, 154, 155, 156, 157, 159, 160, 161, 169, 170, 174, 176, 177, 178, 31 & 183, 184, 185, 186, 187 & 429, 188, 189, 190, 195, 200, 201, 202, 32 & 203, 205, 207, 210, 213, 214, 216 & 428, 217, 218, 219, 220, 221, 222, 223, 224, 226, 228, 4 & 229, 232, 7 & 233, 240, 243, 246, 248, 255, 261, 266, 269, 275, 288, 326, 344, 358, 359, 373, 377, 385, 387, 391, 394, 397, 52 & 398, 399, 400, 403, 409, 434; Courtesy of Galleria Dell'Accademia, Venice/Bridgeman Art Library 19; Courtesy of Private Collection/© Munch Museum/ Munch – Ellingsen Group, BONO, Oslo, DACS, London 2002 36; Courtesy of Private Collection/© Succession Picasso/DACS 2002 37; Courtesy of Private Collection/ © L & M Services B. V. Amsterdam 20020512 38; Courtesy of Private Collection/© DACS 2002 40, 225, 254, 257, 262, 264, 268, 271, 276, 284, 287, 314, 317, 329, 345, 356; © DACS 2002 44; Courtesy of Private Collection/© Salvador Dal´, Gala-Salvador Dal´ Foundation, DACS, London 2002 45, 316; Courtesy of Private Collection/© ARS, NY and DACS, London, 2002 47, 51, 260, 318, 348; Courtesy of Private Collection/© The Estate of Roy Lichtenstein/DACS 2002 49 & 365; Courtesy of Private Collection/2002 © Bridget Riley, all rights reserved Courtesy Karsten Schubert, London 50, 416; Courtesy of Private Collection/© Richard Estes, courtesy, Marlborough Gallery, New York 55; Courtesy of K & B News Foto, Florence/Bridgeman Art Library 77; Courtesy of Galleria Della Uffizi, Florence/Bridgeman Art Library 79, 104; Courtesy of Vatican Museums and Galleries, Rome/ Bridgeman Art Library 87; Courtesy of Kunsthistoriches Museum, Vienna/Bridgeman Art Library 102; Courtesy of Prado, Madrid/Bridgeman Art Library 133, 175; Courtesy of Getty Museum 215; Courtesy of Private Collection/By Courtesy of Felix Rosentiel's Widow & Son Ltd, London on behalf of the Estate of Sir John Lavery 227; Courtesy of Private Collection/Bridgeman Art Library 235, 368; Courtesy of Private Collection/© Estate of Walter R. Sickert 2002. All Rights Reserved, DACS 239; © ADAGP, Paris and DACS, London 2005 241, 308, 401; Courtesy of Private Collection/© ADAGP, Paris and DACS, London 2002 249, 251, 253, 265, 273, 274, 281, 282, 290, 293, 297, 309, 319, 330, 335, 337, 341, 361, 371 & 438, 374, 392; Courtesy of Private Collection/© Estate of Gwen John 2002. All Rights Reserved, DACS 2002 252; Courtesy of Private Collection/© by Dr. Wolfgang & Ingeborg Henze-Ketterer, Wichtrach/Bern 270; Courtesy of The Artists Estate/Bridgeman Art Library 277; © National Gallery of Canada, Ottawa 272; © DACS 2002 289, 312; Courtesy of Private Collection/DACS 2002 © L & M Services B. V. Amsterdam 20020512 292, 367; Courtesy of Private Collection/© ARS, NY and DACS, London 2002 294, 338, 339, 346, 405; © Estate of Thomas Hart Benton 298; Courtesy of Private Collection/© Piet Mondrian 2002 Mondrian/Holtzman Trust c/o Beeldrecht, Hoofddorp & DACS, London 300; Courtesy of Private Collection/© Banco de Mexico Diego Rivera & Frida Kahlo Museums Trust. Av. Cinco de Mayo No. 2, Col. Centro, Del. Cuauhtemoc 06059, Mexico, D.F. 304, 1 & 328; © Succession Picasso/DACS 2002 305; Courtesy of Private Collection/© Estate of Grant Wood/VAGA, New York/DACS, London 2002 310; Courtesy of Private Collection/© Estate of Mrs G. A. Wyndham Lewis 315; Courtesy of Private Collection/© Foundations P. Delvaux-St Idesbald, Belgium/DACS, London 2002 327; Courtesy of Private Collection/Reproduced by kind permission of Carol Lowry, copyright proprietor 332; Courtesy of Private Collection/© Angela Verren-Taunt 2002. All rights reserved, DACS 334; Courtesy of Private Collection/© The Nolde-Foundation 2002/© Nolde-Stiftung Seebüll 343; Courtesy of Private Collection/The Piper Estate 347; Courtesy of Private Collection/© Estate Stanley Spencer 2002. All Rights Reserved, DACS 349 & 427; Courtesy of Private Collection/© Estate of Francis Bacon 2002. All rights reserved, DACS 363; Courtesy of Private Collection/© Foundation Antoni Tàpies, Barcelona/ADAGP, Paris and DACS, London 2002 366; © The Andy Warhol Foundation for the Visual Arts, Inc./ARS, NY and DACS, London 2002 370 & 437; Courtesy of Private Collection/© Jules Olitski/VAGA, New York/DACS, London 2002 372; Courtesy of Art Resource, NY/© Romare Bearden Foundation/VAGA, New York/DACS, London 2002 380; © Robert Rauschenberg/DACS, London/VAGA, New York 2002 382; Courtesy of Private Collection/© Gerhard Richter 383; © David Hockney/Gemini G. E. L 388; Courtesy of Private Collection/© Jasper Johns/VAGA, New York/DACS, London 2002 389; Courtesy of Private Collection/The Artist courtesy of Marlborough Fine Art 402; Courtesy of Private Collection/© DACS, London VAGA, New York 2002 406; Courtesy of Private Collection/© Dedalus Foundation, Inc/VAGA, New York/DACS, London 2002 407; Courtesy of Private Collection/Christie's Images/© Lucian Freud 415.

Sotheby's Picture Library: 360, 375, 376, 390

Other Credits: © Ellsworth Kelly/The Tate, London 2002 48; Courtesy of National Gallery of Canada, Ottawa: 128; © 1992 The Detroit Institute of Arts 139; © 2006 Credit: TopFoto TopFoto.co.uk 167; © The Newark Museum/Art Resource 191; © Smithsonian American Art Museum, Washington, DC/Art Resource, NY 212, 291, 384; Courtesy of The Art Archive 250; Courtesy of © 2005, Digital Image, The Museum of Modern Art, New York, New York/Scala, Florence/© Estate of Ben Shahn/VAGA, New York/DACS, London 2005 303; Courtesy of The Art Archive/© Estate of Ian Fairweather 2002. All Rights Reserved, DACS 306; © Schomberg Center, The New York Public Library/Art Resource, NY 311; Private Collection. Artwork © Gwendolyn Knight Lawrence, Courtesy of the Jacob and Gwendolyn Lawrence Foundation 320; Courtesy of Pinacoteca Digital- de Floria Barrionuevoy Maria Enriqueta Guardia 362; Courtesy of AKG, London © DACS 2002 381; Image with permission of 'The Haenggi Foundation Inc., Johannesburg/Basel' (Gallery 21 London archives) 395; Courtesy of Collection of the Dennos Museum Center, Northwestern Michigan College, Traverse City, Michigan 396; © Ricco/Maresca Gallery/Art Resource, NY 408; © The artist, courtesy of Scottish National Portrait Gallery, Edinburgh 410; Courtesy of Galerie Peter Herrmann, Berlin/ © Chéri Samba 413; Courtesy of National Gallery of Australia, Canberra, purchased with funds from the Moet & Chandon Australian Art Foundation/© The Artist 414; Courtesy of Contemporary American Indian Art Collection, Art Museum of Missoula. Donated by the Artist/© The Artist 417; All Joseph Matar works are © by the artist and LebanonArt – Germinal ltd 420; Courtesy of Private Collection/Artist & Ferner Galleries – New Zealand 421; Courtesy of the Dennos Museum Center, Northwestern Michigan College, Traverse City, Michigan/The Artist 439.

Index by Painting

General Index

Page numbers in *italics* refer to illustrations.
Those in **bold** refer to main entries.